D0023438

ENCYCLOPEDIA OF CONTEMPORARY AMERICAN SOCIAL ISSUES

ENCYCLOPEDIA OF CONTEMPORARY AMERICAN SOCIAL ISSUES

VOLUME 4
ENVIRONMENT, SCIENCE, AND TECHNOLOGY

Michael Shally-Jensen, Editor

ABC-CLIO

Santa Barbara, California • Denver, Colorado • Oxford, England

Copyright 2011 by ABC-CLIO, LLC

All rights reserved. No part of this publication may be reproduced, stored in a retrieval system, or transmitted, in any form or by any means, electronic, mechanical, photocopying, recording, or otherwise, except for the inclusion of brief quotations in a review, without prior permission in writing from the publisher.

Library of Congress Cataloging-in-Publication Data

Encyclopedia of contemporary American social issues / Michael Shally-Jensen, editor.
    v. ; cm.
  Includes bibliographical references and index.
  Contents: Vol. 1: business and economy — Vol. 2: criminal justice — Vol. 3: family and society — Vol. 4: environment, science, and technology.
    ISBN 978-0-313-39204-7 (set : alk. paper) — ISBN 978-0-313-39205-4 (set ebook)
  1. United States—Social conditions—Encyclopedias. 2. United States—Economic conditions—Encyclopedias. 3. United States—Politics and government—Encyclopedias. I. Shally-Jensen, Michael.
  HN59.2.E343   2011
  306.0973—dc22   2010041517

ISBN: 978-0-313-39204-7
EISBN: 978-0-313-39205-4

15 14 13 12 11   1 2 3 4 5

This book is also available on the WorldWideWeb as an eBook.
Visit www.abc-clio.com for details.

ABC-CLIO, LLC
130 Cremona Drive, P.O. Box 1911
Santa Barbara, California 93116-1911

This book is printed on acid-free paper ∞

Manufactured in the United States of America

Contents

VOLUME 2: CRIMINAL JUSTICE

VOLUME 3: FAMILY AND SOCIETY

VOLUME 4: ENVIRONMENT, SCIENCE, AND TECHNOLOGY

Preface

The growing prominence of news, information, and commentary of all kinds, and in every medium, has unfortunately not always been matched by a deepening or a widening of consumers' understanding of the issues at hand. In this era of tweets and peeks (information and video clips), of blogging and befogging (electronic opining), people of all stripes are under increased pressure to make snap judgments about matters about which they may know little. The fact that so many of the issues of the day—corporate misdoings, criminal violence, the condition of the schools, environmental disasters— touch the lives of so many Americans suggests that awareness of them at *any* level is a good thing. At some point, however, one needs to move beyond the news feeds and sound bites and begin to appreciate current issues for the complex matters that they are. This is precisely what the *Encyclopedia of Contemporary American Social Issues* is designed to do.

As with other works of its kind, the present encyclopedia is intended to serve as a bridge between the knowledge of experts and the knowledge of those new to the subjects it covers. We present here, then, scholarly research on a broad array of social issues in a format that is accessible and interesting, yet informative. The contributors have taken care with both the quality of their prose and the accuracy of their facts, the aim being to produce entries that are clear, accurate, and thorough. Contributors and editors alike have paid attention to the language of the entries to ensure that they are written in an intelligible style without losing sight of the terms and conventions employed by scholars writing within their disciplines. Thus, readers will find here thoughtful introductions to some of the most pressing issues currently confronting American society.

Scope

The *Encyclopedia of Contemporary American Social Issues* is divided into four volumes: (1) Business and Economy; (2) Criminal Justice; (3) Family and Society; and (4) Environment, Science, and Technology. Within each volume, the entries are arranged in alphabetical order. There are just over 200 entries in the encyclopedia, the essays ranging in length from about 1,500 words to more than 8,000. Each essay discusses a contemporary issue and ends with suggestions for further reading.

The first problem in compiling an encyclopedia of this type, of course, is determining what constitutes a social issue. It would seem a common enough term about whose meaning there is general consensus. Still, the matter bears a quick review. The *American Heritage Dictionary* defines an issue as:

a. a point or matter of discussion, debate, or dispute;
b. a matter of public concern;
c. a misgiving, objection, or complaint;
d. the essential point, crux.

In other words, not only a matter of public debate or discussion but also a point of concern or matter about which there are misgivings or objections. Included in the mix, moreover, is the idea of a neat summary or something boiled down to its essentials.

In the present encyclopedia, readers will find entries reflecting these varied senses of the term *issue.* There are entries, for example, such as "Health Care," "Oil Drilling," and "Gun Control" whose subjects one often hears debated in public forums. On the other hand, there are entries such as "Globalization," "Sprawl," and "Social Justice" whose subjects are rather harder to identify as clear-cut matters for public debate and seem more like general areas of concern. Of course, more than the general public, it is scholars who routinely examine the ins and outs of various subjects; and for scholars there is little doubt that globalization and the like are key issues requiring careful description and analysis. Fortunately for readers of this encyclopedia, included here are the considered opinions of some 170 scholars and professionals from a variety of different fields, all of whom were asked to lay out "the essential points" for lay readers.

No encyclopedia can encompass the complete spectrum of issues within the contemporary United States. The question of what to include and what to omit is one that has vexed us from the start. The best strategy, we found, was to keep constantly in mind the readers who turn to a work like the *Encyclopedia of Contemporary American Social Issues,* whether in a school or college library or in a public library reference center. We recognize that reference works like this serve a range of purposes for the reader, from gleaning facts to preparing a research paper or introducing oneself to a subject in order to appreciate where it fits within the world at large. In the end, as editors who have been around school curricula and have worked in library reference publishing for many years, we followed our own counsel in deciding upon the contents of this work. We do so knowing that we cannot satisfy all readers; we hope, however, that we have satisfied the majority of those in need of the kind of information presented here.

Although the emphasis is on *contemporary* social issues, the entries generally situate their topics in historical context and present arguments from a variety of perspectives. Readers are thus able to gain an understanding of how a particular issue has developed and the efforts that have been made in the past—including in the most recent times—to address it. Thus, perennial issues such as taxes, education, and immigration are examined in their latest permutations, and newer developments such as cloning, identity theft, and media violence are discussed in terms of both their antecedents and the conversations currently surrounding them. If there is any trend to be noted with respect to contemporary American social issues, it might only be that with each step forward comes the likelihood of further steps yet to be negotiated. We get from point A to point B only by making good use of our democratic heritage and anticipating the prospect of multiple voices or multiple intermediary steps. The *Encyclopedia of Contemporary American Social Issues* reflects that fact and advances the idea that it is useful to know where and how a question first arose before attempting to answer it or move it forward in the public agenda.

There is an established tradition in sociology that focuses on "social problems" and the many means by which these problems can be and have been researched and analyzed. Always something of an eclectic enterprise, and drawing on the collective wisdom of social scientists working in a variety of different fields (including criminology, demography, anthropology, policy studies, and political economy), in recent years the social problems tradition has widened its range still further to include questions about the environment, corporations, the media, gender politics, and even science and technology. It is this expanded version of the sociological traditional that the present encyclopedia takes as its animating vision. Encompassed herein are all of the above fields and more. We welcome the expansion and see it as linked to the broader meaning of the term *social issues.*

The four volumes assembled here—Business and Economy; Criminal Justice; Family and Society; and Environment, Science, and Technology—have benefited from work done earlier by others, work hereby democratically brought forward and expanded in scope. Specifically, we have drawn upon a series of books published previously by Greenwood Press and entitled *Battleground.* Key entries from that series have been updated, revised, rewritten, and in some cases replaced through the efforts of either the original authors or experienced editors knowledgeable in the applicable fields. In addition, some two dozen entries appear here for the first time, the aim being to ensure that issues emerging in the last few years receive the attention they deserve. Among this latter group of entries are "Bank Bailouts," "Cybercrime," "Consumer Credit and Household Debt," and "Airport and Aviation Security."

Acknowledgments

It is to the contributors, then, that I, personally, owe the greatest debt of gratitude. Without their patience and understanding, their expertise and professionalism, this work would not have been possible. An associate editor, Debra Schwartz, and development editor Anne Thompson provided invaluable service in the preparation of entries for publication, and the assistance of Scott Fincher in this regard is happily acknowledged as well. Acquisitions editor Sandy Towers, with whom I first worked in conceiving the project, proved a valuable friend and professional asset throughout the process. Also present from the beginning was Holly Heinzer, whom I thank for her support. Many thanks, too, to the production staffs at both ABC-CLIO and Apex CoVantage for their invaluable assistance in helping to refine the text and set up the volumes for publication. I am grateful to Jeff Dixon for handling the graphics.

—*Michael Shally-Jensen*

A

ACID RAIN

Robert William Collin

When pollution from burning fossil fuel enters the atmosphere, it can react to create acids, which then return to the earth in precipitation, having environmental consequences. Environmentalists and those living in affected communities have challenged industry and government alike over the issue of acid rain.

Acid Rain Dynamics

Moisture in the atmosphere forms small droplets of rain that gradually become larger and heavier and sink to the ground as rain. These droplets can form around dust, particulate matter, and each other. There are many sources for the pollution that forms the acid in rain. The consensus is that it is primarily industrial air emissions that contribute to acid rain. Large coal-fired power plants and factories add to this problem. The prevailing air currents carry these emissions all across the United States and the rest of the world. Airborne emissions from other industrialized and newly industrialized nations also travel long distances to other countries. Thus, the direction of the prevailing winds can determine the deposition of acid onto the earth's surface. Once the acidic gases have been emitted into the atmosphere, they follow prevailing wind circulation patterns. Most industrialized areas of the world are located within the midlatitude westerly belt, and their emissions are carried eastward before being deposited. Acid rain is possible anywhere precipitation occurs. Early scientific controversies were about the number of tree species affected and the long-term ecological impacts. Current controversies are about whether the problem has been solved. It has a greater environmental impact than predicted by early studies. Although sulfur emissions have decreased, other emissions have increased. Some contend that mercury deposition has increased, and others consider the scope of environmental regulation inadequate.

Acidity and Ecosystem Damage

Historical weather data come from precipitation records, ice cores, and tree borings. They show an increase in acid rain starting in the late 1930s and on through the 1940s and 1950s. This was also the approximate time of a large industrial expansion in the United States and before the implementation of clean air policy in the early 1970s. Many U.S. cities used coal and natural gas in their everyday activities, depending on the dominant industry.

Acidity causes metals, such as aluminum or lead, to become soluble in water. Once in the water, acid affects plants and fish and is considered toxic to both. Acid deposition is directly damaging to human health. Its ability to corrode metals—from lead and copper pipes, for example—can be toxic to humans. The sewer and water infrastructures of many older U.S. cities have lead pipes. Increased concentrations of sulfur dioxide and other oxides of nitrogen in the air, common industrial emissions, have been causally related to increased hospital admissions for respiratory illness. In areas that have a large concentration of these airborne industrial emissions, there is an increase in chest colds, asthma, allergies, and coughs in children and other vulnerable populations. Thus, there is a strong public health concern associated with industrial emissions apart from the issue of acid rain.

Acid deposition refers to the process of moving acids to the land within a given ecology. The acids then move through the top surface of the earth, the soil, vegetation, and surface waters. As metals such as mercury, aluminum, and lead are set free owing to the increased acidity from the rain, they can have adverse ecological effects. There is also concern that some of the metals may bioaccumulate and intensify as they move up the food chain. The sustainability of an ecosystem depends on how long it takes for the system to recover, in this case from acid in the rain. The ability of some ecosystems to neutralize acid has decreased because of the cumulative impacts of acid rain over time. This slows the recovery of other parts of the ecosystem. This is why environmentalists contend that recent decreases in some industrial emissions are not likely to bring about full ecosystem recovery. In spite of partial environmental regulation, the cumulative impacts of acid rain pollutants have damaged sensitive areas of the Northeast, such as the Adirondack State Park, by impairing their ability to recover from acid shock events.

Acid rain has a range of effects on plant life. Sensitive species go first. Part of the acid rain controversy is determining which species are affected and the overall scope of the problem. Acid rain falls in any place where it rains or snows. Crops used for food or other purposes can be negatively affected. Acid rain's effects on plants depend on the type of soil, the ability of the plant to tolerate acidity, and the actual chemicals in the precipitation. Soils vary greatly from one location to another. Soils with lime are better able to buffer or neutralize acids than those that are sandier or that contain weathered acidic bedrock. In other soils, increasing acidity causes the leaching of plant nutrients. The heavy metal aluminum causes damage to roots. This can interfere with the plants' ability to absorb nutrients such as calcium and potassium. The loss of these nutrients affects the plants' ability to grow at normal, productive rates, and the intake of metals increases their potential toxicity. For example, acid deposition has increased the concentration of aluminum in soil and water. Aluminum has an adverse ecological effect because it can slow the uptake of water by tree roots. This can leave the tree more vulnerable to freezing and disease.

Many important life forms cannot survive in soils below a pH of about 6.0. The loss of these life forms slows normal rates of decomposition, essentially making the soil sterile. When the acid rain is nitrogen-based, it can have a strong impact on plants. High concentrations of nitric acid can increase the nitrogen load on the plant and displace other nutrients. This condition is called nitrogen saturation. Acid precipitation can cause direct damage to plants' foliage in some instances. Precipitation in the form of fog or cloud vapor is more acidic than rainfall. Other factors such as soil composition, the chemicals in the precipitation, and the plant's tolerance also affect survival. Sensitive ecosystems such as mountain ranges may experience acidic fog and clouds before acid rain forms.

Acid rain falls to the earth and gradually drains to the oceans via rivers, lakes, and streams. Acid deposition erodes the quality of the water in lakes and streams. It causes lakes to age prematurely, speeding up the natural process of eutrophication. It does this in part by reducing species diversity and aquatic life. Fish are considered an indicator species of ecological health. However, ecosystems are made up of food webs of which fish are only one part. Entire food webs are often negatively affected and weakened. Environmentalists and those interested in sustainability are very concerned about ecosystem effects and are much involved in acid rain discussions.

Initial Government Action

On September 13, 2007, in Montreal, Canada, 24 nations signed the Montreal Protocol. Canada is highly motivated to solve air pollution problems because it is highly vulnerable to the effects of acid rain. This landmark environmental treaty required the phasing out of ozone-depleting chemicals and compounds such as chlorofluorocarbons, carbon tetrachloride, and methyl chloroform. There is scientific consensus that these compounds erode the stratospheric ozone layer, which protects the earth from harmful ultraviolet radiation. This radiation can cause cancer, among other environmental impacts. To date, 191 countries have signed the protocol. The United States has implemented many parts of it more quickly and at less cost than expected. The thinning of the ozone layer mostly stopped in 1988 and 1989, almost immediately after treaty reductions began to take effect. The U.S. Environmental Protection Agency estimates that 6.3 million U.S. lives will be saved as a direct result of worldwide efforts to implement the Montreal Protocol's requirements.

The early successes of the Montreal Protocol laid the groundwork for a national approach to acid rain in the United States. The 1990 National Acid Precipitation Assessment Program (NAPAP) concluded that acid deposition had not caused the decline of trees other than the red spruce, which grows at high elevations. This became a significant scientific controversy because of its policy implications for the Clean Air Act Amendments of 1990. Some contended that 20 years of the Clean Air Act had been enough and that air pollution was no longer a severe problem. Others strongly disagreed. Recent research shows that acid deposition has contributed to the decline of red spruce trees and other important trees throughout the eastern United States. Other species, such as black flies, increase under acid rain conditions. Indicator species and mammals at the high end of the food chain show high levels of some of the pollutants in acid rain, indicating the pervasiveness of chemical exposure within the environment. For example, sugar maple trees in central and western Pennsylvania are now also declining. The Clean Air Act Amendments of 1990 included specific provisions concerning acid rain.

THE CLEAN AIR ACT AND ACID RAIN

Early concerns about acid rain provided a strong impetus to early Clean Air Act legislation. The Clean Air Act was strong, groundbreaking environmental policy. It was never complete in its coverage or thorough in its enforcement. Legislative and legal exceptions have developed. Emissions and acid deposition remain high compared with background conditions. The Clean Air Act did decrease sulfur dioxide emissions, yet these emissions remain high. Enforcement on nitrogen oxides and ammonia is sporadic. Emissions of these compounds are high and have remained unchanged in recent years. There are other emissions, such as mercury, that have only recently been regulated. The holes in environmental policy often appear as environmental impacts. Is the Clean Air Act enough? This is still a large controversy, going far beyond the debate about acid rain. Some research shows that the Clean Air Act is not sufficient to achieve ecosystem recovery. In 2003, several states, mostly in the Northeast, sued the U.S. Environmental Protection Agency (EPA) for failing to enforce the Clean Air Act, particularly as it related to greenhouse gases. (The U.S. Supreme Court found in favor of at least one state—Massachusetts—in 2009.) As the debate has moved from acid rain, to clean air environmental policy, to global warming and climate change, this important policy question is certain to be revisited many times.

Canada and the U.S. Acid Rain Controversy

One intrinsic political problem highlighted by acid rain, and involving all air pollution, is that air and water currents do not follow political boundaries. If one country's air pollution goes directly to the neighboring country, little can be done. Canadian concern about the damage from acid rain predates U.S. concern. Canada examines all possible sources for the acid rain problem, including its own contribution. Acid rain resulting from air pollution is severely affecting lakes and damaging forests. Eastern Canada is particularly hard hit because of the prevailing winds. There is a continuing controversy about actual site-specific impacts. Some studies indicate no significant changes in the presence of some degrees of acid rain. Others find that impacts for a given species are significant. Disputes of this kind are typical and tend to be ongoing. U.S.-Canadian relations have overcome some of the initial strain regarding the issue of acid rain. The U.S. government did not make much progress until land was at risk. Those efforts, exemplified by the Clean Air Act Amendments of 1990, put into policy proven measures that could reduce the emissions of pollutants causing acid rain. Since 1990, there have been a number of cooperative environmental programs involving both the United States and Canada.

Acid Rain and Art, Architecture, and Antiquities

Acid rain occurs all over the world. It is most common in areas with a history of industrialization. It has impacts on both the natural and urban environment. The impact of acid rain on the treasures of antiquity all across the planet is difficult to know. Other parts of the world still burn brown coal—that is, coal containing many impurities such as sulfur. Large industrial processes fueled by coal churn large emissions into the atmosphere with little regulation or regard for the environment. The scrubbing of coal is currently expensive but offers a way to remove the sulfur within it.

The negative effects of acid rain on historic buildings and works of art differ depending on the materials of which they are made. The effects are far-ranging, especially over time. Washington, D.C.; Philadelphia; Milan, Italy; Bern, Switzerland; and many other cities feel the impact of acid rain. In terms of traditional Western classical works of art, Italy may face the highest risk of damage from acid rain. In Italy, many works of art are made of calcium carbonate, in the form of marble. As in the case of most choices of building stone, marble was selected because it was locally available. Calcium carbonate reacts upon contact with acid rain, thus gradually tending to dissolve. Italy has a severe acid rain problem owing to its geography, prevailing winds, and the dependence on the burning of coal as a source of energy. Many classic ancient marble structures and statutes are at risk of being corroded by acid rain in Italy's cities. Northern Italy has the worst air quality in western Europe. Some of the smaller sculptures have been encased in transparent cases, which are then filled with a preserving atmosphere. Others have continued to corrode.

In the United States, limestone is the second most commonly used building stone. It was widely used before Portland cement became available. Limestone was preferred because of its uniform color and texture and because it could be easily carved. Limestone from local sources was commonly used before 1900. Nationwide, marble is used much less often than other stone types. Granite is primarily composed of silicate minerals, which are resistant to acid rain. Sandstone is also composed of silica and is resistant to most types of acid rain. Limestone and marble are primarily composed of calcium carbonate, which dissolves in weak acid. Depending on the building materials, many older U.S. cities are suffering damage due to acid rain.

How Much Acid Is There in Rain?

The term *acid deposition* is used to encompass both the dry and wet deposition of acidic compounds in acid precipitation. The most recent term used in place of *acid rain* is *atmospheric deposition,* which includes acidic compounds as well as other airborne pollutants. The term reflects the recognition that air pollution involves the complex interaction of many compounds in chemical stew within the atmosphere.

Unpolluted rain is normally slightly acidic, with a pH of 5.6. Carbon dioxide from the atmosphere dissolves to form carbonic acid, which is why normal rain is slightly acidic. When acidic pollutants combine with the rain, the acidity increases greatly. The acidity of rainfall over parts of the United States, Canada, and Europe has increased over the past 40 years. This is primarily due to the increased emission of sulfur and nitrogen oxides that accompanies increased industrialization.

The sulfur and nitrogen oxides are the common pollutants from coal-burning activities such as power generation. Many if not most of these emissions are legal in that they are within the terms of their permits from the Environmental Protection Agency (EPA) or state environmental agency. Legal or not, these pollutants are oxidized in the atmosphere and converted into sulfuric and nitric acids. These acids are then absorbed by clouds laden with raindrops. As they become heavier, they fall to the earth. This process is called acid deposition. Acidic fog, snow, hail, and dust particles also occur. The acidity of these different forms of precipitation can vary greatly.

Sources of Acid Rain

Part of the controversy about the sources of acid rain has revolved around the question of whether environmental policy could really affect the acidity of rain. Scientific debate about natural, human, and industrial causes engulfed much of the political battleground. Although the policy question was answered in the affirmative—that, yes, environmental policy can make the air cleaner—the debate about sources continues.

All forms of precipitation are naturally acidic because of naturally occurring carbon dioxide; human activities tend to add to the acidity. Nonpolluted rain is assumed to have

ENGINEERING SOLUTIONS TO ACID RAIN

One common concern of industry is that it must meet new and expensive environmental compliance requirements. It is one thing to pass a law, representatives of industry point out, but more difficult to actually implement it at the point of emission. Pollution and abatement engineering firms faced early challenges with aspects of the Clean Air Act because of the concerns raised about acid rain. The enactment of new rules and regulations for emission controls, such as best available control technologies, have required pollution and abatement control engineers to develop new ways to limit the amounts of sulfur and nitrogen in order to comply with their new permit requirements. How do chemical engineers reduce emissions and abate pollution from sulfur dioxide and nitric oxides? Here are some of the basic methods to date.

Pollution-Control Methods for Sulfur Dioxide

GAS ABSORPTION AND CHEMICAL STRIPPING: This is the standard chemical method for removing a substance from a gas stream. It requires a liquid solvent in which the gaseous component is more soluble than the other parts of the sulfur dioxide gas stream. The sulfur dioxide gas enters the absorber where it then flows up and the liquid stream flows down. Once the gas has been chemically stripped of the sulfur dioxide, it is released into the atmosphere. The toxic ash that remains is shipped to a hazardous waste landfill.

LIMESTONE WET SCRUBBERS: Coal- or oil-burning sources that produce pollutants such as sulfur dioxide use this method. First, the solid ash particulates are removed from the waste stream. They are shipped to a hazardous waste landfill. Then, the remaining sulfuric gas goes to a tower where it travels through a scrubbing slurry. This slurry is made of water and limestone particles that react with the sulfuric acid to neutralize it, producing carbon dioxide and a powdery ash. The legal destination for the final waste stream is a hazardous waste landfill.

DRY SYSTEMS: Some pollution abatement and control approaches are called dry because they do not use a wet slurry. In handling sulfur-based emissions, dry systems inject dry alkaline particles into the sulfuric acid gas stream. They neutralize the acid into an ash. The particles are then collected in the particle collection device. Dry systems avoid problems with disposal of wet sludge from wet scrubbers. They increase the amount of dry solids to be disposed of, usually in the form of fly ash. The final destination is again a landfill.

WET/DRY SYSTEMS: These systems are a combination of the wet and dry systems. They remove some pollutants, such as sulfur dioxide, from the waste stream. The sulfur-based emissions are essentially watered down and reduced to a powdery ash. The final destination for this ash is the hazardous waste landfill.

Pollution Abatement and Control Techniques for Nitrogen Emissions

Reducing nitrogen emissions is more challenging in implementation. Basically, there are two ways to reduce NOx emissions:

- Modifying combustion processes to prevent NOx formation in the first place
- Treating combustion gases after flame to convert NOx to N_2

(continued)

(continued)

Both methods incur costs and sometimes liabilities for industry. Pollution abatement and control engineers remain in high demand to assist industrial compliance with environmental laws. The next challenge with acid rain will likely be the removal of atmospheric mercury.

a pH of 5.6. This is the pH of distilled water. Natural sources of these environmentally regulated chemicals may be significant. Emissions due to human activity tend to be concentrated near historic industrial sites and older population centers. The presence of other naturally occurring substances can produce pH values ranging from 4.9 to 6.5. This scientific dynamic has kept other debates alive regarding whether government has an effective role in environmental policy if the sources are natural. pH levels are among the many factors that are monitored.

The relationship between pollutant emission sources and the acidity of precipitation at affected areas has not yet been determined. More research on tracing the release of pollutants and measuring their deposition rates to evaluate the effects on the environment is under way. This is an area of much scientific and legal controversy. If it were possible to show that a given emission definitely came from a given plant, then government would be able to assign liability to the polluter. Governments would also be able to locate sources of acid rain that comes from other countries.

Conclusion

Acid rain as a controversy in the United States has been subsumed by controversies around global warming and climate change. Many of the debates are the same, especially in terms of science and legal issues. Scientific disputes mark the continuing evolution of ways to measure the actual environmental impacts. The controversy around acid rain was an early one, historically documented as a symptom of a larger problem. It is an important historic controversy because it promoted significant, successful policies. It is also a modern controversy because it continues to provide evidence of humans' impact on the environment.

See also **Air Pollution; Climate Change; Coal; Fossil Fuels; Global Warming; Water Pollution; Sustainability (vol. 1)**

Further Reading

Brimblecombe, Peter, *Acid Rain: Deposition to Recovery.* Dordrecht: Springer, 2007.

Ellerman, A. Denny, et al., *Markets for Clean Air: The U.S. Acid Rain Program.* New York: Cambridge University Press, 2000.

Jacobs, Daniel J., *Introduction to Atmospheric Chemistry*. Princeton, NJ: Princeton University Press, 1999.

Oreskes, Naomi, and Erik M. Conway, *Merchants of Doubt: How a Handful of Scientists Obscured the Truth on Issues from Tobacco to Global Warming*. New York: Bloomsbury Press, 2010.

Porter, William F., "Human Impacts from Afar: Acid Rain and Mercury Deposition in the Adirondacks." In *The Great Experiment in Conservation: Voices from the Adirondack Park,* ed. William F. Porter et al. Syracuse, NY: Syracuse University Press, 2009.

Social Learning Group, *A Comparative History of Social Responses to Climate Change, Ozone Depletion, and Acid Rain.* Cambridge, MA: MIT Press, 2001.

Stanitski, Conrad L., et al., "Neutralizing the Threat of Acid Rain." In *Chemistry in Context: Applying Chemistry to Society,* 4th ed. New York: McGraw-Hill, 2003.

Tammemagi, Hans, *Air: Our Planet's Ailing Atmosphere.* Toronto: Oxford University Press, 2009.

AGING INFRASTRUCTURE

Pamela A. Collins and Ryan K. Baggett

In the last decade, the effect of aging infrastructure has become increasingly apparent within the United States. In 2003, the power grid serving the Northeast, much of the Midwest, and parts of Canada failed, leaving an estimated 50 million people without power. In 2005 the levees protecting New Orleans from flooding failed during Hurricane Katrina, and Lake Pontchartrain spilled in to the streets in one of the worst natural disasters in U.S. history. In 2007, the I-35 bridge in Minneapolis, a transportation lifeline for the growing Twin Cities population, collapsed, killing 13 and injuring 145. The degradation of the bridge was attributed to heavy use and age. As author Sydney Liles notes, "These are the infrastructure failures that make headlines. There are numerous other examples seen daily that never make the news because they do not appear to be that serious" (2009). This article analyzes infrastructure in the United States, provides a historical background on the current challenges the nation faces, and highlights several solutions identified by various stakeholders.

The term *infrastructure*, as defined by the *Oxford Pocket Dictionary of Current English* (2008), is the basic physical and organizational structures and facilities (e.g., buildings, roads, and power supplies) needed for the operation of a society or enterprise. Prior to the events of September 11, 2001, this term primarily referred to the U.S. public works system, which included systems such as roadways, bridges, water and sewer systems, airports, seaports, and public buildings. These earlier references often were put in a context of the concern for their "deteriorating, obsolete, and insufficient capacity" (Vaughan and Pollard 1984). Following the tragic events of the Oklahoma City bombing (1995) and the September 11, 2001 attacks on the World Trade Center and Pentagon, more attention was paid to critical infrastructure. Specifically, *critical infrastructure* refers to physical and virtual assets and systems that are so vital to the country that their destruction and/or incapacitation would cause debilitating effects in terms of the nation's security, economy, public health, public safety, or any combination thereof (Collins and Baggett 2009).

U.S. Department of Homeland Security Critical Infrastructure Sectors

The Department of Homeland Security (DHS) has identified 18 separate U.S. critical infrastructure sectors, as displayed in Table 1.

These sectors include the Agriculture and Food Sector, which "comprises more than 2 million farms, approximately 900,000 firms, and 1.1 million facilities." This sector, like many of the others, is predominantly owned privately. It accounts for roughly one-fifth of the nation's economic activity (U.S. Department of Agriculture 2007). The U.S. Department of Agriculture's Agricultural Research Service (USDA-ARS) estimates that one person in eight works in some part of the agriculture/food sector. Cattle and dairy farmers alone earn about $50 billion a year in meat and milk sales. Domestically, about 10 percent of the U.S. annual gross domestic product (GDP) is related to agriculture and food production. Even without agroterrorism, livestock disease costs the U.S. economy about $17.5 billion and crop diseases account for about $30 billion (eXtension 2010).

The Banking and Finance Sector accounts for more than 8 percent of the U.S. annual GDP. This complex and diverse sector ranges from large institutions with assets greater than $1 trillion to the smallest community banks and credit unions. With more than 17,000 depository institutions, 15,000 providers of various investment products, more than 8,500 providers of risk-transfer products, and many thousands of credit and financing organizations, the financial services sector is both large in assets and in the number of individual businesses (National Association of Insurance Commissioners 2005).

The Chemical Sector is an integral component of the U.S. economy, employing nearly 1 million people and earning revenues of more than $637 billion per year. This

TABLE 1. Critical Infrastructure Sectors

Agriculture and Food	Banking and Finance
Chemical	Commercial Facilities
Communications	Critical Manufacturing
Dams	Defense Industrial Base
Emergency Services	Energy
Government Facilities	Healthcare and Public Health
Information Technology	National Monuments and Icons
Nuclear Reactors, Materials, and Waste	Postal and Shipping
Transportation Systems	Water

sector can be divided into five main segments, based on the end product produced: (1) basic chemicals, (2) specialty chemicals, (3) agricultural chemicals, (4) pharmaceuticals, and (5) consumer products. Each of these segments has distinct characteristics, growth dynamics, markets, new developments, and issues. The majority of Chemical Sector facilities are privately owned, requiring DHS to work closely with the private sector and its industry associations to identify and prioritize assets, assess risks, develop and implement protective programs, and measure program effectiveness (U.S. Department of Homeland Security 2010).

The Commercial Facilities Sector is unique because most of the entities in this sector are considered open to the public; in other words, the general public can gain access to these facilities without restrictions. The majority of the facilities in this sector are privately owned and operated and include a variety of venues and establishment within the following eight subsectors: Public Assembly, Sports Leagues, Gaming, Lodging, Outdoor Events, Entertainment and Media, Real Estate, and Retail (U.S. Department of Homeland Security 2010).

The Communications Sector's security strategy is to ensure the nation's communications networks and systems are secure, resilient, and rapidly restored after an incident. The infrastructure includes wire-line, wireless, satellite, cable, and broadcasting and provides the transport networks that support the Internet and other key information systems. Over the past 20 years, the sector has evolved from a predominantly closed and secure wire-line telecommunications network focused on providing equipment and voice services into a diverse, open, highly competitive, and interconnected industry with wireless, satellite, and cable service companies providing many of those same services (U.S. Department of Homeland Security 2010).

The Critical Manufacturing Sector contains those organizations that process iron ore and manufacture steel. It also includes any facility that is involved in smelting, refining, rolling, and extruding nonferrous metals and alloys of nonferrous metals. This sector also includes Engine, Turbine, and Power Transmission Equipment Manufacturing; Electrical Equipment Manufacturing; Vehicle Manufacturing; Aviation and Aerospace Product and Parts Manufacturing; and Railroad Rolling Stock Manufacturing (U.S. Department of Homeland Security 2010).

The Dams Sector includes the vast collection of U.S. dams, totaling approximately 82,640, many of which are privately owned and only about a tenth of which (11 percent) fall under federal regulations. Ten percent of American cropland is irrigated by water stored behind these dams, which have an average age of about 51 years. With the United States second only to Canada in the production of hydropower, U.S. dams produce more than 103,800 megawatts of renewable electricity and meet up to 12 percent of the nation's power needs (U.S. Department of Homeland Security 2010).

The Defense Industrial Base (DIB) Sector includes the Department of Defense (DoD), government, and the private sector worldwide industrial complex, with the capabilities of performing research and development, design, production, delivery, and maintenance of military weapons systems, subsystems, components, or parts to meet military requirements. The DIB Sector includes tens of thousands of companies and their subcontractors who perform under contract to DoD (U.S. Department of Homeland Security 2010).

The Emergency Services Sector (ESS) is a system of response and recovery elements that forms the nation's first line of defense and prevention and reduction of consequences from any terrorist attack. The ESS includes the following first-responder disciplines: emergency management, emergency medical services, firefighting, hazardous materials management, law enforcement, bomb prevention and detection, tactical operations/special weapons and tactics, and search and rescue (U.S. Department of Homeland Security 2010).

The Energy Sector includes nuclear power, oil, coal, natural gas, hydroelectric and alternative sources such as wind. The United States relies on each of these fuel sources to meet the daily demand for energy. Each of these sectors is made up of a series of systems that rely on other energy infrastructure systems to move the energy source to areas as needed. The electricity segment, for example, contains more than 5,300 power plants with approximately 1,075 gigawatts of installed generating capacity. There are 133 operable petroleum refineries that include more than 100,000 miles of product pipeline. Last, there are more than 448,000 gas production and condensate wells and 20,000 miles of gathering pipeline in the country. There are more than 550 operable gas processing plants and approximately 300,000 miles of interstate and intrastate pipeline for the transmission of natural gas (U.S. Department of Homeland Security 2010).

The Government Facilities Sector includes a wide variety of buildings owned or leased by federal, state, territorial, local, or tribal governments; they are located both domestically and overseas. Many government facilities are open to the public for business activities, commercial transactions, or recreational activities. Others not open to the public contain highly sensitive information, materials, processes, and equipment. This includes general-use office buildings and special-use military installations, embassies, courthouses, national laboratories, and structures that may house critical equipment and systems, networks, and functions (U.S. Department of Homeland Security 2010).

The Healthcare and Public Health (HPH) Sector constitutes approximately 15 percent of the GDP, with roughly 85 percent of the sector's assets privately owned and operated (U.S. Department of Homeland Security 2010). Greater emphasis is placed upon the HPH Sector than any one individual hospital or medical facility because of the large number of sector assets, particularly hospitals and clinics. Protecting and preventing damage to any one asset is less vital than the ability to continue to deliver care.

The Information Technology (IT) Sector supports U.S. economic activity and other areas. Many critical infrastructure and key resources (CIKR) sectors rely on the IT Sector for products and services, including the reliable operation of networks and systems, and the movement and storage of critical data. The IT Sector accounts for about 7 percent of the U.S. GDP (World Information Technology and Services Alliance 2006). On a daily basis, more than $3 trillion worth of economic activity (e.g., securities sales settlements, check clearances, and interbank transfers) passes over secure federal financial networks (Federal Reserve Board 2010).

The National Monuments and Icons (NMI) Sector encompasses assets that are listed in either the National Register of Historic Places or the List of National Historic Landmarks. NMI sector assets share three common characteristics:

- They are a monument, physical structure, or object.
- They are recognized both nationally and internationally as representing the nation's heritage, traditions, and/or values or are recognized for their national, cultural, religious, historical, or political significance.
- They serve the primary purpose of memorializing or representing significant aspects of the nation's heritage, traditions, or values and as points of interest for visitors and educational activities.

They generally do not have a purpose or function (U.S. Department of Homeland Security 2008).

The Nuclear Reactors, Materials, and Waste Sector "accounts for approximately 20 percent of the nation's electrical use, provided by 104 commercial nuclear reactors licensed to operate in the United States. The Nuclear Reactors, Materials, and Waste (Nuclear) Sector includes: nuclear power plants; non-power nuclear reactors used for research, testing, and training; nuclear materials used in medical, industrial, and academic settings; nuclear fuel fabrication facilities; decommissioning reactors; and the transportation, storage, and disposal of nuclear material and waste" (U.S. Department of Homeland Security 2010).

The Postal and Shipping Sector processes over 500 million parcels and letters each day. It also maintains a large, geographically dispersed base of assets, systems, and personnel throughout the United States, including approximately 1 million people; 34,000 public and private operating facilities; 300,000 land vehicles; and more than 500 cargo aircraft. The U.S. Postal Service (USPS) receives, processes, transports, and distributes more than 170 billion pieces of mail domestically each year. Currently, there are approximately 1,500 postal inspectors stationed throughout the United States who enforce more than 200 federal laws covering investigations of crimes connected with the U.S. mail and the postal system (U.S. Department of Homeland Security 2010).

The Transportation Systems Sector includes aviation, highways, maritime transportation, mass transit, pipeline systems, and rails. Each of these subsectors has unique infrastructural systems and issues:

1. Aviation includes aircraft, air traffic control systems, and approximately 450 commercial airports and 19,000 additional airfields. This mode includes civil and joint-use military airports, heliports, short takeoff and landing ports, and seaplane bases.
2. The Highway Subsector encompasses more than 4 million miles of roadways and supporting infrastructure. Vehicles include automobiles, buses, motorcycles, and all types of trucks.
3. The Maritime Transportation System consists of about 95,000 miles of coastline, 361 ports, over 10,000 miles of navigable waterways, 3.4 million square miles of Exclusive Economic Zone to secure, and intermodal landside connections, which allow the various modes of transportation to move people and goods to, from, and on the water.
4. Mass Transit includes multiple-occupancy vehicles, such as transit buses, trolleybuses, vanpools, ferryboats, monorails, heavy (subway) and light rail, automated guideway transit, inclined planes, and cable cars designed to transport customers on local and regional routes.
5. Pipeline Systems include vast networks of pipeline that traverse hundreds of thousands of miles throughout the country, carrying nearly all of the nation's natural gas and about 65 percent of hazardous liquids, as well as various chemicals.
6. The Rail Subsector consists of hundreds of railroads, more than 143,000 route-miles of track, more than 1.3 million freight cars, and roughly 20,000 locomotives (U.S. Department of Homeland Security 2010).

The Water Sector includes both drinking water and wastewater utilities. There are approximately 160,000 public drinking water systems and more than 16,000 publicly owned wastewater treatment systems in the United States. Approximately 84 percent of the U.S. population receives their potable water from these drinking water systems, and more than 75 percent of the U.S. population has its sanitary sewerage treated by these wastewater systems (U.S. Department of Homeland Security 2010).

Each of the 18 sectors has a direct impact on personal and economic health of the United States, and events throughout the last decade have pointed toward the paramount need to make improvements in the country's infrastructure system. The system, of which 85 percent is owned by the private sector, is vast, expansive, and oftentimes difficult for most citizens to grasp. To complicate matters, most of these systems are fast approaching the age of 50 years or older.

When these infrastructures were developed, they were designed based upon the population at the time and the available technological resources. For example, our nation's capital has a 150-year-old sewer system; to put this into perspective, 100 years ago there were no automobiles, no airports, trucks, computers, or paved roads. Unfortunately, time and growth have taken their toll on much of the U.S. Critical Infrastructure System. The roads, public transit, and aviation systems continue to worsen, and the U.S water and sewage systems are in their worst condition in nearly 100 years.

Scope of the Problem

The most commonly referred to source on the state of U.S. critical infrastructure is the American Society of Civil Engineers (ASCE) *Report Card for America's Infrastructure*. The report provides grades on 15 categories of infrastructure within the United States. The results from both the 2005 and 2009 reports indicate that the country's infrastructure rates a cumulative grade of D. Ranking among the lowest categories were drinking water, inland waterways, levees, roads, and wastewater. Only one category, energy, improved between 2005 and 2009, going from a D to a D+. In assigning grades, the ASCE council charged with the task considers criteria such as capacity, condition, operations and maintenance, current and future funding, public safety, and resilience. As part of the assessment, the ASCE provides a financial estimate to bring the condition of the nation's infrastructure up to good condition. In 2005 this figure was estimated at $1.6 trillion, while the estimate in 2009 had risen to approximately $2.2 trillion (American Society of Civil Engineers 2009). The following examples, based on the ASCE Report Card Study, represent a snapshot of the extent to which the U.S. infrastructure is aging at alarming rates.

Within the water and environment area, the number of dams determined to be unsafe or deficient has risen from 3,500 in 2005 to 4,095 in 2007. Of that number, high-hazard-potential dams classified as deficient rose from 1,367 in 2005 to 1,819 in 2007. The rate of dam repairs is not keeping pace with the increase in the number of high-hazard dams needing rehabilitation. The gap between dams needing repair and those actually repaired is growing significantly. For example, the number of high-hazard deficient dams increased from 488 in 2001 to 1,826 in 2007. Additionally, the Association of State Dam Safety Officials found that the number of dams in the United States that could fail has grown 134 percent since 1999, to 3,346, and that more than 1,300 of those are considered "high-hazard"—meaning that their collapse would threaten lives (2007).

Within the transportation area, rail is an important component of the nation's transportation network (due to its efficiency and reduced energy consumption), supporting the economy through both commerce and tourism. Approximately 42 percent of all intercity freight in the United States travels via rail, including 70 percent of domestically manufactured automobiles and 70 percent of coal delivered to power plants

(Government Accountability Office 2006) As of 2006, railroads owned and operated 140,249 miles of track (Weatherford, Willis, and Ortiz 2007). However, most traffic travels on approximately one-third of the total network, which totals 52,340 miles.

The Northeast Corridor represents a major infrastructure challenge for Amtrak (a leading commercial rail company) and part of the difficulty with upgrading the infrastructure is the fact that the existing system was installed in the 1930s. Failure of these critical systems could bring the entire line to a halt, which would affect not only Amtrak but also the eight commuter railroads that share the Northeast Corridor (Crosbie 2008). In short, owing to a lack of adequate investment, limited redundancy, intermodal constraints, and energy system interdependencies, the rail system is not resilient.

The transportation area also includes our nation's bridges, which are approximately 43 years old on average and, when built, were estimated to last approximately 50 years (American Association of State Highway and Transportation Officials 2008). There are approximately 600,000 bridges currently being used in the United States. Of those, nearly 15 percent are considered categorized as functionally obsolete and 12 percent designated as structurally deficient. This accounts for about one in four rural bridges classified as deficient and one in three urban bridges as deficient (U.S. Department of Transportation 2010).

Additionally, a 2008 publication by the Pew Research Center compiled several alarming statistics regarding the current challenges with the U.S. Transportation Infrastructure. According to the U.S. Department of Transportation, more than 25 percent of America's nearly 600,000 bridges need significant repairs or are burdened with more traffic than they were designed to carry. The Federal Highway Administration estimates that approximately a third of the nation's major roadways are in substandard condition—a significant factor in a third of the more than 43,000 traffic fatalities in the United States each year. Several factors contribute to the challenges the country faces regarding infrastructure, as noted above. First, by 2007, the U.S. population grew to 303 million, up from 130 million 50 years earlier. Over the next 50 years, the population is expected to grow to 435 million. This represents a serious issue, as infrastructure built decades ago was never designed to handle the frequency of use represented by such a substantial increase in population. For example, in 2007 our highways carried 246 million vehicles, as compared with 65 million vehicles in 1955. This number is expected to reach nearly 400 million by 2055 (Jackson 2009).

The 2007 and 2008 Infrastructure reports detailed not only the dilapidated condition of U.S. infrastructure compared to that in European and Asian nations but also how an insular form of local planning and the lack of a cohesive national policy result in "congenital congestion and diminishing capacity" (American Society of Civil Engineers 2009). Transportation bottlenecks—road, freight, and airport—worsen while, at the same time, water supplies in many regions diminish and the power grid is put under more and more strain. (Ernst and Young 2009).

Potential Solutions

In an effort to remedy the challenges noted above, many stakeholders have proposed solutions to upgrade the status of the nation's infrastructure over the next several years. Commonalities among these solutions include a greater reliance on private sector funding/capital, encouraging elected officials to make infrastructure improvement a top priority, and the development of a national plan or strategy. With regard to a national plan, many present the 1956 Highway Act, developed by President Dwight Eisenhower, as a model for a nationwide critical infrastructure improvement plan. The 13-year, $27.5-billion project resulted in the development of the National Highway System. Eisenhower realized that the availability of skilled labor, the need for highways, and a demand for consumer goods could make the National Highway System a reality (Turnley 2004).

Infrastructure 2009: Pivot Point, produced by Urban Land Institute and Ernst and Young, recommends a four-pronged approach for revamping infrastructure in the United States. First, the setting of national policy (a national infrastructure plan) is encouraged to take into account current and future infrastructure needs as well as increasing population projections. Next, stakeholders are encouraged to plan holistically to reduce congestion, lessen the carbon footprint, rely less on foreign oil, and ensure adequate water supplies. After this strategy is put into place, the authors suggest a careful analysis of the government framework to ensure that the actions are executed and managed. Last, the authors realize that infrastructure improvements, no matter how effective the strategy, will require funding. It is suggested that private capital be attracted and a stronger effort made to advance public/private partnerships. Other tax-restructuring plans and technology implementation advancements are also discussed as an option for revenue generation (American Society of Civil Engineers 2009).

Additionally, the American Society of Civil Engineers report mentioned earlier in this article provides five key solutions for maintaining and improving the nation's infrastructure. First, the authors note that an increase in federal leadership in the area of infrastructure is essential. These leaders must develop a strong national vision to be shared by all levels of government and the private sector. Next, greater efforts toward the promotion of resiliency and sustainability must be undertaken. The nation's infrastructure must be designed to withstand and protect, while using sustainable materials and practices. As noted in the *Pivot Point* article, well-conceived plans and strategies must be developed to "complement our broad national goals of economic growth and leadership, resource conservation, energy independence, and environmental stewardship" (American Society of Civil Engineers 2009, 12). Before significant investment is made in infrastructure development, a detailed cost analysis should be conducted to ensure all costs are anticipated during the lifecycle of the specific infrastructure. Last, the authors contend that infrastructure improvement will be successful only if investments are increased and improved from all stakeholders. These stakeholders include all levels of government, private sector owners, and users (American Society of Civil Engineers 2009).

Providing a homeland security perspective, former U.S. Department of Homeland Security Secretary Michael Chertoff outlines a three-step process that combines both the protection and maintenance of infrastructure. First, he contends that a risk-based approach (similar to the model used to counter terrorist threats) should be implemented to address the need for both the maintenance and protection of infrastructure. Next, he suggests that federal agencies should examine the top 500 to 1,000 high-consequence and high-risk assets to determine their vulnerability. After the vulnerability assessment, he notes that a strategy for maintenance and protection can be developed that effectively estimates the cost of long-term maintenance on the existing infrastructure. Last, the strategy has to be funded, implemented and continued. Chertoff notes that he has observed many "worthy projects begin with a great deal of hoopla and public support, only to watch commitment wane once the television lights are off and the media moves on to the next issue" (Chertoff 2008, 13).

Conclusion

Aging and decaying infrastructure is not only an inconvenience to citizens of the United States; more importantly, it creates public safety issues that are accompanied by potentially devastating economic consequences. In addressing the state of infrastructure in the United States, this article has provided an overview of critical infrastructure sectors, the scope of the existing infrastructure challenges, as well as potential solutions. As awareness of the growing infrastructure problem increases, with events such as growing traffic congestion, airport delays, inadequate school facilities, and rolling blackouts/brownouts, it is hoped that the priority of infrastructure improvements will be increased in federal, state, and local jurisdictions. Despite the varying estimates of financial obligations that loom over the country, the fact remains that infrastructure must be improved with an eye toward population growth, increased infrastructure usage, and the modernization of development strategies, materials, and technologies.

See also **Airport and Aviation Security; Nuclear Energy; Transportation and the Environment; Supply Chain Security and Terrorism (vol. 1)**

Further Reading

American Association of State Highway and Transportation Officials (AASHTO), *Bridging the Gap*. www.transportation1.org/BridgeReport/front-page.html

American Society of Civil Engineers, *2009 Report Card for America's Infrastructure*. http://apps.asce.org/reportcard/2009/grades.cfm

Association of State Dam Safety Officials, "State and Federal Oversight of Dam Safety Must Be Improved." www.damsafety.org

Chertoff, M., "Preserving Infrastructure: A 21st Century Challenge." *Parameters* (Winter 2008): 5–13. www.carlisle.army.mil/USAWC/Parameters/Articles/08winter/chertoff.pdf

Collins, P. A., and R. K. Baggett, *Homeland Security and Critical Infrastructure Protection.* Praeger Security International. Westport, CT: Praeger, 2009.

Crosbie, W. L., Testimony before House Transportation and Infrastructure Committee. October 29, 2008. http://transportation.house.gov/Media/File/Full%20Committee/20081029/Crosbie.pdf

eXtension, *Food Safety Agrosecurity Overview,* 2010. http://www.extension.org/pages/Food_Safety_Agrosecurity_Overview

Federal Reserve Board, "Telling the Fed's Story through Money in Motion." 2010. www.phil.frb.org/publicaffairs/pubs/ar03telling.pdf/

Government Accountability Office, Freight Railroads: Industry Health Has Improved, but Concerns about Competition and Capacity Should be Addressed. October 2006.

Jackson, L., "We Must Do Something Now! Our Nation's Transportation Infrastructure Is Deteriorating." *Defense Transportation Journal* (February 2009).

Kelderman, E., "Look Out Below! America's Infrastructure Is Crumbling." Stateline.org/Pew Research Center, 2008. http://pewresearch.org/pubs/699/look-out-below

McNeil, J. B., *Building Infrastructure Resiliency: Private Sector Investment in Homeland Security.* Washington, DC: Heritage Foundation, 2008.

National Association of Insurance Commissioners, *2004 Insurance Department Resources Report.* Washington, DC: NAIC, 2005.

National Research Council, *Transportation Research Board (TRB) Special Report 27: Deterrence, Protection, and Preparation—The New Transportation Security Imperative.* July 2002.

Turnley, A., *National Strategy for Protecting the Infrastructure: A Visionary Approach.* USAWC Strategy Research Project. Carlisle, PA: U.S. Army War College, 2004.

The Urban Land Institute and Ernst and Young, *Infrastructure 2009: Pivot Point.* Washington, DC: Urban Land Institute, 2009.

U.S. Department of Agriculture, *Agriculture and Food Sector Specific Plan,* 2007. http://www.dhs.gov/xlibrary/assets/nipp-ssp-ag-food.pdf

U.S. Department of Homeland Security, "Critical Infrastructure and Key Resources." 2010. http://www.dhs.gov/files/programs/gc_1189168948944.shtm

Vaughan R., and R. Pollard. *Rebuilding Americas,* Vol. 1: *Planning and Managing Public Works in the 1980s.* Washington, DC: Council of State Planning Agencies, 1984.

Weatherford, B. A., H. H. Willis, and D. S. Ortiz, *The State of U.S. Railroads: A Review of Capacity and Performance Data.* Santa Monica, CA: Rand Supply Chain Policy Center, 2007.

World Information Technology and Services Alliance, "Digital Planet 006: The Global Informant on Economy," 2006. www.witsa.org/digitalplanet/2006/DP2006_ExecSummary.pdf

AIR POLLUTION

Robert William Collin

Smog, acid rain, methane, and other forms of outdoor air pollution, as well as air pollution inside homes and other buildings, can all affect the environment. Cars, trucks, coal-burning energy plants, and incinerators all make controllable contributions to air pollution. New environmental air pollution regulations continue to decrease emissions but with industry resistance.

Air

Air quality has been a driving force for U.S. and global air pollution control. It can be quite different from region to region and over time. Geological features such as deep mountain valleys may facilitate dangerous atmospheric conditions when on the downwind side of industrial emissions, heavy car and truck traffic, and wood and coal stoves. Points of contention in the air quality debate are scientific monitoring of air quality conditions, debate over what chemicals to regulate as pollution, and environmentalists' concerns over weak and incomplete enforcement. Each one of these is a controversy itself.

Public Health

One of the primary criteria for an airborne chemical to be a pollutant is its effect on public health. One of the first areas of public concern about air pollution is breathing.

Asthma is becoming more common. This is true even though some air pollutant concentrations have decreased. The increase in asthma is concentrated in people of color and low-income people. The incidence of acute asthma attacks in children doubled in the last 13 years even as very effective medicines were developed. About five million child hospitalizations were children who had asthma attacks. It is the most frequent cause of childhood hospitalization. Deaths of children with asthma rose 78 percent from 1980 to 1993. It is concentrated in high-population urban areas. This one environmental effect of air pollution can spread to inner-ring suburbs then to air regions over time. Asthma is described as like breathing through a straw. The serious public health issues around air pollution highlight the gravity of the problem as a whole.

Air pollution can have short- and long-term health effects. Asthma from air pollution can have short- and long-term effects. Short-term effects of asthma are irritation to the eyes, nose, and throat. Long-term reactions to air pollution can include upper respiratory infections such as bronchitis and pneumonia. Other symptoms of exposure to air pollution are headaches, nausea, and allergic reactions. Short-term air pollution can aggravate underlying medical conditions of individuals with asthma and emphysema. Long-term health effects are more controversial. Depending on the type of air pollution, there is general consensus that exposure can cause chronic respiratory disease, lung cancer, heart disease, and damage to the brain, nerves, liver, or kidneys. Continual exposure to most kinds of air pollution affects the lungs of growing children by scarring them at early stages of development. Recent studies suggest that the closer one is raised to a freeway in southern California, a notoriously low-quality air region overall, the greater the chance of having one of the listed long-term effects.

WHAT OZONE DOES TO LUNGS

The usual regulatory approach to environmental air pollution policy is the application of cost–benefit analysis to human health and environmental conditions. Although it is value-neutral, this approach can overlook the actual pain and suffering experienced by people in communities. Many communities experience contaminant flows and exposures, some over long periods of time. The application of cost–benefit analysis in the development of air pollution policy generally permits a certain risk of death from cancer per population. There are many other risks and costs, many of a currently unknown nature, short of cancer. They can affect both individual health and the health of a community. Particulate matter is associated with early and unnecessary deaths, aggravation of heart and lung diseases, reduction in the ability to breathe, and increases in respiratory illnesses. This, in turn, can lead to increased school and work absences. Cancer itself can have many causes other than air pollution. Nonetheless, it is known that air pollution can have long-term health effects depending on the type of pollution and the age of the exposed person. The exposure of young people to ozone is particularly controversial because they do not enter into the cost–benefit analysis unless they die of cancer. However, by ignoring this cost, society may face even greater costs later.

Ozone causes chronic, pathologic lung damage. Human lungs are like filters, cleaning the air of whatever contaminants are encountered. What they do not remove can enter the bloodstream. At the levels experienced in most U.S. urban areas, ozone irritates cell walls in lungs and airways. This can cause tissues to be inflamed. This cellular fluid seeps into the lungs. Over time, especially if that time includes early childhood, the elasticity of the lungs decreases. Excessive exposure to high levels of air pollution in childhood can impair lung development for life. Susceptibility to bacterial infections can increase. Scars and lesions can develop in the airways of children chronically exposed to ozone. Ozone's effects are not limited to vulnerable populations. At ozone levels in most warm-weather U.S. cities, average, healthy, nonsmoking young males who exercise can experience ozone impacts. Ozone exposure can shorten life and cause difficult breathing.

Hospital and emergency admissions increase as ozone levels increase. School and work absences increase. The level of human concern, from mother to child, increases as concern for our own and our loved ones' health rises. The intangible psychological factors of dread and fear weigh heavily on those who breathe polluted air. Ozone exposure is one of many.

Cumulative exposure to polluted air does aggravate or complicate medical conditions in the elderly. Some air pollution risk is involuntarily assumed. However, people die prematurely every year in the United States because of smoking cigarettes and voluntarily increasing other risk factors. Members of these communities label this type of risk assessment as blaming the victim. The involuntary assumption of health risks is something most communities strongly object to. With the advent of the Toxics Release Inventory many communities can track airborne industrial emissions. Citizen monitoring of environmental decisions has increased, especially around air quality issues.

State of Air Pollution

The air becomes polluted in different ways. How the air becomes polluted determines the types of problems it causes. Different sources of emissions contain different chemicals. These may interact with other airborne chemicals in unknown ways. As the chemicals mix with moisture in the air they can become rain. The rain can move the chemicals through the ecosystem, including crops and livestock. Mercury, lead, and aluminum all move in this way, with adverse ecological effects. There may be other chemicals with adverse ecological effects that do not last as long as metals do and may therefore be hard to detect while present. Air pollution can expose populations to more than just airborne pollution.

What Is Pollution?

The term *pollution* has important legal and environmental meanings. Legally, it means that a person or business is not complying with environmental laws. Many environmentalists do not think this is extensive enough and believe that large environmental impacts can be considered pollution even if they are legal. Many permits do not in fact decrease emissions but permit more emissions.

Many permits have numerous exceptions to emissions. The petrochemical industry is allowed *de minimus,* fugitive, and emergency emissions beyond the permit, and that industry is leaking a valuable commodity. Industry argues that if it complies with all the environmental laws, then its emissions are not pollution because they are part of the permit issued by the Environmental Protection Agency (EPA) via the respective state environmental regulatory agency. Although state and federal environmental agencies argue with the regulated industries, communities, and environmentalists, the actual environmental impact has worsened. Whereas many environmental decisions are made behind closed doors, more and more communities are monitoring the environment themselves.

One type of air pollution is particulate matter. The particles are pieces of matter (usually carbon) measuring about 2.5 microns or about 0.0001 inches. Sources of particulate matter are the exhaust from burning fuels in automobiles, trucks, airplanes, homes, and industries. This type of air pollution can clog and scar young, developing lungs. Some of these particles can contain harmful metals. Another type of air pollution is dangerous gases such as sulfur dioxide, carbon monoxide, nitrogen oxides, and other chemical vapors. Once in the atmosphere they follow the prevailing winds until they condense and fall to the ground as precipitation. This type of pollution can participate in more chemical reactions in the atmosphere, some of which form smog and acid rain. Other atmospheric chemical reactions are the subject of intense scientific controversy and are part of the debates of global warming and climate change.

Most air pollution comes from burning fossil fuels for industrial processes, transportation, and energy use in homes and commercial buildings. Natural processes can emit regulated chemicals at times. It is a subject of continuing scientific debate, both generally and specifically, how much of a given chemical is naturally emitted versus how much of the emission is from human actions.

The Natural Resources Defense Council closely tracks the air emissions of the biggest polluters. They call it their benchmarking project. They are a nonprofit environmental advocacy organization that believes in keeping track of environmental conditions to establish a baseline. Their research is based on publicly available environmental information, much of it available in the Toxics Release Inventory. Key findings of the benchmarking project's 2004 report include the following:

- Emissions of sulfur dioxide and nitrogen oxides have decreased by 36 percent and 44 percent, respectively, since the stricter pollution-control standards of the 1990 Clean Air Act went into effect.
- Carbon dioxide emissions increased 27 percent over the same period.
- Carbon dioxide emissions are expected to spike in coming years due to a large number of proposed new coal plants.
- Wide disparities in pollution rates persist throughout the electricity industry with a small number of companies producing a relatively large amount of emissions.
- Few power plants use currently available, state-of-the-art emissions control technologies.
- The electric power industry remains a major source of mercury emissions in the United States.

The Natural Resources Defense Council's benchmarking project uses public data to compare the emissions performance of the 100 largest power producers in the United States. They account for 88 percent of reported electricity generation and 89 percent of the industry's reported emissions. Emissions performance is examined with respect to four primary power plant pollutants: sulfur dioxide, nitrogen oxides, mercury, and carbon dioxide. These pollutants cause or contribute to global warming and to environmental and health problems including acid rain, smog, particulate pollution, and mercury deposition.

Indoor Air Pollution

The air inside of buildings can be as polluted as outside air. Indoor air can accumulate gases and other chemicals more quickly than outside air. Cooking, heating, smoking,

THE MOST POLLUTED TOWN IN THE UNITED STATES

The town with the most bad air days per year is Arvin, California. It has averaged about 73 bad air days per year since 1974. It is a small town with very little industry or traffic situated on the valley floor between the Sierra Nevada and Tehachapi Mountains in southern California. Air pollution comes in from the east with the prevailing winds. It comes from the large industrialized California communities of Fresno, Bakersfield, Stockton, and the San Francisco Bay area. The problem has been getting worse for this predominantly Hispanic community. The San Joaquin Valley Air Pollution Control District, where Arvin is located, recently passed a controversial cleanup plan, part of which calls for encouraging cleaner-running vehicles in Arvin and in Fresno. City buses and public vehicle fleets can reduce emissions, but not soon enough for everyone. The community has also considered various legal actions, primarily based on issues of environmental justice and unequal enforcement of environmental laws. Whole communities feel as though their health were threatened. Once this mass of polluted air moves out of the valley, it continues to have environmental impacts. One of the prominent national parks, Sequoia National Park, feels the impact of this waste stream of air pollution. It has among the highest number of bad air days in the country.

painting, new carpeting and glue, and heavy electronic equipment usage can all affect indoor air quality. Large numbers of books without adequate ventilation can cause carbon dioxide to build up. As most people spend most of their time indoors, the exposure to this air is much greater. Vulnerable populations, such as the very young and very old, spend even more time inside. Depending on the pollutants, indoor air pollution can lead to mold and fire hazards.

Conclusion

The controversies around air pollution show no signs of abating. Points of concentrated air pollution are getting more attention and becoming political battlegrounds.

Ports are the latest example of this. On September 5, 2007, the EPA began a research project to test equipment that measures air emissions by equipment used in ports to move goods around docks and on and off cargo ships, trucks, and trains. Most of this equipment burns diesel fuel. The EPA wants to test new equipment that can recapture the energy of hydraulic brakes and thereby use less polluting fuel. They are predicting fuel savings of 1,000 gallons per vehicle per year, with decreased maintenance costs for the fleet. The EPA is working with the Port Authority of New York and New Jersey, Kalmar Industries, Parker Hannifin Corporation, and the Port of Rotterdam. Port authorities are very powerful independent legal entities that can neither tax nor be taxed. They issue bonds. Interest on bonds is not income for federal tax purposes, or for state tax purposes if issued in that state. Wealthy individuals can reduce their tax liability and invest in the country's infrastructure. Historically, this was done in the West with railroad bonds. Authorities are creatures of state law, but very little is required in the way of public participation or environmental planning. Port authorities are able to resist many environmental requirements, especially if they involve several different states. The environment and ecology of ports are often toxic and unappealing. Ports are places where many ships empty their bilges of waste, often illegally. Some states have passed legislation to prevent cruise ships from dumping their wastes in their ports, such as California. Ports have also been the site of land-based waste-dumping practices. Along tidal areas many communities did this with the idea that the tide would take it away. Wastes from fishing and fish processing can also add to the mix. Ports are also the terminus of many rivers that have collected agricultural runoff, municipal sewage, industrial water discharges, and other types of waste. Ports are among the most environmentally challenging ecosystem reconstruction projects in the United States. In early 2000 many port authorities began to incorporate principles of sustainability into their long-range strategic corporate planning. The cumulative effects of waste, the increasing liability for clean up costs and its accounting as a contingent liability, and increasing urban environmental activism all undercut achieving anything sustainable in an environmental, business, or social sense. Port authorities now partner with the EPA around air pollution, expressly motivated by a concern about sustainability. New controversies will also emerge from these new policies, such as how clean is clean.

The environmental policies and laws do have the intended effect of reducing the emissions of some chemicals emitted by most industries. However, asthma rates increase and so too does community concern. It is likely that the costs of further decreasing emissions from industry, from municipalities, and from all of us will be more expensive. The current context of global warming and rapid climate change drives many air pollution controversies to center stage.

See also **Acid Rain; Automobile Energy Efficiencies; Climate Change; Coal; Cumulative Emissions; Global Warming**

Further Reading

Bas, Ed, *Indoor Air Quality: Guide for Facility Managers*, 2d ed. New York: Marcel Dekker, 2004.

Harrap, D., *Air Quality Assessment and Management*. London: Spon Press, 2002.

Lipfert, Frederick W., *Air Pollution and Community Health*. New York: Wiley, 1994.

Moussiopoulos, Nicolas, ed., *Air Quality in Cities*. New York: Springer, 2003.

Schwartz, Joel, *Air Quality in America*. Washington, DC: AEI Press, 2007.

Simioni, Daniela, *Air Pollution and Citizen Awareness*. New York: United Nations Publications, 2004.

AIRPORT AND AVIATION SECURITY

Bartholomew Elias

The terrorist attacks of September 11, 2001, and the response to those attacks have made aviation and airport security a focal issue for the past several years. On that day, teams of hijackers tied to al Qaeda, a radical Islamic terrorist group, commandeered four domestic flights in the United States, crashing two airplanes into the World Trade Center towers in New York City and one into the Pentagon near Washington, DC. The fourth crashed in a farm field in western Pennsylvania, presumably after passengers had learned of the terrorists' intentions and attempted to regain control of the aircraft. Nearly 2,000 people lost their lives in the attacks. Immediately following the attacks, the United States government moved swiftly to pass the Aviation and Transportation Security Act (ATSA) (Public Law 107–171). ATSA established the Transportation Security Administration (TSA), giving it direct responsibility for conducting passenger and baggage screening using a workforce of federal security screeners.

Responsibility for Airport and Aviation Security

Before 9/11, aviation security policies and practices in the United States had evolved out of an emerging need to address increasingly violent hijacking incidents in the early 1970s. Airlines were given the responsibility for mandatory passenger screening, which they, in turn, delegated to contract security firms. Physical security of the airport property, including perimeter security and access control systems for airport workers, however, was placed in the hands of airport operators. The Federal Aviation Administration (FAA) was responsible for regulating airport and airline security, although it had not issued regulations governing the contract security firms that conducted passenger screening. Such regulations had been proposed a year prior to the 9/11 attacks in response to a statutory mandate issued in 1996 (FAA 2000).

Following the 9/11 attacks, the U.S. Congress immediately began examining alternative models for aviation security. Lawmakers expressed considerable concern over low wages and high turnover rates among contract airport screeners. In 1999, the average hourly wage for airport screeners was $5.75, and many screeners did not receive additional benefits. Consequently, at several airports, annual screener attrition exceeded 100 percent (FAA 1999). Policymakers concluded that low pay and inexperience among screeners and lax oversight compromised aviation security. Congress learned that in Canada and in several European countries, both passenger screening and physical security of the airport property were instead the responsibility of airport operators, or in some cases government security forces, and not the airlines. Under these systems, screeners received more training and better pay than contract screeners in the United States, and limited data indicated that they performed better as well (United States General Accounting Office 2001). Under ATSA, the United States established a system under which passenger and baggage screening became the responsibility of the newly formed federal TSA, while airport physical security remained in the hands of the airport authorities. The TSA took over responsibility for regulating all aspects of airport and airline security from the FAA and was given broad authority to implement security measures to detect, prevent, and mitigate threats to aviation.

Passenger and Baggage Screening

Beginning in the early 1970s, the United States and other countries began deploying walk-through metal detectors (WTMDs) and carry-on baggage X-ray systems for pre-boarding screening. These technologies have served as the primary means for screening passengers for more than 30 years. By the mid-1980s, X-ray screening was also being used on a limited basis to screen checked baggage, usually on international flights, as a means to supplement procedures, known as positive passenger bag matching (PPBM), designed to ensure that passengers boarded with their baggage. By the late 1990s, the FAA had deployed about 100 explosives detection system (EDS) machines to screen high-risk baggage on a small number of international flights, but most checked bags were not physically screened (National Research Council 1999).

Following the 9/11 attacks, the United States mandated that all checked baggage undergo explosives detection screening using either EDS machines, which rely on the same principles at computed tomography (CT) scanners widely used in the medical field; explosives trace detection (ETD) systems, which utilize chemical analysis techniques to detect trace amounts of explosives residue or vapors; or other approved methods (see 49 U.S. Code, Sec. 44901). Efforts remain underway to integrate bulky EDS machines into airport baggage handling systems to improve the efficiency of screening the large amount of checked baggage processed at U.S. airports.

While these actions are addressing the threat of explosives placed in checked baggage, there has been growing concern over explosives carried into the aircraft cabin by passengers or in carry-on items. The 9/11 Commission (2004) formally recommended that the TSA give priority attention to implementing technology and procedures for screening passengers for explosives, and provisions to improve checkpoint technologies to detect explosives were included in the Intelligence Reform and Terrorism Prevention Act of 2004 (Public Law 108–458). In response, the TSA initially pilot tested walk-through trace detection portals, or puffer machines, and implemented procedures for conducting pat-down searches of passengers for explosives. Full deployment of the trace detection portals, for use in secondary screening of selected passengers, had been part of the TSA's original strategy for screening passengers for explosives. The machines, however, suffered from reliability issues blamed largely on dirt and humidity in the airport environment (Fiorino, Compart, and Wall 2010).

The TSA has since changed its strategy, focusing instead on whole-body imaging (WBI) technologies, also referred to as advanced imaging technology or AIT, that utilize either X-ray backscatter or millimeter wave imaging techniques to screen passengers and detect threat items concealed underneath clothing. The TSA has implemented procedures, including remote monitoring and privacy filters, to protect passenger identity and dignity and to prevent the storage of passenger images. Privacy advocates have nonetheless raised objections about the use of these screening devices, particularly as a primary screening method (Sparapani 2006).

The TSA is also investing in advanced technology (AT) X-ray equipment, capable of providing multiple view angles and automated threat detection capabilities to improve the screening of carry-on items, and handheld bottled liquids scanners to screen for liquid explosives. The need for bottled liquid screening capabilities emerged following a foiled plot to bomb airliners departing the United Kingdom for North American airports using homemade liquid explosives concealed in soft drink bottles that was uncovered in August 2006. Artful concealment of explosives and other threats carried by passengers remains a key concern. The December 25, 2009, attempted bombing of an international airline flight on approach to Detroit, using an explosive device concealed in the suspect's underwear, reinvigorated debate over policies and strategies for detecting explosives on passengers and in carry-on items. In response, the TSA has pushed for accelerated deployment of WBI systems and other checkpoint screening technologies (Karp 2010).

The cost of passenger and baggage screening and screening technologies, which totaled about $4.5 billion in fiscal year 2010, is paid in part by security fees charged to airlines and airline passengers and in part by general tax dollars collected by the federal government.

Passenger Prescreening and Behavioral Observation

Aviation security measures also rely on intelligence information to prevent suspected terrorists from boarding aircraft or to subject persons that may pose a security threat to additional screening. Prior to the 9/11 attacks, the FAA maintained a small "no-fly" list of known terrorists. Airlines were to deny boarding to any individuals on this list, however none of the 9/11 hijackers were on the list which, at the time, contained only 12 names (9/11 Commission 2004). After 9/11, the list was greatly expanded, and as of 2008 was reported to consist of about 2,500 names (TSA 2008a). The no-fly list is a subset of a larger terrorist screening database (TSDB), a list of about 400,000 individuals maintained by the Terrorist Screening Center (TSC), a unit of the Federal Bureau of Investigation (FBI). The TSDB is comprised of names of suspected and known terrorist compiled from domestic law enforcement databases and information on international terrorists compiled within the Terrorist Identities Datamart Environment (TIDE). The TIDE is a repository of foreign intelligence information on suspected terrorist operatives maintained by the National Counterterrorism Center (NCTC).

The TSA's Office of Intelligence continually updates the no-fly list by reviewing derogatory information contained in the TSDB to pinpoint those individuals believed to pose a specific threat to aviation. It also maintains a second larger list, known as the automatic selectee list, of individuals with possible ties to terrorism who are required to undergo additional checkpoint screening. In the past, the no-fly and automatic selectee lists were provided to the airlines, which were responsible for checking passenger names against these lists. However, the TSA has now implemented a system called Secure Flight, under which airlines provide passenger data, including items such as address and date of birth, to the TSA, which checks this information against the lists and notifies the airlines electronically of a match.

Additionally, airlines continue to utilize the Computer Assisted Passenger Prescreening (CAPPS) system, developed by the FAA in the 1990s, to evaluate passenger records for potentially suspicious characteristics, such as buying a one-way ticket using cash. Passengers determined to be of elevated risk based on the analysis performed by CAPPS may also be selected for secondary screening measures.

The TSA also deploys Behavior Detection Officers (BDOs) to observe passengers for possible indicators of hostile intent as part of a program known as Screening Passengers by Observation Techniques (SPOT). While the TSA has implemented SPOT at most major airports, government auditors found that the program has not been validated (United States Government Accountability Office 2010), and behavioral scientists have raised questions over the merits of the program (Weinberger 2010).

Airport Security

Whereas the TSA is responsible for prescreening and screening airline passengers, airport operators, with the assistance of state and local law enforcement, are responsible for the physical security of airport property including perimeter security and surveillance measures, access controls, and law enforcement support. Although the TSA (2006a) has published guidelines for integrating security elements in the design of airport terminals and facilities, no formal standards exist and solutions are tailored to the needs of specific airports. Since 9/11 many airports have invested in security technologies to enhance surveillance capabilities and improve perimeter protection. Airport security systems may include closed circuit television (CCTV) cameras, infrared sensors and thermal imaging cameras, computer vision systems to detect and alert security personnel regarding possible threats, ground surveillance radar, ground vehicle tracking, and integrated security solutions to tie together assorted sensors and surveillance technologies.

Airport operators also have the responsibility for coordinating law enforcement presence and support to intervene in security incidents as necessary and typically do so through formal arrangements with local or state law enforcement agencies. The TSA has entered into agreements at many airports to partially reimburse these law enforcement agencies for providing federally mandated coverage and law enforcement assistance to checkpoint screeners.

Airport operators are also responsible for implementing access control measures and issuing access credentials to airport workers. Airport workers must pass TSA criminal history records checks (CHRCs) and terrorist threat assessments before gaining unescorted access to secured areas. There has been considerable interest in implementing biometric credentials for airport access controls. While various biometric credentialing systems are being considered and evaluated for authenticating the identities of armed law enforcement officers, airline crews, and airport workers, uniform standards for biometric aviation security credentials have not been established and the use of biometrics in airport security is still relatively limited.

In-Flight Security Measures

ATSA included language requiring the installation and use of reinforced cockpit doors on passenger airliners. Other in-flight security measures used in some cases or under consideration include secondary flight deck barriers, video monitoring of the airline cabin from the cockpit, wireless devices for communication between pilots and flight attendants, and uninterruptable transponders that continuously report aircraft position and cannot be disabled by hijackers. Basic self defense training is provided by the airlines and the TSA offers voluntary advanced self defense training programs for pilots and flight attendants.

Since 9/11, the United States has deployed thousands of armed federal air marshals. Although the total number in the Federal Air Marshal Service (FAMS) is classified, air marshals typically work undercover in teams and, by law, are required to be on every flight considered high risk (49 U.S. Code, Sec. 44917). Prior to the 9/11 attacks, the number of air marshals had been reduced to 33 and deployments were limited to a small number of international flights (9/11 Commission, 2004). While FAMS expanded significantly following 9/11 and had an annual budget of almost $900 million in 2010, some media reports have raised concerns that FAMS cover only a very small percentage of daily flights (Griffin, Johnston, and Schwarzchild 2008).

In addition to deploying FAMS, considerable policy debate following the 9/11 attacks centered on whether allowing pilots to receive special training and authorization to carry firearms in the cockpit could serve to deter and prevent aircraft hijackings. Despite concerns raised by some aviation safety experts over the introduction of firearms in the cockpit, in 2002 the United States enacted legislation creating the Federal Flight Deck Officer (FFDO) program. Under the program, volunteer airline pilots that pass background checks receive firearms training and are issued a handgun to be used only on flights to protect the cockpit from hijackings and other threats. While the program has trained about 10,000 pilots through 2009 at an annual cost of about $25 million, pilot groups have complained that the remote location of the training site and other procedural requirements of the program have discouraged additional pilots from participating.

Options for Protecting Aircraft from Shoulder-Fired Missiles

On November 28, 2002, terrorists launched two shoulder-fired missiles at an Israeli charter jet departing Mombasa, Kenya. Following the incident, the United States Department of Homeland Security (DHS) initiated a program examining the feasibility of adapting missile protection systems deployed on some military aircraft for use on passenger jets. While the program resulted in the certification of two aircraft-based systems that can redirect a heat-seeking missile by focusing a laser on the missile's tracking system, these countermeasures have not been mandated and airlines have not voluntarily installed them on fleet aircraft. Other concepts for protecting airliners, including ground-based missile countermeasures and anti-missile systems installed on unmanned patrol aircraft deployed in airspace around an airport, have also been studied on a limited basis. The future utilization of these technologies remains uncertain, although there is still some particular interest in equipping airliners contracted to carry military troops into hostile areas with certified anti-missile systems. At present, however, the main deterrents against shoulder-fired missile attacks targeting civilian aircraft are law enforcement patrols and surveillance of likely launch sites around airports.

Shoulder-fired missiles remain a considerable security concern because they are widely proliferated on the black market and have the capability to down airliners flying below about 15,000 feet, making them a potential threat at considerable distances from an airport, sometimes as far away as 30 to 40 miles. With increased security to prevent aircraft bombings and hijackings, some experts fear that terrorists may resort to shoulder-fired missile attacks.

Air Cargo Security

Amid heightened security to screen passengers and baggage, concerns have also been raised over the possibility that terrorists may instead attempt to place explosives in air cargo. The Implementing Recommendations of the 9/11 Commission Act of 2007 (9/11 Act, Public Law 110–153) requires the physical screening of all cargo placed on passenger aircraft by August 2010. The TSA has addressed this requirement by developing the Certified Cargo Screening Program (CCSP), an approach that relies heavily on shippers, cargo consolidators, and freight forwarders to carry out much of the operational aspects of screening cargo, often at off-airport sites in conjunction with enhanced supply-chain security measures to prevent tampering with cargo after screening has been conducted. While the TSA maintains that this approach meets the requirements of the legislation, some have argued that the TSA should instead play a more direct role in conducting or overseeing screening operations, and that the screening should take place in closer proximity to locations where cargo is loaded on to passenger airplanes. Owing to the size of bulk and palletized cargo shipments, EDS has a more limited role in cargo screening, particularly at airport locations, and solutions are focusing on extensive use of ETD and canine explosives detection teams to efficiently screen air cargo for explosives.

The 9/11 Commission (2004) also recommended deploying at least one hardened, blast-resistant, cargo container on every passenger airliner. The 9/11 Act required the DHS to complete an evaluation of its hardened cargo container pilot program and, based on this evaluation, carry out a risk-based deployment of hardened cargo containers for use on commercial flights. Under this provision, the cost of acquiring, maintaining, and replacing hardened containers would be provided for by the DHS. While the pilot program has been completed, the future direction for operational deployment of hardened cargo containers remains uncertain.

In addition to improving the screening of cargo placed on passenger aircraft, regulations have been issued to improve security for all-cargo operations and protect against unauthorized access to large all-cargo aircraft. Under existing cargo security rules, secured areas of airports have been expanded to include cargo operations areas. Background checks and security threat assessments are required for all workers with access to air cargo, including an estimated 51,000 off-airport employees of freight forwarding companies. Also, under these regulations, an industry-wide database of known shippers was established and is maintained by TSA to allow freight forwarders and airlines to vet cargo shipments, allowing only cargo received from established known shippers to travel on passenger airplanes (TSA 2006b).

General Aviation Security

Although aviation security measures have focused primarily on protecting passenger airliners, some experts have raised concerns that terrorists may try to avoid detection by using nonairline general aviation aircraft to carry out a 9/11 style attack, deliver a nuclear or radiological weapon to its target, or to dispense a chemical or biological agent over a populated area or major outdoor event. Securing general aviation operations continues to be a significant challenge because of the diversity of operations, aircraft, and airports. Measures put in place thus far, such as the Airport Watch program and the TSA's general aviation security guidelines (TSA 2004), rely heavily on the vigilance of the pilot community to detect and report suspicious activity.

Flight training providers must verify citizenship and confirm that background checks have been properly completed by the TSA before providing training to foreign nationals (see Title 49, Code of Federal Regulations [CFR] Part 1552). Charter pilots operating aircraft weighing more than 12,500 pounds must pass background checks, and charter operators must implement security programs to protect aircraft from unauthorized access. Passengers flying on very large charter jets must be screened, and charter and private aircraft operators must adhere to special security procedures when operating at commercial passenger airports. All inbound and outbound international flights must send advance passenger and crew manifest information to U.S. Customs and Border Protection (CBP) which carries out terrorist watchlist checks and targeted screening of these names.

Security-related airspace restrictions affecting general aviation operators are most prevalent in the Washington, DC, area, where the city is encircled by a 15-mile-radius flight-restricted zone (FRZ) in which general aviation operations are significantly limited, and a larger special flight rules area (SFRA) where pilots must strictly adhere to special air traffic control procedures (Title 49 CFR Part 1562). In August 2005, the TSA implemented a security plan permitting a small number of general aviation flights—mostly large charter and corporate operations—to resume at Washington Reagan National Airport (DCA) which is located at the center of the FRZ. Operations at smaller GA airports located within the FRZ are highly restricted, requiring pilots to undergo background checks and adhere to special airspace security protocols. Since 9/11, flight restrictions have also been put in place at various times over New York City, Chicago, and elsewhere. General aviation pilots have been restricted from flying below 18,000 feet over Disney theme parks and over stadiums during major sporting events, and within 10 miles of a site during a presidential visit.

The TSA remains particularly concerned over the security of large general aviation aircraft. In October 2008, the TSA (2008b) proposed a variety of security measures for operators of all large general aviation aircraft, weighing more than 12,500 pounds, including privately owned, fractionally owned, and corporate aircraft. The measures proposed included CHRCs for all flight crew members, terrorist watch-list checks of all passengers, security inspections of aircraft, and biannual security compliance audits. In addition, operators of all aircraft weighing more than 45,500 kg (roughly 100,000 pounds) would be required to screen passengers and their accessible property. Similar security measures are already required for charter operators. General aviation operators and advocacy groups expressed considerable concern over the burden that would be imposed by these proposals. The TSA has since decided to revise its proposal based on additional input from general aviation interests. This, like many other aspects of aviation and airport security, continues to evolve at a rapid pace in response to changes in threats and vulnerabilities and shifting federal policies and strategies.

Conclusion

Although U.S. policies and strategies regarding aviation security continue to evolve, they have been predicated on a risk-based framework. This risk-based approach relies on expert judgment to evaluate the three core components of security risk: perceived threats, system vulnerabilities, and the potential consequences of various attack scenarios. Based on analyses of these risk factors, policies and strategies continue to evolve to allocate limited resources (including funding, personnel, and technology) in a manner that seeks to minimize security risk across the various sectors of the aviation system. As discussed, these sectors include air cargo operations and general aviation activity in addition to commercial passenger airports and airlines, which remain the primary focus of aviation security policy.

Aviation security relies on a multilayered strategy to protect high-risk components of the air transportation system. For example, commercial airline flights are protected by several layers of security that include passenger prescreening; passenger and baggage screening; and in-flight security measures such as hardened cockpit doors, air marshals, and armed pilots. A multilayered approach is more resilient to potential threats by including complementary security measures which, in combination, significantly reduce the probability that an individual or group could successfully carry out an attack.

Within this risk-based, multilayered framework, aviation security policies and strategies seek to strike a balance between effectively reducing security risk to acceptable levels while minimizing disruptions to air travel and commerce that may arise when various security measures are implemented and while taking appropriate steps to protect the privacy and dignity of the traveling public. Striking an appropriate balance between adequate levels of security and the efficient transportation of passengers and goods through the aviation system remains an ongoing challenge.

See also **Aging Infrastructure; Surveillance—Technological; Supply Chain Security and Terrorism (vol. 1); Patriot Act (vol. 2)**

Further Reading

Elias, Bartholomew, *Airport and Aviation Security: U.S. Policy and Strategy in the Age of Global Terrorism*. Boca Raton, FL: CRC Press, 2010.

FAA, *Draft Regulatory Evaluation, Initial Regulatory Flexibility Determination, Trade Impact Assessment, and Unfunded Mandates Determination: Notice of Proposed Rulemaking, Certification of Screening Companies*. Office of Aviation Policy and Plans, Operations Regulatory Analysis Branch (APO-310), Rulemaking Docket FAA-1999–6673, April 1999.

FAA, Certification of Screening Companies (Proposed Rule). *Federal Register* 65, no. 3 (2000): 560–611.

Fiorino, Frances, A. Compart, and R. Wall, "Technology vs. Terrorism." *Aviation Week and Space Technology* (January 4, 2010): 24–27.

Griffin, Drew, K. Johnston, and T. Schwarzchild, "Sources: Air Marshals Missing From Almost All Flights." *CNN* (March 28, 2010).

Karp, Aaron, "Security in a Post 12/25 World. *Air Transport World* (April 2010): 32–36.

National Research Council, *Assessment of Technologies Deployed to Improve Aviation Security: First Report*. Publication NMAB-482–5. Washington, DC: National Academy Press, 1999.

9/11 Commission [The National Commission on Terrorist Attacks upon the United States], *The 9/11 Commission Report: Final Report of the National Commission on Terrorist Attacks upon the United States* (authorized edition). New York: Norton, 2004.

Price, Jeffrey, and J. Forrest, *Practical Aviation Security: Predicting and Preventing Future Threats.* Burlington, MA: Butterworth-Heinemann, 2009.

Sparapani, Timothy D., Statement of Timothy D. Sparapani, Legislative Counsel, American Civil Liberties Union (ACLU), Before the Senate Committee on Commerce, Science, and Transportation, Regarding U.S. Transportation Security Administration's Physical Screening of Airline Passengers and Related Cargo Screening. Washington, DC, April 4, 2006.

Sweet, Kathleen, *Aviation and Airport Security: Terrorism and Safety Concerns,* 2d ed. Boca Raton, FL: CRC Press, 2008.

TSA, *Security Guidelines for General Aviation Airports.* Information Publication A-001, May 2004.

TSA, *Recommended Security Guidelines for Airport Planning, Design, and Construction.* Revised June 15, 2006a.

TSA, Air Cargo Security Requirements (Final Rule). *Federal Register,* 71 (2006b): 30477–30517.

TSA, *Myth Buster: TSA's Watchlist Is More Than One Million People Strong.* Washington, DC: Author, 2008a.

TSA, Large Aircraft Security Program, Other Aircraft Operator Security Program, and Airport Operator Security Program (Proposed Rule). *Federal Register* 73 (2008b): 64790–64855.

United States General Accounting Office, *Aviation Security: Terrorist Acts Illustrate Severe Weaknesses in Aviation Security.* Statement of Gerald L. Dillingham, Director, Physical Infrastructure Issues, Before the Subcommittees on Transportation, Senate and House Committees on Appropriations, September 20, 2001. GAO-01-1166T. Washington, DC: Author, 2001.

United States Government Accountability Office, *Aviation Security: Efforts to Validate TSA's Passenger Screening Behavior Detection Program Underway, but Opportunities Exist to Strengthen Validation and Address Operational Challenges.* GAO-10-763. Washington, DC: Author, 2010.

Weinberger, Sharon, "Intent to Deceive?" *Nature* 465 (2010): 412–415.

ANIMALS USED FOR TESTING AND RESEARCH

Robert William Collin

The use of animals for research and testing has been part of science since its inception. The lives of research animals of all kinds were often short and painful. In contrast, animal rights activists contend that the lives of animals should be protected as if they were human. They strongly oppose the pain and suffering and killing of animals.

Animals Used in Testing and Research

Animals are used extensively for food and clothing. They are also used in testing and research. Many researchers are most interested in the impact on human of a given chemical in the air or water. Other researchers are working on vaccines and other public health research. Some animals are used in medical diagnosis, such as seeing if a rabbit died after injected with the blood of a pregnant woman. Human subject testing is often illegal and considered unethical. Animals are used extensively and successfully in research and testing. Seventy million animals are used in this manner in the United States each year. Organizations using animals include private research institutions, household chemical product and cosmetics companies, government agencies, colleges and universities, and medical centers. Household goods and cosmetics such as lipstick, eye shadow, soap, waxes, and oven cleaner may be tested on animals. Many of these products now advertise that they do not use animals to test their products. These tests on animals are mainly used to test the degree of harmfulness of the ingredients. Animals are generally exposed to the ingredient until about half die in a certain time period. Animals that survive testing may also have to be euthanized. The primary objections to animal testing are as follows:

- It is cruel in that it causes unnecessary pain and suffering.
- It is outdated; there are more humane modern methods.
- It is not required by law.

Manufacturers justify the use of animal testing to make sure none of the ingredients in their products can pose human risks. By using mammals for their tests, manufacturers are using some of the best tests available. They also claim that the law and regulation almost require them to use animal testing. This is a point of controversy. According to the law, the Food and Drug Administration (FDA) requires only that each ingredient in a cosmetics product be "adequately substantiated for safety" prior to marketing. If it cannot be substantiated for safety then the product must have some type of warning. Furthermore,

- The FDA does not have the authority to require any particular product test.
- Testing methods are determined by the cosmetics and household product manufacturers.
- The test results are mainly used to defend these companies against consumer lawsuits.

Part of this controversy is the issue of humane alternatives, alternatives that do not use animals for testing or research. Animal rights advocates contend that humane alternatives are more reliable and less expensive than animal tests. Computer modeling and use of animal parts instead of live animals are the main humane alternatives. One controversial test uses the eyes of rabbits. The eyes of rabbits are very sensitive to their surroundings. Some Flemish hares (rabbits) were used in the storage silos of Umatilla's biochemical weapon storage facility. If nerve gas was escaping, the eyes of the Flemish hares would dilate. One test involving rabbits' eyes could be replaced by a nonanimal test. The Draize Eye Test uses live rabbits to measure how much a chemical irritates the eye. Instead of using live rabbits for this test, eye banks or computer models can be used to accurately test the irritancy level of a given chemical. However, researchers contest the reliability and cost of these alternatives.

Other alternatives to using animals for research and testing include

- Chemical assay tests
- Tissue culture systems
- Cell and organ cultures
- Cloned human skin cells
- Human skin patches
- Computer and mathematical models

Animal Testing Proponents

Today, scientists are using animal research to

- Study factors that affect transmission of avian flu between birds as well as the genetic and molecular adaptation from wild birds to domestic poultry
- Evaluate whether ducks in Asia are infection reservoirs sustaining the existence of the H5N1 virus
- Develop new and evaluate existing techniques to predict which mild forms of the avian flu virus might transform into more deadly forms
- Develop improved vaccines against avian flu for birds and evaluate vaccines for human use

Heightened animal research is necessary to combat avian flu and other new and emerging animal-borne diseases such as mad cow disease (bovine spongiform encephalopathy [BSE]), SARS, and West Nile virus. Scientists point out that about three-quarters of animal diseases can infect humans. Some call for more collaboration between animal health and public health organizations. Animal research and testing will be required for this collaboration.

Research and Testing of Animals to Achieve Public Health Victories

Major advances in U.S. public health that have increased longevity and the quality of human life were based on research using animals. The decline in U.S. death rates from cardiovascular diseases, infections, and most kinds of cancer since the 1960s is the result of new methods of treatment based on research requiring animals. Researchers claim that others do not understand the long-term results of such research and how it is conducted. Researchers also claim that others do not recognize important differences between using animals for product testing and for biomedical research. Biomedical research is more justified because of the public health benefits to society,

NUMBER OF ANIMALS USED

Information from regulated research facilities establishes some baseline data about the kinds and numbers of animals used in testing and research. Statistics from the Animal Research Database show how animals are used for testing and research.

- There are approximately 56 to 100 million cats and 54 million dogs in the United States.
- It is estimated that every hour 2,000 cats and 3,500 dogs are born.
- Between 10.1 and 16. 7 million dogs and cats are put to death in pounds and shelters annually.
- Approximately 17 to 22 million animals are used in research each year.
- Approximately 5 billion are consumed for food annually.
- Approximately 1.1 percent of dogs and cats from pounds and shelters that would otherwise be euthanized are used in research.
- Fewer than one dog or cat is used for research for every 50 destroyed by animal pounds.
- Rats, mice, and other rodents make up 85 to 90 percent of all research animals.
- Only 1 to 1.5 percent of research animals are dogs and cats.
- Only 0.5 percent are nonhuman primates.
- There has been a 40 percent decrease in the numbers of animals used in biomedical research and testing in the United States since 1968.

Other federal agencies have studied standards of animal care in testing and research. One of them is the United States Department of Agriculture (USDA). According to the USDA, approximately:

- Some 61 percent of animals used suffer no pain.
- About 31 percent have pain relieved with anesthesia.
- Approximately 6 percent experience pain because alleviation would compromise the validity of the data. Much of this work is directed at an understanding of pain.

These figures apply only to those animals covered by the Animal Welfare Act, which currently excludes rats, mice, farm animals, and cold-blooded animals. Some of these are used extensively in animal research.

There are continuing concerns that this reporting underestimates the extent of mortality and suffering.

while product testing is to increase the product safety to the consumer and profit of a manufacturer.

All researchers and research facilities are not the same. Some research sponsors are also concerned about the use of animals in testing and research. There are ways to encourage whenever possible the use of alternatives to live animal testing. The American Heart Association (AHA) sponsors important heart-related research. They have specific guidelines about how research animals are to be used and treated. First, the researcher must demonstrate that the animals are needed, and that there are no viable substitutes for the animal. Second, when animals are needed for association-funded experiments, the animals must be handled responsibly and humanely. Before being approved for Association support, the researchers must show that:

- They have looked at alternative methods to using animals.
- Their research cannot be successfully conducted without the use of animals.
- Their experiments are designed to produce needed results and information.

Together with other responsible and committed research-sponsoring organizations, the AHA hopes to ensure that the use of animals for testing and research will occur more carefully. Many universities have developed ethical guidelines for the use of animals in their research programs.

Not all animal testing occurs in these types of organizations. It is still much more expensive to develop new and untested alternatives than to treat some animals as expendable. A given method of drug testing may be more humane to the animals but less effective as a predictor of the drug's impact on humans.

The Animal Welfare Act of 1966

The main law is the Animal Welfare Act (AWA) of 1966. As such it has been a flash point of controversy for animal rights activists. The AWA is the minimum acceptable standard in most U.S. animal rights legislation. Its original intent was to regulate the care and use of animals, mainly dogs, cats, and primates, in the laboratory to prevent abuse. Now it is the only federal law in the United States that regulates the treatment of animals in research, exhibition, transport, and by dealers. In 1992 a law was passed to protect animal breeders from ecoterrorists. Other laws may include additional species coverage or specifications for animal care and use. Some state and cities have some laws that could be argued to protect against animals' use in research and testing, primarily animal abuse laws. They usually require a cooperative district attorney to file and pursue criminal charges. Because there are so many other types of animal abuse crimes than testing and research the prosecutorial discretion to investigate and enforce abuse laws puts testing and research animal abuse as a low priority.

The AWA is enforced through a federal agency with the usual enforcement powers of investigation, searches, and fines or penalties.

The AWA is enforced by the U.S. Department of Agriculture (USDA), Animal and Plant Health Inspection Service (APHIS) and Animal Care (AC). There is an extensive set of rules and regulations in place. The regulations are divided into four sections: definitions, regulations, standards, and rules of practice.

The definitions section describes exactly what is meant by terms used in the AWA. This section is very important as the legal definition of animal is different than its generally understood meaning. For example, the term *animal* in the act specifically excludes rats of the genus *Rattus* and mice of the genus *Mus* as well as birds used in research. There are many such exemptions in the AWA. These exemptions are controversial among animal rights activists because they consider the exemptions as contrary to the intent of the act. The regulations section of the AWA is quite specific. As noted on the USDA's Web site (USDA 2009), the regulations methodically list subparts for licensing, registration, research facilities, attending veterinarians and adequate veterinary care, stolen animals, records, compliance with standards and holding periods, and other topics such as confiscation and destruction of animals and access to and inspection of records and property. Monitoring these records from large research facilities, both those in compliance and those out of compliance, allowed the USDA to collect large amounts of information. The actual standards for treatment of animals by species are in the next section. Most of the subchapter is the third section that provides standards for specific species or groups of species. Included are sections for cats and dogs, guinea pigs and hamsters, rabbits, nonhuman primates, marine mammals, and the general category of "other warm-blooded animals." Standards include those for facilities and operations, health and husbandry systems, and transportation. This section is the one animal rights advocates most often seek to have enforced. If the animal rights advocates seek legal redress, they must first exhaust their administrative remedies before a court will accept jurisdiction. Their first step in seeking legal redress, generally for the enforcement of the above conditions, is the focal point of the final section of the act. The final section lists the rules of practice applicable to adjudicating administrative proceedings under the AWA. After exhausting administrative remedies under the act, animals rights activists can then go to court. One problem with the administrative agency issue is that it is very time consuming. The administrative agency, a potential defendant, controls the process and hearings format. Many public interest groups feel this is an unfair requirement because it drains the resources of the nonprofit organization before the issue can be resolved.

Animal Care: What Is Humane?

While there may be agreement that inhumane treatment to animals should be regulated, there is more controversy about what specifically is humane treatment. It is generally tied to the activity around the animal. Again, according to the USDA Web site (USDA 2009), the AWA requires that minimum standards of care and treatment be provided for certain animals bred for commercial sale, used in research, transported commercially, or exhibited to the public. People who operate facilities in these categories must provide their animals with adequate care and treatment in the areas of housing, handling, sanitation, nutrition, water, veterinary care, and protection from extreme weather and temperatures. Although these federal requirements do establish a floor of acceptable standards, there is controversy about whether they go far enough. There is also controversy about how well enforced the existing law is under the present circumstances. Regulated businesses are encouraged to exceed the specified minimum standards under the AWA. Some animals are bought and sold from unregulated sources for testing and research, and this remains a concern.

Exemptions

The AWA regulates the care and treatment of warm-blooded animals with some major exceptions, also known as exemptions. As older legislation from the 1960s, such as the AWA, passes through subsequent Congresses, exemptions or categorical exclusions are legislatively added to accommodate powerful interests and changes in public policy. Farm animals used for food, clothing, or other farm purposes are exempt. This is a large exemption representing powerful industrial agricultural interests. If they were included, argue these interest groups, the costs of production would increase the cost of food and clothing. Cold-blooded animals are exempt from coverage under the act, but some advocates are seeking to have them covered. The use of frogs for science courses is traditional. Many cold-blooded animals are used for training, testing, and research. Retail pet shops are another major exemption if they sell a regular pet to a private citizen. They are covered if they sell exotic or zoo animals or sell animals to regulated businesses. Animal shelters and pounds are regulated if they sell dogs or cats to dealers, but not if they sell them to anyone else. The last big exemption is pets owned by members of the public. However, no one is exempt from criminal prosecutions for animal abuse under state and local laws.

Pet Protection from Animal Testing and Research

Selling stolen or lost pets for research and testing is another aspect of this controversy. To help prevent trade in lost or stolen animals, regulated businesses are required to keep accurate records of their commercial transactions. Animal dealers must hold the animals that they buy for 5 to 10 days. This is to verify their origin and allow pet owners an opportunity to locate a missing pet. This also helps suppress the illegal trade in stolen animals for testing and research. Many pets are lost when a natural disaster occurs. Floods, storms, hurricanes, emergency vehicles, and threatening interruptions of food and shelter cause many pets to get lost. Some pets now have a computer chip implanted in them for tracking purposes. Critics point out that many commercial transactions about animals used in testing and research do not always happen with regulated businesses. The legal definition of regulated research facilities specifically includes hospitals, colleges and universities, diagnostic laboratories, and cosmetic, pharmaceutical, and biotechnology industries. Animal dealers complain about the cost of holding animals that long and the other costs of verifying ownership. Many animal shelters operate on a small budget and must euthanize animals to make room for new arrivals faster than the holding period allows. Rigorous enforcement against these groups could put them out of operation, with the net result of no shelter provision or adoption site for animals.

Humane Standards in Research Facilities

Much of the regulation of animal use in testing and research occurs in research facilities. The standards are slightly higher for dogs and primates. All warm-blooded animals, with some major exemptions, get some veterinary care and animal husbandry. This means that a licensed veterinarian examines the health of the animal, and the animal is kept in a clean, sanitary, and comfortable condition. Some animals require a higher standard of care by law. Regulated research facilities must provide dogs with the opportunity for exercise and promote the psychological well-being of primates used in laboratories. According to the USDA's Web site (USDA 2009) researchers must also give regulated animals anesthesia or pain-relieving medication to minimize the pain or distress caused by research if the experiment allows. Regulated entities do express some concern about the cost of these additional procedures. The AWA also prohibits the unnecessary repetition of a specific experiment using regulated animals. The regulated entity itself determines how much repetition is unnecessary. One tenet of science is the ability to repeat a given chain of events, such as corneal exposure to a chemical, and get the same result, such as death or blindness. By prohibiting the repetition of the animal-based tests, some of the results may be weaker. The public protection from a chemical may be weaker, and the industry may be exposed to a large class-action negligence suit. Therefore, research procedures or experimentation are exempt from interference when designated as such. This is a large exemption in an area where animals are thought to suffer pain, and where substitutes or alternatives to animals are not used frequently. This is a continuing battleground in this controversy.

AWA has strict monitoring and record-keeping requirements. The lack of records has been a controversy in the past. By keeping records, information about animals used in testing and research can be gathered. The problem was how to require the regulated entity to comply with the AWA and produce necessary records. The solution in this case was to require a committee at the regulated entity and mandate its membership. The law requires research facilities to form an "institutional animal care and use committee." The purpose of this committee is to establish some place of organizational accountability for the condition of animals at a given research institution. They are primarily responsible for managing aspects of the AWA, especially in regard to the use of animals in experiments. This committee is the point of contact responsible for ensuring that the facility remains in compliance with the AWA and for providing documentation of all areas of animal care. By law, the committee must be composed of at least three members, including one veterinarian and one person who is not associated with the facility in any way.

ANIMAL RIGHTS GROUP CONVICTED OF INCITING VIOLENCE AND STALKING

Those opposed to animal testing have sometimes used violence to make their point, which further inflames this controversy. Criminal prosecution is also a part of it, especially with focused legislation. This, in turn, makes courts one of the battlegrounds.

On March 9, 2006, members of an animal rights group were convicted of two sets of criminal acts. The first was conspiracy to violate the Animal Enterprise Protection Act and the second was interstate stalking. This led to a long and controversial federal jury trial in Trenton, New Jersey. The group itself was also convicted. The jury found the group Stop Huntingdon Animal Cruelty (SHAC) and six of its members guilty of inciting violence against people and institutions who did business with Huntingdon Life Sciences (HLS), a British-based research firm that runs an animal testing laboratory in East Millstone, New Jersey.

SHAC targeted HLS, as well as other companies doing business with HLS, because it uses animals to test the safety of drugs and chemicals. SHAC has claimed responsibility for several bombings and dozens of acts of vandalism and harassment in both the United States and Europe to protest the use of animals in research and testing. Its campaign against HLS has become an international cause among animal rights activists since the late 1990s.

The six defendants—former SHAC spokesperson Kevin Kjonaas; Lauren Gazzola, whom the indictment identified as SHAC's campaign coordinator; Andrew Stepanian, a long-time activist with SHAC and the Animal Defense League; Joshua Harper a self-described anarchist and SHAC activist; and SHAC members Jacob Conroy and Darius Fullmer—were all found guilty of conspiracy to violate the Animal Enterprise Protection Act.

Kjonaas, Gazzola, and Conroy were also found guilty of multiple counts of interstate stalking and conspiracy to engage in interstate stalking. In addition, Kjonaas, Gazzola, and Harper were found guilty of conspiracy to violate a telephone harassment act.

The defendants were arrested in May 2004 by federal agents in New York, New Jersey, California, and Washington. They face three to seven years in prison and fines of up to $250,000. They may also face judgments in civil trials from victims.

The defendants were convicted of conducting a very personal, no-holds-barred campaign of terror against HLS employees and their children. During the three-week trial, prosecutors showed how SHAC's campaign against HLS involved posting personal information on the Internet about its employees and about employees of firms that do business with HLS. The information posted on the Internet included phone numbers, home addresses, and, in some cases, information on where employees' children attended school. Many of those targeted had their cars and homes physically vandalized and received threats against them or their families, according to court testimony.

According to law enforcement officials, one female employee was sent an e-mail from SHAC threatening to "cut open her seven-year-old son and fill him with poison."

(continued)

(*continued*)

The Animal Enterprise Protection Act, signed into law by the first President Bush in 1992, provided animal research facilities with federal protection against violent acts by so-called animal rights extremists. The act gave prosecutors greater powers to prosecute extremists, whose attacks create damages or research losses totaling at least $10,000. Animal enterprise terrorism is defined in the act in part as "physical disruption to the functioning of an animal enterprise by intentionally stealing, damaging, or causing the loss of any property (including animals or records)."

Some critics charged that prosecutors rarely used the Animal Enterprise Protection Act because the penalties were too mild and it was difficult to prove damages of more than $10,000. An antiterrorism bill signed into law by President George W. Bush in 2002 substantially increased the penalties for such actions. Prior to the SHAC trial, there appears to have been only a single successful prosecution under the Animal Enterprise Protection Act. In 1998, a federal grand jury in Wisconsin indicted Peter Daniel Young and Justin Clayton Samuel under its provisions for breaking into several Wisconsin fur farms in 1997 and releasing thousands of animals. Samuel was apprehended in Belgium in 1999 and quickly extradited to the United States. In 2000, Samuel pleaded guilty and was sentenced to two years in prison and ordered to pay over $360,000 in restitution. Young was a fugitive until arrested in March 2005 in San Jose for shoplifting. He was later sentenced to two years in prison.

While there are controversial questions about the enforcement of the Animal Welfare Act, there is little question about the rigorousness of enforcement against those who commit terrorist acts of protest to free animals used for fur, testing, and research.

Conclusion

The controversy around the use of animals for testing will continue because animals will continue to be used for testing. Animal rights groups assert that enforcement of a weak law riddled with exemptions is inadequate and that animals are being abused. One environmental impact of a poorly regulated animal trade is the importation of endangered species under conditions of high mortality. Testing on animals, unlike dogfighting, is done at large institutions often receiving federal research grants. Many of these are universities. When human health considerations are thrown into the equation, animal testing is often justified by researchers despite animal mortality.

See also **Endangered Species; Epidemics and Pandemics; Vaccines**

Further Reading

Bekoff, Marc, ed., *Encyclopedia of Animal Rights and Animal Welfare,* 2d ed. Santa Barbara, CA: Greenwood Press, 2009.

Botzler, Richard George, *The Animal Ethics Reader.* London: Routledge, 2003.

Carbone, Larry, *What Animals Want: Expertise and Advocacy in Laboratory Animal Welfare Policy.* New York: Oxford University Press, 2004.

Garner, Robert, *Animals, Politics, and Morality.* Manchester, UK: Manchester University Press, 2004.

Gluck, John P., Tony DiPasquale, and Barbara F. Orlans, *Applied Ethics in Animal Research: Philosophy, Regulation and Laboratory Applications.* Ames, IA: Purdue University Press, 2002.

Moran, Lisa C., *Science, Medicine, and Animals.* Washington, DC: National Academies Press, 2005.

Regan, Tom, *Defending Animal Rights.* Chicago: University of Illinois Press, 2001.

Rudacille, Deborah, *The Scalpel and the Butterfly: The Conflict between Animal Research and Animal Protection,* Berkeley: University of California Press, 2001.

USDA, "Questions and Answers about the Animal Welfare Act." 2009. http://www.nal.usda.gov/awic/pubs/Legislat/regsqa.shtml

AUTOMOBILE ENERGY EFFICIENCIES

ROBERT WILLIAM COLLIN AND DEBRA ANN SCHWARTZ

Emissions from cars and trucks are central to debates about air pollution and how much of such pollution poses an acceptable risk. The first federal clean air laws were passed in the late 1960s and early 1970s. Pollution-control devices and lead-free gas have decreased some emissions. The onus is on the automobile industry to produce more efficient cars that use less gas and to decrease the environmental impact of vehicles. Emissions from cars and trucks continue to accumulate in land, air, and water. Increased retail sales of fuel-inefficient sport utility vehicles (SUVs) and light trucks, combined with overall increases in number of vehicles, continues to generate emissions that degrade air quality.

Environmentalists want cars with higher fuel efficiency that produce less pollution. Consumers want inexpensive gas and more cars and trucks to drive. Communities want clean air and have valid public health concerns. The petrochemical industry claims it is moving with deliberate speed to comply with environmental standards, garnering tax breaks and profits along the way. However, the near collapse of General Motors and its recent response—to bring hybrid cars to market—suggests a new commitment to social consciousness and less emphasis on Wall Street and profits. For example, in the past, large, luxurious vans turned the largest profit for General Motors, prompting the company to abandon its Saturn brand in favor of gas guzzlers. Many marketing the GM Saturn initially contended that fuel-efficient cars of this kind represented GM's future. However, when bottom lines did not rise fast enough to satisfy stockholders, GM succumbed to pressure and killed the brand.

Fundamental Conflict: Industry and Government

The battle between the government and industry over legislating the production of more efficient vehicles is a long-standing one. Most of this legislation requires minimal compliance by industry at some date years in the future. Manufacturers claim that it takes resources from research and development right now to try to change production technologies to meet those standards. Sometimes they get tax breaks and other public policy–based encouragement to do so. One area of contention is the free market. Market demand is for more cars, trucks, airports, and other petrochemical-based activities. Does legislation from democratically elected representatives constitute market demand? Many economists would say that it does not. Environmentalists claim that the minimal requirements are not fast or stringent enough.

In early April 2010, President Barack Obama changed fuel economy standards in the United States. The administration issued final regulations compromising fuel economy standards set in the Clean Air Act requiring fuel efficiency to increase to over 40 miles per gallon (mpg) by 2015 and 55 mpg by 2025. The compromise, which required an increase instead to 35.5 mpg by 2016, was celebrated by the auto industry for creating a unified national program from a patchwork of varying state and federal standards. It prompted the industry to voluntarily dismiss lawsuits challenging California's motor vehicle greenhouse gas emission standards, which were more stringent than federal standards when adopted a few years ago. With the compromise, California amended its regulations to match federal standards. Rising gas prices, the slowly deepening effects of rising gas prices on food and other consumer goods, and concern about air pollution all increased public involvement. In 2005, California and 16 other states sued the EPA for refusing to allow them to raise fuel economy standards beyond federal limits. Federal law can preempt state law.

Adopting fuel-efficient or alternative fuel technologies to meet the Clean Air Act standards would, in theory, save enormous amounts of gas and oil. A series of environmental disasters involving offshore oil drilling and ocean tankers in 2008 and 2009 may have pushed attention in the direction of acceptance. The sinking of the BP–Deepwater Horizon oil rig in the Gulf of Mexico near Louisiana in April 2010 caused the Obama administration to halt its plans to expand offshore drilling pending further investigation. A major controversy over alternative fuel solutions is whether they would prevent further environmental degradation. Global warming controversies are also pushing this issue into the public view. Some contend the United States needs to do more in terms of addressing mobile emissions sources and their environmental impacts. The exploration of alternative fuels for vehicles can be controversial in terms of environmental impacts. The removal of lead from U.S. gasoline was a major step forward, not yet replicated around the world. It greatly reduced airborne lead emissions. However, with current standards and the volume of driving, assuming complete environmental compliance, U.S. vehicles would still emit 500,000 tons of smog-forming pollution every year.

The United States is among the leading nations for both pollution and pollution-control technology. Diesel-powered vehicles are major polluters. They emit almost 50 percent of all nitrogen oxides and more than two thirds of all particulate matter (soot) produced by U.S. transportation. Because the United States is more reliant on trucks (which tend to be diesel-fueled) for the shipment of goods and raw materials than other nations, diesel emissions can be large contributors to an air stream, along with many other pollutants. Some of these regulated pollutants are from industry and some from the environment.

The scale of diesel usage and its known emissions make it an environmental issue. Nitrogen oxides are powerful ingredients of acid rain. Acid rain can cause nitrogen saturation in crops and wilderness areas. Soot, regulated as particulate matter, irritates the eyes and nose and aggravates respiratory problems including asthma. Urban areas are often heavily exposed to diesel fumes. While diesel is a polluting fuel, regular unleaded gasoline can also pollute. Overall, the environmental impacts of the combustion engine remain largely undisputed. What is disputed is whether the environmental regulations go far enough to mitigate environmental impacts from these sources. The controversy about automobile energy efficiencies opens this aspect of the debate.

Commercial hybrid electric vehicle (HEV) models use both batteries and fuel. In the past few years they have been produced and marketed to the public. More recently, HEV drive trains have been used successfully in heavy-duty trucks, buses, and military vehicles.

Researchers also want to move HEV technology into a more sustainable lifestyle. They would like to produce and market plug-in hybrids that can plug in to household outlets. They want them to be able to store electricity and operate as clean, low-cost, low-environmental-impact vehicles for most of their normal daily mileage. Right now electric cars are limited by their batteries. Combining engines with them and using braking power to recharge the batteries does extend their range and power but also increases their emissions. Transportation is conceptualized as part of a environmental low impact and sustainable lifestyle. These communities unite plug-in hybrids, other low-impact transportation alternatives (bicycles, mass transit stops), zero-energy homes, a range of renewable energy technologies, and sustainable environmental practices. One example of such a community is the Pringle Creek Community in Salem, Oregon.

Hybrid Electric Vehicles

Hybrid electric vehicles, also known as HEVs, are an old idea renewed. In the early 1900s electric cars were popular for their quiet, but did not move as fast as gasoline-driven cars. Present-day hybrids combine both technologies: internal combustion engines and electric motors. The source of the fuel and the electricity may differ from model to model.

The biggest challenge plug-in hybrids face is that even the most rechargeable batteries lose the ability to hold a charge. They then become hazardous waste, There is also a financial and environmental cost to the use of electrical power. Much electrical power in the United States comes from coal-fired power plants. Companies such as Massy Coal are engaged in mountaintop removal practices to separate veins of coal from other rock.

That process involves blowing off the top peaks of mountains and using chemicals such as arsenic and stricnine to loosen the coal. The process creates sludge laced with poison. It is filling rivers and lakes throughout Appalachia, where a large percentage of coal is mined in the United States. That is one environmental impact of using coal-fired electricity. Solar-powered batteries do not represent the same problem.

It is possible to recharge plug-in hybrid vehicles from renewable energy sources. Scientists are extensively researching thermal management, modeling, and systems solutions for energy storage. Scientists and engineers also are researching ways to increase the efficiency of the electrical power.

In addition, researchers seek to make the plug-in electric car reversible. In many areas homes and businesses can sell back energy they do not use or that they create. This is one way to protect the electric grid from brownouts, as well as conserve energy from non-renewable resources. In hybrid vehicles it is called a vehicle-to-grid or V2G. These cars would have a two-way plug that allows the home and vehicle owner and local utility to exchange power back and forth. This could make the batteries accessible backup power in the event of a natural disaster or other power outage. It could also encourage citizens to buy new hybrid cars. Utilities pay for peak, backup, and unused power. Transportation analysts can quantify the potential value of such systems in terms of gas saved, air quality, and other measures. There could be substantial automobile energy efficiencies in these approaches, but many remain untried at a large level. Reversible electrical energy may not be much less environmentally harmful if the source of the electric power and the waste generated have harmful environmental impacts.

Fuel-Cell Vehicles

As research and conceptualization has moved HEVs into production, fuel-cell technology is taking shape. Hydrogen fuel cells have long been used to generate electricity in spacecraft and in stationary applications such as emergency power generators. Fuel cells produce electricity through a chemical reaction between hydrogen and oxygen and produce no harmful emissions. In fuel-cell vehicles (FCVs), hydrogen may be stored as a pressurized gas in on-board fuel tanks. The electricity feeds a storage battery (as in today's hybrids) that energizes a vehicle's electric motor.

An FCV may be thought of as a type of hybrid because its electric battery is charged by a separate on-board system. This underscores the importance of advancing present-day HEV technologies. HEVs help reduce petroleum consumption immediately and provide lessons about batteries, energy storage, fuel advancements, and complex electronic controls that may apply directly to future transportation technologies.

What Is Biodiesel?

Biodiesel is a catchall term used to describe fuel made from vegetable oil or animal fats. These fats are generally converted to usable fuel by a process called *transesterification*.

Biodiesel fuels are usually mixed with conventional diesel. It is estimated that 140 billion gallons of biodiesel could replace all oil used for transportation in the United States. This is an enormous amount of biodiesel, which is creating controversy and innovation in the sources of biodiesel. Large-volume biodiesel use could raise concerns about land-use impacts common to all plant-based fuels. Are there enough plants, such as corn, to meet the fuel needs? Land-use impacts could be much larger if the market demand is driven by fuel needs. Alternative energy sources almost always include renewable energy sources such as solar power. Because most biodiesel is made from plant-based oils or waste-stream sources, it is a renewable fuel. Would there be enough of it?

Waste vegetable and animal fat resources are estimated to be able to produce a billion gallons of biodiesel per year. That prediction is considered speculative by some because it assumes adequate plant and waste production. Collecting the wastes, distilling and cleaning the fat from them, and using the resulting product as fuel can have environmental impacts. Farmers and proponents of biodiesel claim that distribution costs should go down as the first biodiesel stations begin operations and the price of petrochemicals increases. Use of more than a billion gallons per year of biodiesel would require more virgin plant oils and crops for biodiesel production. It would also require the discovery and organization of other waste-stream sources to meet larger demands. More land would be needed to plant necessary crops, such as corn. Crops grown for biodiesel can be grown in a manner that has negative environmental consequences for entire ecosystems. Just as in the case of other crops, they can require pesticides and may be genetically manipulated.

Biodiesel and Global Climate Change

One of the environmental advantages touted with biodiesel is that it has fewer environmentally degrading emissions. Critics have pointed out that biodiesel vehicles require more fuel depending on the mix and may have overall more combustion. Some biodiesel requires chemicals to start up when it is cold. Sometimes the vehicle must warm up to get the grease warm enough to flow. Pure 100 percent biodiesel results in large reductions in sulfur dioxide. However, it can cause 10 percent increases in nitrogen oxide emissions. A popular mix of biodiesel is about 80 percent biodiesel and 20 percent regular diesel, which increases the pollutants emitted proportionally. These pollutants are responsible for acid rain and urban smog. Biodiesel companies are beginning to operate service stations to distribute the fuel. There is controversy about its environmental impacts. Some tailpipe emissions are reduced. However, when the entire life of the vehicle is considered, running on 100 percent biodiesel, some smog-forming emissions can be 35 percent higher than those from conventional diesel.

Are There Other Environmental Attributes of Biodiesel?

One big concern and source of controversy are oil spills and their environmental impacts. Regular petrochemical spills can travel quickly in water and permeate land, depending

ALTERNATIVE FUELS, ETHANOL, AND CORN: POTENTIAL ENVIRONMENTAL IMPACTS

With the rapid increase in demand for ethanol, more corn is being planted in the United States. Ethanol is made from corn. The problem with growing large amounts of corn is the environmental impact. One large concern is the amount of water required for its production. A gallon of ethanol requires about three gallons of water to produce. In locations without reliable water sources it may not be a cost-efficient alternative fuel. Corn requires about 156 pounds of nitrogen, 80 pounds of phosphorus, and differing amounts of pesticides per acre to grow from seed to harvest. Corn requires large amounts of nitrogen because it cannot absorb it from the air. What the corn does not absorb runs off the land into the water table. This causes algae blooms that warm up the water and use up the oxygen, sometimes resulting in large fish kills. Nitrates in the water, largely from agricultural runoff, are also blamed for deaths of livestock, and some suspect them to have played a role in human fatalities. Algae growth can cause other bacteria to grow that are harmful to humans.

Many corn farmers use sophisticated satellite tracking measurements to make sure fertilizer levels are not exceeded. Many keep records of inventory as a condition of bank loans and can keep track of fertilizer expenses. More and more farmers are planting buffer strips between their fields and waterways. These buffer strips are areas of vegetation, usually indigenous, that filter water or runoff from fertilized fields. It is difficult for farmers to leave a buffer strip. Usually the soil near the water is better. Buffer strips can attract animals that dig holes in the fields and destroy crops. Not all farmers are owner–operators. Many commercial agribusinesses lease land to farm. Although their leases often make allowances for buffers and land held in soil and water conservation programs, they are seldom enforced.

on soil structure. Biodiesel is considered less harmful to the environment because it biodegrades four times faster than conventional diesel, so its environmental impacts are not as long-term or ecologically pervasive. It quickly degrades into organic components. Production of petroleum diesel creates much more hazardous waste than production of biodiesel. Biodiesel produces more overall waste depending on the source but generally twice as much as nonhazardous waste. Some of the nonhazardous wastes may be recyclable.

One developing source for biodiesel is algae, grown specifically for this purpose. The specialized algae are grown in a variety of ways. They are vastly easier to grow than most other crops and grow very quickly. While growing, they absorb large amounts of carbon dioxide, a greenhouse gas. Technological entrepreneurship is very much engaged in this, and algae strains are sometimes protected trade secrets. The species used now in the United States is *Botryococcus braunii* because it stores fat that is later used as fuel. The algae must then be broken down to separate fats from sugars. Solvents are used for this, which could be a source of environmental impacts depending on by-products and manufacturing waste streams. Fats cannot be cold pressed out of algae because they are too fragile and disintegrate. The fats are made into biodiesel. One issue is whether they could produce enough to meet demand for biodiesel from vehicles. Aquaflow, a New Zealand algae fuel company, says that it has achieved this.

Oil and Power: Impacts on Automobile Energy Efficiency

The primary resistance to increasing the efficiency of automobile and truck engines is the petrochemical industrial complex. Large oil companies are the backbone of U.S. industry and part of a thriving economy. They are multinational corporations that exert political power here and abroad. Some have revenues larger than those of most nations. Their only legal motivation is to make profit from dispensing a limited natural resource. Environmental and ecological integrity and consumer quality-of-life issues are not their concern. The oil industry has been a strong industrial stakeholder and exerted power at the local, state, and federal levels of government for almost a century. Many state legislatures have passed laws exempting oil companies from releasing their environmental audits or helping oil companies avoid compliance with environmental regulation or enforcement action. Oil companies are not responsive to community concerns and can litigate any issue with vast financial resources. The petrochemical industrial complex has also become part of social institutions such as foundations, churches, schools and universities, and athletic contests. Some employment opportunities, some infrastructure, and the hope of more economic development are offered to communities by oil companies.

Oil politics and the U.S. presidency are closely intertwined as both Bush presidents were major players in the oil industry in Texas and internationally with Saudi Arabia. Since George W. Bush was elected president in 2001, the top five oil companies in the United States have recorded record profits of $342.4 billion through the first quarter of 2006, while at the same time getting substantial tax breaks from a Republican Congress. This is extremely controversial, as gas prices have risen dramatically for most average citizens, and the national debt has gone from a surplus to a large deficit. With the controversial war in Iraq, an oil-producing nation, some people in the United States thought gas prices would decrease domestically. (They did not.) Oil company profit taking during times of natural disaster, such as hurricane Katrina, and war, has attracted much congressional attention. In one congressional hearing in 2006, major oil executives were subpoenaed to testify before Congress and refused to swear to tell the truth.

No oil company seems to be turning their profits into consumer savings. Some are just starting to research more alternative energy sources, but this is controversial. Some environmental groups have recently challenged this assertion. To many U.S. consumers it seems there is a direct correlation between record prices paid by consumers and record profits enjoyed by oil companies. From 1999 to 2004, the profit margin by U.S. oil refiners has increased 79 percent.

Political Controversy: Tax Breaks for Oil Campaign Contributions?

The search for automobile energy efficiency lies in the political maelstrom of the oil industry in Congress. President George W. Bush and the Republican Congress gave $6 billion in tax breaks and subsidies to oil companies in 2006 alone. This is in the face of large oil company profits. From 2001 to 2006 the oil industry gave $58 million in campaign contributions to federal politicians. Eighty-one percent of that went to Republicans. Given the awkward state of campaign financing, it is likely that these numbers would be much higher if travel and other expenses were included. Environmental groups, concerned communities, and taxpaying consumers have all protested this as corruption, misfeasance, and malfeasance in office.

Conclusion

Continued dependence on fossil fuels guarantees increased controversy. As oil becomes depleted, multinational oil corporations exert all their huge influence on the United States to protect their sources, even if it means going to war. The dissatisfaction of environmentalists and communities with the petrochemical industrial complex, the dependence and demand of the United States for oil, the lack of governmental support for alternative energy development, and the inability to keep large environmental impacts secret all fuel this raging controversy.

See also Air Pollution; Biodiesel; Climate Change; Cumulative Emissions; Fossil Fuels; Global Warming; Oil Economics and Business (vol. 1)

Further Reading

Clifford, Mary, *Environmental Crime: Enforcement, Policy and Social Responsibility.* Sudbury, MA: Jones and Bartlett, 1998.

Dobson, Andrew P., *Citizenship and the Environment.* New York: Oxford University Press, 2004.

Fuhs, Allen, *Hybrid Vehicles and the Future of Personal Transportation.* Boca Raton, FL: CRC Press, 2009.

Galambos, Louis, Takashi Hikino, and Vera Zamagni, *The Global Chemical Industry in the Age of the Petrochemical Revolution.* Cambridge, UK: Cambridge University Press, 2006.

Marzotto, Toni, Vicky Moshier, and Gordon Scott Bonham, *The Evolution of Public Policy: Cars and the Environment.* Boulder, CO: Lynne Rienner, 2000.

Miller, Norman, ed., *Cases in Environmental Politics: Stakeholders, Interests, and Policymakers.* New York: Routledge, 2009.

National Renewable Energy Laboratory, "Advanced Vehicles and Fuels Research." www.nrel.gov/vehiclesandfuels

Wells, Peter E., and Paul Nieuwenhuis, *The Automotive Industry and the Environment: A Technical, Business and Social Future.* Boca Raton, FL: CRC Press, 2003.

B

BIODIESEL

Sarah Lewison

Biodiesel, a diesel substitute made from biological materials, can be used directly in a diesel engine without clogging fuel injectors. It is the product of a chemical process that removes the sticky glycerins from vegetable and animal oils. Because it is made from biomass, biodiesel is considered to be a "carbon neutral" fuel. When burned, it releases the same volume of carbons into the atmosphere that were absorbed when the biomass source was growing. Controversy exists, however, in particular over the use of high-quality grains for biodiesel, because land is taken out of food production and devoted to the production of fuel.

Characteristics and Applications

In comparison with diesel, biodiesel has reduced particulate, nitrous oxide, and other emissions and emits no sulfur. Biodiesel is used as a transportation fuel substitute, either at the rate of 100 percent or in smaller percentages mixed with diesel. It mixes completely with petroleum diesel and can be stored safely for long periods of time. Biodiesel is biodegradable and does not contain residuals that are toxic to life forms. It has a higher flash point than diesel and is safer to ship and store. Biodiesel is mixed with kerosene (#1 diesel) to heat homes in New England. It has been used as an additive in aircraft fuel, and because of its oil-dissolving properties, is effective as a nontoxic, biodegradable solvent that can be used to clean oil spills and remove graffiti, adhesive, asphalt, and paint; as a hand cleaner; and as a substitute for many other petroleum-derived industrial solvents. Biodiesel is appropriate as a renewable alternative to petrochemical diesel because it can be produced domestically, lowers emissions, and does not cause a net gain in atmospheric carbon. The overall ecological benefits of biodiesel however, depend on what kinds of oils are used to make it.

Biodiesel is made from the oils in seeds, nuts, and grains or animal fats. Oil sources for biodiesel production are called biomass "feedstock." Agricultural crops are specifically grown to be utilized for biodiesel production. The crops vary according to region and climate; in the northern hemisphere, biodiesel is most often made from soybean, sunflower, corn, mustard, cottonseed, rapeseed (also known as canola), and occasionally, hempseed. In tropical and subtropical regions, biodiesel is made from palm and coconut oils. Experiments have been conducted in extracting oils from microorganisms such as algae to produce the fuel. These algae experiments have raised hopes of converting sunlight more directly into a renewable fuel to be used with existing diesel machinery. Biodiesel offers an efficient use for waste oils that have already been used for frying or otherwise manufacturing food for human consumption. Waste grease biodiesel is made from the oils left over in the fryer and the grease trap as well as from the animal fats and trims left over from the butchering process.

The fuel is manufactured from both fresh and waste oils in the same way, through a chemical reaction called transesterification, which involves the breaking up, or "cracking," of triglycerides (fat/oil) with a catalytic agent (sodium methoxide) into constituent mono-alkyl esters (biodiesel) and raw glycerin. In this process, alcohol is used to react with the fatty acids to form the biodiesel. For the triglycerides to react with the alcohol, a catalyst is needed to trigger a reorganization of the chemical constituents. Most often, a strong base such as sodium hydroxide (lye, NaOH) is used as a catalyst to trigger the reaction between the triglycerides and the alcohol. Either methanol (CH_3OH, or wood alcohol, derived from wood, coal, or natural gas) or ethanol (C_2H_6O, known as grain alcohol and produced from petrochemicals or grain) is used as the alcohol reactant. The chemical name of the completed biodiesel reflects the alcohol used; methanol makes methyl esters, whereas ethanol will produce ethyl esters. Most frequently, methanol is the alcohol used.

Triglycerides are composed of a glycerin molecule with three long-chain fatty acids attached. The fatty acid chains have different characteristics according to the kind of fat used, and these indicate the acid content of the oil. The acid content must be taken into account in order to get the most complete reaction and thus the highest yield of biodiesel. To calculate the correct proportions of lye and methanol needed to transesterify a sample of oil, the acid content of the oil is measured through a chemical procedure called titration. Waste vegetable oil has higher fatty acid content and requires higher proportions of lye catalyst than fresh oil. The titration results determine the proportion of lye to combine with the methanol or ethanol to form a catalytic agent that will complete the reaction fully.

To make biodiesel, the oil is placed in a noncorrosive vessel with a heating element and a method of agitation. The mixture of lye and alcohol is measured and mixed separately. Usually the amount of methanol or other alcohol needed amounts to 20 percent of the volume of oil. The amount of lye depends on the acidity of the oil and is determined by titration and calculation. When the oil reaches 120 to 30 degrees Fahrenheit (48 to 54 degrees Celsius), the premixed catalytic solution is added. The oil is maintained at the same heat while being gently stirred for the next 30 to 60 minutes. The stirring assists in producing a complete reaction. The mixture is then left to cool and settle; the light yellow methyl esters or ethyl esters float to the top and the viscous brown glycerin sinks to the bottom. The esters (biodiesel) are decanted and washed free of remaining soaps and acids as a final step before being used as fuel.

Although transesterification is the most widely used process for producing biodiesel, more efficient processes for the production of biodiesel are under development. The fuel is most simply made in batches, although industrial engineers have developed ways to make biodiesel with continuous processing for larger-scale operations. Biodiesel production is unique in that it is manufactured on many different scales and by different entities. It is made and marketed by large corporations that have vertically integrated supplies of feedstocks to mesh with production, much the same way petrochemical supplies are controlled and processed. There are also independent biodiesel-production facilities operating on various scales, utilizing local feedstocks, including waste oil sources, and catering to specialty markets such as marine fuels. Many independent engineers and chemists, both professional and amateur, contribute their research into small-scale biodiesel production.

Biodiesel can be made in the backyard if proper precautions are taken. There are several patented and open source designs for biodiesel processors that can be built for little money and with recycled materials. Two popular designs include Mike Pelly's Model A Processor for batches of waste oils from 50 to 400 gallons and the Appleseed Biodiesel Processor designed by Maria "Mark" Alovert. Plans for the Appleseed processor are available free on the Internet, and the unit itself is built from a repurposed hot water heater and valves and pumps obtainable from hardware stores. Such open-source plans and instructions available online have stimulated independent community-based biodiesel research and development. In some cases, a biodiesel processor is built to serve a small group of people who decide to cooperate on production within a region, taking advantage of waste grease from local restaurants. The biodiesel fuel is made locally and consumed locally, thus reducing the expenses of transporting fuel.

The use of vegetable oil in diesel engines goes back to Rudolf Diesel, the engine's inventor. The diesel engine demonstrated on two different occasions in Paris during the expositions of 1900 that it could run on peanut oil. (The use of peanut oil was attributed to the French government, which sought to develop an independent agriculturally derived power source for electricity and transportation fuel in its peanut-producing African colonies.)

As transportation fuel, biodiesel can be used only in diesel engines in which a fuel and air mixture is compressed under high pressure in a firing chamber. This pressure causes the air in the chamber to superheat to a temperature that ignites the injected fuel, causing the piston to fire. Biodiesel cannot be used in gasoline-powered internal combustion engines. Because its solvent action degrades rubber, older vehicles running biodiesel might need to have some hoses replaced with those made of more resistant materials. The high lubricating capacity of biodiesel has been credited with improving engine wear when blended at a 20 percent rate with petroleum diesel.

Advantages of Biodiesel

The benefits of burning biodiesel correspond to the percentage of biodiesel included in any formulation. The overall energy gains of biodiesel are also assessed according to the gross consumption of energy required to produce the oil processed into fuel. Biodiesel processed from waste grease that has already been utilized for human food consumption has a greater overall energy efficiency and gain than biodiesel produced from oils extracted from a virgin soybean crop grown with petrochemical-based fertilizers on land previously dedicated to food production.

Biodiesel's emissions offer a vast improvement over petroleum-based diesel. Emissions of sulfur oxides and sulfates (the primary components of acid rain) are eliminated. Smog-forming precursors such as nitrogen oxide, unburned hydrocarbons, and particulate matter are mostly reduced, although nitrogen oxide reduction varies from engine to engine. The overall ozone-forming capacity of biodiesel is generally reduced by nearly 50 percent. When burned, biodiesel has a slightly sweet and pleasant smell, in contrast to the acrid black smoke of petroleum-based diesel.

Biodiesel has the additional and important advantage of carbon-neutrality in that it is produced from the energy stored in living organisms that have been harvested within 10 years of the fuel's manufacture. During their growing cycle, plants use carbon dioxide to process and store the energy of the sun in the form of carbon within their mass. When plants are converted to fuel source and burned, they can release into the atmosphere only the amount of carbon consumed and stored (through photosynthesis) during their life cycle. When petroleum fuel is burned, carbons are released into the atmosphere at a much faster rate. The atmospheric release of the fossilized carbons of petroleum fuel places an impossible burden on existing living biomass (trees and plants) to absorb the massive quantities of carbons being released.

The mass production of biodiesel from biomass feedstock grown specifically for fuel has not been proven to produce a net energy gain because of the energy inputs needed in current industrial farming methods. These include the inputs of petroleum-derived fertilizers and herbicides, fuel for farm machinery, and the energy needed to pump water and transport the fuel. Concerns have also been expressed about taking land and other agricultural resources previously devoted to food production for the production of biomass for fuels such as biodiesel.

See also **Automobile Energy Efficiencies; Fossil Fuels; Global Warming**

Further Reading

Earley, Jane, and Alice McKeown, *Red, White, and Green: Transforming U.S. Biofuels.* Washington, DC: Worldwatch Institute, 2009.
Official Site of the National Biodiesel Board, http://www.biodiesel.org/markets/mar
Pahl, Greg, *Biodiesel: Growing a New Energy Economy,* 2d ed. Burlington, VT: Chelsea Green, 2008.

BIOTECHNOLOGY

CELENE SHEPPARD

Although biotechnology can be defined broadly to include any technological application that uses a biological system or organism, the term has become synonymous with the use of modern technology to alter the genetic material of organisms. The ability to recombine DNA across species has created significant social controversy over the creation of biohazards, "terminator" genes, genetic pollution, "playing God," and the ethics of altering the lives and appearance of animals.

Background and Development

Biotechnology may be considered as any technological application that uses biological systems, living organisms, or their derivatives. The term *biotechnology* covers a broad range of processes and products and can be understood from at least two perspectives. From one perspective, biotechnology (1) is the process of using (bio)organisms to produce goods and services for humans. The use of yeast in the processes of fermentation that make bread and beer and the historical domestication of plants and animals are examples of this kind of biotechnology. From another perspective, biotechnology (2) is the process of using genetic technologies to alter (bio)organisms. This perspective is illustrated by the hybridization of plants, the cloning of sheep, and the creation of genetically engineered food crops. Although both perspectives are debatable endeavors, biotechnology type 2 is inherently more problematic than type 1. Most ethical, moral, and religious criticism of biotechnology focuses on type 2 biotechnology. The United Nations definition, then, focuses on the history and problems associated with type 2 biotechnology.

Biotechnology type 2 began in the late nineteenth century as the rise of the science of genetics established a basis for the systematic and conscious practice of breeding plants and animals. In 1944 Oswald Avery identified DNA as the protein of heredity. In 1953

James Watson and Francis Crick discovered the structure of DNA. Biotechnology blossomed in the late 1960s and early 1970s with the development of recombinant DNA technology and the birth of the biotechnology industry. In 1997 the human genome was mapped and sequenced. Since the 1990s, an increasing number of techniques have been developed for the biotechnological reproduction and transformation of organisms. An examination of controversies associated with biotechnology includes at least the biotechnological modification of microorganisms, of plants, and of animals.

In the early 1970s, researchers across the world began exploring recombinant DNA (rDNA) technology, or the technology of joining DNA from different species. rDNA technology is performed either by a gene-splicing process, wherein DNA from one species is joined and inserted into host cells, or by cloning, wherein genes are cloned from one species and inserted into the cells of another.

In 1972 biochemist Paul Berg designed an experiment allowing him to use rDNA technology to insert mutant genetic material from a monkey virus into a laboratory strain of the *E. coli* bacterium. Berg did not, however, complete the final step of his experiment because he and his fellow researchers feared they would create a biohazard. Because the monkey virus was a known carcinogen and the researchers knew that *E. coli* can inhabit the human intestinal tract, they realized their experiment might create a dangerous, cancer-inducing strain of *E. coli*.

Berg and other leading biological researchers feared that, without public debate or regulation, rDNA technology might create new kinds of plagues, alter human evolution, and irreversibly alter the environment. Berg urged other researchers to voluntarily ban the use of rDNA technologies and sent a letter to the president of the National Academy of Science (NAS). The NAS responded by establishing the first Committee on the Recombinant DNA Molecules. In 1974 that committee agreed to the temporary ban on the use of rDNA technologies and decided that the issue required the attention of an international conference. Scientists worldwide were receptive to the voluntary ban and halted their work on rDNA experiments.

In February 1975, Berg and the NAS organized the Asilomar Conference on Recombinant DNA. Lawyers, doctors, and biologists from around the world convened in Monterey, California, to discuss the biohazard and biosafety implications of rDNA technology and to create a set of regulations that would allow the technology to move forward.

This conference provided a meaningful forum for discussing both whether scientists should use rDNA technologies and how to safely contain and control rDNA experiments. The Asilomar participants were able to identify proper safety protocols and containment procedures for some of these experiments, and they also prohibited some experiments, such as Berg's experiment involving cloning of recombinant DNA from pathogenic organisms.

The Asilomar conference resulted in the first set of National Institutes of Health (NIH) guidelines for research involving recombinant DNA. These guidelines are still the primary source of regulation of recombinant DNA research and have been periodically updated by the NIH.

The Asilomar conference also stimulated further controversy involving rDNA technologies. On one side, concerned citizens and public interest groups that had not participated in the conference began to demand a voice in the regulation of recombinant DNA technologies. The city of Cambridge, Massachusetts, exerted its power to control the rDNA research conducted in its universities, creating the Cambridge Biohazards Committee to oversee DNA experiments. The environmental organization Friends of the Earth even brought a lawsuit demanding that the NIH issue an environmental impact statement on rDNA research. On the other side, biological researchers opposed the inclusion of the public in the rDNA discussion. These researchers feared that public participation in the matter might restrict and compromise the freedom of scientific research.

Ongoing Research and Debate

Humans have for centuries used selective breeding and hybridization techniques to alter food-producing plants. The introduction of recombinant DNA technologies, however, has allowed humans to genetically cross plants, animals, and microorganisms into food-producing plants. There are two basic methods for passing genetic traits into plants. First, biologists can infect a plant cell with a plasmid containing the cross-species genes. Second, biologists can shoot microscopic pellets carrying the cross-species genes directly through the cell walls of the plants. In either case, biologists are reliably able to move desirable genes from one plant or animal into a food-producing plant species.

For instance, scientists have already spliced genes from naturally occurring pesticides such as *Bacillus thuringiensis* into corn to create pest-resistant crops and have genetically altered tomatoes to ensure their freshness at supermarkets.

Genetic technologies allow an increase in properties that improve nutrition, improve the capacity to store and ship food products, and increase plants' ability to resist pests or disease.

In 1994 the U.S. Food and Drug Administration approved the first genetically modified food for sale in the United States. Now genetic modification of food supplies is pervasive, particularly in staple crops such as soy, corn, and wheat. Cross-species gene splicing has, however, created at least two significant controversies.

One controversy arose over the use of "terminator" gene technologies. When biotechnology companies began to produce foods with cross-species genes, they included terminator genes that sterilized the seeds of the plants. This terminator technology served two functions: it kept the plants from reproducing any potential harmful or aberrant effects of the genetic engineering, and it also ensured that farmers who purchased genetically modified plants would need to purchase new seeds from the biotechnology companies each year.

The use of terminator technologies caused an international social debate, especially when biotech companies introduced their genetically modified foods into developing countries. Because farmers in developing countries tend to reseed their crops from a previous year's harvest, the terminator technology created a new and unexpected yearly production expense. Civil and human rights groups urged banning the introduction of genetically modified crops in developing countries, arguing that any potential nutritional or production benefits offered by the genetically modified foods would be outweighed by the technological mandate to purchase expensive, patented seeds each year. In response to this, Monsanto (the biotechnology company that owns the rights to the terminator gene patents) pledged not to commercialize the terminator technology. Human rights groups continue to work toward implementing legal bans on the use of the technology, however.

Another controversy arose with a concern about genetic pollution. Although biologists are reliably able to splice or physically force gene sequences from one species into another, they are not always able to control the reproduction and spread of the altered plants. This has created serious debate over the introduction of genetically modified food from laboratories into natural ecosystems.

One concern is that the genetic alterations will pass from the food-producing crop to weeds that compete for nutrients and sunlight. One good example occurs with pesticide-resistant crops. Some biotechnology companies have modified crops to resist the application of certain pesticides. This allows farmers to apply pesticide to their fields while the modified crop is growing, thus reducing competition from weeds and attacks by pests. However, biologists cannot always control whether the pesticide-resistant gene will stay confined to the food-producing crop. Sometimes the pesticide-resistant gene migrates to surrounding plants, thus creating "super weeds" that are immune to the application of pesticides.

Another concern is that the genetic alterations will unintentionally pass from the modified food-producing crop into another natural strain. Here the concern is that the uncontrolled movement of cross-species genetic alterations may alter evolutionary processes and destroy biodiversity. For example, one controversy focuses on whether the introduction of genetically modified corn has led to the cross-pollination of native Mexican strains of maize. There is also a concern about introducing strains of genetically modified potatoes into areas of Peru, where subsistence farmers safeguard many native strains of potatoes.

The final and perhaps most important social concern is the safety and quality of the food produced by genetically altered plants. There has been a general inquiry into the safety of genetically modified foods. Because few tests have been conducted into the safety of these foods or the long-term effects on human health, there is a strong movement, particularly in western European countries, to ban "Frankenfoods." There has been an even stronger reaction over the labeling and separation of genetically modified foods. Moving genes from one species to another food-producing crop can raise serious allergy and safety concerns. When, for example, one company began splicing desired genes from Brazil nuts into soybeans, it became apparent that the resulting modified soya plant would induce allergic reactions in any person with a nut allergy. However, because food distribution systems, especially in industrialized countries, tend to collectively amass and distribute staple crops, there is no way to tell which foods contain genetically altered plants if no labeling or separating requirement is installed. This raises concerns about the ability to recall products should scientists discover a problem with genetically altered foods.

As with agriculture, humans have long practiced forms of animal biotechnology by domesticating animals and through practices of animal husbandry. However, the use of rDNA technology has allowed humans to clone animals and produce transgenic animals. Scientists now genetically insert genes from cows into chickens to produce more meat per animal, genetically alter research laboratory rats to fit experiments, and genetically modify pigs to grow appropriate valves for use in human heart transplant procedures.

Although all the concerns about plant biotechnology, and particularly the concern about genetic pollution, apply to the genetic manipulation of animals, there are several controversies unique to the application of biotechnology to animals.

The first, and perhaps most fundamental, controversy over the application of biotechnology to animals is the moral reaction against "playing God" with recombinant DNA technologies. Many religious and ethics groups have chastised biologists for violating fundamental limits between species that cannot, without major evolutionary changes, otherwise breed. This has brought a serious debate over whether the biotechnological mixing of species is unnatural or whether it merely demonstrates the arbitrary segregation of our scientific categories of kingdoms and species.

Another controversy unique to applying biotechnology to animals concerns the rights and welfare of genetically modified animals. Genetic technology has, for example, allowed great advances in xenotransplantation (the use of pigs as sources of organs for ailing human beings) and in genetically altering laboratory rats. This enables scientists to "pharm" medical products and laboratory subjects from genetically altered animals. However, this ability to extract resources from animals comes into direct conflict with a growing awareness of ethical duties toward animals and of animal rights. Although few critiques suggest that these ethical duties require us to abandon the practice of applying biotechnology to animals, they have raised serious questions about how genetic modifications alter the lives of animals and what sorts of safeguards or standards should be employed in animal biotechnology.

See also **Genetic Engineering; Genetically Modified Organisms; Stem Cell Research**

Further Reading

Metz, Matthew, "Criticism Preserves the Vitality of Science." *Nature Biotechnology* 20 (2002): 867.

Olmsted, Alan L., *Creating Abundance: Biological Innovation and American Agricultural Development*. New York: Cambridge University Press, 2008.

Patterson, D. J., et al., "Application of Reproductive Biotechnology in Animals: Implications and Potentials." *Animal Reproductive Science* 79 (2003): 137–143.

Quist, David, and Ignacio Chapela, "Transgenic DNA Introgressed into Traditional Maize Landraces in Oaxaca, Mexico." *Nature* 414 (2001): 541–543.

Rodgers, Kay, *Recombinant DNA Controversy*. Washington, DC: Library of Congress, Science and Technology Division, Reference Section, 1978.

Schaller, Barry R., *Understanding Bioethics and the Law: The Promise and Perils of the Brave New World of Biotechnology*. Westport, CT: Praeger, 2008.

BROWNFIELDS DEVELOPMENT

Robert William Collin

Policy aimed at cleaning up contaminated land is called *brownfields*. It is relatively new, with a distinct urban focus. It is controversial because of the displacement of current residents and reliance on market forces to rebuild some sites. Whether the site is cleaned up to a level safe for residential development, or just safe enough for another industrial use, is a community controversy.

Beginning of Brownfields Policy

Since the disaster of Love Canal and the Hooker Chemical Company, U.S. environmental policy has developed a distinct cleanup aspect. It is very controversial. Extremely hazardous sites were prioritized as part of a National Priorities List under the Superfund program. Superfund can assess liability for the cost of a cleanup against the property owner if no other primary responsible parties are around. Huge amounts of unaccounted wastes were produced before the U.S. Environmental Protection Agency (EPA) was formed in 1970, and huge amounts have continued to be produced. As much as 80 percent of Superfund budget allocations have gone to the litigation that can surround these sites. As knowledge and public awareness increased, many more sites were located. Most states had adopted some type of landfill or waste management environmental policy by the late 1980s. Controversies that still simmer today over what is hazardous pushed the EPA into a new phase of cleanup policy. There was a need to prevent nonhazardous sites from becoming hazardous. This can happen at illegal dumps over time. Metals from refrigerators, stoves, cars, cans, and roofing can leach into the water, depending on the site. Many of these sites were in or near densely populated areas, which were not traditional areas for the EPA at this time. In some states this was legal if operated as a dump, no matter where it was located. There were many sites waiting to be verified as hazardous or not for Superfund consideration. Even if the community was successful in getting the site designated as hazardous, there was a complicated and political process of getting on the National Priorities List, a list of about 1,200 or so of the most important sites for the EPA. Getting a site designated as hazardous was not always considered the best thing for the community because it could suppress property values. Sometime local government fought against such a designation, against the community and the EPA. This is often the case in many communities seeking environmental justice. As environmental justice advocacy increased within the EPA in the early 1990s, cleanup policy changed to include more of these sites. In 1993 the EPA first began to address sites that may be contaminated by hazardous substances but that did not pose a serious enough public health risk to require consideration for cleanup under the Superfund program.

The cleanup policy that evolved was conceptualized regionally at first, partially motivated by concerns about sprawl. The idea was to save as much green space as possible by reusing, or infilling, some of these polluted sites. Infill is often proposed as a mitigating solution to sprawl. Municipal boundaries are not related to bioregions or ecosystems, and some municipalities or cities may not want infill. Municipalities have different and sometimes competing priorities. Combating sprawl or environmental protection and cleanup are generally not as important as economic development at this level of government. As a result, there are many polluted sites. When they are abandoned and foreclosed on by the municipality or city for failure to pay property taxes, the city owns them. Cities, such as Milwaukee, for example, then become liable for the cleanup of the polluted sites, and they also lose tax revenue. It is extremely difficult to sell polluted land, and all efforts are made to escape environmental liability in the process. According to the EPA,

> Brownfields are abandoned, idled, or under-used industrial and commercial facilities where expansion or redevelopment is complicated by real or perceived environmental contamination. They range in size from a small gas station to abandoned factories and mill sites. Estimates of the number of sites range from the tens of thousands to as high as 450,000 and they are often in economically distressed areas.

> Portland, Oregon, estimates that it has about 1,000 brownfield sites. Developers avoid them because of cleanup costs, potential liability, or related reasons.

Recent Developments

In 2001, new brownfields policy development authorized granting a liability exemption to prospective purchasers who do not cause or worsen the contamination at a site. It also gave this exemption to community-based nonprofit organizations that seek to redevelop these sites. Most states now have their own brownfields programs. There were substantial differences between some state approaches and the EPA brownfields policy. Some of this has to do with the level of cleanup required for a site to be considered clean. An industrial level is cheaper but still polluted. A residential level is very expensive but not polluted. It is still very controversial. Often no developers or nonprofits are willing to clean up the site. Unlike Superfund, brownfields policy does not attack primary responsible parties for liability. State policy approaches are given some leeway in the 2001 policy changes. The new policy stops the EPA from interfering in the state cleanups. There are three exceptions written into the law:

1. A state requests assistance.
2. The contamination migrates across state lines or onto federal property.
3. There is an "imminent and substantial endangerment" to public health or the environment and additional work needs to be done.

U.S. Urban Environmentalism

The United States is still in the early stages of urban environmentalism, a complex subject with intricate and important histories. The potential for unintended consequences for people, places, and policy is great. Solid wastes are accumulating every day, combined with a century of relatively unchecked industrial waste that continues to pollute our land, air, and water on a bioregional basis. The wastes in our ecosystem respect no human-made boundary, and the consequences of urban environmental intervention through policy or other actions, intended or not, affect us all.

Terms of Art

Brownfields Site

According to the most recent law and policy Public Law 107–118 (H.R. 2869), "Small Business Liability Relief and Brownfields Revitalization Act," signed into law January 11, 2002, the definition of brownfield is as follows: "With certain legal exclusions and additions, the term 'brownfields site' means real property, the expansion, redevelopment, or reuse of which may be complicated by the presence or potential presence of a hazardous substance, pollutant, or contaminant."

Superfund Site

A Superfund site is any land in the United States that has been contaminated by hazardous waste and identified by the EPA as a candidate for cleanup because it poses a risk to human health and/or the environment. There are tens of thousands of abandoned hazardous waste sites in our nation. The implementing edge of the Superfund program is a system of identification and prioritization that allows the most dangerous sites and releases to be addressed, called the National Priorities List.

When outcomes from cleanup and revitalization projects are assessed, the EPA may have unintentionally exacerbated historical gentrification and displacement. EPA funds may have been used to continue private development at the expense of low-income residents.

Urban Environments

Urban areas are complex. For at least a century, urban areas in the United States experienced unrestrained industrialization, with no environmental regulation and often no land-use control. U.S. environmental movements have focused on unpopulated areas, not cities. In addition, U.S. environmental movements did not consider public health as a primary focus. Rather, they emphasized conservation, preservation of nature, and biodiversity. In addition to being the dynamic melting pot for new immigrants, cities became home to three waves of African Americans migrating north after the Civil War. These groups faced substantial discrimination in housing, employment, education, and municipal services. African Americans are the only group in the United States to not have shared in equal opportunity for employment, housing, and education. In addition, people of color and low-income people faced increased exposure to the pollution that accompanied industrialization.

Citizens living in urban, poor, and people-of-color communities are currently threatened by gentrification, displacement, and equity loss on a scale unprecedented since the urban renewal movement of the 1960s. Market forces appear to be the primary drivers of this phenomenon. Spurred by local government attempts to reclaim underutilized and derelict properties for productive uses, residents and business owners who once abandoned the urban core to the poor and underemployed now seek to return from the suburbs. By taking advantage of federal policies and programs, municipalities, urban planners, and developers are accomplishing much of this largely beneficial revitalization. However, from the perspective of gentrified and otherwise displaced residents and small businesses, it appears that the revitalization of their cities is being built on the backs of the very citizens who suffered, in place, through the times of abandonment and disinvestments.

Although these citizens are anxious to see their neighborhoods revitalized, they want to be able to continue living in their neighborhoods and participating in that revitalization.

In addition to facing tremendous displacement pressure, African Americans and other people of color also face difficult challenges in obtaining new housing within the same community (or elsewhere) after displacement. For example, when these populations are displaced, they must often pay a disproportionately high percentage of their incomes for housing. Moreover, they suffer the loss of important community culture. Although it is not fair to suggest that federal reuse, redevelopment, and revitalization programs are the conscious or intentional cause of gentrification, displacement, and equity loss in these communities, it is apparent that the local implementation of these programs is having that net effect. These then become the unintended impacts of such well-intended and otherwise beneficial programs. Brownfields is a pioneering urban environmental policy and unintended consequences could easily result from it.

Community activists should have an educated perspective to decide whether brownfields programs will provide hope and opportunity to their distressed neighborhoods or whether they will exacerbate environmental contamination and/or provide little or no opportunity for their own families to benefit proportionately. Brownfields redevelopment is a big business. Profits are generally more important to brownfields entrepreneurs than community concerns about displacement or reduced cleanup standards. In fact, at the EPA's 2004 National Brownfields Conference, developers reinforced this notion by highlighting their perspective that in order for communities to be players in the redevelopment and revitalization process, they had to be financially vested in the process. This view clearly speaks to the need for EPA intervention to ensure meaningful community involvement irrespective of financial status.

The EPA provides some funding for brownfields to state and local government and to some tribes. As of July 2007, about $2.2 million was awarded to brownfields revolving loan fund recipients. The EPA claims that since 1997 they have awarded about $55 million for about 114 loans and 13 subgrants. The EPA states these loan funds have leveraged more than $780 million in other public and private cleanup and redevelopment investments. Some criticize the program as being underfunded and underresourced. They say the need for cleanup of the places where we live, work, and learn is paramount for any environmental cleanup policy.

How Clean Is Clean?

Cumulative impacts concern the EPA because they erode environmental protection and threaten public health, safety, and welfare. They cross all media—land, air, and water. Independently, media-specific impacts have been the focus of the EPA's work for years. However, if the combined, accumulating impacts of industrial, commercial, and municipal development continue to be ignored, the synergistic problems will only get worse. The cleanup of past industrial practices must be thorough and safe for all vulnerable populations—so say most communities. Another community concern is that long-term industrial use of a given site may decrease the overall value of property in the area, resulting in a loss of wealth over time. However, to clean up the site to a level safe enough for residential development is much more expensive. It is also fraught with uncertainty, which translates into risk for most real estate financial institutions. The state of the law of brownfields cleanup is also very uncertain and dynamic. One thing is certain though: the United States is dotted with contaminated sites generally concentrated in urban areas and multimodal transit nodules (e.g., ports, depots).

By far, the populations most impacted by brownfields decisions are those who live, work, play, or worship near a contaminated site. These people are already in areas with a high pollutant load, with generally higher rates of asthma.

Vulnerable populations such as pregnant women, the elderly, children, and individuals with pre-existing health problems are at increased risk. In many environmental justice communities, a brownfields site may be the only park-like setting available, so it can attract some of the most vulnerable populations.

To the extent members of the community are forced to leave because of increased housing costs, the community loses a piece of its fabric, and sometimes knowledge of its history and culture. This adverse impact must be addressed as part of a cumulative assessment. The sense of identity common to many communities concerned with environmental justice is threatened when communities are displaced.

Conclusion

As part of the first and very necessary wave of urban environmentalism, brownfields unearths many deep-seated environmental and political controversies. U.S. environmental policy and the U.S. environmental movement have ignored cities, where most of the pollution and most of the immigrants and people of color reside. The environment, urban or not, is difficult to ignore as population expands and concepts of sustainability are developed. Citizen monitoring of the environment, environmental lawsuits, and the need to enforce environmental laws equally have driven environmental policy to urban neighborhoods. Cleanup of the environmentally devastated landscape is usually an early priority for any governmental intervention in environmental decision making.

A hard uncertainty underscores the current methods of holding private property owners liable for waste cleanup. What if they cannot afford it? What if they manipulate bankruptcy or legitimately cannot afford it? What if the contamination is so extensive that no one stakeholder alone can afford to clean it up? Ecosystem risk assessment, now mandated at Superfund sites, will unearth only more contamination. The levels of contamination themselves are highly controversial because some believe that as these levels stand now, they do not protect the public enough. How much real estate corporations and banks should be supported by government in developing market-based cleanup strategies is a big policy controversy.

Yet without any intervention these sites accumulate wastes that can spread to water and land. They do not go away but generally get worse. Over time there will be no hiding any of them. With the new and rapidly developing global consensus on sustainability, cleanup of contaminated sites is a natural and necessary first step. This step takes place in a political context of race, class, and awkward histories of human oppression. The immigrants and migrants always lived in the tenements or on the other side of the tracks. (Train toilets dumped directly on the tracks until the late 1990s.) Success was defined as leaving the city for a house in the suburbs, with a better school district. Many but not all immigrant and migrant groups came through polluted and unhealthy urban neighborhoods.

This political step is also a necessary step and one that remains very controversial in the U.S. context. Currently, brownfields is the policy face of that step forward.

BROWNFIELDS PLAYING A ROLE IN THE BIOFUELS INDUSTRY

Many contaminated sites are old gas stations, which often have leaking underground storage tanks. The cleanup costs and liability are much larger when the contamination has spread, especially if it has spread to water. However, without cleanup the contamination can spread. From the city's point of view, such sites unproductive pieces of taxable property. This common scenario has been repeated many times over the last 30 years. Creative new solutions to this difficult and controversial policy issue require collaboration by local government, the EPA, and the property owner.

SeQuential Biofuels opened the first alternative fuel station in Oregon. The United States has a renewed interest in gaining energy security and independence by moving toward producing more of its fuels at home, including biofuels such as ethanol and biodiesel. Biofuels are cleaner fuels that produce fewer pollutants than mainstream fuels. There also is much potential for home-grown economic development in this rising new industry.

Brownfields redevelopment can play an important role in this emerging industry. Brownfields are a good fit because the redevelopment of these contaminated lands protects green space; moreover, the sites often offer an opportunity to reutilize barren urban and industrial space. And often these former gas stations are ideal for such development because they already sit on properties close to roadways.

SeQuential Biofuels has 33 branded pumps around the state with independent retail sites. The company, which owns 60 percent of the biodiesel market share in Oregon, has a large commercial biodiesel production facility that may serve as a model for gathering the fat necessary for biofuel production. Each year, this facility produces a million gallons of biodiesel made from used cooking oil collected from regional restaurants and food processors. It also uses virgin canola oil grown in eastern Oregon. By gathering resources and wastes locally, recycling and processing them, and distributing them locally, the overall ecological production footprint is smaller because of lower energy costs through less transportation. The retail fuel station sits along a commercial corridor adjacent to Interstate 5. The former Franko facility sold gasoline from 1976 until 1991. At that time, the property was turned over to a bankruptcy trustee. Also in 1991, petroleum contamination from the site was observed during trenching along the highway east of the site. Contamination also had migrated to a residential well west of the facility.

In 1996, a private party purchased the property and removed the five underground storage tanks and some contaminated soil. Subsequent assessment identified the former fuel pump islands as the primary source of contamination. Lane County then acquired the property through tax foreclosure and in January 2005 removed more than 400 tires and 15 drums of waste.

SeQuential purchased the property later that year after entering into a prospective purchaser's agreement with the Oregon Department of Environmental Quality (DEQ). The retail fuel station, which sells ethanol and biodiesel blends, opened in the fall of 2009.

Renewable energy, energy efficiency, and sustainable design elements are all part of the business plan. Covering the fueling islands are 244 solar panels that will provide 30 to 50 percent of the electrical power the station requires annually. On the roof of the convenience store is a garden. There are 4,800 plants in five inches of soil.

SeQuential took advantage of several state incentives on this project. Oregon and Washington have played active roles in providing tools to advance biofuels in the private sector. On this project, the Oregon DEQ provided $19,600 for site assessment, the EPA awarded a $200,000 brownfields cleanup grant to Lane County, and the Oregon Economic and Community Development Department provided a $50,000 loan as matching funding for the EPA assessment grant through its Brownfields Redevelopment Fund. The project also qualified for the Oregon Department of Energy's Business Energy Tax Credit, which equals 35 percent of an eligible project's costs, and its Energy Loan Program, which provides low-interest loans.

In its first six months in business, the retail station exceeded volume projections. Its biggest obstacle now is teaching consumers that these biofuels are appropriate for any vehicle.

See also **Cumulative Emissions; Environmental Justice; Land Pollution**

Further Reading

Cohen-Rosenthal, Edward, and Judy Musnikow, *Eco-Industrial Strategies: Unleashing Synergy between Economic Development and the Environment*. Sheffield, UK: Greenleaf, 2003.

Collin, Robert W., *The U.S. Environmental Protection Agency: Cleaning Up America's Act*. Westport, CT: Greenwood Press, 2006.

Hollander, Justin B., *Polluted and Dangerous: America's Worst Abandoned Properties and What Can Be Done about Them*. Burlington, VT: University of Vermont Press, 2009.

Russ, Thomas H., *Redeveloping Brownfields: Landscape Architects, Planners, Developers*. New York: McGraw-Hill, 1999.

Thomas, June Manning, and Marsha Ritzdorf, eds., *Urban Planning and the African American Community: In the Shadows*. London: Sage, 1997.

Thompson, J. William, and Kim Sorvig, *Sustainable Landscape Construction: A Guide to Green Building Outdoors*. Washington, DC: Island Press, 2000.

Witkin, James B., *Environmental Aspects of Real Estate and Commercial Transactions: From Brownfields to Green*. Chicago: American Bar Association, 2005.

C

CANCER

Michael Prentice

Knowledge and understanding of cancer, the leading cause of death in the United States and worldwide, has grown exponentially in the last 20 years. Investment in research and technology has greatly reduced the effects of cancer through advances in prevention, detection, and treatment. Survival rates have never been greater: in 2003, the rate of cancer deaths dropped in the United States for the first time since 1930.

Causes of Cancer

Radically different approaches to prevention and treatment, despite their successes, continue to divide the medical and scientific communities. Developments in cancer research stretch across the medical spectrum. From identifying new drugs to developing new screening tests and implementing more effective therapies, breakthroughs occur every day. Each of the 100 different types of cancers affects the body in unique ways and requires specific prevention, detection, and therapy plans. Understanding the complexities of this disease, which afflicts more than half of all men and a third of all women in the United States, is vital to the medical health of the nation.

The causes of cancer are becoming better understood. Genetics and lifestyle both can contribute to a person's susceptibility to cancer. For example, diet can greatly affect a person's chances of getting cancer. Certain lifestyle choices—such as having excess body fat, eating red meat, not engaging in physical exercise, or consuming alcohol—all seem to increase the likelihood of developing cancer. Many cancers tend to be caused by long-term exposure to cancer-causing agents, such as environmental toxins, rather than by a single incident. Environmental factors and lifestyle choices, however, do not always predict the appearance of cancer; instead, they should be taken as indicators of a higher risk. Understanding how these things interact with genetic factors over the course of a person's life is the front line for future cancer research.

Remedies and Care

The treatment of cancer used to entail surgery, chemotherapy, radiation, or a combination of the three. Although these types of procedures have altered the medical landscape for treating cancer over the past 100 years, new methods have emerged that bypass invasive or problematic surgeries. Researchers have begun to understand how the body fights cancer on its own through the immune system. Many of the developments in fighting cancer have come through the harnessing of the immune system's ability to produce antigens to combat cancerous cells.

Vaccines

Therapy in the form of cancer vaccines has been largely experimental. Recently, however, the U.S. Food and Drug Administration (FDA) approved a major breakthrough in cancer prevention using vaccines.

The development of a vaccine against the human papillomavirus (HPV) marked the first vaccine to gain approval in the fight against cancer since the hepatitis B vaccine. HPV is a leading cause of cervical cancer and, to a lesser degree, other types of cancer. The vaccine, which has gained FDA approval, was shown to be 100 percent effective against two of the leading types of HPV virus. These two strains account for 70 percent of all cervical cancers worldwide.

Vaccines for cancer can either prevent the disease directly (therapeutic vaccines) or prevent its development (prophylactic vaccines). Therapeutic vaccines are used to strengthen the body against existing cancers so as to prevent the reappearance of cancerous cells. Prophylactic vaccines, like the one for HPV, prevent the invasion of viruses that ultimately cause cancer. The HPV vaccine represents a significant breakthrough in cancer research. There are no officially licensed therapeutic vaccines to date, although numerous prophylactic vaccines are being tested by the National Cancer Institute.

Vaccines are part of a growing area of treatment known as biological therapy or immunotherapy. Biological therapy uses the body's immune system to fight cancer or lessen certain side effects of other cancer treatments. The immune system acts as the body's defense system, though it does not always recognize cancerous cells in the body and often lets them go undetected. Furthermore, the immune system itself may not function properly, allowing cancerous cells to recur in a process called metastasis, wherein the

RECENT GOVERNMENT ACTION

Aiming to eradicate cancer, U.S. President Barack Obama earmarked $6 billion for cancer research in his budget proposal for 2010. The funding, which represents around an 8 percent increase from 2009, is aimed at initiating 30 new drug trails in 2011 and doubling the number of novel compounds in clinical trials by 2016. With the additional investment, Obama seeks to stimulate research into breast cancer, melanoma, sarcoma, and pediatric cancers, among others, which in recent years reached a funding plateau that has curtailed further investigation into cures. The National Cancer Institute, part of the National Institutes of Health, expects to receive about $1.3 billion more from Obama's economic stimulus plan to further examine treatment possibilities for restoring health degraded by cancer.

cancerous cells spread to other parts of the body. Biological therapy seeks to step in to enhance or stimulate the body's immune system processes.

Genotyping

One of the new dimensions of cancer research has been the revolution of personalized, or molecular, medicine. Personalized medicine takes into account knowledge of a patient's genotype for the purpose of identifying the right preventive or treatment option. With the success of the Human Genome Project, new approaches have emerged in the field of cancer research. Approaching cancer from the perspective of "disease management" will lead to more customized medical treatments.

The successful implementation of such a revolutionary way of handling the disease will require that a vast amount of genetic data be classified, analyzed, and made accessible to doctors and researchers to determine treatments for individual patients. In 2004, cancer centers across the United States took part in the implementation of the National Cancer Institute's cancer Biomedical Informatics Grid (caBIG), a virtual community that seeks to accelerate new approaches to cancer research. The caBIG community aims to establish an open-access database that provides researchers the necessary infrastructure for the exchange of genetic data.

Gene Expression Profiling

New methods for detecting cancer have also been making headlines. One such method has been gene expression profiling, a process that is capable of identifying specific strains of cancer using DNA microarrays. These microarrays identify the activity of thousands of genes at once, providing a molecular profile of each strain. Research has demonstrated two important guidelines in cancer identification and treatment. Even though certain types of cancer look similar on a microscopic level, they can differ greatly on a molecular level and may require vastly different types of therapy.

The most notable example of this type of process has been used to identify two different strains of non-Hodgkin's lymphoma (NHL), a cancer of the white blood cells. Two common but very different strains of NHL call for radically differing treatments, such that the ability to easily diagnose which strain is active has been a great boon for treatment. In the past, failure to diagnose the different strains has led to therapeutic errors and resulted in lower survival rates.

Proteomics

Another innovation in cancer detection involves the field of proteomics. Proteomics— the study of all the proteins in an organism over its lifetime—entered into the discussion about cancer detection when it was discovered that tumors leak proteins into certain bodily fluids, such as blood or urine. Because tumors leak specific types of proteins, it is possible to identify the proteins as "cancer biomarkers." If such proteins can be linked to cancers, then examining bodily fluids could greatly increase the ability to screen patients for cancer at the earliest stages.

Certain proteins have already been implemented as cancer biomarkers. Levels of certain antigens—types of protein found in the immune system—can indicate cancer of the prostate (in men) or of the ovaries (in women). This method of detection has not yet proved to be 100 percent effective. It may give false negatives in which the test may not detect cancer when it is actually present or even false positives where it may detect cancer in cancer-free patients.

ELECTROMAGNETIC RADIATION AND CANCER

A possible link to cancer from high-tension power lines has researchers looking for a public policy solution to prevent a jump in deadly tumor rates among all animals. At very high frequencies—less than 100 nanometers—electromagnetic particles, also known as photons, have enough power to break chemical bonds in living matter. This is called ionization. One example is x-rays. At lower frequencies, the power of a photon is generally considered too low to be destructive. Most visible light and radio frequencies fall into this range. The scientific community contends that high-frequency sound emissions have a cumulative, synergistic, antagonistic, and chemically interactive effect on humans and other mammals that can cause illness and even death.

That said, there is broad consensus that exposure to high-frequency power lines cannot be proven to be either safe or dangerous. There is a marked divergence in conclusions between U.S. and British research on the danger of electromagnetic fields to humans and other mammals. Technological advances in the near future will form the early contours of this scientific debate; they could open it up to federal legislation, class-action lawsuits, and thousands of land-use ordinances designed to prevent electrical companies from stringing new high-tension power lines.

—Robert William Collin

As processes for detecting cancer improve, the number of cancer diagnoses is likely to increase. Although this would increase the overall incidence of cancer, it would also decrease its lethal consequences.

Improving Outcomes

Traditional forms of cancer treatment—surgery, chemotherapy, and radiation—are also undergoing significant breakthroughs. Developments in traditional cancer treatment involve refining existing procedures to yield better outcomes and reducing the side effects typically associated with such treatments. For example, chemotherapy regimens for head and neck cancers, typically difficult to treat, have improved through recombination of chemotherapy treatments with radiation, the first such major improvement for that type of cancer in 45 years.

Chemotherapy solutions are also being affected by the genetic revolution. A burgeoning field called pharmacogenomics seeks to tailor pharmaceutical offerings to a patient's genetic makeup, abandoning the one-size-fits-all or "blockbuster" drug of previous years. Drugs will now be matched using knowledge of a patient's gene profile, avoiding the trial-and-error method that is often practiced in trying to find the correct treatment for a given patient. Patients will be able to avoid unwanted side effects from unnecessary drugs, as well as lower the cost of health care and reduce repeat medical visits.

Much ground must still be covered before a pharmacogenomics revolution can take place. Drug alternatives must be found for numerous genotypes to avoid leaving patients without any options if their genotypes do not match the drugs available. Drug companies must also have incentives to make specialized drugs, given the exorbitant cost of offering only one single drug.

The effects of cancer and cancer treatments will continue to be studied as more information on the long-term effects of certain diseases becomes available. New examples of long-term complications with cancer have emerged recently in survivors of both breast cancer and childhood cancer. Breast cancer survivors have reported fatigue 5 and even 10 years after their treatment. Similarly, long-term research into childhood cancer survivors has shown that children who survive cancer are much more likely to have other health problems, five times more frequently than their healthy siblings. A large percentage of childhood survivors often developed other cancers, heart disease, and scarring of the lungs by age 45. Such evidence underscores the complicated nature of cancer survival and the fact that long-term studies will continue to play an important role.

There are now more than 10 million cancer survivors in the United States alone. The cancer survival rate between 1995 and 2001 was 65 percent, compared with just 50 percent from 1974 to 1976. As more becomes known about cancer itself, more will also be learned about the effects of cancer after remission. Studies examining cancer survivors 5 to 10 years after surgery are revealing that the effects of cancer and cancer treatment can extend beyond the time of treatment.

Not all research into cancer has been positive: certain types of cancer—namely skin cancer, myeloma (cancer of plasma cells in the immune system), and cancers of the thyroid and kidney—are on the rise. The reasons for the increase in cancers are wide-ranging and require further research to be fully understood.

With the fight against cancer continuing to evolve, new advances continue to converge from different fronts—in the use of human biospecimens, nanotechnology, and proteomics. Each of these fields individually has contributed to the efforts at detecting, preventing, and treating cancer, but if these efforts can be streamlined and pooled, a major battle in the fight against cancer will have been won.

As the fight has taken on a more global character, developments in knowledge sharing and community support have provided cancer researchers, patients, and survivors with new means of battling this life-threatening disease. As the technologies and infrastructures change, however, public policy will also have to change the way advancements in medical science are linked with accessibility for patients, so that financial means will not be a prerequisite for receiving these new treatments.

See also **Children and Cancer; Genetic Engineering; Human Genome Project; Stem Cell Research; Vaccines**

Further Reading

Cantor, David, ed., *Cancer in the Twentieth Century.* Baltimore: Johns Hopkins University Press, 2008.

Faquet, Guy B., *The War on Cancer: An Anatomy of Failure, a Blueprint for the Future.* Dordrecht: Springer, 2005.

Khoury, M. J., and J. Morris, *Pharmacogenomics and Public Health: The Promise of Targeted Disease Prevention.* Atlanta: Centers for Disease Control and Prevention, 2001.

Nass, S., and H. L. Moses, eds., *Cancer Biomarkers: The Promises and Challenges of Improving Detection and Treatment.* Washington, DC: National Academies Press, 2007.

National Cancer Institute, "Cancer Vaccine Fact Sheet. http://www.cancer.gov/cancertopics/factsheet/cancervaccine

Ozols, R., et al., "Clinical Cancer Advances 2006: Major Research Advances in Cancer Treatment, Prevention, and Screening—A Report From the American Society of Clinical Oncology." *Journal of Clinical Oncology* 25, no.1 (2007): 46–162.

Sanders, C., "Genomic Medicine and the Future of Health Care." *Science* 287, no. 5460 (2000): 1977–1978.

CARBON OFFSETS

Robert William Collin and Debra Ann Schwartz

The increasing concentration of carbon dioxide in the air and its part in global climate change have motivated individuals and corporations to consider ways to reduce the amount of it. As a solution, the notion of carbon emissions trading—also known as carbon offsets—came into being and was approved by elected officials. This approach allows people and companies to purchase permission to pollute. It is part of a "cap and trade" system, whereby a certain amount of pollution is deemed allowable, and, within that allowable limit (or cap), it is possible to buy credits. This is intended to prevent or at least curb or delay increases in carbon monoxide emissions from vehicles, for example. Do such offsets work? Or is the system flawed?

What Are Carbon Offsets and How Do They Work?

Carbon offsets are a financial instrument intended to reduce greenhouse gas emissions. They typically are used in the form of investment in a project, such as wind farms, biodiesel plants, or hydroelectric dams or systems for destroying landfill methane, industrial pollutants, and agricultural by-products. Some of the most popular carbon offset projects from a corporate perspective are energy efficiency and wind turbine projects.

Sanctioned by the Kyoto Protocol, the system is a way for governments and private companies to earn carbon credits that can be traded. That means companies will receive a certain amount of credits, allowing them to run their businesses and pollute a certain amount. If their business needs more than the allotted amount, they may purchase emissions credits from a company that does not need as much as its allotment. Therefore one company may sell to another or purchase from another for an unregulated price, creating market competition for pollution credits. This economic stimulation is provided for in the Clean Development Mechanism (CDM) written into the protocol. Organizations unable to meet their emissions quota can offset (supplement) their quotas by buying CDM-approved Certified Emissions Reductions.

The CDM exists to ensure that projects produce authentic benefits. It validates and measures projects to make sure that they involve genuinely "additional" activities, which would not otherwise have been undertaken.

Carbon offsets extended to the level of individual air travelers when companies specializing in brokering emissions trades reached out to them, asking if they might want to pay for their share of the carbon dioxide on a particular flight. Airplane emissions are substantial. Besides fuels and lubricants, airports use wing deicers and other toxic solvents. With acres of paving, the runoff of these pollutants usually affects local water supplies unless treated. The money paid is supposed to go to an activity that uses carbon dioxide to offset the carbon dioxide emitted on the flight, such as tree plantings. Some have estimated that the carbon offset market could be as high as $100 million.

U.S. businesses have also been buying carbon dioxide offsets in order to engage in international business. The Kyoto Protocol set global caps on emissions of greenhouse gases like carbon dioxide. Many nations have devoted substantial resources for many years to the Kyoto process, as did international bodies like the United Nations and the Union of Concerned Scientists. National and international environmental groups, along with community groups and labor unions, all also devoted considerable resources to this process. There is an international movement of cities that sign on with the Kyoto Protocols, including many of the major U.S. cities. U.S. businesses feel strong pressure to reduce the emission of greenhouse gases in order to continue international business transactions, where higher standards are required.

Emerging Questions

There are still some questions about how carbon dioxide emissions are calculated. Although the emissions estimates for most major activities are known, one significant issue concerns how the money for carbon offsets is spent. There is no well-defined offset protocol or policy. If the money goes to develop alternative renewable energy sources like wind and solar power, is the carbon dioxide from the petrochemicals that would have otherwise been used offset? Does it make a difference if the companies assisted make a profit, are nonprofit, or are state operated? Another gray area is home weatherization to save energy costs as a carbon offset. Does it make a difference to an offset program if a single homeowner is benefited? The argument for it counting as a carbon offset is that decreased energy use through conservation measures reduces carbon dioxide emissions by lowering consumption of pollution-causing energy sources. These differences can easily become the basis of public controversy.

Not Enough Regulation to Be Reliable?

The biggest upcoming battleground in this controversy is whether government regulation will help,. There are big differences in program costs and projects. There is a private, nonprofit effort to create a Green-E certification requiring the carbon offsets to meet a prescribed standard. Consumers want their carbon trades to truly reduce the amount of carbon dioxide emitted into the air, but that is not what they often get. There are also concerns that without regulation some offsets may be sold many times or go to projects that occur anyway.

Two powerhouse investigative reporting teams—the *Christian Science Monitor* and the New England Center for Investigative Reporting—have turned up evidence showing the system to be an unreliable form of environmental protection. In April 2010 the *Christian Science Monitor* online reported that individuals and businesses feeding a $700-million global market in carbon offset trading typically are buying vague promises instead of the greenhouse gas reductions they expect.

The team described the system as a scam or con game, one of whose effects was that people and companies were paying for projects that would have been carried out anyway. Their purchases fed middlemen and promoters "seeking profits from green schemes that range from selling protection for existing trees to the promise of planting new ones that never thrive. In some cases, the offsets have consequences that their purchasers never foresaw, such as erecting windmills that force poor people off their farms."

Discoveries made by the investigative reporters showed that carbon offsets are the environmental equivalent of financial derivatives in the banking industry: complex, unregulated, unchecked and, in many cases, not worth their price. And often, the reporters said, those who received "green credits" (among them the Vatican) thinking that their own carbon emissions had been offset, were fooled.

Conclusion

Carbon offsets grew out of ideals to do the right thing to mitigate air pollution. Some feared that the system would attract graft, and their fears seem to have been justified. Others believed the system would favor big polluters, allowing them to pay for the privilege of degrading the environment and contributing to global warming. There is some evidence of that. On the other side of the controversy are those who feel that the criticisms of the carbon offset market are inflated. But no matter what side you are on, the system bears serious scrutiny.

See also **Air Pollution; Carbon Taxes; Climate Change; Emissions Trading; Global Warming**

Further Reading

Bass, Stephen, and D. B. Barry Dalal-Clayton, *Sustainable Development Strategies: A Resource Book.* London: James and James/Earthscan, 2002.

Bayon, Ricardo, Amanda Hawn, and Katherine Hamilton, *Voluntary Carbon Markets: An International Business Guide to What They Are and How They Work.* London: James and James/Earthscan, 2007.

EcoBusiness Links, "Carbon Emissions Offsets Directory." January 20, 2008. www.ecobusiness links.com/carbon_offset_wind_credits_carbon_reduction.htm

Environmental Defense Fund, "Evaluation of Carbon Offset Programs." January 20, 2008. http://www.environmentaldefense.org/page.cfm

Follett, Ronald F., and John M. Kimble, *The Potential of U.S. Grazing Lands to Sequester Carbon and Mitigate the Greenhouse Effect.* Boca Raton, FL: CRC Press, 2000.

Smith, Kevin, *The Carbon Neutral Myth: Offset Indulgences for Your Climate Sins.* Amsterdam: Transnational Institute, 2007.

Struck, Doug, "Buying Carbon Offsets May Ease Eco-Guilt but not Global Warming." April 20, 2010. http://www.csmonitor.com/Environment/2010/0420/Buying-carbon-offsets-may-ease-eco-guilt-but-not-global-warming

CARBON TAXES

Robert William Collin and Debra Ann Schwartz

The carbon content of fuels is the focus of U.S. government strategy to encourage increased use of nonpolluting sources of energy and discourage use of fossil fuels by making them more expensive to use. Lawmakers discerned that placing a tax on fuels using carbon in any form will reduce their attractiveness to consumers. That is known as a *carbon tax*. A carbon tax is a tax on the carbon content of fossil fuels (coal, oil, gas). The Obama administration and Congress currently are considering whether to levy carbon taxes.

The Nature of Carbon Taxes

The intent of carbon taxes is to reduce the amount of greenhouse gases, such as carbon monoxide from vehicles, emitted into the air. Doing so, it is hoped, will help keep intact the various layers of atmosphere supporting life on earth. Carbon taxes are an attempt to make polluters pay cash for the emissions they put into the air. The hope that people will not want to pay the increase to use gasoline, for example, and will seek alternative forms of energy for getting around town or running blenders in the kitchen, for example. Carbon is used to create computer chips, electricity and fuel cars, for example. Carbon taxes are now common throughout the world.

Economists and sustainability proponents have traditionally embraced the idea of having the polluter pay, which means that the polluter pays the costs of cleaning up the contamination. Although in theory this principle is attractive, it is very difficult to implement as an environmental protection policy. Enforcement is weak, coverage of polluters incomplete, and questions about whether money can ever compensate for environmental degradation all prevent environmental regulations from reducing carbon dioxide emissions quickly enough to avoid a global tipping point. The *tipping point* concept is itself debated in the scientific community. It means that once the atmosphere reaches a certain level of carbon dioxide, there will be no way to turn back to lower levels.

Carbon dioxide emissions are a global concern, with the United States leading the world in emissions. Scientists have been examining ways to sequester carbon dioxide under the ground or sea, as is being done by the state oil company of Norway. Many carbon tax advocates feel that the only way to reduce carbon dioxide emissions quickly enough to prevent the tipping point from arising is to tax carbon dioxide emissions. Sustainability advocates also like carbon taxes because they could help move society away from nonrenewable fuels like gas and oil. Critics point out that many of the results sought could be approached by reducing subsidies for nonrenewable energy sources like oil. Politically, a policy of reducing subsidies to nonrenewable energy sources has simply not happened, argue carbon tax proponents, and results are needed. Critics also say that the same results could be attained by use of a cap-and-trade program. Carbon proponents argue that traditional cap-and-trade programs apply only to generators of electrical energy, which account for only about 40 percent of carbon emissions; that carbon taxes are more transparent and easily understood than cap-and-trade arrangements between industry and government; and that carbon taxes will get quicker results in terms of decreased carbon dioxide emissions.

Background

The first country to put a tax on atmospheric carbon dioxide emissions was Sweden in 1991, followed by Finland, Norway, and the Netherlands. Initially applied to combustion-only point sources over a certain size, the tax was equivalent to about $55 (U.S.) per ton of carbon dioxide emitted. Norway has extended the tax to offshore oil and gas production. They found it effective in spurring industry to find cost-efficient ways to reduce carbon dioxide emissions. The European Union began implementing a carbon tax in 2007 and intended to steadily increase the rate over time.

In early June 2010, a panel consisting of representatives of 12 federal agencies provided its climate change analysis to aid lawmakers with deciding what to include in climate change legislation. They estimated that each additional metric ton of carbon dioxide emitted into the earth's atmosphere inflicts at least $21 in damage to agricultural productivity, human health, property damage from flooding, and the value of ecosystem loss due to climate change. According to the U.S. Environmental Protection Agency, the United States contributed 5.6 billion tons of carbon dioxide in 2008. That amounts to $117.6 billion in environmental damage today.

Carbon taxes have been controversial at the city, state, and federal levels. Some environmentally conscious communities have passed their own carbon tax, such as Boulder, Colorado. Boulder's carbon tax applies only to electricity generation and is based on a dollar figure per ton of carbon emitted into the atmosphere. Advocates in Boulder claim the tax will raise almost $7 million over five years.

Direct environmental regulation of carbon by municipalities could occur rapidly in the United States, especially if state legislatures or Congress do not develop a carbon tax policy. Currently, about 330 U.S. mayors are signed on to the U.S. Mayors Climate Protection Agreement. Carbon tax debates could occur in many different localities. Many state legislatures are being exposed to the idea of carbon taxes. In the United States, Massachusetts has formed a study commission on tax policy and carbon emissions reduction. Advocates for a carbon tax say that it will reduce U.S. oil dependence. Nonrenewable energy sources account for much of the U.S. carbon waste stream. Natural gas is responsible for 22 percent, coal burning for 36 percent, and petroleum products for 42 percent of U.S. annual carbon emissions. If the carbon tax is enough to change pollution behavior, then advocates claim it will generate a large amount of revenue, some estimating between $55 billion and $500 billion a year depending on the carbon tax program.

Proposed Legislation

Carbon taxes have made their way into congressional discussions and legislative proposals to reduce pollution. In April 2007 Democratic representatives Peter Stark from California and Jim McDermott from Washington introduced the Save Our Climate Act, a bill to reduce global warming by taxing carbon in fossil fuels. It remains with the

House Ways and Means Committee, which has been discussing this proposal since its introduction. Stark is the primary sponsor of the legislation, with three cosponsors: Mc-Dermott and democrats Bob Filner of California and Raul Grijalva of Arizona.

The bill would charge $10 per ton of carbon in coal, petroleum, or natural gas. It would increase by $10 every year until U.S. carbon emissions decreased by 80 percent of 1990 levels. Stark maintains that this is the level most scientists claim is necessary to slow rapid climate change. Some environmental groups do not endorse it, some influential newspaper columnists do endorse it, and many are leery of anything called a tax. Accepting the concept of carbon taxes requires acceptance of global warming and climate change. These are environmental controversies in themselves. In the United States, they are also political controversies. Because of that, taxes for anything environmental may have difficulty getting enough support to become law.

There is now academic discussion of a global carbon tax. Economists focus on carbon taxes in some of their environmental and policy analyses. It is likely that many nations would find this appealing. Huge issues of enforcement in rich and poor nations would prevent this. No nation likes another nation to tax its citizens in their own country. Nonetheless, the small economics controversy of carbon taxes as environmental policy is receiving serious attention.

Conclusion

Carbon taxes shift environmental policy into the tax policy regulatory arena. Taxes are very strong policy devices and are used here to change the behavior of polluters. As such there are distributional impacts and other taxes to consider. Some have wondered, why not just prohibit carbon dioxide emissions or regulate them out of existence? Carbon taxes do appeal to the basic "polluter pays" principle but suffer some of the same problems. Who does the polluter pay? Who gets the benefit of the new carbon tax revenue? These questions fall into the same category of questions as avoiding carbon taxes by subsidizing renewable energy or withdrawing nonrenewable energy subsidies (for oil companies, for example). The political will of regulatory agencies and federal courts to tax carbon dioxide emissions is not strong enough to reduce the power of industry. The fundamental question is whether carbon taxes will actually reduce carbon dioxide emissions.

See also **Carbon Offsets; Climate Change; Emissions Trading; Fossil Fuels; Global Warming; Sustainability (vol. 1)**

Further Reading

The Carbon Tax Center, "Why Revenue-Neutral Carbon Taxes are Essential." http://www.carbon tax.org

Carraro, Carlo, and Domenico Siniscalco, *The European Carbon Tax: An Economic Assessment.* New York: Springer, 1993.

Dellink, Rob B., *Modeling the Costs of Environmental Policy: A Dynamic Applied General Model.* Northampton, MA: Edward Elgar Publishing, 2005.

EcoNeutral, "Neutralize Your Footprint." www.econeutral.com

FitzRoy, Felix, and Elissaios Papyrakis, *An Introduction to Climate Change Economics.* Sterling, VA: Earthscan, 2010.

Handley, James, "Government Panel Estimates Cost of CO_2 Pollution: $21/t and rising." June 3, 2010. http://www.carbontax.org/blogarchives/2010/06/03/govt-panel-estimates-cost-of-c02–20t-and-rising.

Library of Congress, "Bill Summary & Status, 111th Congress (2009–2010). H.R. 594. Save Our Climate Act of 2009." http://thomas.loc.gov/cgi-bin/thomas

Park, Patricia D., *Energy Law and the Environment.* Boca Raton, FL: CRC Press, 2002.

Serret, Ysé, and Nick Johnstone, *The Distributional Effects of Environmental Policy.* Northampton, MA: Edward Elgar Publishing, 2006.

CHILDHOOD ASTHMA AND THE ENVIRONMENT

Robert William Collin

Recent increases in childhood asthma have created controversies about the environmental causes. Children living in urban areas are especially vulnerable to asthma because of the high number of pollutants and allergens in their environment. Others argue that exposure to pesticides in the air and food helps cause it.

Asthma is a disease that affects breathing. It attacks and damages lungs and airways. Asthma is described as like breathing through a straw; it can be a serious threat to persons of any age. Childhood asthma attracts attention because of its potential developmental consequences. Asthma is characterized by partially blocked airways. It can occur periodically or reactively, and attacks or events can range from mild to severe. The nose, sinuses, and throat can become constricted. Breathing becomes difficult and is accompanied by coughing and wheezing. During an asthma event, the muscles around the breathing passages constrict. The mucous lining of the airways becomes inflamed and swollen. This further constricts air passages. These episodes can last for hours or days. They can be terrifying events for parents and children. Childhood asthma and its disproportionate impact on vulnerable populations is one of the foundational issues of environmental justice in the United States.

Causes of Asthma: Foundations of a Controversy

Asthma is a complex disease with many causes, some known, some contested, and some unknown. Each one presents its own issues. Environmental causes are controversial because they represent a broad, catchall category. Controversies about science, industry trade secrets, and unequal enforcement of environmental laws merge with a very high level of citizen concern. There is an emerging role for public health experts and advocates in urban environmental policies around childhood asthma. There is a greater incidence of asthma among children in U.S. inner cities. Asthma often accounts for a large number of emergency room visits, especially in poor areas underserved by medical insurance. Hospitals, health care administrators, and health insurance corporations are all very interested in the causes of asthma. Employers and educators know that a number of days in school or on the job are lost because of asthma. They also have an interest in understanding the causes. Some stakeholders may fear liability for causing asthma. They have a strong interest in not being named as among those responsible.

Environmental Triggers for Asthma

The policy question posed now is what triggers an asthma attack. Others, such as public health experts and advocates, ask what can prevent it. They are concerned that focus on a trigger overlooks vectors of causality as opposed to last exposure.

Indoor Air Contamination

Dust mites, cockroach droppings, animal dander, and mold are among the environmental conditions that may cause asthma. Exposure to allergens alone may induce the onset of asthma. Exposure to secondhand tobacco smoke is also a contributor. Certain insecticides may also be triggers. Some researchers consider pesticides to be a preventable cause of asthma in children. The quality of indoor air in homes may be made worse by the increasing use of synthetic materials in the form of carpets, carpet glues, curtains, and building materials. There is concern that as these materials age, they release potentially dangerous chemicals. Manufacturers of these items strongly contest any conclusion that their products may be among the causes of childhood asthma. However, concern about release of toxins from synthetic materials has affected market trends in these products. Because many household products are believed to be possible causes of asthma, the marketplace or commerce in these products has become a point of discussion. Large big-box retailers like Walmart are accommodating these consumer concerns about causes of asthma that consumers can control, such as dust mites and animal dander.

Outdoor Air Pollution

There is strong evidence from longitudinal studies that ambient air pollution acts as a trigger for asthma events among persons with this condition. Truck and automotive exhaust is a big part of the polluted air, especially in densely populated urban areas. Combined with industrial and municipal emissions and waste treatment practices (such as incineration), the quality of the air becomes so degraded that the total polluted air load in some urban and nearby suburban areas is a threat to the health of children. It threatens them with the development of asthma due to long-time exposure and poses the risk of initiating an attack at any time.

Children in the City

It is clear that the increasing severity of asthma in the United States is concentrated in cities among children who live in poverty. Children, as compared with adults, are especially vulnerable to air pollution and other toxic exposures, partly because they have more skin surface relative to total body mass. According to Frederica Perera, director of the Columbia Center for Children's Environmental Health:

> They consume more water, more food, and more air per unit body weight than adults by far. Today's urban children are highly exposed to allergens, such as cockroach and rodent particles, and pollutants, such as diesel exhaust, lead and pesticides. And these elements affect them even before they are born. Preliminary evidence shows that increased risk of asthma may start as early as in the womb before birth.

The small particles of soot "are very easily breathed into your lungs, so they really exacerbate asthma," say Peggy Shepard, executive director of the West Harlem Environmental Action, Inc., adding that she believes these diesel particles may also play a role in cancer. Shepard says that New York City is second in the nation when it comes to the amount of toxins released in the air, preceded only by Baltimore.

David Evans, who runs the Columbia Center's "Healthy Home, Healthy Child" intervention campaign, maintains that cockroach particles pose a problem for urban areas nationwide. He says, "Simple housecleaning won't solve the problem, because the cockroach residue tends to be present in many city neighborhoods." According to the Harlem Lung Center, childhood asthma rates increased 78 percent between 1980 and 1993. And according to the Columbia Center, there are an estimated 8,400 new cases of childhood cancer each year nationwide.

Disparities in Asthma Care

Access to health care is an important aspect of the asthma controversy. Many low-income groups do not have health insurance and tend to use the emergency room instead of visits to a primary care physician. An asthma attack often presents that necessity. Language and cultural differences can make a tense medical situation worse. Even with regular medical intervention, differences in asthma treatment by race, gender, and class make this issue an ongoing one, and disparities in the burden and treatment of African Americans and Puerto Ricans with asthma are well documented.

Among African Americans and Puerto Ricans, rates of asthma, hospitalization, and death are higher compared with those of whites. This is especially true among children. Different medicines are prescribed and used for different groups. Research shows that the use of long-term medications to control asthma is lower among African Americans and Puerto Ricans. Cost may be a factor, especially if there is no insurance coverage.

Access to medical care is affected in many ways. There are shortages of primary care physicians in minority communities, and also issues of trust about the role and usefulness of medications.

Costs of Asthma

Asthma is a cause of death among U.S. children. There are 247 deaths each year due to childhood asthma. It is the leading cause of hospital admission for urban children. Asthma is also the leading cause of days of school missed. It is estimated that about 30 percent of acute episodes of childhood asthma are environmentally related.

Air pollution is considered a major cause of asthma, and asthma and public health are major regulatory justifications for clean air laws. The U.S. Environmental Protection Agency (EPA) has estimated the cost savings that resulted from the Clean Air Act. For the years 1970–1990, the EPA calculated that the annual monetary benefits of reductions in chronic bronchitis and other respiratory conditions was $3.5 billion. That is, this figure represents health care costs that would have been incurred if there were no clean air regulations. There are other costs too, of course. Also, if there were no costs and if people with asthma could get free and accessible medical attention, the cost of human resources necessary to handle the scope of the problem could be large. Additional childhood asthma benefits are projected by the EPA to accrue over the years 1990 to 2010, assuming full implementation of the Clean Air Act Amendments of 1990.

Conclusion

This controversy is very salient among communities and public health professionals. Schools, hospitals, nursing homes, and other places where vulnerable people live hold strong views but lack resources. Emissions from traffic, industry, and heating and cooling systems are now part of the U.S. urban landscape. Environmentalists note that the law does not cover all the pollutants and is not enforced equally. Advocates of environmental justice consider childhood asthma as proof of at least one disproportionate environmental impact. Asthma generally has resulted in a substantial increase in the sales and profits of pharmaceutical companies. This controversy is structural in that it pits public health concerns against industrial emissions and is therefore of deep significance.

There will be many ongoing issues. The environmental controversies around childhood asthma will focus on air pollution and use other controversial methods such as ecosystem risk assessment or cumulative risk assessment. Childhood asthma is a big part of the new inclusion of cities by the EPA. In the early 1990s, the visionary EPA administrator Carol Browner reduced the level of particulate matter allowed in urban air districts, effectively banning many diesel and leaded gas vehicles. She started an urban air toxics policy task force to help engage cities and the EPA, along with several other successful policy initiatives. Exxon and other oil companies responded with

FACTS ABOUT ASTHMA

Childhood asthma is an environmental controversy with much saliency in metropolitan areas. The following summary is from the Center of Children's Health and the Environment at the Mount Sinai School of Medicine:

- In 1993–1994, approximately four million children aged 0–14 reported asthma in the preceding 12 months.
- Self-reported prevalence rates for asthma among children ages 0–4 increased by 160 percent from 1980 to 1994; rates among children ages 5–14 increased by 74 percent.
- Asthma was selected as the underlying cause of death among 170 children aged 0–14 in 1993.
- Among children ages 5–14, the asthma death rate nearly doubled from 1980 to 1993.
- Over 160,000 children aged 0–14 are hospitalized for asthma annually.
- Among all age groups, children aged 0–4 had the highest hospitalization rate in 1993–1994 (49.7 hospitalizations per 10,000 persons).
- The cost of illness related to asthma in 1990 was estimated to be $6.2 billion, according to a 1992 study. Of that amount, inpatient hospital services were the largest medical expenditure for this condition, approaching $1.6 billion.

Many more suffer asthma without medical care. There may be rural, institutional, and pockets of urban populations that lack public health resources. Many citizens do not have health care coverage for asthma.

letters to their accounts about the new air pollution regulations. In an unusual step, the American Lung Association and other public health organizations responded in support of the EPA. As U.S. environmental policy matures into comprising all environments, including cities, continued controversy in the area of public health can be expected. Battle lines were drawn then and are much deeper now. Asthma is worse, there is greater consensus that air pollution not only triggers but also causes asthma, there are large documented environmental injustices by race and class, and there is a large overall push for sustainability.

See also **Air Pollution; Children and Cancer; Cumulative Emissions; Environmental Justice**

Further Reading

Akinbami, Lara J., *The State of Childhood Asthma in the United States, 1980–2005*. Hyattsville, MD: U.S. Department of Health and Human Services, 2006.

Bernstein, I. Leonard, *Asthma in the Workplace.* New York: Marcel Dekker, 1999.

Cherni, Judith A., *Economic Growth versus the Environment: The Politics of Wealth, Health, and Air Pollution.* London: Palgrave Macmillan, 2002.

Christie, Margaret J., and Davina French, *Assessment of Quality of Life in Childhood Asthma.* London: Taylor and Francis, 1994.

Institute of Medicine, *Clearing the Air: Asthma and Indoor Air Exposures.* Washington, DC: National Academies Press, 2000.

Naspitz, Charles K., *Pediatric Asthma: An International Perspective.* London: Taylor and Francis, 2001.

CHILDREN AND CANCER

Robert William Collin

A core controversy is whether environmental stressors, such as pollution and pesticides, are responsible for the increase of childhood cancers.

Background

The cause of cancer is always a controversial topic. The rate of cancer among U.S. children has been rising since the 1970s. The mortality rate, however, has decreased since the 1980s. There are scientifically established causes of childhood cancer. Family history of cancer, radiation exposure, genetic abnormalities, and some chemicals used to treat cancer are known causes of childhood cancer. The plethora of new chemicals in food, air, water, clothing, carpets, and the soil is strongly suspected as being part of the cause of cancer in children. The scientific model of causality struggles with proof of the cause of childhood cancer and engages fierce environmental controversy in the process. Some aspects of this controversy have moved into the courtroom. There science struggles both with causality by a certain chemical and liability of a specific person (the defendant).

Childhood Cancer Facts

According to the National Cancer Institute (http://www.cancer.gov/cancer topics/types/childhoodcancers), the following set of statistics measures the expanding parameters of childhood cancer.

A newborn child faces a risk of about 1 in 600 of developing cancer by 10 years of age. The rate of increase has amounted to almost 1 percent a year. From 1975 to 1995 the incidence of cancer increased from 130 to 150 cases per million children. During this time mortality due to cancer decreased from 50 to 30 deaths per million children. In the United States, cancer is diagnosed each year in about 8,000 children below age 15. Cancer is the most common form of fatal childhood disease. About 10 percent of all deaths in childhood are from cancer. There are big differences between types of cancer, and researchers investigate these differences because it may lead them to the environmental stressors. Leukemia was the major cancer in children from 1973 to 1996. About one quarter of all childhood cancer cases were leukemia. Brain cancer, or glioma, increased nearly 40 percent from 1973 to 1994. The overall rate of central nervous system tumors increased from about 23 per million in 1973 to 29 per million children in 1996. These two forms of cancer account for most of the disease in children. Lymphomas are the third most diagnosed category of childhood cancer; they are diagnosed in about 16 percent of cases. There are different kinds of lymphomas; for some categories childhood incidence rates have decreased and for others they have increased. (For example, non-Hodgkin's lymphomas increased from 8.9 per million children in 1973 to 11 per million in 1996.)

According the U.S. Environmental Protection Agency (EPA), Office of Children's Health protection (http://Yosemite.epa.gov/ochpweb.nsf/content/childhood_cancer.htm), there are substantial differences by age and type of cancer:

> Rates are highest among infants, decline until age 9, and then rise again with increasing age. Between 1986 and 1995, children under the age of 5 and those aged 15–19 experienced the highest incident rates of cancer at approximately 200 cases per million children. Children aged 5–9 and 10–14 had lower incidence rates at approximately 110 and 120 cases per million children.

The EPA also reports some ethnic differences in childhood cancer rates:

> Between 1992 and 1996, incidence rates of cancer were highest among whites at 160 per million. Hispanics were next highest at 150 per million. Asian and Pacific Islanders had an incidence rate of 140 per million. Black children had a rate of 120 per million, and Native Americans and Alaska Natives had the lowest at 80 per million.

Also, different types of cancer affect children at different ages. According to the EPA:

> Neuroblastomas, Wilms' tumors (tumors of the kidney) and retinoblastoma (tumors in the eyes) usually are found in very young children. Leukemias and nervous system cancers are most common through age 14; lymphomas, carcinomas, and germ cell and other gonadal tumors are more common in those 15–19 years old.

Scientific Model: Struggling to Keep Up with Policy

The last century saw a drastic lowering of infectious disease rates due to strong public health measures and education. In the United States and other industrialized nations, this has been accompanied by a general rise in systemic, whole-body, or immune system breakdowns. Cancer is considered a possible result of a whole-body immune system breakdown. About 100,000 chemicals are released into the environment. Less than 2 percent of them are tested for public health impacts. The tests are done in constrained laboratory conditions, generally considering a given chemical safe if less than one half or one quarter of the mice exposed to it die. The scientific model requires the isolation of an extraneous possible cause or intervening variables. It ignores cumulative, synergistic, and antagonistic real-world chemical interactions that are the exposure vectors of chemicals for children. The actual biological vulnerability of the affected humans is not taken into account. A developing fetus is much more vulnerable to harm by cancer-causing chemicals. It takes a newborn child at least a year to develop an efficient blood-brain barrier, which works to protect the brain while the central nervous system develops. Before this barrier begins to function fully, the infant could be exposed to whatever the mother is exposed to. There is research indicating that children of people who work with dangerous chemicals have an increased frequency of childhood cancer. The problem of childhood cancer is a driving force behind many other environmental controversies. The real-world number of cancer cases in industrialized nations has increased overall, although it depends on demographics and type of cancer.

Environmental scientists, from government, industry, and environmental groups, have been laboring for many years to unravel some of the exposure vectors to children with cancer and sometimes to endocrine disruption. Many chemicals are much more dangerous when mixed with other chemicals. Children are especially vulnerable to many of the chemicals used around the house, such as cleaners and pesticides. Research has found over twice the risk of brain cancer for children exposed to household insecticide. Some studies have found even higher rates of risk. These early studies focus on just one type of cancer from a few known exposure vectors. The cumulative and synergistic emissions of the past are becoming the cancer risks of the present.

Costs Are Very High: Who Pays?

Health care in the United States is another controversy altogether. Access is difficult, and cancer treatments are very expensive. The annual overall incidence of cancer is 133.3 per million for children under 15 years old in the United States. There were 57.9 million children under 15 years of age in the United States in 1997. About 7,722 cases of childhood cancer are anticipated each year, which is very close to the 8,000 reported. Experts have estimated the cancer-related costs for children to be about $4.8 billion. There are other costs. Psychological stress, transportation, time with medical staff and insurers, and time as a health care provider are all also costs.

The cost of treatment of childhood cancer is controversial in that it is generally too much for an average family to afford. This plays into other controversies about the health care system. If the family cannot afford it or if the insurance company requires it, they file a lawsuit against the most likely cause of the cancer. The litigation hurdles of proof and the burden of proof are often insurmountable obstacles.

What Environmental Stressors Cause Childhood Cancers?

The following brain cancer figures, from the American Cancer Society, show a disturbing trend in the number of cases being found:

1940: 1.95 per 100,000 population
1945: 2.25 per 100,000
1950: 2.90 per 100,000
1955: 3.40 per 100,000
1960: 3.70 per 100,000
1965: 3.85 per 100,000
1970: 4.10 per 100,000
1975: 4.25 per 100,000

These figures show a steady increase for all industrialized nations. To many public policy makers the cancer rates in these countries implicate chemicals used there. Similar increases are occurring in children. Many chemical manufacturing industries would contest this association, stating that in most cases the scientific evidence neither proves nor disproves causality.

Chemicals and Childhood Cancers

As discussed previously, a major form of childhood cancer is brain cancer. Which chemicals have been linked to brain cancers? Chemical workers are often the most exposed to a particular chemical. They make it, store it, and transport it. Sometimes they also use it. Epidemiologists follow the exposure vector to workers of various suspected chemicals. Brain cancer risks follow workers exposed to chemicals used in vinyl and rubber production, oil refineries, and chemical manufacturing plants. Another study by the National Cancer Institute of 3,827 Florida pest-control operators found they had approximately twice the normal rate of brain cancer. Pesticide exposure increases risks for childhood cancer. Because adult workers had higher rates of brain cancer when exposed to these chemicals in their occupations, researchers surmise that because children are more vulnerable, they may get more brain cancer when exposed to these chemicals.

Some chemicals used in pesticides concern public health officials more than others. Chlordane is one of high concern. Research on children who developed brain cancer after their homes were treated with pesticides led officials to this chemical. The debate over this chemical has moved to litigation in many cases. Chlordane is a high-risk chemical for brain cancer. It is a fat-soluble compound, and such compounds are absorbed into the nervous system, which develops rapidly in children from birth to age 5.

Legal chlordane use was stopped in the United States in April 1988. However, the law was and is poorly enforced. One reason it was made illegal was its long-term killing power, which also made it an effective pesticide. The degree to which a chemical persists in the environment is one measure of how dangerous it could be to the environment and to humans. Chlordane is such a persistent chemical that it is still being detected today. Tests of more than 1,000 homes performed by federal agencies found that approximately 75 percent of all homes built before 1988 show air contamination with chlordane. They also found that 6 to 7 percent of such homes are suspected of being over the maximum safe levels for chlordane exposure in residential housing set by the National Academy of Sciences, a limit that some have argued is too low.

Research into this controversial area has increased. Authors Julia Green Brady, Ann Aschengrau, Wendy McKelvey, Ruthann A. Rudel, Christopher H. Schwartz, and Theresa Kennedy from the Boston University School of Public Health in Massachusetts published "Family Pesticide Use Suspected of Causing Child Cancers, I" (1993). In this peer-reviewed article the relationship between family pesticide use and childhood brain cancer was closely examined. The researchers compared brain cancer rates for families using pesticides and those not using pesticides. They concluded that the chemicals did increase the risk of cancer. Significant positive associations with brain cancer rates were observed in families using regular household supplies and pest-control chemicals. Bug sprays for different kinds of insects, pesticide bombs, hanging no-pest strips, some shampoos, flea collars on dogs and cats, diazinon in the garden or orchard, and herbicides to control weeds in the yard were all found by the authors to be part of the chemical vector increasing the risk of brain cancer. These results are still being disputed. Some argue that the sample sizes are very small in some of these studies and the results may not be typical. Unanswered questions fueling the uncertainty that underlies this controversy concern the total range of effects of chemicals. What happens when they combine in water or sunlight over time? Are there possible generation-skipping effects? What happens to the typical child when exposed to these chemicals in their normal environment? What constitutes their regular environment? Does air pollution pose another cancer-causing vector for children? The evidence is fairly conclusive now that secondary tobacco smoke can cause health risks. Originally, tobacco smoking and chewing were considered good for your health. The danger they posed was a conclusion resisted tenaciously by the tobacco industry. Secondary smoke was highly controversial and remains contested when local land-use ordinances restricting the use of tobacco products come into play.

Conclusion

Childhood cancer is a traumatic event for all involved. The costs are very high. Right now it is difficult to overcome scientifically based burdens of proof in litigation. Families with children with cancer often seek legislative recourse to the incidents they believe caused the cancer. Children, as growing beings, naturally absorb more from the environment than adults. The increase in most childhood cancer rates is a cause for alarm for environmentalists and public health officials. Industry tries to cap environmental liabilities through legislation and internal agency advocacy. This all means that this controversy will intensify as more chemicals are linked with childhood cancers.

See also **Cumulative Emissions; Environmental Justice; Pesticides**

Further Reading

Brady, Julia Green, Ann Aschengrau, Wendy McKelvey, Ruthann A. Rudel, Christopher H. Schwartz, and Theresa Kennedy, "Family Pesticide Use Suspected of Causing Child Cancers, I." *Archives of Environmental Contamination Toxicology* 24, no. 1 (1993): 87–92.

Davis, Devra Lee, *The Secret History of the War on Cancer.* New York: Basic Books, 2007.

Hayman, Laura L., ed., *Chronic Illness in Children: An Evidence-Based Approach.* New York: Springer, 2002.

Steingraber, Sandra, *Living Downstream: A Scientist's Personal Investigation of Cancer and the Environment.* New York: Vintage Books, 1998.

CLIMATE CHANGE

Robert William Collin and Debra Ann Schwartz

The consequences of dramatic climate change are uncertain in terms of specific impacts. This uncertainty is everyone's concern. Some general effects, such as rising ocean levels, are known. Specific weather changes that are not yet known could occur abruptly. Many scientific, legal, and international debates are emerging with respect to this issue.

What Is Climate?

Climate is the total of all weather conditions over time.

The difference between climate and weather is specific: climate is average regional weather typically based on a 30-year period. Whether and to what extent there are seasonal changes and when they start and end determines climate. Amount of rainfall, hours of sun, prevailing wind patterns, and temperature are parts of what we call climate. The global warming controversy focuses on the speed of change in climate and the extent humans cause it and can remedy it.

When is climate change too fast or too abrupt? Differing viewpoints exist, however the National Oceanic and Aeronautics Administration (NOAA) notes that shifts historically taking centuries or longer that begin to occur more rapidly, in periods as short as decades, are characterized as "abrupt." Scientists also have couched climate change in terms of effects on ecosystems and social systems and their ability to adapt to climatic shifts.

CAN TECHNOLOGY SOLVE ABRUPT CLIMATE CHANGE?

Environmentalists contend that technology has created many of the pollution problems that are now demanding solutions. Engineers claim that technological intervention solves problems related to increased human population affecting the climate. Human climatic impacts have been labeled accidental. People's faith in technology to solve environmental problems has led to the belief that technological engineering could be used to slow the rate of global warming and the abruptness of climate change. This type of engineering is called geoengineering.

Scientists have offered several untested and controversial ideas about how to slow the rate at which climates are warming and cooling globally to lesser or greater extents that recorded. One idea is to put thin, controllable shields on the edge of earth's atmosphere to block the sun. Other notions include reflective balloons, reflective space dust, iron dust (which absorbs carbon dioxide), reflective roofs and roads, and reforestation. Australian engineers have floated the idea of *terraforming* by building a big pipe that would pump ozone into the stratosphere and plug the hole in the earth's ozone layer, identified many years ago. Another idea is to technologically solve the problem by increasing the amount of light reflected back into space by earth. This approach involves having oceangoing vessels spray saltwater mists into the air to form strong reflective ocean clouds, thus increasing the *albedo*, the amount of solar light absorbed or reflected by water, land, ice, and so on.

Many of these engineering concepts suffer from cost issues, possible unintended impacts like pollution and acid rain, and lack of information and computational power. The response to these concerns is that cost determines priority, and as climatic changes affect more of the earth, more possible solutions are expected to be tried.

Science and Forecasting

Underlying the climate change issue is the matter of contested science. The scale is so large that until the advent of computers, climate change science was theoretical. Now there is consensus among scientists and engineers that climate change is driven by greenhouse gases. There is agreement, for example, that the sun provides about 344 watts of energy per square meter on average. Much of this energy comes in the part of the electromagnetic spectrum visible to humans. The sun drives the earth's weather and climate and heats the earth's water and land surfaces. The earth radiates energy back into space through the atmosphere. Much of this is reradiated energy. Atmospheric gases—including water vapor, carbon dioxide, methane, and particulate matter—exist in a very delicate and dynamic balance. They act like glass windows, letting heat in and holding in some of it to create what is called a *greenhouse effect*. Scientists can now observe atmospheric conditions further in the past by examining deeply embedded ice cores from old ice. Doing so has helped them to isolate the effects of human development on the atmosphere. This research also helped scientists pinpoint large catastrophic natural events in earth's history.

Since as late as 1800, atmospheric concentrations of carbon dioxide have increased by almost 30 percent. With more carbon dioxide and warmer air, more moisture develops in the atmosphere and increases warming trends. Methane concentrations have more than doubled. Nitrous oxide concentrations have risen by about 15 percent. Increases on this scale have enhanced the heat-trapping capability of the earth's atmosphere. They have blurred the windows of the greenhouse. The effect is melting ice caps, rising ocean levels, and in general a warmer planet.

Some scientists contend that human activities are the main reason for the increased concentration of carbon dioxide. They argue that human impacts have affected the usual balance of plant respiration and the decomposition of organic matter, causing them to release large amounts of carbon dioxide. Fossil fuels are responsible for about 98 percent of U.S. carbon dioxide emissions, 24 percent of methane emissions, and 18 percent of nitrous oxide emissions. Increased agribusiness, deforestation, landfills, incinerators, industrial production, and mining also contribute a large share of emissions. In 1997, the United States emitted about one fifth of total global greenhouse gases. This estimate is based on models and industry self-reporting.

Environmental regulation and monitoring are relatively new and dominantly exists only in developed countries. Environmentally regulated countries still allow large amounts of chemicals into the land, air, and water without complete knowledge of short- or long-term ecological risks and impacts. It is difficult to assess these impacts because not all the emissions from humans are regulated. Large amounts of unregulated industrial emissions, municipal emissions, agricultural emissions, and commercial and residential emissions remain unregulated and are a source of uncertainty. Each category represents future stakeholders in a growing controversy. Because so much is still unknown regarding the scale and scope of emissions, it is impossible to predict environmental impacts such as synergistic and cumulative risks. Over time, with an increasing human population and more extensive monitoring, the level of uncertainty about the effects of climate change may decrease. Fear of liability for contamination figures into this equation. Uncertainty about the best policies to follow to mitigate climate changes continues. Many contend mitigation will require better knowledge about actual emissions. The policy need for this information and the stakeholder fear of liability and increased regulation will fuel the first fires of the climate change policy wars. The current state of knowledge is highly dependent on modeling and weather data.

The Case of Methane

Methane remains in the atmosphere for approximately 9 to 15 years. It is more than 20 times as effective for trapping heat in the atmosphere than carbon dioxide. Former U.S. Vice President Al Gore and others conclude that large pockets of methane at the north and south poles will produce more methane than anticipated as the poles warm. The projected consequence is a greatly increased rate of global warming and climate change.

It is estimated that 60 percent of global methane emissions are related to human activities. This gas is emitted during the drilling, refining, use, and transport of coal, natural gas, and oil all over the world. Methane emissions also result from the decomposition of organic wastes. Wetlands, gas hydrates, permafrost, termites, oceans, freshwater bodies, nonwetland soils, volcanic eruptions, and wildfires are natural sources of methane. Some sustainable dairy farms in Vermont began defraying expensive heating costs by collecting and burning methane from cow manure. Now farmer in almost every U.S. state do the same. Methane also collects in municipal solid waste landfills, which are near capacity. Sometimes landfills burn off the methane gas, which can form in a landfill. Methane is a primary constituent of natural gas and an important energy source all over the world.

Other Emissions Affecting Climate Change

As human populations and industrialization increase, several emissions also will increase. Greenhouse gases are expected to escalate substantially. The climate changes that occur could be dramatic. Many experts generally expect

1. Land temperature to increase more than ocean temperature
2. Northern hemisphere sea ice to retreat substantially
3. Sea level to rise more than a meter over the next several hundred years
4. A sharp reduction in the overturning circulation of the North Atlantic ocean
5. Substantial reductions in midcontinent summer soil moisture (about 25 percent)
6. Increases in the intensity of tropical hurricanes and/or typhoons.
7. Sharp increases in the summertime heat index (a measure of the effective temperature level a body feels on a humid day) in moist, subtropical areas

Additional impacts have been speculated upon, including natural disasters and power conflicts between nations.

Climate Data Availability

Climate data provide the basics for characterizing various statistics for temperature, pressure, wind, water amounts, cloudiness, and precipitation as a function of geographical location, time, and altitude. Such data provide invaluable information on the natural variability of climate, ranging from seasons to decades. These data sets have led to important understandings of how the climate system works. They also provide valuable information on how ice ages and warm epochs interact with climatic changes. For example, for meteorological purposes, thousands of observation points collect information continuously for weather forecasting. Most of this information is important to research on longer-term climate change. Climate change data are more expansive than weather forecasting data sets. Some climate change data not usually included in weather data sets are vertical velocity, radiative heating/cooling, cloud characteristics (*albedo*), evaporation, and properties of critical trace species such as particles containing sulfate and carbon. Weather data sets do not provide information on the vegetative cover and its role in governing surface water evaporation. The ocean's currents, waves, jets, and vortices are important climatic measurements that are not included in the usual weather data sets.

Weather often determines human settlement patterns, and as world population increases, the unstable and sometime contradictory computer modeling of climate changes lends itself to controversy. Weather forecasts can also determine financial lending patterns in agricultural areas as well as economic development based on industrial manufacturing. This expands the role of industrial stakeholders from one of being regulated by various international and state governments to one of engagement with the accuracy of the models.

Climate Changes and Their Effects on Animals

The earth is warming and the climate is changing. Climate changes faster than an ecosystem does. Some species in the food chain will be affected first and, unless they evolve or move, will become extinct. Robins, for example, were recently sighted in the Arctic for the first time. Species such as grizzlies and polar bears may move to new territories and interbreed more frequently. Rapidly increasing ice melt is decreasing polar bear habitat and sometimes preventing the bears from getting to the seals they hunt. Consequently, polar bears have moved inland in search of food. More ecosystem aspects will be tested as climate change speeds.

Where Are the Animals Going? Current Research

Vast ecosystem changes cause plants and animals to migrate. They can also cause migrating animals to alter their genetically inbred routes of travel. In the year 2000, scientists from 17 nations examined 125,000 studies involving 561 species of animals around the globe. These investigators found that spring was beginning on average six to eight days earlier than it did 30 years ago. Regions such as Spain saw the greatest increases in temperatures. (This contradicts some climate change models, which forecast the greatest temperature changes at the north and south poles.) Spring season began up to two weeks earlier in Spain. The onset of autumn has been delayed by an average of three days over the same period. Changes to the continent's climate are shifting the timing of the seasons. There is a direct link between rising temperatures and changes in plant and animal behavior.

Recent research examined 125,000 observational series of 542 plants and 19 animal species in 21 European countries from 1971 to 2000. The results showed that 78 percent of all leafing, flowering, and fruiting was happening earlier in the year, while only 3 percent was significantly delayed. When species that depend on each other change at different rates, a breakdown in the food web could result. Current research is based only on indicator species, not entire ecosystems.

WATER AND CLIMATE CHANGE

The National Research Council on April 22, 2010, released a study noting that the earth's oceans currently absorb more than 1 million tons of carbon dioxide per hour. That is contributing to an already unprecedented increase in acid levels in the oceans, threatening to change ecosystems supporting all life in salt water, including red snapper, shrimp, sea bass and every form of life that depends on coral reefs. At the same time, desalinization is taking off around the globe as a means of coping with declining supplies of fresh water. The cost to desalinate has gone down, according to news reports focusing on dollars and cents.

Water is increasingly viewed as the visible face of climate change. Evaporation and drought have been amplified on every continent, along with rising coastlines and increased flooding from Bangladesh to the U.S. Midwest. At the same time, innovative reforestation projects are under way to restore the land and prevent further desertification. Peruvian conservationists, for example, have created a partnership with Heifer International, a nongovernmental organization, to that end.

Further suggesting how water might play the most prominent role in global environmental politics in the next 15 years, Ecuador has become the first nation to emphasize the "rights of nature" in its constitution. Furthering this trend, law schools in the United States have begun adjusting their curricula to train future lawyers in understanding and acknowledging nature's rights.

Global warming's glacial melt is allowing two harvests per year in areas of Tibet where only one was possible before. However, behind that prosperity is the well-supported fear the glacier will disappear, along with the water supply. Measurements show that the glacier is melting at a faster rate than it was 100 years ago. Villagers in Nepal also wonder about their water source. The headwaters of many rivers come from the glaciers of Tibet, which have been called the Third Pole. It is attractive to China at least in part for the fresh water Tibet promises. As reported in *National Geographic* magazine, China has less water than Canada and 40 times more people. China currently aims to build 59 reservoirs north of Tibet to capture glacial melt.

In Africa, the issue is lack of clean water. Medical clinics there report that almost half the illnesses they treat relate to waterborne diseases. In the United States, residues from industry and agriculture run down into the nearest creek if it has not been dried up first by damming, diversion, and irrigation practices. However, a suite of new laws in California mandates water conservation and attempts to restore delta ecosystems there.

Conclusion

Scientific and political controversies about climate change will increase. International environmental responsibilities and choices and rising local concern will raise some inconvenient environmental issues. Industrialization has had and continues to have a large environmental impact, perhaps affecting climate stability. Some of the nations most benefiting from industrialization are now debating policies about sustainability. They ask poorer nations to refrain from using the same fuels that began their own economic

POLITICS AND THE COPENHAGEN ACCORD

In December 2009 the United Nations Climate Change Conference in Copenhagen, Denmark, brought about a nonbinding agreement; this was criticized by the Bolivian delegation as having been reached in an antidemocratic, nontransparent way and as offering no relief to countries most vulnerable to the effects of climate change. In response to what is commonly known as the Copenhagen Accord, Bolivian President Evo Morales hosted the week-long World People's Conference on Climate Change and Mother Earth in April 2010. Indigenous activists and government representatives from 150 nations attended. During the same week, the U.S.-led Major Economies Forum on Energy and Climate was held in Washington, D.C. There, 17 nations responsible for the bulk of global greenhouse gas emissions held closed-door talks. Both gatherings aimed to plan strategies that would direct the 2010 United Nations Climate Change Conference set for December in Cancún, Mexico.

The Copenhagen Accord, whose legality is debated, acknowledges that the notion of global warming and cooling is supported by unassailable science. Although setting limits on emissions was central to the Copenhagen talks, no commitments resulted. China sought to cut carbon dioxide emissions by as much as 45 percent below 2005 levels by 2020. India wanted them cut by only 25 percent, a figure more agreeable to most of those in attendance. Kazakhstan, Iceland, Japan, Monaco, New Zealand, and Russia sought the strictest reductions, hovering around 25 percent below 1990 levels. The United States proposed to reduce emissions to 17 percent below 2005 levels by 2020, 42 percent by 2030, and 83 percent by 2050. In contrast, countries including Costa Rica and the Maldives sought such reductions by 2021 and 2019 respectively.

During the talks and after, China was blamed by developed nations for preventing a better outcome. Others blamed the lack of a binding deal on conservatism in the U.S. Senate and on the part of President Barack Obama. India, China, and other emerging nations were accused of cooperating at Copenhagen only to block attempts to restrict carbon emissions and thereby protect their economic growth. China currently depends on coal for its industry and is facing a severe shortage of fresh water as well.

News analyses of the Copenhagen gathering considered the accord a failure resulting from global recession and conservative domestic pressure in the United States and China. Despite financial woes, the unenforceable accord pledged that the United States would provide $30 billion to the developing world during 2010–2013, increasing this amount to $100 billion per year by 2020. This "fast-start funding" is intended to help poor countries take steps to adapt to climate change. It was central to the forum talks in Washington, D.C. The reality for Fiji, for example, is that glacial melt is shrinking this island nation. Its government is looking for nations who would be willing to accept its people as their land shrinks. Such nations did not get what they wanted in Copenhagen. A parallel can be drawn here to consideration for Louisiana's Cajun culture, which is fast losing neighborhood land to rising salt water in freshwater bayous throughout the area. As a result of this rise, baseball diamonds where children played one year were under water the next.

In mid-April 2010, U.S. President Barack Obama directed the country's National Aeronautic and Space Administration (NASA) to investigate sending astronauts to an asteroid as a training ground for Mars missions. In February 2010, *National Geographic* magazine considered terraforming Mars to make it habitable, noting that we have learned how to warm a planet.

development under free market capitalism. This is the so called North–South debate. Poorer nations want the quality-of-life improvements of free markets and do not like interference from richer nations. This aspect of the issue is global.

The rate of climate change is a continuing element of this discussion. While NASA officials ponder terraforming, concerns about water press toward scarcity. An August 2007 study by NASA climatologist James Hansen predicted that oceans could rise substantially more than predicted. In 2009 Hansen, director of NASA's Goddard Institute for Space Studies in New York and a professor at Columbia University, contended that the two giant reservoirs on the Colorado River—Lake Powell and Lake Mead—had fallen to 50 percent of capacity. These lakes provide water to tens of millions of westerners in the United States. Hansen argued that to stop the cycle we must reduce carbon dioxide emissions to below 350 parts per million from today's 387 parts per million, thus opposing his many colleagues who support stabilizing them at 450 parts per million.

Hansen's argument is based on paleoclimate data published in 2008, showing that the last time atmospheric carbon dioxide concentrations were this high, the earth was ice-free and the sea level was far higher than it is today. His 2007 study argues that because of positive feedback loops in the atmosphere, global warming events could cause oceans to rise much more quickly than predicted. It projected that by 2100, oceans could rise hundreds of feet instead of the smaller predictions of two to four feet by conservative climate-watch organizations. Three years later, Hansen had not changed his position. Recent ice quakes in Greenland, ice core samples from the poles indicating rates of melting, and the rapid release of methane from thawing permafrost all give greater credibility to this still controversial prediction. There will be more controversies surrounding the accuracy of the measurements of climate changes themselves, their rate of change, and their environmental impacts. NASA recorded 2009 as the warmest year on record, but in the following year questions were raised about the validity of climate data generated by a United Nations scientific panel. (The questions were subsequently largely laid to rest.)

Climate change is a local issue as well as a global one. As the push for sustainability rises to a policy level in richer nations, they confront an industrial past. Large programs of waste cleanup and assessments are begun. Environmental regulations are tightened to include all environmental impacts. Local communities begin to adopt environmental principles, like the precautionary principle, in their land-use laws. Climate change concerns may be creating a greater environmental consciousness and in that way create a supportive environment for policies like sustainability and 100 percent waste cleanup.

See also Air Pollution; Coal; Cumulative Emissions; Fossil Fuels; Global Warming; Sustainability (vol. 1)

Further Reading

Archer, David, *The Climate Crisis: An Introductory Guide to Climate Change.* New York: Cambridge University Press, 2010.

Clowney, David, and Patricia Mosto, *Earthcare: An Anthology of Environmental Ethics.* Lanham, MD: Rowman & Littlefield, 2009.

Condon, M. et al., *Urban Planning Tools for Climate Change Mitigation.* Lincoln, NE: Institute of Land Policy, 2009.

Cox, John D., *Climate Crash: Abrupt Climate Change and What It Means for Our Future.* Washington, DC: Joseph Henry Press, 2005.

DiMento, Joseph F. C., and Pamela Doughman, eds., *Climate Change: What It Means for Us, Our Children, and Our Grandchildren.* Cambridge, MA: MIT Press, 2007.

Fagan, Brian M., *The Great Warming: Climate Change and the Rise and Fall of Civilizations.* New York: Bloomsbury Press, 2008.

Hansen, James E., *Storms of My Grandchildren: The Truth about the Coming Climate Catastrophe and Our Last Chance to Save Humanity.* New York: Bloomsbury Press, 2009.

Hulme, Michael, *Why We Disagree about Climate Change: Understanding Controversy, Inaction and Opportunity.* New York: Cambridge University Press, 2009.

CLINICAL TRIALS AND SCIENTIFIC ETHICS

Jill A. Fisher

When new drugs and medical devices are developed, they need to be tested on humans to ensure their safety and effectiveness. Clinical trials—the tightly regulated and carefully controlled tests of pharmaceuticals in large groups of people—raise many ethical challenges. Some of these challenges revolve around the individuals participating in research: Are people being coerced? Are the clinical trials designed appropriately? Are researchers meeting their obligations and behaving ethically?

Other challenges are more difficult to address because they are embedded in existing institutional practices and policies: Is it ethical to include or exclude certain groups as human subjects in clinical trials based on their nationality, income, or health insurance status? What are the responsibilities of researchers to human subjects and to communities after the clinical trials have concluded? Still further challenges arise as the locations of clinical trials shift from university medical centers to profit-based research centers and as more studies are outsourced to developing countries. The history of abuses to human subjects in the United States has profoundly shaped the range of debates regarding ethical research practices and federal regulation of the research enterprise.

Deception and Coercion

Until the 1970s, deception and coercion of human subjects were common strategies used to enroll and retain individuals in medical research. A landmark case was the U.S. Public Health Service's four decades of research on syphilis in rural African American men in Tuskegee, Alabama. In the Tuskegee study, the subjects were told that they were being treated for "bad blood"—the local term for syphilis—even though they were actually not receiving any treatment at all. Instead, the U.S. Public Health Service was interested in watching syphilis develop in these men until their deaths so as to gain an understanding oft the natural course of the disease when left untreated. At the start of the study in the 1930s, there were no cures for syphilis. During the course of the research, however, penicillin was identified as an effective treatment. Still, the men did not receive treatment, nor were they told that they could be cured.

In response to the public outcry following an exposé on Tuskegee as well as other unethical uses of human subjects, the U.S. Congress passed the National Research Act of 1974. It established the National Commission for the Protection of Human Subjects of Biomedical and Behavioral Research, a group charged with outlining ethical principles to guide research and recommending ways to regulate it.

Informed Consent

By the beginning of the 1980s, the U.S. government had enacted regulations to protect human subjects from potential research abuses. These regulations requires that all participants provide their informed consent before participating in any study, that the risks and benefits of each study be analyzed, and that all research protocols be reviewed and overseen by external reviewers. Today's institutional review boards (IRBs) are mandated by this regulation. IRBs are research review bodies at universities and hospitals and in the private sector; they exist to ensure that researchers are following regulations, obtaining informed consent, and conducting ethical and scientifically rigorous research.

The requirement of informed consent is the primary means of protecting against the deception and coercion of human subjects. Researchers are required to provide detailed information about their studies, particularly about any potential risks and benefits, to all participants in the study. The participants or their guardians are required to sign the consent document confirming that they have read and understand the risks and benefits of the trial. Informed consent is meant to ensure that human subjects' participation in clinical research is voluntary. Unfortunately, informed consent has become largely procedural in many research contexts. Although the research trials are often long and complex, human subjects are often informed about the study and prompted for their consent only once, prior to the start of the trial. In response, many bioethicists are calling for a new configuration of informing participants and attaining their consent, a configuration that would treat informed consent as a process that is ongoing throughout the length of a clinical trial.

Although a revision of informed consent may certainly be necessary, it cannot address larger structural issues that must also be examined. Human subjects participate in research for many reasons. Some participate in the belief that research can provide a cure for illness. Others participate because they have limited or no health insurance and can gain access to medical care while participating in the trial. Still others participate for the sake of income in the form of study stipends. These reasons often take precedence over the specific details contained within an informed consent form. In fact, there is currently much debate about the extent to which human subjects should be remunerated for their participation in clinical trials. Because cash incentives may be coercive, many bioethicists argue that the amount of money human subjects receive should cover only those costs—such as transportation and parking, babysitters, time off from work—that are incurred from participation. In any case, the current regulatory environment is not structured to respond to the complex reasons that human subjects might have for enrolling in clinical trials.

Ethics of Study Design

The ethics of clinical trials extend beyond the voluntariness of human subjects' participation. The designs of the clinical trials themselves is also subject to scrutiny for ethical concerns. Nowhere is this more obvious than in discussions about the use of the placebo—or an inert sugar pill with no inherent therapeutic properties—in clinical research. Placebos are valuable tools in clinical research because they provide a controlled comparison to the treatment or therapy being studied. In other words, clinical trials can compare how human subjects' conditions change based on whether they received the treatment under investigation or a placebo. This protocol design becomes problematic because there are instances when it might be considered unethical to give human subjects placebos. Some illnesses should not be left untreated regardless of the scientific merit of the study design. In the case of other illnesses, there are many safe and effective products for treatment already on the market, and some argue that clinical trials should measure investigational products against these other treatments in order to provide the best possible care to human subjects.

In order to determine what is ethical, the medical establishment uses the principle of "clinical equipoise" to guide decisions about clinical trials. Within this framework, the design of clinical trials is considered ethical when the various arms of the study—investigational product, old treatment, placebo, and so on—are considered clinically equivalent. In other words, if researchers have no evidence that the new product is better than a placebo or an older treatment, then it is ethical to compare those groups. If, however, there is evidence that one product might be superior or inferior to another, then it is no longer considered ethical to give human subjects a product known to be inferior.

Like many ethical principles, equipoise can be mobilized to guide the design of clinical trials. There are limitations, however, in its application. Importantly, the definition of what evidence counts to achieve equipoise is fairly loose, and the majority of clinical trials that are conducted are done using a placebo. Part of what shapes decisions regarding equipoise and even informed consent is the broader context of clinical trials, especially their funding sources. Since 1990 the pharmaceutical industry has shifted the location of clinical trials from university medical centers to private-sector settings, such as private practices and for-profit clinical research centers. Although the bulk of most clinical research continues to take place in the United States, the pharmaceutical industry is outsourcing more and more studies to the developing world, including countries in Africa, Asia, eastern Europe, and Latin America.

Ethical Considerations of Globalization

Globalization over the past half century became an important development of economic growth. Proponents stress its benefits in terms of prosperity, while critics highlight the resulting economic disparities and worker exploitation, particularly in low- and middle-income countries. In the realm of clinical trials, pharmaceutical companies and device manufacturers made globalization a core component of their business models. This move raises important questions about the economics and ethics of clinical research. Further questions surface concerning the translation of trial results to clinical practice. At the cutting edge of this quagmire are three main concerns: Who benefits from the globalization of clinical trials? What is the potential for research subject exploitation? Are trial results accurate and valid and can they be extrapolated to other settings?

Some contend the future of the pharmaceutical and device industries is predicated on coming to terms with these questions. Does it sit squarely on the shoulders of the medical research community to voluntarily ensure the ethical and scientific integrity of clinical research globally, or is a law or international policy required? Medical ethicists have suggested that a comprehensive review, perhaps commissioned by the Institute of Medicine or the World Health Organization, is necessary to reach international consensus on these matters.

Conclusion

Both within the United States and abroad, the pharmaceutical industry relies on disenfranchised groups to become human subjects because of their limited access to medical care, their poverty, or their desperation for a cure for illnesses such as HIV/AIDS and other infectious diseases requiring treatment. As a result, the pharmaceutical industry's practices regarding human subjects can sometimes be highly exploitative. The ethical dilemma that is created concerns the distribution of risks and benefits. Those who are most likely to enroll in clinical trials as human subjects are the least likely to benefit from the results of that research. Debates are currently ongoing about the need for researchers to provide care after the close of a clinical trial in order to make those relationships more reciprocal. Clinical trials create many ethical challenges, ranging from the ethical treatment of individual human subjects to the design and implementation of clinical studies and the distribution of risks and benefits of research within society. The design and conduct of clinical trials has been tightly regulated for several decades, but the changing profile of health care and developments in medical research give rise to new questions. Furthermore, as clinical research continues to grow as a profit-driven industry, ethical questions become increasingly challenging. Although there may not be straightforward or standardized answers to these questions, addressing them should be as important as the medical research that generates the need for clinical trials.

See also **Medical Ethics; Off-Label Drug Use; Prescription Drug Costs (vol. 1)**

Further Reading

Applebaum, P. S., and C. W. Lidz, "The Therapeutic Misconception." In *The Oxford Textbook of Clinical Research Ethics,* ed. E. J. Emanuel et al. New York: Oxford University Press, 2006.

Faden, R. R., and T. L. Beauchamp, *A History and Theory of Informed Consent.* New York: Oxford University Press, 1986.

Glickman, S.W., et al., "Ethical and Scientific Implications of the Globalization of Clinical Research." *New England Journal of Medicine* 360, no. 8 (2009): 816–823.

Halpern, S. A., *Lesser Harms: The Morality of Risk in Medical Research.* Chicago: University of Chicago Press, 2004.

Holm, S., "The Concise Argument." *Journal of Medical Ethics* 36, no. 2 (2010): 65.

Jones, J. H., *Bad Blood: The Tuskegee Syphilis Experiment.* New York: Free Press, 1981.

Lorenzo, C., et al., "Hidden Risks Associated with Clinical Trials in Developing Countries." *Journal of Medical Ethics* 36, no. 2 (2010): 111–115.

Petryna, Adriana, *When Experiments Travel: Clinical Trials and the Global Search for Subjects.* Princeton, NJ: Princeton University Press, 2009.

Shah, S., *The Body Hunters: How the Drug Industry Tests Its Products on the World's Poorest Patients.* New York: New Press, 2006.

U.S. National Institutes of Health, "Understanding Clinical Trials." 2007. http://clinicaltrials.gov/ct2/info/understand

CLONING

Heather Bell

To clone is simply to produce an identical copy of something. In the field of biotechnology, however, *cloning* is a complex term referring to one of three different processes. DNA cloning is used to produce large quantities of a specific genetic sequence and is common practice in molecular biology labs. The other two processes, therapeutic cloning and reproductive cloning, involve the creation of an embryo for research or reproductive purposes, respectively, and have raised concerns about when life begins and who should be able to procure it.

DNA Cloning

DNA cloning, often referred to as recombinant DNA technology or gene cloning, is the process by which many copies of a specific genetic sequence are produced. By creating many identical copies of a genetic sequence through a process known as amplification, researchers can study genetic codes. This technology is used to map genomes and produce large quantities of proteins and has the potential to be used in gene therapy.

The first step in DNA cloning involves the isolation of a targeted genetic sequence from a chromosome. This is done using restriction enzymes that recognize where the desired sequence is and "cut" it out. When this sequence is incubated with a self-replicating genetic element, known as a cloning vector, it is ligated into the vector. Inside host cells such as viruses or bacteria, these cloning vectors can reproduce the desired genetic sequence and the proteins associated with it. With the right genetic sequence, the host cell can produce mass quantities of protein, such as insulin, or can be used to infect an individual with an inherited genetic disorder to give that person a good copy of the faulty gene.

Because DNA cloning does not attempt to reproduce an entire organism, there are few ethical concerns about the technology itself. Gene therapy, however, which is currently at an experimental stage because of safety concerns, has raised ethical debates about where the line falls between what is normal genetic variation and what is a disease.

Therapeutic Cloning

Somatic cell nuclear transfer (SCNT) is the technique used in both therapeutic cloning and reproductive cloning to produce an embryo that has nuclear genetic information identical to an already existing or previously existing individual.

During sexual reproduction, a germ cell (the type capable of reproducing) from one individual fertilizes the germ cell of another individual. The genetic information in these germ cells' nuclei combine, the cell begins to divide, and a genetically unique offspring is produced. In SCNT, the nucleus of a somatic cell (the type that makes up adult body tissues) is removed and inserted into a donor germ cell that has had its own nucleus removed. Using electrical current or chemical signals, this germ cell can be induced to begin dividing and will give rise to an embryo that is nearly identical to the individual from which the nucleus came rather than being the result of a combination of two parent cells. This "clone" will not be completely identical to the parent. A small number of genes that reside within mitochondria (small organelles within a cell that convert energy) will have come from the germ cell donor. Therefore the embryo will have nuclear genetic information identical to that of the parent somatic cell but mitochondrial genetic information that is identical to that of the germ cell donor.

SCNT is controversial because it involves the artificial creation of an embryo. Many people who feel that life begins at conception take issue with the technology because a germ cell is induced to divide without first being fertilized.

Similar ethical concerns are raised about therapeutic cloning, also referred to as embryo cloning, which is the production of embryos for the purpose of research or medical treatment. The goal of this procedure is to harvest stem cells from an embryo produced by SCNT.

Stem cells are useful because they are not yet differentiated. Not all cells in the human body are the same; a muscle cell, a bone cell, and a nerve cell have different structures and serve different functions. They all originally arise from stem cells, however, which can be used to generate almost any type of cell in the body. With further research, stem cells may be used to generate replacement cells that can treat conditions such as heart disease, Alzheimer's, cancer, and other diseases where a person has damaged tissues. This technology might provide an alternative to organ transplantation, after which the donated organs are frequently rejected by the receiver's body because the cells are recognized as not being the person's own. With stem cells generated from a person's own somatic cells, rejection would not be an issue.

Because the extraction of stem cells destroys the embryo, people who feel that life begins with the very first division of a cell have ethical concerns about this type of research. Before this technology progresses, it will be important for society to define the rights of an embryo (if rights can be defined) and decide whether embryos can be manipulated for the treatment of other people.

Reproductive Cloning

Reproductive cloning is the process by which a nearly identical copy of an individual is created. In one sense, this type of cloning already occurs in the natural world. Although sexual reproduction of plants and animals involves the genetic information of two individuals combining to create a unique hybrid, asexual reproduction occurring in plants does not involve the combination of genetic information. In this case, an identical copy of the plant is naturally produced. Artificial reproductive cloning has enabled the cloning of animals as well. In this procedure, SCNT is used to create an embryo whose nuclear DNA is identical to that of another individual. This embryo is then cultivated until it is ready to be inserted into the womb of a surrogate parent. The embryo is gestated, and eventually a clone is born. The first mammal to be successfully cloned and raised to adulthood was Dolly, a sheep, in 1997.

Since Dolly, many other animals have been cloned, including goats, cows, mice, pigs, cats, horses, and rabbits. Nevertheless, the cloning of animals remains very difficult and inefficient; it may take over 100 tries to produce a single clone successfully. Previous attempts have also shown that clones have an unusually high number of health concerns, including compromised immune function and early death.

Conclusion

The inefficiency of current cloning technology, along with the compromised health of clones, raises further ethical concerns about the artificial creation of life and the manipulation of individuals for the benefit of others.

The American Medical Association (AMA) has issued a formal public statement advising against human reproductive cloning. The AMA maintains that this technology is inhumane because of both the inefficiency of the procedure and the health issues of clones. The President's Council on Bioethics worries that cloning to produce children creates problems surrounding the nature of individual identity as well as the difference between natural and artificial conception.

Although some individuals and groups have claimed to have successfully cloned a human, these claims have not been substantiated. In the United States, federal funding for human cloning research is prohibited, and some states have banned both reproductive and therapeutic cloning.

See also **Eugenics; Genetic Engineering; Human Genome Project; Medical Ethics; Reproductive Technology; Stem Cell Research**

Further Reading

American Medical Association, http://www.ama-assn.org

Fritz, Sandy, ed., *Understanding Cloning.* New York: Warner Books, 2002.

Haugen, David M., et al., eds., *The Ethics of Cloning.* Detroit: Greenhaven Press, 2008.

Klotzko, Arlene Judith, *A Clone of Your Own? The Science and Ethics of Cloning.* New York: Cambridge University Press, 2006.

The President's Council on Bioethics, http://www.bioethics.gov/reports

Shmaefsky, Brian, *Biotechnology 101.* Westport, CT: Greenwood Press, 2006.

Wilmut, Ian, et al., "Viable Offspring Derived from Fetal and Adult Mammalian Cells." *Nature* 385, no. 6619 (1997): 810–813.

COAL

Hugh Peach

Coal is essentially a kind of "compacted sunlight." It is a combustible material derived from leafy biomass that has absorbed energy from the sun and has been compressed in the earth over geologic time. It is usually found in seams associated with other sedimentary rock. Historically, Earth went through the Carboniferous age about 350 to 290 million years ago. During this period, Earth was like a hothouse, with a higher average temperature than today and a steamy atmosphere that caused plants to grow rapidly. Using sunlight and moving through their life cycles, layer upon layer of plants accumulated on the surface of the earth. These plant materials gradually developed into peat bogs, and many of the bogs became covered with other material and were subjected to pressure over geologic time, eventually turning into coal. The result today is that we find an abundance of coal, often associated with sedimentary rock such as limestone, sandstone, and shale.

What Is Coal?

From a human perspective, coal is a nonrenewable resource. From a geological perspective, coal could be renewed from sunlight and plants over eons, but this would require another carboniferous (hothouse) era, which would not be very congenial to humans.

Peat is the first stage in the development of coal. It has very high water content and is not a good fuel if actual coal is available. When peat is compressed, it first becomes lignite or "brown coal." With further compression, brown coal becomes bituminous coal (soft coal). Finally, with both heat and high compression, we get anthracite or "hard coal," which has the least moisture content and the highest heat value.

Effects of Mining and Storage

Coal mining directly affects the environment. Surface mining produces waste materials, including destroyed trees and plants, but also substantial amounts of waste rock. When a small mountain is stripped for coal, waste rock is often dumped in valleys, and this can generate acid contamination of water. Surface mining also generates considerable dust (the technical name for this is "fugitive dust emissions"). Underground mining occurs largely out of sight but can result in large areas of subsidence. The generation of methane (and other gases) and acid mine drainage into local aquifers can also occur. After coal is mined, the next step is called coal beneficiation. In this step, coal is cleaned of some of the impurities that have interpenetrated it because of surrounding rock formations and geologic activity over several million years. This generates waste streams, including coal slurry and solid wastes that must go somewhere. Then, the cleaned coal has to be stored, handled, and transported. Handling and transportation produce more fugitive dust emissions.

There are examples of both surface and underground mining in which great care has been taken to mitigate these and other environmental effects. However, the effects on local environment can be severe, as shown in many other cases. Coal combustion byproducts (CCBs) are the waste material left over from burning coal. CCBs include fly ash, bottom ash, boiler slag, and flue gas desulfurization (FGD) material. Between 30 and 84 percent of this material can be recycled into other products such as concrete, road construction material, wallboard, fillers, and extenders. The rest is waste, which may include toxic elements that can cause human health problems if they are inhaled (as dust in the wind) or if they get into groundwater.

Emissions from coal combustion include water vapor (steam), carbon dioxide, nitrogen, sulfur, nitrogen oxides, particulate matter, trace elements, and organic compounds. The sulfur dioxide released may transform into sulfur trioxide (sulfuric acid). Nitrogen oxides contribute to the formation of acid rain. Particulate matter causes lessened visibility and, if the particles are breathed, can have serious health consequences, including asthma, decreased lung function, and death. Carbon dioxide is a major component of greenhouse gases. A certain balance of greenhouse gases is necessary to keep the planet habitable, but too much greenhouse gas contributes strongly to global warming. *Carbon sequestration* is the term for capturing carbon dioxide and storing it somewhere.

Carbon sequestration is the attempt to mitigate the buildup of carbon dioxide in the atmosphere by providing means of long-term storage—for example, by capturing carbon dioxide where coal is burned and attempting to inject it into the earth, the oceans, or growing biomass. The questions to ask about proposed methods of carbon sequestration are the following: How long will it stay sequestered before it is released back to the atmosphere? And will there be any unintended side effects of the carbon dioxide in the place in which it is to be put? We also need to be aware of what is sometimes called "silo thinking"—that is, trying to solve an important problem without being aware of interactions and linkages. Right now, fish stocks are declining and ocean coral is dissolving because the oceans are becoming more acidic. Putting huge additional amounts of carbon dioxide in the oceans might help to make power plants "cleaner," but it would more quickly kill off many forms of aquatic life.

Coal Quality

Despite some of these effects, however, coal will continue to be the dominant fuel used to produce electricity because of its availability and lower price compared with other forms of electricity generation. At the same time, carbon dioxide released in the burning of coal is a large contributor to rapid global warming. This is a contradiction without an easy solution. If efficiency, widespread availability, and lowest cost are the relevant criteria, then coal is the best fuel. If we choose in terms of these standard market criteria, we will also move quickly into global warming and climate change. The physical root of the problem is primarily one of scale: a small planet with a small atmosphere relative to the size of the human population and its demand for the use of coal.

It is a simple fact that the use of electricity is increasing all over the planet. The intensity of electricity use is growing gradually, year by year, throughout the economically developed portions of the planet, particularly because of the ubiquitous use of computers and the placing of increasing machine intelligence into other business and consumer devices. The poor and so-called backward regions of the planet continue to electrify, largely in response to their penetration by multinational corporations as an aspect of globalization. At the same time, intermediately developed countries with rapidly growing economies, such as India and China, are experiencing the emergence of strong consumer economies and rapid industrial development. For the near and intermediate future, these (and other) major countries will require substantial numbers of new central generating stations. Meaningfully lowering the demand for electricity would require major changes in our patterns of life, such as moving away from a consumer society and business system and a reorientation of housing and cities to maximize the use of passive solar energy, as well as a transition to local DC power systems in homes.

Historically, the high-quality heat developed from good-quality coal is responsible for much of the success of the industrial revolution in the Western economies. The transition from the stink of agricultural life and the stench and illnesses of early industrial cities to clean, modern living—characterized by the mass production of consumer goods—is highly dependent on clean electricity. Coal kept us warm, permitted the manufacture of steel products, and gave us much of our electricity over the last century. With only a little coal, natural gas, and oil, the human population of the planet would have been limited largely to the possibilities of wind and sun power; history would have developed very differently, and the human population of the planet would be only a small percentage of its size today. It is important to know that doing without coal, gas, and oil would have the reverse implication for the carrying capacity of the planet. At root, the issue is not only the historic and continuing advancement of civilization but also the size and quality of life of populations that are dependent on coal, natural gas, and oil. That is why securing these resources is so integral to the trade and military policies of nations.

Two Levels of Paradox

Whereas coal has been a wonderful resource for human development and the multiplication of the human population, there is a paradox: electricity, which is so clean at the point of use, is associated with extreme carbon loading of the atmosphere if it is generated from coal. This contradiction originally existed only at a local level. As an illustration, Pittsburgh, a major industrial center in America, was long known as a dirty coal and steel town, with unhealthy air caused by the huge steel plants, the use of coal for electricity generation, and the general use of coal for home and business heating in a climate with long cold winters. The air was often dirty and the sky burdened with smoke and dust.

This was initially taken as a sign of economic vigor and prosperity. Pittsburgh's air was cleaned up in the early 1950s by the requirement of very high smokestacks and a shifting away from nonindustrial uses of coal for public health and civic betterment reasons. The tall smokestacks, however, while providing a local solution, simply transferred the problem to places downwind. This is a reality of pollutants: they do not go away; they go somewhere else. Places downwind of the midwestern power plants (such as New York City) experienced more unhealthy air days, and lakes in the mountains downwind began to die because of acid rain. This is the local level of the paradox—clean electricity and efficient large-scale industry produce local or regional pollution problems because of the use of coal.

Similarly, the global level of the paradox is that the use of coal is responsible for significantly fouling the planet, leading to a common future filled with the multiple disasters associated with global warming. Just a few of these experiences we have to look forward to include the submergence of coastal areas, loss of ice at the poles, loss of snowpack on mountains, invasions of species from other areas against weakened natural species, dramatic food shortages, and an increasing number of riots in poor areas where the rising cost of food cannot be met within the local structure of wages— not a war of "all against all" but one of increasing numbers of persons increasingly shut out of the economic system against those still protected by remaining institutional arrangements or by wealth. As resources contract, in addition to the problems of food shortages and new outbreaks of disease, the resulting income gap will likely signal a return to the social inequalities of the Victorian era.

THE TENNESSEE COAL ASH SPILL: IS THERE SUCH A THING AS CLEAN COAL?

On December 22, 2008, a mountain of toxic sludge rising 65 feet in the air and covering 100 acres, which had been accumulating for half a century, burst the dike holding it in. It flowed coal ash packed with poisons—including arsenic, lead, and selenium—over 300 acres of beautiful countryside, moving homes off their foundations and overtaking houses, crops, and sensitive ecosystems. It filled a river.

The sludge is coal ash, also called fly ash. It consists of the concentrated hazardous waste that is left over after power plants burn coal to generate electricity. Coal-fired power plants produce about 130 million tons of fly ash every year—enough to fill a line of boxcars from the United States to Australia—according to Eric Schaeffer, who heads the activist group Environmental Integrity Project.

Some called the 5.4 million cubic yards of ash that spilled from the Tennessee Valley Authority's Kingston Fossil Plant "the Exxon Valdez of coal ash spills." The disaster generated fast-paced questions about whether government regulations for coal ash are strict enough. Until the unstoppable BP-Deepwater Horizon oil gush in the Gulf of Mexico in May 2010, the Tennessee coal ash spill held status as the largest industrial accident in U.S. history. The result is an environmental and engineering nightmare. Cleanup is estimated at $1 billion by the U.S. Environmental Protection Agency, which is overseeing the effort. It is expected to take years if not a lifetime. The spill shows that coal is anything but clean.

Population Needs

An underlying variable, of course, is the size of the human population. If we were facing a few new power plants and limited industrial production, the myth of unlimited resources that underlies conventional economics would be approximately true. It would not matter much if we fouled a few localities if the human population were one-hundredth or one-thousandth of its current size and the planet were covered with vibrant meadows and ancient forests.

With a much smaller human population, the fouling of the planet would be less of an immediate problem. But given the size of the human population, the need is for several hundred new power plants. The demand through market forces for consumer goods, industrial goods, and electricity, particularly from the portion of the human population engaged in unsustainable modern market economies, drives the need for hundreds of new central power plants in the immediate to intermediate future.

Industry in India and China, in particular, is taking off along a huge growth curve, different from but in many ways similar to that of the industrial revolution in the West. In our current situation, coal is, on the one hand, the preferred market solution because it is relatively inexpensive, is a widespread and still abundant resource (in contrast to gas and oil), and can provide power through electricity generation that is clean at the point of use. The problem at the global level is the size of the planet and the limited atmosphere in relation to the size of human population. The scale of what is required will generate far too much pollution for the planet to handle in ways that keep the planetary environment congenial to humankind.

It is possible, however, to talk about "clean coal." This term has two meanings. First, some types of coal emit less carbon into the atmosphere when burned, and some deposits of coal contain much less foreign material than others. Cleaner coal is more expensive than dirty coal. Second, the phrase is a slogan of the coal industry pointing toward the concept of capturing gas emissions from coal burning. As a slogan, it serves the purpose of conveying the image of a future in which commercial-scale coal-burning power plants would emit no carbon dioxide. Research on this problem is ongoing, but there are no such plants at the present time.

The U.S. FutureGen project is on hold after federal funding from the Department of Energy was pulled. The questions to ask about the promised "clean coal" future are these: What is the scale of transfer of carbon dioxide that would be required (if it could be captured)? What would be done with the massive quantities that would have to be sequestered, and would this have any unintended consequences?

Coal is less expensive than other fuels, but this is due in part to the free market system in which the social and environmental costs of coal are treated as what economists like to call "externalities." That is, these costs are left for other people—for regional victims of pollution—and for global society to bear. Several systems have been proposed to transfer all or part of these costs to companies that burn massive amounts of coal, such as electric utilities. In fact, a sector of the electric utility industry is currently campaigning to have some form of carbon trading or carbon tax imposed. It is generally expected that this will occur in the not-too-distant future, given that many industry leaders would like to resolve the ambiguity and uncertainty of what form these costs will take and to speed the new system into place. This may substantially increase the cost of coal as an energy resource.

Conclusion

Coal has had and continues to have a major role in the advancement of civilization. It is currently more abundant and more easily available than other major fuels. Its concentrated energy (high heat content) permits us to create steel products. Without coal, natural gas, and oil, the human carrying capacity of the planet would be a small percentage of the current human population. Yet there is a contradiction inherent in the massive use of coal and in the building of hundreds of new generating stations that depend on coal because carbon release will hasten global warming and also produce other environment effects that are not helpful to human life. This is a contradiction without an easy solution.

See also **Air Pollution; Childhood Asthma and the Environment; Fossil Fuels; Global Warming; Land Pollution**

Further Reading

Brune, Michael, *Coming Clean: America's Addiction to Oil and Coal.* San Francisco: Sierra Club Books, 2008.

Freese, Barbara, *Coal: A Human History.* Cambridge, MA: Perseus, 2003.

Heinberg, Richard, *Blackout: Coal, Climate, and the Last Energy Crisis.* Gabriola Island, BC: New Society Publishers, 2009.

Kilroy, Johnny, "EPA Proposes New Rule to Regulate Coal Ash." Tenthmil. May 5, 2010. http://tenth mil.com/campaigns/policy/epa_proposes_new_rule_to_regulate_coal_ash#ixzz0q7dCdaoh

McKeown, Alice, "The Dirty Truth about Coal." Sierra Club monograph. http://www.sierraclub. org/coal/dirtytruth/coalreport.pdf

Miller, Bruce G., *Coal Energy Systems.* San Diego, CA: Elsevier, 2005.

Shogren, Elizabeth, "Tennessee Spill: The Exxon Valdez of Coal Ash?" National Public Radio. December 31, 2008. http://www.npr.org/templates/story/story.php?storyId = 98857483

"Toxic Tsunami," *Newsweek* (July 18, 2009). http://www.newsweek.com/2009/07/17/toxic-tsunami. html

Ward, Kenneth, Jr., "Mining the Mountains: Tennessee Coal Ash Spill Highlights Broad Gaps in Government Oversight." *Charleston Gazette* (December 30, 2008). http://wvgazette.com/ News/MiningtheMountains/200812290514

Ward, Kenneth, Jr., "EPA Backed Off Tougher Coal-Ash Proposal Amid Industry Complaints, White House Review." *Charleston Gazette* (May 7, 2010). http://blogs.wvgazette.com/coal tattoo/2010/05/07/epa-backed-off-tougher-coal-ash-proposal-amid-industry-complaints-white-house-review

CUMULATIVE EMISSIONS: IMPACTS AND RISKS

Robert William Collin and Debra Ann Schwartz

Since the mid-1850s the results of the industrial revolution have polluted the environment. When industrial manufacturing processes garner raw materials, they produce a product and by-products. These by-products are often wastes and chemicals. They have grown enormously since industrialization first began. In many urban areas, industrial emissions have accumulated for 150 years. These emissions are mixed with other waste streams as they percolate through soil or volatilize into the air. This can result in accumulating impacts to the environment, almost all negative.

Emissions that affect the environment can bioaccumulate in all species, including humans. Bioaccumulation of some chemicals, such as metals, is known to be very harmful and therefore risky to humans. Emissions, impacts, and risks fall under the collective label of *cumulative effects*. No one industry wants to be liable for the emissions of others. Many communities are concerned about the eroding health of their families. Environmentalists want cumulative effects to be accounted for in environmental impact statements. Policy development is weak, yet every day these cumulative effects increase. This is a young controversy that is growing and will drive and divide many other environmental policies.

Several reports have highlighted the importance of understanding the accumulation of risks from multiple environmental stressors. These reports, as well as legislation such as the Food Quality Protection Act of 1996 (FQPA), urged the EPA to move beyond single chemical assessments and to focus, in part, on the cumulative effects of chemical exposures occurring simultaneously. In 1999, the EPA's Risk Assessment Forum began development of EPA-wide cumulative risk assessment guidance.

Cumulative Effects

Cumulative risk means the combined risks from aggregate exposures to multiple agents or stressors. Several key points can be derived from this definition. First, cumulative risk involves multiple agents or stressors, not just one. Second, agents or stressors do not have to be chemicals. They may be, but they may also be biological or physical agents that cause something necessary to decline, such as habitat. Third, the actual risks from multiple agents or stressors require the researcher to determine how the risks interact. It also means an assessment that merely lists each chemical with the corresponding risk but without considering the other chemicals present; this does not provide insight into the full impact the combinations. Cumulative risk may generate interest in a wider variety of nonchemical stressors than do traditional risk assessments.

The EPA Approach

EPA assessments generally describe and, where possible, quantify the risks of adverse health and ecological effects from synthetic chemicals, radiation, and biological stressors.

As part of planning an integrated risk assessment, risk assessors must define dimensions of the assessment, including the characteristics of the population at risk. These include individuals or sensitive subgroups that may be highly susceptible to risks from stressors or groups of stressors due to their age (e.g., risks to infants and children), gender, disease history, size, or developmental stage. There are other risk issues, dimensions, and concerns that the EPA does not address. This broader set of concerns, recognized as potentially important by many participants in the risk assessment process, relate to social, economic, behavioral, or psychological stressors that contribute to adverse health effects. These stressors may include existing health conditions, anxiety, nutritional status, crime, and congestion.

On the important topic of special subpopulations, the EPA and others are giving more emphasis to the sensitivities of children and to gender-related differences in susceptibility and exposure to environmental stressors. The stated focus of the U.S. Environmental Protection Agency (EPA) is on risk assessments that integrate risks of adverse health and ecological effects from the narrower set of environmental stressors. There is a great deal of controversy about what specifically is an adverse impact. The EPA is engaged in several activities that involve working with stakeholders. However, the agency still resists regularly incorporating cumulative risk concerns in most applied policy areas such as environmental impact statements.

Aggregating Risks

Environmental advocacy groups want to make cumulative effects part of the requirements for an environmental impact assessment. Due to the current state of the practice, strongly vested stakeholder positions, and limited data, the aggregation of risks may often be based on a default assumption of additivity in the United States. This simply adds the risk per chemical for a sum total of risk. It also ignores antagonism, which occurs when chemicals mitigate the risk from one another. In many western European markets, synergized risk and risk to vulnerable populations determine entry into commerce. Some emerging cumulative risk approaches in Canada and western Europe may help set up data development approaches in the United States. However, U.S. approaches to emission control still leave many sources completely unregulated, and those that are regulated emit millions of pounds of chemicals per year. For an accurate cumulative risk assessment, all past and present emissions must be counted.

Beginnings

U.S. lawmakers have been setting environmental policy since 1970, when the EPA was created. Research into the cumulative effects of pollution is emerging slowly, and no one is anxious to hear the news. Cumulative effects often represent the environmental impacts of humans when there were no environmental rules or regulations. They can be significant, and represent large cleanup costs. If cumulative effects are an issue in a typical environmental impact statement, then a finding of significant impact on the environment

CASE STUDY: ENVIRONMENTAL JUSTICE

Flint, Michigan, was the site of an early legal challenge based in part on cumulative impacts of lead primarily found in African American children. The case revolves around an industrial plant built by the Genesee Power Company. It was located in a predominantly African American residential neighborhood in Flint. The lawsuit *(NAACP-Flint Chapter et al. v. Engler et al.,* No. 95–38228CZ [Circuit Court, Genesee County, filed 7/22/95])— filed by two community groups, United for Action and the NAACP-Flint Chapter, and several African American women—challenged the state of Michigan's decision to grant a construction permit to the power company on environmental and environmental justice grounds. The complaint alleged that the granting of this permit would allow that facility to emit more than two tons of lead per year into an African American community that already had very high levels of lead exposure and contamination. The Maurice and Jane Sugar Law Center for Economic and Social Justice, a Detroit-based national civil rights organization, represented the community.

A risk assessment presented as evidence demonstrated that African Americans living in Flint constituted the population that would be most affected by the emissions from this incinerator. Health data included public reports, studies from scientific journals, and privately commissioned studies.

Health information specific to children was also very important in this case. Children under age six are especially vulnerable to lead's negative effects because they absorb more lead in proportion to their weight than do adults. Of children ages six months to five years living in the Flint metropolitan area 49.2 percent already had elevated lead levels in their blood. Lead exposure at an early age has been linked to attention-deficit disorder, problems with anger control and management, and other behavioral changes.

The question for the court was whether this new proposed use, a power plant which is really an incinerator that burns and emits even more lead, is an acceptable cumulative risk for an already lead-poisoned community. The lower state court issued an injunction stopping Michigan from granting any air permits for six months. Appeals ensued. They were granted and allowed the incinerator to go into the African American community in Flint.

is made and a larger-scale environmental impact analysis is required. This too is expensive. Cleanup costs and the cost of environmental impact assessments are usually borne by industry. Industry strongly resists assuming responsibility for what they did not cause, based on a weak model of cumulative effects to date. Many of these cleanup costs could affect the profitability of any single corporation in these industries.

Currently, most corporations listed in the stock exchange place these types of environmental issues in a 10B5 Securities Exchange Commission reporting statement under "contingent liabilities." Nonetheless, communities are very concerned about any emissions, especially as they accumulate among them. Public accessibility has increased knowledge about emissions generally and locally, and they become easier to detect as they accumulate over time. As some legislation now contains some cumulative effects provisions, some federal agencies are beginning new policies. The first policy experiments are important in terms of lessons learned. Decisions made now about cumulative environmental and human effects in public policy will have a direct bearing on the future health of communities, the future profitability of corporations, and the place in government that resolves the hard parts of implementing this type of policy. Right now, data and information are being developed through pilot programs. Here are some of them:

- Cumulative acute and subchronic health risk to field workers' infants and toddlers in farm communities as a result of organophosphate pesticide exposure (that is, through respiratory, dermal, dietary, and nondietary ingestion) resulting from agricultural and residential uses in light of the nutritional status of field-worker families.
- Cumulative ecological risk to the survival and reproduction of populations of blue crabs or striped bass in the Chesapeake Bay resulting from water and air emissions from both urban and agricultural sources.
- Cumulative risk under the FQPA may be defined using terms such as *aggregate exposure* (that is, the exposure of consumers, manufacturers, applicators, and other workers to pesticide chemical residues with common mechanisms of toxicity through ingestion, skin contact, or inhalation from occupational, dietary, and nonoccupational sources) or cumulative effects (that is, the sum of all effects from pesticide chemical residues with the same mechanism of toxicity).

The EPA is engaged in several cumulative risk activities. The Superfund program has updated its guidelines on risk assessment to include planning and scoping cumulative risk assessment and problem formulation for ecological risk assessments. The plan for the Office of Solid Waste's Surface Impoundment Study includes both a conceptual model and an analytical plan, per the agency guidance on planning and scoping for cumulative risk.

The Office of Water is planning a watershed-scale risk assessment involving multiple ecological stressors. This approach was developed through collaboration with external scientists.

Several regional offices are evaluating cumulative hazards, exposures, and effects of toxic contaminants in urban environments. In Chicago (Region 5), citizens are concerned about the contribution of environmental stressors to ailments including asthma and blood lead levels. In Baltimore, a regional Office of Prevention, Pesticides, and Toxic Substances/community partnership tried to address the long-term environmental and economic concerns in three neighborhoods that are adjacent to industrial facilities and tank farms. Dallas is developing a geographic information system approach for planning for and evaluating cumulative risks.

The FQPA of 1996 requires that the EPA consider the cumulative effects to human health that can result from exposure to pesticides and other substances that have a common mechanism of toxicity. The Office of Pesticide Programs has developed guidelines for conducting cumulative risk assessments for pesticides and has prepared a preliminary cumulative risk assessment for organophosphorus pesticides.

The air toxics program of the Office of Air and Radiation (OAR) has a cumulative risk focus. Under the Integrated Urban Air Toxics Strategy, OAR will be considering cumulative risks presented by exposures to air emissions of hazardous pollutants from sources in the aggregate. Assessments will be performed at both the national scale (a national-scale assessment for base year 1996 was completed in 2002) and at the urban or neighborhood scale. In partnership with the Office of Research and Development (ORD) and the National Exposure Research Laboratory, the Office of Air Quality Planning and Standards is developing the total risk integrated methodology (TRIM), a modular modeling system for use in single- or multimedia, single- or multipathway human health and ecological risk assessments of hazardous and criteria air pollutants at the neighborhood or city scale.

ORD's National Center for Environmental Assessment (NCEA) has completed ecological risk assessment guidelines that support the cumulative risk assessment guidance. Five watershed case studies are being assessed to demonstrate the guidelines approach. Each of these cases deals with cumulative impacts of stressors (chemical, biological, and, in some cases, physical). In addition, federal agencies have prepared a draft reassessment of dioxin and related compounds.

As emissions, impacts, and effects continue to accumulate in the environment, more chemicals will be reevaluated for their contribution to environmental degradation and public health impacts. This is not happening fast enough for many environmentalists and communities.

Global Developments

The ocean and land absorb about 45 percent of carbon emissions, which are the focus of climate change policy talks today. In general, global efforts to reduce the effects of climate change on crop production, human health and the environment are guided by projections about future temperatures. Scientists are trying to find where the global mean temperature associated with stabilizing levels of greenhouse gas concentrations balances. Greenhouse gases, such as carbon dioxide, are associated with global climate change when they are out of equilibrium. When the balance is tipped, potentially dangerous levels of global warming and cooling can occur.

Recent studies show that peak warming caused by a given cumulative carbon dioxide emission is better constrained than the warming response seen in studies concentrating on stabilization. Researchers also are finding that the relationship between cumulative emissions and peak warming is not particularly sensitive to the timing of emissions. As a result, targets set in new environmental policy that are based on limiting cumulative emissions of carbon dioxide are wrought with scientific uncertainty more than emission-rate or concentration targets.

In today's world of international protocols and accords about how to manage climate change, one pivot point is cumulative emissions. Consideration of what the assessments mean has led to economic environmental policy including the cap-and-trade system and other carbon offset approaches, for example.

Developed nations including the United States are involved in the crucial task of bringing to international climate talks an equal arrangement of emission rights coupled with basic human rights that recognize environmental justice. The United Nations Intergovernmental Panel on Climate Change, the G8, and the Organization of Economic Cooperation and Development organize the talks. This collective currently has assigned developed countries higher emissions quotas than countries that are developing, which remarkably constrains the development interests of poorer countries with, in some cases, less natural resource pollution because of lower industrialization. A global balance is under negotiation, with cumulative emissions at the core.

Conclusion

The public is exposed to multiple contaminants from a variety of sources, and tools are needed to understand the resulting combined risks. The stakes are very high and getting higher every day. The first set of U.S. tools are being tested in the courts. Cumulative effects are receiving much study and are being implemented as policy abroad. With global warming and climate change developing into treaties and U.S. municipal ordinances, these cumulative emissions are increasingly center stage in the United States.

See also **Emissions Trading; Environmental Impact Statements**

Further Reading

Allen, Myles R., et al., "Warming Caused by Cumulative Carbon Emissions Towards the Trillionth Tonne." *Nature* 458 (2009): 1163–1166.

"Assessment of Cumulative Environmental Effects, a Selected Bibliography," November 1995. www.ec.gc.ca/ea-ee/eaprocesses/bibliography_1995_e.asp

Collin, Robert William, *The Environmental Protection Agency: Cleaning Up America's Act.* Westport, CT: Praeger, 2006.

"Considering Cumulative Effects under the National Environmental Policy Act (NEPA)," www.nepa.gov/nepa/ccenepa/ccenepa.htm

"Cumulative Effects Assessment Practitioner's Guide," www.ceaa-acee.gc.ca/ 013/0001/0004/index_e.htm

Lawrence, David Peter, *Environmental Impact Assessment: Practical Solutions to Recurrent Problems.* Hoboken, NJ: Wiley, 2003.

National Research Council, *Cumulative Environmental Effects of Oil and Gas Activities on Alaska's North Slope.* Washington, DC: National Academies Press, 2003.

Noble, Bram F., *Introduction to Environmental Impact Assessment: A Guide to Principles and Practice,* 2d ed. New York: Oxford University Press, 2010.

Social Learning Group, *Learning to Manage Global Environmental Risks.* Cambridge, MA: MIT Press, 2001.

D

DEEP ECOLOGY AND RADICAL ENVIRONMENTALISM

Stephen Potthoff

Coined by the Norwegian philosopher Arne Naess in 1972, the term *deep ecology* designates both a philosophical and social/political movement intended to address the global environmental crisis. On a philosophical level, heavily influenced by Native American and other aboriginal spiritual traditions, deep ecology maintains the fundamental equality and right to flourish of all elements of the earth and living world. Deep ecology's emphasis on the inherent value of the earth and all living things is grounded in the concept of the fundamental unity of human beings with the whole cosmos to which they belong. Much of the debate and discussion inspired by deep ecology centers around the question of how to balance human need with the necessity to preserve and care for the environment on which human (and all other) life depends.

Deep Ecology's Deep Roots

Deep ecology advocates a move away from an anthropocentric (that is, a *human-centered*) perspective to an ecocentric (that is, a *physical world–centered*) worldview that recognizes as primary the continued flourishing of the entire living and natural world (Sessions 1995a, 156–158; Seed, Macy, Fleming 1988, 35–39). This ecocentric perspective at the core of deep ecology has ancient roots in the cosmological and religious systems of indigenous or primal hunter-gatherer cultures, which regard all aspects of the cosmos as sacred, interrelated, and alive. Given that hunter-gatherer life ways have characterized cultures spanning most of human history, associated holistic and ecocentric worldviews rank as the most ancient of human religious and philosophical systems (Sessions 1995a, 158). Indigenous holistic and ecocentric worldviews have inspired the writings and work of many deep ecologists, including Pulitzer prize–winning poet Gary Snyder, whose poetry collection *Turtle Island* grew out of his close work with Native Americans, and rainforest activist John Seed, who draws extensively on the wisdom of indigenous peoples in his work to save the rainforest and heal people's relationship to the earth and living world (Snyder 1995, 457–462; Seed, Macy, Fleming 1988, 9–11).

In its contemporary form, however, the deep ecology movement arose in the 1960s alongside the ecological movement, inspired by the publication of Rachel Carson's book *Silent Spring*. Early deep ecologists found inspiration and direction in the nature writings of Henry David Thoreau and John Muir; Aldo Leopold's land ethic, presented in his *Sand County Almanac;* and the Buddhist perspective of Alan Watts. Gary Snyder, in his synthesis of Native American and Zen Buddhist philosophies, has become a prominent international spokesperson for deep ecology. In the academic sphere, Norwegian philosopher Arne Naess began developing some of the principles of deep ecology as early as 1968, building on the philosophical ideas of Spinoza and Gandhi (Sessions 1995b, 157, 232–234).

Particularly significant in helping to crystallize the ecocentric perspective was UCLA historian Lynn White's seminal 1967 article *The Historical Roots of Our Ecologic Crisis.* White argued that Christianity, characterized by a dangerous anthropocentrism, has desacralized the natural world and encouraged its mindless exploitation as nothing more than a resource to be utilized for purely selfish human ends. Instead of science, technology, or Marxism (which he regarded as a Christian heresy), White advocated as a possible solution a return to the nature mysticism of Saint Francis of Assisi (White 1967, x, 158).

The Defining Principles of Deep Ecology

As defined by philosophers Bill Devall and George Sessions, deep ecology is rooted in two fundamental principles. The first is self-realization, which affirms that each individual (human or otherwise) is part of a larger whole, or Self, which encompasses ultimately the planet Earth and the entire cosmos. Expressed in the Native American (Lakota) prayer *Mitakuye Oyasin* ("I am related to all that is"), the concept of self-realization is embraced in some form by diverse religious traditions worldwide (Badiner 1990, xv; Brown 2001, 89). Many indigenous traditions understand human beings' relationship to the living and natural world in kinship or familial terms: animals and trees as well as rocks and rivers are brothers, sisters, and ancestors belonging to one all-encompassing, all-inclusive interdependent family. As a powerful modern expression of the self-realization concept, many deep ecologists have embraced James Lovelock's *Gaia Hypothesis,* which views the entire planet as a living being (Lovelock 1982, 9; Abram 1990, 75).

The second fundamental principle of deep ecology, as outlined by Devall and Sessions, is biocentric equality, which upholds that all elements of the biosphere have an equal right to live and flourish. In maintaining the principle of biocentric equality, deep ecologists do not deny the apparent inequality of the natural world, as evident in the biological realities of predation or natural selection. Yet deep ecology is concerned primarily with challenging the deeply ingrained anthropocentric notion that human beings have an absolute right to reign supreme over the environment and living things without regard for the welfare of the whole. Deep ecology's insistence on biocentric equality derives from the recognition that all entities in the cosmos live interrelated with and interdependent upon one another. The principle of biocentric equality follows logically from that of self-realization insofar as harming one element of the biosphere harms the whole. Ultimately, deep ecology thus embraces a vision of the cosmos where human beings live in harmony and balance with all entities in the interconnected web of life. In practical terms, this means that humans, as an interdependent part of a much greater Self, should live in ways that encourage the survival of all other species (and the environment) upon which they depend.

In addition to articulating basic principles such as self-realization and biocentric equality, deep ecologists have also sought to distinguish deep ecology from what they see as the more shallow ecology characteristic of environmental policies in the industrialized world. In 1973, Arne Naess critiques what he terms a shallow ecological movement that, though attempting to fight pollution and conserve resources, is primarily concerned with maintaining the health and high living standard of developed countries (Naess 1995b, 151). In a 1986 article, he develops the shallow–deep antithesis further, contrasting the approaches of the two different movements to key issues such as pollution and resource depletion. With respect to pollution, the shallow ecological approach entails the creation of laws that, while seeking to limit pollution, often simply relocate it by exporting high-pollution industry to developing countries. In contrast, the deep ecological approach analyzes pollution in terms of its overall systemic impact on the entire biosphere, looking at health effects on all species and seeking economic and political alternatives to the unjust practice of pollution exportation. With respect to resource depletion, deep ecology rejects the shallow ecological treatment of animals, trees, and the earth merely as resources for human use, insisting that the earth and living world are valuable in and of themselves, independent of their utility to human beings (Naess 1995a, 71–72).

Working together with George Sessions, Arne Naess formulated an eight-point deep ecology platform; a foundational statement embodying both the activist and philosophical commitments of the deep ecology movement (Naess 1995a, 68):

1. The well-being and flourishing of human and nonhuman life on Earth have value in themselves (synonyms: intrinsic value, inherent worth). These values are independent of the usefulness of the non-human world for human purposes.

2. Richness and diversity of life forms contribute to the realization of these values and are also values in themselves.

3. Humans have no right to reduce this richness and diversity except to satisfy vital needs.

4. The flourishing of human life and cultures is compatible with a substantially smaller human population. The flourishing of nonhuman life *requires* a smaller human population.

5. Present human interference with the non-human world is excessive, and the situation is rapidly worsening.

6. Policies must therefore be changed. These policies affect basic economic, technological, and ideological structures. The resulting state of affairs will be deeply different from the present.

7. The ideological change will be mainly that of appreciating life quality (dwelling in situations of inherent value) rather than adhering to an increasingly higher standard of living. There will be a profound awareness of the difference between bigness and greatness.

8. Those who subscribe to the foregoing points have an obligation directly or indirectly to try to implement the necessary changes.

Naess notes that points one to five directly challenge dominant models of economic growth and development in industrialized countries. At the same time, he admits that reducing population growth and wealthy countries' "interference with the non-human world" will take hundreds of years (Naess 1995a, 69). As a way of promoting the deep ecology movement in developing countries, Naess recommends direct grassroots action, which can circumvent government interference.

Critiques of Deep Ecology

One of the most widely discussed critiques of deep ecology is that it is misanthropic: critics have argued that in its critique of anthropocentrism and commitment to biocentric equality, deep ecology advocates the survival and flourishing of nonhuman species at the expense of human beings (Sessions 1995, xiii, 267; Fox 1995, 280). For example, in a remark he subsequently retracted, former Vice President Al Gore charged Arne Naess's deep ecology with treating people as "an alien presence on the earth" (Sessions 1995b, xiii). After giving a speech on overfishing in the Barent Sea, in which Naess advocated viewing the sea as a "whole complex ecosystem" where even microscopic flagellates have intrinsic value, a fishing industry representative is said to have quipped: "Naess is of course more concerned about flagellates than about people" (Naess 1995d, 406).

Deep ecologists respond that such critiques arise from a basic misunderstanding or misrepresentation of deep ecological principles. Al Gore's remark was inspired by a statement from Dave Foreman, a leader of the radical Earth First! environmental group, about "not giving aid to Ethiopians and allowing them to starve"—a remark for which Foreman subsequently apologized (Sessions 1995b, xxvi). Although Earth First! has adopted the deep ecology platform, Sessions points out that such clearly misanthropic statements are fundamentally antithetical to deep ecology's ecocentrism (Sessions 1995b, xiii). Admitting that deep ecology's radical egalitarian stance has often been misunderstood, Naess emphasizes that such egalitarianism does not imply that humans are not extraordinary or that they have no obligations to their own species (Naess 1995a, 76). Deep ecology endeavors to promote "an egalitarian attitude on the part of humans toward all entities in the ecosphere—including *humans*" (Fox 1995, 280).

In developing this point further, Naess explains that deep ecology's ecocentric perspective seeks to promote awareness of human interdependence and interconnectedness within the earth's ecosystem, not to devalue human beings. In response to the charge that he cared more about flagellates than people, Naess explains: "My point was that the present tragic situation for fishermen could have been avoided if policy makers had shown a little more respect for all life, not less respect for people" (Naess 1995d, 406). At the same time, balancing human need with the necessity of preserving the ecosphere is, in practical terms, often very difficult. In addressing such difficult human and environmental issues, some of the most thoughtful challenges to deep ecology have come from scholars and environmentalists in the developing world. Indian environmental scholar Ramachandra Guha, for example, critiques deep ecology on several points, two of which are taken up here.

First, while Guha praises, in a general sense, deep ecology's challenge to human "arrogance and ecological hubris," he rejects the further conclusion "that intervention in nature should be guided primarily by the need to preserve biotic integrity rather than by the needs of humans" (Guha 2003, 555). Encouraging a philosophical shift from an anthropocentric to a biocentric perspective, Guha argues, fails utterly to address the two primary causes of environmental destruction: (1) overconsumption by wealthy nations and Third World elites and (2) militarization, with its threat of nuclear annihilation (Guha 2003, 555). The complex economic, political, and individual lifestyle factors that support militarization and overconsumption cannot be traced back merely to deeply ingrained anthropocentrism (Guha 2003, 556). In essence, then, Guha insists that protecting and preserving the environment necessarily entails addressing the root causes of overconsumption and militarization.

Guha's second critique of deep ecology is that the setting aside of wildlife preserves and wilderness areas, a practice supported by Western deep ecologists, has been thoroughly detrimental in the developing world. As a prominent example, Guha cites Project Tiger in his native India—an effort spearheaded by Indian conservationists in cooperation with international agencies such as the World Wildlife Fund. Project Tiger, by displacing poor rural villagers to preserve endangered tigers, "resulted in a direct transfer of resources from the poor to the rich" (Guha 2003, 556). Guha sees such wilderness preservation efforts, and associated claims by Western biologists that only they are competent to decide how tropical areas are to be used, as a blatant expression of Western neocolonial imperialism (Guha 2003, 556–557).

Deep ecologists have responded to Guha's and similar critiques, at various levels. First, deep ecologists disagree in some respects with Guha over how human beings ought to relate to and live within the natural world. Whereas deep ecology, drawing from the teachings of indigenous and many Eastern religious traditions, promotes a paradigm of cooperative interrelationship with the natural world, Guha sees Eastern religious traditions supporting a model in which humans throughout history in the East have engaged in a "finely tuned but nonetheless conscious and dynamic manipulation of nature" (Guha 2003, 557). From a deep ecological perspective, however, viewing the natural world as something to be manipulated or controlled constitutes in itself a form of imperialism. In an observation with which Guha might well agree, Thomas Birch condemns America's "incarceration" of natural areas into wilderness reservations as another example of the "white imperium" attempting to subdue and control an "adversarial other." Citing Luther Standing Bear, Birch upholds deep ecology's vision of a human relationship with the earth that is not adversarial "but participatory, cooperative, and complementary" (Birch 1995, 348).

Second, from the ecocentric standpoint of deep ecology, the claim that human needs must take precedence over biodiversity illustrates just how deeply ingrained anthropocentrism is in human thinking about the environment (Sessions 1995b, xvi). Third, deep ecologists have pointed out that addressing the widespread social injustice associated with and perpetuated by such things as overconsumption and militarization does not by itself necessarily result in a harmonious or sustainable relationship with the natural world (Fox 1995, 276). Focusing merely on human problems unacceptably relegates the nonhuman world to its traditional secondary position as the "background against which the significant action—human action—takes place" (Fox 1995, 277). In a detailed response to Guha, Naess defends wilderness preservation efforts, clarifying that such a strategy is not intended for export to colonize the developing world but is one of the essential tools in limiting environmental destruction caused by industrial overconsumption in the *West* (Naess 1995d, 401).

Conclusion

Despite such differences in perspective, deep ecologists appear to stand in essential agreement with Guha's analysis. Naess, speaking for many environmentalists, asserts that human beings must set as a universal goal the avoidance of "all kinds of consumerism" and questions whether wealthy nations, given their own environmental record, "deserve any *credibility* when preaching ecological responsibility to the poor countries" (Naess 1995d, 399, 401). Deep ecologists would have very little argument with Guha's call for overconsuming, expansionist western nations to adopt an "ethic of renunciation and self-limitation" (Guha 2003, 558). In addition, deep ecologists and environmental-ists, in general, are well aware of (and are seeking to address) the ongoing environmental (not to mention human) devastation caused by the military industrial complex (Sessions 1995b, xvi–xvii). Naess, Gary Snyder, and many other deep ecologists work with and support indigenous autonomous efforts worldwide to preserve and find ways to live sustainably in relation to the environment (Naess 1995d, 404–405). In this spirit of cooperation and mutual concern, Naess presents deep ecologists with a question to guide future inquiry and action: "How can the increasing global interest in protecting all Life on Earth be used to further the cause of genuine economic progress and social justice in the Third World?" (Naess 1995d, 406). Returning to the core principles of self-realization and biocentric equality, deep ecology thus upholds a vision in which humans take care of themselves by learning to care for Mother Earth.

See also **Endangered Species; Environmental Justice; Wild Animal Reintroduction; Sustainability (vol. 1)**

Further Reading

Abram, D., "The Perceptual Implications of Gaia." In *Dharma Gaia: A Harvest of Essays in Buddhism and Ecology,* ed. A. H. Badiner, 75–92. Berkeley, CA: Parallax Press, 1990.

Badiner, A. H., ed., *Dharma Gaia: A Harvest of Essays in Buddhism and Ecology.* Berkeley, CA: Parallax Press, 1990.

Birch, T., "The Incarceration of Wildness: Wilderness Areas as Prisons." In *Deep Ecology for the 21st Century: Readings on the Philosophy and Practice of the New Environmentalism,* ed. G. Sessions. Boston: Shambhala, 1995.

Bodian, S., "Simple in Means, Rich in Ends: An Interview with Arne Naess." In *Deep Ecology for the 21st Century: Readings on the Philosophy and Practice of the New Environmentalism,* ed. G. Sessions, 26–36. Boston: Shambhala, 1995.

Brown, J. E., *Teaching Spirits: Understanding Native American Religious Traditions.* New York: Oxford University Press, 2001.

Clowney, David, and Patricia Mosto, *Earthcare: An Anthology in Environmental Ethics.* Lanham, MD: Rowman & Littlefield, 2009.

Devall, B., and G. Sessions, "Deep Ecology: Living as if Nature Mattered." Excerpted in *Contemporary Moral Problems,* 7th ed., ed. J. E. White, 545–552. Belmont, CA: Wadsworth/Thomson, 2003.

Fox, W., "The Deep Ecology–Ecofeminism Debate and its Parallels." In *Deep Ecology for the 21st Century: Readings on the Philosophy and Practice of the New Environmentalism,* ed. G. Sessions, 269–289. Boston: Shambhala, 1995.

Grey, W., "A Critique of Deep Ecology." *Journal of Applied Philosophy* 3, no. 2 (June 2008): 211–216.

Guha, R., "Radical American Environmentalism and Wilderness Preservation: A Third World Critique." In *Contemporary Moral Problems,* 7th ed., ed. J. E. White, 553–559. Belmont, CA: Wadsworth/Thomson, 2003.

Lovelock, J. E., *Gaia: A New Look at Life on Earth.* New York: Oxford University Press, 1982.

Naess, A., "The Deep Ecological Movement: Some Philosophical Aspects." In *Deep Ecology for the 21st Century: Readings on the Philosophy and Practice of the New Environmentalism,* ed. G. Sessions, 64–84. Boston: Shambhala, 1995a.

Naess, A., "The Shallow and the Deep, Long-Range Ecology Movements." In *Deep Ecology for the 21st Century: Readings on the Philosophy and Practice of the New Environmentalism,* ed. G. Sessions, 151–155. Boston: Shambhala, 1995b.

Naess, A., "Self-Realization: An Ecological Approach to Being in the World." In *Deep Ecology for the 21st Century: Readings on the Philosophy and Practice of the New Environmentalism,* ed. G. Sessions, 225–239. Boston: Shambhala, 1995c.

Naess, A., "The Third World, Wilderness, and Deep Ecology." In *Deep Ecology for the 21st Century: Readings on the Philosophy and Practice of the New Environmentalism,* ed. G. Sessions, 397–407. Boston: Shambhala, 1995d.

Seed, J., J. Macy, P. Fleming, and A. Naess, *Thinking Like a Mountain: Towards a Council of All Beings.* Montpelier, VT: Capital City Press, 1988.

Sessions, G., "Ecocentrism and the Anthropocentric Detour." In *Deep Ecology for the 21st Century: Readings on the Philosophy and Practice of the New Environmentalism,* ed. G. Sessions. Boston: Shambhala, 1995a.

Sessions, G., ed. *Deep Ecology for the 21st Century: Readings on the Philosophy and Practice of the New Environmentalism.* Boston: Shambhala, 1995b.

Snyder, G. "The Rediscovery of Turtle Island." In *Deep Ecology for The 21st Century: Readings on the Philosophy and Practice of the New Environmentalism,* ed. G. Sessions. Boston: Shambhala, 1995.

White, L., "The Historical Roots of Our Ecologic Crisis." *Science* 155 (1967): 1203–1207.

E

EMISSIONS TRADING

Robert William Collin and Debra Ann Schwartz

Greenhouse gas emissions are a new commodity. The Kyoto Protocol, which the United States did not sign, outlines accepted targets for limiting or reducing emissions that thin or destroy the atmospheric conditions which allow life on Earth as we know it today. The targets are expressed as levels of emissions allowed, or "assigned amounts," per country. They apply to the years 2008–2012. The protocol's jargon divides allowed emissions into "assigned amount units" (AAUs).

The protocol spells out the details in its "Annex B, Parties" and "Article 17" sections. The specifics allow countries with units to spare—that is, that are allotted but not used—to sell their excess capacity to countries that are over their targets or whose industry requires polluting more than is acceptable under the protocol.

As such, the protocol helped to create a new commodity: emission pollution. Mostly, trades are in some form of carbon, such as carbon dioxide, the principal greenhouse gas under discussion. Consequently, carbon now is tracked and traded like any other commodity. This is known as the "carbon market."

The International Emissions Trading Association (IETA) holds regional meetings throughout the world on the matter. In June 2010, the IETA lobbied U.S. senators to pass a bill on climate change after one proposed by Senator Lisa Murkowski (R-AK) failed in the senate.

Definition

Emissions trading is a regulatory environmental policy to reduce the cost of pollution control by providing economic incentives to regulated industries for achieving reductions in the emissions of pollutants. A central authority, such as an air pollution control district or a government agency, sets limits or caps on each regulated pollutant. Industries that intend to exceed their permitted limits may buy emissions credits from entities that are able to stay below their permitted limits. This transfer is normally referred to as a trade. This is a new policy in the United States. Questions that may become controversies include whether all emissions are measured. Another more basic question is whether society can still allow polluters to buy their way out of responsibility for environmental and community impacts.

Harnessing Market Forces for a Safer Environment?

Market-based environmental policies for reducing pollution include many economic or market-oriented incentives. These include tax credits, emissions fees, or emissions trading. There are many types of emissions trading approaches; the one used by Clean Air Market Programs designed by the Environmental Protection Agency (EPA) is called "allowance trading" or "cap and trade" and has the following key features:

1. An emissions cap: a limit on the total amount of pollution that can be emitted (released) from all regulated sources (e.g., power plants); the cap is set lower than historical emissions to cause reductions in emissions.
2. Allowances: an allowance is an authorization to emit a fixed amount of a pollutant.
3. Measurement: accurate tracking of all emissions.
4. Flexibility: sources can choose how to reduce emissions, including whether to buy additional allowances from other sources that reduce emissions.
5. Allowance trading: sources can buy or sell allowances on the open market.
6. Compliance: at the end of each compliance period, each source must own at least as many allowances as its emissions.

U.S. Environmental Policy

According to the EPA, cap and trade is a policy approach to controlling large amounts of emissions from a group of sources at a cost that is lower than if sources were regulated individually. The approach first sets an overall cap, or maximum amount of emissions per compliance period, that will achieve the desired environmental effects. Permits to emit are then allocated to pollution sources, and the total number of allowances cannot exceed the cap. The main requirement is that pollution sources completely and accurately measure and report all emissions. There is grave concern about this premise. Since not all emissions are counted now, many people are concerned that this lack of specific reporting will only hide pollution.

Successes

Cap and trade was first tried in the United States to control emissions that were causing severe acid rain problems over very large areas of the country.

Legislation was passed in 1990 and the first compliance period was 1995. Sulfur dioxide (SO_2) emissions have fallen significantly, and costs have been even lower than the designers of the program expected. The U.S. Acid Rain Program has achieved greater emissions reductions in such a short time than any other single program to control air pollution. A cap and trade program also is being used to control SO_2 and nitrogen oxides (NO_x) in the Los Angeles area. The Regional Clean Air Incentives Market (RE-CLAIM) program began in 1994.

The regulating agency (e.g., EPA) must:

- Be able to receive the large amount of emissions and allowance transfer data and assure the quality of those data
- Be able to determine compliance fairly and accurately
- Strongly and consistently enforce the rule

Allowance trading is the centerpiece of EPA's Acid Rain Program, and allowances are the currency with which compliance with the SO_2 emissions requirements is achieved. Through the market-based allowance trading system, utilities regulated under the program, rather than a governing agency, decide the most cost-effective way to use available resources to comply with the acid rain requirements of the Clean Air Act. Utilities can reduce emissions by employing energy conservation measures, increasing reliance on renewable energy, reducing usage, employing pollution-control technologies, switching to lower-sulfur fuel, or developing other alternate strategies. Units that reduce their emissions below the number of allowances they hold may trade allowances with other units in their system, sell them to other utilities on the open market or through EPA auctions, or bank them to cover emissions in future years. Allowance trading provides incentives for energy conservation and technology innovation that can both lower the cost of compliance and yield pollution-prevention benefits, although this is controversial.

The Acid Rain Program established a precedent for solving other environmental problems in a way that minimizes the costs to society and promotes new technologies.

Allowances

An allowance authorizes a unit within a utility or industrial source to emit one ton of SO_2 during a given year or any year thereafter. At the end of each year, the unit must hold an amount of allowances at least equal to its annual emissions, that is, a unit that emits 5,000 tons of SO_2 must hold at least 5,000 allowances that are usable in that year. However, regardless of how many allowances a unit holds, it is never entitled to exceed the limits set under Title I of the act to protect public health. Allowances are fully marketable commodities. Once allocated, allowances may be bought, sold, traded, or banked for future use. Allowances may not be used for compliance prior to the calendar year for which they are allocated.

Allowances may be bought, sold, and traded by any individual, corporation, or governing body, including brokers, municipalities, environmental groups, and private citizens. The primary participants in allowance trading are officials designated and authorized to represent the owners and operators of electric utility plants that emit SO_2.

Determining Compliance

At the end of the year, units must hold in their compliance subaccounts a quantity of allowances equal to or greater than the amount of SO_2 emitted during that year. To cover their emissions for the previous year, units must finalize allowance transactions and submit them to the EPA by March 1 to be recorded in their unit accounts. If the unit's emissions do not exceed its allowances, the remaining allowances are carried forward, or banked, into the next year's account. If a facility's emissions exceed its allowances, it must pay a penalty and surrender allowances for the following year to the EPA as excess emission offsets.

Emissions trading or marketable rights have been in use in the United States since the mid-1970s. The advocates of free market environmentalism sometimes use emissions trading or marketable rights systems as examples to support the theory that free markets can handle environmental problems.

The idea is that a central authority will grant an allowance to entities based on a measure of their need or their previous pollution history. For example an allowance for greenhouse gas emissions to a country might be based on total population of the country or on existing emissions of the country. An industrial facility might be granted a license for its current actual emissions. If a given country or facility does not need all of its allowance, it may offer it for sale to another organization that has insufficient allowances for its emission production.

Environmentalists point out that this only increases environmental impacts to the carrying capacity, and beyond, of the environment. They observe that industry is supposed to reduce its emissions to the greatest extent possible under current environmental law. Claims that emissions will somehow be reduced now, or at least shifted to where it could saturate another environment, are not viewed as credible. This lays the foundation for controversy. Communities point out that the cumulative impact of already existing industries is a concern and possible public health risk.

Prominent Trading Systems

The most common policy example of an environmental emissions trading system is the sulfur dioxide trading system contained in the Acid Rain Program of the 1990 Clean Air Act. The program mandates reducing sulfur dioxide emissions by 50 percent between1980 and 2010. In 1997, the state of Illinois adopted a trading program for volatile organic compounds in the Chicago area, called the Emissions Reduction Market System. Beginning in 2000, more than 100 major sources of pollution in eight Illinois counties began trading pollution credits. In 2003, New York State proposed and attained commitments from nine northeastern states to cap and trade carbon dioxide emissions. States and regions of the United States are pursuing more of these policies.

The European Union Greenhouse Gas Emission Trading Scheme is the largest multinational, greenhouse gas emissions trading scheme in the world. It started in January 2005 and all 25 member states of the European Union participate in it.

Conclusion

Emissions trading is an experimental policy coming of age in the United States. However, it exposes major flaws in the country's environmental regulatory regime. Most environmental information about some of the biggest and unknown environmental impacts comes from self-reporting and may not be accurate. Many industries self-report whether they emit enough to even require any type of permit or oversight. Once regulated, emissions are simply permitted, and amounts are self-reported by industry. Emissions trading may be seen as a free market band-aid to a young, weak, and incomplete public policy of environmental protection. It opens up large holes in the current system and may inflame environmentalists and the public depending on how it is implemented. In a society moving toward concepts like sustainability, emissions trading may be challenged in its present form.

See also **Carbon Offsets; Cumulative Emissions; Environmental Audits and Industrial Privilege; Sustainability (vol. 1)**

Further Reading

Environmental Economics, "Problems of Emissions Trading." www.env-econ.net/2006/12/problems_with_e.html

FitzRoy, Felix, and Elissaios Papyrakis, *Introduction to Climate Change Economics and Policy.* London: Earthscan, 2010.

Grubb Michael, and Karsten Neuhoff, *Allocations, Incentives and Industrial Competitiveness under the EU Emissions Trading Scheme.* London: Earthscan, 2006.

Hansjürgens, Bernd, *Emissions Trading for Climate Policy: US and European Perspectives.* Cambridge, UK: Cambridge University Press, 2005.

International Emission Trading Association, http://www.ieta.org/ieta/www/pages/index.php

Jong, Cyriel de, and Kasper Walet, eds., *A Guide to Emissions Trading: Risk Management and Business Implications.* London: Risk Books, 2004.

Schreuder, Yda, *The Corporate Greenhouse: Climate Change Policy in a Globalizing World.* New York: Zed Books, 2009.

United Nations Framework Convention on Climate Change, "Emissions Trading." http://unfccc.int/kyoto_protocol/mechanisms/emissions_trading/items/2731.php

ENDANGERED SPECIES

Robert William Collin and Scott M. Fincher

Controversies about endangered species center on the value of species and the cost of protecting and preserving them and their habitats. There are debates about whether a particular species is going extinct and whether a particular policy actually does protect a designated species. Natural resource extraction (logging, mining, grazing), land and road development into wildlife habitats, and increased recreational use are all central issues in this controversy.

Background

Species extinctions have occurred along with evolution. As plant and animal species evolve over time, some adaptations fail. As human population has increased, along with our hunting, farming, and foraging capacities, plant and animal species have begun to disappear faster. Pollution, climate change, and other significant environmental impacts can destroy species in sensitive niches in the food chain. In most cases species are endangered because of human impacts, but each case can present its own issues.

The evidence for human impact on species in the United States is often based on successful eradication programs for problem pests. Knowledge about species extinctions grew as environmentalists, hunters, researchers, and others observed extinctions and near-extinctions of several species, such as the buffalo and pigeon. Endangered species create a great concern for productive bioregions and ecosystem integrity. They can represent a significant part of the food web, and their loss can forever weaken other parts of that food web. Eventually, this great social concern for endangered species found its way into law, now one of the main tools used by advocates on either side of the debate.

Debate over Saving a Species

Debates arise about whether a species is in danger of becoming extinct. When a species is designated endangered, more debate ensues over whether it is worth saving and what governmental polices might help to preserve it. One consideration is the species' habitat. Should activities that might benefit humans—such as mining, logging and grazing—be permitted? Should industrial and residential development continue? Should recreation be limited in wildlife areas?

Species Have Disappeared Naturally

As plant and animal species evolved over hundreds of thousands of years, some became extinct because they failed to adapt appropriately to the natural world. Scientists think that an increasing human population accelerated the process of extinction. Hunting, farming, pollution, climate change, and other human encroachments on species' environments can destroy species in sensitive niches in the food chain. What to do about these activities and conditions is subject to debate.

The evidence for human impact on species in the United States is often based on successful eradication programs for problem pests. Knowledge about dwindling species has resulted from the observations of hunters, researchers, environmentalists, and others. Examples are the much smaller number of American bison and the extinction of the passenger pigeon, which has not been seen in the wild since the 1920s. Endangered species can be a great concern for bioregions and the ecosystem. They can be an important part of the food chain, and their loss can weaken other parts of that chain. Eventually, the concern for species becoming endangered found its way into laws that have become a subject of debate.

U.S. Laws Stir Controversy

The 1966 federal Endangered Species Act (ESA) sets the policy for species preservation. It is controversial and involves issues such as long-term leases of public lands, private property, and defensible science. Scientific controversies include ecosystem risk assessment, the concept of a species and how it has been interpreted for ESA application, and conflicts between species when individual species are identified for protection and others are not. One such controversy is over the preservation of the habitat for the spotted owl in Oregon, which prevented logging. Approximately 60 logging mills subsequently closed. There are current discussions about whether saving the owl's habitat saved the bird (note: why was saving the bird important?). Endangered species designation can affects natural resource extraction such as logging and mining by prohibiting or limiting it.

Before a plant or animal species can receive protection under the ESA, it must first be placed on the federal list of endangered and threatened wildlife and plants. The listing program follows a strict legal process to determine whether to list a species, depending on the degree of threat it faces. The law has levels of designation: An *endangered* species is one that is in danger of extinction throughout all or a significant portion of its range. A *threatened* species is one that is likely to become endangered in the foreseeable future. The federal government maintains a list of plants and animals native to the United States that have potential to be added to the federal list of endangered species.

Small but Important Step

When the U.S. Congress passed the Endangered Species Preservation Act, the law was deemed a small but important first step toward species preservation. The law allows listing of only native animal species as endangered and provided limited means for the protection of species so listed. The Departments of the Interior, Agriculture, and Defense were to seek to protect listed species and to preserve the habitats of such species. Land acquisition for protection of endangered species was also authorized by law. In 1969, another law was passed to provide additional protection to species in danger of worldwide extinction. The next law was the Endangered Species Conservation Act. This law bans the importation and sale of such species in the United States.

World Wakes Up to Problem

The 1969 act also called for an international meeting to adopt a convention on the conservation of endangered species, and in 1973 a conference in Washington led to the signing of the Convention on International Trade in Endangered Species of Wild Fauna and Flora (CITES). It restricts international commerce in plant and animal species believed to be actually or potentially harmed by trade. After that conference, the U.S. Congress passed the ESA of 1973. This law combined and strengthened the provisions of earlier laws. It also had the effect of intensifying the controversy.

Its principal provisions follow:

- U.S. and foreign species lists were combined, with uniform provisions applied to both categories of endangered and threatened.
- Plants and all classes of invertebrates were eligible for protection, as they are under CITES.
- All federal agencies were required to undertake programs for the conservation of endangered and threatened species and were prohibited from authorizing, funding, or carrying out any action that would jeopardize a listed species or destroy or modify its critical habitat.
- Broad prohibitions were applied to all endangered animal species, which could also apply to threatened animals by special regulation.
- Matching federal funds became available for states with cooperative agreements.
- Authority was provided to acquire land for listed animals and for plants listed under CITES.
- U.S. implementation of CITES was provided.

Although the overall thrust of the 1973 act has remained the same, amendments were enacted in 1978, 1982, and 1988. Principal amendments are as follows:

- Provisions were added to Section 7, allowing federal agencies to undertake an action that would jeopardize listed species if the action were exempted by a cabinet-level committee convened for this purpose.
- Critical habitat was required to be designated concurrently with the listing of a species, when prudent, and economic and other effects of designation were required to be considered in deciding the boundaries.

- The secretaries of the Interior and Agriculture were directed to develop a program for conserving fish, wildlife, and plants, including listed species, and land acquisition authority was extended to such species.
- The definition of *species* with respect to *populations* was restricted to vertebrates; otherwise, any species, subspecies, variety of plant, or species or subspecies of animal remained listable under the act.
- Determinations of the status of species were required to be made solely on the basis of biological and trade information, without any consideration of possible economic or other effects.
- A final ruling on the status of a species was required to follow within one year of its proposal unless withdrawn for cause.
- Provision was made for designation of experimental populations of listed species that could be subject to different treatment under Section 4, for critical habitat, and Section 7.
- A prohibition was inserted against removing listed plants from land under federal jurisdiction and reducing them to possession.
- Monitoring of candidate and recovered species was required, with adoption of emergency listing when there is evidence of significant risk.
- A new section requires a report of all reasonably identifiable expenditures on a species-by-species basis that were made to assist the recovery of endangered or threatened species by the states and the federal government.
- Protection for endangered plants was extended to include destruction on federal land and other taking when it violates state law.

Several amendments dealt with recovery matters:

- Recovery plans are required to undergo public notice and review, and affected federal agencies must give consideration to those comments
- Five years of monitoring of species that have recovered are required.
- Biennial reports are required on the development and implementation of recovery plans and on the status of all species with plans.

Roll Call of the Imperiled

As of June 2010, a total of 1,220 species of animals and 798 species of plants in the United States were listed as threatened and endangered or proposed for listing as threatened or endangered. Forty-nine bird and animal species are currently proposed for listing, with 252 species in the United States designated as candidates for endangered status

Over the years, 557 habitat conservation plans (HCPs) have been approved. According to law, a HCP outlines ways of maintaining, enhancing, and protecting a given habitat type needed to protect species. It usually includes measures to minimize adverse affects and may include provisions for permanently protecting land, restoring habitat, and relocating plants or animals to another area.

As of 2010, administrators approved 1,043 species for recovery plans. A recovery plan is a document drafted by a knowledgeable individual or group that serves as a guide for activities to be undertaken by federal, state, or private entities in helping to recover and conserve endangered or threatened species. Recovery priority is also determined in these plans. There can be differences of opinion as to how high a priority certain species should have in a recovery plan. A rank ranges from a high of 1 to a low of 18, and these set the priorities assigned to listed species and recovery tasks. The assignment of rank is based on degree of threat, recovery potential, taxonomic distinctiveness, and presence of an actual or imminent conflict between the species and development activities.

The regulations for protection of endangered species generally require protection of species habitat. As our population grows and development expands into natural areas, the protection of wildlife habitat becomes more important and more difficult. Preservation of riparian (water) migratory pathways, private conservation efforts, and applied scientific research all hold promise for species preservation. However, the need for wildlife habitat preservation will still impair the ability of some property owners use their land as they wish. The controversies around species preservation are likely to be around for a long time.

Conclusion

As human habitation extends into more wild areas, more species are likely to become extinct. Coral reefs are rapidly dying in many parts of the world and with them, many of the species that thrive there. There are strong world conservation efforts for species protection but also strong political conflict when it comes to that kind of preservation. As more information on human environmental impacts on marine environments develops, so too will lists of endangered species.

See also **Deep Ecology and Radical Environmentalism; Federal Environmental Land Use; Logging; Mining of Natural Resources; Wild Animal Reintroduction**

Further Reading

Barrow, Mark V. Jr., *Nature's Ghosts: Confronting Extinction from the Age of Jefferson to the Age of Ecology.* Chicago: University of Chicago Press, 2009.

"Endangered and Extinct Species Lists," eelink.net/EndSpp.old.bak/ES.lists.html

Goble, Dale D., J. Michael Scott, and Frank W. Davis, eds., *The Endangered Species Act at Thirty.* Washington, DC: Island Press, 2006.

Office of Protected Resources, "Species under the Endangered Species Act (ESA)." www.nmfs.noaa.gov/pr/species/esa

Shogren, Jason F., and John Tschirhart, eds., *Protecting Endangered Species in the United States: Biological Needs, Political Realities, Economic Choices.* New York: Cambridge University Press, 2008.

U.S. Fish & Wildlife Service, "Endangered Species Program." June 2010. http://www.fws.gov/endangered/wildlife.html#Species

U.S. Fish & Wildlife Service, "TESS Database Species Report." June 2010. http://www.fws.gov/ecos/ajax/tess_public

Westley, Frances R., and Philip S. Miller, *Experiments in Consilience: Integrating Social and Scientific Responses to Save Endangered Species.* Washington, DC: Island Press, 2003.

ENVIRONMENTAL AUDITS AND INDUSTRIAL PRIVILEGE

Robert William Collin

Industries that perform environmental audits do so for a variety of reasons: by law, voluntarily, and as part of other audits. These audits can disclose whether a particular plant is in compliance with environmental laws, areas of cost savings in environmental compliance, and multifacility environmental compliance measures. Industries want audits kept secret, or privileged. Small and medium-sized businesses especially want this legislation because they want to level the playing field with large industry, which can use its own lawyers and hide information within attorney–client privilege. This secrecy prevents communities, environmentalists, and others from knowing about the environmental audit and any information that would relate to local environmental impacts or risks. Industry is concerned about environmental lawsuits and, if not protected by some legal privilege, would not perform any type of environmental audit. Since most U.S. environmental information about industry is self-reported, an independent audit carries much more credibility than the usual industry and government reports. Access to accurate environmental information is the crux of this controversy.

More than 20 states have enacted environmental audit privilege legislation. It takes different forms and is usually controversial. Regular audits should become a normal business management tool that assists compliance with complex environmental regulations and avoids unnecessary waste. Such audits provide valuable information about potential environmental noncompliance, suggest methods for reducing or eliminating waste streams, inform shareholders and customer queries regarding off-site liability, and can be used to create a green corporate image.

Self-auditing programs generate evidence that could be used against a company in an enforcement action. Any noncompliance reported in such a document may create a paper trail available to both enforcement agencies and private plaintiffs. Consequently, although numerous businesses undertake self-audits, many do not want information suggesting environmental noncompliance to be circulated or written down. The fear that this information will be discovered by a private party or a governmental agency discourages self-auditing programs at various companies. To environmental policy makers, this fear is problematic because it distorts environmental information. Many communities distrust this secret audit process, preferring clear and transparent transactions.

Large industry has always relied on the common-law attorney–client privilege, the work-product doctrine, and, more recently, common-law self-evaluation to argue that audit documentation is privileged. These legal arguments give privileged protection to large companies with environmental self-audit programs. The claim of attorney-client privilege will start a discovery dispute that results in an in-camera review by a judge, who will determine whether to allow the government to use the audit document against the regulated business. In contrast, a small business does not have the financial and strategic capacity to engage a lawyer for an expensive judicial fight for secrecy. The primary controversy between large and small industries here is who gets to privilege environmental information. This is not a controversy shared with communities or environmentalists.

New State Laws on Environmental Privilege

More than 30 states have considered legislation involving environmental audit privilege, and 20 have enacted such laws, including Arkansas, Colorado, Idaho, Illinois, Indiana, Kansas, Kentucky, Michigan, Minnesota, Mississippi, New Hampshire, Ohio, Oregon, South Carolina, South Dakota, Texas, Utah, Virginia, and Wyoming. These state laws essentially codify discovery-dispute procedures that large businesses have always enjoyed. By eliminating the requirement of hiring an attorney, small companies can afford to engage in the same type of self-audit process that most large companies currently take for granted when this legislation is enacted.

The environmental privilege is limited by law and not universally applied or available. A common legislative intent is to encourage owners and operators to conduct voluntary environmental audits of their facilities by offering a limited privilege to audited information. Proponents point out that it is infeasible and unnecessary for state and federal regulators to police each and every business in the state, and therefore self-auditing should be encouraged. Generally, a number of conditions must be met. Some of the conditions that are necessary for the state law on environmental audit privilege to apply are as follows:

1. All noncompliance identified during the audit is corrected in a reasonable manner.
2. The privilege is not asserted for fraudulent purposes.
3. Information in the audit is not otherwise required to be reported.

Some legislation also provides that a person or entity making a voluntary disclosure of an environmental violation is immune from any administrative, civil, and criminal penalties associated with that disclosure. As discussed further on, the compliance focus of environmental law allows for rapid reduction of penalties in return for quick compliance and disclosed and remedied harms.

How Broad Is the Industrial Privilege?

Proponents of audit privilege legislation state that it does not compel secrecy, because no privilege exists unless there is prompt disclosure and correction of the violation. Furthermore, unless the information falls within the very narrow scope of privileged information, it is decidedly vulnerable.

Conclusion

Many states that favor privileging environmental information argue that environmental protection efforts require that businesses, municipalities, and public agencies take self-initiated actions to assess or audit their compliance with environmental laws and correct any violations found. By getting to know all the industries affecting the environment and protecting their information better, compliance with the intent of environmental laws results.

STATE LAWS

Laws can vary from state to state. Some conditions and exceptions of state privilege and immunity laws include:

The audit must be scheduled for a specific time and announced prior to being conducted along with the scope of the audit. (AK)

The company makes available annual evaluations of their environmental performance. (AZ)

In exchange for a reduction in civil and/or administrative penalties a company implements a pollution-prevention or environmental management system. (AZ).

Privilege is not applicable to data, reports, or other information that must be collected, developed, maintained, or reported under federal or state law. (AR)

Audit report is privileged (secret) unless a judge determines that information contained in the report represent a clear, present, and impending danger to public health or the environment in areas outside the facility property. (CO)

An environmental audit report is privileged (secret) and is not admissible as evidence in any civil or administrative proceeding with certain exceptions, if the material shows evidence of noncompliance with applicable environmental laws and efforts to achieve compliance were not pursued by the facility as promptly as circumstances permit. (WY)

The Colorado Environmental Audit Privilege and Immunity Law does not affect public access to any information currently available under the Colorado Open Records Act. This information would include but is not limited to permits, permit applications, monitoring data, and other compliance/inspection data maintained by the Colorado Department of Public Health and Environment.

Additionally, the audit privilege does not affect the Colorado Department of Public Health and Environment's authority to enter any site, copy records, inspect, monitor, or otherwise investigate compliance or citizen complaints.

Community interest in this issue is high, and environmental organizations advocate against these laws. It is likely that state laws on this controversy will change rapidly.

Communities and environmentalists respond that most if not all industrial emissions are self-reported in a context of very weak enforcement. They argue that environmental information is a common good to be shared. Keeping it secret promotes a high degree of distrust and breeds controversy.

Advocates of sustainability and environmentalists want full and complete disclosure of all environmental impacts. The controversy continues to unfold in state and local legislatures and in federal environmental agencies like the EPA. The relationship between states and the EPA on this issue is a developing and somewhat contentious one.

See also **Environmental Impact Statements**

Further Reading

Dietz, Thomas, and Paul C. Stern, eds., *New Tools for Environmental Protection: Education, Information, and Voluntary Measures.* Washington, DC: National Academies Press, 2002.

Martin, Channing J., *Voluntary Disclosure of Environmental Violations: Is Mea Culpa a Good Idea or a Bad Move?* Washington, DC: Environmental Law Institute, 2002.

ENVIRONMENTAL IMPACT STATEMENTS

Robert William Collin

Environmental impact statements (EISs) are powerful regulatory tools that force proponents of projects that have significant impacts on the environment to assess those impacts. Although advisory only, they are used in many environmental controversies.

As knowledge about the environment has grown, so too has concern for the impacts of major projects and processes. Technology and project scale can greatly increase the impact of large-scale development on the environment. Environmental impact statements are advisory in practice but nonetheless required. It is a process fraught with controversies at most of the major stages. The environmental impact process under the National Environmental Policy Act (NEPA) is one that every major project or process with a significant impact on the environment must undergo. Generally, anyone contesting the process must go through the internal agency process first. Some states and tribes have their own environmental impact statement rules and laws.

Flash points for controversies under the EIS requirements are lack of notice, lack of inclusion, and inadequate stakeholder representation. The actual area of impact, called the study area, can shift during the process. Many of the processes of the EIS are time driven, and there is often inadequate time to assess ecosystem or cumulative impacts. The underlying environmental decision, as in the spotted owl controversy, can lend fuel to the EIS process. In the case of the spotted owl, the fact that logging the habitat of this endangered species was a significant environmental impact triggered the requirement for a full EIS. Environmental impact assessment also brings in controversies of risk assessment generally. However, an increase in environmental impact assessment at all levels is inevitable. Assessment is necessary to measure impacts of new projects and to establish baselines with which to measure changes in the environment. Citizen monitoring is also prodding more environmental assessment. Another common frustration with the federal EIS process is that it is advisory only. The decision maker is free to choose more environmentally harmful alternatives. All these controversies are likely to continue as the range of environmental assessments continue to expand into ecosystem and cumulative approaches.

NEPA was signed into law on January 1, 1970. The act establishes national environmental policy and goals for the protection, maintenance, and enhancement of the environment, and it provides a process for implementing these goals within the federal agencies. The act also establishes the Council on Environmental Quality (CEQ). This act is a foundational environmental law. The complete text of the law is available for review at NEPAnet.

NEPA Requirements

Title I of NEPA contains a Declaration of National Environmental Policy that requires the federal government to use all practicable means to create and maintain conditions under which humans and nature can exist in productive harmony. Section 102 requires federal agencies to incorporate environmental considerations in their planning and decision making through a systematic interdisciplinary approach. Specifically, all federal agencies are to prepare detailed statements assessing the environmental impact of and alternatives to major federal actions significantly affecting the environment. These statements are commonly referred to as environmental impact statements (EISs). Section 102 also requires federal agencies to lend appropriate support to initiatives and programs designed to anticipate and prevent a decline in the quality of humans' world environment. In 1978, the CEQ promulgated regulations under NEPA that are binding on all federal agencies. The regulations address the procedural provisions of NEPA and the administration of the NEPA processes, including preparation of EISs.

The NEPA process is an evaluation of the environmental effects of a federal undertaking including its alternatives. Any type of federal involvement, such as funding or permitting, can trigger NEPA regulations. There are three levels of analysis depending on whether or not an undertaking could significantly affect the environment. These three levels include categorical exclusion determination; preparation of an environmental assessment/finding of no significant impact (EA/FONSI); and preparation of an EIS.

At the first level, an undertaking may be categorically excluded from a detailed environmental analysis if it meets certain criteria that a federal agency has previously determined as indicating no significant environmental impact. A number of agencies have developed lists of actions that are normally categorically excluded from environmental evaluation under their NEPA regulations. The U.S. Army Corp of Engineers, the U.S.

Environmental Protection Agency, and the Department of the Interior have lists of categorical exclusions. This is an area of policy controversy. One aspect of these lists is that the cumulative effects of their exclusion are not considered. Another is that some of the categories that were once thought to be insignificant may not be now. Projects having insignificant environmental impacts are not required to perform an EIS.

At the second level of analysis, a federal agency prepares a written environmental assessment (EA) to determine whether or not a federal undertaking would significantly affect the environment. Generally, an EA includes brief discussions of the following: the need for the proposal; alternatives (when there is an unresolved conflict concerning alternative uses of available resources); the environmental impacts of the proposed action and alternatives; and a listing of agencies and persons consulted. It may or may not describe the actual study area. There is no actual requirement for notice to the community. Some communities are environmentally assessed without their knowledge. If the agency finds no significant impact on the environment, then it issues a finding of no significant impact (FONSI). The FONSI may address measures that an agency will take to reduce (mitigate) potentially significant impacts. This is the first notice many communities receive about any evaluation of the impacts. Many communities feel that there are significant environmental issues and, had they known about the EA process, could have directed the agency to them.

If the EA determines that the environmental consequences of a proposed federal undertaking may be significant, an EIS is prepared. Significant environmental impacts can be threats to an endangered species, historic sites, or culturally significant areas. An EIS is a more detailed evaluation of the proposed action and alternatives. The public, other federal agencies, and outside parties may provide input into the preparation of an EIS and then comment on the draft EIS when it is completed.

Interested parties are allowed to submit draft alternatives. The agency calls this scoping. Scoping is when the agency selects the interested parties who can submit an alternative proposal. This is a controversial stage of the process. There may be groups who wanted to participate but were not selected. Often there are communities who did not know about the internal agency scoping decisions. Once interested parties are selected, the alternative selection begins. A controversy can occur about which alternatives are examined. One alternative that is always examined is the no action alternative. The alternatives are compared and contrasted. There may be public hearings and some scientific studies. The agency then produces a draft EIS. This document can be a trove of information because it includes all the alternatives considered. The agency administrator then selects one alternative, and it is published in the final environmental impact statement of the EIS, along with its justification. The final EIS can only be 150 pages in length. The decision maker does not have to prioritize environmental protection over economic considerations. The EIS process seldom stops the decision or project, but it can slow it down and focus the public's attention on the environmental controversy.

If a federal agency anticipates that an undertaking may significantly impact the environment or if a project is environmentally controversial, a federal agency may choose to prepare an EIS without having to first prepare an EA. After a final EIS is prepared and at the time of its decision, a federal agency will prepare a public record of its decision addressing how the findings of the EIS, including consideration of alternatives, were incorporated into the agency's decision-making process. An EIS should include discussions of the purpose of and need for the action; alternatives; the affected environment; the environmental consequences of the proposed action; lists of preparers, agencies, organizations, and persons to whom the statement is sent; an index; and an appendix (if any).

Federal Agency Roles

The role of a federal agency in the NEPA process depends on the agency's expertise and relationship to the proposed undertaking. The agency carrying out the federal action is responsible for complying with the requirements of NEPA. In some cases, more than one federal agency may be involved in an undertaking. In this situation, a lead agency is designated to supervise preparation of the environmental analysis. Federal agencies, together with state, tribal, or local agencies, may act as joint lead agencies. A federal, state, tribal, or local agency having special expertise with respect to an environmental issue or jurisdiction by law may be a cooperating agency in the NEPA process. A cooperating agency has the responsibility to assist the lead agency by participating in the NEPA process at the earliest possible time; by participating in the scoping process; in developing information and preparing environmental analyses including portions of the EIS concerning which the cooperating agency has special expertise; and in making available staff support at the lead agency's request to enhance the lead agency's interdisciplinary capabilities. While there are cooperating federal agencies, there is some controversy about intergovernmental relationships with states and municipalities. Where there is a large federal government land presence, as in the western United States, some communities are excluded from important EIS processes.

EPA's Role

The Environmental Protection Agency, like other federal agencies, prepares and reviews NEPA documents. However, the EPA has a unique responsibility in the NEPA review process. Under section 309 of the Clean Air Act, EPA is required to review and publicly comment on the environmental impacts of major federal actions including actions that are the subject of EISs. If the EPA determines that the action is environmentally unsatisfactory, it is required by section 309 to refer the matter to the CEQ. Also the EPA carries out the operational duties associated with the administrative aspects of the EIS filing process. The Office of Federal Activities in the EPA has been designated the official recipient of all EISs prepared by federal agencies.

The Public's Role

The public has an important role in the NEPA process, particularly during scoping, in providing input on what issues should be addressed in an EIS and in commenting on the findings in an agency's NEPA documents. The public can participate in the NEPA process by attending NEPA-related hearings or public meetings and by submitting comments directly to the lead agency. The lead agency must take into consideration all comments received from the public and other parties on NEPA documents during the comment period.

Public participation can be time-consuming and costly for many stakeholders but especially community members. Receiving actual notice of when they can get involved in a particular EIS is generally a point of contention. Some communities consider the EIS decision already made and their participation a formality. Some EISs use complicated scientific analyses to measure different impacts, and these can be difficult to explain to some citizens. If a particular project is controversial, the agency can find that a significant impact itself, thus triggering the EIS requirement. Demand for community involvement can be part of a particular controversy. There is no public participation in the list of actions categorically excluded from the EIS requirements.

Conclusion

Environmental impact assessment is now an integral part of many environmental decisions. The process forces an assessment and includes the public and interested parties. It can also include human health risk assessments and ecological risk assessments, which can create controversies of their own.

EIS processes are necessary for the development and refinement of environmental policy at all levels. For sustainability purposes these assessments allow us to understand the environment around us. More communities and environmentalists demand them with the expectation of involvement and the hope that they are environmentally meaningful. To the extent these groups become more dissatisfied with both process and product, more controversy will develop.

See also **Cumulative Emissions; Environmental Audits and Industrial Privileges**

Further Reading

Dietz, Thomas, and Paul C. Stern, eds., *Public Participation in Environmental Assessment and Decision Making.* Washington, DC: National Academies Press, 2008.

Glasson, John, et al., *Introduction to Environmental Impact Assessment,* 3rd ed. New York: Routledge, 2005.

Hanna, Kevin, *Environmental Impact Assessment: Practice and Participation,* 2d ed. New York: Oxford University Press, 2009.

ENVIRONMENTAL JUSTICE

Robert William Collin

The term *environmental justice* refers to the distribution of environmental benefits and burdens. It includes fair and equal access to all decision-making functions and activities. Race and income shape the historic and present distribution of many environmental benefits and burdens.

Proximity of Communities of Color to Pollution

African Americans are almost four-fifths more likely than whites to live in neighborhoods where industrial pollution is suspected of posing the greatest health danger. In 19 states, African Americans are more than twice as likely as whites to live in neighborhoods with air pollution. Controversies about racism between whites and African Americans, between other nonwhite groups and African Americans, and within environmental organizations and the government are inflamed by the proximity of African American communities to dangerous industrial pollution.

The Associated Press (AP) analyzed the health risk posed by industrial air pollution using toxic chemical air releases reported by factories to calculate a health risk score for all communities in the United States. The scores are used to compare risks from long-term exposure to industrial air, water, and land pollution from one area to another. The scores are based on the amount of toxic pollution released by each factory, the path the pollution takes as it spreads through the air, the level of danger to humans posed by each different chemical released, and the number of males and females of different ages who live in the exposure paths. The AP study results confirm a long string of reports that show that race maps closely with the geography of pollution and unequal protection. These data do not include many other sources of pollution known to affect all urban residents. They also do not consider possible synergistic and cumulative effects.

Background

Historically, African American and other people-of-color communities have borne a disproportionate burden of pollution from incinerators, smelters, sewage treatment plants, chemical industries, and a host of other polluting facilities. Environmental racism has rendered millions of blacks invisible to government regulations and enforcement.

The risk scores also do not include emissions and risks from other types of air pollution, like trucks and cars. The AP research indicates residents in neighborhoods with the highest pollution scores also tend to be poorer, less educated, and more often unemployed. However, numerous other studies show blacks and other people of color concentrated in nonattainment areas that failed to meet EPA ground-level ozone standards.

This is pollution mainly from cars, trucks, and buses. It is substantial and affects African Americans and Hispanics more than others.

In 1992, 57 percent of whites, 65 percent of African Americans, and 80 percent of Latinos lived in one of the 437 counties that failed to meet at least one of the EPA ambient air quality standards. A 2000 study by the American Lung Association found children of color to be disproportionately represented in areas with high ozone levels.

Hispanics and Asians

According to the AP report, in 12 states Hispanics are more than twice as likely as non-Hispanics to live in the neighborhoods with the highest risk scores. There are seven states where Asians are more than twice as likely as whites to live in the most polluted areas. In terms of air quality, other studies have shown that Hispanic neighborhoods are disproportionately affected by air pollution, particularly in the southwestern United States.

Income

Many hold that environmental proximity is a function of income. This assumes a free and flowing housing market without institutional barriers like racism. Higher-income neighborhoods have more political, legal, and economic power to resist industrial sites. The average income in the highest-risk neighborhoods was $18,806 when the census last measured it (2000), more than $3,000 less than the nationwide average. One of every six people in the high-risk areas lived in poverty, compared with one of eight in lower-risk areas. Unemployment was almost 20 percent higher than the national average in the neighborhoods with the highest risk scores.

Proximity to Pollution Increases Long-Term Exposure to Risk

Short-term exposure to common air pollution worsens existing lung and heart disease and is linked to diseases like asthma, bronchitis, and cancer. Long-term exposure increases these risks. Many potentially synergistic chemical reactions in waste in cities are unknown, and so are their potential or actual bioaccumulative risks to humans. The question is who bears the risk of risks not regulated by the government? Until recently, the costs of public health have been separate from the costs of production for industrial capitalism. As health costs mount, the stakeholders who pay for them are protesting.

Current EPA Response

More than 80 research studies during the 1980s and 1990s found that African Americans and poor people were far more likely than whites to live near hazardous waste disposal sites, polluting power plants, or industrial parks. Other studies of the distribution of the benefits and burdens of EPA environmental decisions also found a clear demarcation along race lines. The disparities were blamed on many factors, including racism in housing and land markets, and a lack of economic and political power to influence land-use decisions in neighborhoods. The studies brought charges of racism. Legally, one must prove the intent to be racist, not just the fact that a given situation is racist. It is very difficult to prove the intent of a city or town when they pass a racially or economically exclusionary zoning ordinance. They are very difficult legal issues to litigate, but litigation still happens. President Clinton responded in 1993 by issuing an environmental justice executive order (EO 12898) requiring federal agencies to ensure that people of color and low-income people are not disproportionately exposed to more pollution. Recent reports suggest little has changed.

The EPA does not intervene in local land-use decisions. The federal government has preemptive power over state and local government to take property it needs. The state governments tend to know about local land-use decisions in relation to environmental agencies. The weak intergovernmental relations between these branches of government allow this controversy to continue to simmer. There are often battles between state environmental agencies and the EPA over the requirements of EO 12898. State environmental agencies are resistant to incorporating environmental justice issues but accommodate regulated industries with one-on-one consultation and permit facilitation.

Racial Disparities

The ways to measure race are themselves very controversial. The U.S. census undercounts urban residents of color frequently, and mayors file lawsuits every 10 years. Significant disparities in health and the actual quality of aspects of the urban environment exist at every level, an indicator of institutionalized racism.

- African Americans represent 12.7 percent of the U.S. population; they account for 26 percent of all asthma deaths.
- African Americans were hospitalized for asthma at more than three times the rate of whites (32.9 per 10,000 versus 10.3 per 10,000) in 2001.
- The asthma prevalence rate in African Americans was almost 38 percent higher than that in whites in 2002.
- African American females have the highest prevalence rates (105 per 1,000) of any group.
- African Americans are more likely to develop and die of cancer than persons of any other racial and ethnic group. During 1992–1999, the average annual incidence rate per 100,000 for all cancer sites was 526.6 for African Americans, 480.4 for whites, 348.6 for Asian/Pacific Islanders, 329.6 in Hispanics, and 244.6 in American Indians/Alaska Natives.
- African Americans are more likely to die of cancer than any other racial or ethnic group in the United States. The average annual death rate from 1997 to

2001 for all cancers combined was 253 per 100,000 for blacks, 200 for whites, 137 for Hispanic Americans, 135 for American Indians/Alaska Natives, and 122 for Asians/Pacific Islanders.

- Cancer kills more African American children than white children. Cancer is surpassed only by accidents and homicides as the number-one killer of African American children.
- Although cancer mortality rates for all races combined declined 2.4 percent each year between 1990 and 1995, the decline for African American children (0.5 percent) was significantly less than that for white children (3 percent).
- African American men have the highest rates of prostate, lung, colon, oral cavity, and stomach cancer.
- African American men are more than 140 percent more likely to die from cancer than white men.
- More white women are stricken with breast cancer than black women, yet black women are 28 percent more likely to die from the disease than white women.
- The overall cancer cure rate, as measured by survival for over five years following the diagnosis, is currently 50 percent for whites but only 35 percent for blacks.
- Cancers among African Americans are more frequently diagnosed after the cancer has metastasized and spread to regional or distant sites.
- Minorities with cancer often suffer more pain owing to undermedication. Nearly 62 percent of patients at institutions serving predominantly African American patients were not prescribed adequate analgesics.
- Many low-income, minority communities are located in close proximity to chemical and industrial settings where toxic waste is generated. These include chemical waste disposal sites, fossil-fuel power plants, municipal incinerators, and solid waste landfills.
- African Americans and other socioeconomically disadvantaged populations are more likely to live in the most hazardous environments and to work in the most hazardous occupations.
- Inner-city black neighborhoods are overburdened with pollution from diesel buses. In a 2002 EPA report, researchers concluded that long-term (i.e., chronic) inhalation exposure to diesel engine exhaust (DE) is likely to pose a lung cancer hazard to humans, as well as damage the lung in other ways, depending on exposure.
- There is a strong relationship between environmental exposure and lung cancer among African Americans, which accounts for the largest number of cancer deaths among both men (30 percent) and women (21 percent).
- People living in the most polluted metropolitan areas have a 12 percent increased risk of dying from lung cancer compared to people living in the least polluted areas.

- Smoking does not explain why lung cancer is responsible for the most cancer deaths among African Americans. Although many black men identify themselves as current smokers, they typically have smoked less and started smoking later in life than white men.
- Rates are higher in urban areas because of increased air pollution and increased particulate matter in the air.
- Minority workers are at a higher health risk from occupational exposure to environmental contaminants.
- African American men are twice as likely to have increased cancer incidence from occupational exposure as white men.

Many feel that belated government efforts to control polluting industries have generally been neutralized by well-organized and well-financed opposition. Industry is challenged in lengthy court battles, during which time industry still has the right to maintain production and exposure of people to suspect materials. Since the environmental regulations themselves and laws apply on a per industrial plant basis, and it is hard to prove any one plant at any one time did directly cause the harm alleged, the process and controversy continue. Communities have also become organized around this issue and have been developing environmental information and data.

PROXIMITY OF COMMUNITIES OF COLOR TO POLLUTION

Environmental Justice Locator

Scorecard.org provides maps at the national, state, county, and census-tract levels that illustrate estimated cancer risks from outdoor hazardous air pollution and the location of three types of pollution-generating facilities: manufacturing firms reporting to the Toxics Release Inventory, facilities emitting criteria air pollutants, and Superfund sites. You can see whether your home, workplace, or school is located in an area where estimated cancer risks are higher, comparable to, or lower than in other communities. You can also see how many polluting facilities are located in your area of interest. Charts associated with the maps provide demographic information about an area, including the percentage of people of color, percentage of families living in poverty, and percentage of homeownership. You can also use Scorecard's mapper to access environmental data at the most local level (i.e., for each individual census tract in the United States).

Distribution of Environmental Burdens

Scorecard uses easy-to-understand bar charts to illustrate which demographic group bears the burden of different pollution problems. Four problems are evaluated: releases of toxic chemicals, cancer risks from hazardous air pollutants, Superfund sites, and facilities emitting criteria air pollutants. Scorecard analyzes the distribution of these problems using seven demographic categories: race/ethnicity, income, poverty, childhood

(*continued*)

(continued)

poverty, education, Homeownership, and job classification. For example, Scorecard calculates whether whites or people of color live in areas with greater toxic chemical releases, and then graphically portrays the extent of the disparity, indicating which group is worse off. Further information about any environmental problems in an area can be found in Scorecard reports listed in the links section.

Locator for Unequal Impacts

For any burden or combination of burdens that you select, or any group you select, this locator will show you every county where that group of people experiences a higher impact than the rest of the population in the same county.

Distribution of Risks by Race, Ethnicity, and Income

Is race or income the driving factor accounting for disparate environmental burdens in your state? Scorecard examines the distribution of estimated cancer risks associated with outdoor hazardous air pollution to illustrate patterns of inequity by race/ethnicity and income. Scorecard calculates a population-weighted estimate of the average lifetime cancer risks imposed on each racial/income group by hazardous air pollutants. The Y-axis shows the estimated cancer risk per million persons, and the X-axis displays nine annual household income categories ranging from less than $5,000 to more than $100,000. Each line in the graph represents one of five racial/ethnic groups: whites, African Americans, Native Americans, Asian/Pacific Islanders, and Latinos. Gaps between the lines indicate potential racial/ethnic disparities in cancer risk burdens. Slopes in the lines indicate potential differences in cancer risk across income categories.

Environmental Hazards

Scorecard provides several measures of environmental hazards that can be used to compare states or counties within a state, including average cancer risks from hazardous air pollutants, the number of facilities per square mile that emit criteria air pollutants, the number of Superfund sites per square mile, and the number of Toxic Release Inventory facilities per square mile. Environmental hazard indicators for counties and states can be compared to demographic profiles in order to assess which communities bear the largest burden from pollution sources.

Conclusion

Racism in U.S. society is not news but remains a fact. Slavery is racist and the United States had African slaves that built the foundations of the country. These facts reach far into many present-day environmental dynamics that are as repulsive as slavery and racism seem to present-day populations. And in the environmental area, just like history, the most pernicious racism is reserved for African Americans. After the Civil War, three waves of African American people migrated north to the cities, seeking freedom and economic opportunity, just as all other immigrants and migrants have done before and since. When urban industrialization expanded, it polluted the city. Many other people of color and migrants were able to melt into U.S. society. In the areas of housing, employment, health, education, and transportation, this has not been the case with African Americans. Instead of moving out of the city, many African Americans stayed because of foreclosed opportunities. Industry has also stayed in these neighborhoods. This controversy is the broken lock to a Pandora's box of unavoidable and necessary controversy. All discussions of cumulative effects, sustainability, and U.S. urban environmentalism must consider the true environmental past of every place. There are many reasons for this, the least of which is to know where to clean up first. The next set of policy controversies involves the prevention of industrial growth in areas that may be irreparably damaged.

Underneath this controversy is another set of issues. The primary reason for most environmental policy is to protect the environment and the public. In most U.S. cities, it is now fairly easy to establish which communities bore the brunt of cumulative and synergistic risks. These communities are now shown to have a disproportionate adverse reaction to environmental stressors, expressing itself in a number of physical ways, such as childhood asthma. New environmental policies such as sustainability and the precautionary principle will require information about past environmental conditions, but the question of reparative public health intervention for proximate communities is left dangling. This is also known as the canary-in-the-coal-mine phenomenon.

Currently, the National Environmental Justice Advisory Committee is meeting with the EPA to recommend ways to limit or mitigate harms to local communities from increased emissions of particulate matter and nitrogen oxide due to increased trade and movement of goods and related transportation infrastructure growth. Some feel that this will focus attention on commercial marine and locomotive engines and their emissions, a current point of contention between environmentalists who want much stricter standards and industry that resists regulation. Ports, railroad depots, airports, and truck depots all create pockets of emissions, and many suspect these disproportionately affect low-income people and people of color. Concern over the impacts of the movement of goods has increased due to recent and projected increases in foreign trade. The assumption is that this increase will require substantial transportation expansion from coasts and ports to inland destinations, likely affecting many environmental justice communities that are already disproportionately affected by past and present pollution. It may be a sign of progress in some areas that the canaries in the coal mine are actively resisting all activities that increase their pollution exposure. It promises to be a significant environmental justice issue in the near future, especially as scientists begin to explore the ecological restoration of coastal waters and rivers. Environmental information will be highly scrutinized, there will be scientific debate about risk and causality, and government regulators will eventually enforce much stricter emission standards at multimodal transportation hubs.

EPA ENVIRONMENTAL JUSTICE SHOWCASE COMMUNITIES

In November 2009, EPA Administrator Lisa P. Jackson announced a national initiative to address environmental justice challenges in 10 communities. The agency allotted $1 million to this effort over the ensuing two years. The amount is relatively small, but the funds are intended primarily as a means of helping communities to organize resources and devise solutions, not as a final remedy for the environmental justice issues facing them.

According to Jackson, "these 10 communities will serve as models for the EPA's committed environmental justice efforts, and help highlight the disproportionate environmental burdens placed on low-income and minority communities all across the nation."

The selected Environmental Justice Showcase Communities will use collaborative, community-based approaches to improve public health and the environment. EPA will provide $100,000 per project to help address concerns in communities disproportionately exposed to environmental risks. These demonstration projects will test and share information on different approaches to increase EPA's ability to achieve environmental results in communities.

The following locations will serve as Environmental Justice Showcase Communities:

Bridgeport, Connecticut: EPA will build on work that has already taken place to develop community capacity and engagement, identify a broad network of partnerships, and connect with the goals of the city government. Using this past work as a foundation, EPA plans to work with a variety of stakeholders to develop projects focused on improving indoor air quality, increasing community capacity for green jobs, increasing recycling rates, and reducing asthma and toxics exposure.

Staten Island, New York: EPA will work with the North Shore of Staten Island, a former industrial community that now contains many abandoned, contaminated, and regulated properties along the waterfront. This neighborhood has seen an increase in the number of kids with elevated lead levels in their blood. EPA, in consultation with key community members and state and local health agencies, will develop a community-based health strategy for the area.

Washington, D.C.: EPA is building on its environmental justice work with a variety of partners, such as the District Department of Environment, the District Department of Health, and local recipients of environmental justice small grant awards.

Jacksonville, Florida: EPA will focus on improving environmental and public health outcomes in an area that consists of a predominantly low income and minority population. This area has a number of Superfund sites, brownfields, vacant and abandoned lots or other properties where contamination is suspected, and impacted waterways. EPA will work with its partners, including environmental justice community representatives, to address sites of concern and turn them into an opportunity for residents to collaborate with developers and revitalize their neighborhoods.

Milwaukee, Wisconsin: EPA will work to further the redevelopment of the 30th Street Industrial Corridor. The corridor, a former rail line in the north-central part of the city, is home to low income communities of color. This project seeks to improve the human, environmental and economic health of these neighborhoods by redeveloping brownfields along the corridor, implementing environmentally preferable storm-water management practices, and developing urban agriculture.

Port Arthur, Texas: EPA has proposed a "cross-media" pilot project in Port Arthur, Texas, a racially and ethnically diverse population along the Gulf Coast of southeast Texas. This community was severely impacted as a result of hurricanes Katrina, Rita and Ike. Through the EJ Showcase Project, EPA will work with partners to strategically target additional work and supplement ongoing efforts.

Kansas City, Missouri and Kansas City, Kansas: EPA has identified 11 neighborhoods in the metropolitan area that have many risk factors including poor housing conditions and increased exposure to environmental hazards. EPA will conduct an assessment to identify specific sources of pollution and will work with neighborhood leaders to prioritize community concerns. Strategies to address these concerns will be developed through these partnerships.

Salt Lake City, Utah: EPA has chosen six neighborhoods in central and west Salt Lake City as the focus of a Children's Environmental Health and Environmental Justice initiative. The areas include Glendale, Jordan Meadows, Poplar Grove, Rose Park, State Fairpark, and Westpointe. EPA selected the areas based on the presence of several environmental risk factors and the community's support and past participation in addressing environmental issues. The multi-agency initiative will seek to identify and reduce children's exposure to contaminants from multiple pathways. EPA will work closely with the community and other federal, state and local agencies to identify issues of concern and develop and apply tools to address those issues. The state of Utah has developed a tracking system that will provide baseline health and environmental data and help the partnership achieve results.

Los Angeles Area Environmental Enforcement Collaborative, California: The densely populated communities closest to the I-710 freeway in Los Angeles County are severely impacted by pollution from goods movement and industrial activity. In a multi-year effort, a collaboration of federal, state and local governments and community organizations will work to improve the environmental and public health conditions for residents along this corridor. Partners will identify pollution sources of concern to the community, review agency data sources and develop action plans. One goal is to improve compliance with environmental laws by targeting inspections and enforcement at the state, federal, and local levels to address community concerns.

Yakima, Washington: EPA will address multiple environmental home health stressors in the Latino and tribal communities in the Yakima Valley. A coordinated effort between state, local, and non-profit partners will be used to address the range of exposures found in the community, with a primary focus on reducing exposure through contaminated private well drinking water. This will be accomplished by assessing homes with contaminated wells, providing "treatment at the tap" mitigation, and reducing pollution sources through available regulatory tools and best management practices.

See also Children and Cancer; Cumulative Emissions; Deep Ecology and Radical Environmentalism; Social Justice (vol. 2)

Further Reading

Bullard, Robert D., ed., *Growing Smarter: Achieving Livable Communities, Environmental Justice, and Regional Equity.* Cambridge, MA: MIT Press, 2007.

Faber, Daniel, *Capitalizing on Environmental Injustice: The Polluter-Industrial Complex in the Age of Globalization.* Lanham, MD: Rowman & Littlefield, 2008.

Rhodes, Eduardo Lao, *Environmental Justice in America: A New Paradigm.* Bloomington, IN: Indiana University Press, 2003.

Schrader-Freschette, K. S., *Environmental Justice: Creating Equality, Reclaiming Democracy.* New York: Oxford University Press, 2002.

EPIDEMICS AND PANDEMICS

Jessica Lyons and Debra Ann Schwartz

The difference between an epidemic and a pandemic rests on the extent to which a disease spreads. When an infectious disease appears in a location where it is not normally present and affects a large number of people, it is known as an *epidemic*. Epidemics can last weeks to years. They are temporary and will eventually disappear. Epidemics are also localized, appearing in villages, towns, or cities. When an infectious disease with these characteristics spreads throughout a country, continent, or larger area, it is known as a *pandemic*. History has documented numerous epidemics and pandemics, including recent outbreaks of H1N1 (swine flu) and severe acute respiratory syndrome (SARS), a serious form of pneumonia. For its long, varied, and at times dramatic history, smallpox, also known as variola, provides an excellent case study in epidemics and pandemics and the debates and issues that surround them.

Early Vaccines

In 430 B.C.E. the population of Athens was hit hard by an unknown plague. The plague, documented by Thucydides, claimed approximately one third of the population. Some contemporary historians speculate that this unknown plague was actually smallpox. Similar plagues thought to be smallpox continued to appear throughout the Roman Empire from 165 to 180 B.C.E. and 251–266 B.C.E. What we now know as smallpox entered western Europe in 581 C.E., and eventually its presence became a routine aspect of life in the larger cities of Europe, such as London and Paris, where it killed 25 to 30 percent of those infected. By the 18th century, smallpox was certainly endemic and responsible for an average of 400,000 deaths per year in Europe and the disfigurement of countless additional individuals.

In 1718 Lady Mary Wortley Montagu brought the practice of variolation to England from Turkey. The procedure was quite simple: a needle was used to scratch a healthy individual's skin, just breaking the surface; a single drop of the smallpox matter was added to the scratch and then loosely bandaged. If this was performed successfully, the individual would progress through an accelerated and mild case of smallpox, resulting in no scars and lifelong immunity.

The mortality rate for smallpox acquired in this manner was 1 to 2 percent, a considerable improvement over smallpox caught in the natural way, which had a mortality rate between 10 and 40 percent. When she returned to England, Lady Montagu variolated both of her children.

Most of London's well-to-do society recoiled in horror at the act of purposely giving an individual the pox. As a result, Lady Montagu was ostracized by all except her closest friends. Her actions sparked hot debates in the chambers of the London Royal Medical Society over the ethics of deliberately exposing an individual to smallpox, of the efficacy of the procedure, and of the methods of the procedure itself. Given the known mortality rate of smallpox and the success of Lady Montague's variolation on her children, however, it was not long before others began requesting that the procedure be performed on themselves and their children. After smallpox claimed the life of Queen Mary in 1692 and almost killed Princess Anne in 1721, members of the royal family became interested in the potential of variolation, influencing the opinions of the royal physicians.

Before members of the royal family could be subjected to the procedure, royal physicians demanded proof of the procedure's success through human experimentation. Several inmates scheduled to be hanged at Newgate Prison, London, who had not had smallpox, as well as one individual who had already had the pox, were chosen and subjected to the procedure. It is not known whether these subjects were chosen or if they volunteered, although it seems doubtful that they would have had a choice in the matter. The manner in which the experiment was performed would certainly be condemned by modern scientists as well as ethicists. The subjects were kept together in a separate cell and monitored daily by physicians. A constant stream of visitors, both medical and civilian, came to observe the infected prisoners in their cell. After all the subjects had made full recoveries, the procedure was considered successful as well as morally acceptable. It is interesting to note that in England, variolation required a specially trained physician, whereas in Turkey, where the practice originated, the procedure was generally performed by an elderly woman in the village.

The case of smallpox raises a number of issues concerning diseases that reach epidemic and pandemic levels. The introduction of a non-Western medical procedure by a nonprofessional, Lady Montagu, created a considerable amount of contention among physicians of the time. Although its long local history in Turkey, as well as its use by Lady Montagu's private physician, indicated that the procedure was successful, it was not until after the favorable outcome of an "official" experiment, executed under the auspices of the

London Royal Medical Society and royal physicians, that the procedure was considered both safe and effective. Individuals who sought to practice variolation put themselves at risk of bodily harm from citizens driven by fear and panic. This was the case until local authorities determined that the practice was safe.

Morally Reprehensible in America

Around the same time, medical controversy spread to America, specifically to Boston. The Reverend Cotton Mather is generally credited with bringing variolation to North America, having "discovered" the practice after a discussion with his slave who responded, "yes…and no" when asked if he had suffered the pox. This slave, Onesismus, provided Mather with the details of variolation as performed by his relatives in Africa. However, it was actually Dr. Zabdiel Boylston who performed the procedure. Whereas Mather might have publicly supported variolation, it was not until several months after it had been in practice that he allowed his children to be variolated, and then it was done in secret.

Boylston, on the other hand, was open with his actions and suffered from repeated threats of imprisonment from the government as well as mob violence. The act of purposely giving an individual such a deadly infection was considered morally reprehensible by both citizens and public officials, regardless of its potential positive outcome. The uproar in Boston over variolation reached fevered levels, with some individuals supporting the practice and others supporting a ban. At various times the selectmen of Boston forbade individuals to enter the city for the purpose of variolation and then banned the procedure itself. On at least one occasion, in an effort to find a legal reason to imprison Boylston, his home was searched by authorities looking for individuals who had purposely been infected by smallpox through variolation.

Eventually, fear of catching smallpox "naturally," combined with the apparent success of variolation and its popularity, forced the local government to legalize the practice. In fact, Boylston was even invited to England for an audience with the king, and he attended a number of variolation procedures during his visit.

Biological Weaponry

Although variolation was a potent weapon against smallpox, it was an expensive procedure; it cost the equivalent of as much as $500 today and was initially available only to the wealthy. As a result, by the time of the Revolutionary War, many Americans were still susceptible to the disease. This posed a problem for both America's soldiers and its civilians. Debates over variolation raged among the commanding generals of the American forces. Smallpox has a two-week incubation period, during which the individual is asymptomatic but still contagious. The possibility that individuals who had undergone the procedure might give smallpox to their fellow soldiers during the infectious incubation period and thus trigger an epidemic among the American forces initially made the procedure look too risky. In 1777, however, George Washington ordered the variolation of the entire Continental Army to prevent further outbreaks of the disease.

British forces were largely immune to smallpox, almost all having been exposed as children. Those who had not been exposed were quickly variolated. During the Revolutionary War, the British crown promised freedom to any American slave who joined their forces. Being American, the majority of freed black slaves were not immune to smallpox. Many acquired it through variolation after joining British forces.

During the contagious incubation period, black patients were allowed to wander the countryside, passing through American villages and towns and leaving smallpox in their wake. Some historians believe that the British simply did not have the inclination or the resources to care for these individuals. Others, however, believe that this represented the deliberate use of a biological weapon by the British to spread smallpox to American citizens and troops.

In July 1763 there was a documented discussion among British forces, during the French and Indian War, of distributing smallpox-infected blankets to the local Native Americans. Whether the plan went into effect was never confirmed, but within six months of the exchange, a violent smallpox epidemic broke out among the local tribes.

The use of infectious diseases as weapons is not innovative. The oldest known use of a biological weapon occurred in the 14th century, when in an attempt to conquer the city of Kaffa, the khan of the Kipchak Tartar army ordered the bodies of plague (*Yersinia pestis*) victims to be catapulted over the city's walls. This event is cited as the catalyst of the Black Death, a pandemic that swept across Europe starting in the 1340s and lasting a century.

The Black Death is believed to have killed as much as one-third of the European population. During World War II, the Japanese attempted to test the effectiveness of such illnesses as *Y. pestis*, smallpox, anthrax, and typhus as biological weapons through experimentation on an unsuspecting Chinese population. It is not beyond the realm of possibility that smallpox, like other infectious diseases, could be weaponized and released, creating a pandemic. Smallpox vaccinations are effective for only 10 years; therefore almost all of the current world population has no immunity to the disease and would be susceptible to such an attack.

Crossing Species

In 1796, in an experiment that would never be permitted today, English doctor Edward Jenner purposely injected an eight-year-old boy with cowpox matter obtained from a pustule on a milkmaid's hand. Following this, he attempted to variolate the boy with smallpox. The results were astonishing. Cowpox, a relatively harmless infection passed from cows to humans, provided potent immunity from smallpox. From this experiment emerged *vaccinia virus*, the modern and more effective vaccine for smallpox. Although there were still skeptics, as illustrated by James Gillray's painting *The Cow*

Pock or the Wonderful Effects of the New Inoculation, which depicted individuals who were half-human and half-bovine, some individuals, including the British royal family, submitted to vaccination. By 1840, variolation was forbidden, and in 1853 vaccination against smallpox in Britain was mandated.

Even with these advancements in prevention, smallpox continued to rage into the 20th century. According to the World Health Organization (WHO), a subcommittee of the United Nations, by the 1950s there were still 50 million cases of smallpox each year. In 1967 the WHO declared that 60 percent of the world's population was still in danger of being exposed to smallpox, with one in four victims dying.

Controversy continued to surround smallpox well into the 20th century when an international group of scientists undertook the task of eradicating smallpox from the world permanently. In the 1950s the Pan American Sanitary Organization approved a program that allocated $75,000 annually toward the extermination of smallpox. In 1958, the WHO took over support of the program, but no action was taken until 1967. At that time the WHO approved $2.4 million for a 10-year program aimed at total eradication of smallpox.

Religion and Disease

Although scientists involved had the support of several international organizations, contention surrounded their project. Some of the most vehement protests were based on religious grounds. Numerous religions, from Hinduism to Christianity, argued that smallpox was divine intervention and judgment and that humans had no right to interfere. During the WHO's quest to eradicate smallpox, individuals who feared that meddling would cause divine retaliation went so far as to hide those suffering from smallpox or who had not yet been vaccinated by Western doctors, making it extremely difficult to treat all cases as the program required. Others disliked the idea of mandatory vaccination, believing that freedom of choice should prevail. The program was ultimately successful, however, and the United Nations declared the world free of smallpox in 1979.

Even though there has not been a reported case of smallpox in almost 30 years, its well-guarded existence in two government facilities continues to generate attention. Governments and organizations argue over the destruction of the last known smallpox specimens. Those arguing for its elimination cite the potential for accidental release onto an unsuspecting public, as well as the need to create an environment where possession and use of smallpox are considered morally reprehensible. Those who argue for its preservation cite its potential in helping future scientists to understand viruses better and the possibility of creating more effective and safer vaccines. Additionally, they question whether it is morally acceptable for humans to purposefully incite the extinction of another living organism. These questions have been debated for almost three decades, and the debate continues.

The implications for health care and disease control policy inherent in that debate is mired in the economic impact associated with epidemics and pandemics. Much research pivots on ways to better assess how much it will cost to produce a vaccine, distribute it, and inoculate those infected. From archeoepidemiologic studies, researchers have helped the health care industry plan for the next influenza pandemic. For example, in 2009 signature features were clarified for three flu pandemics: A/H1N1 from 1918 through 1919; A/H2N2 from 1957 through 1963; and AH3N2 from 1968 through 1970. This detail is expected to contribute to both national and international plans for curbing the disease, drawing international collaboration once again into the health care policy arena.

Lawsuits investigating the line between individual rights and those of the public appear in this arena as well. The recent advent of SARS, swine flu and HIV/AIDS has heightened awareness about dual loyalty conflicts health professionals face when trying to contain epidemics and pandemics. Ethical clashes surface when, for example, a health professional decides it is in the best interest of public health to restrict individual liberties. That might include putting individuals in quarantine when infectious, or revealing to public health authorities confidential information about a patient's sexual partners or health status. Debate continues to offer suggestions for managing dual loyalty conflicts when diseases reach epidemic and pandemic levels.

Conclusion

Disease and the possibility of epidemics and pandemics emerged at the same time that humans began to give up their hunter-gatherer way of life and settle into large communities and cities. Although the specific name of the disease might be in question, these events have been documented in some way since the beginning of written communication. Controversy over treatment has been widespread. Heated debates over the use of eastern prevention and treatment methods in western cultures resulted in new laws, fines, and in some cases arrests. At times religious opposition has helped to spread particular diseases when individuals have refused medical treatment. The use of infectious diseases as biological weapons is always a possibility. This practice has been roundly condemned by the international community. It continues to create fear in the general public and affects decisions about how to manage a particular disease or virus. Once a lethal or contagious disease has been contained, ethical and moral questions inevitably arise as in how to manage the specimen.

See also **Food Safety; HIV/AIDS; Influenza; Vaccines; Globalization (vol. 1); Supply Chain Security and Terrorism (vol. 1)**

Further Reading

Carrell, Jennifer Lee, *The Speckled Monster: A Historical Tale of Battling Smallpox.* New York: Plume, 2003.

Cunha, Burke A., et al., "Swine Influenza (H1N1): Diagnostic Dilemmas Early in the Pandemic." *Scandinavian Journal of Infectious Diseases* 41, no. 11 (2009): 900–902.

Fenn, Elizabeth Anne, *Pox Americana: The Great Smallpox Epidemic of 1775–82.* New York: Hill and Wang, 2001.

Gregor, Michael, *Bird Flu: A Virus of Our Own Hatching.* New York: Lantern Books, 2006.

Koplow, David, *Smallpox: The Fight to Eradicate a Global Scourge.* Berkeley: University of California Press, 2003.

Miller, Mark A., et al., "The Signature Features of Influenza Pandemics—Implications for Policy." *New England Journal of Medicine* 360, no. 25 (2009): 2595–2598.

Price-Smith, Andrew T., *Contagion and Chaos: Disease, Ecology, and National Security in an Age of Globalization.* Cambridge, MA: MIT Press, 2009.

Steel, John, et al., "Transmission of Pandemic H1N1 Influenza Virus and Impact of Prior Exposure to Seasonal Strains or Interferon Treatment." *Journal of Virology* 84, no. 1 (2010): 21–26.

Williams, John, "Dual Loyalties: How to Resolve Ethical Conflict." *South African Journal of Bioethics and Law* 2, no.1 (2009): 8–11.

World Health Organization, "Smallpox." *Epidemic and Pandemic Alert and Response (EPR).* http://www.who.int/csr/disease/smallpox/en

EUGENICS

Gareth Edel

Eugenics was the popular science and associated political movement for state control of reproduction, controversial for its association with the Nazi Holocaust and forced sterilization and racist policies in the United States. In its day it was legitimate science, but today it haunts any discussion of controlling fertility or heredity.

Development of the Field

Broadly considered, eugenics represented not only the scientific study of human heredity and the potential controls of the heredity of the population but also the policies that were created based on these scientific principles. Because of this dual nature, eugenics remains hard to define. Eugenics was a dominant social, scientific, and political philosophy for thinking about differences in population and public health, and controversial as it was even at the time, it represented the state-of-the-art thinking in the 1920s through 1940s. Despite these difficulties in definition, one thing that eugenicists (scientists, philosophers, politicians, and even Christian clergy) had in common was a belief that reproduction should be controlled based on social considerations and that heredity was a matter of public concern. Although both the set of scientific theories and the associated social movement that aimed at the control of human heredity have since been discredited, they were considered acceptable and scientifically credible in their time and have had a lasting impact. Eugenicists were among those who pioneered in the mathematical evaluation of humans, and their influence in turning biology into the quantitative science it is today should not be underestimated.

The eugenics movement reached the zenith of its influence in the 1930s and 1940s, having influenced public health and population control policies in many countries. Its credibility only slowly faded away, even after being popularly associated with the doctrines of anti-Semitism and genocide of the National Socialist Party in Germany during World War II. Because of this connection to the atrocities of World War II, it is easy to forget the extent to which eugenics was accepted as an important science in the United States, which had enacted policies based on its precepts.

The word *eugenics* (from the Greek for "well bred") was coined by Francis Galton in 1883. It represented his participation in a broad cultural movement focused on breeding and heredity throughout the educated middle class of England and the United States. Galton was inspired to work on evolution and heredity by considering the writings of his cousin Charles Darwin and the economist Thomas Malthus, who both had been key contributors to the popular interest in population-level studies in biology during the 19th century. Darwin's theory of evolution stressed the importance of variation within populations, whereas Malthus's work focused on the dangers of overpopulation. From a synthesis of their works, Galton proposed a new science that would study variation and its effect in human populations. Though classification systems based on race and other factors existed, Galton's work advanced and popularized the idea of differing hereditable traits and their potential dangers.

JOSEF MENGELE

Josef Mengele (1911–1979) is mainly remembered for his role as the "Angel of Death" in the Holocaust, supervising atrocities at the Auschwitz-Birkenau concentration camp during World War II, and then as a war criminal in hiding. What is less commonly known are his scientific motivations.

Prior to World War II, he had received his medical doctorate and researched racial classification and eugenic sciences in anthropology. Throughout the war, he provided "scientific samples" (largely blood and tissue samples from victims of the camp) to other scientists. Although he is singled out for his personal direction of the deaths of thousands, his participation in a community of scientists who are not considered war criminals remains controversial. Throughout the war, his position in the medical corps of the notorious military service of the SS kept him apart from colleagues at the prestigious Kaiser Wilhelm Institute, but many there and in the scientific community in the United States were in communication with him. His torture of prisoners was intended to expand German knowledge of such laudable topics as health and the immune system, congenital birth defects, and the improvement of the species.

It is difficult today to balance the dedicated scientist and doctor with the monster capable of cruelties to those he regarded as less than human, but this contrast is often repeated in the history of eugenics and frequently appears in the media when contemporary scientists and doctors seem to cross the line between help and harm.

Although best known for his work in eugenics and genetics, Galton was a Renaissance man. He studied and did research in mathematics, meteorology, and geography; served with the Royal Geographical Society; traveled widely in Africa; and was a popular travel writer. His groundbreaking work on statistics is recognized as some of the earliest biometry (or mathematics of biological variation); his work was crucial in the early development of fingerprinting as a criminal science. Although these activities seem disconnected, Galton's commitment to the idea that mathematical analysis and description would provide deeper understanding has lived on in genetics and biology.

The goal of eugenics both as a scientific practice and as a social philosophy was to avoid what was considered to be the inverse of natural selection, the weakening of the species or "dysgenics," literally "bad birth." As humanity became better able to take care of the weaker, and as wars and revolutions were seen to take a greater toll on the elites and the intelligent, the population was believed to be diminishing in quality. The argument suggested that as the physically fit fought in the two world wars, the disabled remained at home receiving government support, and as the smartest struggled to learn, public schools and factory work allowed the least well adapted to survive. Similarly, racial and economic differences were seen as promoting higher birth rates among these lower classes, whereas the "better born" were seen to be having too few children in comparison. Contemporary fears about birth rates in the developed world (i.e., Japan, France, and the United States) being lower than the birth rates in the less-developed world (i.e., India, China, and Latin America) suggest that these fears remain active.

THE FIRST INTERNATIONAL EUGENICS CONGRESS

Even before the dominance of eugenics at its height in the interwar years, interest was widespread, and the First International Eugenics Congress exemplifies how broad participation was in conversation on eugenics. The congress opened July 24, 1912, a year after the death of Francis Galton, and was presided over by Major Leonard Darwin, the last living son of Charles Darwin. Although his father had carefully stayed away from discussion of eugenics, Leonard was an avid eugenicist, interestingly the only supporter among Charles's five sons, as well as the least accomplished scientist among them. There were more than a thousand registered participants, including luminaries such as Winston Churchill, Thomas Edison, and the Lord Mayor of London. The congress participants argued over new theories and data and the scientific nature and study of heredity as well as the appropriate actions it suggested. Though there was not general agreement on much, there was a shared assumption that some sort of intervention was needed in reproduction and heredity for fear that the weak and undesirable might outbreed the strong and fit.

For Galton and other eugenicists, the disparity between who was reproducing and who should be reproducing demanded intervention. Galton envisioned many ways to intervene, but drawing on the metaphor of domestication and breeding of animals that appeared in Darwin's work, Galton favored what would later be called positive, as opposed to negative, eugenics. The positive–negative model is based on the distinction between encouraging the increase of the reproduction of the favored and preventing the reproduction of the inferior. Galton proposed incentives and rewards to protect and encourage the best in society to increase their birth rates. In the end most national eugenics policies were based on the negative eugenic model, aiming to prevent some people from having children.

Popularization of Eugenics

The control of reproduction by the state has a long history in practice and in theory, appearing in key political works since Plato's *Republic*, wherein the ruler decided which citizens would have how many children, and this history was often cited at the height of popular acceptance of eugenics. Public health, social welfare programs, and even state hospital systems were only beginning to be developed at the middle of the 19th century, and among the social and technological upheavals at the end of the 19th century was an increasingly strong movement to maintain public health through governmental controls. As a result, there was widespread support in the United States for policies that were seen as progressive. In this context, an effort to promote the future health and quality of the population by encouraging the increase of good traits while working to limit the replication of bad traits seemed acceptable.

Broad movements throughout Europe and the United States gave rise to the first public welfare systems and stimulated continued popular concern over evolution. Widely held beliefs about the hereditary nature of poverty and other negative traits led to fear that these new social measures would throw off the natural selection of the competitive world. These debates about welfare and its effect on the population still stimulate concern among citizens of the United States and elsewhere.

Because of popular acceptance and its utility in justifying a range of policies, eugenic science was agreed upon by a wide array of notables who might otherwise have been on different sides of issues. Among those who advocated some form of eugenic policy were President Franklin Delano Roosevelt, the Ku Klux Klan, and the League of Women Voters.

The complex relationship many public figures had with eugenics stems in part from the usefulness of using it as a justification because of its widespread support. Birth control advocate Margaret Sanger publicly supported a rational version of negative eugenics but may have done so only for the credibility she gained as a result. She and other advocates for access to birth control were taken much more seriously by policy makers because they connected the issue with the more popular eugenics movement. In this

MARGARET SANGER

Margaret Sanger (born Margaret Louise Higgins, 1879–1966) was a key figure in the birth and population control movement in the first half of the 20th century. Revered as a central figure in moving the country toward legalizing access to birth control in the United States, she remains a contentious figure for her advocacy of eugenics. Sanger, a nurse, was horrified at seeing women's deaths from botched back-alley abortions. Her sympathy for the plight of women led her to found the American Birth Control League, which would later be known as Planned Parenthood, and open the Clinical Research Bureau, the first legal birth control clinic. A prolific speaker and author, her works include *Woman and the New Race* (1920), *Happiness in Marriage* (1926), *My Fight for Birth Control* (1931), and an autobiography (1938). Although her work on birth control would have been enough to make her contentious, her political support for eugenic policies such as sterilization has led to a fractured legacy, and these beliefs are frequently used as a reason to discredit her more progressive ones. She died only months after the federal decision in *Griswold v. Connecticut* officially protected the purchase and use of birth control in the context of marriage for the first time.

light, Sanger's suggestion that the upper classes were able to get birth control despite the laws and that there was a need to change the laws to slow the breeding of the poor, who were unable to attain birth control, may be seen as a political as opposed to ideological choice.

Eugenics organizations and political movements were started in Germany in 1904, Britain in 1907, and the United States in 1910. At the height of the era of eugenics, there were more than 30 national movements in such countries as Japan, Brazil, and others throughout Europe. In some countries coercive measures were rejected; in others policies were more limited, but in each country the adoption of national eugenics programs and popular movements represented an attempt to modernize and adopt scientific methods for advancing the health and well-being of the populace as a whole. Even the most notorious case of eugenics, the Nazi Germany eugenics program, was associated with discussion of the "greater good." It becomes easy to forget that the Nazi obsession with a healthy nation led not only to genocide but also to national campaigns for healthy eating and the elimination of criminal behavior.

The German eugenics laws were capped by the three Nuremberg Laws in 1935 that signaled the beginning of the Nazi genocide, aimed at "cleansing" the German nation of "bad blood" through negative programs including sterilization and executions while also promoting increased reproduction of those with "good blood" in positive eugenics programs. The Nazi eugenics program sterilized nearly 400,000 people based on the recommendation of the Genetic Health and Hygiene Agency for what were considered hereditary illnesses, such as alcoholism and schizophrenia. Probably the most notorious

THE JUKES AND THE KALLIKAKS

Richard L. Dugdale's 1874 book *"The Jukes": A Study of Crime, Pauperism, Disease and Heredity* and Henry Herbert Goddard's 1912 account *The Kallikak Family: A Study in the Heredity of Feeble-Mindedness* are key examples of what were known as family studies, powerfully convincing stories of the danger of bad heredity that were widely circulated in the first half of the 20th century. Both stories follow the troubles of the members of a family and the passage of harmful traits generation to generation. Dugdale was a progressive, and in the case of the Jukes family, he suggested the problem family was one that demanded rehabilitation, whereas Goddard was more closely associated with the eugenics movement; he saw the problem as one of prevention. These stories were very important in the early days of genetics because they were influential in popularizing the heritability of traits regardless of environment. The comparison in the tale of the Kallikaks between the branch of the family who had been infected with the bad trait and their still pure and good relations resonated and spread the idea of a trait widely. In the end neither story has stood up to scrutiny, as historians have revealed manipulations and fabrications at their sources, but their influence is lasting nonetheless.

manifestation of positive eugenics on record was the Nazi program that paired SS soldiers with unmarried women of "good blood" to increase the birth rate for the benefit of the nation.

Sterilization in the United States

The U.S. program was already under way when the German eugenics program was still beginning, and though state governments in the United States eventually sterilized fewer people, their programs were used as a model by the Germans. The center of the eugenics movement in the United States was the Eugenics Records Office (ERO), located at the Cold Spring Harbor Research Center in New York. The ERO published the *Eugenical News,* which served as an important communications hub and was considered a legitimate scientific publication. By the late 1930s, more than 30 states had passed compulsory sterilization laws and more than 60 thousand people had been sterilized. In 1937 more than 60 percent of Americans were in favor of such program; of the remainder, only 15 percent were strongly against them. In discussions of sterilization, a common consideration was the growing system of institutions and residents. Sterilization was seen as a humane and cost-effective remedy for problems such as alcoholism when compared with lifelong incarceration, and these programs remained a key influence on the development of outpatient treatment for the mentally ill until well into the 1970s.

If there is any practice distinctly associated with the American eugenics movement, it is coerced and forced sterilization. Although Nazi doctors performed these procedures in far greater numbers, in light of the Holocaust their project loses its impact. But in the

United States, this same procedure remains shocking. Many of those who were sterilized were residents of mental hospitals and poorhouses who were forced to undergo the procedure. Others were voluntary or temporary patients at state hospitals. It is difficult to know how many sterilizations were performed and yet more difficult to confirm what percentage of those were coerced. Some patients intentionally sought sterilization as a form of birth control; others chose it as an avenue out of institutionalization; some were tricked or forced. Today documents show that some institutions told patients who were to be sterilized that they were going to have appendectomies; in these and other institutions, high rates of appendectomies were recorded. Forced or coerced surgery on a single individual today would seem shocking, but such procedures were legally mandated in some states for more than 50 years. Because those most likely to have been sterilized were the mentally ill and the indigent, we are likely never to know the full story.

Numerous court decisions challenged the legality of state sterilization, and although several state laws were struck down in court, the Supreme Court decisions in two key cases upheld what was considered a legitimate state interest. In the 1927 case *Buck v. Bell*, the Virginia statute requiring sterilization practices was upheld by the U.S. Supreme Court, and Chief Justice Oliver Wendell Holmes infamously wrote in the decision that the law was necessary because "three generations of imbeciles is enough." Carrie Buck, the plaintiff in the case, had been certified "feebleminded," as had her mother. When Carrie's daughter was "tested" at the age of one month and declared to be "feebleminded," Carrie Buck did have the presence of mind to question the diagnosis and did not want her to be sterilized, but the Court's decision came down against her. Although it was not publicized at the time, Carrie Buck's daughter received further intelligence testing when she was in her early teens and was determined to have above-average intelligence. Whereas many countries slowly rescinded eugenics laws over the course of the second half of the 20th century, in others the laws remain on the books without implementation. The United States and most of the Scandinavian countries are among those that never officially eliminated their eugenics laws, and many others still have public health and hygiene laws from the eugenics period that have simply been modified.

Eugenics and Inheritance

From the 1890s until the late 1930s, a series of laws intending to limit the entry of immigrants into the United States was associated with eugenics, and the laws became increasingly harsh. Although these laws were widely popular among some groups, their explicit racism and isolationism became a growing source of concern for others. This legal link between eugenics and racist immigration policy was associated with the earliest antieugenics responses. Eugenics had initially been associated with the public good and reform, but this association too was tarnished by accusations of racism. Growing segments of the population recognized eugenics as biased against the poor, as noneugenic reformers made social conditions of poverty public and advocated for institutional reform rather than hereditary control of poverty.

In the United States in the late 1930s, in light of the growing upset about the association between eugenics and racism, reformers tried to shift the eugenics movements to a more moderate stance, and many mainstream eugenics groups moved away from hard-line positions. By the late 1940s, the increasing public awareness of Nazi atrocities pushed public opinion even more against eugenics, and the word started to lose its respectability. Eugenics laws were reframed by being called hygiene or public health laws. Many of the reform eugenicists joined other scientists working in the nascent field of genetics, and some were founding members of the American Society of Human Genetics when it was formed in 1948. Although the growing antieugenics sentiment slowly turned eugenics from a dominant scientific field into a discredited memory, scientists who had worked on heredity as eugenicists embedded their study of hereditary diseases and mental and moral traits within Mendelian genetics.

Throughout the rise of eugenics, there was no clear understanding of the mechanism of inheritance within the intellectual community. Although today we have a scientific consensus on the workings of the cell and the importance of DNA, little was known about the inner workings of reproduction and development at the turn of the century. Gregor Mendel (1822–1884) was a Czech monk and biologist whose experimental breeding of pea plants led to his developing a series of scientific laws regarding the segregation, parental mixing, and transfer of traits. The rediscovery and popularization of the work of Mendelian genetics offered an explanation based on finite internal properties of the cell, which appealed to some, but its laws did not appeal to Galton or many eugenicists who saw it as applying only to simple traits such as plant color. The emphasis in Galton's view was on formal Darwinism, the rate of reproduction, and the role of environment and external factors in sorting the fittest and removing the weak. Mendel's theory is no longer associated with eugenics, in part because one of its strongest supporters, geneticist Thomas Hunt Morgan, opposed eugenics, but many other key scientists involved in promoting the acceptance of Mendel's work were doing so because it so clearly defined heritability. It was a powerful argument for the lasting and finite specification of heritable traits, and it worked with the idea of eugenics, whereas other theories argued for more environmental impact and flexibility. Although today there is reason to believe that Mendel's laws oversimplify a more complicated phenomenon, the rediscovery and embrace of these ideas by eugenic science was instrumental in the founding of genetics.

In the early 1970s, around the time the last of the eugenics laws were enacted and only a few years after the latest forced sterilizations in the United States, references in popular press, media, and news sources that suggested that genetic causes of mental and moral defects were at an all time low. In the last 30 years, there has been a steady increase in popular awareness of and interest in genetics and a dramatic resurgence of reference to genetic causes of traits. Between 1975 and 1985, there was 200-fold increase in public references suggesting a genetic cause for crime, mental capacity or intelligence, alcoholism, and other moral and mental traits that had been central concerns under eugenics. This level of interest increased fourfold by the early 1990s and has not decreased. These issues are magnified today in areas where population growth adds to economic and social pressures. Where the use of technology for sex selection and choice of appropriate qualities of one's offspring becomes more active, it leads to controversy. In India and China, the perceived need to extend control to practices and technologies of heredity has garnered accusations of a new eugenics in media coverage.

Lasting interest and study of eugenics is due to its connection to two perennial questions. First, it asks how much of and what parts of who we are come from our heredity, often described as the debate between nature and nurture, and second, how a society should determine, react, and respond to undesirable traits of individuals. These two questions are interlinked in that a trait that is learned may be unlearned, but biological traits have been assumed to be innate and unchangeable, leading to different sorts of responses from society and law.

Today major news sources and media outlets eagerly publicize front-page stories on new scientific findings based on a widespread interest in genetics and biological traits, such as "gay genes" causing homosexuality or "alcoholic genes" passed along from father to son, but few place the corrections and negative evaluations of these findings in view when they are discredited. Stories run about genes that cause diseases such as breast cancer, without discussing any connection to what can be done in response to these discoveries or their connection with the discredited science of eugenics. Little discussion takes place about why these genes are looked for or what good knowing about them does in a culture that emphasizes individual accomplishment as surpassing heredity in determining one's life story.

We do not often ask how a history of eugenics has contributed to the demand for genetic explanations and medical testing today, but the idea of heredity, of unchangeable inherited traits, continues to hold particular power despite or because of its importance at the founding of genetics. One explanation is to be found in the American ethos and legends of the self-made individual. The idea that all people start from a clean slate is ingrained into American society, and the American dream of the ability of anyone to work hard and get ahead is challenged by the failure of so many hard workers to get ahead. The persuasiveness of inherited cause for success or failure shifts the discussion away from systemic environmental constraints on success such as racism, sexism, and class, allowing the focus to remain on the individual. Another concept frequently connected to eugenics and to contemporary genetics is the idea of the easy solution, as exemplified in the lasting presence of the 1950s "better living through chemistry" mentality of the single-drug cure. How much easier to imagine fixing one gene, one trait, than to think through the myriad of causes that might otherwise contribute to something we want to change.

Recent Developments

With the successes and promises for the future of molecular biology and genetic engineering, we are offered new avenues and a new reason to rekindle interest in heredity. The eugenicists believed that heredity was important as a predictive and evaluative tool but did not have the means to alter the traits they attempted to study, whereas contemporary innovations promise to offer the potential to act upon those traits determined to be harmful.

Today approximately 1 in every 16 babies in the United States is born with some birth defect, and although the impacts range in severity, the common conception is that any abnormality or defect creates a victim and represents part of a public health problem. Thinking about the victims of genetic disease, it is very tempting to consider a return to state control or even a voluntary eugenics where parents make the choice presented by their doctor. It is this eugenics of choice that has emerged today. As prenatal tests have been improved and are more widely practiced, they are sometimes compared with eugenics. Amniocentesis, in which genetic testing of unborn babies is performed, has been frequently connected to this history because, for most anomalies found, there is no treatment, leaving parents only with the choice to abort or not. Abortion has been connected with eugenics since Margaret Sanger and others championed birth control legalization at the turn of the century. Medical methods of abortion have become more sophisticated, but fertility control methods have been a presence in most human societies in one form or another and always involve the question of what sort of person the child will be and what sort of life the child will have. Explicit mentions of eugenics in contemporary discussions of abortion appear on both sides: prochoice advocates are concerned about excessive government control of fertility, and antiabortion activists attempt to use eugenic associations with abortion and to compare such procedures with the Holocaust. The language of eugenics is used on both sides to discuss the differential access and use of abortion between the wealthy and poor, between black and white, what sort of people are having abortions, and who is discouraged or encouraged to have children.

The hygiene laws of the first half of the century have faded, and today public health regulations in many states require blood tests before marriage so that couples may be better prepared to choose in having children when they carry some traits. But who decides what traits are to be tested for? If the core of eugenics was a belief that society or the state has an interest in heredity, do we still practice eugenics?

Contemporary premarital blood-test regulations parallel some of the aims and content of the eugenic hygiene laws, though frequently the underlying motivation may be different. In the early part of the 20th century, these rules were enacted based on eugenic arguments against urbanization and growing populations of immigrants and poor and on notions of social purity that we no longer articulate. In recent years, fear of HIV/AIDS and conceptions of personal risk may have taken their place. More than 30 states have evaluated legislation requiring premarital HIV screening, and states including Illinois, Louisiana, Missouri, and Texas have passed such laws. Although later concerns over privacy and the damage done by false positives led all these states to eliminate the laws, some of the state laws had gone so far as to ban marriage for those who had AIDS. While the fear at the heart of this social crisis has passed, we cannot say what is yet to come. Neither were these HIV/AIDS laws unusual; many states still require blood tests for other diseases if one wishes to receive a marriage license, and—in an echo of eugenics—some regulations exempt those who are sterile or forbid marriage until treatment for sexually transmitted diseases has been received.

How will recent court decisions that have legally limited parental rights during pregnancy—for instance criminalizing drug use as child abuse—be expanded as society maintains its claim on control of fertility and heredity, and through them a definition of what sorts of control may be acceptable to society?

See also **Biotechnology; Genetic Engineering; Human Genome Project; Medical Ethics; Reproductive Technology**

Further Reading

Curry, Lynne, *The Human Body on Trial: A Handbook with Cases, Laws, and Documents.* Santa Barbara, CA: ABC-CLIO, 2002.

Duster, Troy, *Backdoor to Eugenics.* New York: Routledge, 1990.

Forrest, Derek Williams, *Francis Galton: The Life and Work of a Victorian Genius.* New York: Taplinger, 1974.

Gould, Stephen Jay, *The Mismeasure of Man.* (New York: Norton, 1981.

Kerr, Anne, and Tom Shakespeare, *Genetic Politics: From Eugenics to Genome.* Cheltenham, UK: New Clarion Press, 2002.

Kevles, Daniel J., *In the Name of Eugenics: Genetics and the Uses of Human Heredity.* New York: Knopf, 1985.

Kluchin, Rebecca M., *Fit to Be Tied: Sterilization and Reproductive Rights in America, 1950–1980.* New Brunswick, NJ: Rutgers University Press, 2009.

Knowles, Lori P., and Gregory E. Kaebnick, *Reprogenetics: Law, Policy, Ethical Issues.* Baltimore, MD: Johns Hopkins University Press, 2007.

Rubenfeld, Sheldon, ed., *Medicine after the Holocaust: From the Master Race to the Human Genome Project.* New York: Palgrave Macmillan, 2010.

F

FEDERAL ENVIRONMENTAL LAND USE

Robert William Collin and Debra Ann Schwartz

Access to public lands plays an increasing role in the exploration and development of hydrocarbon resources and other uses such as recreation. Federal environmental land-use planning is extensive and dictates which lands will be available for leasing and what kind of restrictions will be placed on use of those lands. Public lands are also leased to ranchers, loggers, and miners for natural resource use and grazing. These uses are considered harmful to the environment. Many tenants on public lands have a sense of entitlement due to generations in a given profession, such as ranching or logging, in one place. Many environmentalists press for laws that force the federal government to use these lands sustainably with little or no environmental impact.

Public Landholdings of the U.S. Government

The federal government owns about 29 percent of the land in the United States. There is a maze of federal agencies, and some landholdings controlled by the federal government are not public lands. Four federal agencies administer most of the 657 million acres of federal land. The National Park Service (NPS), the Fish and Wildlife Service (FWS), the Bureau of Land Management (BLM) in the Department of the Interior, and the Forest Service (FS) in the Department of Agriculture make most of the environmental and land-use decisions. The majority of federally owned land (92 percent) is in 12 western states.

One is Utah, where Governor Gary Herbert signed two bills in March 2010 authorizing the state to exercise eminent domain over federal lands. This is clearly unconstitutional, a style of law practiced in several western states including Arizona. Utah legislators set aside $3 million to litigate the frivolous claims the move is expected to generate. They did so at a time of budget shortfalls and other economic burdens taxpayers in the state face.

Challenging Assumptions: Federal Government and Taking of Private Property

Land-use regulation in the United States is done mainly by local government with state oversight. Although the federal government has eminent domain power to control land, it is not exercised at the local level. The federal government has long played a powerful role in local land-use decisions.

Development has scarred U.S. landscapes and destroyed ecosystems. Much of the environmental damage resulted from the federal government's environmental land-use decisions. People are allowed to place developments on federal lands in places that are subject to natural hazards such as fires and avalanches. They are allowed to mine, log, and graze livestock on federal lands in wildlife areas. The most damage is done by the construction of roads needed by loggers, oil drillers, miners, and ranchers. Where the roads go, development often follows. Abuse and lack of federal enforcement of these uses creates and continues to create severe threats to wildlife and wilderness habitat. The Everglades, farmlands where streams and grasses have been ravaged by farm policies, and watersheds degraded by abuse and pollution are some examples.

For 80 years, the federal government has regulated grazing rights across millions of acres of federal land in the West. It has been a controversy between preserving a rural way of life and responding to a growing environmental concern that values watersheds and biodiversity.

Recent regulations make it easier for ranchers to use federal lands without concern for environmental impacts. The new rules give ranchers more time, up to five years, to reduce the size of their herds if the cattle are damaging the environment. Proving that the herds are damaging the environment is a difficult proposition because the ranchers do not let people onto the federal land, treating it as if it were their own private property. Without being able to access the environment, it is impossible to discover abuses and ecological damage until it is severe. The George W. Bush administration gave shared ownership in the water rights and some structures on federal land to private ranchers. The regulations also decrease the opportunities for public involvement in deciding grazing issues on federal lands.

Critics note that the mining, logging, and federal grazing programs cost the United States because they lease areas at below-market rates. It is no simple matter to determine the cost to the United States of the subsidized industries operating on

SCIENTISTS RETALIATED AGAINST FOR RANGE MANAGEMENT REPORT

A major part of federal land management is ranching. Ranches are leased to private corporations and individuals, and these leases are enforced by the landlord—the U.S. federal government. This federally owned land dominates the environment in many western states. These leases cover vast tracts of land and are often controlled by long-term leases held for generations in some communities. Reports from government scientists on the environmental impact of ranching on federal lands are controversial because they stand up to powerful vested special-interest ranching industries. These government reports may be the only reliable information available about the environmental condition of our federal lands because ranchers treat this land as private property. Ranch management scientists work for the federal government and the ranchers to increase the productivity of the range for ranchers. Traditionally they have not focused on ecological preservation or accurate and cumulative environmental impacts. When the environment is rapidly degrading, the productivity of the range for ranchers goes down. These government reports are very powerful documents because they put limits on the abuse of natural resources in federal lands. Some government biologists say the George W. Bush administration interfered with the science of range management to promote its proranching agenda.

In one internal report released to the media, scientists reported that "the cumulative effects...will be significant and adverse for wildlife and biological diversity in the long-term." "The numbers of species listed or proposed for listing under the Endangered Species Act will continue to increase in the future under this alternative." According to the government range scientists, that language was removed from the scientific analysis that accompanied the new grazing regulations.

There are many environmental controversies around government scientists about government censure and misrepresentation. In many environmental controversies scientists follow principles and ethics, often to their own personal detriment in terms of careers and professional black listing. Sometimes government scientists can find protection under a law called whistleblower protection. These are rules and laws designed to protect the independent professional judgment of scientists and other professionals such as lawyers, engineers, and accountants employed by the U.S. government. They coincide with the professional ethics of a given profession because exercising independent professional judgments is the essence of being a professional. The two previous scientists made their statements after they retired. Other scientists in government are laterally transferred. The effectiveness of the whistle-blower protection laws is controversial. They apply only to government professionals. Scientists' ability to exercise independent professional judgment is a very important consideration, especially in the context of federal environmental land-use planning. The manipulation of environmental facts for profit compounds the intensity of this battleground.

federal lands. Part of the cost is the mitigation and cleanup of their environmental impacts. It is a cost that the responsible industries will not voluntarily bear, that the small western communities cannot afford, and that western states allow. Over the last 80 years or so the cumulative environmental effects of large- and small-scale resource exploitation operations on federal lands may begin to undermine their mission of conservation and environmental protection.

Other Uses

In the late 1990s, the Clinton administration allowed the patenting of life forms for the first time in history. That decision had an effect on national park land. It permitted private interests to mine for enzymes, for example, in geyers and hot springs in Yellowstone National Park. Opponents of the practice complained that the nation was not compensated for the takings. They also contended that mining of natural resources was never before permitted in national parks, though support for that position is arguable.

Pharmaceutical companies have a strong interest in the microorganisms taken out of natural resources, as they may be altered slightly and patented. Opponents of this kind of federal land use argue that if this kind of mining is going to be allowed, the public should benefit from any related sales. The money, they argue, could support the park or go toward acquiring more land to protect and conserve as habitat, for ecosystem balance, and the like.

Conclusion

Communities that developed around timber and mining want those jobs to survive and with them a comfortable way of life. Concessions in federal land areas such as national parks exert a strong voice in policy debates about what is more important: ecological communities or human communities. On a national level, environmentalists and proponents of sustainability want the federal landholdings to lead the way in environmental policy development. They press for ecosystem risk assessment, environmental impact statements, and limited environmental impacts. Some demand wilderness areas and then press for the reintroduction of wolves and grizzly bears. Many other diverse federal land users want more access to federal lands. They include snowmobilers, hang gliders, mountain and rock climbers, hunters, and surfers. All these groups have different environmental priorities that will be debated in future federal land policies.

See also Endangered Species; Logging; Mining of Natural Resources; National Parks and Concessions; Stock Grazing and the Environment; Wild Animal Reintroduction

Further Reading

Babbitt, Bruce, *Cities in the Wilderness: A New Vision of Land Use in America.* Washington, DC: Island Press, 2005.

Behan, Richard W., *Plundered Promise: Capitalism, Politics, and the Fate of the Federal Lands.* Washington, DC: Island Press, 2001.

Davis, Charles, ed., *Western Public Lands and Environmental Politics.* Boulder, CO: Westview Press, 2001.

Fretwell, Holly Lipke, *Who Is Minding the Federal Estate? Political Management of America's Public Lands.* Lanham, MD: Lexington Books, 2009.

Nelson, Robert H., *Public Lands and Private Rights: The Failure of Scientific Management.* Lanham, MD: Rowman & Littlefield, 1995.

Public Lands Foundation, www.publicland.org

Public Lands Information Center, www.publiclands.org/home.php?SID =/

Turley, Jonathan, "Utah Governor Signs Law Authorizing Use of Eminent Domain Over Federal Lands." *Salt Lake Tribune* (March 29, 2010). http://jonathanturley.org/2010/03/29/utah-governor-signs-law-authorizing-use-of-eminent-domain-over-federal-lands

Wilderness Society, www.wilderness.org

FOOD SAFETY

Nina E. Redman

Experts disagree about whether food is safer today than it was in the past, but they agree that ensuring safe food has become more complex than at any other point in history. Although we have solved many of the food safety challenges of the past, new problems have developed. We farm, live, and eat differently than we did in the past, and this creates new niches for food-borne illnesses to occupy. In addition, there are other potential threats such as food additives, pesticides, hormones in milk and cattle, overuse of antibiotics in farm animals, genetically engineered plants, and risks associated with bioterrorism.

History

As food safety issues have changed, so have society's methods for making food as safe as possible. Before manufacturing, traditional farming practices and preserving techniques were used to ensure safe food. During the industrial revolution, food began to be processed and packaged. Lacking regulation, manufacturers were free to add whatever they liked to their products. Sweepings from the floor were included in pepper, lead salts were added to candy and cheese, textile inks were used as coloring agents, brick dust was added to cocoa, and copper salts were added to peas and pickles (Borzelleca 1997, 44). In the 1880s, women started organizing groups to protest the conditions at slaughterhouses in New York City and adulterated foods in other parts of the country. In 1883, Harvey W. Wiley, chief chemist of the U.S. Agricultural Department's Bureau of Chemistry, began experimenting with food and drug adulteration. He started a "poison squad," which consisted of human volunteers who took small doses of the poisons used in food preservatives of the time. Wiley worked hard to get legislation passed to regulate what could go into food. Meanwhile, Upton Sinclair spent several weeks in a meat packing plant investigating labor conditions and turned his discoveries into a book, *The Jungle,* published in 1906. Although the focus of that book was the conditions immigrants experienced in the early 20th century, there were graphic descriptions of the filth and poor hygiene in packing plants. These descriptions of packing plants—not the poor working conditions of immigrants—caught the public's attention. People began complaining to Congress and to President Theodore Roosevelt. Pressure was also mounting from foreign governments that wanted some assurances that food imported from the United States was pure and wholesome. Two acts were passed in 1906, the Pure Food and Drug Act and the Beef Inspection Act, to improve food safety conditions.

Regulation came only in response to problems: outbreaks and health hazards were followed by new laws. In 1927, the U.S. Food, Drug, and Insecticide Administration (the name was shortened to the Food and Drug Administration, or FDA, in 1930) was created to enforce the Pure Food and Drug Act. However, in 1937, over 100 people died after ingesting a contaminated elixir. The act proved to have penalties that were too light, and the laws were superseded in 1938 by the Pure Food, Drug, and Cosmetics Act. This act prohibited any food or drug that is dangerous to health to be sold in interstate commerce. The Public Health Service Act of 1944 gave the FDA authority over vaccines and serums and allowed the FDA to inspect restaurants and travel facilities. In 1958, concern over cancer led to the adoption of the Delaney Amendments, which expanded the FDA's regulatory powers to set limits on pesticides and additives. Manufacturers had to prove that additives and pesticides were safe before they could be used. The Fair Packaging and Labeling Act of 1966 standardized the labels of products and required that labels provide honest information. The next major act was the Food Quality Protection Act of 1996. It set new regulations requiring implementation of Hazard Analysis and Critical Control Points (HACCPs) for most food processors. (HACCP is a process where a manufacturing or processing system is analyzed for potential contamination, and systems are put in place to monitor and control contamination at crucial steps in the manufacturing process.) The Food Quality Protection Act also changed the way acceptable pesticide levels are calculated. Now total exposure from all sources must be calculated.

U.S. Department of Agriculture

Growing in parallel to the FDA was the U.S. Department of Agriculture (USDA). The USDA is responsible for the safety of most animal products. In the 1890s, some European governments raised questions about the safety of U.S. beef. Congress assigned the USDA the task of ensuring that U.S. beef met European standards. In 1891, the USDA started conducting antemortem and postmortem inspections of livestock slaughtered in the United States and intended for U.S. distribution. The USDA began using veterinarians to oversee the inspection process, with the goal of preventing diseased animals from entering the food supply.

During World War II, more women entered the workforce and consumption of fast food increased. Ready-to-eat foods like processed hams, sausages, soups, hot dogs, frozen dinners, and pizza increased dramatically. The 1950s saw large growth in meat and poultry processing facilities. New ingredients, new technology, and specialization increased the complexity of the slaughter and processing industry. Slaughterhouses went from being small facilities to large plants that used high-speed processing techniques to handle thousands of animals per day. As a result, food technology and microbiology became increasingly important tools to monitor safety. The Food Safety and Inspection Service, the inspection arm of the USDA, grew to more than 7,000 inspectors. But because of the growth in the number of animals slaughtered and processed, it became impossible to individually inspect each carcass. Without individual inspection, governments and processors must rely on risk-assessment techniques and HACCP to manage these risks. Inspectors must now focus on the production line for compliance, and processing techniques must be strong to compensate for the lack of individual inspection (Schumann et al. 1997, 118).

Risk Assessment

There are several types of food risks. Eating too much of certain types of foods, such as fats, can be harmful. Eating spoiled or contaminated food can be very dangerous, even deadly. Pesticides and food additives can also pose risks. Risk assessment is the process of evaluating the risks posed and determining whether a food ingredient or pesticide can safely be consumed in the amounts likely to be present in a given food.

In order to compute risks, scientists must consider both the probability and the impact of contracting the disease. A disease with high probability but little impact is of less concern than a disease with high probability and high impact. The object is to either reduce the probability of contracting the disease or the severity of impact. Either action will reduce risk. To evaluate risks, a four-step process is used: hazard identification, exposure assessment, dose-response assessment, and risk characterization.

During the first step, hazard identification, an association between a disease and the presence of a pathogen in a food is documented. For example, contracting dysentery is associated with eating chickens contaminated with *Campylobacter jejuni*, a type of bacteria. Information may be collected about conditions under which the pathogen survives, grows, causes infection, and dies. Data from epidemiologic studies is used along with surveillance data, challenge testing, and studies of the pathogen.

After the hazard is identified, exposure is assessed. This step examines the ways in which the pathogen is introduced, distributed, and challenged during production, distribution, and consumption of food. Exposure assessment takes the hazard from general identification to all the specific process-related exposures. For example, chickens might become exposed to *C. jejuni* by drinking unchlorinated water or from other chickens on the farm; the carcass might be exposed during defeathering or on the processing line; the number of pathogens may be reduced in number during the chilling step and increase in number during the packaging step. By examining potential exposure points, the pathogen population can be traced and the likelihood of it reaching the consumer can be estimated.

The third step, dose-response assessment, determines what health result is likely to occur when the consumer is exposed to the pathogen population determined in the exposure assessment step. This step can be very difficult because there may not be good data about what levels of pathogen exposure have health consequences. Another significant factor is the strength of the immune system of the particular consumer. Immune-compromised populations—such as young children, the elderly, AIDS patients, and chemotherapy patients—may react to lower exposure levels and have more severe health consequences.

Risk characterization, the final step, integrates the information from the previous steps to determine the risk to various populations and particular types of consumers. For example, children in general may have a different level of risk exposure than children who consume three or more glasses of apple juice per day. Computer-modeling techniques are often used in this step to ease the computational burden of trying many different scenarios (Lammerding and Paoli 1997). With so many variables, risk assessment does not produce exact, unequivocal results. At best it produces good estimates of the impact of a given pathogen on a population; at worst it over- or underestimates the impact.

Hazard Analysis and Critical Control Points

Hazard analysis and critical control points (HACCP) is a method of improving food safety developed by Pillsbury for the National Aeronautics and Space Administration (NASA) in the late 1950s. HACCP requires determining food safety hazards that are likely to occur and using that knowledge to establish procedures at critical points that will ensure safety. HACCP can be applied at any point in the food cycle from field to fork. The steps, which are modified for each setting, include analyzing the setting for potential problem areas, examining inputs to the system such as suppliers, determining prevention and control measures, taking action when criteria are not met, and establishing and maintaining recordkeeping procedures. Some settings require microbial testing for bacteria.

HACCP is very adaptable to different settings. Rangeland where cattle graze can be managed with HACCP techniques to prevent cattle wastes, which may contain parasites and other potential pathogens, from entering water supplies. The techniques used in this setting include managing stocking rates of cattle to maintain enough vegetative cover, excluding calves from areas directly adjacent to reservoirs, locating water and supplemental feed away from stream channels, maintaining herd health programs, and controlling wild animal populations, such as of deer and feral pigs, that might contaminate the water supply. Regular testing of streams will indicate whether the measures are working, and whether further safeguards need to be undertaken.

Fruit and vegetable producers who grow foods that are often served raw must be especially careful. Their HACCP plans must include worker hygiene plans such as rules for regular handwashing and supplying clean field toilets, adequately composted manure so that pathogens from animal wastes are not spread, testing of incoming water sources, and control of wild animal populations to ensure contaminants are not infecting produce (Jongen 2005).

In a manufacturing plant, HACCP is very compatible with good manufacturing practices (GMPs) that include proper sanitation procedures. HACCP takes GMPs a step further by looking at other potential problem areas. For example, a juice producer following GMPs emphasizes fruit washing, plant cleanliness, and strict adherence to sanitary policies and procedures. To implement HACCP, the plant adds pasteurization to some products, ensures a cold chain by making sure the product always stays cold, and performs microbial testing to make sure the procedures are working.

Jack in the Box restaurants has developed HACCP to a highly refined system since the 1993 *Escherichia coli* outbreak that resulted from tainted meat from one of its suppliers. Now the restaurant chain does extensive microbial testing—testing the ground beef off the production line every 15 minutes. The distribution company has installed time- and temperature-recording boxes that record the temperature in the delivery trucks to ensure that the beef is always stored at the proper temperature (Steinauer 1997).

In retail food service operations such as restaurants, cafeterias, and in-store deli counters, recipes and procedures must be examined to make food as safe as possible. This examination could result in changing a recipe to ensure that foods that are added raw are chopped in a separate place from other items that are chopped before cooking. Suppliers are carefully examined, food is maintained at the proper temperature, and the length of time foods are left out is closely monitored. For example, a policy that unsold chicken nuggets will be thrown out every half hour might be implemented with a timer that beeps on the half hour. Employees might have to initial a log stating that they had disposed of unsold food.

HACCP has been mandatory since the 1970s for the low-acid canned food industry and went into effect for domestic and imported seafood processing in 1997. Meat and poultry processors had to implement HACCP plans in January 2000. Since requiring producers to implement HACCP plans, the USDA's Food Safety and Inspection Service (FSIS) and the FDA have used HACCP as a powerful tool to monitor contaminant levels and require changes to plans in order to reduce hazards. For example, in late 2003, after the FSIS required ready-to-eat-food processors to improve their HACCP plans, the FSIS released data showing that regulatory samples showed a 70 percent decline in the number of samples testing positive for *Listeria monocytogenes*. And in October 2002, the FSIS required all raw beef processing plants to reassess their HACCP plans to reduce the prevalence of *E. coli* O157:H7 bacteria in ground beef. As a result, 62 percent of the plants made major changes to their processing lines. Percentages of regulatory samples testing positive dropped almost two-thirds from 0.86 percent in 2000 to 0.32 percent in 2003 (U.S. Department of Agriculture, Food Safety and Inspection Service 2004).

Epidemiology and Food-borne Illnesses

Most of what is known about food=borne illnesses started with epidemiology, the study of disease in a population. John Snow, a London physician, used deductive reasoning, research, and interviews in the 1880s to determine the cause of a cholera epidemic that had killed more than 500 people in one week. Scientists used Snow's techniques to investigate primarily infectious disease until the 1920s, when the field broadened to include clusters of all factors that apply to the incidence of disease among people.

Epidemiological techniques have improved over the years. In the 1970s, Dr. Paul Blake developed the case-control method. This method compares those who became ill with closely matched individuals who stayed well. By examining what those who became ill did differently from those who stayed well, the source of infection can often be revealed. In the case of food-borne illness, an ill person is questioned about where and what they ate and matched as closely as possible in age, health status, and eating patterns to someone who stayed well in an effort to pinpoint differences.

In the United States, the Centers for Disease Control and Prevention (CDC) works to help treat and prevent disease at the national level, and has increased its scope to lend epidemiological assistance worldwide because of the overlap between the developed and less developed worlds. The people who pick and pack fruits and vegetables in foreign countries that are imported to the United States are handling the U.S. food supply. If foreign workers have illnesses that can be transmitted through food, their illnesses have a direct bearing on our health.

Food-borne illness is most often linked to bacteria, but there are other agents that can cause food-borne illness, including viruses, parasites, prions, and molds. Bacterial illness is the most prevalent, but viruses and parasites are being spread through food more commonly than in the past. Each type of disease agent has different characteristics that must be considered in implementing food safety strategies.

Bacteria and Food

The Centers for Disease Control and Prevention estimate that 79 percent of food-borne illness is caused by bacteria. Bacteria, small microorganisms that do not have a nucleus, can replicate in food, water, or in other environmental media. Some bacteria do not grow well in cold temperatures, while others flourish. Some bacterial strains are extremely virulent, causing infection with as little as two bacteria. Other bacteria must be present in large numbers to cause any problems. The most common way food-borne bacterial illness is transmitted is the fecal–oral route, where fecal matter from an animal or person contaminates foodstuffs. This contamination could result from inadequate handwashing, fecal matter from animals being transferred to meat during the slaughter or processing steps, or even unsterilized manure being used to fertilize crops. Harmful bacteria can also be carried in animals and, even without fecal contamination, can be present in meat or eggs.

One of the most helpful tools scientists have developed to investigate bacterial illnesses is DNA fingerprinting. Each strain of bacteria has a unique genetic fingerprint. By comparing bacteria from ill persons with bacteria from suspected foods, it is possible to definitively conclude whether that particular food is the causative agent of the disease. This tool has helped health departments tremendously to trace the source of infection and limit outbreaks. The following list identifies the major bacterial illnesses.

Campylobacter

Campylobacter is the most common bacterial food contaminant, prevalent in a variety of food animals but most often associated with poultry. Meat becomes contaminated when it comes in contact with fecal matter from an infected animal. In humans, *Campylobacter* can cause bacteremia (bacteria gets into the bloodstream), hepatitis, pancreatitis, septic arthritis (bacteria gets into the joints and causes stiffening), and Guillain-Barré syndrome (GBS).

Listeria

Listeria monocytogenes is a particularly pernicious bacteria found in soil and water that can survive refrigerator temperatures and even freezing. It can be found on some vegetables as well as on meat and dairy products. *Listeria* can cause septicemia, meningitis, encephalitis, and intrauterine or cervical infections in pregnant women that may cause miscarriages or stillbirths. Of the 2,500 cases reported annually in the United States, about 500 die.

Salmonella

Salmonella is the second most common source of food poisoning in the United States after *Campylobacter*. It is most often associated with raw eggs and undercooked poultry, although it also can contaminate vegetables, fruits, and other products. *Salmonella* generally causes sudden headache, diarrhea, nausea, and vomiting. Symptoms may be minor or severe, causing dehydration or even death. The CDC estimates there are 2 to 4 million cases each year resulting in 500 to 1,000 deaths. (U.S. Food and Drug Administration 2005). Some strains of *Salmonella* are becoming resistant to antibiotics.

Escherichia coli

Escherichia coli is a type of bacteria that thrives in our intestines and helps digest food. Most strains are beneficial, but a few release harmful toxins that can cause great discomfort and even death. There are four classes of *E. coli* that cause illness in humans, the most toxic being O157:H7. Scientists believe the toxin first destroys blood vessels in the intestines, causing bloody diarrhea. Most people recover, but about 2 to 7 percent develop hemolytic uremic syndrome (HUS). About 5 percent of those who contract HUS die, and many survivors of the disease are left with lasting problems such as diabetes, kidney damage, visual impairment, or a colostomy (Kluger 1998). *E. coli* O157:H7 is most commonly associated with cattle, transmission usually occurring during the slaughter process when fecal matter from the intestines can contaminate the meat. Heat kills the bacteria, but the cooking of meat must be thorough and must reach an internal temperature of 160 degrees Fahrenheit to be safe.

Shigella

Shigella causes a little less than 10 percent of all food-borne illness in the United States. Shigellosis (the disease caused by *Shigella*) can cause abdominal pain, cramps, diarrhea, fever, and vomiting. It is often found in prepared salads, raw vegetables, milk, other dairy products, and poultry (U.S. Food and Drug Administration 2005).

Yersinia

Yersinia pseudotuberculosis is rare in the United States but can be found in meats, including beef, pork, lamb, oysters, and fish, and also in raw milk. Although most people recover quickly from yersiniosis, about 2 to 3 percent develop reactive arthritis (U.S. Food and Drug Administration 2005).

Staphylococcus

Foods that require lots of handling during preparation and are kept at slightly elevated temperatures after preparation, including prepared egg, tuna, macaroni, potato, and chicken salads, and bakery products like cream-filled pastries, are frequently carriers of *Staphylococcus aureus*. The usual course of the disease is rapid onset of symptoms including nausea, vomiting, and abdominal cramping. Although the number of reported cases is relatively low (usually less than 10,000 per year in the United States), the actual number is probably much higher since many cases go unreported because the duration of the illness is very short, and the symptoms are not that severe (U.S. Food and Drug Administration 2005).

Clostridium perfringens

Clostridium perfringens is an anaerobic bacteria present in the environment and in the intestines of both humans and domestic and feral animals. Since the bacteria are so prevalent, most foods are contaminated with it, especially animal proteins such as meat. However, the small amounts of *C. perfringens* in foods do not cause any problems unless the food is not cooled down quickly enough or stored properly. The CDC estimates that about 10,000 cases occur each year, most of them in institutional settings like hospitals, school cafeterias, prisons, and nursing homes. The illness causes intense abdominal cramps and diarrhea (U.S. Food and Drug Administration 2005).

Parasites, Viruses, and Aflatoxins

Perhaps the best-known parasite in the United States is *Trichinella spiralis,* a small roundworm found in raw pork that causes trichinosis. Early symptoms include diarrhea, vomiting, and nausea. These can be followed by pain, stiffness, swelling of muscles, and swelling in the face. Thiabendazole effectively kills the parasites in the digestive tract, and anti-inflammatory drugs can ease the symptoms (U.S. Food and Drug Administration 2005).

Although *Trichinella* has been well understood for years, it does not cause as much food-borne illness as three other parasites: *Giardia lamblia, Cryptosporidium parvum,* and C*yclospora.* These waterborne parasites can be transferred to food from infected food handlers or from contaminated water used to irrigate or wash fruits or vegetables.

Another source of parasites is raw seafood. The Japanese suffer from high rates of nematode infection resulting from high rates of consumption of raw fish. It occurs less frequently in the United States, where raw fish consumption is moderate. One of the worms, *Eustrongylides* species can be seen with the naked eye and causes septicemia. Other worms are much smaller. Well-trained sushi chefs are good at spotting the large parasites, but other techniques are necessary to protect against the smaller ones.

Blast freezing is one of the techniques that kills parasites. The USDA Retail Food Code requires freezing for all fish that will be consumed raw. The exception is tuna, which rarely contains parasites. Often fish get parasites from eating smaller fish that have the parasites. Fish raised in captivity and fed fish pellets rarely have parasites. High-acid marinades do not affect parasites, so they should not be used as a substitute for cooking or freezing (Parseghian 1997).

Viruses, like parasites, pose great problems for food safety because they are environmentally stable, are resistant to many of the traditional methods used to control bacteria, and have low infectious doses. So virtually any food can serve as a vehicle for transmission. It is not clear just how pervasive food-borne viral illnesses are, partly because viruses are difficult to test for. The most common viral diseases spread by food are hepatitis A and noroviruses.

Over one hundred dogs died early in 2006 from Diamond-brand dog food contaminated by aflatoxins (Aflatoxin Poisoning 2006). Aflatoxins are naturally occurring toxic byproducts from the growth of *Aspergillus flavus* fungi that grow on grains and groundnuts such as corn, wheat, barley, oats, rice, and peanuts. The toxins are a sporadic problem for U.S. farmers.

Mad Cow Disease

Bovine spongiform encephalopathy (BSE) is a disease that strikes cows causing them to develop spongy areas in their brains and suffer neurological damage. It seems likely that the cows get the disease from eating sheep brains contaminated with scrapie, a similar disease found in sheep. (Sheep's brain tissue is rendered into cattle feed.) When BSE was first noticed in the United Kingdom in 1986, some cows were found staggering around in circles, hence the name mad cow disease. By 2006, more than 184,000 cows in 35,000 different herds had been diagnosed with the disease and more than 4 million had been destroyed in an attempt to wipe out the disease (U.S. Department of Health and Human Services 2006). In addition to the toll on cattle, humans began developing a related disease, Creutzfeldt-Jakob disease. Scientists determined that people who had consumed brain or spinal tissue from cows were getting the disease (Easton 2005). Today, both internationally and in the United States, there are safeguards in place to prevent BSE from infecting herds and to keep prions (protein molecules thought to lie at the heart of the disease) from entering the food supply.

Food Additives and Contaminants

Before the U.S. Food and Drug Administration (FDA) approves a new food additive or ingredient, its safety must be demonstrated. Animal feeding studies are performed to determine safety. Large doses are fed to a small number of rats to see whether they develop cancer or other diseases. Olestra and aspartame (marketed as Equal or NutraSweet) have caused the most debate in recent years.

Olestra

Olestra, a fat substitute, was first synthesized at Procter & Gamble in 1968. Chemically, olestra is a table sugar (sucrose) molecule to which as many as eight fatty acid residues are attached. The molecule is so large and fatty that it cannot be broken down by the intestinal enzymes and absorbed by the body. Since it cannot be absorbed by the body, it is used as an indigestible fat substitute in the manufacture of low-calorie foods. Although in the early 1990s researchers discovered that eating even small amounts, such as the quantity in one ounce of potato chips, could cause digestive problems (diarrhea, abdominal cramping, gas, and fecal incontinence), the FDA approved olestra in 1996 for savory snacks such as chips, crackers, and tortilla chips. Because of the adverse effects, however, products had to carry a warning label. Consumer complaints nevertheless began to roll into the FDA; the agency had received almost 20,000 complaints about olestra by 2002, more than all other consumer complaints about other food additives combined (Center for Science in the Public Interest 2006). In 2003 Procter & Gamble lobbied the FDA to remove the warning label for foods containing olestra. The FDA granted the request despite lobbying by consumer groups that wanted the labels to stay.

Aspartame/NutraSweet

Aspartame, sold under the brand NutraSweet, was discovered accidentally by a scientist at Searle in 1965 (Bilger 2006). Today, it is a widely used sweetener that is part of more than 6,000 processed foods including sodas, desserts, candy, and yogurt. There have been some concerns about the safety of aspartame, however. Some people have reported dizziness, hallucinations, and headaches after drinking diet sodas made from aspartame. An independent study confirmed that aspartame can cause headaches in some individuals. Ongoing research suggests that aspartame is probably safe, especially in moderate quantities, like one packet of Equal or one diet soda per day, but individuals who experience headaches or those with the rare disease phenylketonuria (PKU) should avoid it.

Mercury in Fish

Mercury, a toxic metal, makes its way into our oceans from the atmosphere. Mercury is emitted by some natural processes, but it mostly enters the atmosphere from mining and smelting of mineral ores, combustion of fossil fuels, incineration of wastes, and from the use of mercury itself. Mercury is extremely hazardous and causes both neurological and heart problems. The FDA set guidelines for permissible levels of mercury in 1969 (Hawthorne and Roe 2005).

Mercury is a chemical which bioaccumulates, so older fish and fish that live higher on the food chain have higher concentrations of mercury in their systems. In 2004 the EPA and FDA issued a joint warning statement about fish. Children, pregnant women, and women of childbearing age are advised to avoid shark, swordfish, king mackerel, and tilefish because of high levels of mercury and to eat no more than 12 ounces of fish per week total. Further, the agencies recommend that this group of consumers eat only low-mercury fish such as shrimp, canned light tuna, pollock, and catfish. Albacore tuna is higher in mercury and should be avoided by this group.

Many states have issued their own safety warnings to further protect their citizens. Washington State reviewed the FDA's data and concluded that women of childbearing age and children younger than six should not eat fresh or frozen tuna at all, and should limit their canned tuna consumption based on body weight. California requires supermarkets to post warnings in their stores, and Wisconsin and Minnesota recommend at-risk groups limit consumption of halibut, tuna steak, and canned albacore to two meals per month (Hawthorne and Roe 2005).

Salmon

Salmon is the third most popular fish food in the United States behind canned tuna and shrimp. Ninety percent of the salmon consumed is farm raised (Burros 2005b). In 2003, the Environmental Working Group tested farm-raised salmon for PCBs, an industrial pollutant and known carcinogen. These tests revealed that whereas PCB levels in wild salmon averaged 5 parts per billion (ppb), farmed salmon levels averaged 27 ppb. EPA guidelines recommend eating fish with PCB levels that are no higher than 4 to 6 ppb, based on consuming two fish meals per week (Burros 2003a). In follow-up studies, including a large study funded by the Pew Charitable Trust's Environment Program, scientists found large differences in contaminant levels between farmed and wild salmon. The Pew study sampled about 700 salmon from around the world and analyzed them for more than fifty contaminants, including PCBs and two other persistent pesticides, dieldrin and toxaphene. All three of these contaminants have been associated with increased liver and other cancer risk. Using EPA guidelines, the scientists determined how much salmon could be consumed before cancer risks increased to at least 1 in 100,000. For the most contaminated fish, from farms in Scotland and the Faroe Islands, that amounted to 55 grams of uncooked salmon per month, about a quarter of a serving. The cleanest fish are raised in Chile and the state of Washington. One serving can be consumed per month without increasing cancer risk.

Pesticides

There are more than 865 active ingredients registered as pesticides in the United States. These are formulated into thousands of pesticide products. The EPA estimates there are 350 different pesticides that are used on the foods we eat and to protect our homes and pets (U.S. Environmental Protection Agency 2006). Pesticides can be naturally occurring substances such as nicotine, pyrethrum (found in chrysanthemums,) hellebore, rotenone, and camphor, or synthetically produced substances such as inorganic chemicals, metals, metallic salts, organophosphates, carbamates, and halogenated hydrocarbons.

Before a company can market a pesticide in the United States, it must demonstrate to the FDA that it is safe. The FDA determines what concentration levels of a pesticide or its breakdown products are safe. The tolerance levels, the amount allowed to be present on food at harvest, were adjusted by the 1996 Food Quality Protection Act to be based on what levels are safe for children. Some researchers, however, have criticized the methodology used by the EPA and the FDA to determine pesticide safety because it is limited to testing for cancer, reproductive outcomes, mutations, and neurotoxicity. Further, the EPA does not consult the scientific peer-reviewed literature of studies done on pesticides, but relies on the manufacturer's gross feeding studies instead. For example, one meta-study analyzed the results of 63 separate studies that showed that certain pesticides affect the thyroid. (The thyroid controls brain development, intelligence, and behavior.) Yet the EPA has not acted to ban any pesticides due to thyroid effects (Colborn 2006).

Antibiotics

In 1949 Dr. Thomas Jukes, then director of Nutrition and Physiology Research at Lederle Pharmaceutical Company, discovered that animals fed small doses of antibiotics gained weight faster. In the early 1950s farmers began to incorporate antibiotics into livestock feed to both promote growth, and thus cut production costs, and also to treat subclinical diseases—diseases that do not cause obvious symptoms but nevertheless are taxing to the animal. Use of antibiotics remained strong, and according to a 2001 report, approximately 70 percent of the 24.5 million pounds of antibiotics used in the United States are administered to livestock for nontherapeutic purposes (Union of Concerned Scientists 2001). Scientists began to realize that the use of antibiotics in this way was not without consequences, however. In 1969 the Swann committee in England recommended that antibiotics only be used to treat animals when prescribed by a veterinarian. Further, the report stated that penicillin and tetracycline should not be used at subtherapeutic doses for growth promotion. In the early 1970s, most Western European countries banned the two drugs for livestock use, but the United States did not. Since the Swann report, many other research bodies have made similar conclusions about antibiotic use in livestock including the National Research Council Committee on Drug Use in Food Animals, which identified uses of antibiotics in food animals that could enhance development of antimicrobial resistance and its transfer to pathogens that cause human disease (Swartz 2002).

The European Union decided to phase out antimicrobials in food for growth promotion. The final phase went into effect in 2006, and now drugs are no longer allowed. In Denmark, where use of antibiotics in healthy animals was banned years earlier, farmers were able to reduce their use of antibiotics by over 50 percent (some antibiotics are still needed to treat sick animals), and the costs of additional feed were minimal (Wegener 2002). The National Academy of Sciences estimated that eliminating antibiotics in healthy animals would cost consumers from $5 to $10 annually in higher food costs (Keep Antibiotics Working 2006).

In the United States, many groups like the American Medical Association, the American Pediatrics Association, and the American Public Health Association, as well as more than 350 consumer, environmental, and sustainable agriculture groups, do not think the FDA has gone far enough in regulating antibiotics. Two consortium groups, Keep Antibiotics Working and the Alliance for the Prudent Use of Antibiotics, put together a Senate bill in 2007 to ban the use of seven classes of antibiotics for growth promotion that are used to treat humans: penicillins, tetracyclines, macrolides, lincosamides, streptogramins, aminoglycosides, and sulfonamides. It would also restrict any use of a drug that subsequently became important in human medicine. Sick animals, however, could still be treated with the drugs when prescribed by a veterinarian.

Today, four of the nation's top chicken producers, representing 38 percent of the total chicken market, have stopped using antibiotics for growth promotion. Tyson Foods, Gold Kist, Perdue Farms, and Foster Farms also restrict antibiotic use for routine disease prevention. McDonald's Corporation and other large-scale purchasers, such as Bon Appetit Management Company, the fourth-largest food service company in the United

States (the company services colleges and universities as well as corporate food service operations), were part of the impetus to reduce antibiotic use (Weise 2006).

Growth Hormones in Beef Cattle

Since the 1950s, growth hormones have been used to increase meat production. Three naturally occurring hormones—estradiol, progesterone, and testosterone—and their synthetic equivalents—zeranol, melengestrol acetate, and trenbolone—are injected into calves' ears as time-release pellets. This implant under the skin causes the steers to gain an extra two to three pounds per week and saves up to $40 per steer in production costs, because the steers gain more weight with the same amount of feed. Two-thirds of U.S. cattle are treated with hormones, but the European Union banned the practice in 1988 and bans imported beef unless it is certified hormone-free (Raloff 2002).

There is wide disagreement about whether the practice is safe. Hormone-like chemicals (DDT, PCB, dioxin, etc.) in large enough concentrations or at critical points in fetal development disrupt functioning of the natural hormones in both animal and human bodies. The U.S. government has been studying the endocrine disruptive effects of certain estrogenic (estrogen-producing) pesticides and food contaminants known as xeno-estrogens (substances that behave like estrogens), but has only begun to study the effects of hormones in meat and its impact for food safety and the environment. There has been escalating incidence of reproductive cancers in the United States since 1950. However, it is difficult to say whether added hormones in beef are linked to additional cancer cases, as some believe, or whether the causes are from something else entirely, such as eating a diet rich in animal protein. The hormones in meat are trace amounts. Nevertheless, the European Commission Scientific Committee for Veterinary Measures Relating to Public Health concluded that adverse effects from hormones include developmental, neurobiological, genotoxic, and carcinogenic effects. They further concluded that existing studies do not point to any clear tolerance level, and thus banned the hormones outright (European Commission Finds 1999). The U.S. beef industry argues that the natural hormone levels in the aging bulls and dairy cows used for beef in Europe can be many times higher than from steers treated with hormones.

Recombinant Bovine Growth Hormone

Similar controversy surrounds recombinant bovine growth hormone (rBGH), also called recombinant bovine somatotropin (rBST), administered to dairy cattle to help them produce more milk. Developed by the Monsanto Corporation and marketed under the name Posilac, it has generated a lot of debate since it was approved by the FDA in 1993. The United States is the only major industrialized nation to approve rBGH. Health Canada, the food and drug regulatory arm of the Canadian government, rejected rBGH in early 1999 and stirred up more controversy in the process. They rejected the drug after careful review of the same data that was submitted to the U.S. Food and Drug

Administration, finding that it did not meet standards for veterinary health and might pose food safety issues for humans.

The hormone is injected into the pituitary gland of dairy cows every two weeks because it can increase milk production by as much as 15 percent. The mechanism by which rBGH works may, however, create dangerous hormones for people consuming the dairy products from treated cows. As a by-product, rBGH causes cows to produce more insulin growth factor 1 (IGF-1). IGF-1 is present in milk at higher levels in cows that take rBGH. IGF-1 causes cells to divide. Elevated levels have been associated with higher rates of breast, colon, and prostate cancer. Studies show that IGF-1 survives the digestion process, and the added levels in milk may cause additional cancers in humans. As part of the Nurses Health Study conducted by Harvard University, researchers analyzing the study data concluded that "the results raise the possibility that milk consumption could influence cancer risk by a mechanism involving IGF-1" (Burros 2005a).

The U.S. Department of Agriculture (USDA) estimates that approximately 22 percent of the dairy cows in the United States are treated with rBGH, but FDA rules do not permit a dairy to declare its milk rBGH free. Only milk labeled organic is assured to have no rBGH. Most milk is pooled so almost all the U.S. milk supply has at least traces of rBGH.

Genetically Engineered Food

The latest method of improving productivity is genetic engineering: the transfer of DNA from organisms of one species into organisms of a different species. These DNA transfers can be used to make crops pest-resistant, unaffected by herbicides, or with enhanced nutritional qualities. For example, Monsanto inserted a bacterium into potatoes that causes the potato to be starchier. These starchier potatoes absorb less fat during frying, creating lower-fat french fries and potato chips. Monsanto is also currently experimenting with soybeans to change the type of oil found in soybeans to the omega-3 fatty acids found in fish, but without the fish taste, giving consumers the possibility of getting the health benefits of omega-3s without consuming fish. (The American Heart Association recommends consumers eat two servings of fish weekly, yet only 17 percent of the U.S. population eats that much fish) (Melcer 2006).

So far scientific studies have not shown major problems with genetically engineered foods, but there may be long-term, unforeseen consequences when the environment is changed. In many other areas, changes in the ways food is grown and processed have created niches for harmful bacteria and viruses. Genetic engineering has much to offer in increasing the amount of food available to the world's expanding population, but the process should be carefully reviewed and tested to avoid creating new food risks and environmental catastrophes.

Irradiation

Just as science has brought us new food production techniques, it has also brought new food safety strategies, such as irradiation. Irradiation is the process of subjecting food to electron beams or gamma rays to kill bacteria. The radiation damages the bacteria so that it cannot reproduce. By killing the bacteria, spoilage is also delayed. The amount of radiation is not enough to make the food radioactive, only to kill bacteria. Currently irradiation is used to sterilize medical supplies and cosmetics and a limited number of foods.

Irradiation is the only way to kill *E. coli* O157:H7 besides heat. After the four deaths of children from *E. coli* O157:H7 that were traced to Jack in the Box restaurants in 1993, enthusiasm for irradiation grew and the USDA approved irradiation of beef in 1999. Irradiation raises the cost of meat by up to 20 cents per pound (Gersema 2003).

Meat producers have been cautious about introducing irradiated beef because of the added cost and because it can darken meat and change the flavor enough to be noticeable. High-fat foods can develop a rancid smell. Irradiated food must be marked with the Radura symbol or it must say irradiated on the food label. The marketing departments of the grocery and meat trade organizations have found that considerable education of consumers is needed before they will accept irradiated food. The FDA expanded the definition of pasteurization in 2004 to be "any process, treatment, or combination thereof that is applied to food to reduce the most resistant microorganism(s) of public health significance to a level that is not likely to present a public health risk under normal conditions of distribution and storage" (Sugarman 2004). This new definition allows irradiated food to be labeled "pasteurized" as well as food sterilized by a host of new and old technologies such as pulsed electric fields, ohmic heating, high-pressure processing, and regular cooking processes. However, the word irradiation would still have to appear, as in "pasteurized with irradiation." Market demand will have to be seen in order for investment to be made in the large-scale facilities that would be needed to process large quantities of food.

Besides increased cost and potential reduction of food taste, there are several drawbacks to irradiation. When the food is bombarded with radiation, some of the electrons are freed and attach to other atoms forming new compounds, some of which are harmful, like benzene and formaldehyde. There is also significant vitamin loss from irradiation. Vitamins A, B1, B3, B6, B12, C, E, and K and folic acid are affected. In some foods, as little as 10 percent of the vitamins are destroyed, but in others it can be as high as 50 percent. If irradiated foods become a major part of people's diets, overall nutritional quality will suffer. And while irradiation kills most bacteria, it does not affect viruses, and any bacteria that get onto food after treatment suddenly have a food supply without any competitors. This creates the potential for very toxic food (Fox 1998).

Bioterrorism

Since the terrorist attacks of September 11, 2001, all sectors of the United States have considered vulnerability to terrorism, and the food industry is no exception. Food and the agricultural industry do provide a potential avenue for terrorist attacks, although no one knows how likely such an event is to occur. Some researchers think it would be unlikely to occur, but others think there is potential for bioterror depending on the objectives terrorists were trying to achieve.

Agricultural and food-chain assaults do not have the immediacy and impact of human-directed atrocities such as bombings. The impacts are delayed, and may lack a single focus-point for media attention. The hostility and panic surrounding the September 11 attacks were derived in part by the drama of the suicide bombings, whereas agricultural terror and food tampering are slower to get going but can still be quite devastating.

Controlling access, using tamper-resistant or tamper-evident systems such as tape or wax seals, and keeping records so that tracing and recall of animal feeds can occur all enhance food security at the product level. The FDA created industry recordkeeping requirements in 2004 so that in the event of an outbreak officials will be able to track the source of the food (Alonso-Zaldivar 2004).

See also **Genetically Modified Organisms; Industrial Feeding Operations for Animals; Obesity; Persistent Organic Pollutants; Pesticides; Supply Chain Security and Terrorism (vol. 1); Nutrition in Schools (vol. 3)**

Further Reading

"Aflatoxin Poisoning Claims at Least 100 Dogs," Cornell Reports 37, no. 1 (2006):.

Alonso-Zaldivar, Ricardo, "The Nation, Food Supply Is Secure from Bioterrorism, FDA Says; New Rules Require Firms to Keep Records So That Contamination May Be Traced Back to Its Source." *Los Angeles Times* (December 7, 2004): A17.

Bilger, Burkhard, "The Search for Sweet." *New Yorker* (May 22, 2006): 40–46.

Borzelleca, Joseph, "Food-Borne Health Risks: Food Additives, Pesticides, and Microbes." In *Nutrition Policy in Public Health,* ed. Felix Bronner. New York: Springer, 1997.

Burros, Marion, "A Hormone for Cows." *New York Times* (November 9, 2005a): F10.

Burros, Marion, "Stores Say Wild Salmon, but Tests Say Farm Bred." *New York Times* (April 10, 2005b): A1.

Center for Science in the Public Interest, "The Facts about Olestra." 2006. http://www.cspinet.org/olestra

Chalk, Peter, *Hitting America's Soft Underbelly: The Potential Threat of Deliberate Biological Attacks Against the U.S. Agricultural and Food Industry.* Santa Monica, CA: Rand Corporation, 2004.

Colborn, Theo, "A Case for Revisiting the Safety of Pesticides: A Closer Look at Neurodevelopment." *Environmental Health Perspectives* 1 (2006): 10–17.

Easton, Pam, "Man Who Lived Here Has Human Form of Mad Cow: Official Says It's Not a Safety Issue for Texas." *Houston Chronicle* (November 22, 2005): B7.

Edelstein, Sari, *Food and Nutrition at Risk in America: Food Insecurity, Biotechnology, Food Safety, and Bioterrorism.* Sudbury, MA: Jones & Bartlett, 2009.

Entis, Phyllis, *Food Safety: Old Habits and New Perspectives.* Washington, DC: ASM Press, 2007.

European Commission Finds Growth Hormones in Meat Pose Risk, *Journal of Environmental Health* 4 (1999): 34.

FDA Announces Final Decision About Veterinary Medicine, *FDA News* (July 28, 2005). http://www.fda.gov/bbs/topics/news/2005/new01212.html

Fortin, Neal D., *Food Regulation: Law, Science, Policy, and Practice.* New York: Wiley, 2009.

Fox, Nicols, *Spoiled: The Dangerous Truth About a Food Chain Gone Haywire.* New York: Basic Books, 1997.

Gersema, Emily, "School Lunches to Add Irradiated Beef." *Chicago Sun-Times* (May 30, 2003): A8.

Hawthorne, Michael, and Sam Roe, "U.S. Safety Net in Tatters; Seafood Shoppers Are at Risk for Mercury Exposure as Regulators Ignore Their Own Experts, Issue Flawed Warnings, and Set Policies Aiding Industry." *Chicago Tribune* (December 12, 2005): A1.

Jay, James M., Martin J. Loessner, and David A. Golden, *Modern Food Microbiology,* 7th ed. New York: Springer, 2005.

Jongen, Wim, ed., *Improving the Safety of Fresh Fruit and Vegetables.* Boca Raton, FL: CRC Press, 2005.

Keep Antibiotics Working, "Antibiotic Resistance—An Emerging Public Health Crisis." 2006. http://www.keepantibioticsworking.com

Kluger, Jeffrey, "Anatomy of an Outbreak." *Time* (August 3, 1998): 56–62.

Lammerding, Anna M., and Greg M. Paoli, "Quantitative Risk Assessment: An Emerging Tool for Emerging Food-borne Pathogens." *Emerging Infectious Disease* 3 (1997): 483–487.

Melcer, Rachel. "Scientists Work to Fatten Up Soybeans." *St. Louis Post-Dispatch* (April 12, 2006): C1.

Nestle, Marion, *Safe Food: Bacteria, Biotechnology, and Bioterrorism.* Berkeley: University of California Press, 2003.

Parseghian, Pam, "Cook Up Safety Precautions When Serving Raw Fish." *Nation's Restaurant News* 31 (1997): 33.

Pennington, T. Hugh, *When Food Kills: BSE, E. Coli, and Disaster Science.* New York: Oxford University Press, 2003.

Pray, Leslie, et al., *Managing Food Safety Practices from Farm to Table.* Washington, DC: National Academies Press, 2009.

Raloff, Janet, "Hormones: Here's the Beef." *Science News* (January 5, 2002): 10–12.

Rasco, Barbara, and Glyn E. Bledsoe, *Bioterrorism and Food Safety.* Boca Raton, FL: CRC Press, 2005.

Redman, Nina E., *Food Safety: A Reference Handbook.* Santa Barbara, CA: ABC-CLIO, 2007.

Schumann, Michael S., et al., *Food Safety Law.* New York: Van Nostrand Reinhold, 1997.

Steinauer, Joan, "Natural Born Killers." *Incentive* 171 (1997): 24–29.

Sugarman, Carol, "Pasteurization Redefined by USDA Committee." *Food Chemical News* 30 (2004): 21–22.

Swartz, Morton, "Human Diseases Caused by Food-borne Pathogens of Animal Origin." *Clinical Infectious Diseases* Suppl. 3 (2002): 111–122.

Union of Concerned Scientists, 'Estimates of Antimicrobial Abuse in Livestock." 2001. http://www.ucsusa.org/food_and_environment/antibiotics_and_food/hogging-it-estimates-of-antimicrobial-abuse-in-livestock.html

U.S. Department of Agriculture, Food Safety and Inspection Service. "Fulfilling the Vision: Updates and Initiatives in Protecting Public Health." 2004. http://www.fsis.usda.gov/About_FSIS/Fulfilling_the_Vision/index.asp

U.S. Environmental Protection Agency, "Pesticides: Topical and Chemical Fact Sheets: Assessing Health Risks from Pesticides." 2006. http://www.epa.gov/opp00001/factsheets/riskassess.htm

U.S. Food and Drug Administration, *Food-borne Pathogenic Microorganisms and Natural Toxins Handbook.* 2005. http://vm.cfsan.fda.gov/~mow/intro.html

Waltner-Toews, David, *Food, Sex and Salmonella: The Risks of Environmental Intimacy.* Toronto: NC Press, 1992.

Wegener, Henrik, "Veterinary Issues Contributing to Antimicrobial Resistance." In *Proceedings of the Tenth International Conference of Drug Regulatory Authorities,* 24–27. Geneva: World Health Organization, 2002.

Weise, Elizabeth, " 'Natural' Chickens Take Flight." *USA Today* (January 24, 2006): D5.

FOSSIL FUELS

Hugh Peach

In the understanding of the material world provided by physics, *energy* is defined as the ability to do work. Work in this sense means the displacement of an object ("mass") in the direction of a force applied to the object. In everyday life, we use the word *energy* more generally to indicate vitality, vigor, or power. Here, we focus on another definition of energy: a source of usable power. Our homes, our industries, and our commercial establishments from the supermarket to the stock exchange can work because they are provided with sources of usable power. The same is true for hospitals and medical services, schools, fire and police services, and recreational centers. Without usable energy, TVs, the Internet, computers, radios, automobiles and trucks, construction equipment, and schools would not work. To put it transparently and simply, energy is important because doing anything requires energy.

Alternative Fuels

There are many sources of usable power on our planet, including natural gas, oil, coal, nuclear energy, manure, biomass, solar power, wind energy, tidal energy, and hydropower. These energy sources are classed as renewable or nonrenewable. For renewable energy (for example, wind, biomass, manure, and solar power), it is possible to refresh energy supplies within a time interval that is useful to our species. If well planned and

PEAK OIL

In 1956, Shell geologist Dr. Marion King Hubbert accurately predicted that U.S. domestic oil production would peak in 1970. According to his estimates, global production would peak around the year 2000. His calculations have proved accurate.

Everything from microchips to gasoline to highway building consumes energy. Images from the National Aeronautic and Space Administration (NASA) suggest that modern cities cannot exist without unfathomably high consumption of fossil fuels, such as electricity derived from burning coal. Whether they can survive by drawing on solar energy remains to be seen. Scientists and engineers have convinced government leaders to subsidize home installation of solar heating equipment, which could store energy and run a kitchen blender or microwave at night, for example. In some areas, the government formerly paid up to 70 percent of the cost to make this shift. It is an economic policy decision for sustaining life as we know it today.

Some contend that civilization as we know it is coming to an end because of this shift. They have likened it to the ramifications similar to dehydration of the human body. Our bodies are 70 percent water. The body of a 170-pound person is thus 119 pounds of water. A person need not lose 119 pounds of water weight to be dehydrated: just 10 or 15 pounds of such weight loss might be enough to kill the person.

So it is with oil and large urban centers such as New York City, Chicago, Los Angeles, and Houston, for example. And so it is with virtual communities. The Internet consumes tremendous amounts of energy. As a product, it was developed during an era of ultracheap energy. The hardware of the Internet alone, coupled with its worldwide connections, vast server farms, and billions of interlinked computers, consumes around 10 percent of all the electricity produced in the United States. Most of the electricity used to power the Internet is produced from coal or natural gas. Both are near their global production peaks.

In 1977, the Central Intelligence Agency (CIA) prepared a now-declassified report about Hubbert's peak oil notion. Government officials perceived a decline in oil supplies a threat to national security, and they still do. The 1977 report documented government awareness of the potential for the availability of fossil fuels to decline in the near future and permanently. In 1982, the State Department released a report estimating that petroleum production in the United States would peak between 1990 and 2010 at between 80 and 105 million barrels per day.

The catastrophic BP–Deepwater Horizon oil gush in the Gulf of Mexico beginning in the spring of 2010 and the company's inability to cap the offshore well bring nearer, arguably, the last days of life as we have known it in the United States for more than a century. In the long term, the spill may have an economic impact well beyond any immediate environmental effects.

—Debra Ann Schwartz

carefully managed on an ongoing basis, the stock of energy supplied is continuously renewed and is never exhausted. The fossil fuels are forms of nonrenewable energy. For each, the planet has a current supply stock that we draw down. These nonrenewable supplies of fossil fuels are not replaceable within either individual or collective human time horizons. It is not that the planet cannot renew fossil fuels in geologic time—that is, over millions of years—but for all practical purposes, given human life span and our limited abilities, renewal is far beyond our technical and scientific capabilities.

For almost all of human history, our species used very little energy, almost all of it renewable, usually in the form of wood fires for heating and cooking. If we had continued in that fashion, the human population might easily be in the low millions and would be approximately in a steady state in relation to the environment. As the first animal on this planet to learn how to use fire, we were able to establish successful nomadic tribes, small farm settlements, early cities, and the kinds of kingdoms that were typical of medieval and preindustrial civilizations. The associated rise in human numbers and our spread across the planet was also associated with the early use of coal, for example to make weapons. But it is only with the rise of industrial civilization, and specifically and increasingly in the last 500 years, that we learned how to use concentrated forms of energy in industrial processes and to exploit various nonrenewable forms of energy massively for uses such as central heating, industrial processes, and the generation of electricity.

Industry and Globalization

The rise of our current global civilization was dependent on abundant and inexpensive concentrated energy from fossil fuels. All of this energy ultimately derives from sunlight, but as we learned how to use coal (replacing wood as fuel) and then oil and natural gas, there was little concern for energy conservation or for developing rules for limiting energy use. Up until the middle of the last century, and somewhat beyond, the typical discussion of energy would have linked usable energy with progress, as is the case today. The spirit of the presentation would have been celebratory, however, celebrating the daring risks taken and the hard work of miners and oil and gas field workers in dominating nature to extract resources. In addition, it would have celebrated the competence of the "captains of industry" whose business skills and aggressive actions supplied energy to manufacturing industry, and would have implied that this pattern of resource exploitation could go on forever without taking limits into account. Today that era of celebration belongs to the somewhat quaint past, and we are now much more aware of the cumulative damage to the environment from aggressive exploitation of limited fossil fuel resources. We now know that we face an immediate future of global warming, shortages of usable energy, and rising prices. From a material perspective, the planet is a closed system, and the dwindling stocks of nonrenewable but usable energy are critically important. For each fossil fuel, what is left is all we have.

Impact of Extraction

There is currently no social convention to limit the use of nonrenewable energy to essential production or essential services. Under the rules of the neoliberal market system, resources are provided to those who have the ability to pay for them. This is the kind of human behavior that an unregulated or weakly regulated market system rewards. Because the stocks of fossil fuels took millions of years to create, the ability to extract them is inherently short-run when there is no strong social planning to provide for a human future on other than a very short-range basis. We commit the same error with fossil fuels that we commit with fish stocks—as ocean fish dwindle in numbers, and species after species significantly declines, the main response has been to develop more and more efficient methods and machines to kill and extract the remaining fish. The same is true with fossil fuels. As abundance disappears, and the cost of extraction continues to increase, the primary response has been to find more efficient methods of extraction and to open up previously protected areas for extraction. As a general pattern, Georgescu-Roegen and others have pointed out that resources are exploited sequentially, in order of concentration, the easy sources first. After the easy sources of fossil fuels are exhausted, moderately difficult sources are exploited. Then more difficult sources are exploited. Each more difficult source requires the input of more energy (input) in order to extract the sought-after energy resource (output).

In the material world, the process of the energy extraction from fossil fuels requires more and more input energy. And as extraction proceeds to more difficult sources, it is also associated with more and more impurities mixed in with the energy resources. These impurities are often toxic to our species (and other species). Examples include the acidic sludge generated from coal mines and the problem of sour gas in oil and gas drilling (sour gas contains hydrogen sulfide and carbon dioxide). As more and more input energy is required per unit of output energy, we also need to do more work with more and more impurities and toxic waste. Remember now that from our species standpoint the planet is a closed system with respect to nonrenewable forms of usable energy. In physics, the change in internal energy of a closed system is equal to the heat added to the system minus the work done by the system. In this case, *more energy has to be added* to develop a unit of energy output, and more and more work has to be done. For example, as coal, gas, and oil become harder to reach, increasing gross amounts of waste materials are generated.

Beyond this, all of our processes for extracting energy from fossil fuels are inefficient in that energy is lost in the process of doing work. In physics, the measure of the amount of energy that is unavailable to do work is called entropy. (Entropy is also sometimes referred to as a measure of the disorder of a system.) Georgescu-Roegen and others have developed a subfield of economics based on the priority of material reality over conventional economic beliefs. The fundamental insight grounding this subfield of economics is that the earth is an open system with very small (residual) usable energy input. So, like a closed system, it cannot perform work at a constant rate forever (because stocks of energy sources run down).

So if we look at the extraction of energy from finite stocks (of coal, oil, or natural gas), the extraction process must become more and more difficult per unit of energy extracted, become more and more costly per unit of energy extracted, and generate more and more waste per unit of energy extracted.

This understanding, which follows from physics and the nature of the material reality of the planet, does not fit with the conventional capitalist economic theory that currently governs world trade, including the extraction of energy resources. Market economics, sometimes called the "business system," typically advises arranging life so as not to interfere with the operations of markets. This advice comes from a perspective that regularly disregards the transfer of "externalities," costs that must be suffered by others, including pollution, health problems, damage to woodlands, wildlife, waterways, and so on.

Conventional economic thinking employs economic models that assume undiminished resources. That is why it seems reasonable to advise more efficient means of extraction of resources (e.g., with fish and coal) as stocks of resources diminish. Another feature of conventional economic thinking is that it (literally) discounts the future. Depending on the cost of capital, any monetary value more than about 20 years in the future is discounted to equal approximately nothing. These features of conventional economics mean that the tools of economic calculation operate to coach economic agents, including those who own or manage extractive industries, to act for immediate profit as if the future were limited to the very short term.

This is in contrast to a material or engineering viewpoint, the perspective of community-oriented social science, and the humane spirit of the liberal arts. All of these are concerned not simply with the present but with the future of the human community and with the quality of human life and of human civilization in the future as well as today.

Quality of Life and Community

Outside of the limited focus of conventional economics, most disciplines place a high value on the quality of the human community and sustaining it into the distant future. Practical reasoning in everyday life often puts a higher value on the future—most of us would like things to get better and better. One way to understand this difference is to contrast the interest of today's captains of industry with the perspective of a student finishing secondary school or beginning college, just now. For the captains, everything done today has a certain prospect for short-term profit, and the future is radically discounted (progressively, year by year) so that 20 years out, its value is essentially zero.

For the student, the point in time 20 years out has a very high value because the quality of life, the job prospects, the environment (including global warming), the prospects for having a family, and the opportunities for children 20 years out will be of direct personal relevance. The student might argue that the future is more important than today (and should be taken into account without discounting), as would most families that would like a better future for their children. Today's student has a strong interest in having usable energy resources available and the disasters of global warming avoided or lessened. Conventional market economics does not do this; it takes strong regulation, strong central planning, and an engineer's approach to nonrenewable resources to best use and stretch out resources for the future, rather than a conventional economist's approach.

The growth curve of the planetary economy continues to increase. India and China are undergoing rapid economic growth, and the Western economies continue to follow traditional consumption patterns. Capitalist strategies abound in these economies; companies make money by engineering built-in obsolescence into their products. Not only does this require regularly replacing products with new or upgraded versions; it also leaves openings for replacing obsolete products with entirely new lines of products. The computer industry offers numerous examples of this obsolescence imperative. The demand for products of all kinds is soaring in comparison with past decades or centuries. At the same time the human population has increased dramatically over past centuries. All of this requires more and more energy.

Current industry projections for fossil energy suggest that there may be about 250 more years of coal, 67 years of natural gas, and 40 years of oil. These kinds of industry projections change from year to year and are much more generous than projections made by independent university scientists and conservation groups. Several scientists believe we have passed the time of peak oil. The point here, however, is not the specific numbers (it is easy to find more on the Internet) but that these numbers provide a rough indication of remaining stocks. Also, note that the optimistic industry projections are not for millions or thousands of years into the future. From your own perspective, if you knew coal stocks could last for perhaps another 250 years or oil for another 40 years at the outside, would you want fossil energy carefully rationed for specific uses that cannot be easily met by renewable energy (so that it might last 1,000 or 2,000 years)? This is an alternative to the current system of neoliberal market rules that destroy or weaken the institutions of social planning in many small states. Coal, oil, and natural gas are forced onto world markets (by military force, if market pressures and diplomacy do not suffice) with ever more intense extraction for use by those who can afford it (to use as quickly as they like). Which policy is best for you, your family, your community, your country, and the world?

What makes the number of years of remaining stock estimates tricky is that sometimes new resources are found (though this does not happen much anymore), new technical improvements can sometimes increase extraction, and the more optimistic projections tend to use bad math. That is, sometimes the math and statistics fail to take into account factors such as dwindling supply with more and more difficult access, increased percentage of impurities mixed into remaining stocks, increased waste streams, and the entropy factor. When we interpret these estimates, we need to keep in mind that it is not simply that we will "run out" of coal and oil but that remaining stocks will become more and more expensive to extract.

Conclusion

Energy is important because doing anything requires energy. Any area of human civilization largely cut off from fossil fuels (oil, natural gas, or coal in current quantities) will fail to sustain human carrying capacity. Jobs will be lost, businesses will have to close down, and home energy supplies for heating, cooling, and cooking will become sporadic as energy costs spiral beyond people's means. As a secondary effect, the same thing happens to food supplies that are gradually made too costly for increasing numbers of people.

We are currently watching income in the lower and middle to upper-middle sections of society decrease or not increase. By contrast, income in the upper 1 and 5 percent of households is growing rapidly. We are witnessing, in other words, a resurgence of a class division similar to that of the Middle Ages, with a relative handful of privileged households at the apex (enjoying access to usable energy and food supplies) and a vast surplus population and marginalized population of different degrees below them. We have a choice in planning for a long and well-balanced future for the human community in our use of fossil fuel stocks or continuing with neoliberal economics and conventional market rules (supported by military force), which will allow elites to live well for a while and leave most of the rest of us as surplus.

As important as they are, conservation and renewable energy are insufficient to countervail this future unless we make significant changes in lifestyle and gently reduce the number of humans to a level close to that sustainable by renewable technologies. This will take more mature thinking than is typical of the business system or of conventional market economics. In particular, we need an economics in which beliefs are subordinated to the realities of the physics of the material world.

See also **Automobile Energy Efficiencies; Biodiesel; Coal; Nuclear Energy; Oil Drilling and the Environment; Wind Energy; Oil Economics and Business (vol. 1); Sustainability (vol. 1)**

Further Reading

Ayers, Robert U., and Edward A. Ayers, *Crossing the Energy Divide: Moving from Fossil Fuel Dependence to a Clean-Energy Future.* Upper Saddle River, NJ: Wharton School, 2010.

Beard, T. Randolph, and Gabriel A. Lozada, *Economics, Entropy and the Environment; The Extraordinary Economics of Nicholas Georgesçu-Roegen.* Cheltenham, UK: Edward Elgar, 1999.

Brune, Michael, *Coming Clean: Breaking America's Addiction to Oil and Coal.* San Francisco: Sierra Club Books, 2008.

Coming Global Oil Crisis, "Hubbert Peak of Oil Production." 2009. http://www.hubbertpeak.
com

Jensen, Derrick, and Stephanie McMillan, *As the World Burns; 50 Simple Things You Can Do to Stay
in Denial, a Graphic Novel.* New York: Seven Stories Press, 2007.

McQuaig, Linda, *It's the Crude, Dude: War, Big Oil, and the Fight for the Planet,* rev. ed. Toronto:
Anchor Canada, 2005.

Odum, Howard T., and Elisabeth C. Odum, *A Prosperous Way Down: Principles and Policies.* Boulder: University Press of Colorado, 2001.

Savinar, Matt, *Life After the Oil Crash.* http://www.lifeaftertheoil crash.com

G

GENETIC ENGINEERING

Edward White

Genetic engineering has plunged the world into a stunning technological revolution, one that brings great promise, spurs grave fears, and has unquestionably changed humanity's relationship with the very blueprint of life and physical existence. The problem with being in the midst of a revolution is that one can have little idea where one will end up when the revolution is complete.

So far, genetic engineering and gene-based knowledge have lifted biological science from a relatively crude state of inexactitude, have allowed humans to crack the genetic code, and have given researchers the tools to alter human, animal, and plant life to serve human goals.

Already the products of genetic engineering and genetic science are common throughout the developed world: gene therapies to treat human disease, genetically modified foods for people and animals, and pharmaceuticals for humans produced through genetically engineered bacteria.

The wave of potential products is stunning: organs from pigs transplanted into sick humans, drugs for humans produced in cow's milk, plastics produced by plants rather than with fossil fuels, and gene therapies that could extend human life.

Genes and Genomics

What exactly is genetic engineering? In essence, it involves the manipulation of genes using recombinant DNA techniques to modify what the gene does, either by itself or in combination with other genes. *Recombinant* means combining genes from different sources in a different manner than occurs naturally. Genes are the units formed by combinations of the nucleotides G (guanine), A (adenine), T (thymine), and C (cytosine), which lie in two equally long and twisting strings (the famous "double helix") that are attached to each other throughout their length. G, A, T, and C nucleotides combine in pairs across the space between the two strings.

About three billion pairs form the human genome—the string of genes that make up each individual human's genetic structure. The study of genomes—known as *genomics*—aims to discover how genome-scale technologies might be applied to living organisms, including human beings. Genomics currently enjoys strong support, both financial and institutional, within the scientific and medical communities and within the pharmaceutical industry.

Other biological life forms have different numbers of genes than the human genome. A gene is a stretch of A-T and C-G pairs that, by their complex arrangement, lay out the instructions for a cell to produce a particular protein. Proteins are the basic agents, formed from amino acids, that determine the chemical reactions in the cell. This long and complex genome is also incredibly small. It is contained in every cell in the body as a microscopic molecule. Although all of the genetic code is included in each body cell, each cell performs only a relatively tiny number of highly specialized functions, with only a comparatively few genes being activated in the functioning of a cell's production and use of proteins. Each cell may produce thousands of proteins, each the product of a different gene; but most of the genome's genes will never be employed by each cell. The genome can perhaps be understood as an instruction manual both for the construction of a life form and for its functioning once it has formed. It is like a computer operating system that also contains the information that a tiny piece of silicon could use to build itself into the computer that will use the operating system.

Changing Genetic Function

Because genes determine what cells do within an organism, scientists realized that by altering, adding, or deleting genes they could change the functioning of the larger life form of which the genes are a part. To do so they need to use genetic engineering to alter and switch genes.

What scientists have been able to do with genetic engineering is (1) make it possible to "see" the genes in the DNA sequence, (2) understand the functions of some of those genes, and (3) cut into the DNA and remove or add genes and then reform it all as a single strand. Often the genes that are added come not from members of the same animal, plant, or bacterial species but from entirely different species.

Procedure

How is genetic engineering done? Again, there are very simple and exceedingly complex answers to this question, depending on how much detail one wants about the underlying processes.

The recombinant DNA revolution began in the 1970s, led by three scientists from the United States: Paul Berg, Stan Cohen, and Herb Boyer. They knew that certain bacteria seemed to be able to take up pieces of DNA and add them to their own genome. They discovered that even recombinant DNA created in the lab could be taken up by these bacteria. By 1976 scientists had successfully created a bacterium containing a human protein in and later managed to produce human insulin in bacteria. Bacterially produced human insulin, produced using this bacterium-based process, is now the main form of insulin supplied to people suffering from diabetes.

Genetic engineers have discovered ways to isolate a gene in one species that they think could have a useful function in another, insert that gene (with others that make it "stick" to the rest of the DNA strand) into a cell's nucleus, and then make that cell develop into an entire life form. It is comparatively easy for scientists to introduce genes and comparatively much harder to get the altered cell to develop into a larger life form.

Radical Implications

Many fear the implications of this revolution. Not only is it a radically new science with little proof that its many innovations will be entirely safe but, in addition, no one is in control of it. Like all revolutions of knowledge, once the scientific breakthroughs have been achieved and the information has been widely disseminated, human individuals and societies, with all their virtues and vices, will be free to use the knowledge as they see fit. At present nobody is responsible for saying yea or nay to genetic engineering developments on behalf of the human species. History does not suggest that all human beings are either entirely altruistic or completely competent in embracing the possibilities of radical new technology.

Pros and Cons

With all the promise and potential, a wave of beneficial products appears set to wash over the human species and make human existence better.

Since the beginning of the genetic engineering revolution, however, some people have been profoundly concerned about the implications and possible dangers of the scientific innovations now occurring in rapid succession.

From its beginning, genetic engineering has prompted concerns from researchers, ethicists, and the public. For example, Paul Berg, the genetic engineering pioneer, called for a moratorium on molecular genetic research almost simultaneously with his team's early discoveries, so that people could consider the consequences of these new methods. Since then, scientists have debated the positives and negatives of their new scientific abilities while also overwhelmingly embracing and employing those abilities. Many—but not all—of the scientific worries have been alleviated as scientists have improved their knowledge, but the worries of the public and nonscientists conversely have greatly increased.

Some of the concerns of critics about genetic engineering are practical. Is it safe to move genes around from one individual to another? Is it safe to move genes from one species to another? For example, if organs from a pig were genetically altered so that humans could accept them as transplants, would that make that person susceptible to a pig disease? And if that pig disease struck a human containing a pig organ, could that disease then adapt itself to humans in general and thereby become a dangerous new human disease? The actual nuts and bolts of genetic engineering often include many more strands of genetic material than just the attractive characteristic that scientists want to transfer. Different genetic materials are used to combine and reveal changes in genetic structure. What if these elements bring unexpected harm, or if somehow the combination of disparate elements does something somehow dangerous?

Some fear that ill-intended people, such as terrorists or nasty governments, might use genetic engineering to create diseases or other biological agents to kill or injure humans, plants, or animals. For instance, during the years of apartheid, a South African germ warfare program attempted to find diseases that could kill only black people and attempted to develop a vaccine to sterilize black people. During the Cold War, both NATO and Warsaw Pact nations experimented with biological warfare. The program of the Soviet Union was large and experimented with many diseases, including anthrax and smallpox. In one frightening case, an explosion at a Soviet germ warfare factory caused an outbreak of anthrax in one of its cities, causing many deaths. If scientists become able to go beyond merely experimenting with existing diseases to creating new ones or radically transformed ones, the threat to human safety could be grave. Australian scientists alarmed many people when they developed a form of a disease that was deadly to mice. If that disease, which is part of a family that can infect humans, somehow became infectious to humans, science would have created an accidental plague. What if scientists deliberately decided to create new diseases?

This fear about safety is not limited just to humans intentionally creating dangerous biological agents. What if scientists accidentally, while conducting otherwise laudable work, create something that has unexpectedly dangerous characteristics? What if humans simply are not able to perceive all the physical risks contained in the scientific innovations they are creating?

This concern has already gone from the theoretical to the real in genetic engineering. For instance, British scientists got in trouble while trying to develop a vaccine for hepatitis C after they spliced in elements of the dengue fever genome. Regulators disciplined the scientists for breaching various safe-science regulations after some became concerned that a frightening hybrid virus could arise as a result. The scientists had not intended any harm, and no problem appears to have arisen, but potential harm could have occurred, and any victims might have cared little about whether the damage to them was caused deliberately or by accident. Once a disease is out of the laboratory and floating in an ocean of humanity, it might be too late to undo the damage.

Responding to this concern, some argue for an approach they refer to as the "precautionary principle." This suggests that innovations and developments not be allowed out of the laboratory—or even created in the laboratory—until their safety or potential safety has been exhaustively demonstrated. Critics of genetic engineering often claim that the absence of long-term tests of genetic engineering innovations means that they should not be introduced until these sorts of tests can be conducted. This sounds like a good and prudent approach, but if actually applied across the spectrum, this approach would have prevented many innovations for which many humans now are profoundly grateful. If organ transplantation had been delayed for decades while exhaustive studies were conducted, how many thousands of Americans would not be alive today because they could not receive transplants? If scientists were prevented from producing insulin in a lab and forced to obtain it from human sources, how many diabetics would be short of lifesaving insulin? If scientists develop ways to produce internal organs in pigs that could save the many thousands of people who die each year because they cannot obtain human transplant organs in time, how long will the public wish to prevent that development from being embraced? The precautionary principle may appear to be an obvious and handy way to avoid the dangers of innovations, but it is difficult to balance that caution against the prevention of all the good that those innovations can bring.

Some of the concerns have been political and economic. Regardless of the possible positive uses of genetic engineering innovations, do they confer wealth and power on those who invent, own, or control them?

Many genetic engineering innovations are immediately patented by their inventors, allowing them to control the use of their inventions and charge fees for access to them. If an innovation makes a biological product such as a crop more competitive than non-engineered varieties, will farmers be essentially forced to use the patented variety in order to stay competitive themselves? Will the control of life forms changed by genetic engineering fall almost entirely into the hands of wealthy countries and big companies, leaving poor countries and individuals dependent on them? If a researcher makes an innovation in an area that other researchers are working in and then gets legal control of the innovation, can he prevent other researchers from developing the science further? The latter is a question American university researchers have often debated.

Positive Progress or Dangerous Development

Genetic engineering can be seen as radically new, but to some it is merely a continuation of humanity's age-old path of scientific development. Some see it as an unprecedented break with age-old methods of human science and industry and fundamentally different; others see it as the next logical step in development and therefore not fundamentally radical at all.

One's general outlook on scientific development can also color one's view as to whether these developments seem generally positive or negative. Do you see scientific progress as opening new opportunities and possibilities for humans to improve their situation and the world, or do you see it as opening doors to dangers against which we need to be protected? To some degree these different perspectives determine whether one is alarmed and cautious about this new science or excited and enthusiastic about it.

As humanity lives through this stunning revolution, the number of details known will increase. Few believe we are anywhere near the peak of the wave of innovations and developments that will occur because of the ability of scientists and industries to use genetic engineering to alter life. Indeed, most scientists consider this to be a scientific revolution that is only just beginning.

Selective Breeding

Humanity began its social evolution when it began manipulating its environment. Hunter-gatherer peoples often burned bush to encourage new plant growth that would attract prey animals. At a certain point in most cultures, early hunters learned how to catch and domesticate wild animals so that they would not have to chase them or lure them by crude methods such as this. The ex-hunters would select the best of their captured and minimally domesticated animals and breed them together and eliminate the ones that were not as good. Eventually the animals became very different from those that had not been domesticated.

The earliest crop farmers found plants that provided nutritious seeds and, by saving and planting some of those seeds, created the first intentional crops. By selecting the seeds from the plants that produced the biggest, greatest number, or nutritionally most valuable seeds, those early farmers began manipulating those plant species to produce seeds quite different from the uncontrolled population.

The plants and animals created by selective breeding were the result of a very primitive form of genetic engineering by people who did not know exactly what they were doing (or even what a gene was): the attractive animals and plants with heritable characteristics were genetically different from the ones that did not have those characteristics, so when they were bred together, the genes responsible for the attractive qualities were concentrated and encouraged to become dominant, and the animals and plants without the genes responsible for the attractive characteristics were removed from the breeding population and their unattractive genes discouraged.

Over centuries and thousands of years, this practice has produced some stunningly different species from their natural forebears, as deliberate selection and fortuitous genetic mutations have been embraced in the pursuit of human goals. For example, it is hard to imagine today's domestic cattle at one time being a smart, tough, and self-reliant wild animal species capable of outrunning wolves and saber-tooth tigers, but before early humans captured and transformed them, that is exactly what they were. Consider the differences between cattle and North American elk and bison. Even "domesticated" elk and bison on farms need to be kept behind tall wire mesh fences because they will leap over the petty barbed wire fences that easily restrict docile cattle. But in 100 years, after "difficult" animals are cut out of the farmed bison and elk herds, will these animals still need to be specially fenced?

Wheat, one of the world's most common crops, was just a form of grass until humans began selective breeding. The fat-seeded crop of today looks little like the thin-seeded plants of 7,000 years ago. Under the microscope, it looks different too: although the overall wheat genome is quite similar to that of its wild grass relatives, the selective breeding over thousands of years has concentrated genetic mutations that have made to-day's wheat a plant that produces hundreds of times more nutritional value than the wild varieties. Did the farmers know that they were manipulating genes? Certainly not. Is that what they in fact did? Of course. Although they did not understand *how* they were manipulating the grass genome, they certainly understood *that* they were manipulating the nature of the grass called wheat.

In the past few centuries, selective and complex forms of breeding have become much more complex and more exact sciences. (Look at the stunning yield-increasing results of the commercialization of hybrid corn varieties beginning in the 1930s.) But it was still a scattershot approach, with success in the field occurring because of gigantic numbers of failed attempts in the laboratory and greenhouse. Scientists were able to create the grounds for genetic good fortune to occur, but they could not dictate it. They relied on genetic mutations happening naturally and randomly and then embraced the chance results.

This began to change after the existence and nature of deoxyribonucleic acid (DNA) was revealed by scientists in the 1950s. Once scientists realized that almost all life forms were formed and operated by orders arising from DNA, the implications began to come clear: if elements of DNA could be manipulated, changed, or switched, the form and functions of life forms could be changed for a specific purpose.

Milk, Crops, and Cloning

It took decades to perfect the technology and understanding that allows genes and their functions to be identified, altered, and switched. But by the 1990s, products were roll-ing out of the laboratory and into the marketplaces and homes of the public. In animal agriculture the first big product was bovine somatotropin (BST), a substance that occurs naturally in cattle but is now produced in factories. When it is given to milk-producing cows, the cows produce more milk.

Farmers got their first big taste of genetic engineering in produce when various "Roundup Ready" crops were made available in the mid-1990s. Dolly, a cloned sheep, was revealed to the world in 1997. Generally, cloning is not considered genetic engi-neering because a clone by definition contains the entire unaltered gene structure of an already existing or formerly existing animal or cell. The genes can be taken from a fully developed animal or plant or from immature forms of life. Genetic engineering is generally considered to require a change in or alteration of a genome rather than simply switching the entire genetic code of one individual with another. Although not fitting the classic definition of "genetic engineering," cloning is a form of genetic biotechnology, which is a broader category.

Disney and Shelley

Humanity has had grave concerns about new science for centuries. These concerns can be seen in folk tales, in religious concepts, and in literature. Perhaps the most famous example in literature is the tale of Dr. Victor Frankenstein and the creature he creates. Frankenstein, driven by a compulsion to discover and use the secrets to the creation of life, manages to create a humanoid out of pieces of dead people but then rejects his living creation in horror. Instead of destroying it, however, he flees from its presence and it wanders out into the world. The creature comes to haunt and eventually destroy Frankenstein and those close to him. The story of Frankenstein and his creature can be seen as an example of science irresponsibly employed, leading to devastating consequences.

Another tale is that of the sorcerer's apprentice. In order to make his life easier, the apprentice of a great magician who has temporarily gone away uses magic improperly to create a servant from a broomstick. Unfortunately for the apprentice, he does not have the skill to control the servant once it has been created, and a disaster almost occurs as a result of his rash employment of powerful magic.

Both of these tales—popular for centuries—reveal the long-held uneasiness of those hesitant to embrace new technology.

Finding Balance

On a practical and utilitarian level, many people's concerns focus on a balance of the positives versus the negatives of innovations. They are really a compilation of pluses and minuses, with the complication of the known unknowns and unknown unknowns not allowing anyone to know completely what all the eventual pluses and minuses will be.

Balancing complex matters is not an easy task. Innovations in life forms created by genetic engineering can have a combination of positive and negative outcomes depending on what actually occurs but also depending on who is assessing the results. For instance, if genetically altered salmon grow faster and provide cheaper and more abundant supplies of the fish than unaltered salmon, is that worth the risk that the faster-growing genetically engineered salmon will overwhelm and replace the unaltered fish?

A helpful and amusing attempt at balancing the pluses and minuses of genetic engineering's achievements was detailed in John C. Avise's 2004 book *The Hope, Hype and Reality of Genetic Engineering*. In it he introduces the "Boonmeter," which he attempts to use to place genetic innovations along a scale. On the negative extreme is the "boondoggle," which is an innovation that is either bad or has not worked. Closer to the neutral center but still on the negative side is the "hyperbole" label, which marks innovations that have inspired much talk and potential but little success so far. On the slightly positive side is the "hope" label, which tags innovations that truly seem to have positive future value. On the extreme positive pole is the "boon" label, for innovations that have had apparently great positive effects without many or any negative effects.

Throughout his book Avise rates the genetic engineering claims and innovations achieved by the time of his book's publication date using this meter, admitting that the judgments are his own, that science is evolving and the ratings will change with time, and that it is a crude way of balancing the positives and negatives. It is, however, a humorous and illuminating simplification of the complex process in which many people in society engage when grappling with the issues raised by genetic engineering.

Ethical concerns are very difficult to place along something as simplistic as the boon-meter. How does one judge the ethics of a notion such as the creation of headless human clones that could be used to harvest organs for transplantation into sick humans? Is that headless clone a human being? Does it have rights? Would doctors need the permission of a headless clone to harvest its organs to give to other people? How would a headless

SYNTHETIC BIOLOGY

Synthetic biology is do-it-yourself genetic engineering, the kind a building contractor taking a class at City College of San Francisco, a two-year community college, dreamed up for a science competition. Dirk VandePol thought it would be cool to re-engineer cells from electric eels into an alternative source of energy. Instead, his team agreed to try to build an electric battery powered by bacteria for the International Genetically Engineered Machine Competition. The experiment succeeded.

This success required building the bacterium itself; that is, redesigning a living organism, by a process called synthetic biology. Some view the innovation as the 21st century's steam engine.

It is the science of writing a brand new genetic code—assembling specific genes or portions of genes into a single set of genetic instructions. The genes may be made from scratch or drawn from various organisms found in nature. Genetic engineering is developing in this direction as researchers seek to move away from now-traditional cut-and-paste genome technology.

Scientists discovered that implanting the new code into an organism is likely to make its cells do and produce things that nothing in nature has ever done or produced before. Venture capitalists are cutting checks for this kind of science. New commercial applications blossoming from synthetic biology include a sugar-eating bacterium with cells secreting a chemical compound almost identical to diesel fuel. The company responsible is marketing the product as "renewable petroleum." Another company has tricked yeast into producing an antimalarial drug.

Source: Jon Mooallem, "Do-It-Yourself Genetic Engineering." *New York Times* (February 10, 2010).

clone consent to anything? This sounds like a ridiculous example, but at least one scientist has raised the possibility of creating headless human clones, so it may not be as far-off an issue as some may think. Simpler debates about stem cells from embryos are already getting a lot of attention.

Conclusion

As genetically engineered innovations create more and more crossovers with science, industry, and human life, the debates are likely to intensify in passion and increase in complexity. Some biological ethical issues do appear to deflate over time, however. For example, in the 1980s and 1990s, human reproductive technology was an area of great debate and controversy as new methods were discovered, developed, and perfected. Notions such as artificial insemination and a wide array of fertility treatments—and even surrogate motherhood—were violently divisive less than a generation ago but have found broad acceptance now across much of the world. Although there is still discussion and debate about these topics, much of the passion has evaporated, and many young people of today would not understand the horror with which the first "test tube baby" was greeted by some Americans.

Some of these concerns, such as that regarding in vitro fertilization, appear to have evaporated as people have accepted novel ideas that are not fundamentally offensive to them. Other debates, such as those surrounding sperm and egg banks, remain unresolved, but the heat has gone out of them. Other concerns, such as surrogate motherhood, have been alleviated by regulations or legislation to control or ban certain practices. Whether this will happen in the realm of genetic engineering remains to be seen. Sometimes scientific innovations create a continuing and escalating series of concerns and crises. Other crises and concerns tend to moderate and mellow over time.

Even if genetic science is used only to survey life forms to understand them better—without altering the genetic code at all—does that allow humans to make decisions about life that it is not right for humans to make? Some are concerned about prenatal tests of a fetus's genes that can reveal various likely or possible future diseases or possible physical and mental problems. If the knowledge is used to prevent the birth of individuals with, for example, autism, has society walked into a region of great ethical significance without giving the ethical debate time to reach a conclusion or resolution? A set of ethical issues entirely different from those already debated at length in the abortion debate is raised by purposeful judging of fetuses on the grounds of their genes.

A simple, non–genetic engineering example of this type of issue can be seen in India. Legislators have been concerned about and tried to prevent the use of ultrasound on fetuses to reveal whether they are male or female. This is because some families will abort a female fetus because women have less cultural and economic value in some segments of Indian society. Similar concerns have been expressed in North America. Humans have been concerned about eugenics for a century, with profound differences of opinion over the rights and wrongs of purposely using some measure of "soundness" to decide when to allow a birth and when to abort it. These issues are yet to be resolved, and genetic engineering is likely to keep them alive indefinitely.

One area of concern has less to do with the utilitarian, practical aspects of genetic engineering than with spiritual and religious questions. The problem is summed up in the phrase *playing God:* by altering the basic building blocks of life—genes—and moving genes from one species to another in a way that would likely never happen in nature, are humans taking on a role that humans have no right to take?

Even if some genetic engineering innovations turn out to have no concrete and measurable negative consequences, some people of a religious frame of mind might consider the very act of altering DNA to produce a human good to be immoral, obscene, or blasphemous. These concerns are often raised in a religious context, with discussants referring to religious scriptures as the basis for moral discussion. For example, the biblical book of Genesis has a story of God creating humans in God's image and God creating the other animals and the plants for humanity's use. Does this imply that only God can be the creator and that humans should leave creation in God's hands and not attempt to alter life forms? If so, what about the selective breeding that humans have carried out for thousands of years?

On the other hand, if humans are created in God's image and God is a creator of life, then is not one of the fundamental essences of humanity its ability to make or modify life? Because God rested after six days of creation, however, perhaps the creation story suggests there is also a time to stop creating.

The advent of the age of genetic engineering has stirred up a hornet's nest of concerns about the new technology. Some of these concerns are practical and utilitarian. Some are ethical and some are religious in nature. Regardless of whether one approves of genetic engineering, it is doubtless here to stay. The knowledge has been so widely disseminated that it no government, group of governments, or international organizations is likely to be able to eliminate it or prevent it from being used by someone somewhere. The genie is out of the bottle, and it is probably impossible to force it back in.

If they wish to find acceptable approaches before changes are thrust upon them rather than being forced to deal with ethical crises after they have arisen, scientists, politicians, and the public at large will have to develop their ethical considerations about genetic engineering as quickly and profoundly as these new discoveries surface and expand.

See also **Cloning; Eugenics; Genetically Modified Organisms; Human Genome Project**

Further Reading

Avise, John C., *The Hope, Hype and Reality of Genetic Engineering.* New York: Oxford University Press, 2004.

Genetic Engineering & Biotechnology News, http://www.genengnews.com

LeVine, Harry, *Genetic Engineering: A Reference Handbook,* 2d ed. Santa Barbara, CA: ABC-CLIO, 2006.

McCabe, Linda L., and Edward R. B. McCabe, *DNA: Promise and Peril.* Berkeley: University of California Press, 2008.

McHughen, Alan, *Pandora's Picnic Basket—The Potential and Hazards of Genetically Modified Foods.* New York: Oxford University Press, 2000.

Mooallem, Jon, "Do-it-Yourself Genetic Engineering." *New York Times Magazine* (February 10, 2010). http://www.nytimes.com/2010/02/14/magazine/14Biology-t.html

Sherwin, Byron, *Golems among Us—How a Jewish Legend Can Help Us Navigate the Biotech Century.* Chicago: Ivan R. Dee, 2004.

Steinberg, Mark L., and Sharon D. Cosloy, *The Facts on File Dictionary of Biotechnology and Genetic Engineering.* New York: Checkmark Books, 2001.

Vogt, Donna U., *Food Biotechnology in the United States: Science, Regulation and Issues.* Washington, DC: Congressional Research Service of the Library of Congress, 2001.

GENETICALLY MODIFIED ORGANISMS

JASON A. DELBORNE AND ABBY J. KINCHY

Genetically modified plants, microbes, and animals have been a source of controversy since the development of genetic engineering techniques in the 1970s, intensifying with the growth of the life sciences industry in the 1990s. A wide range of critics, from scientists to religious leaders to antiglobalization activists, have challenged the development of genetically modified organisms (GMOs). Controversies over GMOs have revolved around their environmental impacts, effects on human health, ethical implications, and links to patterns of corporate globalization.

A GMO is a plant, microbe, or animal whose genetic material has been intentionally altered through genetic engineering. Other terms often used in place of "genetically modified" are *transgenic* or *genetically engineered* (GE). Genetic engineering refers to a highly sophisticated set of techniques for directly manipulating an organism's DNA, the genetic information within every cell that allows living things to function, grow, and reproduce. Segments of DNA that are known to produce a certain trait or function are commonly called genes. Genetic engineering techniques enable scientists to move genes from one species to another. This creates genetic combinations that would never have occurred in nature, giving the recipient organism characteristics associated with the newly introduced gene. For example, by moving a gene from a firefly to a tobacco plant, scientists created plants that glow in the dark.

Humans have been intentionally changing the genetic properties of animals and plants for centuries, through standard breeding techniques (selection, cross-breeding, hybridization) and the more recent use of radiation or chemicals to create random mutations, some of which turn out to be useful. In this broad sense, many of the most useful plants, animals, and microbes are "genetically modified."

Techniques

The techniques used to produce GMOs are novel, however. To produce a GMO, scientists first find and isolate the section of DNA in an organism that includes the gene for the desired trait and cut it out of the DNA molecule. Then they move the gene into the DNA of the organism (in the cell's nucleus) that they wish to modify. Today, the most common ways that this is done include the following: using biological vectors such as plasmids (parts of bacteria) and viruses to carry foreign genes into cells; injecting genetic material containing the new gene into the recipient cell with a fine-tipped glass needle; using chemicals or electric current to create pores or holes in the cell membrane to allow entry of the new genes; and the so-called gene gun, which shoots microscopic metal particles coated with genes into a cell.

After the gene is inserted, the cell is grown into an adult organism. Because none of the techniques can control exactly where or how many copies of the inserted gene are incorporated into the organism's DNA, it takes a great deal of experimentation to ensure that the new gene produces the desired trait without disrupting other cellular processes.

Uses

Genetic engineering has been used to produce a wide variety of GMOs. Following are some examples:

- Animals: Genetically modified (GM) animals, especially mice, are used in medical research, particularly for testing new treatments for human disease. Mosquitoes have been genetically engineered in hopes of slowing the spread of malaria. Farm animals, such as goats and chickens, have been engineered to produce useful substances for making medicines. Salmon DNA has been modified to make the fish grow faster. Pet zebra fish have been modified to have a fluorescent glow.
- Microbes: GM microbes (single-celled organisms) are in use in the production of therapeutic medicines and novel GM vaccines. Research is under way to engineer microbes to clean up toxic pollution. GM microbes are being tested for use in the prevention of plant diseases.
- Plants: Scientists have experimented with a wide variety of GM food plants, but only soybeans, corn, and canola are grown in significant quantities. These and a small number of other crops (e.g., papaya, rice, squash) are engineered to prevent plant disease, resist pests, or enable weed control. Some food crops have been engineered to produce pharmaceutical and industrial compounds, often called

"molecular farming" or "pharming." Other, nonfood plants have also been genetically engineered, such as trees, cotton, grass, and alfalfa.

History

The research and development of GMOs and other forms of biotechnology have occurred in both universities and corporations. The earliest technologies and techniques were developed by professors in university laboratories. In 1973 Stanley Cohen (Stanford University) and Herbert Boyer (University of California, San Francisco) developed recombinant DNA (rDNA) technology, which made genetic engineering possible.

Although the line between "basic" and "applied" research has always been fuzzy, GMO research has all but eliminated such distinctions. The first release of a GMO into the environment resulted directly from a discovery by Stephen Lindow, a plant pathologist at the University of California–Berkeley. His "ice-minus bacteria," a GM microorganism that could be sprayed on strawberry fields to resist frost damage, was tested by Advanced Genetic Sciences (a private company) in 1986 amid great controversy. In many cases, university professors have spun off their own companies to market and develop practical uses for their biotechnology inventions. Herbert Boyer, for example, cofounded Genentech (NYSE ticker symbol: DNA) in 1976, a biotechnology company that produced the first approved rDNA drug, human insulin, in 1982. Such entrepreneurial behavior by academics has become common, if not expected, but has also attracted criticism from those who mourn what some have called the "commercialization of the university."

The early 1990s witnessed a growth of "life science" companies—transnational conglomerations of corporations that produced and sold agricultural chemicals, seeds (GM and conventional), drugs, and other genetic technologies related to medicine. Many of

UNIVERSITY–INDUSTRY PARTNERSHIPS

Biotechnology firms have begun to invest heavily in university research programs. Such university–industry partnerships have been quite controversial. In one example, the Novartis Agricultural Discovery Institute (a private corporation) and the Department of Plant and Microbial Biology at University of California–Berkeley formed a research partnership in 1998. Supporters of the agreement praised the ability of a public university to leverage private assets for the public good during a time of decreasing governmental support of research and celebrated the opportunity for university researchers to access proprietary genetic databases. Meanwhile, critics warned of conflicts of interest, loss of autonomy of a public institution, and research trajectories biased in the direction of profit-making. An independent scholarly evaluation of the agreement by Lawrence Busch and colleagues at Michigan State University found that neither the greatest hopes nor the greatest fears were realized but recommended against holding up such partnerships as models for other universities to mimic.

GMOS SLIPPING THROUGH THE REGULATORY CRACKS?

In the United States, three agencies are primarily responsible for regulating genetically modified organisms (GMOs): the U.S. Department of Agriculture (USDA), the Environmental Protection Agency (EPA), and the U.S. Food and Drug Administration (FDA). The USDA evaluates the safety of growing GM plants—for instance, to see if GM crops will become weedy pests. The EPA deals with GMOs when they involve herbicides or pesticides that may have an impact on the environment and also reviews the risks of GM microorganisms. The FDA is responsible for the safety of animals, foods, and drugs created using genetic engineering. Some believe that the U.S. system of regulation of GMOs is not stringent enough. Food safety advocates often criticize the FDA because most GM foods are exempted from the FDA approval process. In certain cases, the U.S. government provides no regulatory oversight for GMOs. For example, the "GloFish," a GM zebra fish, has not been evaluated by any U.S. government agencies, yet it is now commercially available at pet stores across the United States. The USDA, EPA, and Fish and Wildlife Service all said that the GloFish was outside of their jurisdiction. The FDA considered the GloFish but ruled that it was not subject to regulation because it was not meant to be consumed.

these companies began as pharmaceutical companies or as producers of agricultural chemicals, especially pesticides (e.g., Monsanto, Syngenta). Companies combined and consolidated in the hope of taking advantage of economic and technological efficiencies, and they attempted to integrate research, development, and marketing practices. By the late 1990s, however, many life science companies had begun to spin off their agricultural divisions because of concerns about profit margins and the turbulent market for GM crops and food. Today there are a mixture of large transnational firms and smaller boutique firms, the latter often founded by former or current university researchers.

The biotechnology industry is represented by lobby groups including the Biotechnology Industry Organization (BIO) and CropLife International. There are also a variety of organizations that advocate for continued research and deployment of GMOs, such as the AgBioWorld Foundation and the International Service for the Acquisition of Agri-Biotech Applications (ISAAA).

Opposition and Regulation

Opposition to GMOs has emerged from many different sectors of society and has focused on various aspects and consequences of biotechnologies. The following list captures the breadth and some of the diversity of critique, although there are too many advocacy organizations to list here.

- Consumers (Consumers Union, Organic Consumers Association): Both as individuals and as organized groups, some consumers have opposed GM food by boycotting products and by participating in campaigns against politicians, biotechnology companies, and food distributors. Reasons include the lack of labeling of GM foods and ingredients (a consumer choice or right-to-know issue), health concerns (allergies, nutritional changes, unknown toxic effects), and distrust of the regulatory approval process (especially in the European Union).

- Organic farmers (Organic Trade Association, California Certified Organic Farmers): Organic agricultural products demand a premium that stems from special restrictions on how they are grown and processed. Under most organic certification programs (e.g., USDA organic), the presence of transgenic material above certain very low thresholds disqualifies the organic label. Organic farmers have therefore sustained economic losses because of transgenic contamination of their crops. Routes of contamination include pollen drift (from neighboring fields), contaminated seeds, and postharvest mixing during transport, storage, or processing. Some conventional farmers have also opposed GM crops (especially rice) because significant agricultural markets in Asia and the European Union (EU) have refused to purchase grains (organic or conventional) contaminated with transgenic DNA.

- Antiglobalization groups (International Forum on Globalization, Global Exchange, Peoples' Global Action): Efforts to counter corporate globalization have frequently targeted transnational biotechnology companies—GM food became a kind of rallying cry at the infamous World Trade Organization protests in Seattle in 1999. Critics oppose the consolidation of seed companies, the loss of regional and national variety in food production and regulation, and the exploitation of human and natural resources for profit.

- Scientists (Union of Concerned Scientists, Ecological Society of America): Scientists critical of GMOs (more commonly ecologists than molecular biologists) tend to emphasize the uncertainties inherent in developing and deploying biotechnologies. They criticize the government's ability to properly regulate GMOs, highlight research that suggests unwanted health or environmental effects, and caution against unchecked university–industry relations.

- Environmental organizations (Greenpeace, Friends of the Earth): Controversy exists over the realized and potential benefits of GM crops. Critics emphasize the negative impacts, dispute the touted benefits, disparage the regulatory process as too lax and too cozy with industry, and point out that yesterday's pesticide companies are today's ag-biotech companies.

- Religious groups (United Church of Canada, Christian Ecology Link, Eco Kosher Network, Directors of the Realm Buddhist Association): Faith-based criticism of GMOs may stem from beliefs against tinkering with life at the genetic level ("playing God"), concerns about inserting genes from "taboo" foods into other foods, or social justice and environmental principles.

- Sustainable agriculture/food/development organizations (ETC Group, Food First/Institute for Food and Development Policy): These nongovernmental organizations (NGOs) bring together ethical, technological, cultural, political, environmental, and economic critiques of GMOs, often serving as clearing-houses of information and coordinating transnational campaigns.
- Indigenous peoples: Because many indigenous groups have remained stewards of eco-regions with exceptional biodiversity, scientists and biotechnology companies have sought their knowledge and their genetic resources ("bioprospecting"). At times, this has led to charges of exploitation and "biopiracy." In some cases, indigenous peoples have been vocal critics of GMOs that are perceived as "contaminating" sacred or traditional foods, as in a recent controversy over GM maize in Mexico.

Advocates and Regulation

Ever since researchers first began to develop GMOs, governments around the world have had to decide whether and how to regulate them. Controversies around GMOs often refer to arguments about the definition, assessment, and management of risk. Promoters of GMOs tend to favor science-based risk assessments ("sound science"), whereas critics tend to advocate the precautionary principle.

Calls for science-based risk assessments often come from stakeholders who oppose increased regulation and want to see GM technologies developed and marketed. Specifically, they argue that before a technology should be regulated for possible risks, those risks must be demonstrated as scientifically real and quantifiable. Although the definition of "sound science" is itself controversial, proponents state that regulatory agencies such as the EPA and FDA have been too quick to regulate technologies without good evidence—arguing that such government interference not only creates financial disincentives for technological innovation but actually causes social harm by delaying or preventing important technologies from becoming available. Such a perspective views government regulation as a risk in itself.

By contrast, advocates of the precautionary principle stress the existence of scientific uncertainties associated with many modern environmental and health issues. They have proposed a framework for decision making that errs on the side of precaution ("better safe than sorry"). Major components include the following: (1) anticipate harm and prevent it; (2) place the burden of proof on polluters to provide evidence of safety, not on society to prove harm; (3) always examine alternative solutions; and (4) include affected parties in democratic governance of technologies. Critics argue that the precautionary principle is little more than a scientific disguise for antitechnology politics.

In line with a precautionary approach to regulation, some governments (England, for example) have focused on genetic engineering as a process that may pose novel environmental or health risks. Other governments (for example, the United States and Canada) focus instead on the product, the GMO itself. Such countries generally do not single out GMOs for special regulation, beyond what is typical for other products. In addition, some governments have restricted the use of GMOs because of concerns about their social, economic, and ethical implications. Austria, for example, requires GMOs used in agriculture to be "socially sustainable."

Global Arena

International law also reflects controversy over regulating GMOs. The agreements of the World Trade Organization, the international body that develops and monitors ground rules for international trade, initially set out an approach similar to that of the United States. In the year 2000, however, more than 130 countries adopted an international agreement called the Cartagena Protocol on Biosafety, which promotes a precautionary approach to GMOs. This conflict has been a matter of much speculation and will likely feature in trade disputes over GM foods in the future.

Labeling of GM foods represents another contentious regulatory issue. Some governments take the position that if GMOs are found to be "substantially equivalent" to existing foods, they do not need to be labeled. In the United States, for example, food manufacturers may voluntarily label foods as "GMO-free," but there is no requirement to note when foods contain GMOs. The European Union and China, on the other hand, require foods made with GMOs to be labeled as such. In countries where labeling is required, there are typically fierce debates about tolerance levels for trace amounts of GMOs in foods meant to be GMO-free.

Philosophical Debate

One dimension of the public debate about GMOs that is difficult to resolve is the question of whether it is morally, ethically, and culturally appropriate to manipulate the genetic makeup of living things. Some people respond with revulsion to the idea that scientists can move genes across species boundaries, putting fish genes into a strawberry, for instance. For some, this feeling stems from a philosophical belief that plants and animals have intrinsic value that should not be subordinated to human needs and desires. Unease with gene transfer may also be based on religious belief, such as the conviction that the engineering of living things is a form of playing God. But where is the line between divine responsibilities and human stewardship of the Earth? Some religious leaders, such as the Pope, have taken the position that if GMOs can be used to end world hunger and suffering, it is ethical to create them.

Evolutionary biologists point out that boundaries between species are not as rigid, distinct, and unchanging as critics of genetic engineering imply. All living things have some genes in common because of shared common ancestors. Furthermore, the movement of genes across species boundaries without sexual reproduction happens in a process called horizontal gene transfer, which requires no human intervention. Horizontal gene transfer has been found to be common among different species of bacteria and to occur between bacteria and some other organisms.

Regardless of the scientific assessment of the "naturalness" of genetic engineering, it is highly unlikely that all people will come to agreement on whether it is right to create GMOs, and not only for religious reasons. Those with philosophical beliefs informed by deep ecology or commitment to animal rights are unlikely to be persuaded that genetic engineering is ethical. Furthermore, many indigenous peoples around the world understand nature in ways that do not correspond with Western scientific ideas.

Given the diversity and incompatibility of philosophical perspectives, should we bring ethics, morality, and cultural diversity into policy decisions, scientific research, and the regulation of GMOs? If so, how? Some have proposed that labeling GMOs would enable people with religious, cultural or other ethical objections to avoid GMOs. Others see widespread acceptance of GMOs as inevitable and judge philosophical opposition as little more than fear of technology. These issues often become sidelined in risk-centered debates about GMOs but remain at the heart of the controversy about this technology.

Seeking Greater Yields

As the world's population continues to grow, many regions may face food shortages with increasing frequency and severity. A variety of groups, including the Food and Agriculture Organization of the United Nations, anticipate that genetic engineering will aid in reducing world hunger and malnutrition, for instance, by increasing the nutritional content of staple foods and increasing crop yields. Such claims have encountered scientific and political opposition. Critics point out that conventional plant-breeding programs have vastly improved crop yields without resorting to genetic engineering and that GMOs may create novel threats to food security, such as new environmental problems.

Whether or not GMOs will increase agricultural productivity, it is widely recognized that greater yields alone will not end world hunger. Food policy advocacy groups such as Food First point out that poverty and unequal distribution of food, not food shortage, are the root causes of most hunger around the world today. In the United States, where food is abundant and often goes to waste, 38 million people are "food insecure," meaning that they find it financially difficult to put food on the table. Similarly, India is one of the world's largest rice exporters, despite the fact that over one-fifth of its own population chronically goes hungry.

Distribution of GM crops as emergency food aid is also fraught with controversy. Facing famine in 2003, Zambia's government refused shipments of corn that contained GMOs, citing health worries and concerns that the grains, if planted, would contaminate local crop varieties. U.S. government officials blamed anti-GMO activists for scaring

GOLDEN RICE

For over 15 years, Swiss researchers have been developing "golden rice," a type of GM rice that contains increased levels of beta carotene, which is converted by the human body into vitamin A. The aim of the research is to combat vitamin A deficiency (a significant cause of blindness among children in developing countries), yet the project has drawn criticism. Some critics see golden rice as a ploy to gain wider enthusiasm for GMOs rather than a genuine solution to widespread malnutrition. Advocates of sustainable agriculture argue that vitamin A deficiency could be ended if rice monocultures were replaced with diverse farming systems that included production of green leafy vegetables, sweet potatoes, and other sources of beta carotene. Scientists also continue to investigate whether golden rice would provide sufficient levels of beta carotene and whether Asian farmers and consumers would be willing to produce and eat the bright orange rice.

Zambian leaders into blocking much-needed food aid to starving people. A worldwide debate erupted about the right of poor nations to request non-GMO food aid and the possibility that pro-GMO nations such as the United States might use food aid as a political tool.

Patenting Life

Patents are government guarantees that provide an inventor with exclusive rights to use, sell, manufacture, or otherwise profit from an invention for a designated time period, usually around 20 years. In the United States, GMOs and gene sequences are treated as inventions under the patent law. Laws on patenting GMOs vary around the world, however. Many legal issues are hotly debated, both in national courts and in international institutions such as the World Trade Organization and the United Nations Food and Agriculture Organization. Should one be able to patent a living thing, as though it were any other invention? Unlike other technologies, GMOs are alive and are usually able to reproduce. This raises novel questions. For instance, do patents extend to the offspring of a patented GMO?

Agricultural biotechnology companies stress that they need patents as a tool for collecting returns on investments in research and development. Patents ensure that farmers do not use GM seeds (collected from their own harvests) without paying for them. Monsanto Company, for instance, has claimed that its gene patents extend to multiple generations of plants that carry the gene. The biotechnology industry argues that the right to patent and profit from genes and GMOs stimulates innovation in the agricultural and medical fields. Without patents, they say, companies would have little incentive to invest millions of dollars in developing new products.

Complicating the issue, however, is evidence that biotechnology patents increasingly hinder scientific research. University and corporate scientists sometimes find their work hampered by a "patent thicket," when the genes and processes they wish to use have already been patented by multiple other entities. It can be costly and time-consuming to negotiate permissions to use the patented materials, slowing down research or causing it to be abandoned.

Advocacy groups, such as the Council for Responsible Genetics, argue that patents on genes and GMOs make important products more expensive and less accessible. These critics worry that large corporations are gaining too much control over the world's living organisms, especially those that provide food. Some disagree with the idea that societies should depend on private companies to produce needed agricultural and medical innovations. Such research, they say, could be funded exclusively by public monies, be conducted at public institutions, and produce knowledge and technology freely available to anyone.

Furthermore, a wide variety of stakeholders, from religious groups to environmentalists, have reached the conclusion that "patenting life" is ethically and morally unacceptable. Patenting organisms and their DNA treats living beings and their parts as commodities to be exploited for profit. Some say this creates a slippery slope toward ownership and marketing of human bodies and body parts.

Many controversies over GMOs center on their perceived or predicted environmental impacts. Although both benefits and negative impacts have been realized, much of the debate also involves speculation about what might be possible or likely with further research and development.

With respect to GM crops, there are a variety of potential benefits. Crops that have been genetically engineered to produce their own pesticides (plant-incorporated protectants, or PIPs) eliminate human exposures to pesticides through hand or aerial spray treatments and may reduce the use of more environmentally harmful pesticides. Crops that have been genetically engineered with tolerance to a certain herbicide allow farmers to reduce soil tillage, a major cause of topsoil loss, because they can control weeds more easily throughout the crop's life cycle. If GMOs increase agricultural yields per unit of land area, less forested land will need to be converted to feed a growing population. Finally, some believe that GMOs represent a new source of biodiversity (albeit human-made).

The potential environmental harms of GM crops are also varied. PIPs may actually increase overall pesticide usage as target insect populations develop resistance. PIPs and herbicide-tolerant crops may create non-target effects (harm to other plants, insects, animals, and microorganisms in the agricultural environment). GM crops may crossbreed with weedy natural relatives, conferring their genetic superiority to a new population of "superweeds." GMOs may reproduce prolifically and crowd out other organisms—causing ecological damage or reducing biodiversity. Finally, because GMOs have tended to be developed for and marketed to users that follow industrial approaches to agriculture, the negative environmental impacts of monocultures and factory farming are reproduced.

MONARCH BUTTERFLIES

Protesters dressed in butterfly costumes have become a regular sight at anti-GMO demonstrations. What is the story behind this ever-present symbol of anti-GMO activism? In 1999 John Losey and colleagues from Cornell University published a study suggesting that pollen from GM corn could be lethal to monarch butterflies. The corn in question had been genetically modified to express an insecticidal protein throughout the plant's tissues, including the pollen grains. The genetic material for this modification came from bacteria that are otherwise used to create a "natural" insecticide approved for use on organic farms. The GM corn thus represented both an attempt to extend a so-called organic method of crop protection to conventional agriculture (an environmental benefit) and a potential new threat to a beloved insect already threatened by human activities. Controversy erupted over the significance and validity of the Losey study, and the monarch butterfly remains symbolic of the controversy over the environmental pros and cons of GMOs.

With regard to GM microorganisms, proponents point to the potential for GMOs to safely metabolize toxic pollution. Critics emphasize the possibility of creating "living pollution," microorganisms that reproduce uncontrollably in the environment and wreak ecological havoc.

GM animals also offer a mix of potential environmental harms and benefits. For example, GM salmon, which grow faster, could ease the pressure on wild salmon populations. On the other hand, if GM salmon escape captivity and breed in the wild, they could crowd out the diversity of salmon species that now exist.

No long-term scientific studies have been conducted to measure the health impacts of ingesting GMOs. As a result, there is an absence of evidence, which some proponents use as proof of GMOs' safety. Critics counter that "absence of evidence" cannot serve as "evidence of absence" and accuse biotechnology corporations and governments of conducting an uncontrolled experiment by allowing GMOs into the human diet. Several specific themes dominate the discussion:

- Substantial equivalence. If GMOs are "substantially equivalent" to their natural relatives, GMOs are no more or less safe to eat than conventional foods. Measuring substantial equivalence is itself controversial: Is measuring key nutrients sufficient? Do animal-feeding studies count? Must every transgenic "event" be tested, or just types of GMOs?
- Allergies. Because most human allergies occur in response to proteins, and GMOs introduce novel proteins to the human diet (new sequences of DNA and new gene products in the form of proteins), GMOs may cause novel human allergies. On the other hand, some research has sought to genetically

modify foods in order to remove proteins that cause widespread allergies (e.g., the Brazil nut).

- Horizontal gene transfer. Because microorganisms and bacteria often swap genetic material, the potential exists for bacteria in the human gut to acquire transgenic elements—DNA sequences that they would otherwise never encounter because of their nonfood origin. Debate centers on the significance of such events and whether genetic material remains sufficiently intact in the digestive tract to cause problems.

- Antibiotic resistance. Antibiotic-resistant genes are often included in the genetic material that is added to a target organism. These DNA sequences serve as "markers," aiding in the selection of organisms that have actually taken up the novel genetic material (when an antibiotic is applied, only those cells that have been successfully genetically modified will survive). Some fear that the widespread production of organisms with antibiotic resistance and the potential for transfer of such traits to gut bacteria will foster resistance to antibiotics that are important to human or veterinary medicine.

- Unpredictable results. Because the insertion of genetic material is not precise, genetic engineering may alter the target DNA in unanticipated ways. Existing genes may be amplified or silenced, or novel functioning genes could be created. A controversial study by Stanley Ewen and Arpad Pusztai in 1999 suggested alarming and inexplicable health effects on rats fed GM potatoes, despite the fact that the transgenic trait was chosen for its nontoxic properties. Unfortunately, most data on the health safety of GMOs remains proprietary (privately owned by corporations) and unavailable to the public for review.

- Second-order effects. Even when GMOs are not ingested, they may have health consequences when used to produce food. For example, recombinant bovine growth hormone (rBGH) was approved for use in increasing the milk production of dairy cows. No transgenic material passes into the milk, but rBGH fosters udder inflammation and mastitis in cows. As a result, milk from cows treated with rBGH includes higher-than-average levels of pus and traces of antibiotics, both of which may have human health impacts.

Segregating GMOs to Avoid Cross-Breeding

Given that most GMOs retain their biological ability to reproduce with their conventional counterparts, there exist a number of reasons to segregate GMOs (to prevent mixing or interbreeding). First, some consumers prefer to eat food or buy products that are made without GMOs. Second, some farmers wish to avoid patented GM crops, for instance, in order to retain the right to save their own seeds. Third, there may be a need for non-GMO plants and animals in the future—for instance, if GM foods are found to cause long-term health problems and must be phased out. Fourth, it is essential that unauthorized GMOs or agricultural GMOs that produce inedible or medicinal compounds do not mix with or breed with organisms in the food supply.

For all of these reasons, the coexistence of GMOs and non-GMOs is a topic of heated debate around the world. There are a variety of possibilities for ensuring that GMOs and conventional organisms remain segregated. One possibility for the food industry is to use "identity preserved" (IP) production practices, which require farmers, buyers, and processors to take special precautions to keep GM plants segregated from other crops, such as using physical barriers between fields and using segregated transportation systems. Thus far, such efforts have proven unreliable, permitting, in some instances, unapproved transgenic varieties to enter the food supply. The biotechnology industry has advocated for standards that define acceptable levels of "adventitious presence"—the unintentional comingling of trace amounts of one type of seed, grain, or food product with another. Such standards would acknowledge the need to segregate GMOs from other crops but accept some mixing as unavoidable.

Critics of biotechnology, on the other hand, tend to see the mixing of GMOs with non-GMOs at any level as a kind of contamination or "biopollution," for which the manufacturers should be held legally liable. Because cross-pollination between crops and accidental mixture of seeds are difficult to eliminate entirely, critics sometimes argue that GMOs should simply be prohibited. For this reason, some communities, regions, and countries have declared themselves "GMO-free zones" in which no GMOs are released into the environment.

One possible technical solution to unwanted breeding between GMOs and their conventional relatives is to devise biological forms of containment. The biotechnology industry has suggested that Genetic Use Restriction Technologies (GURTs), known

GMOs ON THE LOOSE

In August 2006, the U.S. Department of Agriculture (USDA) announced that an unapproved variety of GM rice (Liberty Link Rice 601), manufactured and tested by Bayer CropScience a number of years earlier but never approved for cultivation, had been discovered to be growing throughout the U.S. long-grain rice crop. USDA attempted to reassure the public of the safety of the unapproved variety of rice. But when it was found in food supplies around the world, major importers stopped buying rice from the United States, causing prices for American exports to plummet. Hundreds of U.S. farmers filed a class action lawsuit against Bayer. Although it remains unclear how, exactly, the GM rice got into the seed supply, one possible explanation offered by the company is that it became mixed with "foundation" seeds used to develop seeds that are sold to farmers at a Louisiana State University rice breeding station. Rice breeders there had collaborated on the field trials for the experimental rice. From there, it seems, the rice was reproduced, spreading throughout the food system.

RECENT RESEARCH

In June 2010, a Russian study concerning genetically modified foods indicated long-term sterility as a result. The findings showed that hamsters three generations removed from those eating such foods could not reproduce. Genetically modified foods are in most supermarkets today, even though most Americans say they do not want them. In January 2010, the international *Journal of Biological Sciences* released a study showing the effects that genetically modified foods had on the health of mammals. Researchers analyzing the effects linked agricultural giant Monsanto's GM corn to organ damage in rats.

colloquially as "Terminator Technologies," may aid in controlling the reproduction of GM plants by halting GMO "volunteers" (plants that grow accidentally). GURTs make plants produce seeds that will not grow. Critics have mounted a largely successful worldwide campaign against Terminator Technology, calling attention to its original and central purpose: to force farmers to purchase fresh seeds every year. Other research efforts aim at controlling pollen flow, not seed growth. For instance, a number of EU research programs (Co-Extra, Transcontainer, and SIGMEA) are currently investigating ways to prevent GM canola flowers from opening; to use male-sterile plants to produce GM corn, sunflowers, and tomatoes; and to create transplastomic plants (GM plants whose pollen cannot transmit the transgenic modification).

Conclusion

Should there be more GM crops? Advocates of GMOs argue that currently marketed technologies (primarily herbicide-tolerant and pest-resistant corn, rice, and soy) represent mere prototypes for an expanding array of GMOs in agriculture. Three directions exist, with some progress in each area. First, genetic engineers could focus on incorporating traits that have a more direct benefit to consumers, such as increased nutrition, lower fat content, improved taste or smell, or reduced allergens. Second, existing technologies could be applied to more economically marginal crops, such as horticultural varieties and food crops important in the global south. Third, traits could be developed that would drastically reduce existing constraints on agriculture, such as crops with increased salt and drought tolerance or nonlegume crops that fix their own nitrogen. It remains to be seen how resources will be dedicated to these diverse research paths and who will benefit from the results.

Should there be GM animals? With animal cloning technology possible in more and more species, and some signs of acceptance of cloned animals for the production of meat in the United States, conventional breeding of livestock could veer toward genetic engineering. Scientists around the world are experimenting with genetic modification of animals raised for meat, and edible GM salmon are close to commercialization. GM pets may also be in the future, with one GM aquarium fish already commercially available.

Should there be GM "pharming"? Some companies are pursuing the development of GM crops that manufacture substances traditionally produced by industrial processes. Two directions exist. First, if vaccines or medications can be genetically engineered into food crops, the cost and ease of delivery of such pharmaceuticals could decrease dramatically, especially in the global south (the developing world). Second, crops might be modified to produce industrial products, such as oils and plastics, making them less costly and less dependent on petroleum inputs. A California-based company, Ventria Biosciences, already has pharmaceutical rice in production in the United States. Animals are also being genetically engineered to produce drugs and vaccines in their milk or eggs, raising questions about the ethics of using animals as "drug factories."

Should there be GM humans? Genetic technologies have entered the mainstream in prenatal screening tests for genetic diseases, but the genetic modification of humans remains hypothetical and highly controversial. "Gene therapy" experiments have attempted to genetically modify the DNA of humans in order to correct a genetic deficiency. These experiments have remained inconclusive and have caused unpredicted results, including the death of an otherwise healthy 18-year-old (Jesse Gelsinger). Even more controversial are calls for "designer babies," the genetic modification of sex cells (sperm and eggs) or embryos. Some advocate for such procedures only to correct genetic deficiencies, whereas others see attractive possibilities for increasing intelligence, improving physical performance, lengthening the life span, and choosing aesthetic attributes of one's offspring. Several outspoken scientists even predict (with optimism) that GM humans will become a culturally and reproductively separate species from our current "natural" condition. Critics not only doubt the biological possibility of such developments but also question the social and ethical impacts of embarking on a path toward such a "brave new world."

See also **Biotechnology; Food Safety; Genetic Engineering**

Further Reading

Bailey, Britt, and Marc Lappé, eds., *Engineering the Farm: Ethical and Social Aspects of Agricultural Biotechnology.* Washington, DC: Island Press, 2002.

Charles, Daniel, *Lords of the Harvest: Biotech, Big Money, and the Future of Food.* Cambridge, MA: Perseus, 2001.

Clapp, Jennifer, and Doris Fuchs, eds., *Corporate Power in Global Agrifood Governance.* Cambridge, MA: MIT Press, 2009.

Cook, Guy, *Genetically Modified Language: The Discourse of Arguments for GM Crops and Food.* London: Routledge, 2004.

Kloppenburg, Jack Ralph, Jr., *First the Seed: The Political Economy of Plant Biotechnology 1492–2000.* 2d ed. Madison: University of Wisconsin Press, 2005.

Miller, Henry I., and Gregory P. Conko, *The Frankenfood Myth: How Protest and Politics Threaten the Biotech Revolution.* Westport, CT: Praeger, 2004.

Nestle, Marion, *Safe Food: Bacteria, Biotechnology, and Bioterrorism.* Berkeley: University of California Press, 2003.

Sanderson, Colin J., *Understanding Genes and GMOs.* Hackensack, NJ: World Scientific, 2007.

Schacter, Bernice, *Issues and Dilemmas of Biotechnology: A Reference Guide.* Westport, CT: Greenwood Press, 1999.

Schurman, Rachel, and Dennis D. Kelso, *Engineering Trouble: Biotechnology and Its Discontents.* Berkeley: University of California Press, 2003.

GLOBAL WARMING

Jayne Geisel

Since the 1980s, global warming has been a hotly debated topic in the popular media and among the general public, scientists, and politicians. The debate is about whether global warming has been occurring, whether it is an issue with which the global community needs to be concerned, and whether the current global warming is part of natural cycles of warming and cooling. Currently, the nature of the debate has begun to focus on whether there is anything we can do about global warming. For some, the problem is so insurmountable, and there seems to be so little we can do, that it is easier to entirely forget there is a problem.

In order to understand the changes that need to be made to have any meaningful and lasting impact on the level of global warming, the science behind the greenhouse effect must be understood.

The Scope and Nature of the Problem

The average temperature on Earth is approximately 15 degrees Celsius. The surface of the Earth stays at such a consistent temperature because its atmosphere is composed of gases that allow for the retention of some of the radiant energy from the sun, as well as the escape of some of that energy. The majority of this energy, in the form of heat, is allowed to leave the atmosphere, essentially because the concentrations of gases that trap it are relatively low. When solar radiation escapes the atmosphere, it is largely due to the reflection of that energy from clouds, snow, ice, and water on the surface of the Earth. The gases that trap heat are carbon dioxide, methane, nitrous oxides, and chlorofluorocarbons. These gases are commonly known as greenhouse gases.

In the last 60 years, the percentage of greenhouse gases (in particular, carbon dioxide) has begun to climb. Although the global increase in these gases has been noticed since the beginning of the Industrial Revolution approximately 200 years ago, the increase since the 1950s has been much more dramatic. Carbon dioxide comes from such sources as plant and animal respiration and decomposition, natural fires, and volcanoes. These

RECORDS OF GLOBAL WARMING

The historical record of weather and climate is based on the analysis of air bubbles trapped in ice sheets. By analyzing the ancient air trapped in these bubbles, trends in climate change over very long time periods can be observed. This record indicates that methane is more abundant in the earth's atmosphere now than it was at any time during the past 400,000 years. Since 1750, average global atmospheric concentrations of methane have increased by 150 percent from approximately 700 to 1,745 parts per billion by volume (ppbv) in 1998. Over the past decade, although methane concentrations have continued to increase, the overall rate of methane growth has slowed. In the late 1970s, the growth rate was approximately 20 ppbv per year. In the 1980s, growth slowed to 9 to 13 ppbv per year. The period from 1990 to 1998 saw variable growth of between 0 and 13 ppbv per year. An unknown factor, and a point of controversy, is the amount of methane in the polar ice caps. It is unknown how much methane in a currently inert form could be released as a gas into the atmosphere if the ice caps melt into water. If a large amount of polar methane gas is released faster than current models predict, global warming could accelerate.

natural sources of carbon dioxide replace atmospheric carbon dioxide at the same rate it is removed by photosynthesis. Human activities, however, such as the burning of fossil fuels, pollution, and deforestation, add excess amounts of this gas and therefore disrupt the natural cycle of carbon dioxide.

Scientists have discovered this increase in carbon dioxide and other greenhouse gases by drilling into ice caps at both the north and south poles and in glaciers and by taking ice-core samples that can then be tested. Ice cores have rings, similar to the rings found in trees, which allow for accurate dating. When snow and water accumulate each season to form the ice in these locations, air bubbles are trapped that are now tested for the presence of greenhouse gases. These studies have shown drastic changes in the levels of carbon dioxide.

Global warming is significantly affected by the burning of fossil fuels and the massive loss of vegetation. First, the loss of vegetation removes photosynthetic plants that consume carbon dioxide as part of their life cycle, and second, the burning of fossil fuels releases carbon dioxide that has been stored for thousands of years in decayed plant and animal material into the atmosphere. These two processes have increased significantly globally in the last 100 years.

Although the rate of warming seems small and gradual, it takes only minor temperature fluctuations to have a significant effect on the global scale. During the last ice age, temperatures were less than 5 degrees Celsius cooler than they are today. This small change in temperature is so significant because of the properties of water. Water has a high specific heat, meaning it takes a large amount of heat energy to warm water. The result of this is that it takes a long time to warm or cool large bodies of water. This effect can be noticed in the temperate climate experienced in coastal areas. Once the oceans begin to warm, they will stay warm for an extended period of time. This is critical for life that has adapted to the temperatures currently experienced in the oceans.

The other important and alarming factor related to global warming and the warming of the oceans is the loss of the ice caps at both poles. This melting of ice has the potential to raise the level of the oceans worldwide, which will have potentially disastrous effects for human populations. The largest urban centers worldwide are located in coastal areas, which have the potential to flood. This will displace millions, and possibly billions, of people.

These changes are only gradual when considered within a human time frame. In terms of geological time, the change is extremely fast. This precipitous change will have far-reaching effects on both flora and fauna because most species will not have time to adapt to changes in climate and weather patterns.

The result of this will be extinctions of species on a scale that is difficult to predict. It is certain that changes that have already taken place have had an impact on polar species, such as polar bears, because that habitat is where the changes are most strongly felt right now.

Socioeconomic Disparities

One of the largest issues in the debate on global warming is the difference in the ability to deal with mitigation and the large disparity in the consequences felt between developing and developed nations. The reality faced by many developing nations of poverty and subsistence living means that those populations do not have the ability to withstand some of the changes with which the world is faced. The most vulnerable people living in developed countries will not be able to adapt as easily.

These people, who generally do not contribute as much to the problems associated with an increase in greenhouse gases, will suffer the consequences most severely. Their contributions to global warming are less because many in this segment of the global population do not own cars, do not have electricity or refrigerators with chlorofluorocarbons, do not use air conditioning, and so on. Their lives are generally more closely tied with climate than those more fortunate, however. Their work may involve physical labor outside, they usually are involved in agriculture, or they may not be able to access health care for the inevitable increase in climate-related diseases such as malaria. The large and growing populations of many developing nations live mainly in coastal areas; less privileged people will not have the resources needed to move away from rising water levels. This means there will be a large refugee population that the international community will not easily be able to help.

Rapidly developing nations such as China and India, playing catch-up with the West, are becoming, if they are not already, major contributors to global warming. Older technologies, outdated equipment, and the nature of developing an industrial sector are largely to blame. In the development stage of industry, high carbon dioxide–emitting sectors such as shipping and manufacturing are predominant. Worldwide, work is needed to assist nations in developing their economies without sacrificing the environment to do so.

Global warming is not merely an issue of science and environmental protection; it is also a humanitarian and ethical concern. The methods of mitigation are being debated, and there is no clear answer to the questions concerning the appropriate measures to take. There are generally two appropriate responses. The first is to take any and all steps to immediately reduce the amount of pollution and greenhouse gas emission worldwide, or there will be no life on Earth. The second approach is based on the thought that nothing we do will have a lasting effect on the amount of pollution, so we must better equip the people of the world to deal with the consequences of this crisis. This means breaking

KYOTO PROTOCOL

The Kyoto Protocol, sometimes known as the Kyoto Accord, is an international agreement requiring the international community to reduce the rate of emission of greenhouse gases causing global warming. It was signed in Kyoto, Japan, in 1997, to come into effect in 2005.

The Kyoto Protocol was initiated by the United Nations Framework Convention on Climate Change (UNFCCC) in order to extract a commitment from developed nations to reduce greenhouse gas emissions. The hope was that with developed countries leading the way, businesses, communities, and individuals would begin to take action on climate change.

The Kyoto Protocol commits those countries that have ratified it to reduce emissions by certain amounts at certain times. These targets must be met within the five years from 2008 to 2012. This firm commitment was a major first step in acknowledging human responsibility for this problem, as well as taking a step toward rectifying the crisis. Not all developed countries have ratified the protocol, however, with the United States and Australia among those that have not. This is of great concern, given that the United States is the worst offender when it comes to greenhouse gas emissions.

Criticisms of the protocol are that it puts a large burden for the reduction of greenhouse pollution on developed nations, when developing nations are set to far surpass current levels of emissions. As well, the protocol does not specify what atmospheric levels of carbon dioxide are acceptable, so reduction is not a concrete enough goal to have any real lasting effect. Finally, the Kyoto Protocol is seen as a bureaucratic nightmare and too expensive a solution for this problem compared with the amount of gain that would result.

the poverty cycle, addressing such issues as disease and access to good food and water, and providing appropriate education on a global scale.

Another debate surrounding mitigation of global warming is whether individual effort will have an effect on rates of carbon dioxide and other greenhouse gases. Will one person choosing to ride his or her bike or take public transit reduce the level of emissions across the globe? If one person uses electricity generated by wind instead of coal, is that enough? Critics say that public apathy is so high, and there is such a strong sense of entitlement to resources, that there will never be enough people making the so-called green choice to make any kind of a difference at all. Others feel that all change must happen at a grassroots level and that every step counts and is important. If every single person in North America cut by half the number of hours they spent driving, there would of course be a significant decrease in pollution.

Conclusion

Rising global temperatures are expected to raise the sea level and alter the climate. Changing regional climates alter forests, crop yields, and water supplies. The most recent reports from the United Nations Food and Agriculture Organization indicate that wheat harvests are declining because of global warming. Some experts have estimated that there will be a 3 to 16 percent decline in worldwide agricultural productivity by 2080. Population is expected to rise, however.

The political controversies around global warming focus on the results of climate changes. Equity, value clashes, and uncertainty all promise to make climate change controversial. Some may gain and others will lose. There may be geopolitical shifts in world power. All efforts toward sustainability will be affected by global warming. Closer attention to environmental conditions of the climate, earth, land, air, and water is required to accommodate increasing population growth and concomitant environmental impacts. International treaties, such as Kyoto and the recent Copenhagen Summit, will be pointed to in seeking accords. Both the effects and causes of global warming promise to be a continuing controversy.

See also **Climate Change; Coal; Fossil Fuels; Sustainability (vol. 1)**

Further Reading

An Inconvenient Truth, Documentary directed by David Guggenheim, 2006.

Archer, David, *The Climate Crisis: An Introductory Guide to Climate Change.* New York: Cambridge University Press, 2010.

Broecker, William S., and Robert Kunzig, *Fixing Climate: What Past Climate Changes Reveal about the Current Threat—and How to Counter It.* New York: Hill & Wang, 2008.

Dow, Kirstin, and Thomas E. Downing, *The Atlas of Climate Change: Mapping the World's Greatest Challenge.* Berkeley: University of California Press, 2007.

Flannery, Tim, *The Weather Makers: How We Are Changing the Climate and What It Means for Life on Earth.* Toronto: HarperCollins, 2006.

Houghton, J. T., *Global Warming: The Complete Briefing.* New York: Cambridge University Press, 2009.

McKibben, Bill, *Earth: Making a Life on a Tough New Planet.* New York: Times Books, 2010.

Monbiot, George, *Heat: How to Stop the Planet from Burning.* Toronto: Random House, 2006.

H

HIV/AIDS

LAURA FRY

Human immunodeficiency virus (HIV), a virus affecting the human body and organs, impairs the immune system and the body's ability to resist infections, leading to acquired immunodeficiency syndrome (AIDS), a collection of symptoms and infections resulting from damage to the immune system. Medical confusion and prolonged government indifference to the AIDS epidemic was detrimental to early risk reduction and health education efforts.

Initial facts about AIDS targeted unusual circumstances and unusual individuals, thereby situating the cause of AIDS in stigmatized populations and "at risk" individuals. Although current efforts to curb the spread of HIV/AIDS are based on a more realistic understanding of transmission and infections, government policies and educational campaigns still do not fully acknowledge the socioeconomics, drug use practices, cultural attitudes, and sexual behaviors of populations. Global HIV prevalence stabilized with improvements in identification and surveillance techniques, but reversing the epidemic remains difficult. The pervasive spread of HIV in particular populations and geographic areas continues as economic realities influence infection rates.

Since the first recognized and reported death on June 5, 1981, AIDS has killed more than 25 million people, making HIV/AIDS one of the most destructive epidemics in history. The number of new HIV infections per year peaked in the late 1990s, with over 3 million new infections, but the infection rate never plummeted.

Although the percentage of people infected with HIV leveled off in 2007, the number of people living with HIV continues to increase. The combination of HIV acquisition and longer survival times creates a continuously growing general population. Treatments to decelerate the virus's progression are available, but there is no known cure for HIV/AIDS.

According to 2008 statistics—released in December 2009 by the World Health Organization (WHO) Joint United National Program on HIV/AIDS—60 million people were infected worldwide since the epidemic began. An estimated 33.4 million people were living with HIV, of whom 2.1 million were children under age 15. Within that figure, as many as 610,000 children were born with HIV. Those figures are up slightly from the previous year: about 0.6 percent. Young people account for around 40 percent of new adult (age 15 and above) HIV infections worldwide. In 2008, as many as 3 million people became newly infected, and some 2 million died that year of AIDS-related complications.

Transmission

Two strains of HIV, HIV-1 and HIV-2, infect humans through the same routes of transmission, but HIV-1 is more easily conveyed and more widespread. Transmission of HIV occurs primarily through direct contact with bodily fluids—for example, blood, semen, vaginal fluid, breast milk, and preseminal fluid. Blood transfusions, contaminated hypodermic needles, pregnancy, childbirth, breastfeeding, and anal, vaginal, and oral sex are the primary forms of transmission. There is currently some speculation that saliva is an avenue for transmission, as evidenced by children contracting HIV through prechewed food, but research is ongoing to determine if this hypothesis is correct.

Labeling a person HIV-positive or diagnosing AIDS is not always consistent. HIV is a retrovirus that primarily affects the human immune system by directly and indirectly destroying $CD4^+$ T cells, a subset of T cells responsible for fighting infection. AIDS is the severe acceleration of an HIV infection. When fewer than 200 $CD4^+$ T cells per microliter of blood are present, cellular immunity is compromised; in the United States, a diagnosis of AIDS results. In Canada and other countries, a diagnosis of AIDS occurs only if an HIV-infected person has one or more AIDS-related opportunistic infections or cancers. The WHO grouped infections and conditions together in 1990 by introducing a "stage system" for classifying the presence of opportunistic infections in HIV-positive individuals. The four stages of an HIV infection were updated in 2005, with stage 4 as the indicator of AIDS. Definitions for surveillance and clinical staging were clarified and officially revised in 2006. The symptoms of AIDS do not normally develop in individuals with healthy immune systems; bacteria, viruses, fungi, and parasites are often controlled by immune systems not damaged by HIV.

HIV affects almost every organ system in the body and increases the risk of developing opportunistic infections. *Pneumocystis carinii* pneumonia (PCP) and tuberculosis

(TB) are the most common pulmonary illnesses in HIV-infected individuals. In developing countries, PCP and TB are among the first indications of AIDS in untested individuals. Esophagitis, the inflammation of the lining of the lower end of the esophagus, often results from fungal (candidiasis) or viral (herpes simplex-1) infections. Unexplained chronic diarrhea, caused by bacterial and parasitic infections, is another common gastrointestinal illness affecting HIV-positive people. Brain infections and dementia are neurological illnesses that affect individuals in the late stages of AIDS. Kaposi's sarcoma, one of several malignant cancers, is the most common tumor in HIV-infected patients. Purplish nodules often appear on the skin, but malignancies also affect the mouth, gastrointestinal tract, and lungs. Nonspecific symptoms such as low-grade fevers, weight loss, swollen glands, sweating, chills, and physical weakness accompany infections and are often early indications that an individual has contracted HIV.

Treatment

There is currently no cure or vaccine for HIV/AIDS. Avoiding exposure to the virus is the primary technique for preventing an HIV infection. Antiretroviral therapies, which stop HIV from replicating, have limited effectiveness. Postexposure prophylaxis (PEP), an antiretroviral treatment, can be administered directly after exposure to HIV. The four-week dosage causes numerous side effects, however, and it is not 100 percent effective. For HIV-positive individuals, the current treatment is "cocktails," a combination of drugs and antiretroviral agents administered throughout a person's life span. Highly active antiretroviral therapy (HAART) stabilizes a patient's symptoms and viremia (the presence of viruses in the blood), but the treatment does not alleviate the symptoms of HIV/AIDS. Without drug intervention, typical progression from HIV to AIDS occurs in 9 to 10 years: HAART extends a person's life span and increases survival time by 4 to 12 years. Based on the administration of cocktails and the increase in the number of people living with HIV/AIDS, the prevailing medical opinion is that AIDS is a manageable chronic disease. Initial optimism surrounding HAART, however, is tempered by recent research on the complex health problems of AIDS-related longevity and the costs of antiretroviral drugs. HAART is expensive, aging AIDS populations have more severe illnesses, and the majority of the world's HIV-positive population do not have access to medications and treatments.

Beginnings

In 1981 the U.S. Centers for Disease Control and Prevention (CDC) first reported AIDS in a cluster of five homosexual men who had rare types of pneumonia. The CDC compiled four "identified risk factors" in 1981: male homosexuality, IV drug use, Haitian origin, and hemophilia. The "inherent" link between homosexuality and HIV was the primary focus for many health care officials and the media, with drug use a close second.

The media labeled the disease gay-related immune deficiency (GRID), even though AIDS was not isolated to the homosexual community. GRID was misleading, and at a July 1982 meeting, "AIDS" was proposed. By September 1982 the CDC had defined the illness and implemented the acronym AIDS to reference the disease. Despite scientific knowledge of the routes and probabilities of transmission, the U.S. government implemented no official, nationwide effort to clearly explain HIV mechanics or promote risk reduction until the surgeon general's 1988 campaign. Unwillingness to recognize HIV's pervasiveness or to fund solutions produced both a national fantasy about the AIDS epidemic and sensationalized public health campaigns in the mass media.

Early Prevention: Clean Living

Prevention advice reinforced ideas of safety and distance. The citizenry was expected to avoid "risky" behavior by avoiding "at risk" populations. Strategies to prevent HIV/AIDS were directed at particular types of people who were thought to engage in dangerous behaviors. Homosexual sex and drug use were perceived to be the most risky behaviors; thus heterosexual intercourse and not doing drugs were constructed as safe. Disease prevention programs targeted primarily gay populations but were merely health precautions for everyone else—individuals not at risk.

Citizens rarely considered how prevention literature and advice applied to individual lives because the public was relatively uninformed about the routes of HIV transmission. Subcultures were socially stigmatized as deviant, and at-risk populations were considered obscene and immoral. "Risk behavior" became socially constructed as "risk group," which promoted a limited understanding of how HIV was contracted. The passage of the Helms Amendment solidified both public perceptions and government legislation about AIDS and AIDS education. According to the amendment, federal funding for health campaigns could be renewed each year with additional amounts of money as long as such campaigns did not "promote" homosexuality and promiscuity. Despite lack of funding, much of the risk-reduction information that later became available to the public was generated by advocates within the homosexual community.

Although avoidance tactics were promoted by the national government, precautionary strategies were adopted and utilized by gay communities. Distributing information through newspapers, pamphlets, and talks, the community-based campaigns emphasized safe sex and safe practices. Using condoms regardless of HIV status, communication between sexual partners, and simply avoiding intercourse were universal precautions emphasized in both American and European gay health campaigns. With a nontransmission focus, safe sex knowledge was designed and presented in simple language, not medical terminology, so that the information was easy to understand. Although "don't ask, don't tell" strategies were still adopted by many gay men, the universal safe sex strategy employed by the gay community promoted discussions about sex without necessarily calling for private conversations. The visibility and accessibility to information helped gay men understand HIV and promoted individual responsibility. The national pedagogy, by contrast, banned sexually explicit discussions in the public sphere. Individuals were encouraged to interrogate their partners in private without truly comprehending either the questions asked or the answers received. Lack of detailed information and the inability to successfully investigate a partner's sexual past facilitated a need for an organized method of identifying HIV-positive individuals.

With the intention of stemming HIV, the CDC's Donald Francis proposed, at the 1985 International Conference on AIDS in Atlanta, that gay men have sex only with other men who had the same HIV antibody status; accordingly, he presented a mathematical model for testing. Shortly thereafter, HIV testing centers were established, and the national campaign, centered on avoiding HIV-positive individuals, was implemented. Instead of adopting safe sex education and behaviors, the government merely inserted technology into existing avoidance paradigms. HIV tests were valid only if the last sexual exchange or possible exposure had occurred within six months to a year earlier. However, many people misinterpreted negative test results as an indicator of who was "uninfected," thus merely reinforcing educated guesses. With the test viewed as an ultimate assessment for determining a sexual partner's safety, many individuals relied on HIV test results to confirm individual theories of who was and was not infected. Unrealistic discussions about sexual practices and behaviors were detrimental to the American population, especially adolescents and young adults.

Youth and Economic Stratification

In 1990 epidemiologists confirmed that a wide cross-section of American youth were HIV-positive. Minority and runaway youth were particularly affected, but millions of young people had initiated sexual interactions and drug use in the previous decade. Because health campaigns focused on prevention, there was little and often no help for individuals who were infected. Diagnosing the onset of symptoms and tactics to delay AIDS progression were almost nonexistent. Instead of recognizing the sexual and drug practices of middle-class white kids, society classified young people into categories of "deviance": deviant individuals contracted HIV; innocent children did not. Refusing to acknowledge that young people were becoming infected, many parents and government officials impeded risk-reduction information. Consequently, few young people perceived themselves as targets of HIV infection, and much of the media attention focused on "tolerance" for individuals living with AIDS.

Under the false assumption that infections among youth occurred through nonsexual transmission, HIV-positive elementary school children and teenagers were grouped together and treated as innocent victims. Although drug use and needle sharing were prevalent behaviors in teenage initiation interactions, the public agenda focused on sexuality as the primary transmission route. Knowing about or practicing safe sex was dangerous; ignorance would prevent HIV. Representations of youth in the media reinforced the naiveté and stereotypes that initially contextualized AIDS in the adult population; *New York Times* articles suggested HIV infections in gay youth were the result of liaisons with gay adults or experimentation among themselves. In a manner reminiscent of the initial constructions of AIDS in the 1980s, HIV-infected youth were effectively reduced to deviant, unsafe populations. Securing heterosexuality became, yet again, a form of safe sex and the primary prevention tactic for HIV. Refusal to acknowledge nonintercourse activities as routes for HIV transmission pervaded government policies of the 20th and 21st centuries.

Infected Heterosexual Women

Recommendations for avoiding HIV infections were limited in both scope and funding. Because heterosexual women were increasingly becoming infected, the U.S. Food and Drug Administration (FDA) approved the sale of female condoms in 1993. However, female condoms were largely unavailable, and the price was prohibitive for many women. Approved in 1996 by the FDA, the viral load test measured the level of HIV in the body. As with the female condom, the test was expensive and continues to be cost-prohibitive. Needle exchange programs demonstrated great effectiveness in reducing HIV infections via blood transmission. Although the U.S. Department of Health and Human Services recommended needle exchange programs in 1998, the Clinton administration did not lift the ban on the use of federal funds for such purposes. Needle exchange remains stigmatized, and funding continues to come primarily from community-based efforts. In 1998 the first large-scale human trials for an HIV vaccine began, but no vaccine has been discovered. Despite community and government efforts, people continue to become infected with HIV/AIDS.

With growing numbers of individuals contracting HIV, the government implemented some treatment strategies. The AIDS Drug Assistance Program (ADAP) was established to pay for HIV treatments for low-income individuals. In 1987 azidothymidine (AZT)/zidovudine (ZDV) became the first HIV/AIDS drug to receive the FDA's approval. AZT's toxicity was well documented, but the effectiveness of the long-term monotherapy was questionable. Nevertheless, AZT was administered to the population, and the FDA approved three generic formulations of ZDV on September 19, 2005. AZT continues to be the primary treatment in reducing the risk of mother-to-child transmission (MTCT), especially in developing countries. There were few effective treatments for children until August 13, 2007, when the FDA approved a fixed-dose, three-drug combo pill for children younger than 12 years old. Treatments are improvements for developing awareness of HIV/AIDS, but the realities of transmission and the costs associated with HIV infection remain largely ignored.

People Living with AIDS

People Living With AIDS (PWA, coined in 1983) became the faces of HIV infections, and such individuals provided the impetus for increased attention to the AIDS epidemic. Rock Hudson, an actor world-renowned for his romantic, heterosexual love scenes, appeared on ABC World News Tonight and announced he had AIDS. He died shortly after his October 1985 appearance. President Ronald Reagan, a close friend of Hudson, mentioned AIDS in a public address in 1986, the first time a prominent politician specifically used the words HIV and AIDS. In 1987, the same year the CDC added HIV to the exclusion list, banning HIV-positive immigrants from entering the United States, Liberace, a musician and entertainer, died of AIDS. *Newsweek* published a cover story titled "The Face of Aids" on October 10, 1987, but the 16-page special report failed to truly dispense with the stereotypes of HIV infection. With the growing number of PWAs, government policies toward HIV changed somewhat. In 1988 the Department of Justice reversed the discrimination policy, stating that HIV/AIDS status could not be used to prevent individuals from working and interacting with the population. December 1, 1988, was recognized as the first World AIDS Day. However, even with such social demonstrations of goodwill, recognizable faces remained aloof; the public "saw" HIV but did not associate HIV with the general population until Ryan White, a so-called normal person, grabbed community attention.

Blood Transfusion

Ryan White, a middle-class, HIV-positive child became one of the most public and media-spotlighted individuals. He had hemophilia and contracted HIV through a blood transfusion. His blood-clotting disorder fit existing innocence paradigms and thus provided opportunities for discussions about HIV, intervention, and government aid. At age 13, White was banned from attending school, prevented from associating with his classmates, and limited to classroom interactions via the telephone. The discrimination White endured throughout his life highlighted how "normal" people were affected by public reactions and government policies. In 1990, the year White died at age 18, the Ryan White Comprehensive AIDS Resources Emergency (CARE) Act was passed. With 150,000 reported AIDS cases in the United States, CARE directed attention to the growing incidences of HIV and aroused greater public compassion.

More Celebrities

The teen culture of the 1990s continued to be affected as additional celebrities were added to the seropositive list. Earvin "Magic" Johnson, an idolized basketball player and all-time National Basketball Association (NBA) star, announced his HIV-positive status in 1991. The "perversion" labels normally associated with HIV were momentarily suspended as the public discourse tried to fit Johnson's wholesome role-model status into the existing risk paradigm. Much of the public, including individuals in methadone clinics, referred to positive HIV serostatus as "what Magic's got" and avoided the stigmatized label of AIDS. The compassion and understanding for HIV-positive individuals was short-lived, however. Freddie Mercury, lead singer of the rock band Queen, died in

1991 of AIDS. Because he was a gay man, Mercury's life was quickly demonized, and he did not receive the same "clean living" recognition from the press. Preaching compassion was good in rhetoric but not in practice.

Limited public empathy did not quell the diversity of individuals affected by AIDS. In 1992, tennis star Arthur Ashe announced his HIV status. In the same year, teenager Rick Ray's house was torched (Ray, a hemophiliac, and his siblings were all HIV-positive). During 1993, Katrina Haslip, a leading advocate for women with AIDS in prison, died of AIDS, and Pedro Zamorn, a young gay man living with HIV, appeared as a cast member on MTV's *The Real World*. Zamorn died in 1994 at age 22. Olympic Gold Medal diver Greg Louganis disclosed his HIV status in 1995, which sent shock waves into the Olympic community. Louganis had cut his head while diving during the 1988 Olympics, and concern quickly entered scientific and media discussions about HIV transmission. The discrimination Louganis endured affected athletic policies and issues of participation in sports for HIV-positive athletes. Even though HIV/AIDS was the leading cause of death among African Americans in the United States in 1996, the public continued to focus on individuals whose faces, displayed in the media, informed much of the understanding of HIV in the United States.

Strategies for Improvement

During the June 2006 General Assembly High-Level Meeting on AIDS, the United Nations member states reaffirmed their approval of the 2001 Declaration of Commitment. Efforts to reduce the spread of AIDS focused on eight key areas, including reducing poverty and child mortality, increasing access to education, and improving maternal health. Universal access to comprehensive prevention programs, treatment, care, and support were projected outcomes for 2010. Strategies to improve HIV testing and counseling, prevent HIV infections, accelerate HIV/AIDS treatment and care, and expand health systems were four of the five suggestions WHO expected to implement. The sheer numbers of people infected with HIV, however, tempered the hope and optimism surrounding intervention techniques.

India continues to rank third in the world for HIV. Indonesia has the fastest-growing epidemic, and HIV prevalence among men has increased in Thailand. Eastern Europe and Central Asia have more than 1.5 million people living with HIV, a 10 percent decrease compared with 2007 figures. Sub-Saharan Africa continues to be the most affected region, with an average of 22.4 million people living with HIV. Current infection rates continue to be disproportionately high for women in sub-Saharan Africa. Women are more susceptible to HIV-1 infections, but their partners (usually men) are often the carriers and transmitters of HIV. For women as mothers, MTCT can occur in utero during the last weeks of pregnancy, during childbirth, and from breastfeeding. Although risk behavior has changed among young people in some African nations, the mortality rate from AIDS is high because of unmet treatment needs. Delivery of health service and funding remain inadequate for prevention efforts and HIV treatments. The lowest incidence of HIV infection in the world is in Oceania, where considerably less than 1 percent of adults are infected (around 59,000), compared with Sub-Saharan Africa, where 5.2 percent or around 22.4 million adults carry the AIDS virus.

False Cures, AZT, Politics, and Science

The majority of the world's population does not have adequate access to health care or medical techniques that could prevent HIV infections. Universal precautions, such as avoiding needle sharing and sterilizing medical equipment, are not often followed because health care workers receive inadequate training and there are not enough supplies. Blood transfusions account for 5 to 15 percent of HIV transmissions because the standard donor selection and HIV screening procedures completed in industrial nations are not performed in developing countries. Health care workers' behaviors and patient interactions are affected by the lack of medical supplies, including latex gloves and disinfectants. Approximately 2.5 percent of all HIV infections in sub-Saharan Africa occur through unsafe health care injections. The implementation of universal precautions is difficult when funding is severely restricted or absent.

Education efforts are also constrained by the lack of funding. HIV prevalence has remained high among injecting drug users, especially in Thailand, where HIV rates are 30 to 50 percent. AIDS-prevention organizations advocate clean needles and equipment for preparing and taking drugs (syringes, cotton balls, spoons, water for dilution, straws, pipes, etc.). Cleaning needles with bleach and decriminalizing needle possession are advocated at "safe injection sites" (places where information about safe techniques are distributed to drug users). When needle exchanges and safe injection sites were established, there was a reduction in HIV infection rates. Individuals, especially young people, engaged in high-risk practices with drugs and sex, often because of a lack of disease comprehension. Although aware of HIV, young people continue to underestimate their personal risk. HIV/AIDS knowledge increases with clear communication and unambiguous information.

Questions surrounding HIV/AIDS have stemmed from both a lack of understanding and a desire to understand the complexities of the disease. Early misconceptions about transmission—casual contact (e.g., touching someone's skin), and engaging in any form of anal intercourse—created fear and folklore. Certain populations—homosexual men and drug users—were incorrectly identified as the only people susceptible to HIV. National pedagogy mistakenly proclaimed that open discussions about HIV or homosexuality would increase rates of AIDS and homosexuality in schools. The false belief that sexual intercourse with a virgin would "cure" HIV was particularly detrimental to many young women. Although much of the early fictional rhetoric was rectified through the distribution of scientific information, denial and delusion continue to influence individuals' perceptions of HIV/AIDS.

A small group of scientists and activists questioned the testing and treatment methods of HIV/AIDS, which influenced government policies in South Africa. Established in the early 1990s, the Group for the Scientific Re-Appraisal of the HIV/AIDS Hypothesis launched the Web site virusmyth.net and included a collection of literature from various supporters, including Peter Duesberg, David Rasnick, Eleni Papadopulos-Eleopulos, and Nobel Prize winner Karry Mullis. As a result, Thabo Mbeki, South Africa's president, suspended AZT use in the public health sector. At issue was whether AZT was a medicine or a poison and whether the benefits of AZT in MTCT outweighed the toxicity of the treatment. Retrospective analyses have raised criticisms about Mbeki's interference. The expert consensus is that the risks of AZT for MTCT were small compared with the reduction of HIV infection in children. The South African AZT controversy demonstrates how science may be interpreted in different ways and how politics influences public health decisions.

Scientific Ideology

The biological ideology of most scientific inquiry has influenced HIV investigations, with much research focused on understanding the molecular structure of HIV. During the late 1980s, Canadian infectious-disease expert Frank Plummer noticed that, despite high-risk sexual behavior, some prostitutes did not contract HIV. In spite of being sick, weak from malnourishment, and having unprotected sex with men who were known to have HIV, the women did not become seropositive. The scientific community became highly interested in the women (known as "the Nairobi prostitutes") and hypothesized that the women's immune systems defended them from HIV. Of the 80 women exposed to HIV-1 and determined to be uninfected and seronegative, 24 were selected for immunological evaluation. Cellular immune responses, like T cells, control the infection of HIV; helper T cells seem to recognize HIV-1 antigens. The small group of prostitutes in Nairobi remained uninfected even though their activities involved prolonged and continued exposure to HIV-1. Cellular immunity—not systemic humoral immunity (i.e., defective viral or HIV-antigens)—prevented HIV from infecting them. The Nairobi prostitutes' naturally occurring protective immunity from the most virulent strain of HIV was a model for the increased focus on the development of vaccines.

Historically, vaccine production has concentrated on antibodies and how the human body can be tricked into fighting an infection. A benign form of the virus infects the body, and the immune system's white blood cells respond; antibodies attack the virus in the bloodstream and cytotoxic T lymphocytes (T cells) detect infected cells and destroy them. Vaccines for measles, yellow fever, and pertussis operate within this same paradigm. HIV mutates rapidly, however, and different strains exist within the population. A vaccine for one subtype would not provide immunity to another HIV strain. The unpredictability of HIV requires a scientific transition in the research paradigm and a willingness to use human beings as test subjects.

For the effectiveness of a vaccine to be gauged, thousands of people will have to be part of the research trials. The ethical problems associated with human subjects and the costs of long-term investigations prohibit many researchers from committing to vaccine research. Additionally, the economic market mentality provides more incentive for making a product for mass consumption. The costs and risks of a vaccine limit financial gains for companies; inoculation against HIV reduces the number of consumers who need the product. Instead, antiretroviral medications and treatments are the primary focus for research funding. An AIDS vaccine would benefit the entire world, but no company or country is willing to devote the economic and scientific resources needed for such research. The International AIDS Vaccine Initiative, a philanthropic venture capital firm dedicated to finding a vaccine, has received funding from private and public donations, including significant contributions from the Bill and Melinda Gates Foundation. Researchers, however, continue to reduce the AIDS virus to its genetic components instead of approaching HIV vaccines from new perspectives.

Conclusion

The complexity of HIV creates difficulties in finding a single, permanent solution. Education and prevention have had limited success, and antiretroviral therapies cannot cure the vast number of people infected with HIV/AIDS. A partially effective vaccine or a vaccine that targets only one mutation of HIV is not a solution. Ignoring a population's behaviors, economic situations, and beliefs has proven detrimental to the AIDS epidemic. The difficulties of the disease make HIV/AIDS a formidable problem.

See also **Epidemics and Pandemics; Prescription Drug Costs (vol. 1); Social Justice (vol. 2)**

Further Reading

Abdool Karim, Salim S., and Quarraisha, "AIDS Research Must Link to Local Policy." *Nature* 463 (2010): 733–734.

Barton-Knott, Sophie, "Global HIV Prevalence Has Leveled Off." *UNAIDS.* http://www.unaids.org

Connell, R. W., "Social Class, Gay Men and AIDS Prevention." *Australian Journal of Public Health* 15, no. 3 (2010): 178–189.

Fowke, Keith, et al., "HIV-1-Specific Cellular Immune Responses among HIV-1-Resistant Sex Workers." *Immunology and Cell Biology* 78 (2000): 586–595.

Jakobsen, Janet, and Ann Pellegrini, *Love the Sin: Sexual Regulation and the Limits of Religious Tolerance.* Boston: Beacon Press, 2004.

Kallings, L. O., "The First Postmodern Pandemic: Twenty-Five Years of HIV/AIDS." *Journal of Internal Medicine* 263 (2008): 218–243.

Laumann, Edward, et al., *The Social Organization of Sexuality: Sexual Practices in the United States.* Chicago: University of Chicago Press, 1994.

Patton, Cindy, *Fatal Advice: How Safe-Sex Education Went Wrong.* Durham, NC: Duke University Press, 1996.

Pisani, Elizabeth, *The Wisdom of Whores: Bureaucrats, Brothels, and the Business of AIDS.* New York: Norton, 2009.

UNAIDS, "Overview of the Global AIDS Epidemic." *Report on the Global AIDS Epidemic.* http://www.unaids.org

UNAIDS, Global Facts and Figures, 2009. http://data.unaids.org/pub/FactSheet/2009/20091124_FS_global_en.pdf

U.S. Department of Health and Human Services HIV/AIDS, http://www.aids.gov

Weinel, Martin, "Primary Source Knowledge and Technical Decision-Making: Mbeki and the AZT Debate." *Studies in History and Philosophy of Science* 38 (2007): 748–760.

Whiteside, Alan, *HIV/AIDS: A Very Short Introduction.* New York: Oxford University Press, 2008.

World Health Organization, http://www.who.int/en

HORMONE DISRUPTORS: ENDOCRINE DISRUPTORS

ROBERT WILLIAM COLLIN

The issue of hormone disruption is a significant environmental controversy with many emerging questions and concerns. Some scientists believe that a large number of the chemicals currently found in our air, water, soil, and food supply or added to livestock to increase growth have the ability to act as hormones when ingested by human beings and wildlife. Estrogen-mimicking growth hormones in chicken have been linked to early onset of menses and an increase in female attributes in male humans. The decrease in human sperm counts over the last 50 years may be due to hormone-disrupting chemicals. These chemicals increase profits for livestock producers and chemical manufacturers but may also increase food security and provide public health protection from other environmental risks.

Human Reactions to Chemicals in the Environment

There are many potentially dangerous chemicals in the environment, both human-made and naturally occurring. There is also a range of human reactions to environmental stressors such as these chemicals. The human body has many exposure vectors, such as skin absorption, ingestion, and breathing. There is a large variation in response to chemicals in heterogeneous populations such as that of the United States. This makes it very difficult to predict what dose of a chemical is safe enough for use in different applications, adding fuel to the overall controversy. Children take in more of their environment as they grow than they do when they reach adulthood.

Once in the body, chemicals travel and interact with various bodily systems before they are excreted. Throughout the body there are hormone receptor sites designed specifically for a particular hormone, such as estrogen or testosterone. Hormones are produced primarily in the pituitary gland. Once attached, the hormone controls cell maturation and behavior.

The controversy about endocrine disruption begins because many common chemicals have molecular shapes similar to the shapes of many hormones. This means that these chemicals can fit themselves into cellular receptor sites. When this happens, the chemical either prevents real hormones from attaching to the receptor or alters the cell's behavior and/or maturation. The growth of the cell is seriously disrupted. Which chemicals have this effect, and in what dosages, is a major area of controversy. However, only about 2 percent of the chemicals sold in the United States are tested for public health safety. Even these tests are industry-controlled, critics claim, and their results are not based on vulnerability (e.g., children) or dose–response variations. Of particular concern are chemicals that contain chlorine. Chlorine-containing chemicals are themselves part of a larger class called persistent organic pollutants (POPs), which are also believed to be potential hormone disruptors. They pose a greater risk because they persist in the environment for a long time, taking longer to break down into nondangerous components. Because they take longer to break down, they increase exposure times and vectors to humans. Because exposure is increased, the risk from these chemicals, especially endocrine disruptors, is considered greater.

Endocrine Disruptors: How Do They Disrupt?

Endocrine disruptors are externally induced chemicals that interfere with the normal function of hormones. Hormones have many functions essential to human growth, development, and functioning. Endocrine disruptors can disrupt hormonal function in many ways. Here are some of them:

1. Endocrine disruptors can mimic the effects of natural hormones by binding to their receptors.
2. Endocrine disruptors may block the binding of a hormone to its receptor, or they can block the synthesis of the hormone. Finasteride, a chemical used to prevent male-pattern baldness and enlargement of the prostate gland, is an antiandrogen, since it blocks the synthesis of dihydrotestosterone. Women are warned not to handle this drug if they are pregnant, since it could arrest the genital development of male fetuses.
3. Endocrine disruptors can interfere with the transport of a hormone or its elimination from the body. For instance, rats exposed to polychlorinated-biphenyl pollutants (PCBs; see following) have low levels of thyroid hormone. The PCBs compete for the binding sites of the thyroid hormone transport protein. Without being bound to this protein, the thyroid hormones are excreted from the body.

Developmental toxicology and endocrine disruption are relatively new fields of research. Although traditional toxicology has pursued the environmental causes of death, cancer, and genetic damage, developmental toxicology/endocrine disruptor research has focused on the roles that environmental chemicals may have in altering development by disrupting normal endocrine function of surviving animals.

Environmental Estrogens

There is probably no bigger controversy in the field of toxicology than whether chemical pollutants are responsible for congenital malformations in wild animals, the decline of sperm counts in men, and breast cancer in women. One of the sources of these pollutants is pesticide use. Americans use some two billion pounds of pesticides each year, and some pesticide residues stay in the food chain for decades. Although banned in the United States in 1972, DDT has an environmental half-life of about 100 years. Recent evidence has shown that DDT (dichloro-diphenyl-trichloroethane) and its chief metabolic by-product, DDE (which lacks one of the chlorine atoms), can act as estrogenic compounds, either by mimicking estrogen or by inhibiting the effectiveness of androgen. DDE is a more potent estrogen than DDT and is able to inhibit androgen-responsive transcription at doses comparable to those found in contaminated soil in the United States and other countries. DDT and DDE have been linked to such environmental problems as the decrease in the alligator populations in Florida, the feminization of fish in Lake Superior, the rise in breast cancers, and the worldwide decline in human sperm counts. Others have linked a pollutant spill in Florida's Lake Apopka (a discharge including DDT, DDE, and numerous other polychlorinated biphenyls) to a 90 percent decline in the birth rate of alligators and reduced penis size in the young males.

Dioxin, a by-product of the chemical processes used to make pesticides and paper products, has been linked to reproductive anomalies in male rats. The male offspring of rats exposed to this planar, lipophilic molecule when pregnant have reduced sperm counts, smaller testes, and fewer male-specific sexual behaviors. Fish embryos seem particularly susceptible to dioxin and related compounds, and it has been speculated that the amount of these compounds in the Great Lakes during the 1940s was so high that none of the lake trout hatched there during that time survived.

Some estrogenic compounds may be in the food we eat and in the wrapping that surrounds them, for some of the chemicals used to set plastics have been found to be estrogenic. The discovery of the estrogenic effect of plastic stabilizers was made in an unexpected way. Investigators at Tufts University Medical School had been studying estrogen-responsive tumor cells. These cells require estrogen in order to proliferate. The studies were going well until 1987, when the experiments suddenly went awry. That is, the control cells began to show high growth rates, suggesting stimulation comparable to that of the estrogen-treated cells. Thus it was if someone had contaminated the medium by adding estrogen to it. What was the source of contamination? After spending four months testing all the components of their experimental system, the researchers discovered that the source of estrogen was the plastic tubes that held their water and serum.

TIPS ON AVOIDING HORMONE DISRUPTORS

Many people, especially concerned parents, do not know where to turn to deal with fears of exposure to these chemicals. If the situation is severe enough they may be able to find some medical expertise in this area. In terms of what people themselves can do, there are some basic commonsense steps. To help prevent hormonal disruption, here are some steps some have recommended:

1. Do not use conventional chemical cleaners or pesticides of any type because many contain chlorinated chemicals and other persistent organic pollutants (POPs).
2. Do not consume food that is processed, and eat organic food.
3. Wash all conventional produce well before you prepare it to clean off any pesticide residues, preservatives, or waxes. Wash your hands afterwards because pesticide residues on the skins of produce are easily transferred from the fruit to your hands.
4. Do not heat food in any type of plastic container. Many plastics contain hormone-disrupting chemicals that affect food, especially when heated. Microwave foods in glass or ceramic containers.
5. Avoid fish and shellfish from waters suspected of being polluted. Hormone-disrupting chemicals generally accumulate in animals' fatty tissues and expose people when those animal products are ingested. Some parts of a fish may have very high concentrations of mercury, for example. Cultures that eat the whole fish and fish for subsistence are particularly exposed. Most health risk assessments of food levels that are safe for consumption are based on eating the fillets of fish.
6. Reduce consumption of high-fat dairy products and other high-fat foods like meat (especially beef). Many hormone-disrupting chemicals, including dioxins, accumulate in animal fatty tissues. Some milk is tainted with a dairy growth hormone, which is not currently labeled.
7. Choose unbleached or non-chlorine-bleached paper products. Chlorine bleaching is a major source of dioxin, a particularly toxic POPs. Bleached paper, including coffee filters, can pass its dioxin residues into the food with which it comes in contact.
8. Women should use non-chlorine-bleached, all-cotton tampons. Most tampons are made from rayon, a wood pulp product bleached with chlorine. Scientists have detected dioxins in these products.

Some individuals have very sensitive endocrine systems and can tolerate very little chemical exposure. They claim that their immune systems start breaking down and they become progressively sicker if left exposed to many common chemicals. These individuals must take further precautions by moving to the areas with the cleanest air. All their water is purified and all their food is organic, and even some of that may be limited. Carpets, glues, curtains, drapes, and clothing are all limited. The material must be organic, without any chlorine-based processing. The items must be produced, stored, and shipped in a pesticide-free environment, which is difficult to do. Combustion engines, as in cars, are not allowed because of the chemicals in their emissions and maintenance. Soaps and other toiletries must all be organic and can be limited.

The company that made the tubes refused to tell the investigators about its new process for stabilizing the polystyrene plastic, so the scientists had to discover it for themselves. The culprit turned out to be p-nonylphenol, a chemical that is also used to harden the plastic of the plumbing tubes that bring us water and to stabilize the polystyrene plastics that hold water, milk, orange juice, and other common liquid food products. This compound is also the degradation product of detergents, household cleaners, and contraceptive creams. A related compound, 4-tert-pentylphenol, has a potent estrogenic effect on cultured human cells and can cause male carp (*Cyprinus carpis*) to develop oviducts, ovarian tissue, and oocytes.

Some other environmental estrogens are polychlorinated biphenyls (mentioned earlier). These PCBs can react with a number of different steroid receptors. PCBs were widely used as refrigerants before they were banned in the 1970s, when they were shown to cause cancer in rats. They remain in the food chain, however (in both water and sediments), and have been blamed for the widespread decline in the reproductive capacities of otters, seals, mink, and fish. Some PCBs resemble diethylstilbesterol (DES) in shape, and they may affect the estrogen receptor as DES does, perhaps by binding to another site on the estrogen receptor. Another organochlorine compound (and an ingredient in many pesticides) is methoxychlor. This can severely inhibit frogs' fertility, and it may be a component of the worldwide decline in amphibian populations.

Some scientists, however, say that these claims are exaggerated. Tests on mice have shown that litter size, sperm concentration, and development were not affected by concentrations of environmental estrogens. However, recent work has shown a remarkable genetic difference in the sensitivity to estrogen among different strains of mice. The strain that had been used for testing environmental estrogens, the CD-1 strain, is at least 16 times more resistant to endocrine disruption than the most sensitive strains, such as B6. When estrogen-containing pellets were implanted beneath the skin of young male CD-1 mice, very little happened. However, when the same pellets were placed beneath the skin of B6 mice, their testes shrank and the number of sperm seen in the seminiferous tubules dropped dramatically. This wide range of sensitivities has important consequences for determining safety limits for humans. This is sometimes known as the variance in the dose response to a given chemical.

Environmental Thyroid Hormone Disruptors

The structure of some PCBs resembles that of thyroid hormones, and exposure to them alters serum thyroid hormone levels in humans. Hydroxylated PCB was found to have high affinities for the thyroid hormone serum transport protein transthyretin, and it can block thyroxine from binding to this protein. This leads to the elevated excretion of the thyroid hormones. Thyroid hormones are critical for the growth of the cochlea of the inner ear, and rats whose mothers were exposed to PCBs had poorly developed cochleas and hearing defects.

Deformed Frogs: Pesticides Mimicking Retinoic Acid?

Throughout the United States and southern Canada there is a dramatic increase in the number of deformed frogs and salamanders in what seem to be pristine woodland ponds. These deformities include extra or missing limbs, missing or misplaced eyes, deformed jaws, and malformed hearts and guts. There is speculation that pesticides (sprayed for mosquito and tick control) might be activating or interfering with the retinoic acid pathway. The spectrum of abnormalities seen in these frogs resembles the malformations caused by exposing tadpoles to retinoic acid.

Chains of Causation

Whether in law or science, establishing chains of causation is a demanding and necessary task. In developmental toxicology, numerous endpoints must be checked, and many different levels of causation have to be established. For instance, one could ask if the pollutant spill in Lake Apopka was responsible for the feminization of male alligators. To establish this, one has to ask how the chemicals in the spill might contribute to reproductive anomalies in male alligators and what would be the consequences of that happening. After observing that the population level of the alligators had declined, unusually high levels of estrogens in the female alligators, unusually low levels of testosterone in the males, and a decrease in the number of births among the alligators were reported. On the tissue and organ level, the decline in birth rate can be explained by the elevated production of estrogens from the juvenile testes, the malformation of the testes and penis, and the changes in enzyme activity in the female gonads. On the cellular level, one sees ovarian abnormalities that correlate with unusually elevated estrogen levels. These cellular changes, in turn, can be explained at the molecular level by the finding that many of the components of the pollutant spill bind to the alligators' estrogen and progesterone receptors and that they are able to circumvent the cell's usual defenses against overproduction of steroid hormones.

Human Impacts

It is a matter of debate now as to how to prove the effects of environmental compounds on humans. Scientists claim that genetic variation in the human species, the lack of controlled experiments to determine the effect of any particular compound on humans, and a large range of other multiple intervening factors make any causality difficult to prove. Evidence from animal studies suggests that humans and natural animal populations are at risk from these endocrine disruptors. It may be that the damage is greater than thought because most risk assessments do not compute cumulative effects. Because of the many exposure vectors of chemicals, the cumulative impacts and risks could be far greater and have far-reaching effects on many people.

Conclusion

As chemical emissions accumulate in the environment and bioaccumulate in humans, more controversy will ensue. Loss of fertility, cancer, and other health issues may not be worth the price of increased profits for industries that use or manufacture these chemicals. As more of these chemicals are used and more of their effects become known, this controversy will escalate.

See also **Children and Cancer; Food Safety; Industrial Agricultural Practices and the Environment; Industrial Feeding Operations for Animals; Pesticides**

Further Reading

Guillette, L. J., and D. Andrew Crain, *Environmental Endocrine Disruptors: An Evolutionary Perspective.* New York: Taylor and Francis, 2000.

Hester, R. E., and Roy M. Harrison, *Endocrine Disrupting Chemicals.* London: Royal Society of Chemists, 1999.

Norris, David O., and James A. Carr, *Endocrine Disruption: Biological Basis for Health Effects in Wildlife and Humans.* New York: Oxford University Press, 2006.

Scott, F. Gilbert, and David Epel, *Ecological Developmental Biology.* Sunderland, MA: Sinauer Associates, 2009.

Wittcoff, Harold A., Jeffery S. Plotkin, and Bryan G. Reuben, *Industrial Organic Chemicals.* Hoboken, NJ: Wiley, 2004.

HUMAN GENOME PROJECT

Edward White

The Human Genome Project was an international scientific effort, coordinated by the U.S. National Institutes of Health and the U.S. Department of Energy in 1990, to decode the string of tens of thousands of genes, which are made up of about three billion pieces of deoxyribonucleic acid (DNA) and help find out what they do. In 2003, project scientists announced that they had successfully mapped the entire human genome, two years earlier than expected.

Scientists saw the discovery as starting a golden age of biomedical science that might be able to cure human diseases, extend human life, and allow humans to reach much more of their full genetic potential than ever before. It was reasoned that simply understanding why the human organism works the way it does might help people to understand who and what they are at a fundamental level.

Critics, however, worried about a future in which "designer" people would be purposely created with genetic alterations that would never have naturally occurred. They saw grave dangers in genetic knowledge being used to deny people with potential problems everything from medical insurance to jobs, thus affecting even their ability to survive. They were concerned that new abilities to understand and alter human genes would allow the wealthy and influential to give themselves and their children advantages over poorer and less influential people who could not afford to pay for the manipulation of their genetic makeup.

Questions include the following: Could genetic engineering generate a new basis for a class system, with "supergeniacs" attaining an enduring supremacy over weaker and poorer people? Could wealthy and influential people customize their children's genetic structure to give them advantages over less privileged people? Would these new abilities, if not made equally available, exacerbate the social inequalities that already exist?

Pros and Cons

One possible gain from decoding the human genome is that knowledge about which genes or combinations of genes can cause certain physical diseases, deformations, or other problems; this would allow scientists to produce tests revealing whether individuals have the potential to develop an illness or disability. Many genetic predispositions merely *suggest* that an individual might develop a condition: the finding is not definite or conclusive. Knowledge that an individual has a particular gene or set of genes could offer a heads-up on anemia, multiple sclerosis, or diabetes; yet like diabetes, a person can carry the gene without developing the disease. Similarly, a person might be genetically predisposed to alcoholism but never become an alcoholic. The selling point for the project in part was that it would lead to the reduction of health care costs by nabbing potential conditions before they developed, much like murder was handled in the movie *Minority Report.*

Researchers seek to somehow remove the problem component by replacing it or "turning it off." The purposeful manipulation of human genes to eliminate or minimize the effects of "bad" genes or DNA is called *gene therapy.* Early attempts at using gene therapy to improve human situations have been disappointing, but scientists remain optimistic.

Scientists in 2009 had begun mapping genetic sequences of entire families to study disease and other maladies. As of this writing (mid-2010), scientists were using the human genome to make ancestral connections not only within families but also with Neanderthals, for example. In 2009, *Genetic Engineering & Biotechnology News* reported researchers who sequenced an entire immediate family discovered that parents pass along fewer "genetic mutations" to their children than previously thought. The children were born with two extremely rare conditions: Miller's syndrome and primary ciliary dyskinesia. Scientists were given permission to compare variants in the children's DNA sequences with the Human Genome Project's research. The result confirmed an earlier study that identified four "candidate" gene mutations for causing each disorder.

Certainly some scientists will use the human genome to develop new therapies, drugs, and treatments for human diseases. But what if an insurance company required all applicants for medical or life insurance to submit to a genetic test? The test would reveal potential genetically based diseases or disorders. Would health insurers charge people more or less depending on their predispositions at the time of birth? Or would they simply decline to insure the child? Would this create a class of citizens who could not obtain insurance, not because they actually had a condition but because they might develop one in the future? Could employers, some of whom offer medical insurance coverage, demand such tests and refuse to hire people with potential problems?

Officials elected to the U.S. Congress have introduced legislation attempting to give employees rights in this matter and balance them with those of employers and insurance companies. Around the world, legislators have wrestled with the issue of how to protect rights to employment, insurance, and privacy in an age in which knowledge of someone's genetic makeup can say much about their possible future.

Conclusion

The human genetic code does not yet provide the ability to create Robocop-type or Cylon-like human-machine hybrids. There is no evidence that Data, the peaceful and searching character of the television program Star Trek, will not be developed *before* hybrid military robots. Legislators in the United States are keeping watch on genomics and related ethical considerations. The basic list of genes and their components elucidated by the Human Genome Project is now available to enhance or detract from life as we know it today.

See also **Cloning; Eugenics; Genetic Engineering**

Further Reading

Batra, Karen, "National Academy of Sciences Says Genetic Engineering Could Save Florida's Oranges." *Biotechnology Industry Organization* (March 26, 2010).

Genetic Engineering & Biotechnology News, http://www.genengnews.com

Hubbard, Ruth, and Elijh Wald. *Exploding the Gene Myth: How Genetic Information Is Produced and Manipulated by Scientists, Physicians, Employers, Insurance Companies, Educators, and Law Enforcers.* Boston: Beacon Press, 1999.

Human Genome Project, http://genome.gsc.riken.go.jp/hgmis/project/hgp.html/

Lewontin, R. C., Steven Rose, and Leon J. Kamin, *Not in Our Genes: Biology, Ideology, and Human Nature.* New York: Pantheon, 1984.

Moore, David S., *The Dependent Gene: The Fallacy of "Nature vs. Nurture."* New York: Henry Holt, 2002.

National Academies, "Destructive Citrus Greening Disease Affecting Florida Could Be Combated with Bacteria-Resistant Trees, Early Detection, Coordinated Efforts, Says Report." March 23, 2010a. http://www8.nationalacademies.org/onpinews/newsitem.aspx?RecordID=12880/

National Academies, "Strategic Planning for the Florida Citrus Industry: Addressing Citrus Greening Disease." National Research Council of the National Academies Board on Agriculture and National Resources Division on Earth and Life Studies. National Academies Press: Washington, DC, 2010b, http://www.nap.edu/catalog.php?record_id=12880

Ridley, Matt. *Nature via Nurture: Genes, Experience, & What Makes Us Human.* New York: HarperCollins, 2003.

Simeonidis, Simos. "Biotech Financing Overview and Trends from Last Year's Fourth Quarter." *Genetic Engineering & Biotechnology News.* January 19, 2010. http://tinyurl.com/288c8mc

Stober, Spencer S., and Donna Yarri, *God, Science, and Designer Genes: An Exploration of Emerging Genetic Technologies.* Westport, CT: Praeger, 2009.

I

INCINERATION AND RESOURCE RECOVERY

Robert William Collin

Burning waste for energy purposes is controversial because it may increase the toxicity of the emissions in the form of ash. This is waste that would otherwise go to full U.S. landfills. Many incineration corporations have claimed they were making energy to get status as a utility. At that time utilities were exempt from the right-to-know laws.

Incineration: More Than Just Burning the Trash

Burning the trash is an old custom in many rural areas of the United States. Even today, the EPA estimates that the burning of private residential trash is a major source of pollution in the upper Midwest. Historically, burning trash and waste was an improvement over leaving it around or just placing it in heaps. Burning the trash reduced its volume and risk. Waste can be a vector for many public health risks, and it can attract vermin. Rats, mice, and other rodents can become vectors for diseases such as bubonic plague and spread the risk of deadly disease deep into human populations. Waste can also be fuel and shelter. U.S. pioneers in the Midwest used buffalo chips (waste) to build sod houses. Dried, this waste could be burned for fuel and heat. This type of waste was the main type of waste, as opposed to today's chemically enriched, multisubstance, potentially toxic waste stream.

An estimated 14 to 16 percent of the U.S. waste stream is incinerated. It could be more because many industrial and military wastes are incinerated as well. Generally, waste is delivered to the incinerator. The movement of waste itself is peppered with controversies.

The waste may have come from long distances, from cities and waste transfer stations. As U.S. environmental consciousness has increased, more people have become interested in where their waste goes and what environmental impact it has. Waste transfer stations can become a local land-use issues and sometimes an environmental justice issue. When landfills become full, waste must wait in waste transfer stations. The waste can be hazardous. Many communities fear that the transfer station will become a permanent waste site, as some in fact have. The waste is delivered by truck, ship, and railroad. Sometimes there are spills of hazardous wastes, with severe environmental and community repercussions. Environmental justice communities may have an overconcentration of poorly regulated waste transfer sites. These sites are where many spills occur. When energy is to be used from the incineration, the waste is taken to an energy recovery facility, where it is burned in combustion chambers or boilers. High combustion temperatures can help most of the waste burn thoroughly. This is one goal of incineration—less ash for disposal. Environmentalists are very concerned with air emissions from incinerators. These facilities have large emissions that can accumulate quickly around the site as heavier particulate matter such as metals falls to the ground. Metals are difficult to burn completely. Much of what the incinerators put out reflects what is put into them. Waste stream control is difficult at best, although improvements in recycling have benefited other waste streams. Older, pre-1970 incinerators burned everything they could fit into them. Parts of older buildings painted with lead paint are still burned as hazardous waste. The lead does not burn and drops down as particulate matter, creating a risk of toxicity, as it did in Flint, Michigan. Combustible, explosive, illegal, and other dangerous materials inhabit the waste stream. Evidence of a crime or environmental impact that is burned is usually less recognizable than when placed in a landfill. Medical wastes can include all sorts of waste, including trace amounts of radioactive material. Many older municipal incinerators in the southeastern United States were placed in African American communities, exposing generations to heavy metals such as lead, mercury, and cadmium for decades. Issues such as this surround the movement of waste generally and incineration of it specifically. Industry claims that modern air pollution control devices include electrostatic precipitators, dry and wet scrubbers, and/or fabric; and that these get out everything dangerous. Cumulative emissions are not measured, although their human and environmental impacts can be large.

Current Waste Management in the United States

To say that waste is managed is an overstatement. The main characteristic of U.S. waste trends is the massive increase in volume. Enormous progress in regulating the waste stream is a primary characteristic of the U.S. waste management approach. Federal government financing of the expensive infrastructure, sometimes inclusive of modern pollution-control and abatement technologies, made it possible for local governments to treat solid wastes. The waste stream of the 2000s is very different from that of

50 years ago. It contains inorganic materials that can create risks for people and for the environment. This has increased the overall controversy of siting and permit renewals for incinerator facilities. It has also moved the debate into the courts. Recently, incinerators in the African American community of urban north Florida from the 1920s until the 1970s provided the basis for a successful $76 million tort settlement for wrongful deaths and other environmental impacts. The plaintiffs are quick to point out that money does not replace lost lives of loved ones. These bitter victories only increase the rancor of this controversy.

The Benefits of Resource Recovery through Incineration

Industry claims that by burning the solid wastes into ash, incineration reduces the volume of waste entering the landfill by approximately 90 percent. Recovering some of the energy from burning waste can produce electricity. This can help offset any potential cost

ENERGY VALUE OF PLASTICS, MUNICIPAL SOLID WASTES, AND NATURAL RESOURCES

Plastic Material Energy Value

When material is incinerated, it gives off different levels of energy useful in resource recovery. Emissions from burning these materials, their amount, their toxicity, and the remaining ash are not considered.

Polyethylene terephthalate 9,000–9,700
Polyethylene 19,900
Polyvinyl chloride 7,500–9,000
Polypropylene 18,500–19,500
Polystyrene 17,800

Municipal Solid Waste Material Energy Value

Newspaper 8,000
Textiles 6,900
Wood 6,700
Yard wastes 3,000
Food wastes 2,600
Average for municipal solid waste 4,500

Natural Resources Energy Value

Fuel oil 20,900
Wyoming coal 9,600

Plastics are pervasive in U.S. society. They are used all over the world in agriculture in large amounts. Incineration of wastes such as plastic to create electrical energy could be sustainable depending on the environmental impacts of the ash and air emissions.

of environmental mitigation. Resource recovery by incineration of wastes is considered so efficient that old landfills are being opened up and that waste then incinerated for its energy potential.

Resource Recovery of Plastics

Plastics have a higher energy value and heat content than most municipal solid waste materials. While making up 7 percent of the waste stream by weight and 20 percent by volume, plastics provide incinerators with 25 percent of the recoverable energy from municipal solid wastes. A pound of polyethylene supplies 19,000 British thermal units (Btu), but corrugated paper packaging provides only 7,000 Btu. The incineration of plastics produces more energy.

Another major issue around the incineration of plastics is the environmental impacts of the emissions. Many plastics contain heavy metals such as lead and cadmium, which can increase the toxicity of the incinerator ashes, thus causing the ashes to be hazardous wastes. If they are emitted into the air, they may fall as particulate matter on nearby land and waterways. Currently, incinerator ashes are not categorized as hazardous wastes and can usually be disposed of in landfills. In some communities this can be a significant issue. When that happens, this ash can back up in waste transfer stations. The waste transfer stations are not designed or sited as terminal places for waste of any kind, much less hazardous waste. A small incineration plant processes approximately 300 tons of waste each day, while a large plant can process about 3,000 tons.

Incinerators can produce enough energy to run an industrial facility or a small community, depending on volume and kind of waste stream.

Waste-to-Energy Facilities and Their Operations

The cost of building a waste-to-energy incinerator is very high. The volume of truck traffic will increase. Depending on the facility's permit to operate, it may not be approved to accept all wastes. Trucks delivering wastes are required to display signs that indicate the hazards of their waste loads. Economically, resource-recovery incinerators need a reliable, steady stream of high-energy waste or else processing the waste material will cost more energy than it produces.

Conclusion

Incineration is a waste treatment method sanctioned by the government because research is inadequate to prove it unsafe. This lack of science allows potentially dangerous emissions to enter the environment and communities. The effect of the quantity and types of pesticides in the incineration process has yet to be determined and may present an unaccounted exposure vector to nearby populations and environments. Many communities feel that the burden should be on industry to prove that an emission is safe

INCINERATION AS A METHOD FOR RESOURCE RECOVERY FROM INEDIBLE BIOMASS IN A CONTROLLED ECOLOGICAL LIFE-SUPPORT SYSTEM

In research published by the NASA Ames Research Center, Advanced Life Support Division, Regenerative Systems Branch, Moffett Field, California, waste recovery is serious business.

Resource recovery from waste streams in a space habitat is essential to minimize the resupply burden and achieve self-sufficiency. In a controlled ecological life-support system (CELSS), human wastes and inedible biomass will represent significant sources of secondary raw materials necessary to support of crop plant production (carbon, water, and inorganic plant nutrients). Incineration, pyrolysis, and water extraction have been investigated as candidate processes for recovery of these important resources from inedible biomass in a CELSS. During incineration, carbon dioxide is produced by oxidation of the organic components, and this product can be directly utilized by plants. Water is concomitantly produced, requiring only a phase change for recovery. Recovery of inorganics is more difficult, requiring solubilization of the incinerator ash. The process of incineration followed by water solubilization of ash resulted in the loss of 35 percent of the inorganics originally present in the biomass. Losses were attributed to volatilization (8 percent) and non–water-soluble ash (27 percent). All of the ash remaining following incineration could be solubilized with acid, with losses resulting from volatilization only. The recovery for individual elements varied. Elemental retention in the ash ranged from 100 percent of that present in the biomass for Ca, P, Mg, Na, and Si to 10 percent for Zn. The greatest water solubility was observed for potassium, with recovery of approximately 77 percent of that present in the straw. Potassium represented 80 percent of the inorganic constituents in the wheat straw and, because of slightly greater solubility, made up 86 percent of the water-soluble ash. Following incineration of inedible biomass from wheat, 65 percent of the inorganics originally present in the straw were recovered by water solubilization and 92 percent by acid solubilization. Recovery of resources is more complex for pyrolysis and water extraction. Recovery of carbon, a resource of greater mass than the inorganic component of biomass, is more difficult following pyrolysis and water extraction of biomass. In both cases, additional processors would be required to provide products equivalent to those resulting from incineration alone. The carbon, water, and inorganic resources of inedible biomass are effectively separated and, through incineration, output in usable forms results.

before it is allowed. Currently the burden is on those harmed to prove it is unsafe to a scientific level of certainty, which is quite high. This controversy reopens a more basic question of whether science should control policy. If the scientific methods are underfunded, slow, and not accessible, then environmental policy stagnates. However, political pressure often forces the government to develop new, controversial policies without waiting for the science to catch up. Incineration as an environmental practice by itself may be limited as environmental policy expands to include concepts of sustainability.

However, because it uses the energy from waste and diverts waste from landfills, resource recovery from incineration may see new applications. The larger question is what to do with all the waste, how to stop the generation of waste, and how to clean up the waste already here. Controversies will follow each of these questions.

See also **Air Pollution; Waste Management**

Further Reading

Dhir, Ravindra, Thomas D. Dyer, and Kevin A. Paine, eds., *Sustainable Construction: Use of Incinerator Ash.* London: Thomas Telford, 2000.

Hamerton, Azapagic, Adisa Azapagic, and Alan Emsley, eds., *Polymers: The Environment and Sustainable Development.* Hoboken, NJ: Wiley, 2003.

Holly, Hattemer-Frey, et al., eds., *Health Effects of Municipal Waste Incineration.* Boca Raton, FL: CRC Press, 1991.

Niessen, Walter R., *Combustion and Incineration Processes: Applications in Environmental Engineering.* New York: Marcel Dekker, 2002.

Shevory, Thomas C., *Toxic Burn: The Grassroots Struggle against the WTI Incinerator.* Minneapolis: University of Minnesota Press, 2007.

INDUSTRIAL AGRICULTURAL PRACTICES AND THE ENVIRONMENT

ROBERT WILLIAM COLLIN

Industrial agricultural practices can have large impacts on the environment and entire ecosystem. Environmentalists, small family farmers, downstream communities, and environmental justice communities object to these impacts.

E. COLI IN FOOD AS A RESULT OF INDUSTRIAL AGRICULTURAL PRACTICES?

E. coli is everywhere in the environment. Some strains can be deadly. At the Lane County Fair in Eugene, Oregon, about 140 children contracted a severe strain of *E. coli*. All the children survived, but some were hospitalized for an extended period. All of them now have that strain within them. The cause of this contact was the failure of children to wash their hands after petting the goats and sheep.

Another recent concern is that some strains of *E. coli* could be the result of agricultural industrial practices. This organism has been found in the soil and vegetables from Californian's Central Valley. As these farms are not rigorously regulated for such risks, there is much controversy about who is to blame.

Historically, humans as hunter-gatherers would hunt in an area and then move on. Over time, a human community would settle in a given location and turn to farming. When the game was gone and the soil infertile, the community would move to another location. Human population was so small then, and the environmental impacts of the technology so low, that this allowed the used-up region to regenerate. This method was sustainable only as long as there were new places to move to and environmental impacts remained within the period of time necessary for the regeneration of natural systems. This method was used by European colonial powers all around the planet. In the United States, this method was used by European farmers who moved to the New World. Many European settlers to North America felt a manifest destiny to colonize the continent from coast to coast.

Industrialized Agriculture

Industrialized agriculture can have several meanings. It can mean substituting machines for people in the food production process, increasing the scale of production beyond the regenerative capacity of the land, and using chemicals instead of natural organic materials. In the case of chemicals, when farmers discovered that certain chemicals can replace the older way of fertilizing, they realized that they could save time. The old process of fertilizing was called manuring. It took a large amount of time. Farmers in search of higher productivity industrialized in order to compete on world markets. They used more machines, increased the scale of production, and relied on technology for time-saving efficiency in food production and preparation. Unfortunately, these machines can emit environmentally damaging pollutants, the land can give out, and the chemicals can create public health risks. Each category of industrialization of agriculture is an issue within this controversy and is of concern to environmentalists and others because of its potential environmental impacts and human health risks.

The contours of this controversy are shaped by rapidly developing technology that thrives on large-scale applications and a growing scientific consensus and mobilization of community concern about health risks.

Mainstream agriculture faces enormous controversies and dynamic changes driven in part by environmental issues. The debate around this controversy is affected by the following changing conditions.

- Climate change will have a major impact on agricultural practices in many areas.
- Agriculture will have to find alternative energy sources to sustain productivity because of its current high reliance on nonrenewable energy.
- Environmental waste sinks are increasing in size. The hypoxic zone in the Gulf of Mexico increased to 8,200 square miles in 2002. Most scientists attribute this to runoff from agricultural activities all along the Mississippi River watershed. The same is true for most coastal outlets in industrialized nations.

ANATOMY OF CENTERS FOR DISEASE CONTROL (CDC) RESPONSE TO *E. COLI*

On Friday, September 8, 2006, Centers for Disease Control (CDC) officials were alerted by epidemiologists in Wisconsin of a small cluster of *E. coli* serotype O157:H7 infections of unknown source. Wisconsin also posted the DNA fingerprint pattern of the cluster to PulseNet, thus alerting the entire network. Separately, the state health department of Oregon also noted a very small cluster of infections that day and began interviewing the cases. On September 13, both Wisconsin and Oregon reported to the CDC that initial interviews suggested that eating fresh spinach was commonly reported by cases in both clusters of *E. coli* serotype O157:H7 infections in those states. PulseNet showed that the patterns in the two clusters were identical, and other states reported cases with the same PulseNet pattern among ill persons who also had eaten fresh spinach. The CDC notified the U.S. Food and Drug Administration (FDA) about the Wisconsin and Oregon cases and the possible link with bagged fresh spinach. The CDC and FDA convened a conference call on September 14 to discuss the outbreak with the states.

Quick sharing of information among the states, CDC, and FDA led to the FDA warning the public on September 14, 2006, not to eat fresh bagged spinach. On September 15, the number of reported cases approached 100. Cases were identified by PulseNet and interviewed in detail by members of OutbreakNet. Leftover spinach was cultured at the CDC, FDA, and in state public health laboratories. The epidemiological investigation indicated that the outbreak stemmed from a single plant on a single day during a single shift.

Coordination with the FDA was important for investigating this outbreak. Frequent conference calls relayed the data on spinach purchases and sources to the FDA, guiding the ongoing investigation of production sites of possible interest.

Between August 1 and October 6, a total of 199 persons infected with the outbreak strain of *E. coli* O157:H7 were reported to the CDC from 26 states. Among the ill persons, 102 were hospitalized, 31 had developed hemolytic-uremic syndrome (risking kidney failure), and 3 died. Eighty-five percent of patients reported illness onset from August 19 to September 5. Among the 130 patients from whom a food consumption history was collected, 123 (95%) reported consuming uncooked fresh spinach during the 10 days before illness onset. In addition, *E. coli* O157:H7 with the same DNA matching the tainted strain was isolated from 11 open packages of fresh spinach that had been partially consumed by patients.

This outbreak strain of *E. coli* O157:H7 is one of 3,520 different *E. coli* O157:H7 patterns reported to CDC's PulseNet since 1996. Infections with this strain have been reported sporadically to CDC's PulseNet since 2003, at an average of 21 cases per year from 2003 to 2005. This finding suggests that this strain has been present in the environment and food supply occasionally, although it had not been associated with a recognized outbreak in the past.

(continued)

(continued)

Parallel laboratory and epidemiological investigations were crucial in identifying the source of this outbreak. Rapid collection of standard case exposure information by epidemiologists in affected states led to rapid identification of the suspected food source and public health alerts.

Sustainable Agriculture

Sustainable agriculture is defined as the ability to maintain productivity of the land. In general terms, sustainable agriculture includes the following principles. It must be

- Ecologically restorative
- Socially resilient
- Economically viable

This shifts the emphasis from managing resources to managing ourselves. Agricultural corporations and associated trade groups view this as increased governmental intrusion and do not embrace these ideals in their entirety.

The small farmer is a part of the settlement of the United States. Many laws were written to protect the small family farmer. Currently, many of these laws are used by agribusiness. Some environmentalists think they do so to hide environmental impacts. It has been very difficult to get right-to-know legislation passed in agricultural areas in agricultural states. Agribusiness resists the increased reporting requirements because of the added cost and decreased profitability, especially in regard to pesticides.

Conclusion

The farmer and the cowboy are classical figures in U.S. history and culture. However, they do not fit well with modern industrialization of agriculture. Modern agribusiness is a group of large, powerful corporations and banks. One issue in this controversy is the cultural clash of old and traditional cultures with new ways of producing food.

The industrialization of agricultural practices is not new. Agricultural research at U.S. land grant colleges and universities helped to create the green revolution, which modernized many agricultural practices and pushed them into greater productivity. Now some of the long-term results are more evident. Many people were fed, but some of the long-term consequences may pose risks to public health and the environment. These practices may also not be sustainable, especially with rapid climate change and urban population increases. This entire issue is an emerging political battleground. The technological modernization of food production is continuing. Food can now be produced without soil. Although such techniques still remain at the research stage, their implications for food production are enormous. Food production would no longer have to be tied to the land. These new changes in

WHAT IS *E. COLI*?

E. coli is the abbreviated name of the bacterium in the family Enterobacteriaceae named *Escherichia* (genus) *coli* (species). Approximately 0.1 percent of the total bacteria within an adult's intestines (on a Western diet) is represented by *E. coli*, although in a newborn infant's intestines *E. coli*, along with lactobacilli and enterococci, represent the most abundant bacterial flora. The presence of *E. coli* and other kinds of bacteria within our intestines is necessary for us to develop and operate properly and remain healthy. The fetus of an animal is completely sterile. Immediately after birth, however, the newborn acquires all kinds of different bacteria that live symbiotically with the newborn and throughout the individual's life. A rare strain of *E. coli* is *E. coli* O157:H7, a member of the enterohemorrhagic *E. coli* (EHEC) group. *Enterohemorrhagic* means that this organism causes internal bleeding.

This strain of *E. coli* and all of its progeny produce a toxin. The toxin is a protein that causes severe damage to the cells of the intestinal wall. If this condition is left untreated, internal bleeding occurs, potentially leading to complications and death.

technology will also be highly controversial, opening new environmental possibilities for former farmland.

See also Food Safety; Genetically Modified Organisms; Industrial Feeding Operations for Animals; Pesticides; Sustainability (vol. 1)

Further Reading

Anderson, J. L., *Industrializing the Corn Belt: Agriculture, Technology, and Environment, 1945–1972.* DeKalb: Northern Illinois University Press, 2008.

Bellamy, John Foster, Frederick Butell, and Fred Magdoff, *Hungry for Profit: The Agribusiness Threat to Farmers, Food, and the Environment.* New York: Monthly Review Press, 2000.

Gliessman, Stephen R., *Agroecology: The Ecology of Sustainable Food Systems,* 2d ed. Boca Raton, FL: CRC Press, 2006.

Jansen, Kees, and Sietze Velleme, *Agribusiness and Society: Corporate Responses to Environmentalism, Market Opportunities, and Public Regulation.* London: Zed Books, 2004.

Kimbrell, Andrew, *Fatal Harvest: The Tragedy of Industrial Agriculture.* Sausalito, CA: Foundation for Deep Ecology, 2002.

Manno, Jack P., *Privileged Goods: Commoditization and Its Impact on Environment and Society.* Boca Raton, FL: CRC Press, 2000.

INDUSTRIAL FEEDING OPERATIONS FOR ANIMALS

Robert William Collin

Animal agriculture is switching to industrial practices to meet the needs of a growing world population and increase profits by replacing small to midsize animal farms with large, industrial-scale animal feeding operations (AFOs) that maximize the number of livestock confined per acre of land. Confinement of large numbers of animals in such operations can result in large discharges of animal feed- and waste-related substances (animal residuals) to the environment. The implications of waste management practices at AFOs for ecosystem viability and human health are very controversial. Potential effects of AFOs on the quality of surface water, groundwater, and air and on human health pose controversial issues.

Cattle

Cattle, sheep, hogs, goats, and other animals have been raised for food all over the world for many years. Their environmental impacts are different based on the animal and the particular environment. Goats and hogs can have big impacts on ground cover and do long-term damage to sensitive ecotones such as mountains. Cattle take large amounts of grassland to grow to market maturation. Environmentalists often object to eating beef because the environmental footprint of cattle raising is so large. Some have argued that rain forest deforestation from slash-and-burn techniques is motivated by a desire to expand grazing ranges for cattle. Cattle production is big business. There are about 500,000 concentrated animal feeding operations (CAFOs), about 20,000 of which are regulated under the pollution laws. Three states—Texas, Kansas, and Nebraska—account for two-thirds of all feedlot production of beet cattle in the United States. Ranchers are important political constituencies in these states.

Cattle feedlot operations are financially dominated by large corporations. Industrial feeding operations have refined the process of raising calves to slaughter-ready weight with industrial production methods. These focus on cost-to-profit measures and often prioritize size, weight gain, and time to market.

Environmental Impacts

Large feedlot operations have provoked controversy in their communities, focused on the environmental damage caused by waste runoff and air pollution. Feedlot waste can be found in a watershed up to 300 miles away, depending on the hydrology of that particular watershed.

Lagoons are pools of water used to treat waste from animal feeding operations. They are an older, low-volume, low-cost form of waste treatment but require maintenance. Waste treatment lagoons are often poorly maintained. They have broken, failed, or overflowed. They are prone to natural disasters like floods and hurricanes. When they overflow or break, the waste enters the watershed. Often the waste mixes with high levels of nitrogen and phosphorus from agricultural runoff. This can have major environmental impacts.

CAFOS IN OREGON

EPA's Concentrated Animal Feeding Operation (CAFO) Enforcement: The Case of Oregon

With an estimated 1.5 million head of cattle in Oregon, dairy and beef operations produce at least 7.5 million tons of manure per year; this must be accounted for and kept out of Oregon's waters. Animal waste in water represents an environmental issue and a human health issue. For instance, animal waste is high in nutrients. When it enters a water body, oxygen can be depleted, preventing the breakdown of nutrients and undermining the survival of fish. Animal waste can also contain bacteria and viruses that are harmful to humans, including *E. coli* and *Salmonella*. Additionally, if cattle are allowed into streams, they can trample the streamside vegetation, which reduces shade cover and increases water temperature. It also increases erosion—that is, sediment deposition, which can severely affect the aquatic biota. A number of trout and salmon species found in Oregon are listed or have been proposed for listing as endangered species.

The Clean Water Act was enacted in 1972; however, some cases remain where CAFO owners have done little or nothing to keep animal waste from Oregon waters. CAFOs are defined as point sources under the National Pollutant Discharge Elimination system, and a discharge of animal waste to surface waters is illegal. These discharges often result from overflowing waste storage ponds, runoff from holding areas and concrete pads, or animals having direct access to surface waters. State and EPA regulators have made many efforts to educate the CAFO owners, yet violations persist. EPA's initial efforts began with dairies; they now include cattle feedlots as well as other CAFO operations—for example, hog farms, racetracks, and so on.

The direct involvement of the EPA in the regulation of CAFOs in Oregon is not new. In fact, the EPA has been involved in enforcing these regulations against dairy farms since 1994. The controversy that exists at this time is the result of the EPA's efforts to expand enforcement beyond the Oregon dairy industry to include beef cattle operations, which are a segment of the Oregon CAFO population that has received limited compliance inspections over the last several years, even though they have been subject to the regulations since 1972. In 2007, the EPA directed some attention toward feedlots in eastern Oregon.

The EPA's objectives in taking federal enforcement actions against CAFOs in Oregon are as follows:

- To reduce the environmental and public health threat.
- To level the playing field among CAFOs by eliminating the economic advantage that violators have enjoyed over those who have invested capital to comply with the law.
- To encourage compliance and deter others from violating the law through education and public notice of penalties, thus supporting local efforts.

(continued)

(*continued*)

- To encourage the state of Oregon to reassume its lead role in CAFO enforcement.
- To use the authority of the Clean Water Act as part of the salmon restoration efforts. The EPA is required by law to use this authority under Section 7(a)1 of the Endangered Species Act.

The EPA has been directly involved in the regulation of Oregon CAFOs since 1994. In that time, the EPA has been involved in several activities that have resulted in the education of CAFO owners. These activities include the following:

1. Fact sheets, describing the EPA CAFO requirements and enforcement strategy, mailed annually to producers, assistance providers (NRCS), and industry associations such as the Oregon Dairy Association and the Oregon Cattlemen's Association.
2. Public meetings to discuss EPA requirements and enforcement strategy. These meetings were held in 1999–2000 in Pendleton, LaGrande, Enterprise, Baker City, Portland, Tillamook, Boise, and Tri-cities that were attended by both producers and assistance providers.
3. Several meetings with assistance providers (e.g., local conservation districts) to discuss EPA requirements and enforcement strategy.
4. Public notice of EPA enforcement actions against CAFO operations in Region 10.

What Types of CAFO Operations Are Being Enforced Against?

The EPA is targeting the worst cases first. In the cases filed to date, enforcement actions have been undertaken against operations with confinement areas literally in the stream or where streams run directly through the confinement area with no attempt to keep manure out of the water and sites that have a direct discharge of waste to surface waters. Penalty assessments in Oregon have ranged from $11,000 to $50,000.

The EPA supports voluntary and community efforts to correct these problems, and EPA has supported many of these efforts with grant funds and people in the field. However, some recalcitrant operators remain who seem to need an incentive to do what others have done without having enforcement actions filed against them.

Lagoons and Public Health

One major battleground of industrial feeding operations is the surrounding community. Gases are emitted by lagoons, including ammonia (a toxic form of nitrogen), hydrogen sulfide, and methane. These are all greenhouse gases and pollutants. The gases formed in the process of treating animal waste are toxic and potentially explosive.

Water contaminated by animal manure contributes to human diseases, potentially causing acute gastroenteritis, fever, kidney failure, and even death. According to the Natural Resources Defense Council, nitrates seeping from lagoons have contaminated groundwater used for human drinking water. Nitrate levels above 10 milligrams per liter in drinking water increase the risk of methemoglominemia, or blue baby syndrome, which can cause death in infants.

The Lagoons Harm Water Quality

There are also often cumulative effects from runoff within local watersheds because multiple large-scale feedlots cluster around slaughterhouses.

Watersheds far away are also affected by the atmospheric emission of gases from industrial feeding operations' lagoons, so that the environment is affected by both air and water pathways. Lagoons are often located close to water, which increases the potential of ecological damage. In many places, lagoons are permitted even where groundwater can be threatened. These communities have strong concerns, especially if they use well systems as many rural residents do. If water quantity is a local concern, then lagoons pose another battleground. The lagoon system depletes groundwater supplies by using large quantities of water to flush the manure into the lagoon. As water quantity decreases, pollutants and other chemicals become more concentrated. This decreases the quality of the remaining water dramatically.

The Hog Farm Controversy

One of the biggest controversies over animal feeding operations occurred in South Carolina. Legislation introduced to accommodate hog-farming and hog-butchering operations created some of the controversy. Introduced under the title of a Right to Farm bill, the legislation passed the State House of Representatives without close scrutiny. Controversy began to build during the fall, when it became clear that the legislation would deprive local governments of some power to control land use. National media stories of environmental problems with large-scale hog farms in North Carolina started to get public attention. Those interested in economic development saw large-scale hog operations as a possible substitute for tobacco. Many of the objections to bringing the hog industry into South Carolina have to do with environmental degradation. One factor in the South Carolina hog controversy was how much waste the waterways could absorb. South Carolina water pollution permits have limited availability for waste. They did not want to use that remaining water-pollution capacity for low-return economic development.

South Carolina's legislators decided that if they lost the hog industry, they would not lose many economic benefits, and if they kept it, it would be associated with difficult environmental problems that could hamper economic development over the long run.

EPA Attempts at Regulation

The U.S. Environmental Protection Agency (EPA) recognizes that AFOs pose a variety of threats to human health and the environment. According to the EPA, pollutants from livestock operations include nutrients, organic matter, sediments, pathogens, heavy metals, hormones, antibiotics, dust, and ammonia. In response to increasing community complaints and the industrialization of the livestock industry, the EPA developed water-quality regulations that affect AFOs directly and indirectly, and it is a running battle. The focus of these actions is on the control of nutrient leaching and runoff. The development of this new set of rules is a large battleground.

Concentrated animal feeding operations (CAFOs) are defined as point sources under the Clean Water Act. They are required to obtain a permit to discharge treated and untreated waste into water. Effluent guidelines establish the best available technology economically achievable for CAFOs over a certain size threshold. A threshold is the maximum amount of a chemical allowed without a permit. Thresholds pervade U.S. environmental policy and allow industries that self-report their thresholds to escape environmental scrutiny. A constant regulatory battleground is lowering the threshold to expand the reach of the regulations to include all those with environmental impacts. Many communities and environmentalists complain that the thresholds for water discharges from industrial feeding operations are much too high, thereby allowing risky discharges into water. Industry wants to remain unregulated as much as possible because it perceives these regulations as decreasing profitability. The battleground about effluent thresholds for CAFOs is a major one. The new permitting regulations address smaller CAFOs and describe additional requirements, such as monitoring and reporting.

How Do We Control the Environmental Impacts?

The proposed total maximum daily load (TMDL) regulations and the development of nutrient water-quality criteria will impact AFOs indirectly. States are required to develop TMDLs for water bodies that do not meet the standards for nutrients or other pollutants. A TMDL is a calculation of the maximum amount of a pollutant that a water body can receive and still meet water-quality standards. Through the TMDL process, pollutant loads will be allocated among all permit holders. Animal feedlot operations may have to be slowed down if there is no room for their waste in the water. AFO management practices will be more strictly scrutinized in any event, creating a battleground for enforcement of environmental protection rules. This controversy will include the TMDL controversy when it is implemented at that level.

Conclusion

Industrial feedlot operations provide an efficient means of meat production. Communities and environmentalists are very concerned about their environmental impacts. They want to know more about these operations and usually ask for records on effluent discharges, monitoring systems for air and water, feed management, manure handling and storage, land application of manure, tillage, and riparian buffers. New federal regulations, growing population, community concern over environmental and public health impacts, and emerging environmental lawsuits are part of the battlefield for this controversy.

See also **Cumulative Emissions; Food Safety; Hormone Disruptors; Industrial Agricultural Practices and the Environment**

Further Reading

Clay, Jason W., *World Agriculture and the Environment: A Commodity-by-Commodity Guide to Impacts and Practices.* Washington, DC: Island Press, 2004.

Glasgow, Nina, et al., eds., *Critical Issues in Rural Health.* Ames, IA: Blackwell, 2004.

MacLachlan, Ian, *Kill and Chill: Restructuring Canada's Beef Commodity Chain.* Toronto: University of Toronto Press, 2001.

McNeely, Jeffrey A., and Sara J. Scherr, *Ecoagriculture: Strategies to Feed the World and Save Biodiversity.* Washington, DC: Island Press, 2003.

Pruden, Amy, and Laurence S. Shore, eds., *Hormones and Pharmaceuticals Generated by Concentrated Animal Feeding Operations.* New York: Springer-Verlag, 2009.

Spellman, Frank R., and Nancy E. Whiting, *Environmental Management of Concentrated Animal Feeding Operations (CAFOs).*Boca Raton, FL: CRC Press, 2007.

INFLUENZA

Jessica Lyons

The term *influenza* is derived from the Italian word for "influence" and dates from 1357. Italian astrologers of that time believed influenza was the result of the influence of celestial bodies. Influenza is commonly known today as the flu. It is an infectious disease that affects both birds and mammals. Influenza has been at the center of many debates between private and government scientists and within the government itself, and these debates have become an obstacle to medical scientists and physicians seeking to discover an effective treatment and vaccine.

There are many different strains of influenza, some more dangerous than others, but all are caused by an RNA virus from the Orthomyxoviridae family. Influenza is not a disease natural to humans; it is believed to have originated in birds and spread to humans during the last ice age. There are three types of influenza viruses, classified as A, B, and C. Type C rarely causes disease in humans, and type B causes illness but not epidemics. Only type A is capable of producing an epidemic or pandemic. Individuals suffering from seasonal influenza generally recover in two weeks, with 20,000 to 50,000 individuals dying of influenza viral infections annually within the United States.

The Great Influenza Pandemic of 1918–1919

Although influenza has been known for centuries, it became infamous during the Great Influenza Pandemic of 1918–1919, also known as the Spanish flu (type A, H1N1). Interestingly, it received the name Spanish flu simply because the Spanish newspapers were the first to report it, even though it had appeared in the United States months before. This strain of influenza was particularly lethal and is thought to have originated in Haskell County, Kansas. Although this influenza might have died out, the political state of the country at the time helped to spread it worldwide. America had just entered the Great War (1914–1918) and was preparing to ship thousands of soldiers to France. Before this could be done, the soldiers had to be trained. This training took place in cantonments throughout the country, with each cantonment holding tens of thousands of young men in cramped quarters, and influenza spread rapidly among the soldiers and support staff on the base. The movement of troops between U.S. bases, forts, and cantonments ensured that almost no American community went untouched by the disease.

Shipping men overseas helped to promote the spread of influenza throughout Europe and eventually the world, with cases appearing as far away as the Arctic and on remote islands in the South Pacific. Nearly all residents of Western Samoa contracted influenza, and 7,500 were killed—roughly 20 percent of the total population. As surgeon general of the army, William Gorgas was responsible for ensuring the effective and successful performance of military medicine. But although Gorgas was known internationally as an expert on public health, in reality he was given little authority by the U.S. government. Gorgas recommended that drafts be postponed and that the movement of soldiers between cantonments and overseas cease. President Wilson, however, continued to transfer soldiers from bases throughout the country and to ship them overseas, creating strained relations between the president and his military medical advisers.

Because the natural home of influenza is birds and because influenza can survive in pigs, the survival of humans is not necessary in order for influenza to survive. As a result, mortality rates in humans can reach extremely high numbers. Contemporary estimates suggest that 50 to 100 million individuals were killed worldwide during the Great Influenza Pandemic—2.5 to 5 percent of the world's population—and 65 percent of those infected in the United States died.

A second battle was being fought during the Great War, this one between the scientists and influenza itself. It was no mystery that disease followed war, and on the eve of the United States' entrance into this war, the military recruited the top medical minds in the United States. These included William Welch, founder of Johns Hopkins University; Victor Vaughan, dean of the Michigan medical school; Simon Flexner, Welch's protégé; Paul Lewis from Penn; Milton Rosenau from Harvard; and Eugene Opie at Washington University. Eventually the entire Rockefeller Institute was incorporated into the army as Army Auxiliary Laboratory Number One by Surgeon General of the

Army William Gorgas. As the pandemic raged on, scientists found themselves in a race against time. They worked night and day, at times around the clock, in an attempt to develop a treatment and a vaccine or antiserum for influenza. The risk was great, as more than one scientist was struck down by the disease itself.

The cause of influenza was not known at this time, and two camps emerged: those who believed influenza to be a virus and those who believed that the bacterium *B. influenzae* caused the disease. During this time a number of medical discoveries were made, such as a treatment for three different types of pneumonia. Unfortunately, no true progress toward creating an influenza vaccine was made until 1944, when Thomas Francis Jr. was able to develop a killed-virus vaccine. His work was expanded on by Frank MacFarlane Burnet, who, with U.S. Army support, created the first successful influenza vaccine.

The American Red Cross was another principal player. Given the tremendous number of both civilian and military deaths due to influenza and the cost of the war overseas, the government could not put together the necessary funds and personnel to care for matters on the home front. Assistance was needed, and when it became apparent that this influenza had reached the scale of a pandemic, the Red Cross created the Red Cross National Committee on Influenza to coordinate a national response. The Red Cross proved invaluable. The Red Cross National Committee took charge of recruiting, supplying, and paying all nursing personnel and was responsible for providing emergency hospital supplies when local authorities were unable to do so and for distributing doctors through the U.S. Public Health Service to wherever they were needed. The shortage of medical personnel created by the war meant that the Red Cross was more or less single-handedly responsible for coordinating the movement of medical personnel throughout the country. Between September 14 and November 7, 1918, the Red Cross recruited over 15,000 women with varying degrees of medical training to serve in military and civilian posts. By spring of the following year, the Red Cross had spent more than $2 million in services.

More Recent Decades

The severity of the 1918–1919 epidemic was not forgotten; since then, influenza has been a concern for physicians, scientists, and policy makers. With the exclusion of recent avian viruses passed directly from bird to human, all type A influenza viruses globally have originated from the 1918 H1N1 virus. In the early 1930s, scientist Richard Shope proved that the feared H1N1 virus was alive and thriving in the country's pig population. This is particularly feared because the pig can act as an intermediary animal, allowing avian flu strains to adapt to mammals and then be passed onto humans. This strain of the H1N1 virus in the pig population is often referred to as swine flu. In 1957 the threat of another pandemic appeared. Government and medical officials feared the return of the H1N1 virus, or swine flu. That was not the case. Although the virus killed upward of a million individuals, it was not the H1N1 virus and instead became known as the Asian flu, an H2N2 virus. An earlier, and much less documented, influenza virus had occurred between 1889 and 1890. This pandemic was known as the Asiatic (Russian) flu. The Asiatic flu killed roughly one million individuals, and it is suspected that it too was an H2N2 virus. The most recent pandemic occurred from 1968 to 1969. Known as the Hong Kong virus (H3N2), it infected many, but the mortality rate was low. It was responsible for 750,000 to 1,000,000 deaths. Although there has not been a pandemic since the Hong Kong flu, public officials, hypersensitive to the threat of a flu epidemic, were concerned for the potential of a swine flu epidemic in 1976 and Asiatic flu pandemic in 1977.

In 1976, at Fort Dix, New Jersey, an 18-year-old private, feeling the symptoms of influenza, decided to join his platoon on a night march anyway. A few hours into the hike, he collapsed. He was dead by the time he reached the base hospital. Although the young private's death was the only suspicious death to occur, it was a reminder of the 1918–1919 virus's ability to kill young adults quickly, and officials feared another epidemic was at hand. Simultaneously, a young boy living on a Wisconsin farm contracted swine flu, surviving thanks to the antibodies produced by handling pigs, which were infected with Shope's swine flu virus. Overwhelmed by the potential consequences of being wrong, medical and government officials chose to prepare themselves for the worst and declared the potential for an epidemic. Dr. David J. Sencer, director of the Centers for Disease Control, requested a $134 million congressional allocation for developing and distributing a vaccine. Following a dramatic televised speech given by the President Gerald Ford, Congress granted $135 million toward vaccine development and distribution in a last-minute vote. The president signed Public Law 94–266, allocating funds for the flu campaign on national television, stating that the Fort Dix virus was the cause of the 1918–1919 pandemic. The epidemic never surfaced. The American flu campaign was criticized on both a national and an international level, and Sencer was removed from his position at the CDC in 1977.

Swine Flu and Bird Flu

The most recent influenza scares have centered on swine flu (H1N1) and avian flu (H5N1). Avian influenza, also known as bird flu, is an extremely virulent virus that generally infects only birds. In recent years, however, it has been documented as infecting pigs and most recently, humans. Since April 2009, CDC has received reports of 338 pediatric deaths from the strain, 282 due to H1N1. Both spread rapidly though animal and human populations and can produce a mortality rate of 100 percent within 48 hours. In 1997 the H5N1 virus spread directly from chickens to humans and killed 16 out of 18 infected. It is this particular virus to which the term *avian influenza* most commonly refers. After this incident, all chickens in Hong Kong (1.2 million) were slaughtered in an effort to contain the virus. This protective measure failed because the virus had been able to spread to the wild bird population. In 2003 two more people were infected with avian flu, and one died. When scientists first tried to develop a vaccine for avian flu using the traditional vaccine growth medium, chicken eggs, they found that the virus was too lethal; the virus was killing the eggs in which it was being grown. A vaccine for avian flu now exists, but it took more than a year to develop, and it has not been stockpiled should a pandemic arise. All of those who caught the virus were infected directly by chickens, and the virus did not develop the ability to spread from human to human.

The potential for creation of a new, lethal virus exists, however. If one of the individuals who caught the avian flu had simultaneously been infected with a human influenza strain, it would have been possible for the two different strains of influenza to separate and recombine, using the human individual as an incubator to create a new strain of avian flu capable of being spread through human-to-human contact. It took a year to develop an avian flu vaccine. Should the virus mutate once more, it would have done the majority of its damage by the time a new vaccine could be developed by scientists. In an effort to stem this possibility, the World Health Organization (WHO) established a formal monitoring system for influenza viruses in 1948. Eighty-two countries and 110 laboratories participate by collecting information, which is then processed by four collaborating WHO laboratories. Any mutations in existing viruses are documented and are then used to adjust the next year's vaccine. The surveillance system also actively searches for any signs of a new influenza strain, especially one with the potential to mutate into the next pandemic.

See also **Epidemics and Pandemics; Vaccines**

Further Reading

Barry, John, *The Great Influenza: The Epic Story of the Deadliest Plague in History.* New York: Viking, 2004.

Centers for Disease Control, Key Flu Indicators, 2009, http://www.cdc.gov/h1n1flu/update.htm

Devlin, Roni K., *Influenza.* Westport, CT: Greenwood Press, 2008.

Garrett, Laurie, *The Coming Plague: Newly Emerging Diseases in a World Out of Balance.* New York: Penguin, 1995.

Gregor, Michael, *Bird Flu: A Virus of Our Own Hatching.* New York: Lantern Books, 2006.

Taubenberger, Jeffery, and David M. Morens, "1918 Influenza: The Mother of All Pandemics." *Emerging Infectious Diseases* 12, no. 1 (2006). http://www.cdc.gov/ncidod/EID/vol12no01/05–0979.htm

World Health Organization, "Influenza." *Epidemic and Pandemic Alert and Response (EPR).* http://www.who.int/csr/disease/influenza/en

INTERNET

Michael H. Farris

The Internet is a worldwide system of computers, a network of networks in which someone with one computer can potentially share information with any other computer.

With the number of such linked computers in the billions, the Internet is viewed as one of the most significant technology advances of the 20th century.

Understanding the Internet is not simply a matter of describing how it works, however. It also requires looking at the consequences of using the World Wide Web. The amazing ability of the Internet to hide its complex technologies leads some to think it is easy to understand. Anyone can point and click and traverse the globe. Fewer can speak sensibly about the way modern culture has changed for better and worse in the Internet age.

Today the terms Internet and World Wide Web mean the same thing for most people. Strictly speaking, they are different. The World Wide Web is the collection of documents, files, and media people access through the Internet. The Internet is the network technology that transports World Wide Web content. Put another way, the Internet makes the World Wide Web possible; it is the World Wide Web that makes the Internet essential.

The two terms are a useful way to talk about "the Internet," as most people call it. The first part of the story is the quiet building of the Internet among academics over 25 years. They had no idea of the eventual significance of their inventions. The second part of the story is the rise of the World Wide Web in popular culture, when it seemed everyone knew they had a revolution on their hands.

Origins

Before either story began to emerge, one of the elements of the Cold War between the United States and the Soviet Union was the significance of science. A few years earlier, the United States had established its superiority in science with the development and detonation of the atomic bomb (1945). Each side knew that scientists could win wars, and the A-bomb seemed indisputable proof of this truth at the time. The Soviets raced to develop their own nuclear weapons and then surpassed the United States by launching the first satellite in 1957. Was Soviet science now better than American science? Did the advantage of space mean victory for the Soviets? A shocked U.S. military responded by forming the Advanced Research Project Agency (ARPA), bringing together the best minds in the nation to regain the technological lead. But how could they work together and communicate across the country? In particular, how could their computers talk to each other and share research? The Internet began simply as the answer to that question.

Dozens of innovations mark the way to the Internet wave of the 1990s, but three building blocks stand out, all beginning with the letter *p:* packets, protocols, and the PC (personal computer). None were created with today's Internet in mind, but all three were used to build today's World Wide Web.

"Packets" were designed for a time of war. Planners needed a way to ensure command and control in the event of a nuclear attack. Regular telephone connections would be useless in an attack, and radio broadcasts were too easily intercepted or jammed. ARPA scientists struck on a way to break up all information into packets, each carrying its destination address and enough instructions to reassemble thousands of packets like itself into original information at the end. Breaking down information into thousands of packets meant messages were hard to intercept and useless on their own. Because they were small, they were capable of traveling to their destination through any available route, even by many routes if one was blocked or busy.

Building Blocks

The Internet still works this way. Packets transfer all information, whether that information is Web pages, e-mails, file downloads, or instant messages. Trillions of packets flood through any available network and are routed to their destination by powerful gateway computers. These computers do not examine, filter, or store the packets. They simply send them on to a destination computer that reassembles them perfectly. Imagine a trillion postcards sent out every hour to millions of addresses everywhere in the world and arriving accurately in under a second. This is how the Internet functions, and it works amazingly well. During the 9/11 attack on New York City, regular phone service broke down almost immediately. Cell phone networks were overwhelmed. But e-mails continued to get through because they relied on a method of communication intended to function during a nuclear war.

All elements considered, however, the Internet most certainly would not withstand a real nuclear attack. Although the network itself and the packet method of communication would not fail, the electromagnetic pulse (EMP) of a nuclear explosion would incapacitate 95 percent of the computer chips around the blast zone. The network might continue to work, but the computers hooked up to it would not.

Interestingly, the original military point packets also make it extraordinarily hard to block, filter, or censor Internet content. What was simply a design feature for a time of war has now defined the Internet for those who resist all attempts to censor or to control information. It is ironic that technology for command and control now inspires those refusing any command and control at all over the Internet.

It is not surprising that the efficient method of letting computers talk together through packets caught the attention of university researchers in the 1960s. By the end of the decade, what might be recognizable as an Internet went online under the name ARPANET (Advanced Research Project Agency Network). It only linked a few computers used strictly for research. Private, personal, and commercial uses were not permitted. What was needed for the scientists was simply a way to yoke together multiple computers for solving complex problems. Packet communication was quickly adopted by universities as an excellent way to send large amounts of data through a single network.

The common protocol is the second building block of the Internet (a protocol is an agreed-upon way of doing things). Computer networks spoke the same way (packets);

now they needed a common language in which to communicate. Because networks of the day were built for diverse purposes, many languages were invented. Imagine talking in the United Nations lobby. Vinton Cerf, an ARPA scientist, proposed in 1974 a common protocol for inter-network exchange of information. His invention, called TCP/IP (Transmission Control Protocol/Internet Protocol), meant local computers always communicate with outside networks in a common language. The protocol did not achieve immediate adoption, but the benefit of using a common protocol spurred adoption. With it any computer network could access any other network anywhere in the world, and today TCP/IP is called the glue that holds the Internet together. It was at this time Cerf coined the word *inter-net* as a short form of *inter-network*.

The 1970s and 1980s saw steady growth in Internet connections, but things were still in the hands of researchers. Using the Internet required expensive equipment and mastery of arcane commands for each request. There was little popular awareness of the Internet, and few saw any particular use for it outside academic and military activity. A few small events, in hindsight, provided a catalyst for the eventual explosion of public Internet use in the 1990s.

One was the first e-mail, in 1972. Scientists needed a way to send instructions back and forth. Although this form of communication was officially frowned upon, messages soon involved birthday greetings, weekend plans, and jokes. Soon, the number of e-mails far exceeded the number of research files being exchanged. Another sign of things to come was the first online games played across the network. As early as 1972, administrators started noticing unusually high network traffic on Friday nights after someone uploaded a Star Trek game. People used the network to blast Klingons and compete with friends at other universities. These may have been the first computer nerds, and the significance of their gaming to the development of the Internet today should not be overlooked.

Another tool that in hindsight paved the way for the World Wide Web was USENET (this 1979 term is a contraction of *user network*). Large numbers of users "subscribed" to a special interest topic and were able to conduct two-way discussions. Soon the "news groups," as they were called, went far beyond research and even news and became online communities. They were the precursors of today's discussion forums, chat rooms, and RSS feeds. USENET groups were the watershed development for the shift to having users pull what they wanted personally from the network and then use the medium for the composition of popular content. The first Internet communities thus were born, giving a glimpse of how the World Wide Web would eventually work. USENET also introduced the first spam messages (unwanted communications), the first flame wars (often vicious online disputes), and the first online pornography.

Two more small events had important consequences for the Internet. One was the introduction of the Domain Name System (DNS) in 1984. In place of hard-to-remember numbers such as 74.14.207.99 for network addresses, simple names such as google.com were enough. Now the network was far easier to use, and a name on the network took on potential value. The smallest but most significant event was the lifting of the prohibition against commercial use of the Internet in 1987.

The third building block for today's Internet was the PC (personal computer) introduced by Apple in 1976 and the widespread marketing of business versions by IBM in 1980. The key word here is *personal*. Until then computers were expensive tools for researchers or for the geeks who could build them. The personal computer was aimed at the general public. Soon companies developed graphical user interfaces (GUIs) to replace arcane command languages, and thus simple-to-use software was developed for the novice. The mouse, the icons, and the WYSIWYG (what you see is what you get) interface brought everyday computer use into mainstream society. Anyone could do it. By the end of the decade, personal computers numbered in the millions and were affordable and in the hands of people who played with them in addition to using them at work. With millions of computers in the hands of the utterly uninitiated, everything was ready for an Internet revolution 25 years in the making.

A Physicist's Dilemma

The unintentional revolutionary was Tim Berners-Lee, yet another researcher using the Internet in the late 1980s at the European Laboratory for Particle Physics (CERN) in Switzerland. He relied on the network to collaborate with colleagues around the world. Although the network was fine, the documents and files were not in the same format or easily found. He thought it would be much easier if everybody asking him questions all the time could just read what they wanted to know in his database, and it would be so much nicer if he could find out what these guys were doing by jumping into their similar databases of information. He needed a simple way to format documents and describe their location and some common way to ask for them. It had to be decentralized so that anyone anywhere could get information without asking someone. Ideally the requests could come from inside the documents as links to other documents, so that a researcher did not need to use some other application. Most of all, it had to be easy.

Berners-Lee sat down in 1990 and penned the specifications for a global hypermedia system with now-universal acronyms: HTTP (HyperText Transfer Protocol), HTML (HyperText Mark-up Language), and URL (Uniform Resource Locator). Though originally designed for far-flung researchers to collaborate on projects without bothering each other, the resulting universal information space set in place the keystone of today's Internet. For good measure Berners-Lee even gave his creation a name: the World Wide Web (WWW). He capped off these innovations with a small piece of software called a browser. He intended it only to make it easier for his peers to retrieve and read documents. He did not know it would touch off the modern Internet revolution.

Going to the Cyber Mall

For 25 years the word *Internet* was little known outside of academic circles. As the 1990s unfolded, however, everyone was talking about the Internet, also known as the Information Superhighway, Cyberspace, Infobahn, or simply the Web or the Net, as the technology took hold of popular culture. Everyone wanted to be on the Web, and users who hardly topped 100,000 at the beginning of the decade were on course to surpass 200 million by the end.

Why the sudden growth? In part the Internet was cheap and easy to use. Moreover, it was the effect on people's imagination the first time they clicked around the new frontier. Old rules of geography, money, and behavior did not apply. No one was in charge of the Web. Everything was available in this new world for free. Founded in 1993, the magazine *WIRED* trumpeted a techno-utopianism where the Internet would transform the economy, society, and even humanity itself. The experimental layouts and bold use of fluorescent and metallic inks in *WIRED* sum up the personality of the Internet in those early years, and the magazine is still published today.

For example, Marc Andreessen, one 21-year-old innovator, took Tim Berners-Lee's lowly browser made for research papers and added pictures, color, and graphic design. Others would soon add audio, video, animation, and interactive forms. His company (Netscape, formed in 1994) simply gave the browser away for six months and then went to the stock market with an IPO (initial public offering) worth $2.4 billion on the first day.

No wonder people began saying the Internet had started a "new economy." The Web erased constraints of geography and time. Anything digital could be multiplied a million times and distributed worldwide for free. Entrepreneurs lined up for the new gold rush of the information age. Billions poured in to fund every imaginable innovation, the stock market soared, and for years it seemed true that there was more profit in clicks than in a bricks-and-mortar industry.

What is called the "dot-com bubble" burst in 2000, draining away these billions and delivering the sobering reminder that, even in the "new economy," certain old economy values such as profitability, accountability, and customer service still mattered. Nevertheless, the Internet proved to be a seismic shock to business economics. Even the smallest business, no matter where located, could consider the world its marketplace. Companies that "got the Net" could outmaneuver large corporations. For the most part, traditional businesses did not disappear with the Internet; they adapted their old models to use it. Because most goods and services were physical, traditional business controlled means of production but used the Internet to improve supply management, ordering, and customer service.

Many point to Amazon and eBay, both launched in 1995, as examples of the "new economy." Amazon at first simply sold the old commodity of books. They built success on the frictionless character of Internet access. Books were the same anywhere; the real problem was finding them in a local bookstore. Amazon saw that they could let people find a book easily, review what others thought of it, make payments with a single click, and never have to leave the house. It worked, and today every online seller works on the same principle as Amazon. The Internet enables better selection, cheaper prices, and faster delivery. Nevertheless, although Amazon is 100 percent online, this is still the old economy made better using new technology. To this success should be added industries such as banking, travel, and insurance, all transformed by the Internet within a few years. They migrated online with great success but used Internet technology to enhance existing business rather than to fundamentally change it.

Electronic Commerce

eBay introduced an online version of an economic model as old as society itself: person-to-person trading. The now $50-billion company produced nothing. It simply put buyer and seller together using the Internet. By providing a listing service and payment system and taking a commission, eBay makes a good case for being a "new economy" business. Millions of sellers, not just buyers, were now networked. The stroke of genius in eBay was their rating system for buyers and sellers to keep score on the reputation of each user. Anyone could see another's reputation and make a choice about whether or not to do business with a complete stranger. On the seemingly endless anonymity of the Web, eBay found a way establish old-fashioned reputation as a key economic currency.

It is important to emphasize that the new economy uses information and ease of communication as its currencies. Up to this point, economies were built on the relative scarcity of goods and services. Resources needed to be acquired, marketed, and sold, but they were always finite. The Internet turned this old economic model upside down. Instead of scarcity, it was built on an endless supply. Digital multiplication of information and distribution through the Internet were essentially without limit. What astonished users in the early days of the Web was that people were giving away everything free. Who was paying for this? Who could make money this way? In talking about the "new economy," it may be best to say that the Internet did not create it; rather, the Internet required a new economy.

Google (started in 1997) was an instant and spectacular success in the new economy. It did not enhance an old business; it created an entirely new one, though few saw it at first. The need for powerful search engines on the Web was apparent quite early. Once the problem of access to information on the network was solved, the next problem was finding it. With the growth of the Web, finding a page was like finding a needle in a million haystacks. But even with a search engine, the results could number in the tens of thousands. How could someone find good information?

When Google appeared, it looked like simply a better search engine, but the young graduate students who built it also designed human intelligence into the tool. Instead of only words and titles, Google also analyzed the number and quality of links to each page. Millions of humans chose what pages they visited and what pages they built links to. Google tracked this. The more links to a Web page, the more likely it was that that Web page had good information. It was a surprisingly simple way to judge relevance. Google offered not only an index of the World Wide Web, but also a snapshot of what the world was thinking about it. eBay built a way to track the reputation of users; Google discovered ways to track the reputation of information.

What makes Google worthy of being included in the new economy is that it traffics wholly in information and the power to make sense of it. How can searches be given away free and the company be worth $100 billion? By giving away information and in some cases paying people to take their information, Google gathers intelligence about what is on the Web, what people think about it, and most of all what people are looking for. It is a marketer's dream. Put people and their interests together with products they are looking for, and there is business. The bulk of Google's revenue comes from advertising, which is systematically targeted by demographic, habit, and personal interest. Google does not want only to index the Web; it intends to analyze its users. The larger the Web, the greater the use of it, and the more profitable Google's share of the new economy.

Far different is the situation where an old-style business does battle with the new economy principles of the Internet. The prime example is media. If the Internet means that anything digital can be reproduced instantly across the whole system, is it possible to copy-protect music, movies, and books? Is it even desirable? The only thing that keeps this book from being copied a million times on the Web is the minor inconvenience of transferring the paper-based text to a digital format. If all digital media become potentially free, how will media conglomerates ever make a profit? How will artists earn a living? Software sales are another example. Copying software and posting it for others to use for free is a time-honored use of Internet technology.

Protecting Copyright

One response to unauthorized copying is increasingly sophisticated Digital Right Management (DRM) software, which makes media impossible to use without payment. In turn, clever coders have always found a way to crack the protection and post the media anyway. Various surveys have discovered that up to 50 percent of Internet users believe there is nothing wrong with taking illegal copies of software and music. It is likely that illegal downloads will never go away and that people will pay for media simply for the convenience of downloading from one place and having access to support for their downloads if there are problems. Neither honesty nor technology will have much to do with it. People will pay for not having to root around Warez sites (collections of illegal software) or locate P2P (peer to peer) repositories willing to share.

Another response has been high-profile lawsuits against people and companies with unauthorized media. The purpose is to frighten others into paying for valid copies. Although this works well against business and corporations, it has made barely a dent in the downloading of music and videos by individuals, especially the young. Today sales of CD music are down even as the number of people listening to songs increases, proving the point that the old-style business of media companies is under serious pressure from the "new economy" principles of the Internet.

A third response recognizes that the Internet may have changed the rules. It says that copying is not only allowed but encouraged. It turns the old media economy of control and distribution upside down. Now the artist or programmer wants the widest possible distribution of the media and gives it all away for free. The goal is exposure, increased sales of related items, or simply the desire to create and see others enjoy the creation. Opponents claim the practice will undermine the ability to control and profit from intellectual property. Others point out that art is in good health on today's Internet and that software development has never known such vitality.

The debate over what kind of "new economy" the Internet has helped to spawn leads to no consensus, but there is general agreement that the impact of the Internet on the worldwide economy, whether new or old, cannot be measured. It is somewhere in the trillions of dollars.

The Open Source Movement

There is another dimension of "the new economy" that relates to the economy of ideas on the Web. Here information and ease of communication are the currencies. The slogan "Knowledge wants to be free" is part ideology and part recognition that in digital knowledge, there is no cost of delivery. What is called the Open Source movement in the software industry insists that free distribution, work on projects by unlimited developers, and complete access to source codes will produce the best product. The Web makes it possible. Another vivid example of the new economy of ideas is Wikipedia, an online encyclopedia where anyone can improve articles written by anyone else. Its popularity now rivals that of the famed *Encyclopedia Britannica*.

Discussions of a "new society" built through the Internet follow the same pattern as those on the new economy. Enthusiasts claim that the Internet will inaugurate a golden age of global community. No distance, no border, and no restriction on information will improve education, stimulate communication, spread democracy, benefit rich and poor alike, and level the playing field in a new Internet age. Much of the language about the Internet, from the early years onward, is strongly utopian and uses the word *revolutionary* more often than is wise!

Critics of the so-called Internet revolution fear that the Internet will only take people away from real-world problems and genuine human interaction. Government and corporations will use the technology to snoop on and manipulate citizens. Criminals will invent new high-tech crimes, and at best the world will be no better and at worst much worse.

Neither the dreams nor the nightmares of the Internet age have arrived, but both the enthusiast and the critic have seen hopes and fears realized on the Web.

Impact on Education

For example, education, as old as society itself, finds itself a beneficiary of the Web and an area of major concern. It is true that students now have access to many times the learning content of a few years ago. Books, images, research tools, multimedia, and simulations have been mainstreamed in Western education. Internet literacy is an accepted competency for the educated person. Web-based learning has opened up higher education to greater numbers. The Internet removes many of the physical and time restrictions to learning.

But is the learning available on the Internet good? Where once a teacher could ensure the quality of resources, now the words "found on the Web" can apply to the latest research or to complete nonsense. How will students fulfill the social dimensions of their experience on the Web? Although content-oriented subjects do well in Web-based learning, how can hands-on skills ever be put on the Web? Students find an abundance of information on the Web, but they can also copy and paste it, claiming it as their own. Completion rates for Web-based learning are less than half of those in face-to-face learning, however.

Uses and Gratifications

As it was with the new economy, the new society has turned out to be mainly a version of the old society operating at Web speed. Few things are actually new on the Web. People use the Internet to chat, visit, flirt, and play. Dating, cybersex, marriage, and funerals are all on the Web. Birth still poses a challenge, but in every case there is some version on the Web of what people have been doing for thousands of years. The Web is more of a reflection of society than a force shaping society.

More often than not, quite unforeseen consequences have emerged from the Internet. For example, could the early adopters of e-mail have predicted that more than half the eventual traffic would be spam (unwanted email)? For years visionaries have promised the paperless office, but each year paper use goes up. Office productivity was meant to increase dramatically once everyone was wired into the network. Instead, the Web became the number one source for wasting office time. Dreamers announced whole armies of knowledge workers who would commute via the Internet. Little did they foresee that those knowledge workers would come from halfway around the world, outsourcing or displacing the jobs of local workers.

What should be regarded as "new" in the wired world is the speed with which things happen and the vast increase in the number of people who can be involved. Technology does not change the way people live on the Internet as much as it multiplies its effects. An embarrassing video once circulated among friends and family now can be found by millions of strangers and can never be taken back. A pickpocket could steal a few wallets in a day. A good hacker now can steal a million credit cards in a minute. A rumor or a piece of false information falls into a database or search engine, and suddenly it competes on equal footing with the truth.

A new and dangerously ignored consequence of the Web is the persistence of information. Internet technology not only retrieves data but also keeps it around, perhaps forever. Until now people could trust that their words and written notes simply disappeared or at least could be controlled. This is not so on the Web. Information is kept, and it may be found by anyone in the world.

Privacy, or the lack of it, is certainly an old issue taking a new form on the Web. In the early days, people reveled in the seeming anonymity of their Web browsing. They could hide behind a billion packets and the complex communications of TCP/IP; but not anymore. Online companies track browsing habits. Local Web servers log every request made from a browser. Chat rooms archive information. Governments routinely listen in on the chatter moving across the networks. Unsuspecting users routinely let tracking programs be installed on their computers and give away personal information in exchange for Web-based baubles. Worse, people publish all manner of personal detail on the Web, not grasping that Google and other search engines make this information permanent and findable by anyone. Already employers are searching the history of potential employees on social networking sites. Many people have lost jobs because of some frivolous post made years before. It will not be long before some political candidate for high office will be undone by the record of some indiscreet posting in a forum or visit to an unsavory Web site.

Internet addiction disorder, a distraction causing emotional attachment to and obsessive behavior associated with one's online reputation, is a new wrinkle in the connectivity excitement. Among first-graders in China, A 2010 study revealed that nearly 11 percent showed a preoccupation with surfing the Internet. Documenting the addiction tendency is a new area of psychological research resulting from the "information age." In particular, it has become increasingly relevant for forensic psychiatry because a person's Internet presence can help support or refute a diagnosis presented as part of a court case. For example, the choice of screen name, amount of self-disclosure, and provocative behavior in social media forums can be used to describe a person's credibility and quality of insight or supportable judgment. In this way, the Internet is shaping societies around the globe like a virus. A school of thought about the viral qualities of the Internet is the basis for *memetics,* a branch of cultural anthropology that considers how culture replicates.

It is certain that the World Wide Web has not created the new society some of its cheerleaders proposed. It is also doubtful that society itself has changed that much as a result of the introduction of the Internet to mainstream culture. The idea that technology by itself will determine the character of human life is naïve. It is fair to say, however, that society has not kept up with the consequences of Internet technology. In part this is because the technology is young and people are too close to it. The next wave of the Internet is likely to be the widespread linking not just of personal computers but of things. Phones, media players, and gaming are already widespread online. Someday it could be vehicles, appliances, tools, and parts of the human body linked into a global interactive network.

How then can the significance of the Internet be understood today? First and foremost, it should not be regarded as something entirely new, nor should one listen too closely to either its fans or its cynics. It is one of many innovations dubbed a revolution by some and a threat to society by others. Compare the Internet to electricity, the telegraph, transatlantic cable, telephone, radio, television, satellites, or computers. All struck awe into their first users but were adopted by the next generation as simply the way things are done. None was revolutionary by itself. The social changes that have come with these technologies have as much to do with how people envisioned them, reacted to them, and applied them as they do with the inventions themselves.

Human imagination has a remarkable capacity to adapt technology in ways its inventors did not consider. Therefore society is less likely to be transformed by the Internet than to transform the Internet into areas not yet conceived.

See also **Advertising and the Invasion of Privacy (vol. 1); Conglomeration and Media Monopolies (vol. 1); Intellectual Property Rights (vol. 1); Cybercrime (vol. 2); Identity Theft (vol. 2); Video Games (vol. 3)**

Further Reading

Anderson, Janna Quitney, *Imagining the Internet: Personalities, Predictions, Perspectives.* Lanham, MD: Rowman & Littlefield, 2005.

Aspray, William, and Paul E. Ceruzzi, eds., *The Internet and American Business.* Cambridge, MA: MIT Press, 2008.

Buckley, Peter, and Duncan Clark, *The Rough Guide to the Internet.* London: Penguin, 2007.

King, Elliot, *Free for All: The Internet's Transformation of Journalism.* Evanston, IL: Northwestern University Press, 2010.

Kirkpatrick, David, *The Facebook Effect: The Inside Story of the Company That Is Connecting the World.* New York: Simon & Schuster, 2010.

Negroponte, Nicholas, *Being Digital.* New York: Knopf, 1995.

Scott, Virginia, *Google.* Westport, CT: Greenwood Press, 2008.

Standage, Tom, *The Victorian Internet.* New York, Walker, 1998.

Stoll, Clifford, *Silicon Snake Oil: Second Thoughts on the Information Highway.* New York: Anchor, 1996.

L

LAND POLLUTION

Robert William Collin and Debra Ann Schwartz

Imagine a river running yellow. Or red. Or chemical blue. Military experiments with biological warfare, using explosives, turned rivers red from cadmium, blue from cobalt, and yellow from sulfur during the First and Second World Wars. The rivers deposited the mineral waste along their banks, and the land sucked it in further, creating what is called a plume. Think of British Petroleum's Deepwater Horizon oil well. When it gushed, it created a plume of oil throughout much of the Gulf of Mexico. That plume drifted. When the oil reached coral reefs and shores that collected it from the water, the oil remained on the land, which absorbed it and thus began to create another plume.

Polluted land also results from acid rain, industrialization, body waste, and ecological imbalance. In the case of industrialization, whose production processes have emitted acids into the air, phosphates into the water, and liquid and solid chemicals into the land, a federal law was created in the 1970s to discourage industrial waste dumping. That law is commonly known as Superfund. More formally, it is called the Comprehensive Environmental Response, Compensation and Liability Act, or CERCLA. It exists to create a legal process for finding the polluters responsible for contaminating the land and holding them financially accountable. The law was born out of a chemical waste dump in Love Canal, New York, that made the neighborhood a ghost town.

State, tribal, and local waste programs and policies also exist to prevent pollution by reducing the generation of wastes at their source and by emphasizing prevention over management and subsequent disposal. Preventing pollution before it is generated and poses harm is often less costly than cleanup and remediation. Source reduction and recycling programs often can increase resource and energy efficiencies and thereby reduce pressure on the environment. When wastes are generated, the EPA, state environmental programs, and local municipalities work to reduce the risk of exposures. If land is contaminated, cleanup programs address the sites to prevent human exposure and groundwater contamination. Increased recycling protects land resources and extends the life span of disposal facilities.

Kinds and Types of Waste

The types of waste generated range from yard clippings to highly concentrated hazardous waste. Only three types of waste—municipal solid waste (MSW), hazardous waste (as defined by the Resource Conservation and Recovery Act [RCRA]), and radioactive waste—are tracked with any consistency on a national basis. Other types of waste are not, though they contribute a substantial amount to the total waste accumulated. This is a gaping hole is U.S. environmental policy. These other types of waste contribute a substantial amount to the total waste universe, although the exact percentage of the total that they represent is unknown.

Municipal solid waste, commonly known as trash or garbage, is one of the nation's most prevalent waste types. The EPA has estimated that the U.S. generated 250 million tons of solid waste in 2008, with about 54 percent going to landfills. The new figure represents a nearly 8 percent increase during a 10-year period. In 2000, the United States generated approximately 232 million tons of MSW, primarily in homes and workplaces—an increase of nearly 160 percent since 1960. The EPA updates its statistics every two years. The next update will report 2010 figures.

Between 1960 and 2000, the U.S. population increased by 56 percent, and gross domestic production increased nearly 300 percent. In 1960, with a much smaller population than today, each person in the U.S. generated about 2.7 pounds of waste per day. In 2008, after accounting for recycling and composting, the EPA estimated each person in the United States generated 3 pounds of waste per day. The figures provide that individuals generated 4.5 pounds of waste per day, with 1.5 pounds per person recycled and composted. With that in mind, it can be argued that per-person waste generation today is down from the 2000 estimates of 4.5 pounds of waste per day.

In 2008, Americans recovered about 61 million tons of waste through recycling, with composting recovering 22.1 million tons of waste. About 32 million tons were incinerated for energy recovery. In June 2010, the EPA was seeking public comment on a proposed rule better defining what nonhazardous waste could be incinerated. Residue from waste combustion is emitted into the atmosphere and the remaining ash typically put into an ashfill on land.

The EPA reports that Americans recycled more than 7 million tons of metals (including aluminum, steel, and mixed metals) in 2008, which "eliminated greenhouse gas emissions totaling close to 25 million metric tons of carbon dioxide equivalent (MMT-CO2E). That is like removing more than 4.5 million cars from the road for one year.

Hazardous waste as defined by the EPA is anything containing a material or chemical capable of causing illness, death, or harm to humans and other life forms when mismanaged or released into the environment. The phrase *RCRA hazardous waste* applies to hazardous waste that is ignitable, corrosive, reactive, or toxic, which is regulated under the act. In 1999, the EPA estimated that 20,000 businesses generating large quantities (more than 2,200 pounds each per month) of hazardous waste collectively generated 40 million tons of RCRA hazardous waste. Comparisons of annual trends in hazardous waste generation are difficult because of changes in the types of data collected (e.g., exclusion of wastewater) over the past several years. But the amount of a specific set of priority toxic chemicals found in hazardous waste and tracked in the Toxics Release Inventory (TRI) is declining. In 1999, approximately 69 percent of the RCRA hazardous waste was disposed of on land by one of four disposal methods: deep well/underground injection, landfill disposal, surface impoundment, or land treatment/application/farming.

In 2000, approximately 600,000 cubic meters of different types of radioactive waste were generated, and approximately 700,000 cubic meters were in storage awaiting disposal. By volume, the most prevalent types of radioactive waste are contaminated environmental media (i.e., soil, sediment, water, and sludge requiring cleanup or further assessment) and low-level waste. Both of these waste types typically have the lowest levels of radioactivity when measured by volume. Additional radioactive wastes in the form of spent nuclear fuel (2,467 metric tons of heavy metal) and high-level waste glass logs (1,201 canisters of vitrified high-level waste) are in storage awaiting long-term disposal. EPA fact sheets are available that describe, on a state-by-state basis, the amount of hazardous waste in a state and where it is located.

Extent of Land Used for Waste

Nearly 3,500 acres per year in the U.S. store waste according to the EPA's figures, a clarion call much like the movie WALL*E. Between 1989 and 2000, the number of municipal landfills in the United States decreased substantially to 2,216 from 8,000. Since then the number has increased slightly. According to the EPA, the United States currently has 3,091 active landfills and more than 10,000 old municipal landfills. However, it can be reasoned that there are many more based on U.S. Census figures. As far back as 1997, for example, data show that there are 39,044 general-purpose local governments in the United States.; 3, 043 county governments; and 36,001 subcounty general-purpose governments. Potentially, all of them could have garbage dumps.

Landfills today tend to accept only certain kinds of garbage. Some accept only a specific kind of solid waste, such as food products or fibers. In the past, any kind of waste could be tossed into the local garbage dump. However, as military bases including forts become decommissioned, environmental assessments find everything from typewriters to dead horses in a single landfill. That old landfill typically would not have any kind of liner to protect the land from contamination as the items decomposed. Today, because of products made of petroleum, carbon, synthetics, and other human-made items that leak toxic chemicals into the land as they decompose, landfills are lined. And a single landfill does not accept all kinds of waste. As necessary, some waste is separated out as too toxic for a municipal landfill; it must be sent to a special waste disposal site.

In terms of landfill capacity, in 2000, municipal landfills received approximately 128 million pounds of MSW, or about 55 percent of what was generated. In addition to municipal landfills, the nation had 18,000 surface impoundments—ponds used to treat, store, or dispose of liquid waste—for nonhazardous industrial waste in 2000. Excluding wastewater, nearly 70 percent of the RCRA hazardous waste generated in 1999 was disposed of at one of the nation's RCRA treatment, storage, and land-disposal facilities. Of the 1,575 RCRA facilities, 1,049 are storage-only facilities. The remaining facilities perform one or more of several common management methods (e.g., deepwell/underground injection, metals recovery, incineration, landfill disposal).

The United States also uses other sites for waste management and disposal, but no comprehensive data sets are available. Before the 1970s, waste was not subjected to today's legal requirements to reduce toxicity before disposal and was typically disposed of in open pits. Early land-disposal units that still pose threats to human health and the environment are considered contaminated lands and are subject to federal or state cleanup efforts.

Extent of Contaminated Land

Many contaminated sites must be managed and cleaned up today because of leaking underground storage tanks for gasoline (generally found under gas stations). These are located throughout the country, and their levels of contamination vary. Some sites involve small, nontoxic spills, such as a private garage where someone did an oil change. Others might involve large acreages of potential contamination, such as abandoned mine sites or a dry cleaning business tossing chemicals into the land behind the store. To address this contamination, federal and state programs use a variety of laws and regulations to initiate, implement, and enforce cleanup. The contaminated sites are generally classified according to applicable program authorities, such as RCRA Corrective Action, Superfund, and state cleanup programs.

The most toxic abandoned waste sites in the nation appear on the National Priorities List (NPL). Thus, examining the NPL data provides an indication of the extent of the most significantly contaminated sites. NPL sites are located in every state and several territories. As of May 2010, a total of 61 sites were proposed for listing; 1,279 sites had been finalized by then, and 341 had been deleted from the list. Sites are considered for deletion from the NPL list when cleanup is complete.

The EPA also estimates that approximately 3,700 hazardous waste management sites may be subject to RCRA corrective action, which would provide for investigation, cleanup, and remediation of releases of hazardous waste and constituents. Contamination at the sites ranges from small spills that require soil cleanup to extensive contamination of soil, sediment, and groundwater. Corrective action sites are given high priority and targeted for immediate action by federal, state, and local agencies.

Another type of contaminated land is a brownfield. Brownfields are areas with levels of contamination too low to qualify as Superfund sites. The soil may be highly polluted and carry an estimated cleanup cost of $6 million, while Superfund cleanup status generally starts at $20 million. Brownfields are often found in and around economically depressed neighborhoods. Cleanup and redevelopment puts these often abandoned properties back on the tax roles, benefitting a community financially and potentially providing jobs in the area. Brownfields cannot be redeveloped as community farms because of levels of contamination that the EPA finds acceptable for only redevelopment. The EPA bases its soil toxicity levels and their effect on human health on what would happen if a person ate a certain amount of soil. The EPA calculates "acceptable risk" based on how the property will be used in the future. That is typically determined by local zoning boards.

Human Health Effects and Contaminated Land

Determining the relationship between types of sites and human health is usually complicated. For many types of cancer, understanding is limited by science and the fact that people usually are exposed to many possible cancer-causing substances throughout their lives. Isolating the contributions of exposure to contaminants to incidence of respiratory illness, cancer, and birth defects is extremely difficult—impossible in many cases. Nonetheless, it is important to gain a more concrete understanding of how the hazardous materials associated with waste and contaminated lands affect human populations.

Although some types of potential contaminants and waste are not generally hazardous to humans, other types can pose dangers to health if people are exposed. The number of substances that exist that can or do affect human health is unknown; however, the TRI program requires reporting of more than 650 chemicals and chemical categories that are known to be toxic to humans.

The federal Superfund program identifies sources of common contaminants, including commercial solvents, dry-cleaning agents, and chemicals. With chronic exposure, commercial solvents such as benzene may suppress bone marrow function, causing blood changes. Dry-cleaning agents and degreasers contain trichloroethane and trichloroethylene, which can cause fatigue, depression of the central nervous system, kidney changes (e.g., swelling, anemia), and liver changes (e.g., enlargement). Chemicals used in commercial and industrial manufacturing processes—such as arsenic, beryllium, cadmium, chromium, lead, and mercury—may cause various health problems. Long-term exposure to lead may cause permanent kidney and brain damage. Cadmium can cause kidney and lung disease. Chromium, beryllium, arsenic, and cadmium have been implicated as human carcinogens.

Ecological Effects

Hazardous substances—whether present in waste, on lands used for waste management, or on contaminated land—can harm wildlife (e.g., cause major reproductive complications), destroy vegetation, contaminate air and water, and limit the ability of an ecosystem to survive. For example, if not properly managed, toxic residues from mining operations can be blown into nearby areas, affecting resident bird populations and the water on which they depend. Certain hazardous substances also have the potential to explode or cause fires, threatening both wildlife and human populations.

The negative effects of land contamination and occasionally of waste management on ecosystems occur after contaminants have been released on land (soil/sediment) or into the air or water.

Conclusion

The extent of land pollution is unknown at this time. Cleanup costs are enormous, which results in complex and expensive litigation to determine liability for these costs. In the United States, cities have only recently been included in the environmental protection

---

CLEANUP OF THE EAGLE MINE SUPERFUND SITE

The Eagle Mine, southwest of Vail, Colorado, was used to mine gold, silver, lead, zinc, and copper between 1870 and 1984. After the mine closed, several contaminants—including lead, zinc, cadmium, arsenic, and manganese—were left behind; they spread into nearby groundwater, the Eagle River, and the air, posing a risk to people and wildlife.

Colorado filed notice and claim in 1985 against the former mine owners for natural resource damages under Superfund. In June 1986, the site was placed on the National Priorities List, and shortly thereafter the state and the previous owners agreed to a plan of action. Cleanup operations included constructing a water treatment plant to collect mine seepage and other contaminated water sources, relocating all processed mine wastes and contaminated soils to one main on-site tailings pile, capping that pile with a multilayer clean soil cap, and revegetating all disturbed areas with native plant species.

The water quality in the Eagle River began to show improvements in 1991; as zinc concentrations in the river dropped, the resident brown trout population grew. An October 2000 site review concluded that public health risks had been removed and that significant progress had been made in restoring the Eagle River. Today, biological monitoring is undertaken to evaluate the Eagle River's water quality, aquatic insects, and fish populations.

policy umbrella. Controversies about land pollution generally focus on cleanup of the most serious wastes and/or relocation of the community.

See also **Brownfields Development; Industrial Agricultural Practices and the Environment; Sprawl; Waste Management**

Further Reading

EPA, www.epa.gov

Genske, Dieter D., *Investigation, Remediation, and Protection of Land Resources.* Dunbeath, UK: Whittles, 2007.

Macey, Gregg P., and Jonathan Z. Cannon, *Reclaiming the Land: Rethinking Superfund Institutions, Methods, and Practices.* New York: Springer, 2007.

Nathanail, C. Paul, and R. Paul Bardos, *Reclamation of Contaminated Land.* New York: Wiley, 2004.

Owens, Susan E., and Richard Cowell, *Land and Limits: Interpreting Sustainability in the Planning Process.* New York: Routledge, 2002.

Randolph, John, *Environmental Land Use Planning and Management.* Washington, DC: Island Press, 2004.

Sigman, Hillary, ed., *The Economics of Hazardous Waste and Contaminated Land.* Northampton, MA: Edward Elgar, 2008.

LEAD EXPOSURE

Robert William Collin

Environmental exposure to lead can cause life-impairing if not deadly consequences. Lead is a metal that can harm humans and the environment and is present in many pollutants and consumer goods. Many of the controversial issues surrounding lead exposure relate to scientific disagreement over the extent and severity of exposure. Other controversies relate to political disagreements over who is exposed, when to test for lead exposure, and who will pay for diagnosis and treatment.

What Is Lead?

Lead is essentially a mineral. Minerals are formed by hot solutions working their way up from deep below the earth's rocky crust and crystallizing as they cool near the surface. From early history to the present, lead mining has been part of human culture. Lead has been a key component in cosmetic decoration as a pigment; a spermicide for informal birth control; a sweet-and-sour condiment popular for seasoning and adulterating food; a wine preservative for stopping fermentation or disguising inferior vintages; the malleable and inexpensive ingredient in pewter cups, plates, pitchers, pots and pans, and other household artifacts; the basic component of lead coins; and the material of children's toys. Most important of all was lead's suitability for making inexpensive and reliable water pipes. Lead pipes are still used in many parts of the world and are still present in the United States. Lead pipes kept the Roman Empire supplied with water. From then until now lead has been part of our society.

Human exposure to lead is a serious public health problem. Lead adversely affects the nervous, hematopoietic, endocrine, renal, and reproductive systems of the body. Of particular concern are the effects of relatively low levels of lead exposure on the cognitive development of children. Since the 1970s, federal environmental regulations and abatement efforts have mainly focused on reducing the amount of lead in gasoline, paint, and soldered cans. In addition, some federal programs have supported screening for lead poisoning in children by state and local health departments and physicians as well as lead abatement in housing. Currently, lead exposure usually results from lead in deteriorating household paint, lead at the workplace, lead used in hobbies, lead in some folk medicines and cosmetics, lead in children's toys, and lead in crystal or ceramic containers that leaches into water or food.

Since the late 1970s, the extent of lead exposure in the U.S. population has been assessed by the National Health and Nutrition Examination Surveys (NHANES). These national surveys have measured blood lead levels (BPbs) of tens of thousands of children and adults and assessed the extent of lead exposure in the civilian population by age, sex, race/ethnicity, income, and degree of urbanization. The surveys have demonstrated an overall decline in BPbs since the 1970s, but they also have shown that a large number of children continue to have elevated BPbs (10 μg/dL). The U.S. EPA claims that owing to environmental regulations, airborne lead amounts have decreased by 90 percent from 1980 to 2005.

Sociodemographic factors associated with higher blood lead levels in children were non-Hispanic black race/ethnicity, low income, and residence in older housing. The prevalence of elevated blood lead levels was 21.9 percent among non-Hispanic black children living in homes built before 1946 and 16.4 percent among children in low-income families who lived in homes built before 1946. Overall, blood lead levels continue to decline in the U.S. population. The disproportionate impact on urban people of color makes it an environmental justice issue, although lead can work its way through ecosystems and affect other groups downwind or downstream.

Lead is a highly toxic metal that was used for many years in products found in and around our homes, schools, and workplaces. Lead can cause a range of health effects, from behavioral problems and learning disabilities to seizures and death. Children six years old and under are most at risk because their bodies are growing quickly.

The EPA is playing a major role in addressing these residential lead hazards. In 1978, there were some 3 to 4 million children with elevated blood lead levels in the United States. By 2002, that number had dropped to 310,000 children, and it continues to decline. Since the 1980s, the EPA has phased out lead in gasoline, reduced lead in drinking water and industrial air pollution, and banned or limited lead used in consumer products, including residential paint. States and cities have set up some programs to identify and treat lead-poisoned children and to rehabilitate deteriorated housing. Parents have greatly helped to reduce their children's lead exposure by eliminating lead in their homes, having their children's blood lead levels checked, and learning about the risks of lead for children.

Some population groups continue to be at disproportionately high risk for elevated lead exposure. In general, these are people with low income, people of non-Hispanic black race, and people who live in older housing. Residence in a central city with a population of more than a million people was also found to be a risk factor for lead exposure.

These high-risk population groups are important to recognize for targeting of public health efforts in lead-poisoning prevention. Leaded paint, especially in older homes, is a continuing source of lead exposure. In the United States, approximately 83 percent of privately owned housing units and 86 percent of public housing units built before 1980 contain some lead-based paint. Commercial and industrial structures often have much more lead paint. Bridges are often repainted, and this uses large amounts of lead paint. The areas under the bridges are often contaminated with lead. If the area under a bridge is land, the lead accumulates on the ground and in the dirt. Many bridges of this type are older and in urban areas. Between 5 and 15 million homes contain paint that has deteriorated to the point of being a health hazard. Lead hazard control and abatement costs are highly variable, depending on the extent of the intervention, existing market conditions, type of housing, and associated housing rehabilitation work. Because of the high cost of abatement, the scarcity of adequately trained lead-abatement professionals, and the absence (until 1995) of federal guidelines for implementing less costly methods of containing the hazard of leaded paint, residential lead paint–abatement efforts have focused on homes in which there is a resident child with an elevated BPb rather than on those that have the potential to expose a child to lead. Similarly, publicly funded lead-poisoning prevention programs have focused on screening children to identify those who already have elevated BPbs, so that they may receive interventions, rather than on preventing future lead exposure among children without elevated levels. This is an issue in the public health arena. At least some of the adverse health effects that occur even at relatively low levels of lead may be irreversible. Efforts to prevent lead exposure through screening are important to ensure that children with elevated BPbs receive prompt and effective interventions designed to reduce further lead exposure and minimize health consequences. These types of programs are not consistently well funded.

One source of lead in many countries is vehicle emissions. In the United States these emissions are much lower because lead-free gasoline is used in cars. However, other airborne vehicle emissions, as from diesel, may have a detrimental effect on children. In urban areas near congested roads, exposure to lead via air may be a large vector.

A controversial issue is whether ambient air quality standards are adequate to protect the health of children. Currently a few state environmental agencies are working to identify toxic air contaminants that may cause infants and children to be especially susceptible to risks. In many cases, children may have greater exposure to airborne pollutants than do adults. Children are often more susceptible to the health effects of air pollution because their immune systems and developing organs are still growing. Lead that is inhaled is more easily lodged in the fast-growing bones of children. In a child, it may take less exposure to airborne lead to initiate an asthma attack or other breathing ailment owing to the smaller size and greater sensitivity of the child's developing respiratory system.

Conclusion

As a pervasive material in civilization, lead is ubiquitous. Lead in the water pipes and drinking vessels may have poisoned the people of Rome and contributed to its downfall. Lead still remains in plumbing systems throughout the United States. In Washington, D.C., some of the leaded sewer and water pipes dead end. This means that there is no way to flush them clear of corrosive wastes and debris. This increases the rate of corrosion of these pipes and leaches lead into the water. When the pipe breaks, it may slowly seep lead-contaminated water into the surrounding ground. Such ground can be anywhere the pipe is found, near a road, river, school, factory, or any place connected to or near the break. This is a matter of great concern in chemically polluted older communities and can develop into a land-use issue or an issue around the environmental permits that may be necessary. Refining methods to assess health risks from lead that may exist at proposed and existing school sites is under way. Because lead is found in so many places where vulnerable populations exist, from children's toys to hospitals, controversy around lead exposure and cleanup will increase.

The disposal of lead as hazardous waste is also a controversial issue. Demolition of lead-contaminated houses, factories, and infrastructure creates hazardous waste. If burned in an incinerator, the lead could be spread in the air as particulate matter. The disposal of this type of toxic ash can also become a controversy. If the lead-contaminated structure simply stays in place, the lead can affect the soil and nearby water. The reluctance to expend the resources necessary to protect the most exposed people from lead contamination ensures a continuing controversy. This controversy may not necessarily diminish even as science removes uncertainty about lead contamination.

See also **Air Pollution; Mining of Natural Resources; Transportation and the Environment; Waste Management**

Further Reading

Casas, José S., and José Sordo, eds., *Lead: Chemistry, Analytical Aspects, Environmental Impact, and Health Effects.* Boston: Elsevier, 2006.

Millstone, Erik, *Lead and Public Health: The Dangers for Children.* Washington, DC: Taylor and Francis, 1997.

Moore, Colleen F., *Silent Scourge: Children, Pollution, and Why Scientists Disagree.* New York: Oxford University Press, 2003.

Troesken, Werner, *The Great Lead Water Pipe Disaster.* Cambridge, MA: MIT Press, 2006.

LOGGING

Robert William Collin and Scott M. Fincher

The cutting down of trees, called logging, has severe environmental effects. Attempts at sustainable logging are considered monoculture production, which is the practice of cultivating a single crop in a given area. It is not considered ecosystem preservation. The U.S. Forest Service, a unit of the Department of Agriculture, permits private corporations to cut down trees on public lands. The profits go to the logging company. Permits for cutting trees, salvage logging, and fire-reduction cuts are controversial, in part because of the fees the Forest Service charges.

A Growing Nation and the Need for Land

Historically, clearing land of trees was necessary for human settlement. Clear land was necessary for growing crops. The trees also had provided cover for wildlife, which most American pioneers tried to keep away from their homes and livestock. Today, clearing trees by centuries-old slash-and-burn techniques continues, but modern technology and monoculture pesticide-supported growing techniques make it easier for faster and more extensive deforestation.

Today, logging to clear land for other agriculture is less common although still controversial. Modern logging now treats trees as raw materials for the production of wood and paper among other products.

Environmental Effects

Logging has short- and long-term environmental effects. It affects many parts of the ecosystem because trees are essential components in many ecosystems. They retain water, cast shade over land and water, and provide food and shelter to wildlife.

Although there are many types of trees, only some species are logged. In many ecosystems trees fill unique ecological niches. One example is the Port Orford cedar growing on Oregon's coast. Having adapted to the wet, windy conditions of its ecosystem, it flourished. When it was plentiful, it was logged.

In the 1980s a deadly virus attacked the species. Port Orford cedars grow and communicate through their roots, and the virus moved from tree to tree, wiping out whole groves. State biologists sought preventive solutions, and environmentalists became very concerned. Meanwhile, the U.S. Forest Service permitted logging in and near a wilderness area with some of the last stands of Port Orford cedar. The loggers transmitted the virus to these trees, although they were not logging the Port Orford cedars.

Intense environmental litigation ensued. Among other issues, the court ruled that the loggers were to wash their logging vehicles upon entering and leaving the wilderness area. They do not do this, and the fight over the issue continues.

Logging and Soil Erosion

Another concern about logging is how much soil erosion it causes. Soil erosion degrades the environment in most places because it lowers the ecological productivity of a region. Soil supports plants that wildlife need for food or shelter. When roads are built and heavy loads of logs are moved on them, the stability of the soil on any type of slope is greatly affected. Because many trees are in mountainous areas, logging roads are often built along the sides of valleys or canyons. At the bottoms of these valleys and canyons are usually creeks, streams, and rivers. When the soil becomes unstable, it can cause landslides or allow runoff that hurts fish and other aquatic species. The landslides can occur months or years after the logging operation ceases because the trees are no longer there to hold the soil in place. Some states have more miles of logging roads than paved roads.

Forests also provide a buffer that filters water, and they sustain water and soil resources by recycling nutrients. In watersheds where forests are adversely affected by logging, soil erosion results in silting of the waterways, which, when combined with the loss of shade from trees, increases the temperature of the water, thus threatening aquatic life. Silting can also impede human use of water downstream. This affects agricultural users, cities, and natural systems. In Salem, Oregon, in the late 1990s, overlogging caused the city to close the public water supply. Clear-cutting trees on steep slopes had caused silting of the water in the watershed.

Effects on Climate

Local changes in precipitation are direct and immediate when the forest cover is removed. Trees and forests engage in a natural process of transpiration that modifies water flow, balancing the effects of fluctuations in water volume. Reducing transpiration increases both runoff and erosion.

Loss of Biodiversity

Some scientists and environmentalists assert that logging reduces biodiversity by destroying natural habitats. They fear that that this could lead to the extinction of species, such as the spotted owl in Oregon. The logging industry has developed some replanting and selective harvesting techniques designed to minimize habitat degradation and soil erosion. Some logging corporations say that they try to keep a protected strip of land next to the waterways, a procedure called riparian protection. They limit the number of trees they take from steep slopes so as to prevent soil erosion. They buy land and plant their own trees and then engage in logging there instead of on federally owned land. Logging corporations also prepare environmental impact statements in applying for permits to cut trees on federal land. These corporate techniques are contested by environmentalists, who say that logging corporations do minimal mitigation, create far more damage than they report, and also take trees illegally from federally owned lands.

Many rural western communities are dependent on logging as their only source of income. Since the spotted owl controversy of the 1980s, about 60 logging mills have closed down in Oregon alone.

Sustainable Logging

The idea of sustainable forestry is that the land would never be depleted of its trees. As early as 1936, Weyerhaeuser practiced sustained-yield logging, a practice it continues in the Willamette Valley of Oregon. By logging the forest of its timber and replacing a variety of tree species with a single commercial species, timber companies aim to create a continuing supply of timber. This practice might also result in fewer environmental effects that the logging of virgin or secondary-growth forests.

Critics of this practice say that simply planting your own trees does not necessarily lessen environmental damage, especially to the soil. They say that such monoculture leaves the forests susceptible to disease and that the pesticides used to protect the trees are harmful.

Protests on Both Sides

In some timber states, small property owners have stands of timber they have planted or preserved as a future investment, intended for eventual harvest. Some of these stands can contain unique and irreplaceable old-growth forest. When environmentalists pursue legislation to limit the owners' expectations for the use of this timber, private property activists get involved and open up another front in the logging controversy. When loggers cut old-growth forest, environmental activists increase protest activities such as tree sitting. When timber corporations begin sustainability programs, it is in the context of this entrenched, litigation-heavy controversy.

Roadless Areas and Logging

Many environmental laws protect federal lands and also control multiple uses on them. Roads are a major concern because they erode a "forever wild "status in wilderness areas and can be environmentally detrimental. When roads are built in protected areas so that corporations can log, mine or graze in other areas, recreational users, such as riders of all-terrain vehicles, mountain bikers, and campers on packhorses often begin to use the roads, thus increasing traffic and potentially also the environmental threat.

There are approximately 50 to 60 million acres of roadless areas in the United States, representing about 25 to 30 percent of all land in the national forests; another 35 million acres are congressionally designated wilderness. The rest of the national forests contain 380,000 miles of roads. The vast majority of these rough-cut roads are built by the government to provide access for logging and, to a much lesser extent, mining.

Environmentalists have long accused the Forest Service of simply managing the profits for industry, not protecting the environment. The activists are concerned about watershed protection and restoration and about reforestation. Public opposition to subsidizing logging on public lands by building roads, bridges, and aqueducts in national forests has resulted in budget cuts for the Forest Service.

There is substantial public and political support for permanent protection of the roadless areas. Historically, many people conceived of national parks and wilderness areas as being without any roads. With the increased reliance on automobiles, roads were developed nearly everywhere. Roads greatly affect pristine natural areas, so much so that the need to protect roadless areas is well known. Some experts say environmental policy must establish a ban that protects all roadless national forest areas from road building, logging, mining, grazing, and other activities deemed environmentally degrading.

In 2004 the George W. Bush administration proposed to open up national forests to more logging. The administration had been studying a rule that blocked road construction in nearly one third of national forests designed to prevent logging and other commercial activity. It decided that state governors would have to petition the federal government if they wanted to prevent roads from being build to accommodate logging in remote areas of national forests. The plan covers about 58 million of the 191 million acres of national forest nationwide. The timber industry supported the proposal, maintaining that these decisions are far better made by the local community and state governments than through federal policy.

Conclusion

With the fate of the roadless areas in doubt and industry scientists, environmentalists, and federal agencies intensely studying these issues, the logging controversy will continue. As timber supplies dwindle, governmental agencies may need to take private property to control ecosystem effects from logging. Some logging communities live and die based on local mill operations. Other communities are concerned that their watersheds could be contaminated from runoff or spraying from logging. Logging is also an international environmental issue, and global developments around logging could affect the U.S. controversy.

See also **Environmental Impact Statements; Federal Environmental Land Use; Watershed Protection and Soil Conservation**

CASE STUDY: LOGGING AND ENDANGERED SPECIES

Logging's environmental effect often threatens endangered species such as the spotted owl, which spawned a decade of political and legal controversy. In Oregon and elsewhere in the Pacific Northwest, beginning with George H.W. Bush's campaign for president, the northern spotted owl became the poster bird for the impact of human overpopulation.

A project known as the Sims Fire Salvage timber sale was slated to cut thousands of very large dead trees, called snags, in California's Six Rivers National Forest. Snags serve as homes for all kinds of animals and are considered part of the natural evolution of an old-growth forest. Snags hold fragile soils in place while also providing wildlife habitat.

Around 57 acres of designated critical habitat for the northern spotted owl, marbled murrelet, and coho salmon—all listed as threatened under the federal Endangered Species Act—would have been included in the fire sale. Environmentalists protested that the federal agency overseeing the sale—the U.S. Forest Service—was emphasizing logging projects at the expense of its responsibility to protect fish and wildlife habitat in the public forests.

A federal district court in San Francisco halted the logging project. Since then suggestions for rewriting the National Forest Management Act of 1984, which requires maintaining viable populations of species that indicate the health of an ecosystem, came before judges three times. Beginning in 2000, President George W. Bush's administration systematically worked to increase national forest logging by changing the rules for enforcing environmental laws. Consistently, the courts resisted, noting that the changes proposed did not foster viable populations of endangered species and wildlife.

Shortly after President Barack Obama took office, his administration scrapped a proposal left in the pipeline by the Bush administration that would have boosted logging in Northwest forests and reduced protection for the northern spotted owl. It would have cut the size of critical habitat for the owl and revised recovery plans for the spotted owl to allow logging to increase.

The proposal would have increased the timber harvest by five times. That would amount to only half of what was logged prior to the 1994 Northwest Forest Plan, which dramatically cut logging to protect habitat for owls and salmon. Lawsuits from conservation groups sparked the plan. It reduced logging in Oregon, Washington, and Northern California by more than 80 percent in the name of habitat protection.

This court case and others like it continue to define U.S. environmental policy.

—Debra Ann Schwartz

Further Reading

Alverson, William Surprison, Walter Kuhlmann, and Donald M. Waller, *Wild Forests: Conservation Biology and Public Policy.* Washington, DC: Island Press, 1994.

Berger, John J., *Forests Forever: Their Ecology, Restoration, and Protection.* Chicago: Center for American Places, 2008.

Cox, Thomas R., *The Lumberman's Frontier: Three Centuries of Land Use, Society, and Change in America's Forests.* Corvallis: Oregon State University Press, 2010.

Goble, Dale, and Paul W. Hirt, *Northwest Lands, Northwest Peoples: Readings in Environmental History.* Seattle: University of Washington Press, 1999.

Keiter, Robert B., *Keeping Faith with Nature: Ecosystems, Democracy, and America's Public Lands.* New Haven, CT: Yale University Press, 2003.

Knott, Catherine Henshaw, *Living with the Adirondack Forest: Local Perspectives on Land Use Conflicts.* Ithaca, NY: Cornell University Press, 1998.

MacDonald, Samuel A., *The Agony of an American Wilderness: Loggers, Environmentalists, and the Struggle for Control of a Forgotten Forest.* Lanham, MD: Rowman & Littlefield, 2005.

Rajala, Richard A., *Clearcutting the Pacific Rain Forest: Production, Science, and Regulation.* Vancouver: University of British Columbia Press, 1998.

Roadless Area Conservation, www.roadless.fs.fed.us

M

MEDICAL ETHICS

Joseph Ali

Medical ethics, an offspring of the field of ethics, shares many basic tenets with its siblings: nursing ethics, pharmaceutical ethics, and dental ethics. The definition of medical ethics is itself an issue of some controversy. The term is used to describe the body of literature and instructions prescribing the broader character ideals and responsibilities of being a doctor. Recent sociopolitical and technological changes, however, have meant that medical ethics is also involved with biomedical decision making and patients' rights.

Medical Practitioners and Responsibility

In the first sense of the term, medical ethics consists of professional and character guidelines found in codes and charters of ethics (e.g., the American Medical Association Code of Medical Ethics); principles of ethics (e.g., autonomy, beneficence, nonmaleficence, and justice); and oaths (e.g., the Hippocratic Oath). These formal declarations have the combined effect of expressing an overlapping consensus, or majority view, on how all physicians should behave. It is common to find additional heightened requirements for certain specialties in medicine, such as psychiatry, pain medicine, and obstetrics and gynecology. Moreover, these ethical norms tend periodically to shift as the responsibilities of good doctoring change over time. Such shifts can give rise to heated debates, especially when individuals maintain certain values that have been modified or rejected by the majority.

For example, in the 1980s, the medical profession was forced to consider doctors' obligations in treating HIV/AIDS patients in a climate of discrimination. The American Medical Association (AMA) promulgated ethical rules requiring that physicians treat HIV/AIDS patients whose condition is within the physician's realm of competence. When such rules are violated, boards of medicine, medical associations, hospital and medical school committees, and other credentialing agencies have the difficult task of reviewing alleged breaches and sanctioning misconduct. These professional guidelines begin to clarify the boundaries and goals of medicine as a social good. They attempt to ensure that medical practitioners act humanely as they fight and prevent diseases, promote and restore health, and reduce pain and suffering. The ethical customs found in codes, charters, principles, and oaths form the basis of an entire culture of medicine within the profession.

The practice of medicine is bound by ethical rules for an important reason. In order to fulfill their healing obligation, medical practitioners must often engage in risky procedures interfering with the bodies and minds of vulnerable individuals. Bodily interference, if unconstrained by certain legitimate guiding rules, can be nothing more than assault and battery. Patients must be assured that they will benefit from—or at least not be harmed by—a doctor's care. The establishment of trust is crucial to this end, and once earned, trust marks the doctor–patient relationship.

Perhaps one of the most enduring doctrines in the history of medical ethics is the Hippocratic Oath. The oath dates back to the fourth century b.c.e. and forms the basis of Western medical ethics. It reflects the assumed values of a brotherhood of physicians who charge themselves to care for the sick under a pledge witnessed by the Greek deities. Of great interest to doctors at the time was distinguishing the genuine physician from the fraudulent practitioner. One way in which the oath furthers this goal is by prizing teachers and teaching, requiring that the physician hold his teacher in the "art" of medicine on par with his own parents. It also requires the physician to pledge to help the sick according to his skill and judgment and never do harm to anyone, never administer a deadly drug even when asked to do so, never induce abortion, and never engage in intentional misdeeds with patients (sexual or otherwise). It further requires the physician to keep secret all those things that ought not be revealed about his patients. The good physician, the oath concludes, may enjoy a good life and honored reputation, but those who break the oath shall face dishonor.

To this day, most graduating medical school students swear to some version of the Hippocratic Oath, usually one that is gender-neutral and that departs somewhat from the traditional prohibitions. The mandate of the oath is strong; it directs practitioners to desire what is best for the health of patients. A growing number of physicians and ethicists realize, however, that the Hippocratic Oath and similar ethical codes, though motivational, are inadequate in dealing with the novelties of current practice.

Broader Concerns

Medicine has recently undergone radical shifts in the scientific, technological, economic, social, and political realms, giving rise to artificial life-sustaining devices and treatments, legalized abortions, new artificial reproductive technologies, inventive cosmetic surgeries, stem cell and gene therapies, organ transplantation, palliative care, physician-assisted suicide, and conflicts of interest more powerful than anyone could have predicted just a few decades ago. Many matters previously thought of as "human nature" are continuously being recharacterized to reflect changing knowledge, scientific and otherwise. Medical ethics engages these debates and evaluates the correlative concerns over the definition of death, the moral status of the fetus, the boundaries of procreation and parenting, the flexibility of the concept of personhood, the rights of the dying, and the role of corporations in medicine.

Although physicians' codes play a crucial role in defining the broad parameters of ethical conduct in medicine, in the last few decades sociopolitical demands and market forces have played a much larger role in both shaping and complicating ethics in medicine. Medical ethics then becomes a tool for critical reflection on modern biomedical dilemmas. Ethics scholars and clinical ethicists are regularly consulted when principles or codes appear inadequate because they prescribe unclear, conflicting, or unconscionable actions. Even for ethicists, it is not always obvious what "doing the right thing" means; however, many ethical dilemmas in medicine can be deconstructed using the theoretical tools of medical ethics and sometimes resolved by encouraging decision makers to consider the merits, risks, and psychosocial concerns surrounding particular actions or omissions.

To be sure, clinical ethicists usually do not unilaterally declare right and wrong. But they can ensure that all rightful parties have a fair and informed voice in the discussion of ethically sensitive matters. Medical ethics, as a clinical discipline, approaches decision making through formal processes (e.g., informed consent) and traditional theories (e.g., utilitarianism) that can enhance medical and ethical deliberation. The need for these processes and theories was not just a by-product of technological advances but also a consequence of a movement that has recharacterized the civil status of doctors and patients.

The American Civil Rights Movement of the 1950s and 1960s brought previously denied freedoms to people of color and reinvigorated the spirit of free choice. The unconscionable inferior treatment of marginalized groups was the subject of great sociopolitical concern. Significant legal and moral changes took place both in the ideology surrounding the concepts of justice and equality and in the rigidity of hierarchies found in established institutions of status such as churches, families, schools, and hospitals. Out of the movement came a refreshing idea of fundamental equality based on the dignity of each individual. In the decades that followed, strong criticism arose against paternalism—the practice of providing for others' assumed needs in a fatherly manner without recognizing individuals' rights and responsibilities. It was no longer acceptable for all-knowing physicians to ignore the preferences and humanity of patients while paternalistically doing what they thought was in their "best interests." Doctors were required to respect patients' autonomy, or ability to govern themselves. With this recognition came a general consensus that patients have the legal and ethical right to make uncoerced medical decisions pertaining to their bodies based on their own values.

Autonomy, now viewed by many as a basic principle of biomedical ethics, often translates in practice into the process of "informed consent." Full informed consent has the potential to enrich the doctor–patient relationship by requiring a competent patient and a physician to engage in an explanatory dialogue concerning proposed invasive treatments. By law, physicians must presume that all patients are competent to make medical decisions unless they have a valid reason to conclude otherwise. If a patient is diagnosed as incapable of consenting, the patient's surrogate decision maker or "living will" should be consulted, assuming they are available and no other recognized exception applies. At its core, informed consent must involve the discussion of five elements:

1. the nature of the decision or procedure
2. the reasonable alternatives to the proposed intervention
3. the relevant risks, benefits, and uncertainties related to each alternative
4. an assessment of patient understanding
5. the acceptance of the intervention by the patient

A physician's failure to abide by this decision process can lead to ethical and legal sanctions.

Scholarly questions often arise regarding the diagnosis of incapacity, the determination of how much information must be shared, the definition of "understanding," and the established exceptions to informed consent (e.g., emergency, patient request not to be informed, and "therapeutic privilege"). It is important for informed consent to be an interactive process and not merely the signing of boilerplate forms. The latter does not take the interests of patients into account, it does not further the doctor–patient relationship, and it can result in future conflict or uncertainty if previously competent patients become incapacitated.

Ethical Frameworks

In addition to doctors, many other parties are involved in caring for the ill and facilitating medical decision making. Relatives, spiritual counselors, nurses, social workers, and other members of the health care team all help identify and satisfy the vital needs of patients. Informed consent is a process that can give rise to meaningful dialogue concerning treatment, but like some other tools of practical ethics, it alone may not provide the intellectual means for deeper reflection about values and moral obligations.

To this end, medical ethics makes use of many foundational theories that help situate values within wider frameworks and assist patients, families, and doctors with making ethical choices. These moral theories are typically reduced to three categories: the deontological (duty-based, emphasizing motives and types of action); the consequentialist (emphasizing the consequences of actions); and the virtue-based (emphasizing excellence of character and aspiration for the good life).

The most influential deontological theory is that of Immanuel Kant (1724–1804). Kant derived certain "categorical imperatives" (unconditional duties) that, in his view, apply to the action of any rational being. Generally speaking, the relevant imperatives are as follows: first, individuals have a duty to follow only those subjective principles that can be universalized without leading to some inconsistency and, second, individuals must treat all rational beings as "ends in themselves," respectful of the dignity and integrity of the individual and never merely treating them as a means to some other end. Despite some philosophical criticism, Kant's revolutionary thoughts on the foundations of morality and autonomy are still very timely.

In contrast to Kantian deontology, an influential consequentialist theory is utilitarianism, which states that the moral worth of an action is determined solely by the extent to which its consequences maximize "utility." For Jeremy Bentham (1748–1832), utility translates into "pleasure and the avoidance of pain"; for John Stewart Mill (1806–1873), utility means "happiness." Utilitarianism offers another popular way to conceptualize right and wrong, but it gives rise to the often asked question of how one might accurately calculate the tendency to maximize happiness.

Finally, virtue-based ethics, principally attributed to the Greek philosophy of Plato and Aristotle, generally holds that a person of good character strives to be excellent in virtue, constantly aiming for the *telos* or goal of greater happiness. In leading a virtuous life, the individual may gain both practical and moral wisdom.

These three basic ethical frameworks maintain their relevance today, inspiring many complementary models of ethical reasoning. For example, medical ethics has benefited significantly from scholarship in theological, feminist, communitarian, casuistic, and narrative ethics. These perspectives either critically analyze or combine the language of deontology, consequentialism, and virtue. Together, theories of ethics and their descendants provide some further means of deconstructing the ethically difficult cases in medicine, giving us the words to explore our moral intuitions.

Medical ethics is now often described within the somewhat broader context of bioethics, a burgeoning field concerned with the ethics of medical and biological procedures, technologies, and treatments. Although medical ethics is traditionally more confined to issues that arise in the practice of medicine, both bioethics and medical ethics engage with significant overlapping questions. What are the characteristics of a "good" medical practitioner? What is the best way to oversee the use and distribution of new medical technologies and therapies that are potentially harmful? Who should have the right and responsibility to make crucial moral medical decisions? What can individuals and governments do to help increase access, lower cost, and improve quality of care? And how can individuals best avoid unacceptable harm from medical experimentation? Patients, doctors, hospital administrators, citizens, and members of the government are constantly raising these questions. They are difficult questions, demanding the highest level of interdisciplinary collaboration.

Conclusion

In sum, since the days of Hippocrates, the medical profession has tried to live by the principle of *primum non nocere* (first do no harm). This principle has been upheld by many attentive professionals but also betrayed by some more unscrupulous doctors. To stem potential abuses offensive to human dignity and social welfare, medical ethicists carefully consider the appropriateness of new controversial medical acts and omissions. They try to ensure that medical decision makers do not uncritically equate the availability of certain technoscientific therapies and enhancements with physical and psychosocial benefit. Doctors and patients can participate in a better-informed medical discourse if they combine the dictates of professional rules with procedural formalities of decision making, respecting the diversity of values brought to light. Through this deliberative process, individuals will be able to come closer to understanding their responsibilities while clarifying the boundaries of some of the most difficult questions of the medical humanities.

See also Eugenics; Human Genome Project; Medical Marijuana; Reproductive Technology; Stem Cell Research; Abortion (vol. 3); Euthanasia and Physician-Assisted Suicide (vol. 3)

Further Reading

Beauchamp, Tom L., and James F. Childress, *Principles of Biomedical Ethics,* 5th ed. New York: Oxford University Press, 2001.

Brody, Howard, *The Future of Bioethics.* New York: Oxford University Press, 2010.

Clarke, Adele E., et al., "Biomedicalization: Technoscientific Transformations of Health, Illness, and U.S. Biomedicine." *American Sociological Review* 68 (April 2003): 161–194.

Daniels, N., et al., *From Chance to Choice: Genes and Social Justice.* Cambridge, UK: Cambridge University Press, 2000.

Devettere, Raymond J., *Practical Decision Making in Health Care Ethics,* 3d ed. Washington, DC: Georgetown University Press, 2010.

Illingworth, Patricia, *Ethical Health Care.* Upper Saddle River, NJ: Pearson/Prentice Hall, 2006.

Imber, Jonathan B., *Trusting Doctors: The Decline of Moral Authority in American Medicine.* Princeton, NJ: Princeton University Press, 2008.

Melia, Kath M., *Health Care Ethics: Lessons from Intensive Care.* Thousand Oaks, CA: Sage, 2004.

MEDICAL MARIJUANA

JOSEPH ALI

Whether marijuana should be made legally available for doctors to prescribe as a drug for the treatment of certain medical conditions is hotly debated among politicians, lawyers, scientists, physicians, and members of the general public.

A look at the U.S. legal landscape surrounding medical marijuana shows a complex and rapidly changing scene. Fourteen states—California, Alaska, Oregon, Washington, Maine, Hawaii, Colorado, Nevada, Vermont, Montana, Rhode Island, New Mexico, Michigan, and, most recently, New Jersey—allowed its use in 2010. At least a dozen more were considering eliminating criminal penalties for using marijuana for medical purposes. Its therapeutic use is constantly under fresh review. Recently, the American Medical Association (AMA) adopted a resolution urging review of marijuana as a Schedule I controlled substance.

The cannabis plant (marijuana) has been cultivated for psychoactive, therapeutic, and nondrug uses for over 4,000 years. The primary psychoactive drug in the plant is tetrahydrocannabinol (THC)—a molecule that produces a "high" feeling when ingested and, as is most often the case with cannabis, when inhaled in smoke or vapor form. There are hundreds of other chemical components in marijuana, from vitamin A to steroids, making it somewhat unclear how the human body will react physiologically to short- and long-term use of the substance.

Supporters of medical marijuana argue that the drug is acceptable for medical treatment, citing reports and several scientific peer-reviewed studies. There has been considerable interest in the use of marijuana for the treatment of glaucoma, neuropathic pain, AIDS "wasting," symptoms of multiple sclerosis, and chemotherapy-induced nausea, to name a few. The government opposes the move.

The Food, Drug, and Cosmetic Act—a key law used by the U.S. Food and Drug Administration (FDA) in carrying out its mandate—requires that new drugs be shown to be safe and effective before being marketed in the United States. These two conditions have not been met through the formal processes of the FDA for medical marijuana, and it is therefore not an FDA-approved drug.

The Debate

Proponents of medical marijuana argue that the drug would easily pass the FDA's risk–benefit tests if the agency would give the drug a fair and prompt review. One significant hurdle to obtaining FDA approval is the fact that marijuana has been listed as a Schedule I drug in the Controlled Substances Act (CSA) since 1972. As such, it is considered by the U.S. government to have a "lack of accepted safety," "high potential for abuse," and "no currently accepted medical use." Schedule I drugs, however, have occasionally been approved by the FDA for medical use in the past, with significant restrictions on how they must be manufactured, labeled, and prescribed.

At present, the possession and cultivation of marijuana for recreational use is illegal in all 50 states and in most countries around the world. Further, representatives of various agencies in the current U.S. federal government have consistently stated that there is no consensus on the safety or efficacy of marijuana for *medical* use, and without sufficient evidence and full approval by the FDA, the government cannot allow the medical use of a drug that may be hazardous to health. Some say that the availability of various other FDA-approved drugs, including synthetic versions of the active ingredients in marijuana, make the use of marijuana unnecessary. They claim furthermore that marijuana is an addictive "gateway" drug that leads to abuse of more dangerous drugs and that it injures the lungs, damages the brain, harms the immune system, and may lead to infertility. The use of marijuana for some medical purposes is allowed in Canada, however, though under strict Health Canada regulations.

Proponents maintain that the approved synthetic versions of marijuana are not chemically identical to the actual plant and therefore not as medically beneficial. They further argue that many of the claims of harm either have not been shown to be true or are not at all unique to marijuana but are comparable to the potential side effects of a number of alternative drugs currently on the market. They insist that the government is setting unfair standards for medical marijuana for sociopolitical rather than scientific reasons. They point to a respected scientific report, published in 1999 by the U.S. Institute of Medicine (IOM) and commissioned by the U.S. government through a $1 million grant, which recommends that under certain conditions marijuana should be made medically available to some patients, even though "numerous studies suggest that marijuana smoke is an important risk factor in the development of respiratory disease."

Despite a broad federal stance in opposition to the distribution, possession, and cultivation of marijuana for *any* drug-related use, many U.S. states have enacted their own "medical use" laws. The level of permissibility for marijuana use in state laws varies. Some states, such as California, allow doctors to prescribe marijuana very liberally, whereas others, such as New Mexico, allow access to medical marijuana only for patients suffering pain as a result of a few specific conditions. The enactment of medical marijuana state statutes that conflict with the federal Controlled Substances Act has given rise to lawsuits brought by both sides in the controversy.

The issue has gone so far as to reach the U.S. Supreme Court in the case of *Gonzales v. Raich*. In that 2005 case, the Court ruled that Congress has the authority to *prohibit* the cultivation and use of marijuana in California and across the United States despite laws in California allowing the use of medical marijuana. the court did not require California to change its laws, however. As a result, both the California medical-use statutes and the conflicting federal laws remain in force today. Some doctors in California continue to prescribe medical marijuana through the state's program, and the federal government's Drug Enforcement Administration (DEA) continues to enforce the federal statute in

California against those who choose to prescribe, possess, or cultivate marijuana for medical use. The issue remains largely undecided in law.

In *Gonzales v. Raich*, the Supreme Court did state that Congress could change the federal law to allow the medical use of marijuana if it chose to do so. Congress has voted on several bills to legalize such use, but none has been passed. Most recently, a coalition has petitioned the U.S. government to change the legal category of marijuana from "Schedule I" to a category that would permit physicians to prescribe marijuana for patients they believe would benefit from it. Given recent trends, it is unlikely that the federal government will respond entirely favorably to this petition; it is equally unlikely, however, that supporters of medical marijuana will be quick to abandon their cause.

See also **Medical Ethics; Off-Label Drug Use; Drugs (vol. 3)**

Further Reading

Chapkis, Wendy, and Richard J. Webb, *Dying to Get High: Marijuana as Medicine.* New York: New York University Press, 2008.

Controlled Substances Act, U.S. Code Title 21, chapter 13.

Federal Food, Drug, and Cosmetic Act, U.S. Code Title 21, chapter 9.

Fielding, Amanda, ed., *Cannabis Policy: Moving Beyond Stalemate.* New York: Oxford University Press, 2010.

Gonzales v. Raich (previously *Ashcroft v. Raich*), 545 U.S. 1 (2005).

Hoffman, D., and Webber, E., "Medical Marijuana and the Law." New England Journal of Medicine 362, no. 16 (2010): 1453–1457.

Joy, Janet Elizabeth, Stanley J. Watson, and John A. Benson, *Marijuana and Medicine: Assessing the Science Base.* Institute of Medicine Report. Washington, DC: National Academies Press, 1999.

MINING OF NATURAL RESOURCES

Robert William Collin and Debra Ann Schwartz

Mining is the process of extracting ores and other substances from the earth. It can have enormous and irreparable environmental impacts, especially with technological improvements in the industry. These impacts affect national parks, indigenous peoples, and nearby communities. In the United States, many large mines are on land leased from the government to private corporations. Some communities are dependent on the mining industry, such as those around some coal mines.

Background

The 1872 Mining Law allowed the mining of valuable minerals on federal land with minimal payments to the U.S. government. Its purpose was to encourage westward expansion of European settlement. Some of the oldest roads in the West are old mining roads. Mining for gold, silver, and other minerals was extremely dangerous work in the late 1800s. The mines were very warm, collapsed frequently, were subject to fires and floods, and were filled with toxic gases. Long-term leases, low-cost sales, and other arrangements allowed mining interests to develop a basic natural resource in the West. While they were doing so, some of the basic road infrastructure was developed. The profits for these government-protected risks is one of the controversial issues. Critics of the 1872 Mining Law contend that the profits generated by mining federal lands are very large and no longer need any government subsidization. Environmental concerns about roads generally, and about the increasing scale and environmental impacts of mining and loss of habitat, enter the battleground.

Speculation on Federal Lands: Environmental Impacts and Controversies

Mining is restricted by local land-use regulations, state environmental laws, and federal environmental rules and regulations. Many more restrictions are imposed on the timing of mining activities on federal land. Generally, environmentalists would like to see more mitigation and cleanup of environmental degradation. Many environmentalists would like to see absolutely no mining in areas where there are endangered species. In terms of land speculation with federal mineral rights leases, the issue is how long the lease can be held without mining. This makes it difficult for things such as conservation easements or for any private property owner to simply not develop his or her mineral rights. It is a use-it-or-lose-it proposition that works to increase mining and the environmental impacts of mining. Diligence requirements in the leases limit how long a lease can be held without any development and how long it can be held after production is shut down. Moreover, regular expenditures are required by the terms of the lease. Environmentalists and others maintain that those restrictions are not rigorous enough to constrain development. Others think that restrictions are a good idea but that existing restrictions are more than adequate.

Sharing the Wealth: What to Do with Mining Revenues

Mining fees are distributed primarily to residents of sparsely populated western states because Congress allocates half of gross mining receipts to the state in which the mining occurs. That is one reason why many state environmental agencies and communities in these states support the mining industry. Many environmentalists would like to use some of that money to restore the ecology to its premining ecological condition.

Sustainability and Mining

Many question whether mining can be described as sustainable. Of all the earth and ore disturbed for metals extraction, only a small amount is actual ore. For example, in

SURFACE MINING

The term *surface mining* refers to the removal of material, such as coal or tar sand, from veins lying at or near the earth's surface rather than deep inside it. In this form of mining, there is no need to drill a shaft or bore hole, because the substance being mined can be excavated more or less directly from the surface. There are three main varieties of surface mining. In *strip mining*, a layer of earth lying immediately above a vein of coal, for example, is removed by giant excavating machines and discarded to provide access to the coal, which is then mined directly. Illinois initiated strip mining in the United States in the 1850s. It turned the state's lush land where the Kickapoo Native Nation lived into ash and spoil piles, stagnant mine ponds and pits. Machines clear-cut forests in the Prairie State and detonated explosives across the Illinois landscape to remove anything overlying the mineral seams. Eventually, the practice also cost the miners their jobs, leaving them with polluted communities and devastating the region for any other economic development, since the environment had been defiled. Development attempts on reclaimed mine sites have included prisons, small-town airports, golf courses, and waste disposal sites for sludge.

In *open-pit mining*, material is extracted from the earth by means of a vast pit, up to two miles wide and a half-mile deep, dug at the surface. Open-pit mines lay claim to large areas and leave in their wakes toxic residues including sulfides, created during the ore processing stage. The Berkeley Pit in Butte, Montana, which closed in 1982 after operating for nearly 30 years, is now a toxic lake filled with heavy metals and acid compounds. Such toxins can and do leach into the surrounding soils and pose risks to aquifers, or ground water supplies. Nevertheless, some open-pit mines have been successfully rehabilitated following their closure.

Mountaintop removal is a third form of surface mining. Companies such as Massey Energy, the largest producer of Central Appalachian coal, blast away the tops of mountains to gain access to veins of coal. Once this has been done, the company will loosen the coal from its bed with chemicals such as arsenic, which often runs into the rivers and soaks into the soil, creating plumes that sometimes move into aquifers. This process creates excessive mining waste, which fills in nearby valleys, rivers, mountain streams, hollows, and other ecosystems.

The environmental impact of surface mining was described in detail in a 2010 report in the journal *Science*. No way has been found to completely restore the ecological balance left by this kind of mining. Valley fills from explosions frequently bury the headwater streams from which rivers originate. The result is permanent ecosystem loss. In addition, the loss of large tracts of deciduous forest through surface mining threatens several endangered species. It will take a lot of effort by the best minds available to solve the riddle of how to supply needed minerals and other materials while not permanently damaging the environment.

1995, the gold-mining industry moved and processed 72.5 million tons of rock to extract 7,235 tons of gold. The rest, 99 percent, was left as waste. Mine tailings can be hazardous and build up quickly in the host community. Cleanup of radioactive uranium tailings is a significant environmental issue. Some Native American environmental justice issues revolve around the cleanup of low-level radioactive waste, often piles of mine tailings.

An initial environmental question is whether it is acceptable to mine at all. For example, it is held that in some instances, even an operation with state-of-the-art environmental design should simply not be built because it is planned for a location that is not appropriate for mining. Environmental critics claim that mining companies want to engage sustainability only in terms of how to mine, not whether to mine.

Community Concern

While nations and multinational corporations profit from mining operations around the world, local communities face the resulting environmental impacts. Mining communities have begun to exercise their right to prior informed consent to mining operations.

The concept of prior informed consent involves the right of a community to be informed about mining operations on a full and timely basis. It allows a community to approve an operation prior to commencement. This includes participation in setting the terms and conditions and addressing the economic, social, and environmental impacts of all phases of mining and postmining operations. Some environmentalists oppose this type of community rule because communities' short-term economic interests may outweigh long-term environmental implications. They wonder how well all the terms and conditions in the prior informed consent would really be enforced.

Conclusion

Communities, environmentalists, mining companies and their employees, and government all decry the environmental impacts of mining. Yet consumer demand for products made from mined materials and a rapid increase in technology allow the scope and scale of mining to increase. This will increase environmental impacts and also future controversy.

See also Coal; Cumulative Emissions; Environmental Impact Statements; Water Pollution; Sustainability (vol. 1)

Further Reading

Burns, Shirley Stewart, *Bringing Down the Mountains: The Impact of Mountaintop Removal Surface Coal Mining on West Virginia Communities, 1970–2004.* Morgantown: West Virginia University Press, 2007.

Crow, Peter, *Do, Die, or Get Along: A Tale of Two Appalachian Tows.* Athens: University of Georgia Press, 2007.

Crowder, Ad'aele A., Earle A. Ripley, and Robert E. Redmann, *Environmental Effects of Mining.* Boca Raton, FL: CRC Press, 1996.

Hartman, Howard L., and Jan M. Mutmansky, *Introductory Mining Engineering.* New York: Wiley, 2002.

LeCain, Timothy, *Mass Destruction: The Men and Giant Mines that Wired America and Scarred the Planet*. New Brunswick, NJ: Rutgers University Press, 2009.

U.S. Department of the Interior, Office of Surface Mining, Environmental Assessments, www.osmre.gov/pdf/streambufferea.pdf

MISSILE DEFENSE

Steven T. Nagy

Ever since the advent of long-range weapons, militaries have been concerned with defending themselves against objects falling from the sky. Developing technologies in the 1950s brought a new threat in the form of ballistic missiles. Governments and their armed forces sought defensive measures, culminating recently in the United States in a National Missile Defense (NMD) program. There are three main concerns with NMD: destabilization, functionality, and who should be in charge of decisions about its development and deployment. The discussion currently centers on general versus immediate deterrence and international conflict.

Historical Background

The first attempt at missile defense in the United States came in the late 1950s with the Nike-Zeus interceptor. Because the United States lacked advanced guidance technology, the only reasonable path to interception lay in arming the defensive missile with a nuclear warhead. This system was unsuccessful and was replaced in 1961 by the Ballistic Missile Boost Interceptor (BAMBI). Housed in satellite platforms, BAMBI would intercept enemy missiles shortly after launch (the "boost" phase) by deploying a large net designed to disable intercontinental ballistic missiles (ICBMs). Again, because of technical difficulties, it was never deployed.

In 1963, U.S. Defense Secretary Robert McNamara unveiled the Sentinel program. This program differed from its predecessors by layering defensive missiles. Made up of both short- and long-range interception missiles and guided by radar and computers, the system would protect the entire United States from a large-scale nuclear attack. Political concerns about the destabilizing influence of this system, along with the technical difficulties involved in tracking and intercepting incoming ICBMs, ensured that the Sentinel fared no better than its predecessors.

In 1967 the Sentinel was scaled back and renamed Safeguard. With this reduction in scale, the entire United States could not be protected, and Safeguard was installed only around nuclear missile sites. This enabled launch sites to survive a first strike and then retaliate. For the first time in U.S. missile defense theory, survival of retaliatory capability outweighed the defense of American citizens.

While the United States worked at developing NMD systems, the USSR did the same. It became obvious to the two superpowers that this could escalate into a defensive arms race. In an effort to curb military spending, the two countries agreed in 1972 to limit their defensive systems, creating the Anti-Ballistic Missile (ABM) treaty. Under this agreement, each country could deploy one defensive system. The United States chose to defend the Grand Forks Air Force Base in North Dakota and the USSR chose Moscow.

In 1983 President Ronald Reagan revived the NMD debate by announcing the Strategic Defense Initiative (SDI), known derisively as "Star Wars." Although previous missile defense systems had used ground-based control systems, Star Wars called for an elaborate series of nuclear-pumped x-ray laser satellites to destroy enemy missiles. This program would provide complete protection to the United States in the event of an all-out attack by a nuclear-armed adversary. Unfortunately, the technical problems were too great, and with the collapse of the USSR and the end of the Cold War, the program was canceled.

Recent Developments

Under the administration of George W. Bush, SDI morphed into NMD. This project was less ambitious than SDI, and its goal was the defense of the United States against nuclear blackmail or terrorism from a "rogue" state. The system consisted of ground-based interceptor missiles in Fort Greely, Alaska, and at Vandenberg Air Force Base in California. By 2005, there had been a series of arguably successful test launches from sea- and shore-based launchers against a simulated missile attack. (The results of these tests are themselves debated.)

As with its predecessors, there were three current concerns with the NMD program: destabilization, functionality, and who should be in charge of decisions about its development and deployment.

Under the doctrine of Mutually Assured Destruction (MAD), both sides avoided launching missiles because the enemy would respond in kind. Neither side could win; therefore neither would go to war. Developing an effective NMD would eliminate the retaliatory threat, destabilizing the balance of power by making a nuclear war winnable and thus increasing the chance that one might occur. Even the fear that one side might field such a system could cause a preemptive strike.

The concept a successful NMD assumes a system that works. To date, missile defense systems have posed numerous technical problems and have never achieved true operational status. Critics of NMD argue that this current system has fared no better than others, whereas supporters claim that the successful tests of the recent past show that the technology is viable.

Finally, there is the question of who is in charge. Given post-9/11 security issues, the main concern is defending against launches from countries that have possible links to terrorists. As the developer of NMD, the United States would want the final say in its deployment and use. Unfortunately, to maximize interception probabilities, NMD requires sites in other countries, mostly members of the North American Treaty Organization (NATO). Poland and the Czech Republic, because of their position along possible missile flight paths, figured prominently in U.S. strategies under President Bush. The administration's plan called for up to 54 missiles to be based in Poland and the controlling X-band radar to be sited in the Czech Republic.

These and other NATO countries, however, believe that participating in NMD makes them into potential targets of both terrorists and countries unfriendly to NATO. They feel they should have the authority to launch missiles in their own defense should the need arise. In fact, as a result of the plans to deploy NMD in Eastern Europe, tensions between the United States and Russia grew. Both in order to relieve these tensions and confront the economic and technical difficulties of NMD, the incoming Obama administration announced that it would not be going forward with deployments in Eastern Europe and had begun investigating alternatives to NMD generally.

Conclusion

NMD remains an unproved system. Despite over 50 years of work, the probability of successful ballistic missile defense remains low. Add to this the concerns over destabilization, costs, and the utility of the system in light of the changing landscape of warfare in the 21st century (where "small wars" and tactical weapons are the norm), and the future of NMD is far from certain. A growing number of skeptics and realists are beginning to regard NMD as just another entry in a long list of failed or cancelled projects.

See also **War and the Economy (vol. 1)**

Further Reading

Cimbala, Stephen J., *Shield of Dreams: Missile Defense and U.S.-Russian Nuclear Strategy.* Annapolis, MD: Naval Institute Press, 2008.

Lettow, Paul Voerbeck, *Ronald Reagan and His Quest to Abolish Nuclear Weapons.* New York: Random House, 2005.

Mockli, Daniel, "U.S. Missile Defense: A Strategic Challenge for Europe." *CSS Analyses for Security Policy* 2, no. 12 (2007): 1–3.

O'Hanlon, Michael E., *Budgeting for Hard Power: Defense and Security Spending under Barack Obama.* Washington, DC: Brookings Institution Press, 2009.

Peoples, Columba, *Justifying Ballistic Missile Defense: Technology, Security, and Culture.* New York: Cambridge University Press, 2010.

Quckenbush, Stephen L., "General Deterrence and International Conflict: Testing Perfect Deterrence Theory." *International Interactions* 36, no. 1 (2010): 60–85.

N

NATIONAL PARKS AND CONCESSIONS

Robert William Collin and Debra Ann Schwartz

National parks are predominantly in the western United States, where vast tracts of land were set aside and protected as settlers and development pressed beyond the Mississippi River. Significant national parks and monuments exist in every state. An old park service policy of granting private concession monopolies, without open bidding, caused uproars about injustice early on. The U.S. National Park Service (NPS) also operated concessions in the form of lodging, guides, and so forth as the parks were created. In many areas the national parks provided needed jobs and tourist revenue, especially during the Great Depression of the 1930s. Still a revenue corridor to the local economy, most forms of recreation—including snowmobiling, river rafting, skiing, and the use of all-terrain vehicles—impact the environment and have been argued as activities in conflict with the overall mission of the NPS.

The U.S. national park system is often the focus of environmental controversies. One current example is the extent to which scenic preservation and environmental quality in the parks is surrendered in favor of money that concession stands contribute to keep the parks open. Concessions, for example, require electricity. Bringing electrical lines into the parks has an environmental and scenic impact. Consequently, some environmentalists oppose the stands as business operations in national parks.

Emerging Issue: Electricity

The Energy Policy Act of 2005 gave the U.S. secretary of energy the authority to designate public and private lands as National Interest Electric Transmission Corridors

(NIETCs). Two regions served as the starting point for creating the corridors: the southwestern United States, passing through southern California, Arizona, and Nevada; and the Mid-Atlantic states, through Pennsylvania, New Jersey, New York, Virginia, West Virginia, Maryland, and Washington, D.C.

Weaker environmental impact assessments are allowed for projects within these designations, which pass through five national parks, at least 13 national wildlife refuges, and many other nature preserves. Environmentalists argue that the designations clash with the National Wildlife Act. Concessions almost always need electrical power; as they expand, so too will their need for electrical energy. When the source of the electrical energy is a coal-fired power plant, environmental activists have publicly chided the government for supporting nonrenewable energy sources that pollute the environment instead of cleaner and more sustainable fuel sources, such as solar power.

Taking sides with environmental activists yet presenting a different argument, landowners from surrounding communities have also objected to the corridors, citing documented impacts to livestock health from waves of electricity. As well, there is similar research indicating that electromagnetic radiation causes negative health effects in people and plants. This aspect of the concessions controversy will expand as more projects are proposed and begun in designated areas.

Many requests for concessions were denied amid this controversy after the 2005 law. However, in early December 2007, the Department of Energy granted rehearings to further consider arguments from all who filed timely requests in the Mid-Atlantic and Southwest corridors. In January 2008, eleven environmental organizations from both areas filed suit against the Department of Energy (DOE) over its corridor designations. Led by the National Wildlife Federation and the Piedmont Environmental Council, the groups challenged the designation as violating the National Environmental Protection Act and Endangered Species Act by failing to study the potential harmful impacts of the corridor on air quality, wildlife, habitat, and other natural resources. They also restated that the NPS is mandated to conserve the scenery in national parks, and that having energy corridors run through them is inappropriate. According to the suit, DOE overstepped what Congress called for in the 2005 Energy Policy Act and designated lands that lie outside of the identified congestion area. Three months later, on March 6, 2008, the DOE issued an order denying all applications for rehearing. As of May 2010, corridors in Grand Teton National Park in Wyoming, Hot Springs National Park in Arkansas, and Volcanoes National Park in Hawaii awaited approval.

In addition to health and fuel source concerns, local control of land also is part of this issue. Because federal law supersedes state and local land-use controls when it is more strict, communities tend to fight federal land grabs. In the many jurisdictional controversies around the fear of federal encroachment on states' rights, the issue of concessions to local residents and their businesses is one of the most significant. Generally, compromises have to be made on both sides—sometimes following a public hearing.

Despite the congressional mandate to protect the scenic beauty and environmental quality (about which the Transcendentalists and American Romantics waxed poetic), entrepreneurs have long sought to create recreational ski areas in Colorado's Rocky Mountain National Park, for example, one of the oldest national parks. Park Service philosophy has maintained that all outdoor sports, including winter sports, should be encouraged there. Early powerful park administrators believed that to get appropriations from a parsimonious Congress they had to publicize the recreational potential of the park system. Others contended that visitors should be allowed to use the parks to the fullest no matter what the environmental impacts. As a result, ski lifts were eventually built in the Mt. Rainier, Sequoia, Yosemite, Lassen Volcanic, and Olympic national parks. To implement these directives in Rocky Mountain National Park without marring the scenery became the special problem of more than one superintendent, and the fact that a winter sports complex was built there suggests that the Park Service was bowing to political pressures.

Perennial Issue: Campgrounds

Park officials regularly grapple with controversies surrounding campgrounds and inholdings—privately owned land contained within a national park. The existence of both is considered ecologically unsound by some, since they irrevocably alter the environment for wildlife. Thus it seemed logical to buy out privately developed lands within areas acquired for national parks. To replace developed areas with campgrounds was a politically realistic policy. Pressures from politicians and chambers of commerce demanding more campgrounds, roads, and trails are ever present for many park administrators. Allowing campgrounds within national parks also presented a business challenge for hotel, inn, and motel owners who could not compete profitably with such campgrounds.

Another Environmental Impact: Noise Pollution

Noise generated by human activities is another ongoing issue. Large recreational vehicles often need to run generators, so their use in large campgrounds tends to compromise the wilderness experience. Some communities want to expand their airports to take economic advantage of the presence of a national park, thereby also contributing to noise pollution. Larger airports mean bigger planes and more tourist revenue. They also mean extending the environmental impacts of noise and air pollution into the community. Some wonder what existing land-use policies involving concessions will bring in the future.

Controversy and litigation have increased in the case of parks where visitors hear touring planes and helicopters, snowmobiles, watercraft, off-road vehicles, and even the NPS's own equipment and concessions. Members of environmental groups, off-highway vehicle groups, the air tourism industry, tribal nations, and some of the major government agencies that oversee public lands all spar over noise control. Will the national parks allow racecar driving, manufacturing industries, or tall office buildings?

Conclusion

As park users increase their demand for the national park experience, conflict and controversy are increasing as well. Strong economic and political pressure from logging, mining, and ranching opportunists could arise once concessions for in-park businesses are made. The NPS's mission clashes with many of the special interests that drive economic pressure for concessions stands; it also collides with ranchers, for example, who resent wildlife reintroduction programs—including for wolves, which eat livestock, and grizzly bears.

It is likely that national parks will continue generate strong and controversial issues around noise, electricity lines, and other activities disrupting wildlife and issues that relate to businesses operating concessions in the parks. Ecosystem risk assessments, endangered species, and cumulative impacts are themselves all environmental controversies that are heightened within the confines of a national park.

See also **Federal Environmental Land Use; Logging; Mining of Natural Resources; Stock Grazing and the Environment; Wild Animal Reintroduction**

Further Reading

Bowersox, Joe, *The Moral Austerity of Environmental Decision Making.* Durham, NC: Duke University Press, 2002.

Buckley, Ralf, Catherine Pickering, and David Bruce Weaver, *Nature-Based Tourism, Environment and Land Management.* London: CABI Publishing, 2003.

Fretwell, Holly Lippke, *Who Is Minding the Federal Estate? Political Management of America's Public Lands.* Lanham, MD: Lexington Books, 2009.

Machlis, Gary E., and Donald R. Field, *National Parks and Rural Development: Practice and Policy in the United States.* Washington, DC: Island Press, 2000.

National Park Service Concession Program, www.concessions.nps.gov

National Park Service Concessions Assessment, www.whitehouse.gov/OMB/expectmore/detail.10003716.2005.html

National Parks Conservation Association, www.npca.org

National Park Service, History, www.cr.nps.gov/history/hisnps/NPSHistory/timeline_annotated.htm

O'Brien, Bob R, *Our National Parks and the Search for Sustainability.* Austin: University of Texas Press, 1999.

U.S. Department of Energy, National Interest Electric Transmission Corridors and Congestion Study, 2010, http://nietc.anl.gov

Vaughn, Jacqueline, *Conflicts over Natural Resources: A Reference Handbook.* Santa Barbara, CA: ABC-CLIO, 2007.

The Yellowstone Case, 2009, http://www.edmonds-institute.org/yellowstone.html

NATURE VERSUS NURTURE

Jennifer Croissant

"Nature versus nurture" is the popular phrase depicting the debate between proponents of sociobiology (biological or genetic determinism) and proponents of behaviorism (social determinism) over the reasons adult humans come to behave the way they do.

In his 1930 classic *Behaviorism*, John B. Watson (1878–1958), father of behavioral psychology, wrote perhaps the strongest formulation of a view of nurture, with development through learning and environment represented as the determinant of human possibilities. He said, "Give me a dozen healthy infants, well-formed, and my own specified world to bring them up in and I'll guarantee to take any one at random and train him to become any type of specialist I might select—doctor, lawyer, artist, merchant-chief and, yes, even beggar-man and thief, regardless of his talents, penchants, tendencies, abilities, vocations, and race of his ancestors."

In opposition to such sentiments, especially after the foundations of inheritance changed with the discovery of DNA, other scientists looked for physical rather than social explanations for human characteristics and achievements. Sociobiology (biological or genetic determinism) is a field in which human behaviors are studied to clarify how they might emerge from evolutionary mechanisms. For example, altruism (in which an individual sacrifices for a greater good at the expense of his or her own genetic success) may be explained as advancing the genetic fitness of a group. Specifically, one's genes are often shared with relatives; therefore if a behavior advances the evolutionary success of the larger group, the genes are propagated even if not by a specific individual. Other behaviors then are considered based on similar assessments of individual and group fitness and thus the ability to pass on genes to subsequent generations.

Genetic Markers

Sociobiology rests on ideas about genetic determinism, a theory that attempts to link complex behaviors to genes at more individual levels. Attempts have been made to connect alcoholism, homosexuality, mental illness, and many other behaviors and conditions to specific genetic mechanisms. Despite occasional features in the popular media, however, careful scrutiny of genetic attributions rarely hold up; either the statistical measures are re-examined and dismissed by other scholars or (more frequently) dismissed when a broader population is sampled inconclusively for a specific genetic marker.

Despite current problems, certain genetic diseases are still good models for genetic determinism. For example, Huntington's disease is a heritable neurological illness marked by loss of motor control and physical and psychological decline. It is unambiguously linked to a kind of mutation (a repeated amino acid sequence) on chromosome four. Even that mutation has variations in the number of repeated sequences, and the severity and progression of the disease is strongly, though not exactly, linked to the scope of the mutation. Similarly, although BRCA1 and BRCA2 (breast cancer 1 and 2, early onset) genes are statistically linked to increased risk of breast cancer in women, the detection of either gene in any particular woman does not necessarily mean that she will definitely develop breast cancer. This leads to a great deal of uncertainty and anxiety for women who carry these genes because they have to consider preventive treatments such as drugs, which have serious side effects, or even removal of the breasts to try to avoid cancer. It is further complicated by the fact that many breast cancers are not linked to the BRCA markers, meaning that being screened negatively for these markers does not guarantee that any woman so screened will not eventually develop breast cancer. Thus, for many diseases, such as breast cancer, such a focus on genetics is sometimes seen as a distraction from research on environmental contributions—such as exposure to toxins or dietary factors that might cause breast cancer—because it focuses attention on cure rather than prevention.

Although the popular appeal of genetic determinism is hard to counteract, the attribution of apparently straightforward medical conditions to genetic inheritance leads to a critique of "nature" by the proponents of social determinism. Twin studies, for example, are taken to "prove" the heritability of many things, from weight and height to spirituality or political affiliation. One of the most important factors, probability, is rarely considered. Suppose, for example, that a researcher found that twins who were separated at birth and now live 150 miles apart in Iowa both drove red pickup trucks and liked a particular brand of beer and hot dogs. He might see these facts as proof that the observed behaviors were caused by genes. However, one must also sort out the probability of any two adult men driving red trucks and liking particular brands of beer and hot dogs. In Iowa, that may not be a very surprising correlation. If one of our twins had been raised in Ireland rather than Iowa, nearer his twin, and liked a particular beer (rather than stout) and hot dogs (rather than haggis) and drove a red pickup truck, then that might be a more interesting finding. That is, environments are often assumed to be completely dissimilar, neglecting the facts of broadly shared culture and parenting practices. There are no systematic or agreed-upon measures of "environment" in twin studies; therefore so results are necessarily inconclusive.

It is clear that genetic theories of characteristics such as intelligence or athletic ability can easily be associated with racism and eugenics and can have complicated political and social justice implications. Stereotypes such as "white men can't jump" or "blacks can't do math" become taken as facts rather than as phenomena that may or may not be true or that may have social explanations ranging from the demographic to the psychological. For example, if people believed that white people cannot jump, white people might not put themselves in situations where they would have a chance to improve their jumping, thus creating a self-fulfilling prophecy that is only superficially true, and so on.

Society and Social "Types"

Social determinist explanations also have their racist counterparts, however. Stereotypes about "the black family" are an environmental, rather than genetic, explanations of the dynamics of urban black poverty. Adopting a view that something such as homosexuality is a product of nature (genes in contemporary theories) can be an attempt to argue that because it is not chosen and is a natural part of human existence, it therefore should not be subject to discrimination. A theory of homosexuality as genetic, however, does not prevent people from discriminating: skin color is natural, and yet people still use it as a basis for discrimination. Thus a genetic theory does not prevent continued pathologization, and a search for "treatments" or "cures" may in fact enhance efforts to try to eliminate a behavior or kind of person. Although theories about nurture or the social construction of behavior and identity are often interpreted as more socially progressive, they are also not immune to producing justifications for discrimination or medical intervention.

In addition to ambiguous political outcomes, theories of nature or nurture both share a tendency toward a fundamental attribution error or typological thinking. That is, a behavior is extrapolated to be an expression of the "true self" or of a "type" of person distinct from other types. For example, there is little correlation between whether or not people keep their rooms neat and also turn in neat homework. Yet most people will examine either the state of the room or the homework and infer that the one matches the other. In terms of human behaviors such as homosexuality, many persons engage in same-sex behaviors yet do not self-identify as homosexual. Not only can sexual orientation change across the life course but, in addition, the context (ranging from the local, such as prisons, to the historical, such as Sparta in Ancient Greece) shapes the meaning, frequency, and persistence of the behavior. These things greatly complicate the attribution of either a genetic foundation or an environmental "cause" that holds across time or context.

Conclusion

In an obvious sense, nature matters: children generally look like their biological parents, and populations of people do have common features, whether facial features, skin color, or tendencies toward risk factors in illnesses. But because genes require expression to have their effects, it is impossible to separate nature and nurture in any meaningful sense. Theories such as dynamic systems theory are proposed to explain the complexity of human development, considering both the genetic and biological features and their interaction within environmental contexts. For example, many genes contribute to height, but the expression of those genes is strongly influenced by nutrition and exercise.

There is no way to completely untangle the multiple factors affecting human characteristics and behavior except in the broadest statistical sense, which makes it extremely difficult to infer anything about a specific individual. Both researchers and the lay public, however, will continue to try to single out either nature or nurture as determining factors for behavior, illness, and identity because these theories support important political narratives and projects that shape the distribution of goods, services, and social justice in contemporary culture.

See also Eugenics; Gender Socialization (vol. 3); Mental Health (vol. 3)

Further Reading

Fausto-Sterling, Anne, *Sexing the Body.* New York: Basic Books, 2000.

Gillette, Aaron, *Eugenics and the Nature-Nurture Debate in the Twentieth Century.* New York: Palgrave Macmillan, 2007.

Parens, Erik, et al., eds., *Wrestling with Behavioral Genetics: Science, Ethics, and Public Conversation.* Baltimore: Johns Hopkins University Press, 2006.

Ridley, Matt, *Nature via Nurture: Genes, Experience, and What Makes Us Human.* New York: HarperCollins, 2003.

Watson, John B., *Behaviorism,* rev. ed. Chicago: University of Chicago Press, 1958.

Wilson, E. O. *Sociobiology: The New Synthesis,* 25th anniversary ed. Cambridge, MA: Belknap/Harvard University Press, 2000.

Wright, Lawrence, *Twins: And What They Tell Us about Who We Are.* New York: Wiley, 1997.

NUCLEAR ENERGY

Robert William Collin

Nuclear energy has always been controversial because of its long-term environmental impacts and community concerns about the safety of nuclear plants. In addition, its use and threat of use in war creates a powerful aura of fear around this energy source. Other controversial issues related to environmental regulation of industry, such as disclosure of chemicals and audit privileges, attract much more attention from the public when the industry is nuclear power. Many countries (e.g., France) increasingly rely on this form of energy.

In the United States, no nuclear plants have been built since the late 1970s, although U.S. utilities have become much more commercially aggressive about nuclear energy. Some environmental groups have supported nuclear energy as less environmentally harmful than petrochemical energy. Owners of existing plants are seeking renewal of operating licenses and are getting ready to upgrade power output or restart closed reactors. Some observers predict that during the next few years there could be applications for 10 or more new U.S. reactors producing approximately 40,000 megawatts of energy.

Several events form the basis of this controversy. They have shaped the public's image of risk and of the credibility of nuclear risk assessments and assessors.

- During the 1970s, Pennsylvania's Three Mile Island experienced an overheated reactor core.
- During the 1980s, the Soviet Union's Chernobyl plant experienced an uncontained meltdown, the worst such accident ever to have occurred anywhere in the world.
- The U.S. Nuclear Regulatory Commission has issued formal alerts or declared site emergencies at least 10 times between 1979 and the present.
- Since September 11, 2001, public fear has increased regarding security risks at nuclear sites.

The risk of a nuclear meltdown with a potentially devastating range of human and ecological impacts and the general issue of plant security underscore modern tensions around nuclear energy.

The United States Today

Today, about 103 nuclear reactors are operating in 31 states. They generate about one fifth of the nation's electricity. Major expansions are planned, and each will be an issue in this controversy. With this growth comes a much closer scrutiny of the environmental costs and benefits of nuclear energy by environmentalists, government agencies, and competing energy sources.

In general, today's market forces support nuclear power. The electricity industry is being deregulated, allowing consumers and their cities to avoid the forced contracts of hydroelectric power companies. Existing nuclear plants appear to be a low-cost alternative energy source. Many power plants run on coal or petrochemicals, with high levels of emissions into the air. This has a powerful impact on global warming and climate change. A main cause of climate change, global warming, air pollution, and acid rain is carbon dioxide emissions. Nuclear reactors do not emit any carbon dioxide. Industry proponents tout the new and improved safety of modern plants to alleviate regulator and consumer fears. In the United States, electricity produced by nuclear power plants has been greater than that from oil, natural gas, and hydropower. Coal accounts for 55 percent of U.S. electricity generation. Nuclear plants generate more than half the electricity in at least six states. According to industry statistics, average operating costs of U.S. nuclear plants dropped substantially during the 1990s and 2000s. Expensive downtime for maintenance and inspections has been steadily reduced. Licensed commercial reactors generated electricity at a record-high average of more than 87 percent of their total capacity in the year 2000, which indicates increasing demand.

Although nuclear energy is gaining international and domestic appeal in the marketplace, environmentalists and those living near plant sites remain concerned. They are concerned about human and environmental impacts due to exposure from transit of nuclear waste, spills, and other environmental sources. Nuclear environmental impacts are among the most powerful ones humans can create, and such effects can destroy any resiliency in a given ecosystem. They last a very long time and can move through the soil and water to contaminate other parts of an ecosystem. Radiation may remain unstable and lethal for 100,000 years. Nuclear waste is currently stored in holding pools and casks alongside the power plants. Some people have expressed concern with leaking casks. Radiation is a potential problem in every phase, from mining the uranium to operating the plant and finally disposing of the waste. Low-level radioactive waste is also the source of a pressing environmental controversy.

Cleaning up severe environmental problems at U.S. nuclear weapons production facilities alone is expected to cost at least $150 billion over the next several decades. Cleaning up old nuclear energy plants is another large expense. Each of these projects is followed by community controversy about exposure and adequacy of cleanup.

New Power Plants

Because of the powerful environmental impacts of nuclear energy, this controversy will persist. There is as yet no solution to the waste problem. Old power plants generate public concern about safety. Building new plants will be expensive. If recent history is a reliable indicator, cost overruns can be expected that will affect the price of electricity. Also, the will probably be community resistance, which can effectively block the building of new nuclear power generators. Community resistance can take the form of refusing to finance any aspect of design, construction, or operation. When the Washington Public Supply System tried to build five nuclear power plants during the mid-1970s, environmental lawsuits for violations of the required environmental impact statements and community resistance to taking or paying contracts from the Bonneville Power Administration led to the plan's collapse. More than $3 billion of default on taxpayer bonds then occurred, resulting in 43 lawsuits in five states. Many investors lost substantial sums of money. The courts were clogged with long, complicated lawsuits involving municipal finance as well as the environmental lawsuits that followed the project.

Thermal Pollution Controversy

Thermal pollution, the addition of heated water to the environment, has recently come to public attention. In England the largest single industrial use of water is for cooling purposes, while in the United States in 1964, some 49,000 billion gallons of water were used by industrial manufacturing plants and investor-owned thermal electric utilities. Ninety percent, or 44,000 billion gallons, of this amount was used for cooling or condensing purposes primarily by electric utilities. With the increased demand for greater volumes and less expensive electric power, the power companies are rapidly expanding the number of generating plants, especially nuclear-powered plants.

To the power companies, nuclear plants offer many advantages over conventional plants, but they have one major drawback that seriously affects the environment: losses

THE CASE FOR SAFE REACTORS

Since the occurrence of accidents in the 1970s and 1980s, researchers have developed newer and safer reactors known as Generation III (and 3+). Japan was the first country to implement advanced reactors in the late 1990s. According to the World Nuclear Association (2006), the third-generation reactors tend to have the following characteristics: a standardized design for each type to expedite licensing, reduced capital costs, and reduced construction time; a simpler and more rugged design, making them easier to operate and less vulnerable to operational upsets; higher availability and longer operating life (typically 60 years); reduced possibility of core melt accidents; minimal effect on the environment; higher burnup to reduce fuel use and the amount of waste; and burnable absorbers to extend fuel life.

Many of the new designs incorporate passive or inherent safety features that require no active controls or operational intervention to avoid accidents in the event of a malfunction. They may rely on gravity, natural convection, or resistance to high temperatures. The safety systems on second-generation reactors require active electrical or mechanical operations. (Malfunction of a pump was the initial cause of the problems at Three Mile Island.) Generation III reactors are a transitional step toward full implementation of the prototypes currently being developed through international partnerships and agreements.

An international collective representing 10 countries formed the organization known as the Generation IV International Forum (GIF) in 2001. The members are committed to the development of the next generation of nuclear technology and in 2002 identified six reactor technologies that they believe represent the future shape of nuclear energy. In 2005 the United States, Canada, France, Japan, and the United Kingdom agreed to undertake joint research and to exchange technical information. India, though not part of the GIF, is developing its own advanced technology to use thorium as a fuel and a three-stage processing procedure utilizing three different types of reactors.

With the current style of reactor, the supply of uranium may last 50 years, but with the newer breeder-style reactors being developed, that time frame would extend to thousands of years. Per gram, the uranium used in breeder reactors has 2.7 million times more energy than coal. Making the supply of fuel last longer is one aim, but reusing spent fuel is another.

Of the six technologies identified by the GIF for development, most employ a closed fuel cycle to maximize the resource base and minimize high-level waste products that would be sent to a repository. Most of these reactors actually use as fuel material that was considered waste in older reactor technology.

There are six types of new GIF reactor designs. Gas-cooled fast reactors' (GFR) fuels include depleted uranium, with spent fuel reprocessed on site and actinides recycled to minimize long-lived waste (actinides are radioactive elements such as uranium, thorium, and plutonium). In lead-cooled fast reactors (LFRs), the fuel is depleted uranium metal or nitride, and actinides are recycled from regional or central reprocessing plants. In Molten Salt Reactors (MSRs), the fuel is uranium, and actinides are fully recycled. In Sodium-cooled Fast Reactors (SFR), depleted uranium is used as the fuel as well as a mixed oxide fuel (a blend of plutonium, uranium, and/or reprocessed uranium). In Supercritical Water-cooled Reactors (SCWRs), the fuel is uranium oxide, although there is an option of running them as fast reactors using an actinide recycle based on conventional reprocessing. Finally, Very High Temperature Gas Reactors (VHTRs) have flexibility in the types of fuels used, but there is no recycling of fuels.

The spent fuel contained and stored as waste through today's reactor technology retains 95 percent of its energy. Using reprocessed spent fuel would reduce the amount of new fuel required while decreasing the amount sent to long-term storage. Fuel reprocessing, which was banned in the United States by President Jimmy Carter, involves separating the uranium and plutonium, the latter being the prime ingredient in nuclear weapons. If the actinides are kept in the fuel, it can no longer be used for weapons. Generation IV reactors will burn fuel made from uranium, plutonium, and all other actinides, leaving very little to entice possible terrorists. The spent fuel can be continuously recycled, leaving only short-lived and low-level-toxicity materials for waste. Underground repositories will still be necessary, but the waste will be much less radioactive and up to 1,000 times less in quantity. Canadian studies predict that vitrification of spent fuels (encasing waste in solid glass) will last 100 million years. Increasingly, this sounds like "sustainable" nuclear energy.

One of the public's greatest fears is a nuclear meltdown and spill, like the Chernobyl accident. All of the new reactor technologies incorporate characteristics that will make meltdowns and other catastrophes virtually impossible. The reactors will be designed to shut down at excessive temperatures. Problems with pumps breaking down, as was the case at Three Mile Island, will be eliminated. In brief, the new reactor designs prevent these plants from becoming hot enough to split open the fuel particles. If there is a coolant failure, the reactor shuts down on its own, without any human intervention.

The proposed new reactor designs under development will address some of the major concerns expressed by opponents of nuclear energy, but there are still other issues to tackle. The important thing, according to advocates, is for opponents to recognize that nuclear energy is one extremely important part of a system of technologies. Once properly developed, it should allow society to finally move away from our crippling dependence on fossil fuels as the major sources of energy. There is no one magic solution, but there are a lot of exciting possibilities.

—Jerry Johnstone

of excess heat. These plants are only 40 percent as efficient as conventional plants in converting fuel to electricity; that and loss of efficiency manifest themselves as waste heat. As the number of nuclear power plants and other industrial plants increases, an estimated ninefold increase in the output of waste heat will result.

Liquids released by nuclear power plants may be either nonradioactive or slightly radioactive. Water that has been used to cool the condenser and various heat exchangers used in the turbine-generator support processes or that has passed through the cooling towers is considered nonradioactive. The cooling towers remove heat from the water discharged from the condenser, so that the water can be discharged to a river or recirculated and reused.

The water that goes through the cooling towers differs from plant to plant. Some nuclear power plants use cooling towers as a method of cooling the circulating water that has been heated in the condenser. Nuclear powers plants also differ in when they emit hot water into the environment. During colder months, the discharge from the condenser may be directed to a river. Recirculation of the water back to the condenser's inlet occurs during certain fish-sensitive times of the year, when the plant is supposed to limit its thermal emissions. Many environmentalists contend that such plants do not do this, and even when they do, the environmental impacts of hot water on the aquatic ecosystem are too severe. The thermal emissions of a nuclear plant are powerful and can heat up large bodies of water. They can heat the circulating water as much as 40°F. Some nuclear power plants have placed limits on the thermal differential allowed in their coolant water emissions. For example, they may have limits of no more than 5°F difference between intake and outflow water temperatures. Cooling towers essentially moderate the temperature to decrease the thermal impact in the water, but they also decrease power plant efficiency because the cooling-tower pumps consume a lot of power.

Some or all of this water may be discharged to a river, sea, or lake. One way to reduce thermal pollution is to make use of the hot water and steam using cogeneration principles.

Usually water released from the steam generator is also nonradioactive. Less than 400 gallons per day is considered low leakage and may be allowed from the reactor cooling system to the secondary cooling system of the steam generator. This is an issue because of concerns that radioactivity might seep out. By law, where radioactive water may be released to the environment, it must be stored and radioactivity levels reduced below certain levels. These levels themselves can be controversial. Citizens frequently challenge experts over nuclear risk issues.

In terms of the environmental impacts of thermal pollution, much remains unstudied. Water that is too warm can damage endangered species, such as some types of salmon. This thermal pollution causes a variety of ecological effects in the aquatic ecosystem. More must be learned about these effects to ensure adequate regulation of thermal discharges.

Industry proponents claim that the small amounts of radioactivity released by nuclear plants during normal operation do not pose significant hazards to workers, the community, or the environment. What concerns many communities is the potential for long-term hazardous waste disposal. There could be deadly cumulative effects. There is scientific uncertainty about the level of risk posed by low levels of radiation exposure. Problems inherent in most risk assessments, such as failure to account for population vulnerability or dose–response variance, do little to assure communities they are safe. Human health effects can be clearly measured only at high exposure levels, such as nuclear war. Other human health effects are generalized from animal studies. In the case of radiation, the assumed risk of low-level exposure has been extrapolated from health effects among persons exposed to high levels of radiation. Industry proponents argue that it is impossible to have zero exposure to radiation because of low levels of background radiation. There is public and community concern about the cumulative impacts of radiation generally.

Industry and Government Responsibility

Because of the high level of public concern, there are strict protocols for safety. Responsibility for nuclear safety compliance lies with nuclear utilities that run the power plants and self-report most of the environmental information. By law, they are required to identify any problems with their plants and report them to the Nuclear Regulatory Commission (NRC). These reports, or the lack of them, have been points of contention. Nuclear power plants last about 40 years and t must then be closed in a process called decommissioning. The NRC requires all nuclear utilities to make payments to special trust funds to ensure that money is available to remove all radioactive material from reactors when they are decommissioned. Several plants have been retired before their licenses expired, whereas others could seek license renewals to operate longer. Some observers predict that more than half of today's 103 licensed reactors could be decommissioned by the year 2016.

There may be an issue looming as to whether there is enough money in the trust funds to clean up the sites adequately. The decommissioning of these power plants will be an issue because of the controversies surrounding the disposal of low-level radioactive waste. It will also be very expensive and fraught with scientific uncertainty. By law, the federal government is responsible for permanent disposal of commercial spent fuel and federally generated radioactive waste. The choosing of sites for this waste is part of the larger controversy surrounding nuclear power. States have the authority to develop disposal facilities for commercial low-level waste. This is often an issue at the state level. The siting process for these types of waste sites then becomes an issue at the local level, often engaging strong community protests. Generally the federal government can preempt state authority, which can preempt local authorities. In this controversy, lawsuits are common.

Nuclear Waste: Is There a Solution?

One of the controversies surrounding nuclear power has to do with the disposal of radioactive waste. It must be sealed and put in a place that cannot be breached for thousands of years. It may not be possible to make warning signs that last long enough. Thousand-year time scales are well beyond the capability of current environmental models. A whole range of natural disasters could ensue and breach the waste site. Few sites can withstand an earthquake or volcanic eruption. Wastes are stored on-site, then moved to a waste transfer station, then to a terminal hazardous waste site. There are political battles at each step in the process. Each nuclear reactor produces an annual average of about 20 tons of highly radioactive spent nuclear fuel and 50 to 200 cubic meters of low-level radioactive waste. Over the usual 40-year permits granted to nuclear power plants by the NRC, this amounts to a total of about 800 tons of radioactive spent fuel and 1,000 to 8,000 cubic meters of low-level radioactive waste. There are additional hazardous materials used in the operation of the power plant. Upon decommissioning, contaminated reactor components are also disposed of as low-level waste. When combined with any hazardous waste that was stored on the site, the waste produced can be quite large.

The cradle-to-grave exposure to radiation, the increased regulation of hazardous vehicle routes in cities, and the likely expansion of nuclear energy to more community sites all portend a larger controversy.

Conclusion

As climate change becomes a more salient political issue, the push for nuclear energy becomes stronger. There is still no policy to deal with the dangerous waste this energy process produces, which is a source of growing controversy. Scientific controversies about dose–response levels with radiation exposure, cancer causation, and effects on vulnerable populations close to communities all continue. Environmentalists have traditionally opposed nuclear energy as a source of power, but some groups have recently begun to question this in light of global warming and greenhouse gas emissions from coal and oil sources.

See also **Acid Rain; Coal; Cumulative Emissions; Solar Energy; Wind Energy; Sustainability (vol. 1)**

Further Reading

Bodansky, David, *Nuclear Energy: Principles, Practices, and Prospects,* 2d ed. New York: Springer, 2004.

Cravens, Gwyneth, *Power to Save the World: The Truth about Nuclear Energy.* New York: Knopf, 2007.

Garwin, Richard L., and Georges Charpak, *Megawatts and Megatons: The Future of Nuclear Power and Nuclear Weapons.* Chicago: University of Chicago Press, 2002.

Greenberg, Michael R., et al., *The Reporter's Handbook on Nuclear Materials, Energy, and Waste Management.* Nashville, TN: Vanderbilt University Press, 2009.

Hore-Lacy, Ian, *Nuclear Energy in the 21st Century.* Burlington, MA: Academic Press, 2006.

Muller, Richard, *Physics for Future Presidents: The Science Behind the Headlines.* New York: Wiley, 2008.

Murray, Raymond L., *Nuclear Energy: An Introduction to the Concepts, Systems, and Applications of Nuclear Processes,* 6th ed. Burlington, MA: Butterworth-Heinemann, 2008.

Vanderbosch, Robert, and Susanna Vanderbosch, *Nuclear Waste Stalemate: Political and Scientific Controversies.* Salt Lake City: University of Utah Press, 2007.

O

OBESITY

Jennifer Croissant

Obesity, like malnutrition, is a worldwide health problem. Many adults and children of various socioeconomic classes and ethnicities are overweight or obese. Disproportionately more lower-income people are considered too heavy, women are more frequently overweight than men, and there are variations among ethnic groups.

Scope of the Problem

The usual metric for obesity is body mass index (BMI), which is a numerical relationship between height and weight that correlates well with percent of body fat. BMI is an imperfect measure, however; it is often inaccurate for very muscular or big-boned people or those with atypical builds (people who have very broad shoulders or who are very tall or very short, for example).

The Centers for Disease Control and Prevention (CDC) defines adults with a BMI over 25.0 as overweight and over 30.0 as obese. Children and teens have adjusted calculations to account for growth and size changes. Using these measures, in 2004 approximately 66 percent of U.S. adults were overweight or obese—an increase from the 47 percent who were overweight in 1976. Seventeen percent of children ages 2 to 19 are overweight or obese, up from approximately 6 percent. Across the globe, despite the prevalence of malnutrition and starvation in some areas, the World Health Organization (WHO) estimates that there are approximately 1 billion overweight or obese individuals.

The health impacts of obesity are numerous. They include increased susceptibility to type II diabetes (formerly known as adult-onset diabetes but now emerging in younger children), cancer, cardiovascular disease and stroke, and respiratory diseases. These illnesses cause untold suffering and billions of dollars in lost work and medical expenses. Older women who are overweight or obese show lower rates of osteoporosis (bone thinning), but this advantage is offset by the increased rate in the number of falls and injuries.

Contributing Factors

Dietary reasons for the increase in obesity include the prevalence of low-cost, calorie-dense, but nutritionally poor foods—such as "fast foods" and sodas containing high fructose corn syrup (HFCS)—and the inaccessibility of fresh foods such as high-quality fruits and vegetables. These dietary concerns are coupled with increasing hours spent at work (reducing time for home cooking or exercise), increasingly sedentary activities such as sitting in front of televisions and computers, lack of exercise facilities, and a decline in walking and bicycling as forms of transportation.

These multiple factors all contribute to variations in obesity rates as well as to the growing prevalence of obesity. For example, poor urban areas have fewer good food options—with less fresh food and more fast-food restaurants—as well as fewer playgrounds, exercise facilities, and opportunities to walk safely. Gender and cultural factors play into this as well. For example, despite the rapid increase in women's sports over the last 30 years in the United States, it is still acceptable for women not to play sports (in some subcultures, vigorous exercise is actually discouraged), leading to lower activity levels and deteriorating fitness.

Environmental factors make nutritious eating and adequate exercise difficult to achieve; therefore these have become the focus of renewed public health efforts to improve the lifestyles of overweight persons. The focus on environmental factors makes it impossible to use a "fat gene" explanation for the rapid increase in obesity or more simplistic explanations that blame overweight persons for their own lack of willpower. When calorie-rich foods are more easily available and lower in cost than healthful foods and exercise is difficult to schedule, "willpower" is insufficient to change health opportunities and behavior.

Responses

The complete failure of the weight-loss industry, despite nearly $40 billion in annual expenditures by U.S. consumers on diet programs and aids, furthers skepticism about explanations that blame overweight people for their condition, such as "healthism." *Healthism* is defined by obsessive attention to the body and the medicalization of bodily differences that creates an individualistic response, rather than a social or political response, to dietary issues. Healthism is both a public ideology and a private obsession that may have an influence on the rise of eating disorders such as bulimia or anorexia and that prevents a critical examination of contextual definitions of health. For example, the U.S. military is concerned about obesity rates among youth because it affects the availability of eligible recruits. Those who question the role of the military may be skeptical about such "obesity crisis" assertions.

For similar reasons, those in the size-acceptance or fat-acceptance community reject the representation of obesity trends as a crisis or the idea that a person's size is anybody else's business. Activists and food industry respondents argue that the BMI is not a good measure, asserting the current crisis may merely reflect more accurate statistics. Measurable increases in chronic disease over the past 30 years, however, mean that at least some dimensions of increasing obesity are real and represent a crisis in public health. Approximately 300,000 U.S. deaths per year are attributable to the effects of obesity, making it a more significant cause of death than tobacco use.

Healthism leads to what scholar Joan Brumberg (1997) termed "body projects," the relentless search for perfection particularly aimed at women (and increasingly, at men), resulting from intense media saturation of thin, flawless bodies and perfect complexions. A purely individualistic focus on obesity fosters healthism and body projects, enhancing guilt and stress for those whose BMI is not in line with medical standards; thus too, healthism avoids scrutiny of the social and political factors that make healthier dietary choices and vigorous exercise unattainable for many adults and youth.

Some doctors contend that the weight problem is attributable to family fragmentation at mealtime. Preparing meals together and sitting down and enjoying them together will make a difference, they argue. This position holds that fast and already prepared foods dominate the kitchen table and are filled with preservatives and empty calories that pack on weight without nourishing the body.

For all of these reasons, U.S. First Lady Michelle Obama made promoting healthful lifestyles and fighting childhood obesity the focus of her agenda. In May 2010, calling childhood obesity an epidemic, she unveiled her action plan for the newly formed Childhood Obesity Task Force. In the following February she launched the "Let's Move!" campaign to solve childhood obesity within a decade. That effort concentrates on schools and families.

See also **Nature versus Nurture; Marketing to Children (vol. 1); Nutrition in Schools (vol. 3)**

Further Reading

Albritton, Robert, *Let Them Eat Junk: How Capitalism Creates Hunger and Obesity.* New York: Pluto Press, 2009.

Brumberg, Joan Jacobs, *The Body Project: An Intimate History of American Girls.* New York: Random House, 1997.

Cardello, Hank, with Doug Carr, *Stuffed: An Insider's Look at Who's (Really) Making America Fat.* New York: Ecco Press, 2009.

Centers for Disease Control and Prevention, "BMI—Body Mass Index." http://www.cdc.gov/nccdphp/dnpa/bmi

Finkelstein, Eric. *The Fattening of America: How the Economy Makes Us Fat, If It Matters, and What to Do about It.* Hoboken, NJ: Wiley, 2008.

Liu, Davis. "McDonald's Will Impact Obesity Issue More Than Docs," *Basil and Spice.* May 2010. http://www.basilandspice.com/weight-loss/52010-mcdonalds-will-impact-obesity-issue-more-than-docs.html

National Center for Health Statistics Centers for Disease Control and Prevention., "Obesity Still a Major Problem." http://www.cdc.gov/nchs/pressroom/06facts/obesity03_04.htm

Obama, Michelle, "Childhood Obesity Task Force Unveils Action Plan: Solving the Problem of Childhood Obesity Within a Generation." Press Release, The White House. May 11, 2010. http://www.whitehouse.gov/the-press-office/childhood-obesity-task-force-unveils-action-plan-solving-problem-childhood-obesity

Stern, Judith S., *Obesity: A Reference Handbook.* Santa Barbara, CA: ABC-CLIO, 2009.

World Health Organization, "Obesity and Overweight." http://www.who.int/dietphysicalactivity/publications/facts/obesity/en

OFF-LABEL DRUG USE

Nancy D. Campbell

Off-label use of pharmaceuticals is common in cancer treatment for many reasons, including targeting certain kinds of tumors. It is employed in many other medical situations as well. Yet such use raises sticky ethical questions and muddies legal liability, because clinical trials will not have shown the drug to be effective for conditions other than those for which it has been approved. Some regard off-label drug use as an unethical form of human experimentation, yet it often becomes the standard of care and may sometimes be state-of-the-art therapy.

Off-label use is legal in the United States, where the practice is so widespread that some studies show that 60 percent of prescriptions in the United States are written for unapproved uses. It is mainly older, generic medicines that fall into this category because often new uses for them are found. Frequently, there is medical evidence to support the new use. But the makers of the drugs have not put them through the formal, lengthy, and often costly studies required by the U.S. Food and Drug Administration (FDA) to officially approve the drug for these new uses. Insurance companies are reluctant to pay for drugs for uses that are not FDA-approved. Reimbursement is the biggest problem with off-label drug use. Denials of payment are common because insurance companies view off-label drug use as "experimental" or "investigational."

According to the American Cancer Society, in cancer treatment these issues have been largely addressed through 1993 federal legislation that requires coverage of medically appropriate cancer therapies. This law includes off-label uses if the treatment has been tested in careful research studies and written up in well-respected drug reference books or the medical literature. And in 2008, Medicare rules were changed to cover more off-label uses of cancer treatment drugs.

History

In efforts to avert drug-related public health disasters, the U.S. Congress amended the 1938 Food, Drug, and Cosmetic Act in 1962. Still in effect, the 1962 amendments require that the FDA approve new drugs coming onto the market for specific conditions. Pharmaceutical companies must specify the exact conditions for which the drug is to be used; must show its safety, efficacy, and effectiveness; and must keep marketing and promotional materials within that scope. The "fine print" required on printed pharmaceutical advertisements, the warnings that accompany broadcast advertisements, and the "patient package inserts" (or PPIs) you get at the pharmacy may mention only the approved uses. Even if the unapproved uses of the drug have become commonplace, so-called off-label uses may not be mentioned

The FDA has been careful not to regulate the practice of medicine and has left physicians free to use their own clinical judgment in prescribing drugs. Patients who have so-called orphan diseases, those suffered by small numbers of people, almost always rely on off-label prescriptions, and cancer patients are also often prescribed drugs off-label. Even common conditions such as acne can be treated with off-label drugs. Hormonal contraceptives have been prescribed for their "side effects" in cases of severe acne because Accutane, the drug approved for acne, causes birth defects and is strictly controlled. Male and female users must certify that they are using at least two forms of contraception while on Accutane.

Case Study

Although physicians may prescribe off label, pharmaceutical companies are strictly barred from marketing drugs for off-label uses and can be sued if they mention off-label uses in marketing and promotions or try to persuade physicians to prescribe drugs for unapproved conditions. A high-profile case involved Parke Davis, then a division of Warner-Lambert, maker of the antiseizure drug Neurontin, which was approved in 1994 to treat epilepsy as an "add-on" after other drugs had failed to control seizures. Parke Davis undertook a successful campaign to get physicians to prescribe Neurontin not just to reduce seizures but also for pain. This campaign made Neurontin a blockbuster drug—until a sales representative blew the whistle on the off-label marketing strategy in 1996.

Conclusion

It is always to a company's financial advantage to widen the market for its products. The question that remains unsettled is when pharmaceutical companies should go back and seek FDA approval for off-label uses.

See also Medical Ethics; Medical Marijuana; Prescription Drug Costs (vol. 1); Drugs (vol. 3)

Further Reading

American Cancer Society, Off-Label Drug Use. Feb. 23, 2010. http://www.cancer.org/docroot/
    eto/content/eto_1_2x_off-label_drug_use.asp

Angell, Marcia, *The Truth about the Drug Companies.* New York: Random House, 2004.

Eaton, Margaret L., and Donald Kennedy, *Innovation in Medical Technology: Ethical Issues and
    Challenges.* Baltimore: Johns Hopkins University Press, 2007.

Loughlin, Kevin, et al., eds., *The Guide to Off-Label Prescription Drugs: New Uses for FDA-Approved
    Prescription Drugs.* New York: Free Press, 2006.

National Cancer Institute, Understanding the Approval Process for New Cancer Treatments.
    Q&A: Off-Label Drugs. www.cancer.gov/clinicaltrials/learning/approval-process-for-cancer-
    drugs/page5

United States General Accounting Office, Off-label drugs, reimbursement policies constrain
    physicians in their choice of cancer therapies (report GAO/PEMD-91–14). September 1991.
    Washington, DC. http://archive.gao.gov/d18t9/144933.pdf

OIL DRILLING AND THE ENVIRONMENT: THE CASE OF ANWR

Robert William Collin and Debra Ann Schwartz

The Arctic National Wildlife Refuge (ANWR) is a vast, protected wildlife habitat in Alaska where oil and natural gas have been found. Because of this, environmentalists representing the interests of pristine wilderness and endangered species are pitted against oil and gas corporations. Federal, state, tribal, and community interests are heavily involved. For many years there have been contentious legislative sessions in Alaska and Washington, D.C., over drilling for oil in the Arctic Wildlife Refuge and other parts of Alaska. The issues in this controversy may well end up being addressed in the courtrooms.

Political Dimensions

In June 2010, Tea Party Libertarian activist Sarah Palin, who resigned as Alaska's governor shortly after a failed attempt at the vice presidency, blamed environmentalists' tactics for British Petroleum's massive oil spill in the Gulf of Mexico. Palin contended that the ban on oil drilling in pristine areas such as the ANWR and shallow onshore waters forced the United States to pursue risky deep-ocean drilling for economic purposes.

The U.S. Fish & Wildlife Service (FWS), which has authority over the ANWR, is currently revising its Comprehensive Conservation Plan for the refuge. This multiyear effort involves much public comment officially presented during public hearings before elected officials.

The plan's intent is to guide stewardship of the land for the next 15 years or more. It will include requiring a wilderness review of the entire refuge. Researchers with FWS currently are studying the Smith's longspur, a rare bird making its home in the refuge. Changing climate is causing large parts of the refuge to be redefined by birds, fish, and mammals that did not make their home there until recently. For example, robins have appeared in northern Alaska for the first time, as have other warm-weather species.

In May 2010, the fight over oil drilling in the ANWR heated up at a hearing in Anchorage over the possibility that the FWS's new management plan could put the refuge and its billions of barrels of crude off limits for good. If the ANWR is designated as wilderness by the FWS, no drilling for oil could occur there. The FWS expects to finalize the plan in 2012.

For decades, ANWR has been a point of contention between environmentalists—who oppose drilling there—and oil companies and Alaska's elected and appointed officials, who see money in their pockets from tapping ANWR's oil, although publicly they will argue for drilling as a means of relief from foreign oil dependency.

The U.S. Environmental Protection Agency (EPA) during the presidency of George W. Bush opposed drilling in ANWR, arguing instead that increasing the minimum gas mileage requirement for vehicles by at least three miles per gallon would eliminate U.S. dependence on foreign oil. (Hybrid vehicles that use a combination of gasoline and electricity for fuel have gone beyond the three-mile increase, with further fuel efficiencies required by the Obama administration.) U.S. Senators Lisa Murkowski and Mark Begich contend that it is a waste of taxpayer dollars to investigate whether to make the ANWR forever wild. Pamela Miller of the Northern Alaska Environmental Center, on the other hand, has said that what is needed is to consider the environmental disaster unfolding in the Gulf of Mexico. This is not the time, says Miller, to be "contemplating BP waltzing into our nation's premier wilderness area."

Background

Federal lands in Alaska are vast. Roads and people are scarce. Wildlife abounds, unseen by human eyes. The weather can stop most human activities for days at a time, also making travel uncomfortable, risky, and expensive. Economic development around most types of activities such as agribusiness, oil or mineral drilling, logging, tourism, and shipping is equally constrained by the cold, inclement weather and the expense of dealing with it. Without good roads and transportation infrastructure, most economic development suffers, making the prospect of such improvements attractive to many Alaskan communities. However, the federal government was and is the largest land-owner and has exerted its power to create and protect its interests.

Ever since Alaska was recognized and accepted by the United States as a state, environmental protection and natural resource use have been at odds. Although Alaska has seemingly limitless natural resources, these exist in fragile tundra and coastal environments. Without roads, logging, mining, or any substantial human development is very difficult. Indigenous peoples of Alaska have, in the past, been self-sufficient, subsisting on the land and water. Subsistence rights to fish, game, and plants as well as ceremonial rights to this food are very important to many indigenous peoples, including bands and tribes in the United States. Therefore Congress passed the Alaska National Interest Lands Conservation Act (1980) and established the ANWR. At that time Congress specifically avoided a decision regarding future management of the 1.5-million-acre coastal plain. The controversy pitting the area's potential oil and gas resources against its importance as wildlife habitat, represented by well-organized environmental interests, was looming large then.

This was the not the first or last experience pitting oil companies against environmentalists, state interests in economic development against federal interests in preserving wilderness areas, and other opposing interests. Numerous wells have since been drilled and oil fields discovered near the ANWR. Also, the characteristics of the ecosystem and measures of environmental impacts to date have been documented in very similar places nearby.

Global warming and climate change greatly affect this particular controversy. Most scientists agree that for every one degree of global warming, the Arctic and Antarctica will warm up by three degrees. The planet has been warming and the Arctic ice is melting. In September 2004 the polar ice cap receded 160 miles away from Alaska's north coast, creating more and more open water. This has had dramatic environmental impacts in the Arctic because many species from plankton to polar bears follow the ice for survival. The implications of global warming for the ANWR oil-drilling controversy are developing. Environmentalists think such development may make an already sensitive ecosystem even more sensitive. Mosquitoes are now seen further north than ever before. They attack nesting birds that do not leave the nest for long periods and have never been exposed to mosquitoes before. There are many anecdotal reports of species impacts in the Arctic.

The focus of the controversy about oil drilling in the ANWR is its coastal plain. It is a 25-mile band of tundra wetlands that is of key interest to both oil interests and environmentalists. This area provides important nursing areas for Arctic wildlife. Damaged tundra takes a long time to recover and is generally considered a sensitive ecosystem. Tundra is very sensitive to many of the activities around oil drilling. The wetlands, where food can be moved around the coast efficiently, can also allow the movement of hazardous materials in the same way.

But the refuge's coastal plain also contains oil. Exactly how much and where is a subject of dispute. Controversies about the sensitive ecological character of the refuge; the amount, kind, and accessibility of oil that lies beneath it; and the environmental impact that oil development would have on it all abound. The primary concern about its impact is the threat to species and other parts of the ecosystem.

Environmental Characteristics

ANWR's brutal winters and glorious summers characterize its seasonal extremes. Given its inaccessibility to humans, many species of wildlife thrive here. The ANWR is located between the rugged Brooks Mountain Range and the Beaufort Sea in northeast Alaska. This large area, with ecotones ranging from mountains to the coastal plain, allows many species to adapt to seasonal extremes. The seasonal migration of the caribou plays a large part in the food chain here.

The coastal plain's rich ecosystem is easily affected by both local and global environmental forces. The ANWR's coastal plain alone supports almost 200 wildlife species, including polar bears, musk oxen, fish, and caribou. Every year, millions of tundra swans, snowy owls, eider ducks, and other birds migrate to the coastal plain to nest, raise their offspring, molt, and feed. Other species give birth there, and many others migrate through the area.

Some environmental scientists consider the coastal plain to be the biological heart of the entire refuge. They maintain that any oil drilling in the refuge would irreparably harm the wildlife by destroying this unique habitat. Oil development, with its drilling, road building, water and air emissions, noise, and waste — could irreparably degrade this pristine, fragile wilderness. The fact that the plan involves exploration and drilling for oil and gas, the very substances that cause so much pollution, heightens the controversy. Environmental groups are making a stand because this is one of last remaining untouched wilderness areas of this type in the United States.

Oil's Industrial Impact

When the Exxon Valdez spilled millions of gallons of fresh black crude oil into the healthy, clear waters of Prudhoe Bay, a pristine area—known for its rich fisheries and traditional native lifestyle, a way of life that had sustained people and wildlife for hundreds of years—disappeared. The oil spill of the Valdez, its environmental impacts, and subsequent protracted litigation are well known. Environmentalists point to other nearby similar areas that have allowed oil development, arguing that the environmental impacts in the ANWR are not worth the oil. They point to the controversial Alaskan

North Slope, where oil extraction occurs on a massive scale, as well as to the 2010 BP–Deepwater Horizon oil spill in the Gulf of Mexico.

The Alaskan North Slope was once part of the largest intact wilderness area in the United States. It is similar to the ANWR. With controversy, the North Slope was opened up to oil drilling and a pipeline was built, which continues to leak through Alaska and Canada as it brings oil to the United States.

Alaska's North Slope oil operations expanded. This enterprise now comprises one of the world's largest industrial complexes. The oil operations and transportation infrastructure are vast, covering about 1,000 square miles of land. Not so long ago, most of this land and environment was wilderness, as the ANWR is now. There are oilfields, oil tankers, a few basic oil refineries, oil storage, and oil spills. Roads and airstrips are often built. These activities drastically increase environmental impacts in wild areas.

On the Alaskan North Slope, Native Americans have important interests, and some locations there are considered sacred by them. Industrial development land rights, allegedly existing for the public good, may extend to a limited set of natural resources, such as timber or seasonal harvesting. Wilderness destruction has sometimes moved ahead without protection for the land held sacred by traditional residents.

Sometimes local communities are in favor of infrastructure development as a means of economic development, despite the environmental consequences. The scale of industrial operations here affects all these interests. Prudhoe Bay and 26 other oilfields on the Alaskan North Slope include the following:

- 28 oil production plants, gas processing facilities, and seawater treatment and power plants
- 38 gravel mines
- 223 production and exploratory gravel drill pads
- 500 miles of roads
- 1,800 miles of pipelines
- 4,800 exploration and production wells

This large-scale industrial operation is taking place in a comparably fragile region much like the ANWR. In the modern context of global warming and climate change, the caribou that play such an important role are affected by the retreating ice. They cannot feed on the lichen on rocks in places formerly covered by ice. Their migratory route is being altered. The same is true for many species. The environmental impact alone is a controversy now fueling the ANWR controversy. Ecosystem resiliency is defined as the length of time it takes an ecosystem to recover from stress. Because of the same factors that affect the ANWR, the North Slope is considered fragile.

The crucial factors are a short, intense summer growing season, bitter cold in the long winter, poor soils, and permafrost. The North Slope, like ANWR today, was originally a wildlife area with little human intrusion. Environmentalists contend that any physical disturbance to the land—such as roads, oil spills, and drilling—has long-term, perhaps irreparable environmental impacts. The National Academy of Sciences has concluded with regard to the North Slope that "it is unlikely that the most disturbed habitat will ever be restored and the damage to more than 9,000 acres by oilfield roads and gravel pads is likely to remain for centuries." Many environmentalists contend that the cumulative impacts of oil development have affected Prudhoe Bay negatively. Environmentalists use the North Slope experience to argue for the protection of the ANWR. They use it to show that it is impossible to drill for oil without irreversible environmental consequences.

Of particular concern is spilled oil and other petrochemical waste products from engine maintenance. According to environmentalists, oil operations spill tens of thousands of gallons of crude oil and other hazardous materials on the North Slope every year. Environmentalists worry that not all spills are reported, as most industry environmental impact information is self-reported. Spills can occur when companies are drilling for new oil, storing it, and transporting it. Conditions for all these activities can be physically rough in Alaska. Weather conditions can become severe for days at a time, making them conducive to spills. According to industry and government reports, from 1996 to 2004, there were at least 4,530 spills on the North Slope of more than 1.9 million gallons of diesel fuel, oil, acid, biocide, ethylene glycol, drilling fluid, and other materials. Some of these chemicals can rapidly percolate, or move through, soil to reach water tables. Conditions in Alaska, particularly in the northern reaches of Alaska, can make it difficult to contain and clean up a spill of any size.

Oil Operations and the Air

Coal-burning power plants and petrochemical refineries emit large quantities of regulated pollutants into the air. Diesel generators and vehicles, trucks, and airplanes also emit pollutants. According to the Toxics Release Inventory, oil operations on Alaska's North Slope emit more than 70,000 tons of nitrogen oxides a year. Sulfur and nitrogen are air pollutants, which contribute to smog and acid rain. North Slope oil operations also release other pollutants, which are major contributors to air pollution. Each year, they admit to emitting 7 to 40 million metric tons of carbon dioxide and 24,000 to 114,000 metric tons of methane in the North Slope. This is probably within the terms of their air permit and may exclude de minimus or fugitive emissions.

Emissions caused by natural disasters such as hurricanes and tsunamis are also exempt. Sustainability advocates point out that the methane emissions do not include the methane released because of the melted permafrost. All these impacts are in the context of larger controversies such as global warming and climate change, which also affect sensitive Alaskan ecosystems. Emissions will be higher in the ANWR as North Slope oil is transported by tanker from the site to a refinery. It is refined and distributed off

POLAR BEARS AND GLOBAL WARMING

All over the southernmost part of their Arctic range, polar bears are thinner, lower in number, and producing fewer offspring than when the ice was thick. As the ice has retreated, polar bears have been forced to get food from human garbage. Some say that the lack of ice due to global warming has disrupted the ability of polar bears to hunt for seals, forcing them to swim further in search of food. Some are not successful. In 2004, researchers found four dead polar bears floating about 60 miles off Alaska's north shore. Although polar bears are capable of swimming long distances, 60 miles is considered unusual.

The polar bear is at the top of the food chain in the Arctic. At least 200 species of microorganisms grow in Arctic ice floes. They form curtains of slimy algae and zooplankton, and when they die, they feed clams at the bottom, which feed the walruses and seals, which feed polar bears.

Polar bears also act as storehouses of the heavy metals they consume when they eat fish and other animals that have eaten creatures lower in the food chain. This is called bioaccumulation. Cancer-causing chemicals and heavy metal compounds in great concentrations become stored in the fish and animal's fat cells and increase in quantities as more is consumed. This is especially true for mercury and polychlorinated biphenyls (PCBs) generated by polluting industries such as oil drilling, paper making, and textile mills.

Scientists closely examine apex animals, such as polar bears and humans, living in the places where the effects of climate change are first observable. The North Slope polar bears are now monitored by radio collaring and the mapping of dens.

the drilling site. ANWR oil and gas could still be refined on site if oil exploration and drilling is approved.

Airborne pollution from Prudhoe Bay has been detected as far away as Barrow, Alaska, about 200 miles distant. The environmental impact of industrial oil operations on the North Slope is widespread. The Canadian government has experimented with oil companies and cumulative impacts research in neighboring northern Alberta. In the sensitive Arctic environment of northern Alberta, the government has allowed drilling and refining operations on the condition that the involved companies account for all impacts, including cumulative impacts. Because vast areas of Alaska are undeveloped, the potential exists for a large environmental impact before it can be discovered or contained, as in BP's Gulf of Mexico disaster. (In the latter case, the company did not have sufficient well-capping measures in place to prevent the catastrophe that occurred, and the well leaked 60,000 barrels per day for two days before it was discovered. By the end of the nearly three-month period during which the leak was active, close to 5 million barrels of crude had been discharged into the gulf.)

Hazardous Waste and Its Impacts on Water and Wetlands

Drilling for oil includes digging large pits in the ground. As these pits become obsolete, they are used as waste dumps. Pits holding millions of gallons of wastes from oil and gas drilling and exploration can still be found all over the North Slope. These pits were a stew of toxic chemicals, many with long-lasting environmental impacts in any ecosystem. Deep well injection, as this waste disposal method is called, was stopped because of

LONG-LASTING ENVIRONMENTAL DISASTER

BP (formerly British Petroleum), whose Deepwater Horizon offshore oil rig succumbed to an explosion and gushed tens of thousands of barrels of crude oil into the Gulf of Mexico each day between April 20, 2010, and July 15, 2010, was obliged to set up a $20-billion recovery fund for businesses, organizations, and individuals harmed by the spill and its environmental effects. That is in addition to the $9.5 billion the company incurred in working to cap the well head and seal off the reservoir lying below.

In May 2010, BP announced that it would spend up to $500 million over 10 years to research how oil spills in the ocean affect marine and shoreline life. BP's 10-year research plan includes studying the effects of oil on land and on life in general as well as the impact of chemical dispersants used to break up oil on the seabed and along the shore, ways to improve technology to detect oil, and ways to clean up the ooze.

Meanwhile, wetland scientists, both during and after the crisis, have considered ways to protect the environment. Some have suggested that the most effective tool for eliminating an oil spill from an offshore rig is a box of matches in the context of a controlled burn. This method had had a history of success before the gulf spill, and it ended up being used to good effect by the U.S. Coast Guard in managing the Deepwater Horizon slick.

Another possible approach is to fertilize the microbial community with nitrogen and phosphorus to increase its size. The thinking is that activity by more microbes would degrade the oil. A third possibility for protecting a delta ecosystem is to build artificial barrier islands, or sand berms, to prevent the oil from coming onshore. And in cases where it does make landfall, it has been proposed that one may cut the oil-coated marsh grasses at the surface, leaving their roots intact for future growth. Although all of these methods were tried to one degree or another during the gulf spill, it was controlled burning and chemical dispersants that became the two workhorses of the containment effort. Neither one of these, however, has had its long-term effects well documented.

In response to the spill, the Society of Wetland Scientists has created an online repository of resources related to the impacts of oil on wetland ecosystem at http://sws.org/oilspill/. This repository aims to document the ecological impacts of the spill on wetlands and the experiences of the wetland science community as it responds to this latest disaster. News articles, science conferences, personal experiences, and professional opinions are posted there.

its impact on underground aquifers. As aquifers dry up, as around San Antonio, Texas, they pull in the waste injected in deep wells.

Of the known and undisputed pit sites, more than 100 remain to be cleaned. *Clean* is a relative term. In this case, it generally means pumping out the toxic materials and removing them for treatment as hazardous waste. *Clean* does not mean restoring the ecological integrity of the place. This is why some environmentalists claim that the impacts of oil exploration and drilling cannot be mitigated and it should therefore not be allowed. There could be many more. Many of the sites that have already been cleaned had pervasive environmental impacts because the wastes had migrated into the tundra and killed it. The oil company pit sites contain a variety of toxic materials and hazardous chemicals. Typically, they include acids, lead, pesticides, solvents, diesel fuel, caustics, corrosives, and petroleum hydrocarbons. If the pit sites are not adequately closed, they can become illegal sites for more trash.

This second wave of trash can include vehicles, appliances, batteries, tires, and pesticides. Oil industry trade groups point out that deep well injection has been an accepted method of waste disposal for oil operations. It was the prevailing practice in Texas and Alaska for many years. Environmentalists respond by noting that the industry may have been acting within the bounds of its permits, but the environmental impacts are still too large. Politically, the oil operations expanded revenue for the state and built some infrastructure in a large state with a low population. Communities differ greatly on aspects of this controversy. State environmental agencies do not strictly or overzealously enforce environmental laws against large corporations. In fact, Alaska voluntarily relinquished its control of the Hazardous Waste Cleanup Program, and the EPA took it over.

This aspect of the ANWR controversy, the hazardous waste cleanup, is an issue for state and federal environmental agencies. Most state environmental agencies get most of their revenue from the federal environmental agencies such as the EPA. However, in federally mandated environmental programs, such as the Clean Air Act, the states must either do it to some minimal standards or the EPA will do for them. In most instances states are free to choose the best method to meet the federally mandated result. However, in Alaska results were not meeting federal standards. This confrontation heightens the intensity of the ANWR controversy for industry, community, and environmental interests. It is seen by some as a test of federal sovereignty over states rights, which removes some of the environmental issues from the discussion. Similar tussles between federal, state, and corporate entities regarding duties and responsibilities occurred in the case of the Deepwater Horizon disaster in the Gulf of Mexico (until, that is, the federal government, on June 16, 2010, made clear that BP was responsible for shouldering the full cost of the cleanup and that the cleanup would be done to EPA standards).

If oil drilling is allowed in the ANWR, then more impacts to the environment from hazardous and toxic waste can be expected. Environmentalists point out that most past mitigation efforts were not successful or mandatory. There is no legal requirement to mitigate the impacts of mitigation, which could themselves be considerable in large-scale projects.

Current and Past Controversial Policies

Generally, the George W. Bush administration facilitated processes for the energy industry to drill for oil and gas in many sensitive public lands. Across the western United States, federal agencies such as the Department of the Interior leased these areas for oil and gas development. The tenants are oil and gas companies setting up operations on millions of acres of previously wild and open federally owned land. Proponents of this change in public policy contend that there is an energy crunch and that, with rising gas prices, the country needs to access to all possible U.S. oil sources. This position goes against everything two major social movements in the United States have sought to protect: wilderness. The Romantic Movement and the American Transcendentalists fought industrialists and politicians in the 1800s to protect and conserve wilderness. It provides peace, rapture and restores the soul, they argued. The National Park System resulted from their efforts, and state parks followed along with wilderness protection areas such as the Adirondacks in New York State, overwhelmingly voted to stay forever wild by state residents.

According to the Natural Resources Defense Council, the Bush administration granted faster, almost pro forma, drilling approvals for requests to drill for oil on public lands. They also relaxed rules and policies to make it easier for oil interests to drill on public lands such as in national parks. In addition to reducing the number of environmental restrictions, they also reduced the amount of royalty payments companies paid to the government if oil was tapped on public land, thereby allowing private interests to take in more money for themselves without honoring their full obligation to the country or its citizens. (In the aftermath of the BP–Deepwater Horizon spill, similar "sweetheart deals" were discovered to have been in place for companies operating in the Gulf of Mexico under the now defunct Minerals Management Service.)

During the Bush administration, officials from the Bureau of Land Management (BLM), the Interior Department agency that manages the vast majority of federal lands and onshore energy resources, directed field staff to expand access to public lands for energy development and to speed related environmental reviews. BLM data show that the number of leases for oil, gas, and coal mining on public lands increased by 51 percent between 2000 and 2003—from 2.6 million acres to more than 5 million acres. The BLM has also repeatedly suspended seasonal closures designed to protect wildlife and is rushing to update numerous western land use plans to permit even more leasing and drilling. In the interior West, where most of the nation's oil and gas resources lie, more than 90 percent of BLM-managed land is already open for energy leasing and development.

There is much controversy about how much oil exists in ANWR. Critics say that if it were the only source, it would yield less than a six-month supply of oil. Supporters of drilling, based on national security, say that all resources need to be marshaled. Overreliance on foreign oil sources leaves us dependent on other countries and vulnerable while at war, proponents of drilling contend. The United States is a large consumer of oil. As a country it has 5 percent of the world's population but consumes almost 25 percent of all the oil produced worldwide every year. The United States has only 3 percent of the world's proven oil reserves, making drilling in the ANWR a higher-stakes battlefield. Federal agencies have assessed the issue. The U.S. Geological Survey (USGS) estimates that the amount of oil that might be recovered and profitably brought to market from the refuge's coastal plain is only 5.4 billion barrels, based on the U.S. Energy Information Administration's (EIA) average forecast price of $28 a barrel over the next 20 years.

At $40 per barrel, the USGS estimates that there would be only 6.7 billion barrels that could be profitably brought to market from the coastline reserves. The United States uses about 7.3 billion barrels of oil per year. Drilling proponents claim that at least 16 billion barrels of oil could be recovered from the refuge's coastal plain. They point out that there could be recoverable oil and gas in other parts near the coastal plain.

But the USGS says there is less than a 5 percent possibility that the coastal plain and adjacent areas contain that much recoverable oil. They maintain that only a small part of that oil could be economically produced and transported to markets. Drilling proponents are accused of ignoring the fact that the costs of exploration, production, and transportation in the Arctic are substantially higher than in many other regions of the world. Shipping, pipelines, and rail are all challenged by rough weather, earthquake-prone landscapes, and wilderness conditions. Extreme weather conditions and long distances to market would make much of that oil too expensive to produce at current market conditions.

Drilling supporters claim that once the roads are built and the infrastructure is set up, costs will decrease, and oil demand is almost always increasing. They point out that the North American continental natural gas pipeline is expanding and that technology may make oil transport cheaper and safer for people and the environment. They also consider global warming to have one positive impact in that shipping lanes will be more reliably open because of the receding ice. The ice has drastically receded at the coastal plain in ANWR.

To many rural Alaskan communities, getting infrastructure and the promise of an oil-company job are large benefits. With new roads, airstrips, and ports, other forms of economic development would be able to occur. Tourism is a growing industry without the environmental impacts of oil drilling but requires a safe transportation network. The area's Inupiat Eskimo and Gwich'in Athabaskan-speaking Native American inhabitants are actively involved in the controversy. Their respective views are significantly shaped by the nature of their relationship to the economy, the land, and its natural resources. Some of the oil reserves are on tribal lands. Some tribes are in favor, some are divided, and others are against oil exploration.

Conclusion

The environmental effects of the Exxon Valdez oil spill in Alaska's Prince William Sound on March 24, 1989, are still visible on the land and in the wildlife there. Just as Exxon was caught unprepared for an emergency, so BP is wearing those shoes today. While scientists try proven techniques to deal with the situation, one problem persists: they have never been tried in 5,000 feet of water. How was the oil industry allowed to build offshore rigs without a set of proven remediation tools in place appropriate to the environment in which it was working? Lisa Jackson, administrator for the EPA, observed that the oil industry has improved its techniques for getting oil out of the ground but not its skill at containing it. Seemingly, BP had no plan for a worst-case scenario. Looking at the industry running through the same set of solutions it did in 1979 when a well blew up in the Bay of Campeche off of Mexico, the solution seems to be to change the way the industry calculates risks. New regulations that will fill technological gaps revealed by the BP–Deepwater Horizon spill in the Gulf of Mexico are expected.

The controversy over drilling in the ANWR swirls around questions of how much oil is there and whether any drilling at all is acceptable in a pristine wilderness area. It may be that there is more oil and much more gas there than currently known. It may also be that oil cannot be reached without irreversible environmental impacts. As other global petrochemical resources dry up, the pressure to drill for oil and gas in the ANWR will increase.

Petrochemical controversies around protected parts of nature also affect other controversies. Declining air quality from burning petrochemicals touches all aspects of this controversy, from local neighborhoods, tribes, and communities to global warming concerns. Political concerns about oil company profits right after Hurricane Katrina and all during the Mideast conflicts also inflame oil drilling issues in the Arctic. The earlier controversy concerning North Slope oil exploration and drilling provided evidence of severe environmental impacts. The potential for future controversy in ANWR drilling is very great.

See also **Endangered Species; Land Pollution; Mining of Natural Resources; Transportation and the Environment; Water Pollution; Oil Economics and Business (vol. 1)**

Further Reading

Arctic Wildlife Refuge, arctic.fws.gov/issues1.html

Federal Agency North Slope Science Initiative, www.mms.gov/alaska/regs/mou_iag_loa/2005_BLM.pdf

Fischman, Robert L., *The National Wildlife Refuges.* Washington, DC: Island Press, 2003.

McMonagle, Robert J., *Caribou and Conoco: Rethinking Environmental Politics in Alaska's ANWR and Beyond.* Lanham, MD: Rowman & Littlefield, 2008.

Mowbray, Rebecca, "Deepwater Horizon Oil Spill Revealed an Industry Ill-Prepared to Deal with 'Black Swan' Event." *Times-Picayune* (May 21, 2010). http://www.nola.com/news/gulf-oil-spill/index.ssf/2010/05/deepwater_horizon_oil_spill_re.html

Pemberton, Mary, "ANWR Coastal Plain Hearing Draws Standing-Room Crowd." *Anchorage Daily News* (May 11, 2010). http://www.adn.com/2010/05/11/1273779/anwr-coastal-plain-hearing-draws.html

Reed, Stanley, and Alison Fitzgerald, *In Too Deep: BP and the Drilling Race That Took It Down*. New York: Bloomberg Press, 2011.

Sacred Lands: Arctic Wildlife Refuge, www.sacredland.org/endangered_sites_ pages/arctic.html

Spotts, Pete, "BP Oil Spill: How to Save Wetlands—Set Them on Fire, Maybe." *Christian Science Monitor* (May 24, 2010). http://www.csmonitor.com/USA/2010/0524/BP-oil-spill-How-to-save-wetlands-Set-them-on-fire-maybe

Standlea, David M., *Oil, Globalization, and the War for the Arctic Refuge*. New York: SUNY Press, 2006.

Truett, Joe C., and Stephen R. Johnson, *The Natural History of an Arctic Oil Field*. London: Elsevier, 2000.

U.S. Fish & Wildlife Service. Potential Impacts of Proposed Oil and Gas Development on the Arctic Refuge's Coastal Plain: Historical Overview and issue of Concern. http://arctic.fws.gov/issues1.htm

U.S. Fish & Wildlife Service, Arctic National Wildlife Refuge, http://arctic.fws.gov

U.S. PIRG Education Fund, *The Dirty Four: The Case against Letting BP Amoco, ExxonMobil, Chevron, and Phillips Petroleum Drill in the Arctic Refuge*. Washington, DC: U.S. PIRG Education Fund, 2001.

P

PERSISTENT ORGANIC POLLUTANTS

Robert William Collin

Persistent organic pollutants present environmental and health risks despite their effectiveness in their uses and applications. There is a strong international movement to ban them from food sources, but some countries still use them, and chemical manufacturing corporations still produce them for profit.

Why Are Persistent Organic Pollutants a Controversy?

These chemicals cause controversy because they last a long time in the environment. Their presence can be damaging to other parts of the soil and water. Since they persist, or last, in the environment, annual reapplication of pesticides increases cumulative exposures dramatically. Persistent organic pollutants (POPs) are several groups of chemicals. Polychlorinated biphenyls (PCBs) are industrial chemicals. The two remaining groups are dioxins and furans. POPs have one common characteristic: their persistence in the environment. Some early pesticide applications wanted this characteristic because it was presumed that stronger chemicals that lasted longer performed their task better. They last longer than required for their intended use, however, and it is always an issue as to exactly how long they do last. Over time, the accumulation of POPs eventually made the case that they do persist. All 12 POPs listed are chlorinated compounds, 9 of them having been developed as pesticides. Their use is decreasing, but controlling international use is controversial. Farm workers and others who live near POP applications can suffer from overexposure. This can cause acute poisoning. If acute poisoning occurs, no

PERSISTENT ORGANIC POLLUTANTS

Polychlorinated Biphenyls (PCBs) in New York's Hudson River

General Electric (GE) is responsible for PCBs on the bottom of the Hudson River in New York. GE is an old company that existed well before any environmental regulation. It has long contended that natural processes, including reductive dechlorination, substantially reduce the risk of PCB exposure to humans and the environment and that these processes should be allowed to continue. The U.S. Environmental Protection Agency (EPA), however, designated the area a Superfund site in the 1980s, and in 2000 began considering a large-scale dredging operation to clean up the contaminated sediments, with GE as the primary responsible party. Environmentalists filed several lawsuits against the company and other parties to force a cleanup. Community groups along the historic Hudson River were also concerned.

The EPA concluded that dechlorination would not naturally remediate contaminated sediments. Although GE continues to maintain that a number of natural processes, viewed together, stand to dramatically reduce the risk from contaminated sediments, saying that "Anaerobic dechlorination reduces toxicity; aerobic degradation reduces the overall mass; and sorption onto organic particles reduces bioavailability."

Nevertheless, community and environmental groups maintain that Hudson River PCBs are a serious health risk.

- PCBs can damage the immune, reproductive, nervous, and endocrine systems. They can impair children's physical and intellectual development.
- PCBs cause cancer in animals and are strongly linked to human cancer, according to studies by leading health agencies.
- GE maintains that PCBs do not hurt people, citing a study it commissioned on workers at its Hudson Falls plant. The New York State Department of Health and many independent scientists have critiqued the research, saying that it does not support GE's claims.
- According to the EPA, cancer risks from eating upper-river PCB-contaminated fish are 1,000 times over its goal for protection and 10 times the highest level generally allowed by Superfund law.

Hudson River PCBs will not go away naturally. There is deep distrust from the community that people are safe from harm from these PCBs.

- PCBs were designed not to break down. They are persistent organic pollutants that remain in the environment indefinitely.
- GE claims that river microbes eliminate PCBs naturally, but the EPA found that less than 10 percent had broken down. After breakdown, PCBs remain toxic and are more readily spread throughout the ecosystem.
- GE claims that Hudson River PCB pollution has dropped 90 percent, a deceptive statistic because the drop occurred when discharges were banned in the late 1970s. Since the mid-1980s, levels have remained quite constant and well

above acceptable limits. The EPA's independent, peer-reviewed science pre-dicted that, without remediation, the problem would last into the foreseeable future.

- GE's PCBs are responsible for "eat-none" health advisories for women of child-bearing age as well as for children for all fish from all Hudson River locations.

Hudson River PCBs are not safely buried by sediments, contend community members and scientists. This is a pervasive controversial issue in environmental cleanups. Does disturbing the site cause more environmental damage? Often this question is compli-cated by cost-cutting measures that affect the environmental decision. The early days of "don't ask, don't tell" environmental policy are replaced by ecosystem risk assessment at Superfund sites. In the case of the Hudson River and GE,

- Of the estimated 1.3 million pounds of PCBs dumped by GE, about 200,000 pounds remain in upper-river sediments. Every day, through resuspension by currents, boats, bottom-dwelling animals, and so on, the sediments release PCBs. About 500 pounds wash over the Troy Dam annually.
- The EPA's peer-reviewed science has found that PCBs are not being widely bur-ied by sediments.

Current Dredging Technology Is Safe, Effective, and Efficient

- Dredging stands to cut in half the flow of PCBs over the Troy Dam, and the EPA forecasts safe fish levels 20 years earlier after dredging.
- The EPA's proposal does not rely on a local landfill.
- Under the EPA's worst-case scenario, dredging might stir up 20 pounds of PCBs annually. However, the cleanup will immediately and dramatically reduce the 500 pounds moving downstream already. In the long term, dredging can virtu-ally eliminate upriver sediment releases of PCBs.
- A recent Scenic Hudson national study of 89 river cleanup projects found that dredging was preferred 90 percent of the time. Dredging reduced PCB levels in rivers and fish in locations such as the Fox River (Wisconsin), Manistique Harbor (Michigan), Cumberland Bay (New York), and Waukegan Harbor (Illinois).
- Dredge operations at rivers nationwide were minimally disruptive to lifestyle and recreation.
- River ecosystems will not be devastated and will quickly re-establish themselves in a clean and healthy environment.

In 2002 the EPA ruled that dredging was the best solution. GE was given the option of doing the work itself or having the EPA do it at GE's expense. After further delays, the first phase of the operation got under way in 2009, with GE choosing to perform the work itself according to EPA specifications. The EPA's PCB-removal plan combines plan-site source control with removing 100,000 pounds of PCBs from the river. Dredging is expected to reduce cancer and noncancer dangers by up to 90 percent compared with just stopping contamination from GE's old plants.

antidotes are available for the internationally banned POPs. POP exposure can follow other vectors of exposure because they are so persistent in the environment. They eventually reach the top of the food chain—humans.

Human Exposure

The greatest part of human exposure to the listed POPs comes from the food chain. The contamination of food, including breast milk, by POPs is a worldwide controversy. In most of the world, breast milk is the sole source of food for most infants. Edible oils and animal products are most often involved in cases of POP contamination. Food contaminated by POPs can pose chronic health risks, including cancer. The long-term implications of low-level exposure are not known. There is controversy on this point within the scientific community. Some researchers are concerned that long-term low-level exposure to POPs may have more cumulative impacts because of their persistence. Others maintain that low-level exposures do not cause any risk, but these individuals do not engage the cumulative-risk concerns.

Vectors for food contamination by POPs occur through environmental pollution of the air, water, and soil or through the use of organochlorine pesticides. Food contamination by POPs can have a significant impact on food exports and imports. At the international level, limits for residues of persistent organochlorine insecticides have been established for a range of commodities. They are recognized by the World Trade Organization as the international reference in assessing nontariff barriers to trade. Because of this, international bodies are major players in the controversies over POPs.

Disposal of POPs

Most countries are facing the problem of disposal of some remaining POPs. This is a large controversy because of the cost of such disposal and the environmental and public health risks of not implementing it.

The strict requirements for proper disposal of these chemicals create an enormous burden for a developing country and its industries, both economically and technologically. Legal aspects of transboundary movement of POPs are very specialized and time-consuming. The temptation to dispose of POPs illegally can be strong.

Do POPs Ever Degrade Naturally?

There have been recent claims that POPs can degrade naturally. Some say it is a type of bioremediation. If this is the case, the cost of cleanups decreases dramatically because POPs can be left to degrade in place. Environmentalists generally prefer bioremediation because it usually has lower environmental impacts.

The controversy over whether POPs can be naturally degraded by microbial action is a long-standing one. New research indicates that this occurs for DDT. Research also indicates that naturally occurring organisms in sediments play an important role in breaking down the chlorinated compounds. The finding that DDE, a toxic by-product of the pesticide DDT, can naturally degrade comes from laboratory experiments performed by researchers from Michigan State University's Center for Microbial Ecology. They used marine sediments collected from a Superfund site off the coast of southern California. Their research samples came from the Palos Verdes Shelf, the subject of one of the largest Natural Resources Damage Assessment cases in the United States. More than 20 years after they were deposited, DDT compounds are still present in surface sediments at levels harmful to life. But according to the Michigan State University microbiologist, the experiments do not prove that dechlorination is taking place at a significant rate in the sediments at the site. They do demonstrate that there are sediment microbes that can dechlorinate what was previously considered a terminal product.

The EPA's most likely plan for the Superfund site is to cover part of the ocean floor with a cap of thick sand, a project that could cost as much as $300 million.

Conclusion

The POPs list is likely to expand as our use and knowledge of them increases. So too will the list of potential alternatives to some POPs. Eliminating them from food chains and human breast milk will be a big first step when it eventually happens, but other more inclusive policy approaches will be more controversial. Waste disposal, bioremediation, cost of cleanup and who pays for it all remain debated and growing areas of environmental policy. The main front for the POPs controversy will remain the international environmental community in the form of treaties and international bodies like the United Nations. The issue of mandatory disposal is an emerging one and could shape the cleanup policies of hosting countries. Environmentalists fear an increase in illegal ocean dumping.

See also **Industrial Agricultural Practices and the Environment; Land Pollution; Pesticides; Water Pollution; Watershed Protection and Soil Conservation**

Further Reading

Bargagli, Roberto, *Antarctic Ecosystems: Environmental Contamination, Climate Change, and Human Impact.* New York: Springer, 2005.

Downie, David, *Northern Lights against POPs: Toxic Threats in the Arctic.* Montreal: McGill-Queen's Press, 2002.

Fiedler, H., ed., *Persistent Organic Pollutants.* New York: Springer, 2003.

Hanson, Larry G., and Larry W. Robertson, *PCBs: Human and Environmental Disposition and Toxicology.* Urbana: University of Illinois Press, 2008.

Harrad, Stuart, *Persistent Organic Pollutants: Environmental Behaviour and Pathways of Human Exposure.* New York: Springer, 2001.

Johansen, Bruce Elliott, *The Dirty Dozen: Toxic Chemicals and the Earth's Future.* Westport, CT: Praeger, 2003.

Mehmetli, Ebru, and Bogdana Koumanova, *The Fate of Persistent Organic Pollutants.* Dordecht: Springer Science/Business Media, 2007.

PESTICIDES

Robert William Collin

Chemicals used to kill insects, fungi, rats, and weeds are called pesticides. They can enter ecosystems and create damage. They can bioaccumulate up food chains and affect humans. Their widespread use makes environmentalists and communities uneasy despite improvements in public health due to their use. Some pesticide manufacturers label their products in confusing ways, which creates distrust. Some chemical manufacturers claim trade secrets when registering their pesticides with the EPA. Agribusiness points to high levels of productivity with their use. Many retail pesticides are sold every day to households. While pesticides are everywhere, many people are concerned about exposure and health risks from them.

People are also concerned about multiple exposures to pesticides. When those concerned are dismissed as hysterical housewives, the uneducated public, or extremist environmentalists, the seeds for controversy are sown. These are very serious concerns that demand explanation, and inadequate responses from government and industry do little to alleviate these concerns. Food and drinking water are sometimes contaminated from the same agricultural runoff. Some of the same pesticides used in industrial agriculture are also used in homes, hospitals, churches, schools, and day care centers. These are also places where vulnerable populations of the young, pregnant, and old can be more exposed. The human health effects from pesticide exposures are large. The large numbers of potentially affected people and the financial and social costs of exposure have not been considered in the formation of environmental policy around pesticides.

Questions about who is exposed to how much become questions about how much is safe for whom. There is a high level of concern around cumulative impacts and vulnerable populations that drives this controversy. Every niche of this controversy is laden with debating scientists, successful and unsuccessful lawsuits, agonizing government regulation and enforcement, and victims who will fight this issue to their literal death. The nature of the debate shows the intensity of this particular controversy. Some of the basic parameters of the current raging controversy about pesticide exposure of children are described by the Natural Resources Defense Council, a national U.S. environmental group. The summary findings of their research conclude as follows:

- All children are disproportionately exposed to pesticides, compared with adults, due to their greater intake of food, water, and air per unit of body weight, their greater activity levels, narrower dietary choices, crawling, and hand-to-mouth behavior.

- Fetuses, infants, and children are particularly susceptible to pesticides compared with adults because their bodies cannot efficiently detoxify and eliminate chemicals, their organs are still growing and developing, and they have a longer lifetime to develop health complications after an exposure.
- Pesticides can have numerous serious health effects, ranging from acute poisoning to cancers, neurological effects, and effects on reproduction and development.
- Many pesticides that are never used indoors are tracked into the home and accumulate there at concentrations up to 100 times higher than outdoor levels.
- In nonagricultural urban or suburban households, an average of 12 different pesticides per home have been measured in carpet dust and an average of 11 different pesticide residues per household have been measured in indoor air in homes where pesticides are used.
- In an early 1990s nationwide survey of pesticide residues in urine in the general population, metabolites of two organophosphate pesticides, chlorpyrifos and parathion, were detected in 82 percent and 41 percent, respectively, of the people tested.
- In a rural community, all 197 children tested had urinary residues of the cancer-causing pesticide pentachlorophenol; all except 6 of the children had residues of the suspected carcinogen p-dichlorobenzene, and 20 percent had residues of the normally short-lived outdoor herbicide 2,4-D, which has been associated with non-Hodgkins lymphoma.

Pesticides in Agricultural Areas

The Natural Resources Defense Council did a special study of agricultural children and their exposure to pesticides, called *Trouble on the Farm: Growing Up with Pesticides in Agricultural Communities* (October 1998). Following is a summary of their conclusions.

- Children living in farming areas or whose parents work in agriculture are exposed to pesticides to a greater degree and from more sources than other children.
- The outdoor herbicide atrazine was detected inside all the houses of Iowa farm families sampled in a small study during the application season and in only 4 percent of 362 nonfarm homes.
- Neurotoxic organophosphate pesticides have been detected on the hands of farm children at levels that could result in exposures above levels designated safe by the U.S. Environmental Protection Agency (EPA).
- Metabolites of organophosphate pesticides used only in agriculture were detectable in the urine of 2 out of every 3 children of agricultural workers and in 4 out of every 10 children who simply live in an agricultural region.

- On farms, children as young as 10 can work legally, and younger children frequently work illegally or accompany their parents to the fields owing to economic necessity and a lack of child-care options. These practices can result in acute poisonings and deaths. (See http://www.nrdc.org/health/kids/farm/exec. asp/May 15, 2007.)

Kinds of Pesticides

Many different kinds of pesticides are in use today. Pesticides are referred to according to the type of pest they control.

Chemical Pesticides

Some examples of chemical pesticides follow. Other examples are available in sources such as *Recognition and Management of Pesticide Poisonings* (Reigart and Roberts 1999).

Organophosphate Pesticides

These pesticides affect the nervous system by disrupting the enzyme that regulates a chemical in the brain called acetylcholine. Most organophosphates are used as insecticides. Some are very poisonous. Both manufacturers of pesticides and government claim they are not persistent in the environment. Others claim they could be responsible for endocrine disruption in humans, as well as other nervous system impacts.

Pesticides and Public Health Protection

Pesticides have had a strong historical role in limiting threats to the public health. Many states and localities use them for this purpose. Pests that are public health threats are eradicated or contained by the application of pesticides. When the government is applying the pesticides, some members of the resident community may object. Some people simply want to be free from any chemical intrusion and want that choice respected. Controversy can flare up at this point with public pest-eradication programs reliant on widespread application of persistent pesticides. Some members of the public want such a program to eliminate pestilence. Exactly what is a pest for these purposes?

The central front in this type of pesticide controversy will often be the state agencies with responsibilities that include the use of pesticides. There are often the transportation departments that spray the side of the road with herbicides to keep weeds down. Weeds along a road can create a fire hazard in the hot, dry summer months of the United States.

When Is a Pest a Public Pest?

Protecting public health goes beyond the general mandate to ensure the required safety of pesticides sold on the market for pest control. The Federal Insecticide, Fungicide, and

THE LANGUAGE OF PESTICIDES

Whether a given pesticide is safe partially depends on the application. Pesticides are application-specific, and changes from these applications may pose hazards to people and the environment. Although many of these terms have complex legal meanings, a working knowledge of the basic terms gives depth to this controversy. These are basic terms in the pesticide literature and can be found in the references and Web resources at the end of this entry. Pesticides that are related because they address the same type of pests include the following:

Algicides: Control algae in lakes, canals, swimming pools, water tanks, and other sites.

Antifouling agents: Kill or repel organisms that attach themselves to underwater surfaces, such as boat bottoms.

Antimicrobials: Kill microorganisms (such as bacteria and viruses).

Attractants: Attract pests (for example, to lure an insect or rodent to a trap; however, food is not considered a pesticide when used as an attractant).

Biocides: Kill microorganisms.

Biopesticides: Certain types of pesticides derived from such natural materials as animals, plants, bacteria, and certain minerals.

Disinfectants and sanitizers: Kill or inactivate disease-producing microorganisms on inanimate objects.

Fumigants: Produce gas or vapor intended to destroy pests in buildings or soil.

Fungicides: Kill fungi (including blights, mildews, molds, and rusts).

Herbicides: Kill weeds and other plants that grow where they are not wanted.

Insecticides: Kill insects and other arthropods.

Microbial pesticides: Microorganisms that kill, inhibit, or outcompete pests, including insects and other microorganisms.

Miticides (also called acaricides): Kill mites that feed on plants and animals.

Molluscicides: Kill snails and slugs.

Nematicides: Kill nematodes (microscopic, wormlike organisms that feed on plant roots).

Ovicides: Kill eggs of insects and mites.

Pheromones: Biochemicals used to disrupt the mating behavior of insects.

Repellents: Repel pests, including insects (such as mosquitoes) and birds.

Rodenticides: Control mice and other rodents.

The term *pesticide* also includes these substances:

Defoliants: Cause leaves or other foliage to drop from a plant, usually to facilitate harvest.

Desiccants: Promote drying of living tissues, such as unwanted plant tops.

Insect growth regulators: Disrupt the molting, maturity from pupal stage to adult, or other life processes of insects.

Plant growth regulators: Substances (excluding fertilizers or other plant nutrients) that alter the expected growth, flowering, or reproduction rate of plants.

Rodenticide Act (FIFRA) requires the EPA, in coordination with the U.S. Department of Health and Human Services (HHS) and U.S. Department of Agriculture (USDA), to identify pests of significant public health importance and, in coordination with the Public Health Service, to develop and implement programs to improve and facilitate the safe and necessary use of chemical, biological, and other methods to combat and control such pests. FIFRA defines the term *pest* as meaning "(1) any insect, rodent, nematode, fungus, weed or (2) any other form of terrestrial or aquatic plant or animal life or virus, bacteria, or other microorganism (except viruses, bacteria, or other microorganism on or in living man or other living animals) that the Administrator declares to be a pest under section 25(c)(1)."

The EPA has broadly declared the term *pest* to cover each of the organisms mentioned except for the organisms specifically excluded by the definition. Following is a brief description of the identified pests or categories of pests and an explanation for designating each as a public health pest.

- Cockroaches. Cockroaches are controlled to halt the spread of asthma, allergies, and food contamination.
- Body, head, and crab lice. These lice are surveyed for and controlled to prevent the spread of skin irritation and rashes, and to prevent the occurrence of louse-borne diseases such as epidemic typhus, trench fever, and epidemic relapsing fever in the United States.
- Mosquitoes. Mosquitoes are controlled to prevent the spread of mosquito-borne diseases such as malaria; St. Louis, Eastern, Western, West Nile, and LaCrosse encephalitis; yellow fever; and dengue fever.
- Various rats and mice. The listed rats and mice include those that are controlled to prevent the spread of rodent-borne diseases and contamination of food for human consumption.
- Various microorganisms, including bacteria, viruses, and protozoans. The listed microorganisms are the subject of control programs by public health agencies and hospitals for the purpose of preventing the spread of numerous diseases.
- Reptiles and birds. The listed organisms are controlled to prevent the spread of disease and the prevention of direct injury.
- Various mammals. The listed organisms have the potential for direct human injury and can act as disease reservoirs (i.e., rabies, etc.).

It is possible that this list may need to be changed. Should any additional species be found to present public health problems, the EPA may determine that it should consider them to be pests of significant public health importance under FIFRA. The EPA is supposed to update the list of pests of significant public health importance.

Pesticides and Food Quality

The Food Quality Protection Act placed requirements on the EPA related to public health and pesticides. The EPA considers risks and benefits of pesticides that may have public health uses. The EPA regulates certain pesticides that might be found in drinking water by setting maximum contaminant limits.

Pesticide Spray Drift: Another Case of Involuntary Exposure

Another controversial risk to public health is from pesticide spray drift. The EPA defines pesticide spray drift as the physical movement of a pesticide through air at the time of application or soon thereafter, to any site other than that intended for application (often referred to as off-target). This can affect the health of neighboring communities and farms, especially organic farms.

Pesticide drift can affect human health and the environment. Spray drift can result in pesticide exposures to farm workers, children playing outside, and the ecosystem. Drift can also contaminate a home garden or another farmer's crops.

There are many reported complaints of pesticide spray drift each year. Reports of exposures of people, plants, and animals to pesticides due to off-target drift are called drift incidents. They are part of an important component in the scientific evaluation and regulation of the uses of pesticides. The EPA is supposed to consider all of these routes of exposure in regulating the use of pesticides. A major criticism of the EPA approach is that it does not measure the cumulative effects of pesticide exposure. Another issue is the weak enforcement of this environmental protection policy. EPA policy relies on complaints of drift incidents and on labeling. This is often seen as a weak and ineffective response by many who are subject to repeated drift incidents. If no people are nearby, the environmental impacts of drift incidents may accrue over years, eventually working their way into land and water systems. This underscores the necessity of a cumulative and ecosystem risk analysis. The EPA allows some degree of drift of pesticide particles in almost all applications. It assumes pesticide applications are made in responsible ways by trained operators. This is not the case in many instances. In making their decisions about pesticide applications, prudent and responsible applicators must consider all factors, including wind speed, direction, and other weather conditions; application equipment; the proximity of people and sensitive areas; and product label directions. A prudent and responsible applicator must refrain from application under conditions that can cause pesticide drift. They decide whether or not to apply a pesticide. It is their responsibility to know and understand a product's use restrictions, but most do not. The practical result is potential human health effects from chemical overexposure.

The EPA conducts ecological risk assessments to determine what risks are posed by a pesticide and whether changes to the use or proposed use are necessary to protect the environment. Many plant and wildlife species can be found near or in cities, agricultural fields, and recreational areas. Before allowing a pesticide product to be sold on the market, the EPA ensures that the pesticide will not pose any unreasonable risks to wildlife and the environment. They do this by evaluating data submitted in support of registration regarding the potential hazard that a pesticide may pose to nontarget fish and wildlife species.

Pesticides, Water Quality, and Synergy

When pesticides are applied on fields, gardens, parks, and lawns, some of the chemicals run off the treated site. More than 80 percent of urban streams and more than 50 percent of agricultural streams have concentrations in water of at least one pesticide, mostly those in use during the study period, that exceed a water-quality benchmark for aquatic life. Water-quality benchmarks, set by the EPA, are estimates of pesticide concentrations that the agency says may have adverse effects on human health, aquatic life, or fish-eating wildlife. Insecticides, particularly diazinon, chlorpyrifos, and malathion, frequently exceed aquatic-life benchmarks in urban streams. Most urban uses of diazinon and chlorpyrifos, as on lawns and gardens, have been phased out since 2001 because of an EPA-industry agreement. In agricultural streams, the pesticides chlorpyrifos, azinphosmethyl, p,p'-DDE, and alachlor are among those most often found above benchmarks. While the standard benchmarks were not exceeded for human health, recent studies and decades of incomplete risk assessments suggest that EPA benchmarks are severely underestimated. This is a very controversial scientific issue. If synergy and cumulative impacts increase public health risk, then new regulations with different standards could become law.

Pesticides seldom occur alone in the real world, but rather almost always as complex mixtures. Most stream samples and about half of well samples contain two or more pesticides, and frequently more. The potential effects of contaminant mixtures on people, aquatic life, and fish-eating wildlife are still poorly understood. Most toxicity information and the water-quality benchmarks are developed for individual chemicals. The common occurrence of pesticide mixtures, particularly in streams, means that the total combined toxicity of pesticides in water, sediment, and fish may be greater than that of any single pesticide compound that is present. Studies of the effects of mixtures are still in the early stages, and it may take years for researchers to attain major advances in understanding the actual potential for effects. A recent study by researchers at the University of California–Berkeley finds that pesticide mixtures harm frogs at levels that do not produce the same effects alone, often levels 10 to 100 times below EPA standards. This has implications for local governments and other water providers. Drinking water providers are faced with a dilemma about how to deal with the twin problem of killing dangerous bacteria while not increasing the chemical health risks for pregnant women and healthy infants. Pesticides are getting into the drinking water sources for

PESTICIDES: THE FIGHT IN CONGRESS

Pesticide regulation and control are very controversial issues in Congress. Presidential administrations also affect this controversy in different ways. One very controversial issue is whether pesticides should be tested on people. Most scientific studies generalize from mice or rats to humans. Some are concerned that this species generalization may be inaccurate, especially if the effects of other chemicals in the environment are considered. As the EPA and other governmental agencies struggle to develop standards and regulations around pesticides, the need for exact data increases. As environmentalists and toxic tort lawyers challenge industry in the courts, the need for data that support human injury also increases. However, most individuals, when given a free choice, choose not be tested for pesticide safety. A core question is whether safe standards for humans can be developed without testing pesticides on humans. Scientifically this may be difficult, but it is demanded by the public.

On June 29, 2005, one day after the George W. Bush administration's proposal to allow industry to test pesticides on people was leaked to the media, the Senate acted to block such testing. By a vote of 60 to 37, the Senate adopted a bipartisan amendment to the 2006 Interior and Environment appropriations bill, which blocks the U.S. Environmental Protection Agency from spending tax dollars to fund or review studies that intentionally expose people to pesticides. The U.S. Senate also voted 57 to 40 to adopt another amendment that requires the EPA to review the ethical ramifications of human pesticide testing.

millions of people in the United States. These contaminants combine with disinfectants, such as chlorine (added by drinking water providers to kill dangerous viruses, bacteria, and pathogens), forming disinfectant by-products that are associated with increases in birth defects and miscarriages. This drives the concern that the pesticides in our drinking water cannot be addressed by the chemical-by-chemical regulatory approach of government.

Research Needed

While the effects of pesticides increase, there is a continued need for more research. Pesticide controversies are tied to cumulative risk controversies and therefore will not decrease. Given recent scientific evidence of pesticide synergy, it is likely that public policy development will require more data and information to react and to plan for pesticide public health issues. This is an emerging issue that pits public health interests against chemical manufacturers of pesticides. It will be difficult for scientists to exercise independent professional judgment given the disparity of power and resources between the two interests.

PESTICIDES: INERT INGREDIENTS IN PESTICIDE PRODUCTS—ABOUT TOLERANCE REASSESSMENT

Pesticide Tolerances

How much of a chemical an individual can take before an adverse response occurs is called a tolerance limit, or a dose response. In investigating the safety of pesticides, researchers determine the tolerance limit for an average person. This model person was usually a 155-pound white male, among the healthiest demographic groups in U.S. society. There are two controversial problems with this method. There is a large dose-response variance in the U.S. population. Something as simple as aspirin can have a 100-fold dose-response difference. This model does not take vulnerability into account and thus underestimates actual risk from pesticides for many segments of the U.S. population. The second problem is that the approach of the U.S. Environmental Protection Agency (EPA) does not take into consideration the accumulated pesticide impacts on a given person. From the human health perspective, this is very important. One dose of a chemical may not kill you, but 10,000 small exposures could. The difference to the human body or to the environment—whether the exposure comes from one bad episode of pesticide drift or 10,000 exposures to residential lawn pesticides—is small.

The EPA sets limits on the amount of pesticides that may remain in or on foods. These limits are called tolerances. The tolerances are set based on a risk assessment and are enforced by the U.S. Food and Drug Administration. More information on tolerances is provided at the Web site for Pesticide Tolerances (www.epa.gov/pesticides/regulating/tolerances.htm).

Conclusion

Pesticide controversies will continue to dominate environmental policy in the courts, legislatures, agencies, and communities. They affect private households, local and state governments, big and small industries, agribusiness, the public health of communities, and many who rely on them. They have large impacts on the environment that may accumulate and bioaccumulate. Many do pose risks to vulnerable populations, and many more could if they mix with other chemicals in the real world. Who is to bear the risk of unknown harm, whether from pesticides or the lack thereof? Science will have a big role to play in this controversy, and there are politically powerful forces in opposition to each other about it.

See also **Cumulative Emissions; Food Safety; Industrial Agricultural Practices and the Environment; Land Pollution; Persistent Organic Pollutants; Water Pollution**

Further Reading

Beres, Samantha, *Pesticides: Critical Thinking about Environmental Issues.* Farmington Hills, MI: Greenhaven Press, 2002.

Levine, Marvin J., *Pesticides: A Toxic Time Bomb in Our Midst.* Westport, CT: Praeger, 2007.

Matthews, Graham A., *Pesticides: Health, Safety and the Environment.* Oxford, UK: Blackwell, 2006.

Nash, Linda Lorraine, *Inescapable Ecologies: A History of Environment, Disease, and Knowledge.* Berkeley: University of California Press, 2007.

Reigart, J. Routt, and James R. Roberts, eds., *Recognition and Management of Pesticide Poisonings.* Washington, DC: U.S. Environmental Protection Agency, 1999.

Wargo, John, *Green Intelligence: Creating Environments that Protect Human Health.* New Haven, CT: Yale University Press, 2009.

R

REPRODUCTIVE TECHNOLOGY

Anne Kingsley

In 1978 Louise Brown became the first "test tube" baby to be born using in vitro fertilization (IVF). Her birth marked the advent of a rapidly advancing reproductive science, and it also became a testament to a changing concept of creation. Her birth was not only a moment of celebration but also one of controversy. For some, IVF opposed traditional or religious beliefs about family and reproduction. Conception took place outside the body and outside the family and was altered through medical intervention. Many of the practices used in IVF and other assisted reproduction technologies (ART) challenged what was commonly thought of as the standard or normal family: one mother, one father, and children. A process such as egg or sperm donation, both of which take a third-party donor to create a fertilized embryo that will then be introduced into the female body using IVF, was therefore seen as counter to traditional family ideology and practice.

The success of IVF, however, opened new possibilities in the treatment of infertility. Proponents continued to see the practice as a means of conceiving a child where it otherwise may not have been possible. Many women who sought the treatment also supported this notion, considering the ability to conceive a child as their right. Today, the predominant public attitude toward assisted reproduction has shifted from wavering opposition to general acceptance. It is widely recognized and practiced as a standard treatment for infertility.

IN VITRO FERTILIZATION (IVF)

IVF is a process that enables a human embryo to be conceived outside the body. In IVF, eggs are collected using ovulation induction: hormonal drugs are given to induce the production of eggs. These are then removed from the ovary and placed in a lab dish (the "vitro" or glass) and fertilized. After several days, the fertilized eggs are transferred into the woman's uterus to continue growing. The practice of IVF introduced an exceptional level of human intervention into the reproductive process. It also suggested that life can be "altered" in the process. Although there are many assisted reproductive technologies available to women, IVF is the most utilized and successful.

Choices and Controversies

The phenomenal increase in the number of babies born using alternative methods of fertilization over the past 20 years testifies to the changing outlook on once controversial medical procedures. Furthermore, the demand for reproductive options opens the door to more avenues of scientific exploration to both refine existing reproductive technologies and search for new methods. Accompanying the unprecedented rate of scientific growth, however, is a growing concern over the extent of new plateaus in reproductive technology and their costs. As a result, a new set of controversies and a new set of medical, ethical, and social questions have emerged to shape debate over assisted reproduction.

The new story of reproduction is located at the intersection of shifting social values and a rapidly advancing scientific understanding. New technologies afford women the decision to postpone reproduction. Hypothetically, a woman in her thirties, working toward a successful career or further education, is well aware that with each year the possibility of having a healthy child and an uncomplicated pregnancy diminishes. She is also aware that alternative procedures such as freezing one's eggs give her the tentative option of conceiving at a chosen future date. The process does not guarantee reproduction, but it does open new considerations in terms of family planning. In a society where fertility and pregnancy are at odds with "career ladders" for women, proponents of new advancements in reproductive technology see it as affording more lifestyle and body choices without sacrificing the desire to also have a family.

Yet skeptics argue that the original design of the fertility treatment was meant to offer infertility options, not lifestyle choices. A controversy over age limits emerges in this conversation because some critics worry how far medical practice will go to allow older women to conceive, even after menopause. Since ART is a relatively unregulated field of practice, no restrictions in age exist thus far. Many of these questions carry both scientific and social implications. On the one hand, reproductive technology has allowed women at many age levels to conceive and start a family. On the other hand, the increasing tendency to treat reproduction and conception as a medical issue has changed the traditional social narrative of the family. As prevalent as many of these controversies may be, their lack of resolution has not slowed the accelerating pace of further research and development.

New advancements and research in assisted reproductive technologies seek to make existing procedures more successful and more available to larger numbers of women. Newer processes mark not only how far we have come but also how far we may yet go. Advancements in reproductive technology create new controversies, many of which remain unaddressed.

Risks and Benefits

One of the predominant issues with infertility treatments is the long-term effect on both the woman and the child. As standard as many of the procedures in ART are, long-term results are relatively unstudied. After all, Louise Brown, who turned 30 in 2008, is still relatively young. New measures are being taken to set up systems of surveillance that track and record the progress, the effects, and the health of the constituents involved. Some critics question how far we should advance medicine without knowing the full set of risks to mother and child. Proponents of the advancement in reproductive technologies see such suspicion of potential risks as a means of limiting female choice, undercutting the availability of IVF.

One of the known complications of ART is the predominance of multiple births. To ensure that pregnancy takes place, multiple embryos can be placed within the woman's uterus, potentially resulting in multiple births. Newer technologies can help predetermine healthy embryos, thus reducing the possibility of multiple births before implantation takes place. Yet the same technology used to prescreen the embryos can also be applied to screening for a predisposition to genetic diseases and for sex. The prescreening allows the parents to make decisions before fetal pregnancy occurs. The process of prescreening and selection of healthy embryos raises questions about the role of medical selection and the alteration of life outside the body. Some critics fear that the list of prescreening traits may grow longer, resulting in the institution of *Brave New World* tactics, where "designer babies" and "designer families" are the results of "quality control."

Interestingly, one of the more pressing quandaries generated by ART is its proximity to cloning. The laboratory techniques generated by ART are the same as those used in cloning. However, in a process such as IVF, the fertilized egg is the result of two biological parents, whereas with cloning, the cloned cell is the exact copy of one parent. Regulations controlling both cloning and stem cell research may also pose restrictions to ART, given that all are seen as working within the embryonic stages of life.

New advancements in reproductive technology carry risks along with the benefits. Although the technology is often heralded as necessary progress, critics point out that progress must be accompanied by bioethical responsibility. In other words, scientific research and its applications must be carefully understood and monitored for its ethical and moral implications.

Bioethical Considerations

Much of the current controversy in ART involves larger institutional practices rather than simply the medical procedures themselves. One such concern is the disposal of unused embryos. Here, the controversy intersects with the dialogue concerning post-coital contraceptive practices (such as the morning-after pill) and research practices in stem cell research—where does life begin? Proponents see the unused embryos, especially in stem cell research, as an opportunity for developing new treatments against disease. Opponents of using or destroying embryos, however, express concern over the increased power for science to manipulate fundamental definitions of life. Some critics even fear that the line between ethical and unethical practice gets ever more slippery as the limitations of embryonic research are further extended. Thus, ART again comes under scrutiny, requiring that more attention be given to regulations and limitations.

In order to address bioethical responsibility in assisted reproductive technology, some critics call for new measures in regulation. Those who call for regulation wish to monitor research practices more closely, including experimenting with new forms and methods of ART and medical practices actively applying existing methods of ART. Some women fear that "regulation" will equate to "restriction" of bodily rights, however, and certainly, determining bodily rights versus moral concerns is a difficult process.

An issue that may be overlooked is the potential of politicizing infertility as discussions of reproduction take place within scientific and political discourse. Reproductive technology, at one point, opened up a new agenda for women wanting both family and career. It was seen as a progressive move in the women's rights struggle. And yet, the politicization of the practice and the resultant discourse on "property rights" in terms of the female body, and the objectifying of women's bodies as a scientific or political event, may also be seen as regressive. It may be seen as counterproductive, as a woman's body becomes a space of experimentation—a scientific workplace.

Another pressing issue as ART moves into the arena of private industry is the blurring of the distinction between consumer and patient. Certainly, the capitalization of the reproductive technology market raises some concerns. ART is a $3-billion-a-year industry at the intersection of medical practice and private business.

Profit incentives facilitate the process of freezing, storing, and thawing eggs. That eggs have become a commodity is evidenced by the advertisements that blanket college newspapers offering to pay women for egg donations. For consumers, the concern or emphasis of the practice is on product. For patients, there is not only the health and practice concern but also an emotional concern. Skeptics say that a business is not equipped to handle a woman who, despite ART, cannot conceive a child. They question whether a business attitude toward reproduction can answer and identify her needs. Supporters of ART maintain that the right technology, even if driven by economics, offers the best possible means of addressing infertility. On either side of the issue, the word *embryo*, not just as a scientific term but as a business one as well, takes on new connotations.

Many social implications result from considering fertility as a commercial business; one of these is that fertility becomes a question of affordability. Access to treatment becomes a question of who can pay and who can not. ART procedures are extremely costly. The fee for freezing eggs can be almost $10,000. The cost of hormone treatments to stimulate egg production can be another $4,000. The future in vitro fertilization of the eggs will cost around $15,000 to $20,000. Critics of the view that technology brings choice point out that financial cost can actually eliminate choice.

For example, infertility rates are much greater outside the United States; yet, because of the high cost, fewer people have access to the technology or treatment. In many countries, infertility comes at the cost of social exclusion, raising questions, again, about the intention of ART to provide an answer to a social need. Even inside the United States, many insurance policies do not provide for ART, excluding families who cannot afford the thousands of dollars the treatments often incur.

In addition, high costs do not necessarily equate to success. The process of assisted reproduction can offer only a possibility of a healthy pregnancy, not a guaranteed assurance of conceiving a child and bringing it to term. Less than half of the procedures performed result in infants carried to term. Critics point out that there is no reimbursement financially or emotionally for undergoing a process that fails in the end. At the same time, proponents maintain that ART practices offer the best possible solution to infertility.

Conclusion

Public dialogue on reproductive technologies is both steeped in controversy and pressingly necessary as our understanding and advancement of the science continues to move forward, creating many medical, ethical, and social questions along the way. Do these technologies oppose traditional family structures? Do lifestyle choices come at the cost of natural, biological practice? What should be the limits of ART as the biological and ethical implications become better understood? Whether for skeptics or for proponents, the advancement of reproductive technology will certainly challenge the intersection of science and society as social and ethical institutions come face to face with medical and scientific exploration.

See also **Biotechnology; Cloning; Eugenics; Genetic Engineering; Medical Ethics**

Further Reading

De Jonge, Christopher, and Christopher L. R. Barratt, eds., *Assisted Reproduction Technology: Accomplishments and New Horizons*. Cambridge, UK: Cambridge University Press, 2002.

Merrick, Janna C., *Reproductive Issues in America: A Reference Handbook.* Santa Barbara, CA: ABC-CLIO, 2003.

Mundy, Liza, *Everything Conceivable: How Assisted Reproduction Is Changing Men, Women, and the World.* New York: Knopf, 2007.

Naam, Ramez, *More Than Human: Embracing the Promise of Biological Enhancement.* New York: Broadway Books, 2005.

Winkler, Kathleen, *High Tech Babies: The Debate over Assisted Reproductive Technology.* Berkeley Heights, NJ: Enslow, 2006.

ROBOTS AND SOCIAL ROBOTICS

JENNIFER CROISSANT AND SELMA SABANOVIC

Long an inspiration for science fiction novels and films, the prospect of direct, personal, and intimate interaction between humans and robots is the focus of contemporary debate among scientists, futurists, and the public. The term *robot* comes from the play *R.U.R.*, for "Rossum's Universal Robots," written by Czechoslovakian author Karel Capek in 1920. In this play, humanoid automata overthrow and exterminate human beings, but because the robots cannot reproduce themselves, they also face extinction. This play was internationally successful at the time, engaging public anxieties produced by rapid industrialization, scientific change, and the development of workplace automation.

In the play, inventor Rossum's robots are fully humanoid. These forms of robot are sometimes referred to as androids, or gynoids for machines with feminine characteristics. Humanoid or anthropomorphic robots represent only one kind of robot, however. Robots vary in the degree of automation, as well as the extent to which they are anthropomorphic. The sophisticated animatronic human figures of amusement parks represent some of the best imitations of human movement, although these robots' programming controls all of their actions. Social robotics focuses on the representation of human communication and social interaction, although no systems to date are capable of independent locomotion, and they resemble human forms and faces only slightly. Industrial robots are designed not to mimic the human form at all but to efficiently conduct specific manufacturing processes. Industrial robots are the least humanlike in form and movement of all the forms of robots.

Levels of Control

The degree to which a robot is capable of autonomous or self-directed responses to its environment varies. Many if not most robotic systems are extremely limited in their responses, and their actions are completely controlled by programming. There are also robots whose actions are controlled directly by a human operator. For example, bomb-squad robots are controlled by a human operator who, using cameras and radio or other wireless connections, can control the detailed operations of the robot to defuse a bomb.

Only a handful of experimental systems have more than a very limited range of preset responses to environmental stimuli, going beyond rote conversations for social robots to simple algorithms for navigating obstacles for mobile robots. It has been, for example, very difficult to develop a reliable robot that can walk with a human gait in all but the most controlled environments.

These different levels of control connect robotics to cybernetics or control theory. The term *cybernetics* comes from the Greek term *kybernos,* or governor. There are many kinds of cybernetic systems. For example, the float in the tank of a toilet that controls water flow and the thermostat on the wall that controls temperature are simple forms of cybernetics where information about the environment (feedback) is translated into a command for the system. For floats, the feedback is of a straightforward mechanical nature. Thermostats use a very simple electrical signal to tell a furnace or air conditioner to turn on or off. Animatronics at amusement parks or complex robotic toys use information about the balance of the device and its location in relation to obstacles to compute changes in position, speed, and direction. The more complex the desired behavior or system and the more independent the robot is supposed to be, the more complex, and thus costly, the information needed in terms of sensors for collecting data, and the greater the computing power needed to calculate and control the possible responses of the device to its environment.

Debating Limits and Social Values

The cost and complexity of a robot with a broad range of responses to the environment point to the first of two controversies surrounding robotics. The first controversy surrounds the limits to automation on a theoretical level. Is there anything that cannot be done by a robot or automated system? The second set of controversies is about the desirability of robotic systems, particularly in terms of their impact on labor and economics. That is, even if we can automate something, should we? These two sets of controversies overlap in several places.

Debates about the limits to automation within the robotics and artificial intelligence communities have many dimensions. There are debates, for example, as to whether certain kinds of knowledge or action can be successfully automated. For example, can medical knowledge be fully captured in automatic diagnosis systems? There are also intense technical debates as to what algorithms or programs might be successful. Simple mimicry or closed programs that map out every possibility are considered weak in comparison with cost-effective and reliable substitutes for developing algorithms that can generate appropriate responses in a more open-ended system. One of the continuing debates has to do with the balance between anthropomorphism and specificity. Human beings are good at a lot of different tasks, so it is very difficult, and perhaps inefficient, to try to make robot systems with that degree of generalizability. A robot that can do one very specific thing with high accuracy may be far superior and cost-effective, if less adaptable (and less glamorous) than a generalized machine that can do lots of things.

The most publicly debated controversies surrounding robots and robotics concern economics and labor. Superficially, robots replace human workers. But because robots lower production costs, their implementation can also expand production and possibly increase employment. The workers displaced may not get new jobs that pay as well as the jobs taken over by automation, however, and they may also be at a point in their working lives where they cannot easily retrain for new work. Robots as labor-saving technologies do not make sense in places where there is a surplus of labor and wages are very low.

The first implementations of robots into workplaces did displace human workers and often degraded work. Work was deskilled, as knowledge and technique was coded into the machine. This deskilling model holds for some cases of automation, but it also became apparent that these automatic systems do not always or necessarily deskill human labor. It is possible to adapt automation and computer systems to work settings in which they add information to work processes rather than extracting information from people and embedding it in machines. In the information systems approach, human labor is supported by data collection and robotics systems, which provide more information about and control over processes. The automation-versus-information debate has been complicated by office automation systems, which lead to debates about whether new technologies in the workplace centralize managerial control or decentralize decision processes in organizations.

Marx's labor theory of value is best at explaining the nuances of the economics of robotics implementation. In this theory, workers do not get the full value of their efforts as wages. The surplus is extracted by owners as profit. As the size of the labor pool increases, wages are driven downward and automation becomes economically undesirable. Skilled labor is the ideal target for automation because of the higher proportional wage costs, yet complex work is the most expensive to implement. Routine labor, often perceived to be low-skill, is targeted for replacement by robotic systems, but the economic benefits of automation for routine labor are ambiguous. To paraphrase Norbert Wiener, one of the fathers of modern cybernetics, anything that must compete with slave labor must accept the conditions of slave labor, and thus automation generally depresses wages within the occupational categories automated. Of course new jobs also emerge, to build and maintain the machines, and these are generally high-skill and high-wage jobs with a high degree of work autonomy. So, consider the automatic grocery-store checkout system. There are usually four stations and one clerk, and it seems to save the wages of at least three checkout clerks to have customers themselves using the automatic system. But the costs of design, implementation, and upkeep of these systems may be very high: the wages of one programmer may be more than that of the four clerks replaced. So it is not clear in the long term whether automatic checkout systems will save money for grocery stores or for customers.

Practical Considerations

There are two continuing problems confronting the implementation of robotics and automatic systems. The first is the productivity paradox, where despite the rapid increases in computing power (doubling approximately every 18 months) and the sophistication of robotics, industrial productivity increases at a fairly steady 3 percent per year. This huge gap between changes in technology and changes in productivity can be explained by several factors, including the time needed to learn new systems by human operators, the increasing costs of maintaining new systems, and the bottlenecks that cannot be automated but have the greatest influence on the time or costs associated with a task.

The second problem with robotics implementation is the perception of the level of skill of the tasks targeted for automation. For example, robots are seen by some groups of roboticists and engineers to be somehow suited for use in taking care of the elderly. The work of eldercare is perceived as low-skill and easy to conduct; it is also seen to be undesirable and thus a target for automation. Although the work is definitely low-paying and difficult, there may be a serious mismatch between the actual complexity of the work and the wages, leading to the labor shortage. The work of taking care of the elderly may not be as routine as it is perceived to be by outsiders and thus may be extremely difficult to automate with reliability or any measure of cost-effectiveness.

So perceptions about work as much as economic issues shape the implementation of robotic systems. These perceptions about the nature of work and the nature of robots play themselves out in popular media. In the 1920s, whether in Capek's *R.U.R* or the film *Metropolis* by Fritz Lang, robots on stage and screen represented sources of cultural anxiety about the rapid industrialization of work and the concentration of wealth. More recent films, such as the *Terminator* and *Matrix* series, are similarly concerned with our dependence on complex technological systems and robotics, and the extent to which robots take on lives of their own and render human beings superfluous. The media representations magnify real problems of worker displacement and questions about human autonomy that are embodied in robotic systems.

Social Robotics

Autonomous machines that can interact with humans directly by exhibiting and perceiving social cues are called social robots. They are the materialization of futuristic visions of personable, socially interactive machines popularized by fictional characters like *Star Wars*' R2-D2 and C-3PO, *The Terminator*'s T-800, and *AI*'s David. Topics of contention in social robotics concern the capability of machines to be social, the identification of appropriate applications for socially interactive robots, their potential social and personal effects, and the ethical implications of socially interactive machines.

Since the 1960s, the primary use of robots has been for repetitive, precise, and physically demanding jobs in factories and dangerous tasks in minefields, nuclear "hot spots," and chemical spills. In contrast, today's social robotics projects envision new roles for robots as social entities—companions and entertainers, caretakers, guides and receptionists, mediators between ourselves and the increasingly complex technologies we encounter daily, and tools for studying human social cognition and behavior. Although social robotics projects have their start in academic, corporate, and government labs, social robots are coming into closer contact with the general public. In 2003, Carnegie Mellon University (CMU) unveiled the world's first Roboceptionist, which gives visitors to the Robotics Institute information and guidance as it engages in humorous banter. Researchers in Japan have developed a number of different social robot prototypes and working models.

Human-Robot Interactions

Social robots are built with the assumption that humans can interact with machines as they do with other people. Because the basic principles of human–human interaction are not immediately obvious, roboticists have developed a variety of approaches for defining social human–robot interaction. In some cases, social roboticists use a range of individual traits to define social machines: the capacity to express and perceive emotion; the skill to engage in high-level dialogue; the aptitude to learn and recognize models held by other agents; the ability to develop social competencies, establish and maintain social relationships, and use natural social cues (gaze, gestures, etc.); and the ability to exhibit distinctive personality and character. Cynthia Breazeal describes Kismet, the first robot designed specifically for face-to-face interaction, as a "sociable robot." By using the term *sociable,* Breazeal emphasizes that the robot will be pleasant, friendly, and fond of company. Such robots, though potentially agreeable assistants, cannot be fully social because they would not be capable of the range of social behavior and affective expression required in human relationships. In qualifying robot sociality, Kerstin Dautenhahn uses a more systemic view and emphasizes the relationship between the robot and the social environment. She differentiates between "socially situated" robots, which are aware of the social environment, and "socially embedded" robots, which engage with the social environment and adapt their actions to the responses they get.

Although roboticists cite technological capabilities (e.g., processor speed, the size and robustness of hardware and software components, and sensing) as the main barrier to designing socially interactive robots, social scientists, humanities scholars, and artists draw attention to the social and human elements that are necessary for social interaction. Philosophers John Searle and Daniel Dennett contest the possibility of designing intelligent and conscious machines. Psychologist Colwyn Trevarthen and sociologist Harry Collins argue that humans may interpret machines as social actors, but the machines themselves can never be truly social. Social psychologist Sherry Turkle shows how social robots act as "relational machines" that people use to project and reflect on their ideas of self and their relationships with people, the environment, and new technologies. Other social scientists argue that the foundation for human and possibly robot sociality is in the subtle and unconscious aspects of interaction, such as rhythmic synchronicity and nonverbal communication. These approaches suggest that gaining a better understanding of human sociality is an important step in designing social robots. Both social scientists and roboticists see robots as potentially useful tools for identifying the factors that induce humans to exhibit social behavior towards other humans, animals, and even artifacts.

Although it is generally agreed that a robot's appearance is an important part of its social impact, the variety of social robot shapes and sizes shows that there is little agreement on the appropriate design for a robot. David Hanson's K-bot and Hiroshi Ishiguro's Actroid and Geminoid robots resemble humans most closely, including having specially designed silicone skin and relatively smooth movements. These robots are known as androids. Along with humanoid robots, which resemble humans in shape, androids express the assumption that a close physical resemblance to humans is a prerequisite for successful social interaction. This assumption is often countered by the hypothesis that human reactions to an almost-but-not-quite-human robot would be quite negative, commonly known as the "uncanny valley" effect. In contrast, Hideki Kozima's Keepon and Michio Okada's Muu robots are designed according to minimalist principles. This approach advocates that a less deterministic appearance allows humans to attribute social characteristics more easily. Researchers often use a childlike appearance for robots when they want to decrease users' expectations from machines and inspire people to treat them like children, exaggerating their speech and actions, which makes technical issues such as perception easier. Surprisingly, research in human–robot interaction (HRI) has shown that machines do not have to be humanlike at all to have social

THE UNCANNY VALLEY

The "uncanny valley" hypothesis, proposed by Japanese roboticist Mori Masahiro, suggests that the degree to which a robot is "humanlike" has a significant effect on how people react to the robot emotionally. According to Masahiro, as a robot is made more humanlike in appearance and motion, humans will have an increasingly positive emotional response to the robot up to a certain point. When the robot resembles a human almost completely but not quite, people will consider it to be repulsive, creepy, and frightening—much as they do zombies and corpses. Once it becomes impossible to differentiate the robot from a human, the response becomes positive again. Although it is widely discussed and cited in social robotics literature, the uncanny valley hypothesis has not been experimentally tested. One of the difficulties is that the main variables involved, humanlike qualities and familiarity, are themselves quite complex and not easily defined.

characteristics attributed to them. People readily attribute social characteristics to simple desktop computers and even Roomba vacuum cleaners.

Finding a Place for Robots

Roboticists claim that social robots fundamentally need to be part of a society, which would include both humans and machines. What would a future society in which humans cohabit with robots look like? Information technology entrepreneurs such as Bill Gates forecast robotics as the next step in the computing revolution, in which computers will be able to reach us in ever more intimate and human ways. Ray Kurzweil, futurist and inventor, sees technology as a way for humanity to "transcend biology," and Hans Moravec claims that, by the year 2040, robots will be our cognitive equals—able to speak and understand speech, think creatively, and anticipate the results of their own and our actions. MIT professor Rodney Brooks views the robots of the future not as machines but as "artificial creatures" that can respond to and interact with their environments. According to Brooks, the impending "robotics revolution" will fundamentally change the way in which humans relate to machines and to each other. A concurring scenario, proposed by cognitive scientists such as Andy Clark, envisions humans naturally bonding with these new technologies and seeing them as companions rather than tools. In his famous *Wired* magazine article "Why the World Doesn't Need Us," Bill Joy counters these technologically optimistic representations of technological advancement by recasting them as risks to humanity, which may be dominated and eventually replaced by intelligent robots.

Views echoing Joy's concerns are common in American fiction, film, and the media. This fear of robots is colloquially known as the "Frankenstein complex," a term coined by Isaac Asimov and inspired by Mary Shelley's novel describing Dr. Frankenstein's loathing of the artificial human he created.

Robotics technologies are regularly suggested as viable solutions for social problems facing developed nations, particularly the steady increase in the elderly population and attendant rising demand for caretaking and domestic assistance services. The Japanese Robotics Association (JARA) expects advanced robotic technologies to be a major market by 2025. In May 2004, Japan's Ministry of Economy, Trade and Industry (METI) made "partner robots" one of seven fields of focus in its latest industrial policy plan. Visions of a bright future for commercial robots have been put into question by difficulties in finding marketable applications. Sony's AIBO, which was credited with redefining the popular conception of robots from that of automated industrial machines to a desirable consumer product, was discontinued in 2006. Mitsubishi did not sell even one unit of its yellow humanoid Wakamaru. Honda's ASIMO has opened the New York Stock Exchange, visited the European Parliament, shaken hands with royalty, and been employed by IBM as a $160,000-per-year receptionist, but Honda has yet to find a viable application for it in society at large.

ROBOTS AS CULTURAL CRITIQUE

Artists engage in robotics to provide cultural and social critiques and to question common assumptions. White's Helpless Robot upends our expectations of robots as autonomous assistants by getting humans to aid the immobile robot by moving it around. In the Feral Robotic Dogs project, Natalie Jeremijenko appropriates commercial robotic toys and turns them into tools that the public can use for activist purposes, such as exploring and contesting the environmental conditions of their neighborhoods. The Institute for Applied Autonomy's Little Brother robot uses cuteness to distribute subversive propaganda and circumvent the social conditioning that stops people from receiving such materials from humans. Simon Penny's Petit Mal and Tatsuya Matsui's robots Posy and P-Noir engage the assumptions of the robotics community itself and ask them to question their motives and approaches to building robots that interact with humans.

Similar concerns about applications have kept NEC from marketing its personable robot PaPeRo. In the United States, social robots such as Pleo and Robosapiens have been successful as high-tech toys. The most commercially successful home robotics application to date, however, is the iRobot vacuum cleaner Roomba, which had sold over 2.5 million units as of January 2008.

Ethical Concerns

Social robots bring up novel ethical challenges because both roboticists and critics envision them to have profound and direct, intended as well as unintended, impacts on humans as well as the environment. Even with their current limited capabilities, interactions with social robots are expected to change not only our understanding but also our experiences of sociality. Although social roboticists overwhelmingly focus on the potential positive influences of these machines, their emphasis on the technical challenges of making social machines can produce designs that have unanticipated consequences for their users, individuals who perform jobs for which the robots were designed, and society in general. Critics have questioned the effects that interaction with machines rather than humans can have on the quality of interaction, especially in the case of vulnerable populations such as children and the elderly. The introduction of robots into certain occupations—such as nursing, the caregiving professions in general, and teaching—is not always seen as a benefit to existing employees. People are concerned that they may have to work harder to compensate for the robot's deficiencies or that their work has been devalued and reduced to an unskilled, mechanical operation. The rise of unemployment that was experienced as a result of factory automation raises further concerns about the effects of robots taking over service sector jobs. The development of socially oriented robotic technologies also calls on us to consider the limitations and capabilities of our social institutions (family, friends, schools, government) and the pressures they face in supporting and caring for children and the elderly (e.g., extended work hours for both parents, dissolution of the extended family and reliance on a nuclear family model, ageism and the medicalization of the elderly).

See also **Airport and Aviation Security; Biotechnology; Surveillance—Technological; Supply Chain Security and Terrorism (vol. 1)**

Further Reading

Breazeal, Cynthia, *Designing Sociable Robots (Intelligent Robotics and Autonomous Agents).* Cambridge, MA: MIT Press, 2002.

Noble, David, *Forces of Production: A Social History of Industrial Automation.* New York: Oxford University Press, 1986.

Reeves, Byron, and Clifford Nass, *The Media Equation: How People Treat Computers, Television, and New Media Like Real People and Places.* CSLI Lecture Notes. Stanford, CA: Center for the Study of Language and Information Publications, 2003.

Siciliano, Bruno, and Ousamma Khatib, eds., *Springer Handbook of Robotics.* Berlin: Springer, 2008.

Thomas, Robert J., *What Machines Can't Do: Politics and Technology in the Industrial Enterprise.* Berkeley: University of California Press, 1994.

Volti, Rudi, *Society and Technological Change,* 6th ed. New York: Worth, 2009.

Wallach, Wendell, *Moral Machines: Teaching Robots Right from Wrong.* New York: Oxford University Press, 2009.

Wood, Gaby, *Edison's Eve: A Magical History of the Quest for Mechanical Life.* New York: Anchor Books, 2002.

Zuboff, Shoshana, *In the Age of the Smart Machine: The Future of Work and Power.* New York: Basic Books, 1988.

Zylinska, Joanna, ed., *The Cyborg Experiments: Extensions of the Body in the Media Age.* New York: Continuum, 2002.

S

SOLAR ENERGY

Robert William Collin and Scott M. Fincher

As nonrenewable energy sources become depleted, proponents of investing in solar energy say the sun's daily presence justifies its development as an energy source. Questions about solar energy include economic arguments that it are not always cost-effective, and that location restrictions, such as the amount of sunlight in the North versus the South, impedes its use.

A tenet of U.S. environmentalism is conservation of natural resources. When electricity comes from burning gas, coal, or other materials, the cost of electricity can increase dramatically in a short time because many of these resources cannot be renewed. Fossil fuels and other power sources such as nuclear fission greatly affect environment in ways that range from damage during resource extraction to pollution and dangerous by-products, including nuclear waste. The Deepwater Horizon oil rig disaster in the Gulf of Mexico in 2010 is an example.

Many developing nations adopt solar power because that is the only electricity available. Many countries have limited hours of electricity, if any at all. Power sources can be unreliable, with frequent brownouts. Solar power combined with low-power LED lights is currently bringing light to the night in villages in developing nations. Instead of relying on a complicated grid of wires to carry electricity from distant generating stations, solar power can be produced on site. This also greatly reduces its ecological footprint.

Discussion of alternative energy sources triggers debate about cost-effectiveness. These can be complex matters including utility rate structures; bond recovery rates;

local, state, and federal regulatory accommodations, and safety. Most measures of cost-effectiveness compare the new source with petrochemical sources. Because petrochemical depletion is contested, it remains an unknown factor in cost-effectiveness computations. Another debated assumption in these measures is the provider of the power. Solar energy can be home-generated, which is called "off the grid" power generation. In some areas the power company is required to buy back the excess power generated provided the correct monitoring mechanisms are in place.

Another tenet of environmentalism is saving power. Using less power is considered to reduce human effects on the environment. Frugal homeowners also find it a convenient way to save money.

Solar Energy Basics

The sun is our major source of energy. The conversion of sunlight to electricity or heat uses solar energy. There are many technologies and technological variations for this process. The most basic way is the use of photovoltaic systems to convert sunlight directly into electricity. Photovoltaic (PV) arrays commonly are used to generate electricity for a single residential or commercial building. Large PV arrays covering many acres can be combined to create a solar power plant, and large mirror arrays can be used to generate heat. In the latter, sunlight is focused with mirrors to create a high-intensity heat source. This heat then produces steam to run a generator, which creates electricity.

Solar water-heating systems for most residential and commercial buildings usually have two main sections. The first is a solar collector that is aimed so that it faces the sun as much as possible. Generally the longer and more direct the sunlight, the more power is created. The second section, which is connected to the solar collector, is a storage tank of liquid, generally water. It retains the heat generated by the solar collector. This heated water can then be used for heating, washing, cleaning, and other daily tasks.

Solar power can be used for anything that requires electricity. For the most part, it is used to heat water, which uses a lot of energy. Many residential and commercial buildings can use solar collectors to do more. Solar energy systems can heat buildings. A solar ventilation system can be used in cold climates to preheat air before it enters a building. Other than for buildings, solar power supplies energy to space missions, remote viewing and sensing outposts in wilderness areas, home motion-detector lights, and many other applications.

Passive Solar Heating

When architects design a building, they can develop an energy plan for it that incorporates using the sun. To use the sun efficiently requires strict compliance with the rules of nature at the particular site. If a design does this, it is considered to be using passive solar energy; once the building is built, the solar energy system demands little maintenance.

In the Northern Hemisphere, buildings designed to use solar energy require features such as large south-facing windows, building materials that absorb and slowly release the sun's heat, and a structure that can support tanks that might be holding water heated by the sun. Passive solar designs should include natural ventilation for cooling.

The way a building sits on a lot can have a large effect on the efficiency of passive solar energy. Many municipal zoning and land-use laws restrict how buildings, especially for residential structures, sit on a lot. Buildings often must be set back from the front, back, and side, creating an envelope around them. On a small lot, this will greatly constrain the direction the building can face, which can limit passive solar efficiency. This is one of many land-use issues related to solar power.

Environmental Requirements

The environmental requirements for solar power differ based on power usage. Often they are site-specific and not always readily available to a home buyer or builder. Essential environmental information is how much solar energy is available to a particular solar collector. The availability of or access to unobstructed sunlight for use both in passive solar designs and active systems is protected by zoning laws and ordinances in some communities.

Property Rights and the Sun

Access to the sun in cities has been controversial, whereas access to light and air is part of U.S. private property law. Solar access means having unobstructed, direct sunlight. Solar access issues emerged in the United States when commercial property owners sought to ensure that their investment in solar power was not obscured by shadows from a later nearby development. This can be contentious because solar access needs can clash with development rights of nearby property owners. Solar energy advocates say that communitywide solar access can greatly increase the efficiency of the solar collectors and lower the cost of energy.

Several communities in the United States have developed solar access land-use guidelines or ordinances; most have not done so. Many communities are entangled in debates over other issues, such as the erection of cellular telephone towers and ways of economic development. Powerful interests—such as real estate, banking, and mortgage-lending institutions—prefer traditional private property approaches, and many private property owners see mandatory solar access as an infringement on their rights. As a result, mandatory solar access can encounter community resistance. Environmentalists would like to see more protection for investment in solar energy. Many states now offer tax incentives for the development of alternative energy sources.

In the absence of access laws, landowners using solar power can avoid shadows by buying surrounding development rights, but that is a costly alternative. Governmental entities can also exercise their power of eminent domain to achieve public purposes related to solar energy development.

Traditional zoning ordinances and building codes can create problems for solar access. Most pertain to the zoning envelope mentioned previously:

- Height
- Setback from the property line
- Exterior design restrictions
- Yard projection
- Lot orientation
- Lot coverage requirements

The most important solar access rule is making sure an installation faces the sun in a predominantly east–west direction. Common problems that landowners or developers who want to install solar power have encountered with building codes include the following:

- Exceeding roof load
- Unacceptable heat exchangers
- Improper wiring
- Unlawful tampering with potable water supplies.

Potential zoning issues include the following:

- Obstructing side yards
- Erecting unlawful protrusions on roofs
- Siting the system too close to streets or lot boundaries.

Special area regulations such as local community, subdivision, or homeowners' association covenants also demand compliance. These covenants, historic district regulations, and floodplain provisions can easily be overlooked.

Turning Solar Energy into Chemicals

How to store energy derived from the sun has been a central drawback to its use. In April 2010, microbial scientist Derek Lovley of the University of Massachusetts at Amherst found a way that turns 90 percent of carbon dioxide, a greenhouse gas, and some bacteria into fuel without further processing. His method, called "microbial electrosynthesis," is carbon-neutral—which means that it does not add greenhouse gases to the atmosphere. In addition, it is believed to use solar energy more efficiently than is done by plants. As such, it provides a solution to the storage problem because it immediately turns solar power directly into chemicals, which are then readily stored with existing infrastructure and distributed on demand.

Excitement over this innovation stems in part from the fact that no biomass or feedstock or arable land is required for the process. Similarly, far less water is required of the process than, say, energy generated by nuclear means. And, no elaborate postproduction fermentation is required. Consequently this process does not produce any known toxic waste.

Conclusion

Voluntary consumer decisions to purchase electricity supplied by renewable energy sources are a powerful market-support mechanism for renewable energy development. Beginning in the early 1990s, a small number of U.S. utilities began offering green power options to their customers. Since then, these products have become more available, both from utilities and in states that have introduced competition into their retail electricity markets. Today, more than 50 percent of all U.S. consumers have an option to purchase some type of green power product from a retail electricity provider. Currently, about 600 utilities offer green power programs to customers in 34 states.

This burgeoning economic growth will push at the current constraints on the use of solar energy. As more information emerges about the environmental costs of petrochemical production, the amount of oil left, and the record-breaking profits made by multinational petrochemical corporations, communities and residents seeking more self-sufficiency will pursue solar power.

See also **Wind Energy; Sustainability (vol. 1)**

Further Reading

Asplund, Richard W., *Profiting from Clean Energy.* Hoboken, NJ: Wiley, 2008.

Inslee, Jay, and Bracken Henry, *Apollo's Fire: Igniting America's Clean-Energy Economy.* Washington, DC: Island Press, 2008.

Oldfield, Frank, *Environmental Change: Key Issues and Alternative Perspectives.* Cambridge, UK: Cambridge University Press, 2005.

Scheer, Hermann, *A Solar Manifesto.* London: James and James/Earthscan, 2005.

Simon, Christopher A., *Alternative Energy: Political, Economic, and Social Feasibility.* Lanham, MD: Rowman & Littlefield, 2007.

SPRAWL

Robert William Collin

Sprawl is the unconstrained growth of real estate and unplanned land development. It has detrimental environmental effects. Controlling sprawl requires land-use regulation that can decrease the value of some properties.

Problems with Sprawl

Sprawl refers to the inefficient use of natural resources and especially open land on the outskirts of communities. Antisprawl groups say it increases avoidable and unnecessary environmental degradation. Poorly planned development threatens our environment, our health, and our quality of life in many ways. Sprawl spreads development out over large amounts of land, paving much of it. Because many of Americans do not live near where they work and because industrial, commercial, and residential lands tend to be separated, there are long distances between homes, services, and employment centers. This increases dependency on automobiles, a major source of pollution. Sprawl decreases routine pedestrian or bicycle traffic and can have a negative effect on individual and public health.

Because sprawl requires more paved roads and use of cars, it increases air and water pollution. Sprawl destroys more than two million acres of parks, farms, and open space each year.

The owners of the parks, farms, and open space sell their property on the private real estate market or have it taken unwillingly by government through eminent domain. Sprawl can begin when landowners in rural areas subdivide large tracts into smaller parcels for residential or commercial development. After this, counties or other governmental entities decide the minimum lot size allowed for development. Residential projects, called subdivisions, can be large or small, built all at once or in phases, and they increase demand for government services. Having more roads is one such service.

Sprawling development increases traffic on side streets and highways. It pulls economic resources away from existing communities and often puts them far away from a community's core. Local property taxes subsidize new roads, water and sewer lines, and schools as well as increased police and fire protection. An underlying concern about sprawl is that it leads to degradation of older towns and cities and to higher taxes. There also is concern that services like fire, police, sanitation, and education cost more because development is more spread out.

Critics assert that sprawl is an institutional force that combines tax policies, land speculation and an unrestrained profit motive. Others claim sprawl is simply the result of unrestrained market dynamics applied to land development for profit: they reason that people move to outlying areas because land is cheaper there.

Sprawl-Threatened Cities

U.S. cities are suffering from sprawl. Many municipalities may make up a given metropolitan area, and they can compete with one another to develop a high tax base with low service delivery. These communities seldom act with their region in mind except for some transportation planning. As a result, development can be a hodgepodge.

What are the actual descriptions of sprawl? What are the environmental effects? How do sprawl controversies unfold? Below are some examples.

Washington, D.C.

The District of Columbia has steadily lost population since 1970. The outermost suburbs have experienced growth. Open space is being rapidly allocated to commercial and residential structures, roads, parking lots, and strip malls.

A 2009 study by the Texas Transportation Institute of Texas A&M University ranked Washington second, behind Los Angeles, for time stuck in traffic.

Cincinnati, Ohio

Although the number of people moving into the Cincinnati metro area has not risen significantly in recent years (7.22 percent between Census 2000 and the 2008 Census population estimate), its land area has spread out steadily over the years: from 335 square miles in 1970 to 512 square miles in 1990, a 53 percent increase. The area grew by another 12 percent between 1990 and 1996. The Texas Transportation Institute estimates that the average rush-hour traveler spent an extra 25 hours in his or her car in 2007 because of congestion.

Kansas City, Missouri

The metro area has also been influenced by an extensive regional freeway system planned in the 1940s and white flight. Kansas City has paved miles of roads, sidewalks, curbs and even streambeds. Kansas City has more freeway lane miles per capita than any other city in the country. The percentage of work trips made by people driving alone is 79.7 percent, above the national average of 73.2 percent. Public transit is poor, and public transit ridership per capita in Kansas City is one-third the average of most other cities the same size.

Seattle, Washington

The Seattle metropolitan region is moving southward along the coast and eastward, closer to the Cascades mountain range. The metropolitan area grew in population by 13 percent from 1990 to 1996, much of it in the outer suburbs. During the same period, population grew by only 1.6 percent in Seattle's center city. Seattle's four-year-old urban growth boundary has helped slow down some of the unplanned sprawl.

Minneapolis–St. Paul, Minnesota

Between 1982 and 1992, Minnesota lost 2.3 million acres of farmland to development. Hennepin County, where Minneapolis is located, lost the greatest proportion: 29 percent. The rate of open space destroyed by development increased by almost 25 percent in the Minneapolis–St. Paul metro area overall. The number of people moving to the city's surrounding areas increased 25 percent in the 1980s and another 16 percent in the early 1990s. Few urban areas have experienced a faster-growing traffic problem than Minneapolis/St. Paul. The average rush-hour driver burned 14 gallons of extra fuel in 1992; that rose to 27 gallons in 2007, according to the Texas Transportation Institute.

Sprawl is a development pattern that affects all sizes of cities. It can have the same effects and controversies as in large cities.

**The Five Most Sprawl-Threatened Medium-Size Cities
(population 500,000–1 million)**
Orlando, FL
Austin, TX
Las Vegas, NV
West Palm Beach, FL
Akron, OH

The Five Most Sprawl-Threatened Small Cities (population 200,000–500,000)
McAllen, TX
Raleigh, NC
Pensacola, FL
Daytona Beach, FL
Little Rock, AR

Alternatives to Sprawl

Hundreds of urban, suburban, and rural neighborhoods are using smart-growth solutions to address the problems caused by sprawl. Examples of smart-growth solutions include the following:

- More public transportation
- Planning pedestrian-friendly developments with transportation options; providing walking and bicycling facilities around services and parks
- Building more affordable housing close to transit and jobs
- Requiring greater public involvement in the transportation and land-use planning processes
- Requiring developers to pay impact fees to cover the costs of new roads, schools, and water and sewer lines and requiring environmental impact studies on new developments

Smart Growth

In response to sprawl, a movement to emphasize planning in land development exists under the name *smart growth*. Smart growth is development that serves the economy, the community, and the environment. It changes the terms of the development debate away from the traditional growth/no growth divide to "how and where new development should be accommodated." Underscoring the smart-growth movement is the premise of preserving open space, farmland, wild areas, and parks as necessary for a healthy environment and community. The question of how to stop sprawl is complicated, new in the United States, and controversial. Smart growth has garnered the support of some state legislatures. However, any loss of profit in the sale of private property because of the local land-use rules required by smart growth will encounter stiff resistance from powerful lobbies of realtors, home builders, mortgage bankers, and others with a financial interest in land.

Ecosystem Preservation

Given the current U.S. checkerboard pattern of many competing municipalities in any given metropolitan area, any shift toward ecosystem preservation will be extremely difficult, but many claim that it is necessary. The shift is prompted by the realization that ecosystems are the appropriate units of environmental analysis and management. Wildlife must be managed as a community of interrelated species; actions that affect one species affect others. The open-space plan emphasizes connections to off-site habitat and preservation of corridors rather than isolated patches. It helps to preserve patches of high-quality habitat, as large and circular as possible, feathered at the edges, and connected by wildlife corridors.

Patches preserved in an urbanizing landscape should be as large as possible. In general, the bigger the size of land, the more biodiversity of species it can accommodate. Patches of 15 to 75 acres can support many bird species, smaller mammals, and most reptiles and amphibians. Wildlife corridors should be preserved to serve as land bridges between habitat islands. Riparian strips along rivers and streams are the most valuable of all corridors, used by nearly 70 percent of all species.

When land is developed, a large volume of storm water that once seeped into the ground or nourished vegetation is deflected by rooftops, roads, parking lots, and other impervious surfaces; it ends up as runoff, picking up urban pollutants as it goes. This change in hydrology creates four related problems. Peak discharges, pollutant loads, and volumes of runoff leaving a site increase as compared with predevelopment levels. By reducing groundwater recharge, land development also reduces base flows in nearby rivers and streams.

To mitigate the adverse impacts of development, there are two options: storm water infiltration and storm water detention. With infiltration, storm water is retained on site in basins, trenches, or recharge beds under pavements, allowing it to infiltrate into the ground. With detention, storm water runoff is slowed via swales, ponds, or wetlands but ultimately discharged from the site. Experts are beginning to favor infiltration as the only complete approach to storm-water management.

Where soils and water table elevations permit, infiltration can maintain the water balance in a basin and runoff before and after development using infiltration trenches, swales, different dams, and/or permeable pavements. Infiltration rates can be increased by means of infiltration basins and vegetated swales, created prairies, created wetlands, and a storm water lake to reduce runoff volumes. The swales and prairie lands clean and infiltrate runoff, while the wetlands and lake mitigate the effects of the remaining discharge. Turf is used only where it serves a specific purpose, such as erosion control or recreation, rather than as fill-in material between other landscape elements. One visual preference survey found that lawns with up to 50 percent native groundcover are perceived as more attractive and less work (as well as much more natural) than are conventional turf lawns. Plants with similar irrigation requirements are grouped together into water-use zones (so-called hydrozones). Irrigation systems can then be tailored to different zones rather than operating uniformly. It is recommended that high-water-use zones (consisting of turfgrasses and plants that require supplemental watering year 'round) be limited to 50 percent of total landscaped area, and that drip or bubbler irrigation be used on trees, shrubs, and ornamentals. Even some of the most manicured developments are beginning to experiment with native plantings. One may expect to see more of the same as other developers discover that a palette of native and adapted plants is more economical and visually pleasing than is endless turfgrass.

The required environmental changes in our approaches to sprawl are severe in our current context. Many are nonetheless required. This assures that as they become more operational in education, business, and governmental practices they will also be controversial.

Conclusion

The land-use decisions made today could have the most important, long-term environmental consequences for future sustainability. Innovative thinking and foresight can facilitate the creation of green space in development plans and how urban communities can create green space from previously ignored areas. The vast majority of land is privately owned. As a result, individual landowners, developers, and local governments are the principal land-use decision makers. They do not always have the same vision and foresight regarding the environment if it affects their profit from the sale of the land.

U.S. metropolitan areas are spreading outward at unprecedented rates, causing alarm from Florida to California, from New Jersey to Washington State. Without changes in policy and practice, most new development will take the form of suburban sprawl, sprawl being this nation's now-dominant development pattern. The economic and social costs will be large. By designing with nature, developers can further the goals of habitat protection, storm water management, water conservation, and aquifer protection. Ways of furthering another environmental goal—air quality—can include natural amenities such as woodlands, hedgerows, slopes, rock outcroppings, and water bodies, which cost nothing in their pure state and are preferred by residents. Wild places (natural areas with nothing done to them at all) are a particular favorite with children. Greenbelts and other open spaces, if designed for physical and visual access, can enhance property values of nearby developable lands.

With increasing population and a strong, car-based transportation infrastructure, sprawl will continue. But strong environmental and public health values oppose the negative impacts of sprawl. With a long tradition of respecting private property but with a need more brass-tacks environmental policies, controversies will continue to develop.

See also **Aging Infrastructure; Air Pollution; Transportation and the Environment; Water Pollution; Sustainability (vol. 1)**

Further Reading

Flint, Anthony, *This Land: The Battle over Sprawl and the Future of America*. Baltimore: Johns Hopkins University Press, 2006.

Garreau, Joel, *Edge City: Life on the New Frontier*. New York: Random House, 1991.

Gonzales, George A., *Urban Sprawl, Global Warming, and the Empire of Capital*. Albany: State University of New York Press, 2009.

Hayden, Dolores, *A Field Guide to Sprawl*. New York: W. W. Norton, 2004.

Mitchell, John G. "The American Dream: Urban Sprawl." *National Geographic Magazine Online Extra* (July 2001). http://ngm.nationalgeographic.com/ngm/data/2001/07/01/html/ft_20010701.3.html

O' Toole, Randal. *A Libertarian View of Urban Sprawl*. Cato Institute. March 18, 2010. http://www.cato-at-liberty.org/2010/03/18/a-libertarian-view-of-urban-sprawl

Soule, David C. ed., *Remaking American Cities: A Reference Guide to Urban Sprawl*. Lincoln: University of Nebraska Press, 2007.

Wolch, Jennifer, Manual Pastor, and Peter Dreier, eds. *Up Against the Sprawl*. Minneapolis: University of Minnesota Press, 2004.

STEM CELL RESEARCH

Anne Kingsley

The stem cell debate is high-profile science and front-page news. In 1998 scientists at the University of Wisconsin were able to purify and successfully culture embryonic stem cells that could be used to replace or regrow human tissue. These rare cells, with the ability to differentiate into a variety of other specialized cells in our bodies, evoke both wonder and skepticism as they dominate headlines. On the one hand, they promise new therapeutic opportunities for the treatment of destructive and debilitating diseases, including Parkinson's and Alzheimer's. On the other hand, the research raises many questions about the ethical responsibilities and limitations of scientific practice.

The discussion surrounding the use of these cells involves scientific, medical, moral, and religious concerns. Political considerations also enter the debate as people turn to policy to define, structure, and regulate the use of embryonic stem cells. In turn, vast attention to the debate captures a wide audience and accelerates passionate rhetoric from all sides. Even Hollywood has jumped into the debate, and spokespersons such as Michael J. Fox and the late Christopher Reeve have fueled media attention. Perhaps the best way to approach the stem cell debate is first to untangle its notoriety.

CELL DIFFERENTIATION

Cell differentiation is the process through which a stem cell becomes a more specialized cell. Embryonic stem cells are especially unique in that they can become all types of cells. Scientists work to direct stem cell differentiation to create cell-based therapies for diseases. This new research proposes methods to develop differentiated stem cell lines for replacement cells that could potentially be administered for clinical use.

Conflicting Views

Among the many contemporary controversies in science and medicine, that regarding stem cells stands out as one of the most discussed and least understood. The research discussion ranges from science and sociology to theology. In all of these arenas, no single consensus has been reached on the use of embryonic stem cells. What exactly is at stake?

All sides in the debate make religious, moral, and ethical claims. Interestingly, in the terminology of the debate, it is *immoral* to destroy life in any form, and it is simultaneously *immoral* to deny scientific advancement that could potentially cure devastating diseases. In this situation, government policy becomes a regulating force.

The body is made up of many different cells. Each cell is programmed for a specific function—for example, to form part of our skin, liver, or blood. Stem cells, however, are unique in that they have the ability to give rise to many different types of cells. A bone cell and a brain cell are not the same, but they originate from differentiated stem cells. Potentially, these cells can be used to grow new tissue. If science can understand how to control these cells, they could be used to replace damaged cells or even grow new organs in a petri dish. Scientific progress is motivated by the possibility of these medical benefits. For example, damaged neurons in Alzheimer's patients could possibly be replenished by healthy neuron cells produced by using stem cells.

The most effective stem cell for growing tissue is the embryonic stem cell; for this reason, it is at the heart of the controversy. It is not the stem cell itself that is controversial; rather, it is the practice of isolating these cells that fuels debates. Some stem cells are obtained from the tissue of aborted fetuses. Most embryonic stem cells to date, however, are acquired from unused embryos developed from eggs that have been fertilized. In vitro fertilization (IVF) can cause multiple embryos to develop, but only some are actually used to create pregnancy. The leftover embryos are frozen and often remain unused in fertility clinics. Researchers use these "spare" embryos to generate stem cell lines, a process that involves the destruction of the embryo.

The use of embryonic stem cells motivates the most publicly known debate: Should we destroy human embryos for the sake of research? The "moral status" of the stem cell is frequently under discussion. For proponents of embryonic stem cell use, the embryo itself does not constitute a fully formed life because it has not developed in the womb.

Furthermore, even if it is defined as life, other advocates see it as a justified means to an end. The use of these embryos could result in more lives saved, which is, overall, considered beneficial. For opponents, the fertilized egg marks the process of conception and therefore the onset of life. Even the embryonic stage is seen as a form of consciousness. Although it might be easy to divide the debate between science and religion—and this is often done—there is actually no consensus and no easy division between those who advocate and those who oppose stem cell research. For example, there are many religious advocates *for* stem cell research.

The first major government regulation of embryonic stem cell research was announced in 2001. Under federal funding policy, only existing lines of embryonic stem cells can be used for scientific purposes if researchers wish to be eligible for federal funding in the United States. These stem cells must come from unused embryos created under IVF, and the donor must consent to their use. No new lines can be produced, and no new embryos can be used.

Although these are national policies, the question of regulation is an international concern. Ethical debates over the concept of human life take place in multinational venues. In countries such as Great Britain, Japan, Brazil, and Korea there is still much debate over the limitations and regulations of embryonic stem cell research programs. These laws, worldwide, will undergo constant transformation depending on scientific breakthroughs, public acceptance, and political motivations.

These political demands motivate some researchers to find different means of producing stem cells. New practices often create new controversies, however. Adult stem cells may provide an alternative source, although they too have issues of their own. For one, they are difficult to isolate in the body, whereas a large subset of the cells in the embryo are stem cells. Even once they are found, adult stem cells are difficult to control and produce. In addition, many of the adult stem cells generate only particular tissues, usually determined by where the cell originated in the body. Despite these hurdles, scientists continue to make advancements using these cells.

Other research labs are turning to cell nuclear replacement, the same process used in cloning, to produce embryos without fertilization. Through this development, the research labs seemingly bypass the ethical debate of where life begins by creating unfertilized embryos. Because it is aligned with cloning, however, many people have regarded this procedure with uncertainty. Articles in the journal *Bioethics* suggest that current laws against federal funding of human cloning preclude going down this slippery slope. These articles also acknowledge that public concern may not be so easily assuaged.

There is concern about the value of continuing stem cell research in the midst of these heated debates. What is certain is that researchers are motivated by the hope of producing scientific breakthroughs that could offer advances in the areas of research and medicine. Yet there is also concern over the line between principle and practice. How does research become effective and safe clinical practice? Will it? These questions

CELL NUCLEAR REPLACEMENT

Cell Nuclear Replacement in stem cell research involves removing the DNA of an unfertilized egg and replacing it with the DNA of a cell from the body of the patient. Scientists can then force the egg to develop and divide as though it has been fertilized. The stem cells formed in the new embryo will have an exact DNA match to the patient, therefore reducing the risk of rejection. The process of cell nuclear replacement is also the same process that was used to clone Dolly the sheep. Although the method may steer away from the debate about the destruction of life, it is right in the middle of the debate on human cloning. In that light, the technique has been referred to as "therapeutic cloning," thereby associating the research with the clinical use of stem cells to treat disease.

propose that potential benefits may remain only possibilities. One real issue facing the clinical use of embryonic stem cells is the body's acceptance of the replacement cells. If the patient's body does not recognize the cells, the organs produced may be rejected.

There is also growing discussion of the economics behind stem cell use. Certainly the production of stem cell lines, the production of patents for procedures, and the potential profit for accumulating embryos for research all pose ethical questions. Stem cell research is an emerging moneymaking industry. We can see the guiding hand of economic influence when we look to a stem cell–friendly state such as California. Although federal laws maintain certain restrictions, individual regions can use their state funds to promote and recruit scientists for stem cell research. State policies could potentially create a disparity in where active stem cell research takes place. Funding measures in California have made it a hotbed for stem cell research and, in turn, a promising venue for large economic profits. Disparate funding measures across the country raise concern about the real goals of stem cell research, as science and business intersect.

One question of particular concern to bioethicists in the stem cell debate is to whom the benefit will accrue. Many bioethicists believe in the very real possibility of society benefiting from embryonic stem cell research. They still maintain concern about who will have access to these therapies if they are produced, however. Celebrities and influential figures might be able to afford treatment, but there would be many who could not. In this light, stem cell research has the potential of reinforcing existing social divisions or creating new ones. Despite these social concerns, the possible benefits of stem cell use continue to push stem cell research forward.

State of the Research

Rensselaer Polytechnic Institute in May 2010 received $2.45 million from the New York Stem Cells Science Program of the Empire State Stem Cells Board to create a sophisticated, state-of-the-art lab for basic stem cell research. Growing the cells and learning how to control their differentiation is the goal. Researchers will attempt to guide the stem cell's development into specialized cell types used by the human body. This is the key scientific challenge of stem cell research today.

Conclusion

For many people, stem cells are the symbol of scientific innovation. They represent cutting-edge research at the frontiers of science. They also represent concern over the limits of science and the ability of science to determine the status of life. Perhaps most eye-opening, however, is the debate's representation of the intersecting lines of thought within scientific research. The stem cell controversy invites the languages of research, religion, ethics, and politics into one (as yet inconclusive) conversation.

See also **Biotechnology; Genetic Engineering**

Further Reading

Bellomo, Michael, *The Stem Cell Divide: The Facts, the Fiction, and the Fear Driving the Greatest Scientific, Political, and Religious Debate of Our Time.* New York: AMACOM, 2006.

Collins, Francis S., *The Language of Life: DNA and the Revolution in Personalized Medicine.* New York: Harper, 2010.

Fox, Cynthia, *Cell of Cells: The Global Race to Capture and Control the Stem Cell.* New York: Norton, 2007.

Holland, Suzanne, Karen Lebacqz, and Laurie Zoloth, eds., *The Human Embryonic Stem Cell Debate: Science, Ethics, and Public Policy.* Cambridge, MA: MIT Press, 2001.

Kass, Leon, "Ethical Issues in Stem Cell Research." In *Technology and Values: Essential Readings,* ed. C. Hanks. Malden, MA: Wiley-Blackwell, 2010.

Martialay, Mary, "$2.45 Million Grant To Support Stem Cell Research." *Medical News Today* (May 27, 2010). http://www.medicalnewstoday.com/articles/189976.php

Ruse, Michael, and Christopher A. Pynes, eds., *The Stem Cell Controversy: Debating the Issues,* 2d ed. New York: Prometheus Books, 2006.

Waters, Brent, and Ronald Cole-Turner, *God and Embryo.* Washington, DC: Georgetown University Press, 2003.

STOCK GRAZING AND THE ENVIRONMENT

Robert William Collin

The grazing of cattle, sheep, and goats provides food but also has environmental impacts. In some environments, stock grazing can be destructive. Stockmen use 70 percent of the U.S. West for raising livestock, and most of this land is owned by the public. Experts and environmental activists consider ranching to be the rural West's most harmful environmental influence.

Many animals naturally graze or eat plants such as grasses and leaves. Some animals and plants develop strong symbiotic relationships in the natural environment. Grazing animals in nature can fill important parts of the food chain in a given ecosystem. Many predators rely on them for food. Humans learned that raising your own animals was easier and more reliable than hunting them. Since early civilization, humans have grazed animals such as sheep, cattle, and goats. With the advent of large moving herds of the same grazing animal, environmental impacts increased, especially over time and in the context of increasing human population. Increasing population and expanding development reduce the amount of pastureland available and can increase the environmental impacts on the pastureland that is left. Increasing population also increases demand for food. The demand for meat and animal products drives the overall production of meat and the need for efficient industrial production processes. Part of these more efficient processes is producing the most meat per acre, which may have environmental impacts. Producing meat from pastures generally requires a minimum pasture size, depending on pasture quality and grazing animal.

Global Context

Not all pastureland is affected by large stock grazing systems. Approximately 60 percent of the world's pastureland is covered by grazing systems. This is just less than half the world's usable surface. The grazing land supports about 360 million cattle and over 600 million sheep and goats. Grazing lands supply about 9 percent of the world's production of beef and about 30 percent of the world's production of sheep and goat meat. For an estimated 200 million people, grazing livestock is the only source of livelihood. For many others, grazing animals provide the basis for a subsistence lifestyle and culture.

U.S. Context

Ranching is big business in the United States. Although it is concentrated in the western United States, other states have some ranching interests. (Hawaii, for instance, has one of the biggest ranches in the United States in the Parker Ranch on Hilo.) One issue is the use of federal land for grazing. The federal government is a large landowner is western ranching states. In the western United States, 80 percent of federal land and 70 percent of all land is used for livestock grazing. The federal government grants permits to ranchers for their herds to use federal lands. The mean amount of land allotted per western grazing permittee is 11,818 acres. Many ranchers own both private property and permits from the federal government for ranching public land. The public lands portion is usually many times larger than the private one.

Cattle and sheep have always comprised the vast majority of livestock on public land. Cattle consume about 96 percent of the estimated total grazed forage on public land in the United States. There are some small public lands ranchers, but corporate ranchers and large individual operators control the market now. This is also an issue because some say that ranchers are exploiting the land with the aid of the U.S. government. Many of the permits involve long-term leases at below-market rates. Forty percent of federal grazing is controlled by 3 percent of permittees. On the national scale, nearly 80 percent of all beef processing is controlled by only three agricultural conglomerates.

Environmental Challenges and Benefits

Stock grazing can damage the environment by overgrazing, soil degradation, water contamination, and deforestation. Seventy-three percent of the world's 4.5 billion hectares of pasture is moderately or severely degraded already. Livestock and their need for safe pastures is one reason for the cutting down of tropical rain forests.

Prolonged heavy grazing contributes to species extinction and the subsequent dominance by other plants, which may not be suitable for grazing. Other wild grazing animals are also affected by the loss of plant biodiversity. Such loss of plant and animal biodiversity can have severe environmental impacts. In sensitive environments, such as alpine and reclaimed desert environments, the impacts of overgrazing can be irreversible. Livestock overgrazing has ecological impacts on soil and water systems. Overgrazing causes soil compaction and erosion and can dramatically increase sensitivity to drought, landslides, and mudslides.

Actions to mitigate environmental impacts of overgrazing include preservation of riparian areas, place-sensitive grazing rotations, and excluding ranchers from public lands. Each one of these actions is controversial. Ranchers do not like being told by the government how to run their businesses and resist taking these steps because their implementation costs money. Excluding ranchers dramatically increases the intensity of the debate, but that is the preferred solution for many conservationists. The areas that benefit from these types of mitigation include the following:

- Grasslands, grassy woodlands, and forests on infertile, shallow, or skeletal soils
- Grassy woodlands and forests in which trees constrain grass biomass levels and prevent dominant grasses from outcompeting smaller herbs
- Other ecosystems on unproductive soils that occur among grassy ecosystems within managed areas

Conclusion

Given climate change, population growth, and the dependence of people on grazing animals, it is likely that this controversy will become more intense. In the United States, perceptions of a vested property right in U.S. land by ranchers, their families, and their communities clash with the reality that this is land held in trust for all citizens of the United States. As environmental restrictions on grazing on public and private lands challenge this perception, courts and federal agencies will be front-and-center issues in this controversy. As concern about endangered species and sustainability rises, so too will these issues enter this controversy.

See also **Climate Change; Endangered Species; Federal Environmental Land Use; Global Warming**

Further Reading

Davis, Charles E., *Western Public Lands and Environmental Politics.* Boulder, CO: Westview Press, 2000.

Robbins, William G., and William Cronon, *Landscapes of Conflict: The Oregon Story, 1940–2000.* Seattle: University of Washington Press, 2004.

Vaughn, Jacqueline, *Conflicts over Natural Resources: A Reference Handbook.* Santa Barbara, CA: ABC-CLIO, 2007.

SURVEILLANCE—TECHNOLOGICAL

Kathryn E. Scarborough, Pamela A. Collins, and Ryan K. Baggett

Surveillance, especially technological surveillance, has been and continues to be one of the most controversial of tactics being used by law enforcement authorities today. In the world after the attacks of September 11, 2001, we have been bombarded with new concerns of terrorism that have caused us to rethink our positions concerning what we will accept for safety and security in a seemingly more threatening world than we knew prior to 9/11. We have decided in some cases to allow practices that were once considered invasions of our privacy, as it is contended that they contribute immensely to our safety and security. In other cases, however, we have decided that while our safety and security are of the utmost importance, certain practices reach beyond the scope of what is acceptable and infringe upon our most basic guarantees granted by the various legal instruments that have survived the test of time.

Surveillance has been a popular tactic for police, security, and other public safety personnel for decades. Since the earliest forms of surveillance were utilized, which primarily relied on humans for their operations, both professionals and the public have supported the tactic of monitoring people, places, and things and gathering information in a variety of settings. As technology has advanced, so have the forms of surveillance. Beginning with Signals Intelligence (SIGINT) during World War I, technological surveillance has expanded into a virtual catalogue of equipment of varying levels of complexity for numerous uses.

Background

Technological Surveillance (TS) refers to technologies that are used for the sole purpose of identification, monitoring, tracking, and control of assets, individuals, and information. Although surveillance can also refer to simple, relatively no- or low-technology methods such as direct observation, it is used in this context to describe the various technological methods used for the purpose of recording information. The literal translation of the word *surveillance* (in French) is "watching over," and the term is often used to describe various forms of observation.

There are many views as to the application and effectiveness of TS, especially in a post-9/11 environment. For example, many often argue that in order to have greater safety and security, we must place a greater reliance on the use of TS. In other words, they accept the notion that there is a trade-off between privacy and enhanced security. Others believe that there does not necessarily have to be a trade-off or sacrifice between increased surveillance and security and individuals' civil liberties. Still others argue that these are actually the wrong questions to ask and serve more to cloud the real issue, which is how surveillance serves as a trade-off that promotes "spatial segregation and social inequality" (Monahan 2006).

A distinction must be made with regard to the specific type of technology being used. Based upon the works of both David Lyon (2006) in his article "Surveillance after September 11, 2001" and Kirstie Ball and Frank Webster (2003) in their text, *The Intensification of Surveillance,* technological surveillance can be categorized into four distinct typologies: categorical suspicion, categorical seduction, categorical care, and categorical exposure.

Categorical suspicion relates specifically to surveillance that focuses on the identification of threats to law and order by common criminals, organized crime, dissidents, and terrorists. Categorical seduction addresses the tactics used by marketers and their attempts to study and predict customer behavior in attempts to hone their advertising and methods for luring in customers. Categorical care surveillance is used primarily by the health and welfare services, for example, to manage health care records in an attempt to monitor "at-risk" groups, study geographic health trends, and collect and manage extensive records of clients. Finally, categorical exposure was coined to describe the development of the ever-increasing intrusive character of the media. This is best illustrated by the tabloid press and the antics of many in the media, such as those that contributed to the automobile crash and subsequent death of Diana, Princess of Wales.

Types of Technological Surveillance

There are numerous technologies used for surveillance applications, such as eavesdropping, wiretapping, closed circuit television, global positioning systems, computer surveillance, and radio frequency identification device (RFID) tracking. Eavesdropping refers to the process of gaining intelligence through the interception of communications. This interception can include audio, visual, and data signals from various electronic devices. Generally, eavesdropping consists of three principal elements: a pickup device, transmission link, and listening post. The pickup device, usually a microphone or video camera, picks up sound or video and converts them to electronic impulses. The transmission link can be a radio frequency transmission or wire that transmits the impulses to a listening post. Finally, a listening post is a secure area where the signals can be monitored, recorded, or retransmitted to another area for processing (Rao 1999).

Wiretapping is the monitoring of telephone and Internet conversations by a third party, often by covert means. *Lawful interception* refers to legalized wiretapping by law enforcement or other recognized governmental authorities. In 1994, the Communications Assistance for Law Enforcement Act (CALEA) was passed. This legislation gave law enforcement agencies the authority to place wiretaps on new digital wireless networks. CALEA also requires carriers to make their digital networks able to support law enforcement wiretapping activities (CALEA 2007). A covert listening device (commonly referred to as a "bug") is a combination of a miniature radio transmitter and a microphone. Bugs come in various shapes and sizes and can be used for numerous applications. While the original purpose of a bug was to relay sound, the miniaturization of technology has allowed modern bugs to carry television signals. Bugs can be as small as the buttons on a shirt, although these have limited power and operational life (Pinpoint Productions 2005).

Closed circuit television (CCTV) is a visual surveillance technology designed for monitoring a variety of environments and activities. CCTV systems typically involve a fixed (or "dedicated") communications link between cameras and monitors. The limits of CCTV are constantly extended. Originally installed to deter burglary, assault, and car theft, in practice most camera systems have been used to combat "antisocial behavior," including many such minor offenses as littering, urinating in public, traffic violations, obstruction, drunkenness, and evading meters in town parking lots (Davies 1996, 183).

A global positioning system (GPS) tracking unit determines the precise location of a vehicle, person, or other asset to which it is attached and has the ability to record the position of the asset at regular intervals. The recorded location data can be stored within the tracking unit, or it may be transmitted to a central location database, or Internet-connected computer. This allows the asset's location to be displayed against a map backdrop either in real time or when analyzing the track later, using customized software (Clothier 2004).

A bait car is a vehicle that has been equipped by a law enforcement agency with the intent of capturing car thieves. Special features may include bulletproof glass; automatic door locks; video cameras that record audio, time, and date; and the ability to disable the engine remotely. Some law enforcement agencies have credited bait-car programs with reducing auto thefts by more than 25 percent. Additionally, insurance companies have begun buying cars for police, because over a million automobiles are stolen each year in the United States (Eisler 2005).

Surveillance aircraft are used for monitoring activity from the sky. Although these aircraft play a major role in defense operations, they are also being used in the civilian world for applications such as mapping, traffic monitoring, and geological surveys. These aircraft have also been used by law enforcement for border surveillance to prevent

JAMES PATRICK BULGER

On February 12, 1993, James Patrick Bulger was abducted from a Merseyside (United Kingdom) shopping mall and subsequently murdered. James was a two-year-old toddler and his murderers were two 10-year-old boys, Jon Venables and Robert Thompson. As expected with a crime of this nature, the tragedy caused shock and grief throughout Liverpool and the surrounding towns. Additional attention was paid to this case because the abduction of the two-year-old from the mall was caught on closed-circuit television (CCTV). The fuzzy images from the abduction were replayed night after night on the national news. While CCTV had not managed to prevent the killing, the ghostly images at least held out the prospect that the culprits would be caught.* The two boys were arrested and sentenced to a minimum of 10 years in prison. Thompson and Venables were released in June 2001, after serving eight years (reduced for good behavior).

Due to the anxiety brought about by the Bulger tragedy, the number of surveillance systems in the United Kingdom dramatically increased. One example was a "City Challenge Competition" sponsored by the home secretary, who allocated government money to fund open street CCTV. The home office was overwhelmed by applications and ultimately increased both the amount of allocated funding as well as the number of cities that were funded.**

*D. Smith, *The Sleep of Reason: The James Bulger Case.* London: Century Arrow Books, 1994.

**C. Norris, M. McCahill, and D. Wood, "The Growth of CCTV: A Global Perspective on the International Diffusion of Video Surveillance in Publicly Accessible Space." *Surveillance and Society CCTV Special* 2, nos. 2/3 (2004): 110–135.

smuggling and illegal migration. Surveillance aircraft can be both manned or unmanned planes, such as the unmanned aerial vehicle (UAV). A UAV is a powered aerial vehicle sustained in flight by aerodynamic lift and guided without an on-board crew. It can fly autonomously or be piloted remotely (UAV RoadMap Meeting 2005).

Computer surveillance is the act of monitoring computer activity without the user's knowledge by accessing the computer itself. The majority of computers in the United States are equipped with network connections that allow access to data stored on the machine. Additionally, malicious software can be installed on the machine that provides information on the user's activity. One way to conduct computer surveillance is through packet sniffing, whereby data traffic is monitored coming into and out of a computer or network. Also, a keystroke logger can be implanted in the keyboard, perhaps broadcasting the keystroke sequence for pickup elsewhere. Finally, with the miniaturization of electronics, hidden cameras can be used to monitor keystrokes and display images (Bonsor, n.d.).

Radio frequency identification (RFID) tracking devices can be embedded in clothing or in devices or objects that are carried, such as building access badges. The RFID's capabilities set this technology apart from traditional identification devices such as bar codes. For example, RFID tags can be read at a longer distance, because this technology does not require a line of sight. Additionally, the technology is relatively invisible to others (Stapleton 2005).

Technological Surveillance Theories and Research over Time

Although surveillance as a topic for research and study has increased in popularity and interest in just the years following the events of 9/11, this is not a new area of study. What has changed are the advances in various technology systems and the scope and reach of technological surveillance (Webster and Robins 1986). Some of the early researchers that began to examine the implications of TS included Michel Foucault, who is best known for his book titled *Discipline and Punish*, published (in English) in 1979 and credited with being critical to the dialogue and debate surrounding electronic surveillance. Others that followed criticized Foucault and suggested that a greater analysis and understanding of contemporary electronic technology-dependent surveillance was needed (Zuboff 1988).

During this earlier period of debate there was a discussion of Foucault's panopticon (Foucaultian panopticon) and its application to the design and construction of prisons. He presented this approach as a model for understanding the operation of power in contemporary society (Foucault 1979). Foucault's work, along with the 17th-century writings of Jeremy Bentham on the panopticon (1995), resulted in the panopticon being considered the leading scholarly model or metaphor for analyzing surveillance.

Traditionally, panoptic surveillance related primarily to the monitoring of people rather than more general surveillance. For example, panoptic surveillance has not been used to describe other types of technological surveillance, such as environmental surveillance. Environmental surveillance involves the use of satellites and imaging, which now allows for very detailed analysis of both dramatic changes to the earth's surface following tsunamis as well as subtle changes that measure migration or water levels. Therefore it has been suggested that panoptic surveillance has not kept pace with the significant changes taking place in technological surveillance, such as the use of sensors, satellites, biometric devices, DNA analysis, chemical profiling, and nanotechnology, all of which have been described as tangentially panoptic. Another limitation of panoptic surveillance is that is does not account for the role or importance of the watchers. Nevertheless, this postpanoptic surveillance theory remains an important historical model for the early debate on surveillance and continues to be referred to in ongoing technological surveillance research studies (Haggerty 2006).

Another theory worth noting is the "space and time in surveillance theory," which suggests that there are "zones of indistinction" that unlike the postpanoptic surveillance theory, which was a distinct and bounded area, there is a shift from spaces of surveillance as territories to deterritorialization and time is seen not as an outcome of computerization or social sorting in "real time" (Bogard 2006). In other words, surveillance is important not in what it captures in real time but for its importance in "capturing" the future before it's "already over" (Genesko and Thompson 2006). For example, casinos use facial recognition software to identify known suspects who have been banned because of techniques used to "cheat the system."

Authors such as Elmer and Opel (2006) make the argument that we now live in a "survivor society" in which citizens are called upon to suspend disbelief, a preemptive requirement to act, a movement from "what if" scenarios to "what then" scenarios that accept that the U.S. administration has things well under control. They argue that using a "what then" approach, rather than a "what if" approach, presupposes an event will occur rather than the latter approach, which allows for the possibility of preventing an event from occurring at all. The "what then" approach removes all control from the citizenry and assumes that in spite of all of our best efforts we cannot prevent the inevitable, and therefore a higher authority must intervene that knows what is in the best interest of the society or organization. Space and time surveillance theorists argue that technological surveillance functions in an environment in which evidence is not needed to act or set national policy. The danger with this theory is that because the future is "deemed inevitable," instead of a forecasting model approach, we now rely on an approach that is not focused on tracking and monitoring behavior but that stymies social critique and political debate.

Moving from the theoretical studies and research to the more applied research and evaluation, studies reveal that there has been little work done to evaluate the overall effectiveness of many of the technological surveillance systems. We need only turn to the United Kingdom (UK) to look for research on the effectiveness and widespread use of CCTV systems. The tipping point, if you will, for the greatest expanse and proliferation of the use of CCTV in the UK, came after the 1993 James Bulger killing. In this case two 10-year-old boys kidnapped and killed two-year-old James Bulger. The shopping mall where James was kidnapped had CCTV in place and the two older boys were seen leading him by the hand out of the mall. At the time of this incident there was broad sweeping support for the proliferation of public surveillance, and since that time the UK now has one of the most extensive and high-density CCTV systems in the world. There are estimated to be nearly 4 million cameras throughout the UK, and approximately half a million of those cameras are located in London (Norris 2002).

In spite of the widespread use of CCTV in the UK, much of the research that has been done on the effectiveness of this type of technological surveillance system has been inconclusive. For example, a recent study on CCTV in the UK by the *Christian Science Monitor* suggests that after 10 years of research projects at a publicly funded expense of $420 million dollars, the research does not support the use of CCTV. Moreover, the study concluded that although cameras were effective in reducing vehicular crime, they had little to no effect on other crimes; in fact, street lighting appeared to be more effective in reducing other crimes (Rice-Oxley 2004).

Research on CCTV and other TS systems in the United States is not as prevalent because the use of CCTV is not as widespread, nor is it a public initiative. The private sector, the military, and the government primarily use CCTV in the United States In cases where it is used by public safety organizations, and more specifically law enforcement, there is little to no evaluation conducted to assess its effectiveness. The study that is most often cited as demonstrating that the use and application of CCTV was not effective in reducing crime was the study by Musheno, Levine, and Palumbo (1978) of low-income housing. They concluded that the use of video surveillance in New York City's public housing did not reduce crime or fear of crime. According to these authors, the system failed on two levels, conceptual deficiencies and technical limitations.

In a more recent study of a public housing complex in Buffalo, New York, researchers found that drug dealers were not deterred by the CCTV system in place but instead used the system to assist in the expansion of their operation by monitoring the arrival of customers and watching for local police (Herbeck 2004). Another recent study demonstrated benefits of a CCTV traffic light system in Washington, D.C., which reduced red light traffic violations by 63 percent. With the expansion of technological surveillance in the United States following 9/11, there will be greater opportunities to research and evaluate the many systems that are being put into place.

Conclusion

Knowing the theoretical underpinnings of any technology usually benefits the user and those taking advantage of the technology. Research helps consumers understand how the technology improves and in some cases is made more versatile for numerous situations. As we frantically searched for reactive tactics and procedures to allow us to improve the safety and security after 9/11, knowing the range of availability with respect to different types for different circumstances gave us some sense of solace as we struggled with living in our "new" world. Recognizing the evolution of technological surveillance and understanding that, with time, it will only continue to improve and reach beyond what we know now also gives us a sense of comfort as we wait for whatever challenges we may face. At the same time, however, we are reminded as to just how much intrusion we will or can allow in order to maintain those privileges that we so cherish as the basic foundations that make us Americans, in the land of the free and the home of the brave. Now we struggle with these issues while we anxiously await the next threat to our safety and security in our ever-changing world. Our immediate reactions to incidents tend to be radical, and once time passes, we take a step back and reconsider what is best to accomplish the goals of our public safety and law enforcement professionals. We expect to be saddled with decisions like this for the remainder of time. In retrospect, it is necessary, or better yet imperative, that we challenge ourselves with the wealth of information that we are afforded and make the best decision, for greater good, to maintain what makes us Americans in the nation we so highly value.

See also Airport and Aviation Security; Supply Chain Security and Terrorism (vol. 1); Border Fence (vol. 2)

Further Reading

Ball, Kirstie, and Frank Webster, eds., *The Intensification of Surveillance: Crime, Terrorism and Warfare in the Information Age.* Sterling, VA: Pluto Press, 2003.

Bentham, J., *The Panopticon Writing,* ed. M. Bozovic. London: Verso, 1995.

Bogard, W., "Surveillance Assemblages and Lines of Flight." In *Theorizing Surveillance: The Panopticon and Beyond,* ed. D. Lyon. Portland, OR: Willan, 2006.

Bonsor, K., "How Workplace Surveillance Works." n.d. http://computer.howstuffworks.comwork place-surveillance.htm

Clothier, J., *GPS Surveillance to Keep Kids Safe.* 2004. http://www.cnn.com

Communication Assistance to Law Enforcement Act, 2007. http://www.askcalea.net

Davies, S., *Big Brother: Britain's Web of Surveillance and the New Technological Order.* London: Pan Books, 1996.

Eisler, P., "High-Tech 'Bait Cars' Catch Unsuspecting Auto Thieves." *USA Today* (November 2005).

Elmer, G., and A. Opel, "Pre-Empting Panoptic Surveillance: Surviving the Inevitable War on Terror." In *Theorizing Surveillance: The Panopticon and Beyond,* ed. D. Lyon. Portland, OR: Willan, 2006.

Farren, Mick, and John Gibb, *Who's Watching You? The Truth about the State, Surveillance, and Personal Freedom.* New York: Disinformation Company, 2007.

Foucault, M., Discipline and Punish: The Birth of the Prison. New York: Vintage, 1979.

Genesko, G., and S. Thompson, "Tense Theory: The Temporalities of Surveillance." In Theorizing Surveillance: The Panopticon and Beyond, ed. D. Lyon. Portland, OR: Willan Publishing, 2006.

Haggerty, K. D., "Tear Down the Walls: On Demolishing the Panopticon." In Theorizing Surveillance: The Panopticon and Beyond, ed. D. Lyon. Portland, OR: Willan, 2006.

Herbeck, D., "Raids Target Drug Dealing in Housing Projects." Buffalo News (February 26, 2004).

Heymann, Philip B., and Julliette N. Kayyem, *Protecting Liberty in an Age of Terror.* Cambridge, MA: MIT Press, 2005.

Hier, Sean P., and Josh Greenberg, *Surveillance: Power, Problems, and Politics.* Vancouver: UBC Press, 2009.

Lyon, David, ed. *Theorizing Surveillance: The Panopticon and Beyond.* Portland, OR: Willan Publishing, 2006.

Monahan, Torin, *Surveillance and Security: Technological Politics and Power in Everyday Life.* New York: Routledge, 2006.

Monahan, Torin, *Surveillance in the Time of Insecurity.* New Brunswick, NJ: Rutgers University Press, 2010.

Musheno, M. C., J. P. Levine, and D. J. Palumbo, "Television Surveillance and Crime Prevention: Evaluating an Attempt to Create Defensible Space in Public Housing." *Social Science Quarterly* 58, no. 4 (1978): 647–656.

Norris, C., "From Personal to Digital: CCTV, the Panopticon and the Technological Mediation of Suspicion and Social Control." In *Surveillance and Social Sorting: Privacy Risk and Automated Discrimination,* ed. D. Lyon. London: Routledge, 2002.

Pinpoint Productions, Inc., "Bugs, Bugging and Covert Listening Devices." 2005. http://www.tscmvideo.com/Articles%20and%20Reports/bugs-listening-device.html

Rao, S., "Executive Secrets." *Forbes* (October 4, 1999).

Rice-Oxley, Mark, "Big Brother in Britain: Does More Surveillance Work?" *Christian Science Monitor* (February 6, 2004). http://www.csmonitor.com/2004/0206/p07s02-woeu.htm

Stapleton, R., "Researching RFID's Surveillance Potential." *RFID Journal* (July 28, 2005). http://www.rfidjournal.com/article/articleview/1765/1/1/

UAV RoadMap Meeting, 2005. http://www.defenselink.mil

Webster, F., and K. Robins, *Information Technology: A Luddite Analysis.* Norwood, NJ: Ablex, 1986.

Zuboff, S., *In the Age of the Smart Machine: The Future of Work and Power.* New York: Basic Books, 1988.

T

TRANSPORTATION AND THE ENVIRONMENT

ROBERT WILLIAM COLLIN

Transportation is a major contributor to air pollution, with motor vehicles accounting for a large share of nearly all the major pollutants found in the atmosphere. Trains, planes, trucks, and cars define the transportation system and have large environmental effects. As these effects become known and begin to accumulate in communities, many urban communities resist transportation enlargements such as roads.

The movement of people, goods, and materials requires large amounts of energy. Much of this energy is reliant on nonrenewable fuel reserves such as gas and oil. They also produce pollution that affects the land, air, and water. It is the issue of air pollution that creates some of the most intense controversy.

Bus and railway depots in urban areas can be sinks of polluted air. These sinks will increase as these facilities expand to meet transportation demands. Increased transportation demand is reflected in longer and bigger traffic jams and gridlock. These themselves increase the amount of emissions that spew into the surrounding air. Many urban communities are already overloaded with transportation modalities that tend to benefit those outside the city. The notorious electrified third rail of the New York City subway system poses a deadly hazard wherever it is exposed. That subway tends to run underground in wealthy areas and above ground in generally lower-income and diverse communities.

Many large cities east of the Mississippi have similar mass transit approaches. Mass transit has often left these communities more exposed to transportation hazards. Some maintain that rich and powerful white communities get better-designed roads with higher safety margins than poor, African American and Hispanic communities. As these emissions have accumulated, and these communities become environmentally self-empowered, the resistance to enlargements in transportation infrastructure is vigorous. Local political battlegrounds may include land-use hearings, environmental impact assessments, and the courts. For example, Portland, Oregon, would like to add a fifth lane to the four-lane interstate highway to accommodate commuters from the outlying, predominantly white suburbs. They want to add a lane in a Portland community that is lower income and very diverse and that already has large amounts of air pollution. These issues have been debated in a series of community and city meetings, with the city trying to persuade the community that the land expansion is important. The neighborhoods strongly resist and do not think anything could mitigate environmental effects enough to reduce the area's 14 percent asthma rate.

Another example is in Seattle, Washington. After years of controversy and public ballots, Seattle is building a better mass transit system. Because there are significant environmental effects, the U.S. Department of Transportation had to perform an environmental impact assessment. Early plans replicated the U.S. East Coast pattern of delivering infrastructural improvement based on the wealth and race of the community. Because the environmental impact assessment did not adequately address environmental justice effects, they had to do it all over again and make significant changes in the transit plan. The litigation and result held up about $47 million in federal aid until the environmental assessment was performed to a satisfactory level.

The environmental effects of mass transit and private transportation are well known. Both transportation types are increasing, and communities are increasing their resistance because of the environmental effects. There have been attempts to handle aspects of this problem with federal legislation. Although the Intermodal Surface Transportation Efficiency Act of 1991 strongly reinforced the Clean Air Act requirements through its planning requirements and flexible funding provisions, technical uncertainties, conflicting goals, cost-effectiveness concerns, and long-established behavioral patterns make achievement of air quality standards a tremendous controversy. Techniques of estimating (and forecasting) emissions from transportation sources in specific urban areas are still controversial and generally inaccurate at the individual level. The number of monitoring stations and sites remains low, which often forces the citizens to monitor the air themselves. The lack of monitoring sites is a key issue for most U.S. environmental policy. Most industry self-reports its environmental effects, and many industries are not even required to get any kind of permit. The more monitoring sites the more potential liability the corporation faces. Communities and environmentalists do not trust government and industry when monitoring is not allowed or is insufficient. This greatly inflames any controversy but particularly air pollution controversies around transportation's environmental effects.

Transportation activity contributes to a range of environmental problems that affect air, land, and water—with associated effects on human health and quality of life.

Noise

Noise is probably the most resented form of environmental impact. Despite the money devoted to noise abatement, these measures are still limited in their effects. Numerous studies have been conducted from economic points of view, but their findings can be seen as somewhat controversial. Environmental effects of noise can affect nesting sites for birds, migration pathways and corridors, and soil stability. Noise can also decrease property values.

Sprawl and Cars

U.S. cities are characterized by a separation of work and home, connected mainly by cars and some mass transit systems in denser urban and older suburban areas. The desire for a single-family detached home away from work, and increasingly away from other trips like shopping and school, requires large amounts of land and therefore has greater environmental effects. Cars and trucks on the road today are some of the heaviest contributors to poor air quality and global warming. Illnesses such as cancer, childhood asthma, and respiratory diseases have become increasingly linked to emissions from transportation. This problem is furthered by poorly designed transportation systems that contribute to sprawl, causing freeways to become more congested and polluted. Despite improvements in technology, the average fuel economy of vehicles is less than it was in the 1980s, which also means they generate more pollution. The expansion in the production of hybrid vehicles and technological improvements in conventional vehicles could raise the fuel efficiency of new vehicles to 40 miles per gallon within a decade and 55 miles per gallon by 2020 according the Natural Resources Defense Council, an environmental organization.

Freeways' Tainted Air Harms Children's Lungs

Southern California contains some of the dirtiest air in the United States. There are enormous traffic problems, large polluting industries, and a rapidly increasing population. The smog can extend for hundreds of miles out in the Pacific Ocean, and hundreds of miles inland to the majestic Sierra Mountains. The public health risks extend to wherever the smog accumulates. The regional air quality control boards have been the subject of intense debates. At one time all 15 scientists in the Los Angeles air basin quit, resigned, or were terminated because of the failure to set enforceable and strong clean air standards. The issue of air pollution harm is therefore a very intense controversy.

University of Southern California (USC) researchers found in January 2007 that children living near busy highways have significant impairments in the development of

CONTEXT SENSITIVE SOLUTIONS

Context Sensitive Solutions (CSS) is a forward-thinking notion aimed at solving environmental pollution problems associated with transportation. It is a policy-making process. The approach has four core principles applying to transportation processes, outcomes, and decision making. They are:

1. Strive toward a shared stakeholder vision to provide a basis for decisions.
2. Demonstrate a comprehensive understanding of contexts.
3. Foster continuing communication and collaboration to achieve consensus.
4. Exercise flexibility and creativity to shape effective transportation solutions while preserving and enhancing community and natural environments.

The Center for Transportation and Environment at North Carolina State University and the Federal Highway Administration (FHWA), part of the U.S. Department of Transportation, recently joined forces to stimulate dialog about the environment and transportation. They are using this innovative method to facilitate discussion and arrive at a solution.

It is the latest and hottest approach to a solution that is generating cutting-edge workshops, conference sessions, and new courses at universities throughout the United States. At the 2010 Transportation Research Board Environment and Energy Research Conference, more than 400 revolutionary transportation, environmental, and planning professionals met to investigate plans, process applications and delivery, and data/information management in an effort to minimize transportation effects on natural habitats, ecosystem and environmental quality.

The FHWA publishes case studies of projects resulting from the CSS national dialog at http://www.contextsensitivesolutions.org/content/newsletter/mar-2010/. Additional information is available at http://itre.ncsu.edu/cte/EEConference/index.asp Center for Transportation and the environment.

—*Debra Ann Schwartz*

their lungs. These impairments, or tears and scars in the lung tissue, can lead to respiratory problems for the rest of their lives. The 13-year study of more than 3,600 children in 12 central and southern California communities found that the damage from living within 500 yards of a freeway is about the same as that from living in communities with the highest pollution levels. For communities in high-pollution areas and living near highways there is a huge increase in risk of respiratory illness. The greatest human damage is in the airways of the lung and is normally associated with the fine particulate matter emitted by automobiles. The research is part of an ongoing study of the effects of air pollution on children's respiratory health. Previous study findings show that smog can slow lung growth, and highway proximity can increase the risk of children getting asthma.

Groups of fourth-grade students began the study, average age 10, in 1993 and 1996. The USC research team collected extensive information about each child's home, socio-economic status, and health. Once each year, the team visited the schools and measured the children's lungs. Results from the study in 2004 indicated that children in the communities with the highest average levels of pollution suffered the greatest long-term impairment of lung function. In the new study, children who lived within 500 yards of a freeway had a 3 percent deficit in the amount of air they could exhale and a 7 percent deficit in the rate at which it could be exhaled compared with children who lived at least 1,500 yards, or nearly a mile, from a freeway. The effect was statistically independent of the overall pollution in their community. The most severe impairment was in children living near freeways in the communities with the highest average pollution. According to the USC study, those children had an average 9 percent deficit in the amount of air they could expel from the lungs. Lung impairment was smaller among those who moved farther from the freeways.

Environmental Effects

Each major highway or other transportation project effects the environment in a variety of ways. The most immediate negative impact on the human environment is the destruction of existing homes and businesses. Longer-term effects include noise, air pollution, and potential loss of living quality. Wildlife and plants suffer from habitat destruction and various forms of pollution.

In addition, ecosystems suffer fragmentation; habitats and ecosystems that had worked together are divided. Migratory species may be separated into genetic islands, reducing future biodiversity and leading to local extinctions. Transportation projects may also necessitate the draining or contamination of wetlands, which are important for flood control and filtering and cleaning water. Current laws require that wetlands be reclaimed or created somewhere else. Critics claim these laws are poorly enforced and have many exemptions.

Conclusion

Transportation systems show little signs of abating in size and scale. Their environmental effects have serious public health consequences and implications for sustainability. The air emissions from these systems accumulate, and more communities are now knowledgeable about some of their effects. The environmental impact statements required by many of these projects are issues in their own right. Mass transit and low-impact transportation modalities (like bicycles) are not accommodated in the United States. The current lack of integrated environmental land-use planning in the United States also prevents the development of alternative modalities on the scale necessary to reduce environmental effects. The current healthy-community movement and policies do emphasize low-impact and healthy alternatives and the physical design necessary for people to engage in these activities safely, but all these are still theoretical.

HAWAII: PARADISE LOST?

Without public comment, transportation officials exempted the Hawaii Superferry from an environmental review required of projects that use federal government money and have significant environmental effects. This has generated enormous controversy among many stakeholder groups. In September 2007 the Kauai Surfers Association protested the first day of operation and successfully blocked the Superferry's physical progress.

The first ferry is a four-story, 900-passenger, 250-car catamaran built especially for Hawaii at a shipyard in Mobile, Alabama. The second is being built. The first Superferry is to make daily trips between Honolulu and the islands of Kauai and Maui with one-way fares of $42 per person and $55 per vehicle. The second ferry would add service to the Big Island. Currently, the only regular interisland travel is by air, with one-way fares ranging from $79 to more than $100.

Environmentalists resist the Superferry because of traffic congestion, collisions with humpback whales, the spread of invasive species, and strains on limited harbor space. A recent opinion by the state Environmental Council said the Department of Transportation erred when it granted the exemption for an environmental impact review. Superferry officials argue they have exceeded environmental requirements.

Two lawsuits calling for environmental evaluations, one before the Hawaii Supreme Court and another in Maui Circuit Court, are also pending. At issue is whether the Superferry would be exempt. The law states in relevant part as follows:

Section (b) of 11–200–8 . . . no exemption shall apply "when the cumulative impact of planned successive actions in the same place, over time, is significant, or when an action that is normally insignificant . . . may be significant in a particularly sensitive environment."

The DOT previously had found that successive actions relating to a proposed intraisland ferry (on Oahu) in the early 1980s did require preparation of an environmental impact statement, and thus there was a distinct inconsistency in their application of an exemption in the case of the Superferry. Both the cumulative and secondary effects evidenced through numerous resolutions of county officials in Maui, as well as the established sensitivity of the environment in which the Superferry will operate (conservation district, shoreline, endangered species, etc.) meet the explicit terms of §11–200–8(b).

The ultimate concern here lies in the avoidance of systematic environmental review. No amount of after-the-fact study or mitigation undertaken by the Superferry reverses the failure to abide by the intent of the law that there should be public disclosure and consideration of serious environmental concerns as part of a process that is concluded prior to approval of a major project. One of the three lawsuits filed, specifically challenging the exemption, is under appeal to the Hawaii Supreme Court.

Source: Hawaii Environmental Council, http://hawaii.gov/health/oeqc/envcouncil.html

Controversies about roadway development and expansion will continue as environmental controversies.

See also **Acid Rain; Aging Infrastructure; Automobile Energy Efficiencies; Climate Change; Environmental Impact Statements; Sprawl**

Further Reading

Environmental Stewardship and Transportation Infrastructure Project Reviews, Executive Order 13274. www.dot.gov/execorder/13274/eo13274/index.htm

Forman, Richard T. T., *Road Ecology: Science and Solutions.* Washington, DC: Island Press, 2002.

Kutz, Myer, ed., *Environmentally Conscious Transportation.* Hoboken, NJ: Wiley, 2008.

National Research Council Transportation Research Board, *Surface Transportation Environmental Research: A Long-Term Strategy.* Washington, DC: National Academies Press, 2002.

Pavel, Paloma, ed., *Breakthrough Communities: Sustainability and Justice in the Next American Metropolis.* Cambridge, MA: MIT Press, 2009.

Rietveld, Piet, and Roger R. Stough, *Barriers to Sustainable Transport: Institutions, Regulation and Sustainability.* New York: Spon Press, 2005.

Root, Amanda, *Delivering Sustainable Transport: A Social Science Perspective.* Boston: Pergamon, 2003.

Schäfer, Andreas, et al., *Transportation in a Climate-Constrained World.* Cambridge, MA: MIT Press, 2009.

Sherwood, Bryan, David Frederick Cutler, and John Andrew Burton, *Wildlife and Roads: The Ecological Impact.* Singapore: Imperial College Press, 2002.

Sightline Institute, Sprawl and Transportation: Research and Publications, www.sightline.org/research/sprawl/res_pubs

V

VACCINES

Karl F. Francis

Vaccination against disease has saved millions of lives, yet controversy about their efficacy continues. Researchers have claimed evidence of a link between vaccines and autism, fueled by studies of the effects of mercury poisoning. They also have speculated that increases in attention deficit/hyperactivity disorder may be associated with the high doses of mercury in vaccines for controlling influenza, for example. That is why a citizens movement developed to challenge the safety of vaccines in the 1990s.

Many people in the United States and in other countries take vaccination for granted. When vaccines work, no apparent misery is endured by the patient. Nothing noticeable happens—except that the person has no symptoms of illness of any kind. No polio. No smallpox. No measles. No scarlet fever. No plague. Millions of people have died from smallpox, diphtheria, mumps, and tetanus, for example. We think of vaccinating ourselves as a sign of progress, a triumph over epidemic diseases.

Yet the real or hypothetical side effects of viruses remain a medical contention. Some researchers and critics shake a finger at organisms that have adapted to antibiotics and rendered them ineffective and viruses that have evolved beyond current treatments (e.g., HIV infection). They blame vaccines for causing the disease strains to mutate and persist.

It has been suggested that the problem with human disease epidemics is related to the way we have organized our society economically and politically. The theory is that if society gives priority to accumulating land, resources, and wealth over public health concerns, this in turn creates problems for those who want to control pandemics. Even the political agendas of some governments play a role in the distribution of vaccines, as was illustrated in recent years in the controversy surrounding the human papillomavirus vaccine.

State of the Research

Scientists are beginning to think that vaccines would work better in protecting children from flu if they included both strains of influenza B instead of just one. Further, researchers are reporting that a novel vaccine strategy using viruslike particles (VLPs) could provide stronger and longer-lasting influenza vaccines with a significantly shorter development and production time than current ones, allowing public health authorities to react more quickly in the event of a potential pandemic.

The quest for a universal flu vaccine continues, but researchers at the Mt. Sinai School of Medicine in May 2010 reported new findings suggesting that the day is near when there will not be a need for seasonal flu shots. There will be one vaccine, and it will guard against all kinds of influenza. Current flu shots are strain-specific, making it necessary to adjust the vaccine each year. A patent application for the universal flu vaccine has been filed. (The new findings were reported in the inaugural issue of *mBio,* the first online, open-access journal published by the American Society for Microbiology.)

Germs and Toxins

There are two central concerns regarding vaccines. First, there is the problem of suspected contaminants or toxins that accompany the vaccines, and the safety of the vaccines themselves, as vaccines are often made from weakened, inactive, or "killed" viruses.

Second, there are concerns about the efficacy of vaccines: Do they actually threaten the appearance of germs? There is worry about emerging "superbacteria" and rapidly mutating viruses. In the wake of public anxieties regarding ongoing and emergent diseases (e.g., HIV, SARS, resistant strains of TB, and now avian, or bird, flu), one wonders if vaccination programs and public health systems in the United States and abroad are sufficient to meet a real pandemic—a disease moving around the globe affecting millions, maybe billions, of people and the animals they depend on. So it is interesting that some people see vaccines themselves as an emerging problem, whereas others see vaccines as a necessary solution to epidemic diseases. The concern remains that the vaccines, and treatment systems in general, may be inadequate given the natural evolution of microorganisms.

The two problems may be interrelated: those who are worried about government-enforced vaccination programs have some grounds for concern because governments themselves are caught up in contradictory demands from citizens in general on one hand and business concerns on the other.

Background

Historically speaking, epidemic diseases are not inevitable or natural events, such as earthquakes or hurricanes. The notion that collectively humans are in part responsible for what literally plagues them has been addressed in popular nonfiction. Jared Diamond, author of a popular book on the history of civilization, notes the central role disease plays in our history and how our societies have helped our diseases. For instance, there is his discussion of our relationship with domestic animals, including pets. Infectious diseases picked up from pets and other animals are usually small nuisances. But some have developed into major killers—smallpox, TB, malaria, the plague, cholera, and measles, to name just a few.

Many of the diseases that have plagued us began early in the agricultural revolution thousands of years ago. Pests such as mosquitoes—which transmit malaria, anthrax, and foot-and-mouth disease—are among the important examples. Such pests are attracted by us and large groups of animals in close captivity.

The maintenance of a stable society over time, involving hundreds or thousands of people, has often required people to own property, tools, and animals and later other people. So-called crowd diseases that would not have gotten a foothold in hunter-gatherer societies flourished in the increasingly large and dense populations of humans and their domesticated animals. Life spans actually decreased as humans transitioned to agricultural communities, where they were subjected to such new maladies as measles, smallpox, TB from cattle, flu and pertussis from pigs, as well as plague and cholera.

The history of vaccines is indicated in part by the very term. *Vaccine* is derived from *vaccinus,* a Latin word meaning "of or from cows." The English naturalist Edward Jenner, hearing that milkmaids working with cows reportedly were less likely to contract smallpox, eventually developed a theory that exposure to the less virulent cowpox conferred some type of resistance to the often lethal human disease. He used variolation, a procedure whereby some pus or lymph from a pox lesion was introduced into a cut made by a lancet, quill, or other sharp object. He inoculated first a child and then others, including his family, with viral particles of cowpox. His theories may have been flawed, but it is interesting that although cowpox and later smallpox inoculations using this method were effective, there were often terrible side effects similar to the disease itself, and occasionally deaths occurred. It is also noteworthy that there was no informed consent. Seldom were people told what could happen or what the risks were. When an epidemic was threatening Boston, Reverend Cotton Mather was eager to introduce variolation to the colonies. This was met with considerable resistance, and those gentlemen heads of households who were persuaded to try the procedure tended to use it on the slaves, women, and children of the household first. It was often the case that women, children, slaves, and servants were the original test subjects. Perhaps this was one historic origin of the controversies over vaccine safety and the distrust of manufacturers and eventually government health programs in the United States.

Case Studies and Lawsuits

The history of vaccines has many dark pages—for example, the U.S. government's rush to inoculate the U.S. population against swine flu in the 1980s and the famous Cutter debacle that introduced a toxic vaccine responsible for thousands of lost lives due to an improperly prepared polio vaccine. (The latter incident was, not surprisingly, responsible for increasing public suspicion of vaccines.)

Although, in the wake of the swine flu vaccine program, the swine flu of the 1980s never became a pandemic, reports began to emerge in late November 1976 of a paralyzing neurological illness. This condition, called Guillain-Barré syndrome, was connected to an immune response to egg proteins in the swine flu vaccine. According to historical accounts, federal courts had 4,000 injury claims. It is not known how many injuries were due to vaccination, but the government had to pay out around $100 million.

Given the history of vaccines, it may not be surprising that there have been responses such as the vaccine safety movement in the United States. Arthur Allen, a self-described vaccine advocate, reports the accidents, debacles, and incompetencies that have haunted the history of vaccination. The swine flu incident during the presidency of Gerald Ford came at a time not only of questioning and distrust of the government—in the wake of Vietnam protests and the Watergate scandal, among other important events—but also of a more general distrust of science. In his book, Allen describes the forming of a movement of citizens resisting vaccination, especially compulsory vaccination. In particular, there was resistance to the diphtheria/tetanus/pertussis (DTP) vaccination given in a series of shots to infants. The vaccine does have side effects, especially stemming from the manufacture of the pertussis, or "whooping cough," vaccine. Side effects have been mild to severe in some infants. The release of the television documentary *DPT: Vaccine Roulette* in 1982 provoked a grassroots movement of opponents to compulsory vaccinations.

In a report covering a winning lawsuit against a vaccine manufacturer, a spokesperson for the Centers for Disease Control (CDC) had to publicly attempt to stem fears that the vaccine was related to (or a cause of) autism. (The evidence remains far less conclusive than supporters of the vaccination theory would like it to be.) Sociologist Barry Glassner criticizes the American media and other organizations for helping to create what he calls "metaphoric illness"—maladies that people can focus on instead of facing larger, more pressing issues. For instance, we have given much attention to Gulf War syndrome, rather than looking at the reasons for the Gulf War and its consequences. A focus on DTP (also referred to as DPT) deflects the public's attention from larger concerns, perhaps about the credibility of government itself. The DTP vaccine does have some side effects, however, and a newer version is now being used. Glassner points to a similar scare in Japan, and whooping cough, once responsible for the deaths of thousands of infants, may be making a comeback in Japan and the United States. As noted previously, there is more than metaphoric illness going on, whatever fears safety-movement opportunists may be amplifying. The history of vaccination reveals that there are relevant concerns, issues, and problems on both sides of the vaccine debate.

Improperly prepared or contaminated vaccines have resulted in sickness and death. Many vaccines comprise weakened or neutralized germs. One method of making them is to grow microbes in chicken eggs. People allergic to egg products are warned about using vaccines before their annual flu shots. Concerns about some vaccines causing disorders such autism, as noted, have led to an increased resistance.

Yet anyone who reads firsthand accounts of smallpox epidemics, the current ravages of HIV, or the limited attacks of bird flu will probably want to receive the latest vaccination, even if there are specific risk factors. Other issues have been raised, however, about the overall impact on society of vaccine use. For instance, there is the recent controversy about inoculating under-age women against the strains of human papillomavirus that are linked to cervical cancer. This cancer causes the deaths of thousands of women each year in the United States and the United Kingdom. Because the virus can be sexually transmitted, some critics believe that vaccinating young people may be sending the message that it is acceptable to have sex while legally a minor or to have sex outside of marriage. It remains to be seen whether the use of such vaccines will contribute to an increase in sexual activity in any age group. Whatever our thoughts on this debate, it is easy to see that vaccination involves ethical as well as medical concerns.

Why Vaccinate?

The point of vaccination programs is to prevent sickness and death. What various debates on safety and toxicity overlook (or even obscure) is the social arrangements that often promote epidemics and pandemics. For example, the concern over avian flu has probably spurred historical research into past pandemics and our collective reactions. Further, researchers want to know to what extent human action contributes to pandemics. Would we have had the great flu pandemic that followed the World War I (1914–1918) if we had not had the war to begin with? There are good reasons to think that social and economic organization are causative factors in pandemics and our inability to overcome them. A parallel can be found in treatment responses. Antibiotics were once thought to be a road to the ultimate triumph over bacterial infections. Yet the way they are produced and distributed, combined with the evolution of bacteria, have produced bacteria with resistance to these drugs. In effect, the medical and economic organization of treatment has helped to produce "superbugs" that are far more lethal than their genetic ancestors.

Many people are worried that the influenza strain H5N1, or "bird flu," will become a pandemic. So far, this flu has been largely contained, although whole populations of pigs and chickens have been eliminated in the effort to contain it. One would think that because treatment for this flu is limited in supply and because it is so potentially lethal, those countries that have outbreaks would do everything possible to contain the disease.

The flu may not appear as such initially, and the countries involved may have insufficient supplies and treatment facilities.

These factors, combined with the increasing demand for chicken and pork, allow for increased exposure between wild fowl and domestic chickens and ducks on one hand (a viral reservoir) and agricultural workers and farm animals on the other. This, in turn, creates the conditions for new strains to develop, including strains that can spread from human to human. If this happens and a pandemic occurs, it will no longer be a "bird flu" except in origin. It will then be a human influenza that can mutate further into something similar to the flu that killed millions worldwide after 1918.

Social influences are also reflected in the fact that drug companies dislike flu vaccines because they are hard to produce, are seasonal, and are subject to variable demand. The production process has changed little over the last half century (since Francis and Salk), and although the newer, safer cell-culture technology would eliminate the contamination risk associated with using fertile chicken eggs, drug companies have not upgraded to this process.

Although numerous observers have pointed to the economic problems associated with pandemics—some blaming "corporate capitalism," others more general economic problems—Tamiflu, or oseltamivir, the one effective treatment for avian flu, is in short supply in the United States. Only two corporations in the United States were making flu vaccine in early 2004, in comparison with the 37 companies making vaccines in 1976.

The 1968 "mild" influenza pandemic killed approximately 34,000 people in the United States. An HN1 (bird flu) pandemic today would very likely kill many more. Sooner or later, an influenza pandemic will happen, but the timing is open to speculation. Given that, why would supposedly advanced societies not prepare for a pandemic with a more powerful virus?

Even a relatively mild pandemic would pressure the United States health care system to the point of collapse. Far fewer hospital beds are available per capita today than in 1968. Shortages of key items, such as mechanical respirators and stores of antibiotics for secondary infections, would quickly develop. Cutting costs is usually a way to save money and bolster profits for investors, or a response to decreased funding from state and federal sources. Responses to cost-cutting efficiency occur on the level of individual practitioners and group practice as well, in great part because of a managed care system that supplies reimbursements and referrals. (The lymphocytic choriomeningitis virus in a pregnant woman, for example, can cause hydrocephalus in her infant. Very little is known about the prevalence of this virus, but running diagnostics for it can raise a doctor's "cost profile" and cause his or her professional ranking as determined by insurance organizations to drop.)

Philosophical Perspective

One other issue about vaccines is philosophical, involving our understanding of the nature of disease and our attitudes toward it. The history of vaccination, along with the history of responses to pathogenic organisms that led to the development and use of antibiotics, involves the presupposition that disease is bad and that health involves the avoidance or prevention of disease. As we learn more about the immune system, the socially constructed character of such a conclusion is called into question. Although no one is going to argue that smallpox is a good thing, the "kill the enemy" metaphor in response to pathogens of all types and sorts rests on very weak foundations. A much more effective and useful understanding comes out of viewing the immune system as one would a system of muscles; properly built up and maintained, the immune system can handle the environmental pathogens that people encounter unknowingly every day. Vaccines then can have a role in building up immunological "strength" as long as they do not overstress the system and cause it to break down.

Vaccination for all diseases and reasons, however, reflects economic and social reasoning rather than a medical or scientific indication. A crucial example of this problem is the use of a vaccination for the varicella zoster virus, or chickenpox. Very few children—at least with healthy immune systems—who contract chickenpox have symptoms serious enough to require hospitalization as long as the disease is contracted early in childhood. If exposure to chickenpox is deferred to the late teens or early twenties, the chances of serious infection, hospitalization, or even death among patients skyrockets. The disease is endemic worldwide; thought to be one of the oldest human diseases, it recurs in older people as the painful, though again not usually deadly, condition called shingles (herpes zoster). Vaccination for chickenpox has been promoted for two reasons: (1) to protect our children from disease (the philosophical rationale) and (2) because of the financial implications of parents or caregivers having to take several days off from work so as to care for their sick children. Nowhere in this equation is the danger acknowledged of a vaccination that has an indeterminate effectiveness over time; perhaps we are merely extending the inevitable infection until a later point in adolescence or young adulthood when the benign childhood disease becomes serious or lethal. (Although losing a couple of days of work is irritating, most parents of young children would likely prefer this to the alternative of having a very sick—or dead—teenager.) The public pressure for the new vaccine, however, particularly when marketing focuses on the philosophical rationale of protecting children from disease, is enormous, and the vaccine manufacturers, naturally, have a vested economic interest in promoting such a rationale.

Conclusion

Given the history of vaccines—the experimentation on vulnerable people without informed consent, the problems with their manufacture and distribution, and the rapid evolution of new strains that our economic activity may be assisting—skepticism about vaccination will continue, especially in times where cost cutting and poor production override concerns for safety or when corporate economics, rather than public health, drive the research and manufacturing of new vaccines.

Skepticism may also continue in the social response to metaphoric illnesses. Metaphoric illness is a way of dealing with social problems that people are unable or unwilling to face head on, perhaps because of the apocalyptic visions of superbugs that no vaccine or health policy can address. Vaccines involve governments making policy about public health and how to intervene directly in the lives—and bodies—of individuals. The intervention of vaccination occurs across a lifetime, involving knowledge and expertise that most people do not have; that is, they do not understand the history, production, and distribution of vaccines, nor do they have medical professional expertise to administer them. Vaccination encompasses a large system of health care, which has become an industry run by remote corporations and technicians with esoteric knowledge. Vaccination is an intervention in the patient's body by this system; it symbolizes a host of interventions beyond the control and understanding of most people. Failure to address the metaphoric dimensions of anxieties about vaccines, fueled by the inevitable side effects and mistakes of any widespread medical undertaking, fosters a public anxiety that may have little foundation in medical science but is nonetheless influential.

See also **Cancer; Epidemics and Pandemics; Influenza**

Further Reading

Allen, Arthur, *Vaccine: The Controversial Story of Medicine's Greatest Lifesaver.* New York: Norton, 2007.

Barry, John M., *The Great Influenza: The Story of the Deadliest Pandemic in History.* New York: Penguin Books, 2004.

Colgrove, James, *State of Immunity: The Politics of Vaccination in Twentieth-Century America.* Berkeley: University of California Press, 2006.

Glassner, Barry, *The Culture of Fear: Why Americans Are Afraid of the Wrong Things.* New York: Basic Books, 1999

Levy, Elinor, and Mark Fischetti, *The New Killer Diseases: How the Alarming Evolution of Germs Threatens Us All.* New York: Three Rivers Press, 2004.

Maugh, Thomas H., and Andrew Zajek, "'Vaccines Court' Rejects Mercury-Autism Link in Three Cases." *Los Angeles Times* (March 13, 2010). http://articles.latimes.com/2010/mar/13/science/la-sci-autism13–2010mar13

Peters, C. J., and Mark Olshaker, *Virus Hunter: Thirty Years of Battling Hot Viruses around the World.* New York: Anchor Books, 1997.

Pringle, Evelyn, Autism, ADD, ADHD—Vaccine Related. Independent Media TV. June 27, 2007. http://www.autism99.org/articles/Autism_ADD_ADHD__Vaccine_Related.htm

Steel, John, et al., "An Influenza Virus Vaccine Based on the Conserved Hemagglutinin Stalk Domain." *mBio* 1 (May 18, 2010). http://mbio.asm.org/content/1/1/e00018-10.full

VOTING TECHNOLOGIES

Ruth Ann Strickland

Controversy over voting technologies in U.S. politics came about in the 2000 presidential election. The inability to obtain a reliable vote count in Florida in the close presidential contest between Al Gore and George W. Bush triggered electoral reform, with a particular focus on election voting machinery. The 2000 presidential election illustrated to all the vulnerability of U.S. voting systems and how voting machines could play havoc with voter intent and electoral results. States today use five different voting technologies, and some jurisdictions employ more than one type. Because of heightened awareness and increased media attention to voting problems, choosing among these various voting technologies has become problematic and controversial.

A Range of Choices

State governments, being primarily responsible for election administration, have used a variety of balloting procedures and voting hardware, including oral voting, paper ballots, mechanical lever machines, punch-card systems, mark-sense or optical scanning ballots, and electronic systems. One of the least complex systems—the hand-counted ballot—was the first voting mechanism used. Hand-counted ballots allow voters to mark boxes next to the preferred candidates' names. Even more simplistic, in the late 1700s and early 1800s, southern male voters would go before a judge and, when their names were called, would publicly state which candidates they supported. Because of voter coercion and intimidation, the secret paper ballot was introduced and became the primary voting device (Alvarez and Hall 2008, 15). Given the time-intensive nature of hand-counting paper ballots, the use of paper ballots has greatly declined. Paper ballots are used primarily in less populous counties; nationwide, the number of voters using them has been reduced from 2 million in the year 2000 to 300,000 (or 0.2 percent) in 2006 (Percy 2009, 2).

Mechanical Lever Systems

The mechanical lever machine, invented in 1892, was adopted by states to obtain quicker and more reliable election results. In using this machine, voters indicate their voting decisions by pulling a lever near a candidate's name. The levers, connected to counting wheels, maintain a running tally of the votes cast for each candidate. Election officials obtain vote totals by reading the number of votes recorded by the counting device. Devised to alleviate problems associated with paper ballots, mechanical lever machines were also vulnerable to fraud and corruption. For example, election administrators with access to the storage devices could manipulate stored vote totals at any time during the election cycle. Mechanical lever machines make it difficult for the disabled to vote because, being large machines (comparable in size to a refrigerator), they can be hard to access by those with physical handicaps or those who are visually impaired. Also, lever devices are not easily adapted to provide ballots in multiple languages (Alvarez and Hall 2008, 16). By 1998, only about 15 percent of counties still used mechanical lever machines, affecting about 18 percent of the voting population. In 2006, mechanical voting systems were used in just 62 counties and covered less than 7 percent of the nation's voting-age population (Knack and Kropf 2002).

Punch-Card Systems

In the 1960s, punch-card voting machines emerged. They were cheaper and allowed election officials to purchase more machines to accommodate larger precincts. Punch-card systems employ two types of ballots. The simpler ballot design—Datavote—allows voters to punch a hole on a card beside the candidate's name using a punching tool with a metal shaft. The second type—Votomatic—provides the candidate's name in a booklet attached to a mechanical holder under which voters insert a prescored punch card. Each hole on the punch card has a corresponding number. Voters punch a hole corresponding to the number of the candidate they wish to support. With a stylus or other device, voters punch holes at the appropriate spots on the card, forcing out the marked areas (also known as "chads"). In 1998 about 20 percent of counties, comprising 35 percent of the population, used punch-card technology. Following the 2000 election, in which this technology became an issue, the use of punch cards rapidly declined, and by 2006 only 13 counties used punch-card systems, affecting less than 0.5 percent of voters (Saltman 2006, 7–13).

In Florida, during the 2000 presidential election, use of punch-card voting systems led to undervoting (failure to vote in a race that the voter was eligible to vote in) and overvoting (or voting more times than permitted). Votomatic systems in particular were subject to alignment failures and malicious tampering with instructions. Also, voters with visual impairments found it hard to see the ballot with the punch card, and those with physical impairments found it difficult to use the stylus to mark their ballots (Alvarez and Hall 2008, 18). In 2000, punch-card voting systems, compared to optical scan, paper ballot, and machine lever ballots, had the highest rejection rate in Florida. In a study of rejected ballots in that state, approximately 4 percent of punch-card ballots were rejected. In such a situation, when different voting systems are used, voters in one jurisdiction do not have the same chance that their votes will be counted as do voters who live in another jurisdiction—effectively denying some voters the right to vote (Percy 2009, 7). An additional limitation to punch-card voting is that this type of equipment may influence the racial gap in proportion to voided ballots. African Americans cast invalid ballots more frequently than whites. Voting records from Louisiana and South Carolina, the only states to report voter turnout by race, indicate that punch-card voting systems produce a wider gap in frequency of voided ballots between blacks and whites than do mechanical lever and electronic machines. These findings have given jurisdictions further incentive to upgrade their voting systems (Tomz and Houweiling 2003, 58–60; Buchler et al. 2004, 523).

Optical Scan Ballots

Marksense, or optical scan, ballots were introduced in the 1980s for computing election results, but the technology had been around for decades, as these machines were frequently used to grade standardized examinations. Similar to paper ballots, marksense ballots require voters to use a black marker to fill in a circle or box beside the names of preferred candidates. A scanning machine reads the dark marks on ballots and records the results. Although similar to a paper ballot, a marksense ballot is larger, allowing jurisdictions to provide information about candidates directly on the ballot rather than in a separate booklet. Two types of optical scanners in use are precinct-count optical scanning and central-count marksense equipment. Precinct-count optical scanning equipment allows voters to feed ballots directly into a reader, which can be programmed to return the ballot to the voter if the voter has mistakenly selected more than one candidate for the same office (Saltman 2006, 13). With central-count marksense equipment, on the other hand, voters drop ballots into a box, and election officials then feed the ballots into the counting machine. With this system, voters do not have an opportunity to correct faulty ballots. Increasing in popularity in the 1990s, the technology reached peak use in 2006, with 56 percent of all counties and almost 50 percent of the nation's voting-age population embracing optical scan equipment (Utter and Strickland 2008, 46).

Like punch-card technology, optical scan ballots require voters to mark their choices on paper, and the paper is then scanned by an electronic device. Likewise, optical scanning voting systems face similar problems to those of punch-card voting. Voters are prone to undervote or overvote and may make mistakes with write-in candidates or find some other way to deface or spoil the ballot. Precinct-count machines can reduce these errors. Still, disabled voters may find it difficult to use optical scan technology if they have a handicap that makes using a pen or marking device unworkable. Voting with assistance raises concerns about coercion and fraud, because those who provide the assistance could potentially record preferences that do not match those of the actual voter. Because optical scan voting systems require that information specific to each precinct be printed on ballots to reflect all the possible choices voters would face and that the paper used be of high quality, it is hard to implement these systems in large, complex election jurisdictions. The increased complexity of printing these types of ballots across a large jurisdiction—which may require multiple formats and possibly multiple languages—raises the costs of using this technology. Because the technology is paper-based, some argue that this establishes a voter-verified paper trail and a means for recounting ballots for accuracy. However, the 2000 election demonstrated that having a marked ballot and interpreting voter intent are two different things. Voters may mark their ballots in ways that make their intent indiscernible, leading to delay in obtaining election results or no change in the recount of the vote (Alvarez and Hall 2008, 22).

Electronic Systems

Based on the microprocessor technology that emerged in the 1970s, electronic voting machines or direct recording electronic (DRE) devices allow voters to use touch-screen technology to vote. A ballot, displayed on an electronic device, displays vote choices. Then voters push buttons or touch spots on the surface of a computer screen to indicate their vote choices. Voters may write in a candidate, using the keyboard to type the name. Some DRE machines count votes as soon as they are cast, while others record ballot images that compute vote totals when the polling stations close (Jones 2001). Voter preferences are stored electronically, and if the machine is programmed correctly, voters have no chance to overvote. DRE systems can be programmed to display ballots in any language to accommodate minority voters for whom English is a second language. These systems can be designed to aid the disabled, granting improved access. Compared to punch-card and lever machines, DRE systems can reduce voter rolloff—the failure to indicate a vote choice for all offices and measures on a ballot—by up to 26 percent in judicial elections (Fischer 2001). In 2006, about 38.4 percent of voters (or 65.9 million voters) used DRE voting systems (Percy 2009, 8).

This type of technology has also generated its share of controversy. After the 2000 elections, manufacturers of DRE machines lobbied states to purchase their technology as a panacea for all their voting system problems. In conjunction with this, Congress passed the Help America Vote Act (HAVA), which gave states incentives to replace their punch-card and lever machines. In their rush to get the HAVA monies, many state governments did not engage in comprehensive evaluations of the DRE machines. If they had done so, they would have found various security and reliability problems. Critics argue that under DRE voting technology, only a very small number of individuals can inspect and verify the machines' correct operation. Thus the integrity of a jurisdiction's voting system rests with very few people. Some believe that the machines are subject to manipulation and error and that even the machines that print out a complete record of the votes cast can be trusted only to the extent that the software is transcribed in a valid fashion (Percy 2009, 8–9). The Caltech/MIT Voting Technology Project expresses numerous concerns including the following: (1) no longer being able to "see" the vote count (no auditable trail), (2) the inability of numerous people to examine the various stages of the voting process, (3) the vesting of authority in electronic machine manufacturers with little federal oversight on the technology, (4) companies that produce the machines can program them to record and count votes according to their partisan political interests, and (5) failures in the DRE machines that have led to lost votes and altered election outcomes (Alvarez and Hall 2008, 35).

Conclusion

As of 2009, about 89 percent of localities across the United States used either optical scan paper ballots or an electronic system. Less than 7 percent of election jurisdictions used lever machines and paper ballots. With almost $1.26 billion spent through HAVA to replace other voting technologies such as punch-card, mechanical lever, and paper ballots (Wolf 2008), clearly a possibly irreversible shift has occurred in the use of voting technologies in the United States.

See also **Election Campaign Finance (vol. 1)**

Further Reading

Alvarez, R. Michael, and Thad E. Hall, *Electronic Elections: The Perils and Promises of Digital Democracy.* Princeton, NJ: Princeton University Press, 2008.

Buchler, Justin, Matthew Jarvis, and John E. McNutty, "Punch Card Technology and the Racial Gap in Residual Votes." *Perspectives on Politics* 2 (September 2004): 517–524.

Fischer, Eric A., "RL 30733: Voting Technology in the United States: Overview and Issues for Congress." Congressional Research Service Report for Congress. March 21, 2001. usa.us embassy.de/etexts/gov/voting.pdf

Jones, Douglas W., "Evaluating Voting Technology." Testimony before the United States Civil Rights Commission, Tallahassee, FL, January 11, 2001. http://www.cs.uiowa.edu/~jones/voting/uscrc.html

Knack, Stephen, and Martha Kropf, "Who Uses Inferior Voting Technology?" *PS: Political Science and Politics* 35 (September 2002): 541–548.

Percy, Herma, *Will Your Vote Count? Fixing America's Broken Electoral System.* Westport, CT: Praeger, 2009.

Saltman, Roy G., *The History and Politics of Voting Technology: In Quest of Integrity and Public Confidence.* New York: Palgrave Macmillan, 2006.

Tomz, Michael, and Robert P. Houweiling, "How Does Voting Equipment Affect the Racial Gap in Voided Ballots?" *American Journal of Political Science* 47 (January 2003): 46–60.

Utter, Glenn H., and Ruth Ann Strickland, *Campaign and Election Reform,* 2d ed. Santa Barbara, CA: ABC-CLIO, 2008.

Wolf, Richard, "Voting Equipment Changes Could Get Messy on November 4." *USA Today* (October 29, 2008). http://www.usatoday.com/news/politics/election2008/2008–10–28-voting equipment_N.htm

W

WASTE MANAGEMENT

Alexandre Pólvora

Waste management has been a part of our human-built worlds from the time of the earliest cultures and civilizations. Only in the late 19th century, however, owing to an increase in human population and therefore the amount of waste generated, did widespread awareness about issues such as recycling and landfills emerge in Western political and economic arenas. When New York City produced so much waste that nearby Staten Island could no longer accept trash from the city—there was no place to put it—the world watched in amazement as garbage from U.S. cities began to be shipped overseas and out of the country for disposal. This awareness became a central concern of everyday life beginning in the mid-20th century.

What Is Waste?

The word *waste* refers to junk, scrap, trash, debris, garbage, rubbish, and so on. For the most part, it is understood as those materials resulting from or rejected by a particular production activity. Waste is also a more or less inclusive concept for such matters as energy losses, pollution, and bodily fluids. Waste is what we no longer need or want, as individuals or groups, and what emerges from sorting activities where parts of our worlds are discarded and others are not.

Waste has always existed and will continue to exist. The exact definition of waste is not necessarily always the same, even if we share common notions of waste in dealing with it daily, or even if most institutions and experts agree on how to define it functionally.

For example, we may find dissimilar notions of waste just by observing how substances currently judged as waste are the target of contrasting views, by different people or social groups, in distinct places or even in the same place. Present debates are frequently localized or regionalized, and waste has distinct configurations in southeast urban Brazil, northern rural India, and San Francisco Bay, for example.

Furthermore, we can also find dissimilar notions of waste by looking backward through archeological records, which show us how the earliest human settlements began to separate their residues and assume a need to control some of them. In doing so, we can see how these records distinguish between the notions regarding waste of the first human settlements and those of previous human groups mainly engaged in hunting and gathering activities.

Hunters and gatherers did not stay put long enough to deal with remains of slow dissolution. Waste should be seen constantly as a dynamic notion, socially constructed and without the same meanings shared by everybody, everywhere, across time, space, and culture.

Classifications of Waste

Waste can be classified along a spectrum from extremely hazardous to potentially non-hazardous. In addition, based on its type, waste can occur as a gas, liquid, or solid. Based on origin, it may be commercial, household, industrial, mining, medical, nuclear, construction, or demolition waste. Based on their physical nature, waste streams can be organic or inorganic. Some putrefy, some do not. Based on possible outcomes, waste can be categorized as possibly reusable, returnable, recyclable, disposable, or degradable.

These categories distinguish how dangerous, expensive, or complicated each type is to eliminate. Almost all of our waste is framed as a problem in today's terms because of the quantity our society generates. If our society practiced a lifestyle that did not waste anything, or generated little waste and of the kind not harmful to the environment, it

ORGANIC BREAKDOWN

The Waste Management Corporation recently determined that the best way to manage waste today is to invest in increasing the rate at which biodegradable waste composts or decomposes. This waste hauler collects nearly 66 million tons of garbage every year. The company has put its money into a small firm with a means to create conditions in which the kinds of bugs that break down organic waste material thrive.

In January 2010, Waste Management announced a partnership with Harvest Power, a venture-capitalized company with a process to break down trash fast and turn it into natural gas, electricity, or nontoxic compost rich in soil nutrients that make plants grow well. The output from that digestion process is the same as what one gets from a cow: natural gas and good fertilizer.

would not be considered a problem. Decomposition would turn the problem into an asset just based on chemistry alone.

Our main way of dealing with waste is to assemble technical strategies. Those strategies become the core of waste management. Each grouping under a strategy corresponds to a material and symbolic technical world, based on large-scale processes with linked stages such as the identification, removal, control, processing, packaging, transportation, marketing, and disposal of wastes.

Waste is viewed in hierarchies, often ordered from the most to the least favored kind of waste to manage. For example, waste that does not contaminate water, land, or air would carry most-favored status for landfills. Waste that is toxic would carry least-favored status for incineration, for example, because burning the residue would contaminate the air. The sustainability mantra of "reduce, reuse, and recycle" applies. Depending on types of waste and intentions, strategies such as prevention, minimization, reduction, reutilization, retrieval by recycling or composting, energy recovery by incineration, and disposal to landfills or other legal depositories are employed.

Waste hierarchies guide the disposal approaches followed by most industrial, business, or government institutions. Modern paths to successful waste management policies, sustained by worldwide case studies, have been grounded not only on straightforward arrangements between some or all possible strategies but also on the perception that sometimes a lower option can be better than a higher one. Leading experts at the present time argue against these hierarchies, however observe that no strategy should be linearly pursued one after another but rather should be used in synergistic or complementary fashion. These hierarchies are now seen more as guidelines, able to provide basic information on the relative benefits brought by each of the strategies, rather than as preassembled processes.

The world of waste management tends to present situations merely as applied, or ready to be dealt with by engineers or chemists, as its performance is constructed in a technologically integrated way that often depends on this practical standard. Waste management is mostly nourished by endogenous technical talks rather than by health, environmental, economical, cultural, or other social debates on waste impacts and causes. There are now more joint efforts between manufacturers, merchants, activists, and lay people. Recent waste-management strategies have benefited from enlarged and exogenous joint frameworks, supported by institutional procedures that also take into account nontechnical issues and actors, notwithstanding the technical strategies that tend to be privileged.

Calculating the Risk and Cost

Risk management and cost assessment are among the approaches known for including the impacts and causes of waste. Using qualitative and quantitative research methods, these approaches acquire vital information needed to manage not only waste and its required disposal but also the potential effects or costs. Moreover, these methods are able to inform particular decision-making processes on the adoption, construction, and location of particular technical strategies or to structure thematic disputes. Should the costs of handling waste be borne by public entities, or are they the producers' responsibility? This leads to legal questions that address the "polluter pay" principle, and the "product lifespan stewardship" associated with life-cycle analyses.

There are other general approaches that carry waste management into larger contexts such as ecological modernization. Such approaches mostly point to steady economic growth and industrial developments, overlapped with environmental stances and legal reforms concerning waste. Even so, within them we may always find extreme positions, framing waste in strict economic terms on the principle that it should always be rationalized into the building of competitiveness policies or market efficiency. On the other extreme, there are those who frame waste in conservationist terms and see it narrowly as a hazard that, above all, affects biological and social sustainabilities.

These and similar approaches make it hard to talk about waste management without regarding it and its debates as parts of a broader controversy involving social equality and environmental sustainability. For almost every waste management strategy there is an equal and opposite counterstrategy—or at least opposition against it. Perhaps the most prominent today is the social justice movement, which focuses on equity, empowering the disadvantaged and creating environmentally sustainable practices that bring economic development to a community without causing negative health effects. We can always find crucial issues within waste disposal, such as toxic emissions from incineration, persistent organic pollutants, permanence of radioactive sludges, landfill locations, end-of-life vehicles, electronic-waste increases, ocean dumping, energy inefficiencies, and large scale littering, as well as toxic coal ash spills and unstoppable oil gushing.

Critical Discussions

Waste management has grown as a topic of general concern, with most critical discussions emerging around its various technicalities. Debates on such a subject have played a substantial part in catalyzing public reflections about the links between, on one hand, technical interests, and on the other hand, public and private safety and welfare. Some of these debates even gain legitimacy, not only by helping to erect regulatory procedures in national and local domains but also by influencing the emergence and ratification of international treaties in relation to waste.

Examples of this include the 1989 Basel Convention on the Control of Transboundary Movements of Hazardous Wastes and Their Disposal, or the inclusion of waste in broader agreements about sustainable global politics, as in the 1992 Rio Declaration on Environment and Development.

The emergence of social g roups and movements addressing concerns about waste management has been equally significant. Since the antinuclear and antitoxics oppositional movements of the 1960s, waste issues have grown to be an arena for civic participation. We now have an engaged landscape of groups and movements, ranging from health to ecological justice, that has not yet stopped confronting or shifting the settings of waste management. In such a landscape we can observe resistance trends such as "not in my backyard" or "not in anyone's backyard," ideas such as "want not, waste not," or concepts such as "zero waste." We may also identify movements and projects that, in recent years, have engaged in the recovery of waste, at times ideologically associated with "freeganists" (people who limit their involvement with the conventional economy), at other times coupled to public interventions, as in the "Basurama" collective (a loose network of those interested in trash and its social effects). Other groups are based on the bricolage of "do it yourself," or even on artistic recovery activities, such as the "WEEE Man" project (Waste Electrical and Electronic Equipment Directive, which drew attention to itself by erecting a large humaniform sculpture made out of electronic waste).

Conclusion

No assessment of waste management has ever been deemed to be completely consensual. Major disputes involve questions about the extent to which we should limit ourselves in surveying waste-management strategies. As a result, we find "throwaway" ideologies that leave society and culture overflowing with the costs of producing goods and services. Managing waste is considered impossible or inadvisable when and where regular economic growth seems to depend on "planned obsolescences" promoting waste itself, with junk piles of devalued residues matched by stockpiles of commodities. Most of these outlooks have not been consistently considered appropriate in major waste-management approaches, but their persistence has often helped to support various critiques concerning the source of what is wasted in our mass systems of invention, production, distribution, and consumption.

See also **Incineration and Resource Recovery; Sustainability (vol. 1)**

Further Reading

Kinnaman, Thomas C., ed., *The Economics of Residential Solid Waste Management.* Burlington, VT: Ashgate, 2003.

Melosi, Martin V., *The Sanitary City: Environmental Services in Urban America from Colonial Times to the Present,* abridged ed. Pittsburgh: University of Pittsburgh Press, 2008.

Rathje, William, and Cullen Murphy, *Rubbish! The Archaeology of Garbage.* New York: Harper Collins, 1992.

Scanlan, John, *On Garbage.* London: Reaktion Books, 2005.

Strasser, Susan, *Waste and Want: A Social History of Trash.* New York: Owl Books, 2000.

Thomas, Vivian E., *Garbage In, Garbage Out: Solving the Problems with Long-Distance Trash Transport.* Charlottesville: University of Virginia Press, 2009.

WATER POLLUTION

Robert William Collin

Water is essential for life, and water quality is often at odds with the demands of increased development. Conflicting laws, poorly enforced environmental regulations, and increased citizen monitoring are the ingredients for powerful and long-lasting controversy.

Water pollution is a term that describes any adverse environmental effect on water bodies (lakes, rivers, the sea, groundwater) caused by the actions of humankind. Although natural phenomena such as volcanoes, storms, and earthquakes also cause major changes in water chemistry and the ecological status of water, these are not pollution. Water pollution has many causes and characteristics. Humans and livestock produce bodily wastes that enter rivers, lakes, oceans, and other surface waters. These wastes increase the solids suspended in the water and the concentration of bacteria and viruses, leading to potential health impacts.

Increases in nutrient loading may lead to eutrophication, or dead zones, in lakes and coastal water. Organic wastes deplete the water of oxygen, which potentially has severe impacts on the whole ecosystem. Industries and municipalities discharge pollutants, permitted and sometimes unpermitted, into their wastewater, including heavy metals, organic toxins, oils, pesticides, fertilizers, and solids. Discharges can also have direct and indirect thermal effects, especially those from nuclear power stations, and also reduce the available oxygen. Human activities that disturb the land can lead to silt running off the land into the waterways. This silt can have environmentally detrimental effects even if it does not contain pollution. Silt-bearing runoff comes from many activities, including construction, logging, mining, and farming. It can kill aquatic and other types of life. Salmon, for example, do not spawn if the temperature of the water is too high.

Another environmental controversy around water quality is that when water becomes polluted, native species of plants and animals fail to flourish in rivers, lakes, and coastal waters. Depending on how exactly the water quality is impaired, some of these species may be threatened with extinction. If, for example, the water quality is impaired through agricultural runoff containing nitrogen and other chemical fertilizers, this may precipitate algae blooms. These blooms can warm up the water as well as rapidly deplete oxygen in the water.

Pollutants in water include chemicals, pathogens, and hazardous wastes. Many of the chemical substances are toxic. Many of the municipal water supplies in developed and undeveloped countries can present health risks. Water quality standards consist of three elements: the designated uses assigned to those waters (such as public water supply, recreation, or shellfish harvesting), criteria to protect those uses (such as chemical-specific thresholds that should not be exceeded), and an antidegradation policy intended to keep waters that do meet standards from deteriorating from their current condition.

Water regulations control point sources of pollution. Some environmentalists consider the definition of *point source* to be too narrow because it allows smaller discharges into the water. It has been estimated that between 50 and 80 percent of water pollution comes from non-point sources. Non–point source (NPS) pollution comes from many sources, including human habitation and industrial emissions currently unaccounted for. NPS pollution begins with precipitation moving on and through the ground. As the force of gravity pulls the water down, it carries with it natural and human-made pollutants. Many of these pollutants end up in lakes, rivers, wetlands, coastal waters, and underground sources of drinking water. These pollutants include the following:

- Excess fertilizers, herbicides, and insecticides from agricultural lands and residential areas
- Oil, grease, and toxic chemicals from urban runoff and energy production
- Sediment from improperly managed construction sites, crop and forest lands, and eroding stream banks
- Salt from irrigation practices and acid drainage from abandoned mines
- Bacteria and nutrients from livestock, pet wastes, and faulty septic systems

Atmospheric deposition is also a source of NPS pollution. An incinerator next to a lake could be a source of water pollution.

NPS Pollution

States report that NPS pollution is the leading remaining cause of water quality problems. The effects of NPS pollutants on specific waters vary and may not always be fully assessed. These pollutants have harmful effects on drinking water supplies, recreation, fisheries, and wildlife. With only about 20 percent of lakes and rivers being monitored in any way and much to learn about the movement of underground water and aquifers, the degree of uncertainty as to non–point sources is currently very large. Even water areas that are monitored still allow permits to industries and cities to discharge treated and untreated waste and chemicals.

NPS pollution results from a wide variety of human activities on the land. These activities touch upon debates in areas from private property to corporate environmental responsibility. Governmental responses to water pollution from NPSs are spread across the spectrum. Some activities are federal responsibilities, such as ensuring that federal lands are properly managed to reduce soil erosion. Some are state responsibilities, for example, developing legislation to govern mining and logging and to protect groundwater. Others are local, such as land-use controls like erosion control ordinances. The coordination of intergovernmental relations and communication between these levels of government about water pollution approaches are poor, contributing to the controversy.

The United States developed new environmental policies in the past 35 years to clean up water pollution by controlling emissions from industries and municipal sewage treatment plants. This last 35-year period was preceded by 500 years of urbanization and then industrialization and waves of immigration from every coast. There was little in the way of enforceable environmental legislation in the United States until 1970. Navigable waterways have been intentionally and unintentionally altered in drastic ways, such as the rechanneling the Mississippi River by the U.S. Army Corp of Engineers. Modern plumbing devices, such as backflow regulators, help keep wastewater separate from drinking water. Urbanized areas without backflow regulators on industry eventually taint the entire watershed. In many areas, it is often the case that as water quantity goes down so does water quality. In places such as Texas, which practiced a form of waste discharge called deep well injection, some of the water sources may be contaminated. The accumulated wastes from the water pollution both before and after the formation of the U.S. Environmental Agency (EPA) will themselves foster cleanup controversies. Fear of liability for past acts of environmental contamination is a powerful motivator, but it can lead to either forward thinking or attempts to sweep the problem under the rug.

NPS pollution is the largest source of water quality problems in the United States. It remains the catchall term for all other than point sources of water pollution. Point sources are regulated by the EPA, which in 2010 announced an overhaul of regulations that would allow officials to keep a close watch on dozens of contaminants simultaneously and tighten rules on chemicals used by industry. Each watershed is allowed to have a limited overall amount of water pollution. If all sources were counted, including non–point sources, the overall amount of permissible chemical discharges into the watershed would decrease. This could result in fewer permits being issued. The fewer permits issued generally means less industrial economic development. Industries and governments prefer more industrial and manufacturing economic development. Some industries prefer not to compete with other industries in the same watershed and may not want to share a water permit. Uncertainty of the water permit can deter financial investors from long-term investments in a plant or real property.

Other stakeholders—like farmers, agribusiness, and Native Americans—all hold various rights and expectations for the same water. NPS of water pollution have serious unresolved environmental issues that involve many stakeholders. Accurate environmental monitoring is a necessity as the foundation of sound environmental policy, especially if sustainability is the goal. The range of disrespect for the environment from some stakeholders shocks other stakeholders, who feel reverence for the environment when it comes to water pollution. The wide range of environmental expectations becomes controversial when accurate environmental monitoring and research reveal the true extent of the environmental impacts of water pollution.

Known NPSs of Water Pollution

Agribusiness is the leading source of water quality impairments, degrading 60 percent of the impaired river miles and half of the impaired lake acreage surveyed by states, territories, and tribes. Runoff from urban areas is also a very large source of water quality impairments. Roads, parking lots, airports, and other impervious paved surfaces that occur with U.S. land development increase the runoff of precipitation into other parts of the watershed. The most common NPS pollutants are soil sediment and chemical nutrients. Other NPS pollutants include pesticides, pathogens (bacteria and viruses), salts, oil, grease, toxic chemicals, and heavy metals.

Role of Communities

Communities play an important role in addressing NPS pollution. When coordinated with federal, state, and local environmental programs and initiatives, community-based NPS control efforts can be highly successful. More than 500 active volunteer monitoring groups currently operate throughout the United States. Monitoring groups may also have information about other NPS pollution projects, such as beach cleanups, stream walks, and restoration activities. More than 40 states now have some type of program to help communities conserve water. NPS pollution starts at the household level. Households, for example, can water lawns during cooler hours of the day, limit fertilizer and pesticide applications, and properly store chemicals to reduce runoff and keep runoff clean. Pet wastes, a significant source of nutrient contamination, should be disposed of properly. Communities can also replace impervious surfaces with more porous surfaces.

Runoff from Urban Areas

NPS pollution often come from paved, impermeable road surfaces. These can be in urban, suburban, or rural areas. Many vehicle emissions run off from the pavement with water when it rains. Effective drainage systems can remove this water to city water systems, but these do not necessarily treat the runoff for its load of pollutants. In many cities, the consolidated sewer overflow system, means that when it rains heavily the sewers simply overflow into the nearest river or lake. Many urban sewer and water systems are old and need repair, especially those made with lead pipes.

Cities with storm sewer systems that quickly channel runoff from roads and other impervious surfaces increase their environmental impacts with large flow variations. Runoff gathers speed in the storm sewer system. When it leaves the system, large volumes of quickly flowing runoff erode riparian areas and alter stream channels. Native fish, amphibians, and plants cannot live in urban streams impacted by urban runoff.

Conclusion

Water pollution will become more controversial. As water pollution standards mature, environmental impact assessment and pollution accountability will increase. Many stakeholders now assume they have the right to fresh, clean water, and as much of it as they want. Where the water begins to run out, violent confrontations can occur. In Klamath, Oregon—the site of a furious water controversy between farmers, various agencies of the federal and state government, and environmentalists—violence erupted in 2006 as Native American children were assaulted on their school bus by farmers angry at their loss of water. Although the Klamath tribe tried to avoid the controversy, they do have water rights by treaty and law. The farmers' property rights lawsuit, claiming that they owned the water as a property right, was dismissed in a 57-page opinion in federal court. In 2007, Vice President Dick Cheney was investigated by a House committee to see if he had illegally intervened in this dispute and commanded federal agencies to let agribusiness get the water. The committee was unable to find conclusive proof that Cheney directly gave incriminating orders. In 2010, the governors of Oregon and California, the U.S. secretary of the interior, and leaders of Native American tribes signed an agreement in part establishing water-sharing rights between farmers and fishers.

As more and more of the aquatic environment becomes known, the issue of who pays for cleanup and for dredging becomes increasingly salient. There are controversies over the environmental impacts of these activities alone. In arid developing areas where water can become scarce, those who use it and pollute it affect many other groups. There will be an increase in stakeholder accountability for pollution sources as environmental law enforcement works its way upstream. Litigation and community engagement will increase in the controversy over water pollution.

See also **Acid Rain; Cumulative Emissions; Industrial Agricultural Practices and the Environment; Pesticides; Transportation and the Environment**

Further Reading

Best, Gerry, *Environmental Pollution Studies.* Liverpool, UK: Liverpool University Press, 2000.

Helmer, Richard, *Water Pollution Control.* London: Spon Press, 1998.

Natural Resources Defense Council, Issues: Water. www.nrdc.org/water/pollution/default.asp

Pagenkopf, James R., et al., *Municipal Waste-Water Treatment.* New York: Wiley, 2002.

Sources of Water Pollution, www.soest.hawaii.edu/GG/ASK/waterpol3.html

Spellman, Frank R., *The Science of Water: Concepts and Applications.* Boca Raton, FL: CRC Press, 2008.

Sullivan, Patrick J., Franklin J. Argady, and James J. J. Clark, *The Environmental Science of Drinking Water.* Burlington, MA: Butterworth-Heinemann, 2005.

U.S. Environmental Protection Agency, Polluted Runoff (Nonpoint Source Pollution). www.epa.gov/nps

Wargo, John, *Green Intelligence: Creating Environments that Protect Human Health.* New Haven, CT: Yale University Press, 2009.

WATERSHED PROTECTION AND SOIL CONSERVATION

ROBERT WILLIAM COLLIN

Watersheds are tracts of land that feed pools of water both above and below ground. They funnel rainfall and snowmelt, for example, through wetlands, which are natural filtration systems. The spongy soil constituting a wetland traps sediment sometimes carrying pollutants. The water trickling down becomes increasingly free of contaminants as it makes its way down to replenish underground aquifers, which humans draw on for drinking water. Land composition varies in a watershed. A single watershed may consist of mountains, prairie and/or rolling hills.

Watersheds left unprotected from development may suffer environmental impacts that deplete soil resources. Logging, grazing, some types of mining, paving over land with impervious surfaces, and excessive rechanneling of major watercourses have affected watersheds in negative ways. Many farmers and environmentalists want to prevent soil depletion by protecting watersheds. Communities want to protect watersheds for water quality. For watershed protection to work as a policy it may require the taking of private property or the terminations of long-term leases given to loggers, ranchers, and mining corporations. Water use and quality are generally becoming controversial.

Watershed protection is increasingly seen by some as excessive government intervention. Others see it as a necessary component of any successful sustainability program or policy.

Considering the value of one watershed to the residents of Montana, on March 3, 2010, Montana Senator Max Baucus introduced the North Fork Watershed Protection Act of 2010, which prohibits mining on federally owned lands and interests in the North Fork Flathead Watershed and protects this vital natural resource from corruption and contamination from mineral mining or geothermal leasing. It also prohibits anyone from patenting any life form or material found in the area in its original form or by slight alteration such as changing an innocuous enzyme in the item. On April 28, 2010 the bill was referred to the U.S. Energy and Natural Resources Subcommittee on Public lands and Forests, which held hearings to help consider the measure.

Background

Visions of hurricanes and floods tearing the Midwest's luscious black top soil downstream prompted many to ask the federal government to intervene in the 1930s. The early legislation set the tone for today's policy. Most of the federal legislation for watershed protection emerged in this time to protect rural and agricultural interests. The Watershed Protection and Flood Prevention Act of 1954, as amended, authorized Natural Resources Conservation Service (NRCS) to cooperate with states and local agencies to carry out works of improvement for soil conservation and for other purposes including flood prevention; conservation, development, utilization, and disposal of water; and conservation and proper utilization of land. NRCS implements the Watershed Protection and Flood Prevention Act through the following programs:

- Watershed Surveys and Planning
- Watershed Protection and Flood Prevention Operations
- Watershed Rehabilitation
- Watershed Surveys and Planning

The NRCS cooperates with other federal, state, and local agencies in making investigations and surveys of river basins as a basis for the development of coordinated water resource programs, floodplain management studies, and flood insurance studies. NRCS also assists public sponsors to develop watershed plans. The focus of these plans is to identify solutions that use conservation practices, including nonstructural measures, to solve problems. Each project must contain benefits directly related to agriculture, including rural communities that account for at least 20 percent of the total benefits of the project.

Watershed Operations

Watershed Operations is a voluntary program that provides assistance to local organizations sponsoring authorized watershed projects, planned and approved under the authority of the Watershed Protection and Flood Prevention Act of 1954, and 11 designated watersheds authorized by the Flood Control Act of 1944. NRCS provides technical and financial assistance to states, local governments, and tribes (project sponsors) to implement authorized watershed project plans for the purpose of watershed protection; flood mitigation; water quality improvements; soil erosion reduction; rural, municipal, and industrial water supply; irrigation water management; sediment control; fish and wildlife enhancement; and wetlands and wetland function creation and restoration. There are over 1,500 active or completed watershed projects. As communities become more involved in environmental issues they quickly learn about their particular watershed.

Flood Prevention Program

The Flood Control Act of December 22, 1944, authorized the Secretary of Agriculture to install watershed improvement measures (http://www.nrcs.usda.gov/pro grams/watershed/pl534.html).

This act authorized 11 flood prevention watersheds. The NRCS and the Forest Service (FS) carry out this responsibility with assistance from other bureaus and agencies within and outside the U.S. Department of Agriculture (USDA). Watershed protection and flood prevention work currently under way in small upstream watersheds all over the United States sprang from the exploratory flood prevention work authorized by

TABLE 1. Flood Prevention Watersheds

Watershed Name	State	Watershed Size
Buffalo Creek	New York	279,680 acres
Middle Colorado River	Texas	4,613,120 acres
Coosa River	Georgia, Tennessee	1,339,400 acres
Little Sioux River	Iowa	1,740,800 acres
Little Tallahatchie River	Mississippi	963,977 acres
Los Angeles River	California	563,977 acres
Potomac River	Virginia, W. Virginia, Maryland, Pennsylvania	4,205,400 acres
Santa Ynez River	California	576,000 acres
Trinity River	Texas	8,424,260 acres
Washita River	Oklahoma, Texas	5,095,040 acres
Yazoo River	Mississippi	3,942,197 acres

the Flood Control Act of 1944, and from the intervening 54 pilot watershed projects authorized by the Agriculture Appropriation Act of 1953. These projects are the focus of much study as watershed protection and soil conservation have become increasingly high-profile issues following the impact of Hurricane Katrina on New Orleans in 2006. Many accuse these types of projects as too little too late for prevention of risk to urban areas from natural disasters. The 11 watershed areas are listed below in Table 1.

Because the authorized flood prevention projects include relatively large areas, work plans are developed on a subwatershed basis. Surveys and investigations are made and detailed designs, specifications, and engineering cost estimates are prepared for construction of structural measures. Areas where sponsors need to obtain land rights, easements, and rights-of-way are delineated. This can present an issue when private property owners do not want to cooperate with flood prevention and soil conservation. There are presently over 1,600 projects in operation.

Watershed Projects Provide Thousands of Acres of Fish and Wildlife Habitat

There are 2,000 NRCS-assisted watershed projects in the United States, with at least one project in every state. Some projects provide flood control, while others include conservation practices that address a myriad of natural resource issues such as water quality, soil erosion, animal waste management, irrigation, water management, water supplies, and recreation. Whatever the primary purpose, watershed projects have many community benefits such as fish and wildlife habitat enhancement. Over 300,000 acres of surface water have been created by the construction of 11,000 watershed dams.

Lakes generally range in size from 20 to 40 surface acres and provide a good mix of deep water and shoreline riparian areas. Some lakes have up to several hundred acres of surface water, and many had recreational areas developed around them. Lakes formed by the watershed dams have created thousands of acres of open water providing excellent fish and wildlife habitat and areas for migrating waterfowl to rest and feed. Conservation practices in watershed projects such as buffers, pasture and rangeland management, tree plantings, ponds, conservation cropping systems, and conservation tillage provide cover, water, and food for a variety of birds and animals.

Thousands of people enjoy fishing, hiking, boating, and viewing wildlife in these very scenic settings each year. NRCS-assisted watershed projects provide a wide diversity of upland habitat landowners in watershed projects with technical and sometimes financial assistance in applying conservation practices. Many of these practices create or improve wildlife habitat and protect water quality in streams and lakes.

Although watershed projects may offer benefits to recreational users, others wonder about their environmental impacts. To what end is the soil being conserved? What if the area is a natural floodplain? What are the impacts of recreational users on endangered or threatened species? These questions and others abound in the traditional soil conservation and floodplain protection policies.

Creating and Protecting Wetlands: Watershed Program Results

According to the Natural Resources Conservation Service, they have assisted in creating the following:

- Upland wildlife habitat created or enhanced: 9,140,741 acres
- Wetlands created or enhanced: 210,865 acres
- Stream corridors enhanced: 25,093 miles
- Reduced sedimentation: 49,983,696 tons per year

The 2,000 watershed projects have established a $15 billion national infrastructure, by their own estimate that is providing multiple benefits to over 48 million people.

- Agricultural flood damage reduction: $266 million
- Nonagricultural flood damage reduction: $381 million
- Agricultural benefits (nonflood): $303 million
- Nonagricultural benefits (nonflood): $572 million
- Total monetary benefits: $1.522 billion
- Number of bridges benefited: 56,787
- Number of farms and ranches benefited: 154,304
- Number of businesses benefited: 46,464
- Number of public facilities benefited: 3,588

- Acres of wetlands created or enhanced: 210,865
- Acres of upland wildlife habitat created or enhanced: 9,140,741
- Miles of streams with improved water quality: 25,093
- Number of domestic water supplies benefited: 27,685
- Reduced soil erosion (tons per year): 89,343,55
- Tons of animal waste properly managed: 3,910,10
- Reduced sedimentation (tons per year): 49,983,696
- Water conserved (acre feet per year): 1,763,472

The Watershed Program has been used by communities for over 50 years. The authorizing legislation has been amended several times to address a broader range of natural resource and environmental issues, and today the program offers communities more assistance to address some environmental issues. There are watershed projects in every state. Over 2,000 projects have been implemented since 1948. New projects are being developed each year by local people.

Conclusion

As water resources become scarce, the competition for water will force water users to exert all rights in water and the land. In places where floods occur, property owners will want flood control as watershed protection. Communities want clean and safe drinking water, and this is becoming a scarce resource even in communities with water. Watersheds absorb all past and present wastes, by-products, emissions, discharges, runoff, and other environmental impacts. Their protection will require increasingly stringent controls on all water users and residents of the watershed. Private property owners and land developers object to this because they may have planned for a more profitable use. Without water it is difficult to make a profit in developing land. Sustainable sources of safe water are essential to many stakeholders. Watershed protection will become increasingly controversial as it moves from 1940s and 1950s soil erosion prevention policy to one that incorporates accurate monitoring of water and precepts of sustainability in urban and suburban settlements as well as rural ones.

See also **Logging; Mining of Natural Resources; Pesticides; Sprawl; Water Pollution; Sustainability (vol. 1)**

Further Reading

deGraaff, Jan, et al., eds., *Monitoring and Evaluation of Soil Conservation and Watershed Development Projects.* Enfield, NH: Science Publishers, 2007.

Hirt, Paul W., *A Conspiracy of Optimism: Management of the National Forests since World War Two.* Lincoln: University of Nebraska Press, 1994.

Mastney, Lisa, and Sandra Postel, *Liquid Assets: The Critical Need to Safeguard Freshwater Ecosystems.* Washington, DC: Worldwatch Institute, 2005.

Morandi, Larry, Barbara Foster, and Jeff Dale, *Watershed Protection: The Legislative Role*. Washington, DC: National Conference of State Governors, 1998.

Open Congress, S.3075—North Fork Watershed Protection Act of 2010. http://www.opencongress.org/bill/111-s3075/show

Riley, Ann Lawrence, *Restoring Streams in Cities: A Guide for Planners, Policymakers, and Citizens.* Washington, DC: Island Press, 1998.

Sabatier, Paul A., *Swimming Upstream: Collaborative Approaches to Watershed Management.* Cambridge, MA: MIT Press, 2005.

Sanderson, James, and Larry D. Harris, eds., *Landscape Ecology: A Top-Down Approach.* Boca Raton, FL: Lewis Publishers, 2000.

U.S. Environmental Protection Agency, Monitoring and Assessing Water Quality: Volunteer Monitoring. www.epa.gov/owow/monitoring/vol.html

U.S. Environmental Protection Agency, Watersheds. www.epa.gov/owow/water shed

WILD ANIMAL REINTRODUCTION

Robert William Collin

To prevent wolves from becoming extinct, the National Park Service has reintroduced them on park lands. Nearby ranchers protested this, claiming the wolves prey on their herds. Environmentalists claim ranchers killed some of the wolves. Grizzly bears may be reintroduced in national parks next.

One of the biggest reasons for the reintroduction of wolves back into Yellowstone was that this was part of their original habitat. Wolves had originally roamed from Yellowstone all the way down to Mexico. While many environmentalists and wildlife agencies were in favor of the reintroduction of the wolves, many other groups were against it. The main people who were against the reintroduction of the wolves were the ranchers who made a living in the areas surrounding the park. During its 70 years of absence from the Rockies, the grey wolf had been protected under the Endangered Species Act, which was passed in 1973. Therefore, a person could be punished with up to a $100,000 fine and up to one year in jail for killing a wolf. Back in the 1850s, there was a major population increase of the wolves in the United States, stemming from the westward movement of settlers. These settlers killed more than 80 million bison, and the wolves started to scavenge on the carcasses left behind. By the 1880s, most of the bison were gone, so the wolves had to change food sources. This meant that they turned their attention to domestic livestock, causing farmers and ranchers to develop bounties and other vermin-eradication efforts. Owing to the lack of a food source as well as the bounties being offered, the wolf population plummeted in the lower 48 states.

When the numbers in an animal population become low, the genetic diversity of that species decreases dramatically, which can hasten the species' extinction. One of the premises of governmental intervention in these environmental controversies around species reintroduction is to prevent extinction. An important aspect of this is gene pool diversity. This requires active animal management by humans, including an in-depth knowledge of the genes of specific animals and packs. One aspect of this controversy is the need for more scientific monitoring of animals facing extinction.

When the wolf population dropped, there was still a safe place. That was Yellowstone National Park, established in 1872. In 1916 the National Park Service started to eliminate all predators in Yellowstone National Park, which meant killing 136 wolves, 13,000 coyotes, and every single mountain lion. By 1939, this program was shut down, but all the wolves were dead.

What Is a Wolf Pack?

A wolf pack is very hierarchical and organized. Dominance and submission establish the order of power in the pack. A pack consists of an alpha male, an alpha female, and their descendants. The alpha pair are the only two that breed. The natural pattern of breeding within a wolf pack works to protect their genetic diversity if populations are healthy.

The Reintroduction Program

In January 1995, some 14 wolves from many separate packs were captured in Canada and brought into Yellowstone Park. The next step in their reintroduction was to place them in one-acre acclimation pens. Capturing wolves from different packs helped protect their genetic diversity. Biologists then created packs from these captured wolves.

While in captivity, the wolves were fed large amounts of meat in the form of roadkill or winter carrion from the area. This often consisted of deer, elk, and smaller animals. Each pack was fed once every 7 to 10 days, which is how frequently they eat in the wild. A small wolf pack of six in the wild will consume on average 800 pounds of meat per month. In Yellowstone National Park, that would average out to two adult elk and maybe a small deer per small pack per month. Today, 90 percent of all wolf kills are elk; the other 10 percent consist of bison, deer, moose, and other small game.

Ranchers' Resistance to Wolf Reintroduction

In the West, ranchers control large tracts of land. Sometimes they own the land outright, and sometimes the land is leased from the U.S. government. The ranchers' concerns are basic. The wolf is a predatory animal that finds the easiest type of food source available. An animal that has been domesticated and no longer has natural predators is very easy prey.

From 1995 to 1998, for example, 9 head of cattle and 132 sheep were killed by wolves. The wolves that killed the livestock were mainly traveling from Canada to Yellowstone, across Montana. Defenders of Wildlife, an organization dedicated to wildlife preservation (including predator preservation), has worked to compensate ranchers financially for cattle and sheep lost to wolves. Many environmentalists fear that ranchers will kill off all of the newly introduced wolves. Only a small number of wolves have died legally, while many more have died of unknown causes. The reintroduction of the wolf has caused many problems, ranging from lawsuits to loss of livestock. The two lawsuits that have been filed contended that it was unconstitutional to reintroduce the wolves into the park. The judge who was looking over these lawsuits said that the wolves needed to be returned to Canada, but Canada did not want them. Then the judge said that all the introduced wolves were to be sent to a zoo, but no zoo had room for them. Finally the judge said all of the introduced wolves needed to be destroyed, but the environmentalists protested. In the end, nothing was done.

The Role of States

As of 2009, the population of the wolf was 98 individuals in 12 packs, the recovery goal of 10 breeding pairs having been met a decade earlier (2000). This means that the states are now trying to get the wolf off the endangered species list and under state control. Back around 1998, all of the states (Wyoming, Idaho, and Montana) started to make plans for how they were going to manage the wolf populations in their states. Each plan was then reviewed by wolf specialists and depredation specialists to see what they thought of the plans. Each state had its plans finished by 2002. Wyoming was the first to send its plan to be reviewed by the U.S. Congress. The other two states waited to see what would come of Wyoming's plan before they sent theirs in. In 2003 the Wyoming Grey Wolf Management Plan was sent back to the state, saying that it would not work. Most people probably felt the plan did not go through because Wyoming was planning on managing the wolves as if they were a predator species. This meant that the wolves could be hunted freely as long as they were off national forest or national park property and on private property. Many environmentalists did not want this, since they felt this was the reason all the wolves had been lost in the first place. The Montana and Idaho plans were different from Wyoming's. These states were planning on putting a trophy hunting season out on the wolf. At present, Wyoming has not made any changes to its plan, even though Congress wants them to change it to better manage the wolf population. Wyoming intends to take this matter to the courts.

Conclusion

This is a highly controversial topic at the local level that will continue to be debated in courts, legislatures, and federal agencies. As more species become endangered and protected, successful reintroduction programs around national parks and other federal lands will be initiated. The debate in this controversy may move to legislatures. As federal and state wildlife and park agencies seek more funding for reintroduction programs, others will seek to prevent this. Ranchers and others in surrounding communities will continue to resist the siting of dangerous animals among them. These very communities have often benefited from the presence of nearby national parks as well as long-term grazing leases from the federal government at very favorable rates.

See also **Endangered Species; Stock Grazing and the Environment**

Further Reading

Lowry, William R., *Repairing Paradise: The Restoration of America's National Parks.* Washington, DC: Brookings Institution Press, 2009.

Maehr, David S., et al., eds., *Large Mammal Restoration: Ecological and Sociological Consideration in the 21st Century.* Washington, DC: Island Press, 2001.

Smith, Douglas, and Gary Ferguson, *Decade of the Wolf: Returning the Wild to Yellowstone.* Guilford, CT: Lyons Press, 2005.

Urbiqkit, Cat, *Yellowstone Wolves: A Chronicle of the Animal, the People, and the Politics.* Granville, OH: McDonald & Woodward, 2008.

WIND ENERGY

Robert William Collin and Scott M. Fincher

Wind power comes from turbines that generate electricity. Proponents assert that wind power can be harnessed to be a nonpolluting, renewable source of energy to meet electric power needs around the world, but some communities do not want the turbines near homes or schools. The turbines can create noise that studies show causes headaches in some people and death for some animals, including goats and wildlife. In cold climates a turbine's blades can throw ice and snow. Sometimes the variation in wind turbulence can cause traditional fan blades to come off.

Wind power is a form of renewable energy. As portions of the earth are heated by the sun, the heated air rises, and air rushes to fill low-pressure areas, creating wind. The wind is slowed as it brushes the ground so it may not feel windy at ground level. The power in the wind might be five times greater at the height of the blade tip on a large, modern wind turbine. Entire areas of a region might be very windy while other areas are relatively calm. The majority of people do not live in high-wind areas, although climate change could increase that number.

Wind into Electricity

Wind generates electricity as it moves the blades of a windmill or wind turbine. In a modern, large-scale wind turbine, the wind is converted to rotational motion by a rotor, which is a three-bladed assembly at the top of the wind turbine. The rotor turns a shaft that enters a gearbox that greatly increases the rotational shaft speed. The output shaft is connected to a generator that converts the rotational movement into electricity.

WIND FARMS AND NOISE

One common controversy with earlier wind turbines was their noise. Noise issues are difficult because it is hard to measure noise in real-life conditions. The following are measurements in decibels of some common noises:

Source/Activity	Indicative noise level dB
Threshold of hearing	0
Rural nighttime background	20–40
Quiet bedroom	35
Wind farm at 350 m	35–45
Car at 40 mph at 100 m	55
Busy general office	60
Truck at 30 mph at 100 m	65
Pneumatic drill at 7 m	95
Jet aircraft at 250 m	105
Threshold of pain	140

Although modern turbines are quieter, no research has been undertaken about the cumulative effects of constant noise from wind turbines.

The wind resource in the United States is vast. Proponents claim there is theoretically enough wind flowing across the United States to supply all of our electricity needs if today's technology is used to harness it. Assuming access to the national electric grid, windy North Dakota alone could supply over 40 percent of the nation's electricity. Offshore sites in the mid-Atlantic region were recently identified by Google and various other corporate partners as forming the basis of a proposed 6,000-MW wind energy system to be developed beginning in 2013. Currently, however, less than 1 percent of U.S. electricity is supplied by wind power.

Environmental Effects

One of wind energy's important benefits is its minimal effect on the environment. In the United States, most electricity is produced from coal and other fossil fuels (70 percent), nuclear energy (20 percent), and hydroelectric sources (dams), which have a greater effect on the environment. There has been some controversy about the noise the wind turbines make.

Recently there has been major technological innovation in the design of multidirectional, conical turbines. Some engineers claim to have designed them small enough to fit on top of rooftops in urban areas. Cities such as Chicago have great interest in these "microturbines," but there are many skeptics. An emerging issue is the government regulation of microturbines on urban rooftops. Given the density of the unit in urban areas it is unlikely that every building could harness the wind energy. The buildings

THE CAPE WIND PROJECT

In 2001, Massachusetts approved a measure putting a windmill farm in Nantucket Sound off Cape Cod, one of the country's environmental jewels. Known as the Cape Wind Project, it was proposed by Cape Wind Associates, owned by developer Jim Gordon. In response, the Alliance to protect Nantucket Sound formed that year to block the project. The farm is expected to cost between $1 billion and $2 billion to construct. Once completed, it will be the first offshore wind energy farm in coastal waters under U.S. jurisdiction. It would be located on Horseshoe Shoal.

The first six months of 2010 saw decisions on the project. The opposition publicized its cause and sought support, the government and the developer maneuvered and solidified the backing they had received.

Supporting the opposition, the National Park Service determined that Nantucket Sound is eligible for listing on the National Register of Historic Places, which would prevent any change in the area's character due to development. The Park Service ruled that because of the sound's cultural and spiritual significant to two Native American nations, it could not be adulterated. On January 4, 2010, U.S. Interior Secretary Ken Salazar gathered stakeholders together to discuss an agreement on how to mitigate potential impacts on historic and cultural resources if the project went forward. He set March 1 as a deadline for a decision, and threatened to "take the steps necessary to bring the permit process to conclusion" if an agreement was not reached by then. The deadline was not met.

On March 22, 2010, all sides delivered testimony at a hearing before the Advisory Council on Historic Preservation. On April 28, 2010, Salazar approved the Cape Wind project. Opponents vowed court action.

On May 7, 2010, Cape Wind announced a power purchase agreement with National Grid to sell half the project's output for more than twice current retail rates for electricity. The deal is subject to approval by the state government.

Ten days later, on May 17, 2010, the Federal Aviation Administration (FAA) resolved its concerns that windmills could cause interference with radar systems at nearby Otis Air Force Base. Cape Wind was cleared for construction by the FAA. Cape Wind agreed to make adjustments to the base's radar system to ensure its effectiveness after the wind farm was developed.

In June, the Alliance to Protect Nantucket sound filed a lawsuit claiming that the federal approval process had violated the Endangered Species Act and other laws. In late August, the Massachusetts Supreme Judicial Court ruled that state has the power to override community opposition and issue building permits for the project. Unless further holds are placed on the project, building should begin in 2011.

—*Debra Ann Schwartz*

would have to be able to take both the weight of the units and the stress of wind turbulence. Nonetheless, many engineers and builders think that lighter and stronger materials will address these problems. There is promise of rapid technological advancement increasing the efficiency and safety of wind power.

New Technology Raises Appeal

Technological advancements in wind turbines and in other ways to increase their efficiency may could them more appealing. Some experts say they can make them function on a building. Globally, wind markets are growing. The Global Wind Energy Council analyzed wind energy data from 70 nations. It reports that in 2006 total installed wind energy capacity was 74,223 megawatts (MW). In 2005, it was 59,090 MW. The wind energy market grew by 41 percent in 2006. Europe has the largest market share, with 65 percent of the total. Germany and Spain are especially involved in wind energy, and alternative, renewable energy generally. Asia had 24 percent of new installations in 2006, according to the council report. Canada increased its wind power capacity from 683 MW in 2005 to 1,459 MW in 2006. The United States has the highest new installed wind power capacity, reporting 2,454 MW in 2006. Google's proposed Atlantic Wind Connection will, when completed, nearly triple that capacity and likely spur interest in other, similar projects.

Conclusion

As nonrenewable sources of energy dwindle, alternative sources must be found to replace them. Wind power is an alternative. If developed on a large scale, wind turbines could encounter community resistance because of concerns over noise and documented health effects to humans and animals.

With the development of a national policy on alternative fuels, other issues are emerging. How much money should the government invest in supporting wind power? Can a government use its power to take private property for wind turbines to generate power for community use? Would it matter if it were a private company, a utility, or a city that owned the wind turbines and/or land underneath it?

Concern about energy independence and environmental effects influences the use of wind power. Given the recent advancements in technology of wind turbines and the robust increases in global wind energy markets, it is likely that environmental controversies associated with them will increase. However, technology may be able to overcome concerns about noise and other issues.

See also **Climate Change; Global Warming; Solar Energy; Sustainability (vol. 1)**

Further Reading

Asmus, Peter, *Reaping the Wind: How Mechanical Wizards, Visionaries, and Profiteers Helped Shape Our Energy Future.* Washington, DC: Island Press, 2001.

Gipe, Paul, *Wind Energy Comes of Age.* New York: Wiley, 1995.

Hills, Richard Leslie, *Power from Wind: A History of Windmill Technology.* Cambridge, UK: Cambridge University Press, 1994.

Pasqualetti, Martin J., Paul Gipe, and Robert Righter, *Wind Power in View: Energy Landscapes in a Crowded World.* St. Louis, MO: Elsevier, 2002.

Patel, Mukund R., *Wind and Solar Power Systems.* Boca Raton, FL: CRC Press, 1999.

Pimentel, David, ed., *Biofuels, Solar, and Wind as Renewable Energy Systems: Benefits and Risks.* New York: Springer, 2008.

Union of Concerned Scientists, Wind Power: Clean, Sustainable, and Affordable. www.ucsusa.org/clean_energy/coalvswind/index.html

U.S. Department of the Interior, Wind Energy Development Programmatic EIS Information Center. windeis.anl.gov

Wind Power: Environmental and Safety Issues, Wind Energy Fact Sheet 4. www.dti.gov.uk/files/file17777.pdf

Bibliography

Energy

Asmus, Peter, *Reaping the Wind: How Mechanical Wizards, Visionaries, and Profiteers Helped Shape Our Energy Future.* Washington, DC: Island Press, 2001.

Asplund, Richard W., *Profiting from Clean Energy.* Hoboken, NJ: Wiley, 2008.

Ayers, Robert U., and Edward A. Ayers, *Crossing the Energy Divide: Moving from Fossil Fuel Dependence to a Clean-Energy Future.* Upper Saddle River, NJ: Wharton School Publishing, 2010.

Bass, Stephen, and D. B. Barry Dalal-Clayton, *Sustainable Development Strategies: A Resource Book.* London: James and James/Earthscan, 2002.

Bayon, Ricardo, Amanda Hawn, and Katherine Hamilton, *Voluntary Carbon Markets: An International Business Guide to What They Are and How They Work.* London: James and James/Earthscan, 2007.

Beard, T. Randolph, and Gabriel A. Lozada, *Economics, Entropy and the Environment: The Extraordinary Economics of Nicholas Georgescu-Roegen.* Cheltenham, UK: Edward Elgar, 1999.

Bodansky, David, *Nuclear Energy: Principles, Practices, and Prospects,* 2d ed. New York: Springer, 2004.

Brune, Michael, *Coming Clean: America's Addiction to Oil and Coal.* San Francisco: Sierra Club Books, 2008.

Carraro, Carlo, and Domenico Siniscalco, *The European Carbon Tax: An Economic Assessment.* New York: Springer, 1993.

Coming Global Oil Crisis, Hubbert Peak of Oil Production, 2009. http://www.hubbertpeak.com

Cravens, Gwyneth, *Power to Save the World: The Truth about Nuclear Energy.* New York: Knopf, 2007.

Earley, Jane, and Alice McKeown, *Red, White, and Green: Transforming U.S. Biofuels.* Washington, DC: Worldwatch Institute, 2009.

EcoBusiness Links, Carbon Emissions Offsets directory. www.ecobusinesslinks

Freeman, Jody, and Charles D. Kolstad, eds., *Moving to Markets in Environmental Regulation: Lessons from Twenty Years of Experience.* New York: Oxford University Press, 2007.

Freese, Barbara, *Coal: A Human History.* Cambridge, MA: Perseus, 2003.

Fuhs, Allen, *Hybrid Vehicles and the Future of Personal Transportation.* Boca Raton, FL: CRC Press, 2009.

Galambos, Louis, Takashi Hikino, and Vera Zamagni, *The Global Chemical Industry in the Age of the Petrochemical Revolution.* Cambridge, UK: Cambridge University Press, 2006.

Garwin, Richard L., and Georges Charpak, *Megawatts and Megatons: The Future of Nuclear Power and Nuclear Weapons.* Chicago: University of Chicago Press, 2002.

Gipe, Paul, *Wind Energy Comes of Age.* New York: Wiley, 1995.

Greenberg, Michael R., et al., *The Reporter's Handbook on Nuclear Materials, Energy, and Waste Management.* Nashville, TN: Vanderbilt University Press, 2009.

Hansjürgens, Bernd, *Emissions Trading for Climate Policy: US and European Perspectives.* Cambridge, UK: Cambridge University Press, 2005.

Heinberg, Richard, *Blackout: Coal, Climate, and the Last Energy Crisis.* Gabriola Island, BC: New Society Publishers, 2009.

Hills, Richard Leslie, *Power from Wind: A History of Windmill Technology.* Cambridge, UK: Cambridge University Press, 1994.

Hore-Lacy, Ian, *Nuclear Energy in the 21st Century.* Burlington, MA: Academic Press, 2006.

Inslee, Jay, and Bracken Hendricks, *Apollo's Fire: Igniting America's Clean-Energy Economy.* Washington, DC: Island Press, 2008.

International Emissions Trading Association, www.ieta.org/ieta/www/pages/index.php

Jensen, Derrick, and Stephanie McMillan. *As the World Burns; 50 Simple Things You Can Do to Stay in Denial, A Graphic Novel.* New York: Seven Stories Press, 2007.

Jong, Cyriel de, and Kasper Walet, eds., *A Guide to Emissions Trading: Risk Management and Business Implications.* London: Risk Books, 2004.

Marzotto, Toni, Vicky Moshier, and Gordon Scott Bonham, *The Evolution of Public Policy: Cars and the Environment.* Boulder, CO: Lynne Rienner, 2000.

McMonagle, Robert J., *Caribou and Conoco: Rethinking Environmental Politics in Alaska's ANWR and Beyond.* Lanham, MD: Rowman & Littlefield, 2008.

McQuaig, Linda, *It's the Crude, Dude: War, Big Oil, and the Fight for the Planet,* rev. ed. Toronto: Anchor Canada, 2005.

Miller, Bruce G., *Coal Energy Systems.* San Diego, CA: Elsevier Academic Press, 2005.

Miller, Norman, ed., *Cases in Environmental Politics: Stakeholders, Interests, and Policymakers.* New York: Routledge, 2009.

Muller, Richard, *Physics for Future Presidents: The Science Behind the Headlines.* New York: Wiley, 2008.

Murray, Raymond L., *Nuclear Energy: An Introduction to the Concepts, Systems, and Applications of Nuclear Processes,* 6th ed. Burlington, MA: Butterworth-Heinemann, 2008.

National Biodiesel Board, http://www.biodiesel.org/markets/mar

National Renewable Energy Laboratory. Advanced Vehicles and Fuels Research, www.nrel.gov/vehiclesandfuels

Odum, Howard T., and Elisabeth C. Odum, *A Prosperous Way Down: Principles and Policies.* Boulder: University Press of Colorado, 2001.

Pahl, Greg, *Biodiesel: Growing a New Energy Economy,* 2d ed. Burlington, VT: Chelsea Green, 2008.

Park, Patricia D., *Energy Law and the Environment.* Boca Raton, FL: CRC Press, 2002.

Pasqualetti, Martin J, Paul Gipe, and Robert Righter, *Wind Power in View: Energy Landscapes in a Crowded World.* St. Louis, MO: Elsevier, 2002.

Patel, Mukund R., *Wind and Solar Power Systems.* Boca Raton, FL: CRC Press, 1999.

Pimentel, David, ed., *Biofuels, Solar, and Wind as Renewable Energy Systems: Benefits and Risks.* New York: Springer, 2008.

Savinar, Matt, Life After the Oil Crash. http://www.lifeaftertheoil crash.net

Scheer, Hermann, *A Solar Manifesto.* London: James and James/Earthscan, 2005.

Simon, Christopher A., *Alternative Energy: Political, Economic, and Social Feasibility.* Lanham, MD: Rowman & Littlefield, 2007.

Smith, Kevin, *The Carbon Neutral Myth: Offset Indulgences for Your Climate Sins.* Amsterdam: Transnational Institute, 2007.

Standlea, David M., *Oil, Globalization, and the War for the Arctic Refuge.* New York: SUNY Press, 2006.

Truett, Joe C., and Stephen R. Johnson, *The Natural History of an Arctic Oil Field.* London: Elsevier, 2000.

Union of Concerned Scientists, Wind Power: Clean, Sustainable, and Affordable, www.ucsusa. org/clean_energy/coalvswind/index.html.

U.S. Department of the Interior, Wind Energy Development Programmatic EIS Information Center, windeis.anl.gov

Vanderbosch, Robert, and Susanna Vanderbosch, *Nuclear Waste Stalemate: Political and Scientific Controversies.* Salt Lake City: University of Utah Press, 2007.

Wells, Peter E., and Paul Nieuwenhuis, *The Automotive Industry and the Environment: A Technical, Business and Social Future.* Boca Raton, FL: CRC Press, 2003.

Wind Power: Environmental and Safety Issues, Wind Energy Fact Sheet 4. www.dti.gov.uk/files/file17777.pdf

Environment

Akinbami, Lara J., *The State of Childhood Asthma in the United States, 1980–2005.* Hyattsville, MD: U.S. Department of Health and Human Services, 2006.

Alverson, William Surprison, Walter Kuhlmann, and Donald M. Waller, *Wild Forests: Conservation Biology and Public Policy.* Washington, DC: Island Press, 1994.

An Inconvenient Truth. Documentary. Directed by David Guggenheim, 2006.

Anderson, J. L., *Industrializing the Corn Belt: Agriculture, Technology, and Environment, 1945–1972.* DeKalb: Northern Illinois University Press, 2008.

Archer, David, *The Climate Crisis: An Introductory Guide to Climate Change.* New York: Cambridge University Press, 2010.

Babbitt, Bruce, *Cities in the Wilderness: A New Vision of Land Use in America.* Washington, DC: Island Press, 2005.

Barrow, Mark V., Jr., *Nature's Ghosts: Confronting Extinction from the Age of Jefferson to the Age of Ecology.* Chicago: University of Chicago Press, 2009.

Bas, Ed, *Indoor Air Quality.* New York: Marcel Dekker, 2004.

Behan, Richard W., *Plundered Promise: Capitalism, Politics, and the Fate of the Federal Lands.* Washington, DC: Island Press, 2001.

Bellamy, John Foster, Frederick Butell, and Fred Magdoff, *Hungry for Profit: The Agribusiness Threat to Farmers, Food, and the Environment.* New York: Monthly Review Press, 2000.

Beres, Samantha, *Pesticides: Critical Thinking about Environmental Issues.* Farmington Hills, MI: Greenhaven Press, 2002.

Berger, John J., *Forests Forever: Their Ecology, Restoration, and Protection.* Chicago: Center for American Places, 2008.

Bernard, Ted, *Hope and Hard Times: Communities, Collaboration, and Sustainability.* Gabriola Island, BC: New Society Publishers, 2010.

Bernstein, I. Leonard, *Asthma in the Workplace.* New York: Marcel Dekker, 1999.

Best, Gerry, *Environmental Pollution Studies.* Liverpool, UK: Liverpool University Press, 2000.

Bowersox, Joe, *The Moral Austerity of Environmental Decision Making.* Durham, NC: Duke University Press, 2002.

Brimblecombe, Peter, *Acid Rain: Deposition to Recovery.* Dordrecht: Springer, 2007.

Broecker, William S., and Robert Kunzig, *Fixing Climate: What Past Climate Changes Reveal about the Current Threat—and How to Counter It.* New York: Hill & Wang, 2008.

Buckley, Ralf, Catherine Pickering, and David Bruce Weaver, *Nature-Based Tourism, Environment and Land Management.* London: CABI Publishing, 2003.

Bullard, Robert D., ed., *Growing Smarter: Achieving Livable Communities, Environmental Justice, and Regional Equity.* Cambridge, MA: MIT Press, 2007.

Burns, Shirley Stewart, *Bringing Down the Mountains: The Impact of Mountaintop Removal Surface Coal Mining on West Virginia Communities, 1970–2004.* Morgantown: West Virginia University Press, 2007.

Casas, José S., and José Sordo, eds., *Lead: Chemistry, Analytical Aspects, Environmental Impact, and Health Effects.* Boston: Elsevier, 2006.

Cherni, Judith A., *Economic Growth versus the Environment: The Politics of Wealth, Health, and Air Pollution.* London: Palgrave Macmillan, 2002.

Clowney, David, and Patricia Mosto, *Earthcare: An Anthology of Environmental Ethics.* Lanham, MD: Rowman & Littlefield, 2009.

Collin, Robert W., *The U.S. Environmental Protection Agency: Cleaning Up America's Act.* Westport, CT: Greenwood Press, 2006.

Condon, Condon M. et al., *Urban Planning Tools for Climate Change Mitigation.* Lincoln, NE: Institute of Land Policy, 2009.

Cox, John D., *Climate Crash: Abrupt Climate Change and What It Means for Our Future.* Washington, DC: Joseph Henry Press, 2005.

Cox, Thomas R., *The Lumberman's Frontier: Three Centuries of Land Use, Society, and Change in America's Forests.* Corvalis: Oregon State University Press, 2010.

Crow, Peter, *Do, Die, or Get Along: A Tale of Two Appalachian Tows.* Athens: University of Georgia Press, 2007.

Crowder, Ad'aele A., Earle A. Ripley, and Robert E. Redmann, *Environmental Effects of Mining.* Singapore: CRC Press, 1996.

Davis, Charles, ed., *Western Public Lands and Environmental Politics*. Boulder, CO: Westview Press, 2001.

Dernbach, John C., ed., *Agenda for a Sustainable America*. Washington, DC: Environmental Law Institute, 2009.

Dhir, Ravindra, Thomas D. Dyer, and Kevin A. Paine, eds., *Sustainable Construction: Use of Incinerator Ash;* London: Thomas Telford Publishing, 2000.

Dietz, Thomas, and Paul C. Stern, eds., *Public Participation in Environmental Assessment and Decision Making*. Washington, DC: National Academies Press, 2008.

DiMento, Joseph F. C., and Pamela Doughman, eds., *Climate Change: What It Means for Us, Our Children, and Our Grandchildren*. Cambridge, MA: MIT Press, 2007.

Dow, Kirstin, and Thomas E. Downing, *The Atlas of Climate Change: Mapping the World's Greatest Challenge*. Berkeley: University of California Press, 2007.

Downie, David, *Northern Lights against POPs: Toxic Threats in the Arctic*. Montreal: McGill-Queen's Press, 2002.

Ellerman, A. Denny, et al., *Markets for Clean Air: The U.S. Acid Rain Program*. New York: Cambridge University Press, 2000.

Endangered and Extinct Species Lists, eelink.net/EndSpp.old.bak/ES.lists.html

Environmental Defense Fund, www.edf.org/home.cfm

Faber, Daniel, *Capitalizing on Environmental Injustice: The Polluter-Industrial Complex in the Age of Globalization*. Lanham, MD: Rowman & Littlefield, 2008.

Fagan, Brian M., *The Great Warming: Climate Change and the Rise and Fall of Civilizations*. New York: Bloomsbury Press, 2008.

Fiedler, H., ed., *Persistent Organic Pollutants*. New York: Springer 2003.

Flannery, Tim, *The Weather Makers: How We Are Changing the Climate and What It Means for Life on Earth*. Toronto: HarperCollins, 2006.

Flint, Anthony, *This Land: The Battle over Sprawl and the Future of America*. Baltimore: Johns Hopkins University Press, 2006.

Fretwell, Holly Lipke, *Who Is Minding the Federal Estate? Political Management of America's Public Lands*. Lanham, MD: Lexington Books, 2009.

Genske, Dieter D., *Investigation, Remediation, and Protection of Land Resources*. Dunbeath, UK: Whittles, 2007.

Glasson, John, et al., *Introduction to Environmental Impact Assessment*, 3d ed. New York: Routledge, 2005.

Gliessman, Stephen R., *Agroecology: The Ecology of Sustainable Food Systems*, 2d ed. Singapore: CRC Press, 2006.

Goble, Dale D., J. Michael Scott, and Frank W. Davis, eds., *The Endangered Species Act at Thirty*. Washington, DC: Island Press, 2006.

Gonzales, George A., *Urban Sprawl, Global Warming, and the Empire of Capital*. Albany: State University of New York Press, 2009.

Hanna, Kevin, *Environmental Impact Assessment: Practice and Participation*, 2d ed. New York: Oxford University Press, 2009.

Hansen, James E., *Storms of My Grandchildren: The Truth about the Coming Climate Catastrophe and Our Last Chance to Save Humanity*. New York: Bloomsbury Press, 2009.

Hanson, Larry G., and Larry W. Robertson, *PCBs: Human and Environmental Disposition and Toxicology*. Urbana: University of Illinois Press, 2008.

Harrad, Stuart, *Persistent Organic Pollutants: Environmental Behaviour and Pathways of Human Exposure*. New York: Springer, 2001.

Harrap, D., *Air Quality Assessment and Management*. London: Spon Press, 2002.

Harris, Jonathan M. *A Survey of Sustainable Development: Social and Economic Dimensions*. Washington, DC: Island Press, 2001.

Hartman, Howard L., and Jan M. Mutmansky, *Introductory Mining Engineering*. New York: Wiley, 2002.

Hayden, Dolores, *A Field Guide to Sprawl*. New York: Norton, 2004.

Helmer, Richard, *Water Pollution Control*. London: Spon Press, 1998.

Hirt, Paul W., *A Conspiracy of Optimism: Management of the National Forests since World War Two*. Lincoln: University of Nebraska Press, 1994.

Hollander, Justin B., *Polluted and Dangerous: America's Worst Abandoned Properties and What Can Be Done about Them*. Burlington: University of Vermont Press, 2009.

Holly, Hattemer-Frey, Janos Szollosi, Lajos Tron, et al., eds., *Health Effects of Municipal Waste Incineration*. Boca Raton, FL: CRC Press, 1991.

Houghton, J. T., *Global Warming: The Complete Briefing*. New York: Cambridge University Press, 2009.

Hulme, Michael, *Why We Disagree about Climate Change: Understanding Controversy, Inaction and Opportunity*. New York: Cambridge University Press, 2009.

Institute of Medicine, *Clearing the Air: Asthma and Indoor Air Exposures*. Washington, DC: National Academies Press, 2000.

Jansen, Kees, and Sietze Velleme, *Agribusiness and Society: Corporate Responses to Environmentalism, Market Opportunities, and Public Regulation*. London: Zed Books, 2004.

Johansen, Bruce Elliott, *The Dirty Dozen: Toxic Chemicals and the Earth's Future*. Westport, CT: Praeger, 2003.

Kabat, Geoffrey C., *Hyping Health Risks: Environmental Hazards in Daily Life and the Science of Epidemiology*. New York: Columbia University Press, 2008.

Keiter, Robert B., *Keeping Faith with Nature: Ecosystems, Democracy, and America's Public Lands*. New Haven, CT: Yale University Press, 2003.

Kimbrell, Andrew, *Fatal Harvest: The Tragedy of Industrial Agriculture*. Sausalito, CA: Foundation for Deep Ecology and Island Press, 2002.

Kinnaman, Thomas C., ed., *The Economics of Residential Solid Waste Management*. Burlington, VT: Ashgate, 2003.

Knott, Catherine Henshaw, *Living with the Adirondack Forest: Local Perspectives on Land Use Conflicts*. Ithaca, NY: Cornell University Press, 1998.

Lawrence, David Peter, *Environmental Impact Assessment: Practical Solutions to Recurrent Problems*. Hoboken, NJ: Wiley, 2003.

LeCain, Timothy, *Mass Destruction: The Men and Giant Mines That Wired America and Scarred the Planet*. New Brunswick, NJ: Rutgers University Press, 2009.

Levine, Marvin J., *Pesticides: A Toxic Time Bomb in Our Midst*. Westport, CT: Praeger, 2007.

Lipfert, Frederick W., *Air Pollution and Community Health*. New York: Wiley, 1994.

Lowry, William R., *Repairing Paradise: The Restoration of America's National Parks*. Washington, DC: Brookings Institution Press, 2009.

MacDonald, Samuel A., *The Agony of an American Wilderness: Loggers, Environmentalists, and the Struggle for Control of a Forgotten Forest*. Lanham, MD: Rowman & Littlefield, 2005.

Macey, Gregg P., and Jonathan Z. Cannon, *Reclaiming the Land: Rethinking Superfund Institutions, Methods, and Practices*. New York: Springer, 2007.

Machlis, Gary E., and Donald R. Field, *National Parks and Rural Development: Practice and Policy in the United States*. Washington, DC: Island Press, 2000.

Maehr, David S., et al., eds., *Large Mammal Restoration: Ecological and Sociological Consideration in the 21st Century*. Washington, DC: Island Press, 2001.

Maser, Chris, *Ecological Diversity in Sustainable Development: The Vital and Forgotten Dimension*. New York: Lewis Publishers, 1999.

Mastney, Lisa, and Sandra Postel, *Liquid Assets: The Critical Need to Safeguard Freshwater Ecosystems*. Washington, DC: Worldwatch Institute, 2005.

Matthews, Graham A., *Pesticides: Health, Safety and the Environment*. Oxford: Blackwell Publishing, 2006.

Mazmanian, Daniel A., and Michael E. Kraft, eds., *Towards Sustainable Communities*, 2d ed. Cambridge, MA: MIT Press, 2009.

McKibben, Bill, *Eaarth: Making a Life on a Tough New Planet*. New York: Times Books, 2010.

Mehmetli, Ebru, and Bogdana Koumanova, *The Fate of Persistent Organic Pollutants*. Dordecht: Springer Science/Business Media, 2007.

Melosi, Martin V., *The Sanitary City: Environmental Services in Urban America from Colonial Times to the Present*, abridged ed. Pittsburgh: University of Pittsburgh Press, 2008.

Millstone, Erik, *Lead and Public Health: The Dangers for Children*. Washington, DC: Taylor and Francis, 1997.

Monbiot, George, *Heat: How to Stop the Planet from Burning*. Toronto: Random House, 2006.

Moore, Colleen F., *Silent Scourge: Children, Pollution, and Why Scientists Disagree*. New York: Oxford University Press, 2003.

Morandi, Larry, Barbara Foster, and Jeff Dale, *Watershed Protection: The Legislative Role*. Washington, DC: National Conference of State Governors, 1998.

Moussiopoulos, Nicolas, ed., *Air Quality in Cities*. New York: Springer, 2003.

Nash, Linda Lorraine, *Inescapable Ecologies: A History of Environment, Disease, and Knowledge*. Berkeley: University of California Press, 2007.

Naspitz, Charles K., *Pediatric Asthma: An International Perspective*. London: Taylor and Francis, 2001.

Nathanail, C. Paul, and R. Paul Bardos, *Reclamation of Contaminated Land*. New York: Wiley, 2004.

National Research Council, *Cumulative Environmental Effects of Oil and Gas Activities on Alaska's North Slope*. Washington, DC: National Academies Press, 2003.

National Park Service Concession Program, www.concessions.nps.gov

National Park Service Concessions Assessment, www.whitehouse.gov/OMB/ expectmore/detail.10003716.2005.html

National Parks Conservation Association, www.npca.org

Natural Resources Defense Council, Issues: Water, www.nrdc.org/water/pollution/default.asp

Nelson, Robert H., *Public Lands and Private Rights: The Failure of Scientific Management.* Lanham, MD: Rowman & Littlefield, 1995.

Niessen, Walter R., *Combustion and Incineration Processes: Applications in Environmental Engineering.* New York: Marcel Dekker, 2002.

Noble, Bram F., *Introduction to Environmental Impact Assessment: A Guide to Principles and Practice,* 2d ed. New York: Oxford University Press, 2010.

Norden, Bengt, *Interaction Mechanisms of Low-Level Electromagnetic Fields in Living Systems.* Oxford: Oxford University Press, 1992.

O'Brien, Bob R., *Our National Parks and the Search for Sustainability.* Austin: University of Texas Press, 1999.

O'Toole, Randal, *A Libertarian View of Urban Sprawl.* Cato Institute. March 18, 2010. http://www.cato-at-liberty.org/2010/03/18/a-libertarian-view-of-urban-sprawl

Office of Protected Resources, Species under the Endangered Species Act (ESA), www.nmfs.noaa.gov/pr/species/esa

Oreskes, Naomi, and Erik M. Conway, *Merchants of Doubt: How a Handful of Scientists Obscured the Truth on Issues from Tobacco to Global Warming.* New York: Bloomsbury Press, 2010.

Owens, Susan E., and Richard Cowell, *Land and Limits: Interpreting Sustainability in the Planning Process.* New York: Routledge, 2002.

Pagenkopf, James R., et al., *Municipal Waste-water Treatment.* New York: Wiley, 2002.

Public Lands Foundation, www.publicland.org

Public Lands Information Center, www.publiclands.org/home.php?SID=/

Rajala, Richard A., *Clearcutting the Pacific Rain Forest: Production, Science, and Regulation.* Vancouver: University of British Columbia Press, 1998.

Randolph, John, *Environmental Land Use Planning and Management.* Washington, DC: Island Press, 2004.

Rao, P. K., *Sustainable Development.* Oxford: Blackwell, 2000.

Rathje, William, and Cullen Murphy, *Rubbish! The Archaeology of Garbage.* New York: HarperCollins, 1992.

Rhodes, Eduardo Lao, *Environmental Justice in America: A New Paradigm.* Bloomington: Indiana University Press, 2003.

Riddell, Robert, *Sustainable Urban Planning: Tipping the Balance.* Oxford: Blackwell, 2004.

Roadless Area Conservation, www.roadless.fs.fed.us

Russ, Thomas H., *Redeveloping Brownfields: Landscape Architects, Planners, Developers.* New York: McGraw-Hill, 1999.

Sabatier, Paul A., *Swimming Upstream: Collaborative Approaches to Watershed Management.* Cambridge, MA: MIT Press, 2005.

Sanderson, James, and Larry D. Harris, eds., *Landscape Ecology: A Top-Down Approach.* Boca Raton, FL: Lewis Publishers, 2000.

Scanlan, John, *On Garbage.* London: Reaktion Books, 2005.

Schrader-Freschette, K. S., *Environmental Justice: Creating Equality, Reclaiming Democracy.* New York: Oxford University Press, 2002.

Schwartz, Joel, *Air Quality in America.* Washington, DC: AEI Press, 2007.

Shevory, Thomas C., *Toxic Burn: The Grassroots Struggle against the WTI Incinerator*. Minneapolis: University of Minnesota Press, 2007.

Shogren, Jason F., and John Tschirhart, eds., *Protecting Endangered Species in the United States: Biological Needs, Political Realities, Economic Choices*. New York: Cambridge University Press, 2008.

Sigman, Hillary, ed., *The Economics of Hazardous Waste and Contaminated Land*. Northampton, MA: Edward Elgar, 2008.

Simioni, Daniela, *Air Pollution and Citizen Awareness*. New York: United Nations Publications, 2004.

Smith, Douglas, and Gary Ferguson, *Decade of the Wolf: Returning the Wild to Yellowstone*. Guilford, CT: Lyons Press, 2005.

Social Learning Group, *A Comparative History of Social Responses to Climate Change, Ozone Depletion, and Acid Rain*. Cambridge, MA: MIT Press, 2001.

Social Learning Group, *Learning to Manage Global Environmental Risks*. Cambridge, MA: MIT Press, 2001.

Soule, David C. ed., *Remaking American Cities: A Reference Guide to Urban Sprawl*. Lincoln: University of Nebraska Press, 2007.

Sources of Water Pollution, www.soest.hawaii.edu/GG/ASK/waterpol3.html

Spellman, Frank R., *The Science of Water: Concepts and Applications*. Boca Raton, FL: CRC Press, 2008.

Spellman, Frank R., and Nancy E. Whiting, *Environmental Management of Concentrated Animal Feeding Operations (CAFOs)*. Singapore: CRC Press, 2007.

Strasser, Susan. *Waste and Want: A Social History of Trash*. New York: Owl Books, 2000.

Sullivan, Patrick J., Franklin J. Argady, and James J. J. Clark, *The Environmental Science of Drinking Water*. Burlington, MA: Butterworth-Heinemann, 2005.

Tammemagi, Hans, *Air: Our Planet's Ailing Atmosphere*. Toronto: Oxford University Press, 2009.

Thomas, Vivian E., *Garbage In, Garbage Out: Solving the Problems with Long-Distance Trash Transport*. Charlottesville: University of Virginia Press, 2009.

Troesken, Werner, *The Great Lead Water Pipe Disaster*. Cambridge, MA: MIT Press, 2006.

U.S. Department of the Interior, Office of Surface Mining, Environmental Assessments, www.osmre.gov/pdf/streambufferea.pdf

U.S. Environmental Protection Agency, Monitoring and Assessing Water Quality: Volunteer Monitoring. www.epa.gov/owow/monitoring/vol.html

U.S. Environmental Protection Agency, Polluted Runoff (Nonpoint Source Pollution), www.epa.gov/nps

U.S. Environmental Protection Agency, Watersheds, www.epa.gov/owow/water shed

U.S. Fish & Wildlife Service, Endangered Species Program. June 2010. http://www.fws.gov/endangered/wildlife.html#Species

Urbiqkit, Cat, *Yellowstone Wolves: A Chronicle of the Animal, the People, and the Politics*. Blacksburg, VA: McDonald & Woodward, 2008.

Vaughn, Jacqueline, *Conflicts over Natural Resources: A Reference Handbook*. Santa Barbara, CA: ABC-CLIO, 2007.

Wargo, John, *Green Intelligence: Creating Environments that Protect Human Health*. New Haven, CT: Yale University Press, 2009.

Wilderness Society, www.wilderness.org

Wolch, Jennifer, Manual Pastor, and Peter Dreier, eds., *Up Against the Sprawl.* Minneapolis: University of Minnesota Press, 2004.

Health and Medicine

Albritton, Robert, *Let Them Eat Junk: How Capitalism Creates Hunger and Obesity.* New York: Pluto Press, 2009.

Allen, Arthur, *Vaccine: The Controversial Story of Medicine's Greatest Lifesaver.* New York: Norton, 2007.

American Medical Association, http://www.ama-assn.org

Angell, Marcia, *The Truth about the Drug Companies.* New York: Random House, 2004.

Barry, John M., *The Great Influenza: The Story of the Deadliest Pandemic in History.* New York: Penguin, 2004.

Barry, John, *The Great Influenza: The Epic Story of the Deadliest Plague in History.* New York: Viking, 2004.

Beauchamp, Tom L., and James F. Childress, *Principles of Biomedical Ethics,* 5th ed. New York: Oxford University Press, 2001.

Cantor, David, ed., *Cancer in the Twentieth Century.* Baltimore: Johns Hopkins University Press, 2008.

Cardello, Hank, with Doug Carr, *Stuffed: An Insider's Look at Who's (Really) Making America Fat.* New York: Ecco Press, 2009.

Centers for Disease Control, http://www.cdc.gov

Chapkis, Wendy, and Richard J. Webb, *Dying to Get High: Marijuana as Medicine.* New York: New York University Press, 2008.

Colgrove, James, *State of Immunity: The Politics of Vaccination in Twentieth-Century America.* Berkeley: University of California Press, 2006.

Devettere, Raymond J., *Practical Decision Making in Health Care Ethics,* 3d ed. Washington, DC: Georgetown University Press, 2010.

Devlin, Roni K., *Influenza.* Westport, CT: Greenwood Press, 2008.

Eaton, Margaret L., and Donald Kennedy, *Innovation in Medical Technology: Ethical Issues and Challenges.* Baltimore: Johns Hopkins University Press, 2007.

Entis, Phyllis, *Food Safety: Old Habits and New Perspectives.* Washington, DC: ASM Press, 2007.

Faquet, Guy B., *The War on Cancer: An Anatomy of Failure, a Blueprint for the Future.* Dordrecht: Springer, 2005.

Finkelstein, Eric, *The Fattening of America: How the Economy Makes Us Fat, If It Matters, and What to Do about It.* Hoboken, NJ: Wiley, 2008.

Fortin, Neal D., *Food Regulation: Law, Science, Policy, and Practice.* New York: Wiley, 2009.

Fox, Nicols, *Spoiled: The Dangerous Truth About a Food Chain Gone Haywire.* New York: Basic Books, 1997.

Garrett, Laurie, *The Coming Plague: Newly Emerging Diseases in a World Out of Balance.* New York: Penguin, 1995.

Glassner, Barry, *The Culture of Fear: Why Americans Are Afraid of the Wrong Things.* New York: Basic Books, 1999

Gregor, Michael, *Bird Flu: A Virus of Our Own Hatching.* New York: Lantern Books, 2006.

Halpern, S. A., *Lesser Harms: The Morality of Risk in Medical Research.* Chicago: University of Chicago Press, 2004.

Hayman, Laura L., ed., *Chronic Illness in Children: An Evidence-Based Approach.* New York: Springer, 2002.

Hester, R. E., and Roy M. Harrison, *Endocrine Disrupting Chemicals.* London: Royal Society of Chemists, 1999.

Illingworth, Patricia, *Ethical Health Care.* Upper Saddle River, NJ: Pearson/Prentice Hall, 2006.

Imber, Jonathan B., *Trusting Doctors: The Decline of Moral Authority in American Medicine* Princeton, NJ: Princeton University Press, 2008.

Jakobsen, Janet, and Ann Pellegrini, *Love the Sin: Sexual Regulation and the Limits of Religious Tolerance.* Boston: Beacon Press, 2004.

Jones, J. H, *Bad Blood: The Tuskegee Syphilis Experiment.* New York: Free Press, 1981.

Jongen, Wim, ed., *Improving the Safety of Fresh Fruit and Vegetables.* Boca Raton, FL: CRC Press, 2005.

Khoury, M. J., and J. Morris, *Pharmacogenomics and Public Health: The Promise of Targeted Disease Prevention.* Atlanta: Centers for Disease Control and Prevention, 2001.

Laumann, Edward, et al., *The Social Organization of Sexuality: Sexual Practices in the United States.* Chicago: University of Chicago Press, 1994.

Levy, Elinor, and Mark Fischetti, *The New Killer Diseases: How the Alarming Evolution of Germs Threatens Us All.* New York: Three Rivers Press, 2004.

Loughlin, Kevin, et al., eds., *The Guide to Off-Label Prescription Drugs: New Uses for FDA-Approved Prescription Drugs.* New York: Free Press, 2006.

Melia, Kath M., *Health Care Ethics: Lessons from Intensive Care.* Thousand Oaks, CA: Sage, 2004.

Nass, S., and H. L. Moses, eds., *Cancer Biomarkers: The Promises and Challenges of Improving Detection and Treatment.* Washington, DC: National Academies Press, 2007.

National Cancer Institute, http://www.cancer.gov

Nestle, Marion, *Safe Food: Bacteria, Biotechnology, and Bioterrorism.* Berkeley: University of California Press, 2003.

Norris, David O., and James A. Carr, *Endocrine Disruption: Biological Basis for Health Effects in Wildlife and Humans.* New York: Oxford University Press, 2006.

Patton, Cindy, *Fatal Advice: How Safe-Sex Education Went Wrong.* Durham, NC: Duke University Press, 1996.

Pennington, T. Hugh, *When Food Kills: BSE, E. Coli, and Disaster Science.* New York: Oxford University Press, 2003.

Peters, C. J., and Mark Olshaker, *Virus Hunter: Thirty Years of Battling Hot Viruses around the World.* New York: Anchor Books, 1997.

Pisani, Elizabeth, *The Wisdom of Whores: Bureaucrats, Brothels, and the Business of AIDS.* New York: Norton, 2009.

Pray, Leslie, et al., *Managing Food Safety Practices from Farm to Table.* Washington, DC: National Academies Press, 2009.

Redman, Nina E., *Food Safety: A Reference Handbook.* Santa Barbara, CA: ABC-CLIO, 2007.

Schumann, Michael S., et al., *Food Safety Law.* New York: Van Nostrand Reinhold, 1997.

Steingraber, Sandra, *Living Downstream: A Scientist's Personal Investigation of Cancer and the Environment.* New York: Vintage Books, 1998.

Stern, Judith S., *Obesity: A Reference Handbook.* Santa Barbara, CA: ABC-CLIO, 2009.

UNAIDS, Global Facts and Figures. 2009. http://data.unaids.org/pub/FactSheet/2009/20091124_FS_global_en.pdf

U.S. Department of Health and Human Services, HIV/AIDS, http://www.aids.gov

Whiteside, Alan, *HIV/AIDS: A Very Short Introduction.* New York: Oxford University Press, 2008.

World Health Organization, http://www.who.int/en.

World Health Organization, "Obesity and Overweight." http://www.who.int/dietphysicalactivity/publications/facts/obesity/en

Science and Ethics

Bellomo, Michael, *The Stem Cell Divide: The Facts, the Fiction, and the Fear Driving the Greatest Scientific, Political, and Religious Debate of Our Time.* New York: AMACOM, 2006.

Botzler, Richard George, *The Animal Ethics Reader.* London: Routledge, 2003.

Brody, Howard, *The Future of Bioethics.* New York: Oxford University Press, 2010.

Carbone, Larry, *What Animals Want: Expertise and Advocacy in Laboratory Animal Welfare Policy.* New York: Oxford University Press, 2004.

Collins, Francis S., *The Language of Life: DNA and the Revolution in Personalized Medicine.* New York: Harper, 2010.

Curry, Lynne, *The Human Body on Trial: A Handbook with Cases, Laws, and Documents.* Santa Barbara, CA: ABC-CLIO, 2002.

Daniels, N., A. Buchanan, D. Brock, and D. Wikler, *From Chance to Choice: Genes and Social Justice.* Cambridge, UK: Cambridge University Press, 2000.

Davis, Devra Lee, *The Secret History of the War on Cancer.* New York: Basic Books, 2007.

Duster, Troy, *Backdoor to Eugenics.* New York: Routledge, 1990.

Faden, R. R., and T. L. Beauchamp, *A History and Theory of Informed Consent.* New York: Oxford University Press, 1986.

Fausto-Sterling, Anne, *Sexing the Body.* New York: Basic Books, 2000);

Forrest, Derek Williams, *Francis Galton: The Life and Work of a Victorian Genius.* New York: Taplinger, 1974.

Fox, Cynthia, *Cell of Cells: The Global Race to Capture and Control the Stem Cell.* New York: Norton, 2007.

Fritz, Sandy, ed., *Understanding Cloning.* New York: Warner Books, 2002.

Garner, Robert, *Animals, Politics, and Morality.* Manchester, UK: Manchester University Press, 2004.

Genetic Engineering & Biotechnology News, http://www.genengnews.com

Gillette, Aaron, *Eugenics and the Nature-Nurture Debate in the Twentieth Century.* New York: Palgrave Macmillan, 2007.

Gluck, John P., Tony DiPasquale, and Barbara F. Orlans, *Applied Ethics in Animal Research: Philosophy, Regulation and Laboratory Applications.* Ames, IA: Purdue University Press, 2002.

Gould, Stephen Jay, *The Mismeasure of Man.* New York: Norton, 1981.

Haugen, David M., et al., eds., *The Ethics of Cloning*. Detroit: Greenhaven Press, 2008.

Holland, Suzanne, Karen Lebacqz, and Laurie Zoloth, eds., *The Human Embryonic Stem Cell Debate: Science, Ethics, and Public Policy*. Cambridge, MA: MIT Press, 2001.

Hubbard, Ruth, and Elijh Wald, *Exploding the Gene Myth: How Genetic Information Is Produced and Manipulated by Scientists, Physicians, Employers, Insurance Companies, Educators, and Law Enforcers*. Boston: Beacon Press, 1999.

Human Genome Project, http://genome.gsc.riken.go.jp/hgmis/project/hgp.html

Kerr, Anne, and Tom Shakespeare, *Genetic Politics: From Eugenics to Genome*. Cheltenham, UK: New Clarion Press, 2002.

Kevles, Daniel J., *In the Name of Eugenics: Genetics and the Uses of Human Heredity*. New York: Knopf, 1985.

Klotzko, Arlene Judith, *A Clone of Your Own? The Science and Ethics of Cloning*. New York: Cambridge University Press, 2006.

Kluchin, Rebecca M., *Fit to Be Tied: Sterilization and Reproductive Rights in America, 1950–1980*. New Brunswick, NJ: Rutgers University Press, 2009.

Knowles, Lori P., and Gregory E. Kaebnick, *Reprogenetics: Law, Policy, Ethical Issues*. Baltimore: Johns Hopkins University Press, 2007.

Lewontin, R. C., Steven Rose, and Leon J. Kamin, *Not in Our Genes: Biology, Ideology, and Human Nature*. New York: Pantheon, 1984.

Moore, David S. *The Dependent Gene: The Fallacy of "Nature vs. Nurture."* New York: Henry Holt, 2002.

Moran, Lisa C., *Science, Medicine, and Animals*. Washington, DC: National Academies Press, 2005.

Olmsted, Alan L., *Creating Abundance: Biological Innovation and American Agricultural Development*. New York: Cambridge University Press, 2008.

Parens, Erik, et al., eds., *Wrestling with Behavioral Genetics: Science, Ethics, and Public Conversation*. Baltimore: Johns Hopkins University Press, 2006.

Petryna, Adriana, *When Experiments Travel: Clinical Trials and the Global Search for Subjects*. Princeton, NJ: Princeton University Press, 2009.

The President's Council on Bioethics, http://www.bioethics.gov/reports

Regan, Tom, *Defending Animal Rights*. Chicago: University of Illinois Press, 2001.

Ridley, Matt, *Nature via Nurture: Genes, Experience, and What Makes Us Human*. New York: HarperCollins, 2003.

Rubenfeld, Sheldon, ed., *Medicine after the Holocaust: From the Master Race to the Human Genome Project*. New York: Palgrave Macmillan, 2010.

Rudacille, Deborah, *The Scalpel and the Butterfly: The Conflict between Animal Research and Animal Protection*. Berkeley: University of California Press, 2001.

Ruse, Michael, and Christopher A. Pynes, eds., *The Stem Cell Controversy: Debating the Issues*, 2d ed. New York: Prometheus Books, 2006.

Schaller, Barry R., *Understanding Bioethics and the Law: The Promise and Perils of the Brave New World of Biotechnology*. Westport, CT: Praeger, 2008.

Scott, F. Gilbert, and David Epel, *Ecological Developmental Biology*. Sunderland, MA: Sinauer Associates, 2009.

Shah, S., *The Body Hunters: How the Drug Industry Tests Its Products on the World's Poorest Patients.* New York: New Press, 2006.

Shmaefsky, Brian, *Biotechnology 101.* Westport, CT: Greenwood Press, 2006.

Stober, Spencer S., and Donna Yarri, *God, Science, and Designer Genes: An Exploration of Emerging Genetic Technologies.* Westport, CT: Praeger, 2009.

U.S. National Institutes of Health, Understanding Clinical Trials. 2007. http://clinicaltrials.gov/ct2/info/understand

Waters, Brent, and Ronald Cole-Turner, *God and Embryo.* Washington, DC: Georgetown University Press, 2003.

Wilson, E. O., *Sociobiology: The New Synthesis,* 25th anniversary ed. Cambridge, MA: Belknap/Harvard University Press, 2000.

Wittcoff, Harold A., Jeffery S. Plotkin, and Bryan G. Reuben, *Industrial Organic Chemicals.* Hoboken, NJ: Wiley, 2004.

Wright, Lawrence, *Twins: And What They Tell Us about Who We Are.* New York: Wiley, 1997.

Technology

Alvarez, R. Michael, and Thad E. Hall, *Electronic Elections: The Perils and Promises of Digital Democracy.* Princeton, NJ: Princeton University Press, 2008.

American Association of State Highway and Transportation Officials (AASHTO), *Bridging the Gap.* July 2008. www.transportation1.org/bridgereport/front-page.html

American Society of Civil Engineers, *2009 Report Card for America's Infrastructure.* www.infrastructurereportcard.org/report-cards

Anderson, Janna Quitney, *Imagining the Internet: Personalities, Predictions, Perspectives.* Lanham, MD: Rowman & Littlefield, 2005.

Aspray, William, and Paul E. Ceruzzi, eds., *The Internet and American Business.* Cambridge, MA: MIT Press, 2008.

Association of State Dam Safety Officials, *State and Federal Oversight of Dam Safety Must Be Improved.* www.damsafety.org

Avise, John C., *The Hope, Hype and Reality of Genetic Engineering.* New York: Oxford University Press, 2004.

Bailey, Britt, and Marc Lappé, eds., *Engineering the Farm: Ethical and Social Aspects of Agricultural Biotechnology.* Washington, DC: Island Press, 2002.

Ball, Kirstie, and Frank Webster, eds., *The Intensification of Surveillance: Crime, Terrorism and Warfare in the Information Age.* Sterling, VA: Pluto Press, 2003.

Breazeal, Cynthia, *Designing Sociable Robots (Intelligent Robotics and Autonomous Agents).* Cambridge, MA: MIT Press, 2002.

Buckley, Peter, and Duncan Clark, *The Rough Guide to the Internet.* London: Penguin, 2007.

Chalk, Peter, *Hitting America's Soft Underbelly: The Potential Threat of Deliberate Biological Attacks Against the U.S. Agricultural and Food Industry.* Santa Monica, CA: Rand Corporation, 2004.

Charles, Daniel, *Lords of the Harvest: Biotech, Big Money, and the Future of Food.* Cambridge, MA: Perseus, 2001.

Chertoff, M., "Preserving infrastructure: A 21st Century Challenge." *Parameters* (Winter 2008): 5–13.

Cimbala, Stephen J., *Shield of Dreams: Missile Defense and U.S.-Russian Nuclear Strategy.* Annapolis, MD: Naval Institute Press, 2008.

Collins, Pamela A. and Ryan K. Baggett, *Homeland Security and Critical Infrastructure Protection.* Westport, CT: Praeger Security International, 2009.

De Jonge, Christopher, and Christopher L. R. Barratt, eds., *Assisted Reproduction Technology: Accomplishments and New Horizons.* Cambridge, UK: Cambridge University Press, 2002.

Edelstein, Sari, *Food and Nutrition at Risk in America: Food Insecurity, Biotechnology, Food Safety, and Bioterrorism.* Sudbury, MA: Jones & Bartlett, 2009.

Elias, Bartholomew, *Airport and Aviation Security: U.S. Policy and Strategy in the Age of Global Terrorism.* Boca Raton, FL: CRC Press, 2010.

Farren, Mick, and John Gibb, *Who's Watching You? The Truth about the State, Surveillance, and Personal Freedom.* New York: The Disinformation Company, 2007.

Forman, Richard T. T., *Road Ecology: Science and Solutions.* Washington, DC: Island Press, 2002.

Genetic Engineering & Biotechnology News, http://www.genengnews.com

Hier, Sean P., and Josh Greenberg, *Surveillance: Power, Problems, and Politics.* Vancouver: UBC Press, 2009.

Jackson, L., "We Must Do Something Now! Our Nation's Transportation Infrastructure Is Deteriorating." *Entrepreneur Magazine* (2009).

Kelderman, E., "Look Out Below! America's Infrastructure Is Crumbling." Stateline.org/Pew Research Center. January 22, 2008. http://pewresearch.org/pubs/699/look-out-below

Kloppenburg, Jack Ralph, Jr., *First the Seed: The Political Economy of Plant Biotechnology 1492–2000,* 2d ed. Madison: University of Wisconsin Press, 2005.

Kutz, Myer, ed., *Environmentally Conscious Transportation.* Hoboken, NJ: Wiley, 2008.

Lettow, Paul Voerbeck, *Ronald Reagan and His Quest to Abolish Nuclear Weapons.* New York: Random House, 2005.

LeVine, Harry, *Genetic Engineering: A Reference Handbook,* 2d ed. Santa Barbara, CA: ABC-CLIO, 2006.

McCabe, Linda L., and Edward R. B. McCabe, *DNA: Promise and Peril.* Berkeley: University of California Press, 2008.

McHughen, Alan, *Pandora's Picnic Basket—The Potential and Hazards of Genetically Modified Foods.* New York: Oxford University Press, 2000.

McNeil, J. B., *Building Infrastructure Resiliency: Private Sector Investment in Homeland Security.* Washington, DC: The Heritage Foundation, 2008.

Merrick, Janna C., *Reproductive Issues in America: A Reference Handbook.* Santa Barbara, CA: ABC-CLIO, 2003.

Monahan, Torin, *Surveillance in the Time of Insecurity.* New Brunswick, NJ: Rutgers University Press, 2010.

Mundy, Liza, *Everything Conceivable: How Assisted Reproduction Is Changing Men, Women, and the World.* New York: Knopf, 2007.

Naam, Ramez, *More Than Human: Embracing the Promise of Biological Enhancement.* New York: Broadway Books, 2005.

National Research Council Transportation Research Board, *Surface Transportation Environmental Research: A Long-Term Strategy.* Washington, DC: National Academies Press, 2002.

Negroponte, Nicholas, *Being Digital*. New York: Knopf, 1995.

Nestle, Marion, *Safe Food: Bacteria, Biotechnology, and Bioterrorism*. Berkeley: University of California Press, 2003.

Noble, David, *Forces of Production: A Social History of Industrial Automation*. New York: Oxford University Press, 1986.

O'Hanlon, Michael E., *Budgeting for Hard Power: Defense and Security Spending under Barack Obama*. Washington, DC: Brookings Institution Press, 2009.

Peoples, Columba, *Justifying Ballistic Missile Defense: Technology, Security, and Culture*. New York: Cambridge University Press, 2010.

Percy, Herma, *Will Your Vote Count? Fixing America's Broken Electoral System*. Westport, CT: Praeger, 2009.

Price, Jeffrey and J. Forrest, *Practical Aviation Security: Predicting and Preventing Future Threats*. Burlington, MA: Butterworth-Heinemann, 2009.

Reeves, Byron, and Clifford Nass, *The Media Equation: How People Treat Computers, Television, and New Media Like Real People and Places*. CSLI Lecture Notes. Stanford, CA: Center for the Study of Language and Information Publications, 2003.

Rietveld, Piet, and Roger R. Stough, *Barriers to Sustainable Transport: Institutions, Regulation and Sustainability*. New York: Spon Press, 2005.

Root, Amanda, *Delivering Sustainable Transport: A Social Science Perspective*. Boston: Pergamon, 2003.

Saltman, Roy G., *The History and Politics of Voting Technology: In Quest of Integrity and Public Confidence*. New York: Palgrave Macmillan, 2006.

Schacter, Bernice, *Issues and Dilemmas of Biotechnology: A Reference Guide*. Westport, CT: Greenwood Press, 1999.

Schäfer, Andreas, et al., *Transportation in a Climate-Constrained World*. Cambridge, MA: MIT Press, 2009.

Schurman, Rachel, and Dennis D. Kelso, *Engineering Trouble: Biotechnology and Its Discontents*. Berkeley: University of California Press, 2003.

Scott, Virginia, *Google*. Westport, CT: Greenwood Press, 2008.

Siciliano, Bruno, and Ousamma Khatib, eds., *Springer Handbook of Robotics*. Berlin: Springer, 2008.

Standage, Tom, *The Victorian Internet*. New York, Walker, 1998.

Stoll, Clifford, *Silicon Snake Oil: Second Thoughts on the Information Highway*. New York: Anchor, 1996.

Sweet, Kathleen, *Aviation and Airport Security: Terrorism and Safety Concerns*, 2d ed. Boca Raton, FL: CRC Press, 2008.

Thomas, Robert J., *What Machines Can't Do: Politics and Technology in the Industrial Enterprise*. Berkeley, CA: University of California Press, 1994.

Turnley, A., *National Strategy for Protecting the Infrastructure: A Visionary Approach*. USAWC Strategy Research Project. Carlisle Barracks, PA: U.S. Army War College; 2004.

The Urban Land Institute and Ernst & Young, *Infrastructure 2009: Pivot Point*. Washington, DC: Urban Land Institute, 2009.

U.S. Department of Homeland Security, *Critical Infrastructure and Key Resources*. 2010. http://www.dhs.gov/files/programs/gc_1189168948944.shtm

Vaughan, R., and R. Pollard, *Rebuilding Americas, Volume 1: Planning and Managing Public Works in the 1980's*. Washington, DC: Council of State Planning Agencies, 1984.

Vogt, Donna U., *Food Biotechnology in the United States: Science, Regulation and Issues*. Washington, DC: Congressional Research Service of the Library of Congress, 2001.

Volti, Rudi, *Society and Technological Change*, 6th ed. New York: Worth, 2009.

Wallach, Wendell, *Moral Machines: Teaching Robots Right from Wrong*. New York: Oxford University Press, 2009.

Weatherford, B. A., H. H. Willis, and D.S. Ortiz, *The State of U.S. Railroads: A Review of Capacity and Performance Data*. Santa Monica, CA: Rand Supply Chain Policy Center, 2007.

Winkler, Kathleen, *High Tech Babies: The Debate over Assisted Reproductive Technology*. Berkeley Heights, NJ: Enslow, 2006.

Wood, Gaby, *Edison's Eve: A Magical History of the Quest for Mechanical Life*. New York: Anchor Books, 2002.

Zuboff, Shoshana, *In the Age of the Smart Machine: The Future of Work and Power*. New York: Basic Books, 1988.

Zylinska, Joanna, ed., *The Cyborg Experiments: Extensions of the Body in the Media Age*. New York: Continuum, 2002.

About the Editor and Contributors

Editor

Michael Shally-Jensen is former editor-in-chief of the *Encyclopedia Americana,* executive editor of the *Encyclopedia of American Studies,* and editor of numerous other books and reference publications. He received his Ph.D. in cultural anthropology from Princeton University, having specialized in aspects of American culture and society. He lives in Amherst, Massachusetts.

Contributors

Joseph Ali is a research scientist with the Johns Hopkins Berman Institute of Bioethics, in Baltimore, Maryland. He came to the Institute in 2007 as coordinator of the Johns Hopkins–Fogarty African Bioethics Training Program, an NIH-funded research ethics training program for researchers and scholars from sub-Saharan Africa. In addition to his work with the Fogarty program, he provides project coordination for an NIH challenge grant exploring the U.S. research oversight system and facilitates an NIH-funded project focusing on informed consent. He is also a Pennsylvania licensed attorney.

Ryan K. Baggett is the deputy director of technology and information services at the Eastern Kentucky University Justice and Safety Center in Richmond, Kentucky. In this capacity he manages programs from the U.S. Department of Homeland Security. Additionally, he is an adjunct instructor for the Eastern Kentucky University Department of Safety, Security, and Emergency Management. He holds a master's degree from Eastern Kentucky University and a bachelor's degree from Murray State University.

Heather Bell is a freelance writer based out of Winnipeg, Manitoba. She has a BSc from McGill University and a diploma in creative communications from Red River College in Winnipeg, Manitoba.

Nancy D. Campbell is an associate professor of science and technology studies at Rensselaer Polytechnic Institute in Troy, New York. She is the author of *Using Women: Gender, Drug Policy, and Social Reproduction* (2000); *Discovering Addiction: The Science and Politics of Substance Abuse Research* (2007); and, with J. P. Olsen and Luke Walden, *The Narcotic Farm: The Rise and Fall of America's First Prison for Drug Addicts* (2008). She has also written on the history of harm reduction drug policy; sweat-patch drug testing; and feminist science studies.

Robert William Collin is the senior research scholar at Willamette University Center for Sustainable Communities in Salem, Oregon. His published works include *Battleground: Environment; The EPA: Cleaning Up America's Act;* and, with Robin Morris Collin, *The Encyclopedia of Sustainability,* all published by Greenwood Press.

Pamela A. Collins is the executive director of the Justice and Safety Center, housed in the College of Justice and Safety at Eastern Kentucky University in Richmond, Kentucky. She is a professor of both undergraduate and graduate security studies. Currently she serves as the principal investigator on three key Department of Homeland Security projects. She has written numerous publications relating to security and homeland security/crime prevention, campus security, drug testing, physical security, and workplace violence.

Jennifer Croissant is associate professor in the Department of Women's Studies at the University of Arizona. Her research interests fall into the area of the sociology and anthropology of knowledge, science, and technology.

Jason A. Delborne is assistant professor of liberal arts and international studies at the Colorado School of Mines in Golden, Colorado. His research and teaching focus on the intersections of science, technology, society, and policy.

Gareth Edel is a graduate student in science and technology studies at Rensselaer Polytechnic Institute. He has worked in medical advertising and social work education. His research interests include the history of medicine and the biological sciences as well as and studies of knowledge and authority.

Bartholomew Elias is a specialist in aviation policy for the U.S. Congressional Research Service (CRS) in Washington, DC. He is the author of *Airport and Aviation Security: U.S. Policy and Strategy in the Age of Global Terrorism* (2009).

Michael H. Farris is manager of the Learning Technologies Group at Red River College in Winnipeg, Manitoba. He holds a Ph.D. from the University of Toronto.

Scott M. Fincher is a news- and photo-editing veteran of the *Chicago Tribune* and *Chicago Sun-Times*. His photos are collected internationally. Scott's work has received many awards, including a certificate of excellence in *Applied Arts* magazine because of his work in Canada's 2009 sports photo competition. He also received a judge's prize in the University of Chicago's "City of Man" exhibition.

Jill A. Fisher is assistant professor in the Center for Biomedical Ethics & Society at Vanderbilt University. She is author of *Medical Research for Hire: The Political Economy of Pharmaceutical Clinical Trials* (2009).

Karl F. Francis lives and works in the Capital District of New York State. He has completed graduate work in both science and technology studies and social welfare. His interest in public health and policy is related in part to his current work as a community advocate for people with disabilities.

Laura Fry is currently researching the social construction of the HPV virus as a doctoral student at the University of Arizona and is an adjunct instructor in sociology at Northern Arizona.

Jayne Geisel is a horticulturist and landscape architect and is an instructor in the Greenspace Management program at Red River College in Winnipeg, Manitoba.

Jerry Johnstone is an instructor and project coordinator for the Technology Solutions industry training initiative in the civil engineering technology department at Red River College in Winnipeg, Manitoba.

Abby J. Kinchy is assistant professor in the science and technology studies department at Rensselaer Polytechnic Institute. She has a variety of research interests, including food, agriculture, biotechnology, and rural communities; environmental politics and history; social movements and participatory science; and expertise and democracy.

Anne Kingsley is a Ph.D. candidate and undergraduate writing/composition instructor at Northeastern University. She is interested in gender and cultural studies, 20th-century women's writing, and the history of women's rhetoric.

Sarah Lewison is an interdisciplinary artist and writer interested in economics and ecology. She is assistant professor in radio and television at Southern Illinois University, Carbondale. Her teaching and research areas include media and social change, ecological pedagogy, and experimental performance. Her video work includes the documentary *Fat of the Land*, which screened on PBS and elsewhere.

Jessica Lyons is a doctoral student in science and technology studies at Rensselaer Polytechnic Institute. Her current research examines contemporary whaling as a case study for global environmental policy. She is a graduate of New York University's John W. Draper Interdisciplinary Master's Program in Humanities and Social Thought.

Steven T. Nagy holds a BSc (Hons.) in chemistry and physics and an MA in war studies (military history) from the Royal Military College of Canada. He is currently an instructor in air force history and doctrine at the Canadian Forces School of Aerospace Studies.

Hugh Peach is president of H. Gil Peach & Associates/ScanAmerica and provides strategic policy, planning, and evaluation support primarily to utilities and regulatory authorities.

Alexandre Pólvora is a Ph.D. researcher at CETCoPra/Center for the Study of Techniques, Knowledge and Practices, the philosophy department at the Université Paris 1—Panthéon-Sorbonne, and also a Ph.D. researcher in the sociology department of ISCTE/Lisbon University Institute.

Stephen Potthoff is assistant professor of religion and philosophy at Wilmington College, in Wilmington, Ohio. His most recent research involves an archaeological project in Carthage, Tunisia.

Michael Prentice is a graduate of Brown University with a degree in linguistics and anthropology. He currently lives in New York City and works in the advertising and branding industry.

Nina E. Redman is a reference librarian at Glendale Community College, Glendale, California. She is the author of *Food Safety: A Reference Handbook* (ABC-CLIO, 2007).

Selma Sabanovic is assistant professor in the School of Informatics and Computing at Indiana University. Her research explores how robotic technologies are designed and perceived in different cultural contexts and how human–robot inter-action research can be used to develop and evaluate models of social cognition. She is currently working on a book project about culturally situated robot design.

Kathryn E. Scarborough received her doctorate at Sam Houston State University. She has authored or coauthored numerous journal articles and three textbooks, including *Police Administration* (2010), with Gary W. Cordner. She is currently on leave from the department of safety, security, and emergency management at Eastern Kentucky University. Her primary areas of interest are homeland security, intelligence, cybersecurity, police administration, and law enforcement and security technology.

Debra Ann Schwartz is a veteran reporter specializing in science and the environment. She holds a doctorate in journalism and public communication from the University of Maryland, where she acquired expertise in scholarly editing and personal narrative writing. She is listed on the Fulbright Specialists Roster, which allows businesses and schools to request an individual's services and receive partial funding from the Fulbright Commission. She currently lives in Tempe, Arizona.

Celene Sheppard is a recent graduate of the University of Colorado's dual-degree graduate program in law and environmental studies and is an associate at the law firm of Snell & Wilmer in Phoenix, Arizona.

Ruth Ann Strickland is a professor of political science at Appalachian State University, Boone, North Carolina. Her areas of interest include American government, public policy, the judicial process, and administrative law. She is the author of five books, including *Campaign and Election Reform* (ABC-CLIO, 2008), with Glenn H. Utter.

Edward White is a Winnipeg-based reporter and columnist for *The Western Producer,* Canada's largest farm newspaper. He has won numerous awards for his journalism, including being named Agricultural Journalist of the Year in 2000 by the (U.S.) National Association of Agricultural Journalists. He has an MA in journalism from the University of Western Ontario.

Index

For reference

Not to be taken from the room.

DATE DUE
